John O'Grady and Peter

Ecumenics from

Theology, Ethics and Interreligious Relations

Studies in Ecumenics

Edited by

The Irish School of Ecumenics

Volume 1

LIT

Ecumenics from the Rim

Explorations in
Honour of John D'Arcy May

edited by

John O'Grady and Peter Scherle

LIT

Gedruckt auf alterungsbeständigem Werkdruckpapier entsprechend
ANSI Z3948   DIN ISO 9706

Cover Picture: 'Blue Marble' – Earth View, from NASA's Earth Observatory
(NASA Goddard Space Flight Center)

Bibliographic information published by the Deutsche Nationalbibliothek
The Deutsche Nationalbibliothek lists this publication in the Deutsche
Nationalbibliografie; detailed bibliographic data are available in the Internet at
http://dnb.d-nb.de.

ISBN 978-3-8258-0637-8

A catalogue record for this book is available from the British Library

© LIT VERLAG Dr. W. Hopf Berlin 2007
Auslieferung/Verlagskontakt:
Fresnostr. 2   48159 Münster
Tel. +49 (0)251–62 03 20   Fax +49 (0)251–23 19 72
e-Mail: lit@lit-verlag.de   http://www.lit-verlag.de

Distributed in the UK by: Global Book Marketing, 99B Wallis Rd, London, E9 5LN
Phone: +44 (0) 20 8533 5800 – Fax: +44 (0) 1600 775 663
http://www.centralbooks.co.uk/acatalog/search.html

Distributed in North America by:

Transaction Publishers
New Brunswick (U.S.A.) and London (U.K.)

Transaction Publishers
Rutgers University
35 Berrue Circle
Piscataway, NJ 08854

Phone: +1 (732) 445 - 2280
Fax: + 1 (732) 445 - 3138
for orders (U. S. only):
toll free (888) 999 - 6778
e-mail:
orders@transactionspub.com

Table of Contents

Acknowledgements ix
Preface xi

Part 1 Ecumenics – Introduction

John O'Grady and Peter Scherle
Ecumenics in the 21st Century 3

Part 2 Christian Theology as Ecumenics

Ann Aldén
The Christian Church – Focal Point for Identity and Experience 23

Ursula Baatz
Anthropology of Spirituality 29

François Bousquet
An Open Christology: Kierkegaard for Interreligious Dialogue 37

Gabriel Daly OSA and Andrew Pierce
Christian Theology, Imagination and 'Religious Fundamentalism' 43

Alan D. Falconer
The Holy Trinity: A Living Reality, Linked to Our Human Existence 53

Antje Fetzer
The Concept of 'Service' from a Diaconal and Theological Viewpoint 61

Robert Gascoigne
Christian Identity and Social Commitment 71

Norman C. Habel
The Beginning of Violence: An Ecological Reading of Genesis 4 79

Cathy Higgins and Johnston McMaster
Towards a Life-Giving Ethic 87

Maureen Junker-Kenny
Out of Their Depth: Cultural Conquest, Debt and Renewal 95

Hedwig Meyer-Wilmes
Transformations of Spirituality in a Post-Modern Culture 103

Paul O'Grady
Two Dogmas and Empiricism 111

Joseph S. O'Leary
Forgiveness 119

Aloysius Pieris
Vatican II: Glimpses into Six Centuries of its Prehistory 127

John Robinson
Is There a Future for the Anonymous Christian? 137

Simone Sinn
Human Dignity and Remembrance 143

Geraldine Smyth OP and Lesley Carroll
Wisdom to Know the Difference 151

Eugene Stockton
Truth of God 169

Garry Trompf
Of Colligation and Reification in the Representation of Religion 179

Martin Wilson MSC
Gsell Centenary: Missiological Reflections 187

Part 3 Interreligious Relations as Ecumenics

Raquel Bouso García
Emptiness as Compassion 197

Terry Duffy
Transcending Violence and Constructing Memory 205

Georg Evers
Personal Reflections on Mysticism in Christianity and Buddhism 215

Frank Fletcher MSC
The Long Rejection yet Survival of the Koorie People 221

Kieran Flynn
At the Heart of Islam 229

Gideon Goosen
Towards a Theory of Dual Religious Belonging 237

Paul F. Knitter
'What's Next? — What's Now?' The 'Now' is the 'Next' 247

Brendan Leahy
Between Logos and Nothingness 253

Karl-Wilhelm Merks
Wie viel Glauben hat die Moral nötig? 261

Gerry O'Hanlon
Muslims in the Free Society 271

Martin Rötting
Christian Process and Buddhist Reference? 279

Joseph Salihu
Uniqueness and Interreligious Dialogue in Northern Nigeria 287

Jacques Scheuer
The Buddha's Entering into *Nirvāna* and the Death of Christ 295

Perry Schmidt-Leukel
Uniqueness: A Pluralistic Reading of John 14:6 303

Parichart Suwanbubbha
Speaking of Mary from a Buddhist Perspective 311

David Thomas
The Trinity in Christian-Muslim Relations 317

Abraham Vélez de Cea
Interreligious Dialogue through Comparative Studies 325

Carolina Weening
D.T. Suzuki – From *Genesis* to Jesus 335

Part 4 Peace Studies as Ecumenics

Theodor Ahrens
Reconciliation – Leitmotif of Christian Mission 345

Iain Atack
NGOs as Agents of Cosmopolitan Values or Parochial Interests 353

Thomas Bremer
Peace-Building in the Balkans – Do the Churches Contribute? 363

Jude Lal Fernando
God of Plentitude and Meditation on Conscience 369

Gladys Ganiel
Religious Dissent and Reconciliation in Northern Ireland 379

Elizabeth J. Harris
Transforming Conflict: Can Religion Help? 387

Gerhard Köberlin
Coming Home: The Place of the Other in Religious Peace Work 395

Kristin Kwasniewski
Developing a Muslim Modernity 403

Aasulv Lande
Dialogue, for Heaven's sake 411

Fiachra Long
The Challenge of Tactility 419

David R. Loy
The Attention-Deficit Society 427

Bill McSweeney
In Praise of Fuzzy Boundaries 435

Eda Sagarra
Dumb Believers and Clever Jesuits 441

Sulak Sivaraksa
No River Bigger Than *Tanha* 451

Jørgen Skov Sørensen
Modernity, Diversity and Coexistence in Contemporary Society 459

David Stevens
Look if You Like But You Will Have to Leap 467

Part 5 John D'Arcy May and Ecumenics

Heinz-Günther Stobbe
Between Melancholy and Anger – Looking Back on Common Days 475

Robyn Reynolds
Australian Accent 479

Published Work by John D'Arcy May 481

Contributors' Biographies 493

Acknowledgements

John D'Arcy May DTh DPhil FTCD and Associate Professor of Interfaith Dialogue is retiring this year from the Irish School of Ecumenics, Trinity College Dublin. It has been our privilege and pleasure to work with many scholars and practitioners in composing this Festschrift in John's honour. He has been and will continue to be our friend and mentor.

We hope that the essays herein will contribute to the ongoing debate about and development of the field of ecumenics. The reader will quickly see that John himself has contributed greatly to the field and its development…and he is not finished yet! Serendipitous connections between some of the essays here may inspire him to critical and nuanced tilling of old ground and to fresh thoughts and new avenues for exploration.

We wish to thank the many people whose help has been invaluable. The contributors in the first place; they – all busy and over-committed – willingly gave their energies to this enterprise. They have opened a dialogue amongst themselves, one that will grow, blossom and ripen in the years to come.

Our typesetter, Martine Maguire-Weltecke, has dealt with John O'Grady's manias and lapses with equanimity and unswerving purpose. All her efforts were then added to warmly by Dr Michael Rainer and Frank Weber of LIT Verlag. Earlier on, though, others, like Seán O'Boyle, gave us much of their time and helpful advice.

The money to finance this venture was provided by the Trust of the Irish School of Ecumenics. Fr John Dardis SJ as President of the Trustees and Henry Saville as Chair of the Steering Committee have whole-heartedly supported us. This publication is yet one more testimony to their and the Trust's commitment to the work of ecumenism and the publication of worthwhile contributions to research and teaching.

Professor of Ecumenics and Head of School, Linda Hogan, graciously prefaced this text. Not surprisingly, when extra hands were needed on deck to help with proofreading or counsel, it was to Linda's fellow staff that we could always turn, especially, Andrew Pierce and Geraldine Smyth. Behind the obvious structures of ISE, there are many who should also be recalled; in particular, the Jesuits, who, Provincial after Provincial to member after member, have supported ISE in good times and bad; they have been committed to ISE because they have first been committed to an ecumenical vision of the world. It was one such, Fr Michael Hurley SJ, now in less than leisurely retirement, who founded ISE in 1970.

Dr Martin Mansergh TD, one of Ireland's keenest intellectuals, readily agreed to spend his holidays reading this text in advance of his launching of the Festschrift.

If, as they say, there is a man in front of every woman, we have preferred the less controversial 'behind every (good) man there is a (better) woman'. In this, John May is luckier than most for he has two women: Margret, John's partner in life, and their daughter Katrin. It is thanks to Margret's happy scheming, practical assistance and willing advice at crucial moments that we were able to accomplish our aim.

To all, our sincere thanks,

The Editors

Preface

Although John D'Arcy May had a significant academic career before he arrived at the Irish School of Ecumenics in 1987, his critical role in defining the contours of the field of ecumenics has been associated with his work here. Indeed, he has had a considerable impact on the manner in which the School has defined the subject and constructed its curriculum. Also, as colleagues in the field will attest, John has been to the front in the debates about how best to capture the fundamental nature of ecumenics so that its inter-denominational, interreligious and socio-political dimensions are understood.

As the editors of this volume indicate, and as the contributors to this *Festschrift* illustrate, John had, by 1982, already begun to challenge the conventional understanding of the field of ecumenics and he was one of a number of scholars who were to the fore in developing the discipline in new directions, taking the study of ecumenics into the domains of interreligious and ethical analysis. Twenty years on, one can see that John's academic work in the ISE and beyond has been fundamental to the way in which the concept of ecumenics has been reframed. Thus, we now conceptualize the field in terms of an intellectual paradigm rather than in terms of a discrete discipline. Moreover, the essence of this paradigm is that it places the encounters between distinctive religious, cultural and social worlds centre-stage, it reflects on the implications of these encounters for their respective identities and it promotes modes of engagement that are reconciling rather than conflictual. Whereas traditionally the *oikoumene* of ecumenics had been understood in terms of the encounters between Christian denominations, ecumenics in this new mode is concerned not only with the unity of Christians but also with interreligious understanding and with international peace and reconciliation. This characterization of the field restores to ecumenics the full and proper meaning of the *oikos* – originally, the household – that is at the heart of *oikoumene*, the one inhabited earth.

That so many scholars of repute have contributed to this *Festschrift* is itself a testament to the international significance of John's research. Furthermore, in Ireland too John has been a pioneer. Long before Ireland became a multi-religious society John was preparing the ground, educating generations of students in interreligious understanding and raising questions that today have social and political significance.

As an academic, and as a former Director of the ISE, John has provided dynamic leadership in the School. He has been a creative, thoughtful and generous colleague and a loyal and supportive friend. His commitment to his students is unsurpassed and his personal dedication to the vision and mission of the School is long acknowledged and appreciated. He has been a corner-stone of the academic life of the School for two decades. As John marks his sixty-fifth birthday and enters a new phase in his life we are glad of this opportunity to celebrate his achievements thus far and we look forward to savouring the gifts of his scholarship and friendship for many years to come.

Linda Hogan

Part 1

Ecumenics – Introduction

John O'Grady and Peter Scherle

Ecumenics in the 21st Century
Plumbing the relationships of theology, interreligious dialogue and peace studies

> *Only life has a way out*
> *And the human soul is fated to wide-eyed responsibility*
> *In life.*
>
> D.H. Lawrence

An Etymological Introduction

A central metaphor for our developing understanding of what ecumenics is about is taken from the mundane world of household piping. One of the earliest materials used in piping was the ductile metal, lead, which in Latin is *plumbum*. Hence such terms as plumbing and plumb-line. Here, we are concerned mainly with the verb *to plumb*, which enjoins notions of measuring (of water's depth), exploring fully (the depths of one's feelings), and assessing accuracy (of the vertical). Perhaps now is a good time to take the measure of this field of studies and branch of knowledge that we call ecumenics and see where it leads us.

John May and Ecumenics

In 1980 the Australian research fellow John May contributed to the book *Ecumenical Theology*, edited by his German professor Peter Lengsfeld, the director of the Roman-Catholic Ecumenical Institute at the University of Münster.[1] John D'Arcy May contributed three articles which in their interrelatedness from today's perspective can be seen as an agenda for the years to come. Even more – and this demonstrates how much John created research questions in the field himself – they can be taken as an outline of the field of ecumenical studies that as such becomes a starting point for ecumenics in the 21st century.

In the first of his articles John tackled the issue of 'racism as a test case of ecumenical communication' focusing on the problem of 'language as a means of unity and of dispute'.[2] The second article, written together with his friend Heinz-Günther Stobbe, focused on the 'foundations of ecumenical consensus-building and the search for truth' trying to work out the possibilities of 'agreement and capability for action'.[3] These two articles reflected the doctoral work John had done and published on 'Language of Ecumenism – Language of Unity' (1976) trying to work out the basis of a theological ethic.[4]

---

1 Peter Lengsfeld (ed.), *Ökumenische Theologie. Ein Arbeitsbuch*, Stuttgart, Kohlhammer, 1980.
2 John May, 'Sprache der Einheit – Sprache der Zwietracht. Der Rassismus als Testfall ökumenischer Kommunikation', in Lengsfeld, *Ökumenische Theologie*: 251-284.
3 Heinz-Günther Stobbe and John May, 'Übereinstimmung und Handlungsfähigkeit. Zur Grundlage ökumenischer Konsensbildung und Wahrheitsfindung', in Lengsfeld, *Ökumenische Theologie*: 301-337.
4 John May, *Sprache der Ökumene – Sprache der Einheit. Die Einheit der Menschheit: Zukünftige Grundlage der ökumenischen Ethik der Katholischen Kirche und des Ökumenischen Rates der Kirchen*, Bonn, Verlag Linguistica Biblica, 1976.

The third article, 'From inner-Christian to interreligious dialogue',[5] reflected the research area John had moved into in these years, viz., the 'wider ecumenism' of interreligious relations, especially the focus on Christian-Buddhist encounter.[6] First hints are detectable of interest in 'primal religions' as a reference point for understanding the so-called world religions, their identity, their social reality and their interaction.

In these articles John had covered all aspects of the ecumenical approach he later encountered in the Irish School of Ecumenics[7] of which he became director in 1987. By then he was a renowned expert in the area of *inner-Christian communication and conflict*, especially in relation to hermeneutics and the conditions of the possibility of church unity. He also had established himself in the field of *interreligious studies*, especially focusing on the Pacific[8] and on the 'encounter of Buddhist, Christian and Primal traditions'.[9] His interest in matters ethical, as documented in the article tackling the issue of racism, covered both the whole area of *peace studies*, especially the interrelatedness of religion and conflict,[10] and research into the possibility of an 'interreligious ethic'.[11] Since the late 1980s the way in which these three areas are part of 'ecumenics' was a matter of dispute, a dispute that reflects the dynamics of our social, religious and ecclesial realities. Ecumenics could best be described as a meta-reflection on all the aspects of human life on planet earth with the aim of enhancing all life on earth. Ecumenics, therefore, is reflection on the inter-cultural, interreligious and inner-religious construction of world-views and their social impact in service of the flourishing of life.[12] This indicates that we will have to plumb new ways in which to describe the study of ecumenics, identify respective research areas and point out what relevance that might have for the emerging world society.

We do not claim to encapsulate or gauge fully the rich depths of John's research and insights in just a few pages.[13] We want, rather, to take his work as an exploratory *sketching of the study that is ecumenics*: ecclesial communities and their interrelations, the Christian encounter with other religions and its own forms of primal religiosity (popular religion), the social, cultural and political realities of which Christians and Christian churches are part and parcel. John May's work is significant and can guide us into the next phase of ecumenics. Here we are already faced with the fact that ecumenics, though a meta-reflection, is always aware of presupposed religious world-views and political commitments that it must both take seriously and deconstruct at the same time. We also

---

5 John May, 'Vom innerchristlichen zum interreligiösen Dialog', in Lengsfeld, *Ökumenische Theologie*: 419-432.
6 John D'Arcy May, *Meaning, Consensus and Dialogue in Buddhist-Christian Communication: A Study in the Construction of Meaning*, Berne, Frankfurt/Main, Nancy and New York, Peter Lang, 1984.
7 For an account of the early history of the School, see Michael Hurley SJ, *Christian Unity: An Ecumenical Second Spring?*, Dublin, Veritas, 1998, especially 265-291; Hurley was the founder of ISE, in Dublin in 1970.
8 John D'Arcy May, *Christus Initiator. Theologie im Pazifik*, Düsseldorf, Patmos, 1991.
9 John D'Arcy May, *Transcendence and Violence: The Encounter of Buddhist, Christian and Primal Traditions*, New York and London, Continuum, 2003.
10 John D'Arcy May (ed.), *Pluralism and the Religions: The Theological and Political Dimensions*, London and Herndon VA, Cassell, 1998.
11 John D'Arcy May, *After Pluralism: Towards an Interreligious Ethic*, Münster, Hamburg and London, LIT, 2000.
12 See Raimon Panikkar's notion of intra-religious dialogue, in his *The Intrareligious Dialogue*, New York and Mahwah, Paulist, 1999^2.
13 A list of his publications is given at the end of this volume.

take John's work as exploring and assessing *theories that can be applied to the study of ecumenics*, especially the conditions of the possibility of mutual understanding through language and the encounter with the (primal) other. Finally, we want at least to appreciate, if unable to measure fully, the *efforts to validate these theoretical approaches to the study of ecumenics through research,* as John has done so masterfully and with aplomb in his latest book *Transcendence and Violence* (2003).

Sketching the Study of Ecumenics

In sketching the study of ecumenics one has to take account of *a new perception of the interrelatedness of ecumenical, interreligious and peace studies*. Although the Greek term *oikoumene* always had the potential to mean the whole inhabited world, it took the modern ecumenical movement from the beginning to the latter half of the 20th century to put this meaning at the heart of the ecumenical enterprise. Christians were responding to the different crises of western Christian civilization – two world wars, colonialism, the Shoah, etc. – while trying to renew Christianity by re-envisioning the churches mission (encountering other major religions in the East and experiencing secularization in the West), striving for church unity by working on the issues of faith and order (struggling with doctrinal and non-doctrinal factors of church-division) and re-defining the churches' place in the modern world (trying to demonstrate their relevance for the 'unity of humankind' and their transformative quality in civil society). The ecclesial context of the social phenomenon of 'ecumenism' and of the academic 'ecumenical studies' can still be seen in the term 'wider ecumenism' that tried to incorporate the relations to people of other 'living faiths and ideologies'. In the same way the earlier approach to peace and conflict studies was in fact Church-centred and had to be revised in the light of a more complex analysis of the role of religion in the social sphere, though one must also challenge tendencies to ignore the religious dimension as such.

It is in the light of this history that we have to develop a new understanding of the study of ecumenics and a useful academic approach. Thus, in the context of ecumenical, interreligious and peace studies it is first of all necessary *to question the hidden assumption of the churches, religions and societies as distinct realities, which may or may not interact.* The social reality we live in cannot be divided. Society consists (though, not only) of religion. Religion is a social reality. Christian churches, for example, are result from inter-Christian, interreligious and intercultural communication and conflict. Even fundamental religious convictions, canonical texts, rituals and symbols, forms of piety and ways of living are informed by an ongoing encounter. The way in which churches are developing on the other hand is inseparable from the transformations of societies.

Ecumenics, the reflection on the interaction of all these factors, is 'more' than ecumenical, interreligious or peace studies, though it shares their field-orientation and interdisciplinary character. Its focus, however, on the dynamic of real encounter and on the social construction as well as the social effects of religious world-views, invites a unique way of relating inside and outside perspectives. It needs to be familiar with and take seriously the respective 'theologies' and at the same time be a 'social theory'.

Theology and Religion

The difficulty with the terms 'religion' and 'theology' is that they both emerged from a Christian cultural and philosophical background. However, if we understand *'religion' as a form of communication of human beings, in which a specific coherent meaning of the world as a whole is expressed through speech, acts and artefacts,*[14] *and which assumes the participation of a divine reality in this human communication*, we can perceive Christianity as a religion amongst other religions. Theology or its equivalents, then, is a certain way of reflecting that takes place within religion where language and a canon of sacred scriptures have become the central medium by which the divine message can be perceived. *Theology is rooted in a religious community and is a critical self-reflection on the way in which communication of the divine takes place within religious communication.* Theology, reflecting on God talking within human God-talk, seeks to offer, as it were, a vertical dimension that keeps the horizontal true. It is a form of human wisdom and, so, can take place in the academic sphere applying modern sciences to critically reflect on our human God-talk. However, as theology, it is more than historical, philosophical or empirical research, since it is done in the interest of a present communication of the divine in the service of faith.

Theology cannot be determined by relating it to the functional sphere of religion or by trying to transform it into a cultural theory of a religion. It is always related to the praxis of a specific religion and reflects from the respective normative perspective (self-communication of the divine) on the life-world. Let's take Christian theology: theology is dependent on Christian life and the communication of the Gospel, not on its place at university, its status as an academic discipline or its acceptance in society.[15] In all its historical, systematic, critical and practical academic disciplines it is a praxis-theory that reflects in a coherent way on the ways in which Gospel and culture interact. By taking the trans-cultural, in-cultural (contextual), counter-cultural and cross-cultural dimensions of that interaction seriously[16] it withstands the fundamentalist and culturalist temptation. Christian theology is reflection *coram Deo* in which an ongoing process of interpretation of human experiences takes place. It interprets the interpretations of interpretations and follows certain rules by relating its reflection back to the normative horizons of interpretation: the biblical canon and the Christian creed.[17] Therefore, it is a Christian interpretation of Christian interpretations of the Christian faith. Faith itself is commun-

---

14 Here we follow Fritz Stolz, *Grundzüge der Religionswissenschaft*, Göttingen, Vandenhoeck & Ruprecht, 1997²: 101-113; he responds to Plutarch's distinction between 'legomena', 'dromena' and 'deiknymena'.

15 See Ingolf U. Dalferth, *Evangelische Theologie als Interpretationspraxis. Eine systematische Orientierung*, Leipzig, Evangelische Verlagsanstalt, 2004: 52. For the debate on the nature and organisation of Christian theology, see also B.G. Wheeler and E. Farley (eds.), *Shifting Boundaries: Contextual Approaches to the Structure of Theological Education*, Louisville, Westminster/John Knox, 1991; Bernard J.F. Lonergan, *Method in Theology*, Minneapolis, Seabury, [1972] 1979; David Tracy, *Blessed Rage for Order: The New Pluralism for Theology*, Chicago, University of Chicago, 1975; Gerhard Ebeling, *Studium der Theologie. Eine enzyklopädische Orientierung*, Tübingen, Mohr, 1975; Charles M. Wood, *Vision and Discernment: An Orientation in Theological Study*, Atlanta, Scholars, 1985; Edward Farley, *Theologia: The Fragmentation and Unity of Theological Education*, Philadelphia, Fortress, 1989²; J. Astley, L. J. Francis and C. Crowder (eds.), *Theological Perspectives on Christian Formation: A Reader on Theology and Christian Education*, Grand Rapids, Eerdsman, 1996.

16 For this fourfold dynamic, see 'Nairobi Statement on Worship and Culture: Contemporary Challenges and Opportunities', in S. Anita Stauffer (ed.), *Christian Worship: Unity in Cultural Diversity*, Geneva, Lutheran World Federation, 1996: 23-28.

17 The Gospel is the (pragmatic-effective) power of God that transforms human lives and all creation and not a (semantically fixed) doctrine or deposit of faith, see Dalferth, *Evangelische Theologie*: 117. What we consider to be the Gospel for us today therefore has to be discovered. It may, in fact, be revealed especially in dialogue with people who believe and live differently.

icated through a variety of media (from speech to printed media to the internet) and cultural practices that – from a theological perspective – are used by God to mediate Godself. Since the self-communication of God takes place (sacramentally) 'in, with and under' human cultural practices, theology has to use all academic disciplines that reflect on such cultural practices (history, sociology, language theory, etc.) and yet respond to the presence of the divine in these practices today, in order to enhance understanding. The aim of theology is not to generate faith; rather, it is faith that seeks understanding in service of understanding the way in which faith emerges.

As a result Christian theology has created a plurality of perspectives, organized in different academic disciplines with respective methods taken from and shared with neighbouring (secular) faculties. The temptation of theology in the modern university is twofold: on the one hand, it could be locked into its Christian 'God-talk' and become irrelevant, and, on the other, just melt into the other faculties and become superfluous. Therefore, it has to be seen as an academic discipline *coram mundo* in the public sphere of the university (with its rules, research- and teaching-standards) and at the same time be a coherent multi-disciplinary reflection in the public *coram deo*.[18] Theology operates then, with two perspectives at the same time: the (formal-)academic and the (material-)theological.[19] The combination of both distinguishes theology from other academic disciplines and modes of reflection. Thus, Christian theology cannot only be an explication of the Christian faith and it cannot be reduced to empirical-historical religious studies.

Theology and Interreligious Relations[20]

On this basis efforts to develop a 'pluralist theology of religions'[21] are faced with a major problem. If we perceive this formula to be a *genetivus objectivus* then it would assume that the respective theology use the perspective of a certain religion. As *genetivus subjectivus*, however, it would claim a theology that is able to free itself from a determined religious perspective. The problem arises because the three fundamental positions exhibited in the discussion – exclusivism, inclusivism and pluralism[22] – operate on different levels. Whereas 'exclusivism' and 'inclusivism' are mainly understood as *genetivus objectivus*, 'pluralism' is defined as *genetivus subjectivus*. Yet, the claim to do theology above and beyond particular religious communities and commitments can itself be both exclusivist, in its claim to present a perspective by which the truth of religions can be judged, and inclusivist, in its claim to embrace all religious approaches to this truth. Such a pluralist theology of religions in fact ignores its dependence on a religious community on the one hand and the impossibility to judge a religion from outside

---

18 The concept of the three publics (church, university, society) by David Tracy does not emphasize enough the double perspectivity of Christian theology, see Dalferth, *Evangelische Theologie*: 134.
19 See Dalferth, *Evangelische Theologie*: 137 and 180.
20 In this section we follow and critically discuss the argument put forward by Andreas Feldtkeller, *Theologie und Religion. Eine Wissenschaft in ihrem Sinnzusammenhang*, Leipzig, Evangelische Verlagsanstalt, 2002.
21 See the discussion in Gavin D'Costa (ed.), *Christian Uniqueness Reconsidered: The Myth of a Pluralistic Theology of Religions*, Maryknoll, Orbis, 1990.
22 Perry Schmidt-Leukel, 'Zur Klassifikation religionstheologischer Modelle', in *Catholica* 47 (1993): 163-183; he discusses this threefold scheme that can be traced back to lectures given in Oxford in 1936 by the Indian philosopher Sarpavelli Radhakrishnan, see the latter's, *Eastern Religions and Western Thought*, London, OUP, 1940^2: 341-348) and adapted for a Christian theology of religions by Alan Race, *Christians and Religious Pluralism: Patterns in the Christian Theology of Religions*, London, SCM, 1983.

such religious communities on the other.²³ Therefore, *a theology of religions, or better, of interreligious relations, requires a distinction between the theological reflection from within its own religion and reflections on the observation of other religions from the outside.*

However, the task is even more complex: it is carried out by theologians who consider the dominance of language and scripture as constitutive for religion, even as they deal with forms of religion, which we call primal or primary, because they belong to a fundamental level of human religiosity. *This 'primary religion'*²⁴ *cannot only be perceived in primal religion but is also an ongoing part of the scripture-based religions.* Human 'communities of origin' are the basic form of a religious community. Based on the sequence of generations, the ordering of time and space and the presence of the divine enacted in ritual and symbolic expressions this primary religiosity focuses on the good life of the community and is fundamentally about 'being whole in community'. Without being rooted in this primary religion no religion could survive.

On the other hand, a religion would not become dynamic enough to stretch beyond these communities of origin if it would not have developed a 'secondary religiosity', triggered by religious founders who opened up a new understanding of the '*vera religio*' in times of crisis when the very existence of the community of origin was endangered (e.g., by natural disasters, wars, fundamental social change). This 'secondary religion' generated a scriptural communicative memory, hermeneutic rules and concepts of truth, and it tried to attract individuals to this notion of truth and specific ways of life. Religion is no longer just handed on within a community of origin. It is spread out and its 'missionaries' try to make converts who then have to make sense of the truth that is presented to them.²⁵

Secondary religion is critical about aspects of the primary religion. This *innerreligious critique of religion* focuses on images and representations of the divine, religious practices, the way in which the world and inner-worldly life are seen, and the limitation to a community of origin. In all religions this theological critique of religion itself takes on determinate forms.

These forms bind some religions to one other if their mutual development has been a 'parting of the ways'. *This is the case for Christianity in relation to Judaism and for Islam in relation to Christianity (and Judaism); a conflictual definition of the respective identities has been engraved into the canonical scriptures.* To avoid spiritual arguments for generating violence a self-critique of one's own religious tradition has to plumb the depths of violence perpetrated against other religions (this is necessary in relation to Christian claims of replacing Israel by the Church as the people of God). Also, the external critique of one's own religious tradition should be incorporated in such a way that it helps one rephrase one's own theological considerations so that they become more meaningful for today's world (this is necessary in relation to Islamic criticism of the fundamental trinitarian and christological considerations).

---

23 See Theo Sundermeier, 'Evangelisation und die Wahrheit der Religionen', in Reinhold Bernhardt (ed.), *Horizontüberschreitung. Die pluralistische Theologie der Religionen*, Gütersloh, Gütersloher Verlagshaus Gerd Mohn, 1991: 175-190.

24 Here we follow Theo Sundermeier, *Was ist Religion? Religionswissenschaft im theologischen Kontext. Ein Studienbuch*, Gütersloh, Gütersloher Verlagshaus Gerd Mohn, 1999: 34-42.

25 John May tells of a colleague in Papua New Guinea who offered this test of successful inculturation: 'The best sign of inculturation is that the missionary won't like it', see John D'Arcy May, 'Visible Unity as Realised Catholicity', in *SMT* [Swedish Missiological Trends] 92,1 (2004): 55-61: 55.

In relation to other religions these forms of inner-religious critique can also be activated. Interreligious relations, then, may be determined in Christianity by identifying them either as paganism, as a mistaken, enforced way of life, or as heresy. Similar mechanisms are operative in other religions. In any case, this way of determining relations does not allow for valid theological interpretations of other religions. *What is needed is a comparison of the ways in which the respective religions exercise religious critique of their own primary religion.* Christian theology could then understand the Islamic perspective as familiar: for instance, Islam is radical in its insistence on the unity and transcendence of God as well as in separating the religious calendar of festivals from the natural cycle of the year; and it is less critical in making religion normative for the sphere of politics and the way of life of individuals. Similar considerations can be made in relation to Hinduism (less critical about the divinization of inner-worldly realities) or Buddhism (more radical than any form of inner-worldly primary religion and less critical in relation to the way of life of the non-enlightened).

Christian theology is not only bound to specific religious communities, it is also academic in its character. It has inherited this connection between religion and science: in the ancient world Jewish, Christian and Muslim religious learning also encompassed the ancient sciences and out of these the idea of the 'university' emerged and became institutionalized in Europe. In medieval universities theology was the mother of the sciences, the first faculty on which the other faculties were modelled. In time, the initial conflict between theology and the early modern sciences was a conflict within the framework of Christendom, a conflict between the authority of an ecclesial theology (related to the ecclesial *magisterium*) and of the emerging university theology (with its own academic standards).

Protestant university theology can be seen, then, as part of the emancipation of all sciences from the claims of the Roman Catholic religious authority. This may explain to some extent why Protestant theology saw itself as part of the academic community and lost contact with its own religious grounding. The importance of continental European Protestant theology around the turn of the 20th century is very much related to a biblical scholarship with its historical-critical approach based on the assumptions of a European rationalism that was not aware of its own cultural and ideological perspective. Similarly, it denied the social and communicative aspect of religion, in which the divine reality is involved, by defining it as a reality of the inner psyche reachable, not through religious media (speech, acts, artefacts), but by the immediate 'word of God'.

Today's reflections on the nature of science have opened up the possibility of redefining theology as an academic discipline. Only approaches that are aware of the fact that they use certain perspectives, that they are self-referential[26] and need a second-order observation of their own discipline, can be seen as academic. *Theology* in this respect is not different from physics. However, *its unique and specific contribution to the modern university lies in its relation to the all-embracing meaning given to the world by religion.* Human reason and academic-scientific work are always rooted in and dependent on fundamental assumptions about the meaningfulness of the natural world, states of 'normality', underlying 'laws', etc. They remain embedded in cultural and religious point of views. For instance, theology would be mistaken were it to read its own scriptures as revelations and codifications of scientific insights; the canonical scriptures

---

[26] See Niklas Luhmann, *Social Systems*, translated by John Bednarz, Jn., with Dirk Baeker, Foreword by Eva M. Knodt, Stanford, Stanford University, 1995: 32-38.

reflect the state of science at the time. Yet, theology, as an academic discipline that reflects its own religious affiliation, is necessary for any scientific deliberation that would render an account of the plurality of horizons of meaning.

This may indeed still justify theology as the first faculty of the modern university. *Certainly, theology cannot be replaced by religious studies in this respect.* Indeed, religious studies itself is highly dependent on such theological perspectives. The challenge today is better described as that of the plurality of theological perspectives and their different religious backgrounds. Thus, developing theological faculties in which chairs, say, of Jewish, Islamic or Buddhist 'theology', would be established beside chairs in Christian theology may well become necessary.[27] Students of diverse religious affiliations would be then challenged to develop 'their' theology in relation to theological questions raised from outside their theological system. It is easy to see how enriching this could be – if, of course, it is seen as an academic challenge, and not a missionary contest.

(Meta-)Theories for research

This requires us to understand *'ecumenics' as a theory of processes of dynamic interrelations, of communications and conflicts* that are taking place within Christianity and between churches, between and within religions as well as within the emerging and ruptured world society. John May's contributions in the articles mentioned were truly part of an effort to develop a 'collusion theory', that identified 'truth', the 'social being' and the 'identity' of churches as three factors which were tackled in 'dialogue' (e.g., the bi- and multilateral talks on doctrinal issues like baptism, Eucharist or justification), 'cooperation' (e.g., agencies centred on common ethical concerns) and 'transformations' of identity (that were taking place in encounters and unification processes). Unfortunately, this theory and the research on collusions and collisions of the three factors in the 'narrow' ecumenical field of inner-Christian relations has not been taken up in the past two decades or developed further.

This is but one indicator of the lack of coherent views of the study of ecumenics. There is a great variety of approaches available drawing on a wide range of theories from many different academic disciplines that have informed ecumenical, interreligious and peace studies. Nevertheless, the *work on meta-theories that hold the study of ecumenics together* has not been pushed ahead to the extent that 'ecumenics' is seen as a coherent, valuable and necessary academic enterprise. The following three theoretical approaches, given their respective strengths, may indicate possible directions for sounding out such a (meta-)theoretical basis for ecumenics.[28]

First, from the theories applied to the 'narrow' field of inner-Christian relations, i.e., ecumenical studies, the *market theory* that was first put forward in 1963 by Peter Berger deserves mention.[29] He observed that ecumenical convergence was somehow connected

---

27 This is presently done in the university of Frankfurt on the Main. An earlier (temporary) chair of Jewish studies within the Protestant (Evangelische) faculty of theology had already existed for some time. The establishment of two chairs of Islamic studies, funded by the Turkish state-related religious authorities, in the same department of theology has raised a major controversy in relation to the status of theological faculties in German universities.
28 These three models have been outlined by Friedrich Wilhelm Graf in his *Die Wiederkehr der Götter. Religion in der modernen Kultur*, München, C.H. Beck, 2004^2: 14ff.
29 Peter Berger, 'A Market Model for the Analysis of Ecumenicity', in *Social Research* 30 (1963): 77-93.

with the (re-)invention of confessional identities. His micro-sociological research on Protestant 'main line churches' led him to propose a macro-sociological model, which perceived the churches 'as economic units which are engaging in competition within a free market' (79). Cooperation served to reduce costs and to improve services, but it also required 'marginal differentiation'. Competition raised quality and so on. Berger's approach contributed to the development of a 'religious economics', especially in the context of the neo-liberal Chicago school of economics. 'Rational choice theory' was also used to explain the 'rise of Christianity',[30] as was 'winners and losers'[31] in the religious economy of the United States. The market-metaphor, especially with North American sociologists of religion, is considered useful for describing the religious field: churches exchange 'symbolic capital' and 'sell God'.[32] This outside perspective on religion seems to explain some of the dynamics in situations of religious pluralism and takes religious organizations seriously as social agents. It also explains the 'success' of aggressive forms of 'God selling' and of strict forms over against liberal forms of religion and their open interpretation of fundamental truths. Nevertheless, it seems too narrow to be useful for the study of ecumenics precisely because it lacks the necessary complexity in relation to the social, especially the inter-cultural and interreligious, construction of religion. Similarly, the way in which the relations between religious organizations are seen as a market phenomenon seems too reductive.

Another theoretical approach – let's call it the *shared history theory* – can be detected in those efforts that understand religions and religious organizations as establishing a collective memory, which informs world-views, ways of life, moral attitudes and practical behaviour and which develops in a history shared with other faith-communities.[33] Religious discourse is hybrid. Religious rituals and symbols, their canonical texts and interpretative cultures create insiders and outsiders. This social dynamic of inclusion and exclusion is a way of determining relations between religions and responds to the process of modernization: it redefines the respective religion, its role in society, its visions of political structures and of the modern world.[34] This approach has proved very useful in analysing conflict-situations with a 'tribal' dimension (i.e., where religion cannot be separated from other factors of a group-identity) and their possible transformation. It also explains, why the (re-)invention of religious identities takes place in the process of modernization, part of which was the process of inner-denominational differentiation (e.g., the High and Low Church in Anglicanism; the orthodox, conservative and reform movements in Judaism) as well as the emergence of comparative confessional studies and the construction of (essentialist) confessional principles.[35] It even allows for a theory of fundamentalism as a modern

---

30 Rodney Stark, *The Rise of Christianity: A Sociologist Reconsiders History*, Princeton, Princeton University, 1996.
31 Roger Finke and Rodney Stark, *The Churching of America 1776- 1990: Winners and Losers in our Religious Economy*, New Brunswick NJ, Rutgers University, 1992.
32 See, e.g., Robert Laurence Moore, *Selling God: American Religion in the Market-Place of Culture*, Oxford and New York, OUP, 1994; Laurence R. Iannaccone, 'Religious Markets and the Economics of Religion', in *Social Compass* 39 (1992): 123-131; and, 'Introduction to the Economics of Religion', in *Journal of Economic Literature* 36 (1998): 1465-1495.
33 See Graf, *Die Wiederkehr der Götter*: 30ff.
34 The formation of Irish confessional and national identities is a well-researched example.
35 One could claim the (re-)invention of Judaism as a 'monotheist' religion and the (re-)invention of a 'non-Jewish' Christianity are mutually connected ways of identity formation. The 'other' religion thereby is engraved into one's own identity, see Shmuel Feiner, *Haskalah and History:*

form of religion that shares the absolutist claims of modernity and is anti-traditional in religious terms, because the re-invented tradition disrupts the pluralist diversity of the interpretative religious cultures.[36] This theory of a shared history analyses the ecumenical and interreligious field and explains the paradoxical interrelationship of osmotic and delineating strategies, of communication and conflict about symbolic resources and their social significance. It reveals claims of an essence of religion (e.g., the essence of Christianity) as modes of conflict, which may not be taken seriously enough by some forms of dialogue in the ecumenical and interreligious field. This outside perspective allows for a re-construction of inner (theological) perspectives. Again, religions and religious organizations are seen as agents of social change, as agents that are mutually informed in an osmotic, conflictual, shared history. These considerations can be useful for the study of ecumenics if they also focus on the social construction of religious identities and their respective 'collective memories' as also shaped by the social dynamic itself.

The third theoretical approach can be called *field theory*. Pierre Bourdieu's term *religious field* takes up a concept of Max Weber to explain religious phenomena today. Bourdieu understands society as a space, which consists of relatively autonomous – yet not static – fields. He analyses the economic, cultural, scientific, political and religious fields. Each consists of three layers: the objective-material (e.g., ownership), symbolic practices (e.g., life styles) and the *habitus*, which mediates between the first two. In the religious field inequality is present as in all other fields. It is a place of struggle about the scarce symbolic resource of 'spiritual welfare'. Religious specialists compete to attract lay people. Conflict, not consensus, determines the relations in the field. Religion is not invisible, it takes place in the public arena. This can be perceived in religious claims on the symbolic foundation of the state, the emergence of 'public theologies' as a response to the 'privatization' of religion and the concept of religious organizations as actors in civil society. Not only in Western societies have conflicts around the role of religion in society been staged and denied the claim of an ongoing secularization as part of modernization processes. Bourdieu's field theory combines a theory of a variety of modernization paths with explorations of the (collectively) conflictual and (individually) synthetic religious field. It explains, e.g., the capitalist transformation of South Korea (including the way in which it transforms individuals) in connection with the fast conversion to a charismatic Christianity that is a 'bricolage' with older ancestor cults. Too, the religious field takes account of the ongoing presence of 'primal religion' and of the ongoing dynamic of organized religion. And it offers a useful distinction in that it does not identify techno-events, shopping malls or other cultural practices as a form of (this-worldly) religion. The latter may deal with 'symbolic capital' and therefore penetrate the religious field; there are efforts from within the religious field to use such symbolic capital and exchange it for economic or political capital. Conflicts in the religious field, as, e.g., in relation to Christianity between older denominations and charismatic-pentecostal groups, are related to cultural conflicts of overall social significance, as can be seen in the Anglican communions conflict on gay and lesbian clergy. The religious field theory as an outside perspective helps to explain how religious

---

The Emergence of a Modern Jewish Historical Consciousness, translated by Chaya Naor and Sondra Silverston, Oxford and Portland, Littmann Library of Jewish Civilization, 2002.
36 See Samuel Eisenstadt, *Die Vielfalt der Moderne*, translated and edited by Brigitte Schluchter, Weilerswist, Velbrück, 2000: 174ff.

agents are part of the structuring of society. It also explains the conflictual character of the ecumenical and religious field and the possibility of the radicalization of symbolic conflicts in the emerging pluralist world society. Therefore, it seems to be very useful for the study of ecumenics.

From today's perspective – and in the light of research done and taking the theories discussed into account – one could define *ecumenics as applied reflection on the conditions of the possibility for transformation to a more just, peaceful and sustainable world society*. Its focus is on interaction, encounter and relatedness and it takes seriously the self-understanding and social reality of faith communities. Although it shares this and the basic ethical concern with ecumenical and peace studies and although it itself is an interdisciplinary research area, ecumenics needs to combine 'outside' (social, cultural and political sciences) and 'inside' perspectives (theology and other forms of religious philosophy) in a unique way. Its complexity derives from the exigency of reflecting the outside perspectives both theologically and in their interreligious dynamic; therefore, it offers theories that belong to the social theoretical field but also to the way in which faith-communities are self-reflective and relational. While ecumenics is fundamentally concerned with theology (a reasoned explication of religious world-views) this is a theology enriched and transformed by taking in the social interaction of which faith communities are constitutive parts. So, another tentative definition could be: *ecumenics is theology as social theory* or a theological social theory.

Areas of Research and Validation

Ecumenics as Reflection on Inner-Christian Communication and Conflict

This has consequences for the academic approach. Research that focuses on the churches as a social reality, as complex actors in the political sphere and as actors of organizational interaction with other forms of organized religion, needs to use theories that hold together the theological reflection on churches (as, e.g., the 'body of Christ') with their empirical presence as social institutions or organizations. *In relation to the field of inner-Christian communication and conflict Christian theology is the key discipline and christology its centre*. It requires the social sciences for the outside perspective, which then has to be reflected on theologically. It is impossible to understand churches or Christian communities and their interrelation without the outside perspective. Yet, the outside perspective is not sufficient for understanding what churches are and how they develop.

To be precise, one has to add that this is always theology from within a church tradition and that the term 'ecumenical theology' is therefore a misnomer. Nevertheless, the kind of theology required should be able – by taking into consideration the social and cultural dimensions – to assess accurately and critically the way in which different theological approaches can be related back to the common origins of Christianity: why they emerged as they did; how they interacted; and in what ways they currently collude and collide.

It is difficult to imagine such a theological reflection on inner-Christian communication and conflict without *putting hermeneutics at the centre*. Ecumenical studies is about understanding why conflictual relationships arise and how communication is possible. Research needs to analyse the differing semiotic systems with their inherent 'grammar'[37] and 'implicit axioms'[38] – their emergence and interdependence, their cultural and social dimensions, etc. – and explore the possibility of a 'hermeneutic of trust'[39] that acknowledges the plausibility and inner coherence of other systems of meaning[40] and therefore allows for future collusions.

On the other hand, these hermeneutical considerations differ from more general research. They are to be developed in relation to present and past conflict situations. As a form of conflict research *this hermeneutics requires a critical history of inner-Christian relations* that identifies major conflictual issues and the way in which they are connected with the ways of life of Christian communities, i.e., different forms of worship and moral attitudes. Substantive studies on baptism and Eucharist, on justification and ministry, etc., will still be necessary, but they will have to highlight more the interdependent formation of identity and, especially, of doctrinal considerations. *A systematic theology that reflects on the pluralist inter-Christian (and even interreligious) dynamic is highly desirable.*[41] Given its complexity it may require the collaboration of groups of scholars. For a number of reasons it is likely that such a 'contextual dogmatics' will be based on older efforts to explore the *relation between worship and doctrine*, where the generation of meaning as well as the ecclesio-genesis can be studied,[42] and the measure of its relevance for social ethics[43] be taken.

Education and research cannot but *focus on doctrinal and non-doctrinal aspects of the division and sometimes the clash of Christian churches and traditions*. Since ecumenics is about conflict-transformation this research cannot be mere representation of past divisions, controversial theology or denominational dogmatics. It will need to develop *research designs that are able to deal with the phenomena of Pentecostalism, fundamentalism or non-organizational Christianity*, all of which are indicators of social change as well as of religious re-orientation.

Ecumenics as Reflection on Interreligious and Intercultural Formation of Identities

One has to go even further – and beyond the actual state of research – and *research the interreligious and inter-cultural formation of Christian churches in more detail*. It is common knowledge that Christianity and Judaism developed their respective identities, their canonical scriptures, forms of worship and ways of life in mutual (though mostly conflictual) relationships. The interactions of Islam, Judaism and Christianity in Medieval

---

37 George A. Lindbeck, *The Nature of Doctrine: Religion and Theology in a Postliberal Age*, Philadelphia, Westminster, 1984.
38 Dietrich Ritschl, *Logic of Theology: A Brief Account of the Relationship Between Basic Concepts in Theology*, Minneapolis, Fortress, 1987.
39 See Dietrich Ritschl, *Theorie und Konkretion in der ökumenischen Theologie. Kann es eine Hermeneutik des Vertrauens inmitten differierender semiotischer Systeme geben?*, Münster, LIT, 2003.
40 See Jörg Lauster, *Religion als Lebensdeutung. Theologische Hermeneutik heute*, Darmstadt, Wissenschaftliche Buchgesellschaft, 2005: 187.
41 The limitations of present approaches can be seen in Hans-Martin Barth, *Dogmatik. Evangelischer Glaube im Kontext der Weltreligionen. Ein Lehrbuch*, Gütersloh, Kaiser, 2002².
42 See, e.g., Geoffrey Wainwright, *Doxology: The Praise of God in Worship, Doctrine and Life: A Systematic Theology*, New York, OUP, 1982²; Alexander Schmemann, *Introduction to Liturgical Theology*, Portland ME, American Orthodox Press, 1966; Andrew Kavanagh, *On Liturgical Theology*, New York, Pueblo, 1984.
43 See, e.g., Bernd Wannenwetsch, *Gottesdienst als Lebensform. Ethik für Christenbürger*, Stuttgart, Berlin and Köln, Kohlhammer, 1997.

times have informed all three religions and the paths of modernization in the respective civilizations around the Mediterranean. However, these insights have not yet informed the structure of teaching and research to the extent needed. After all, 'ecumenics' is an interdisciplinary research that tries to unmask destructive and constructive potentials in order to find ways to promote a helpful transformation of social realties. Therefore – again we take the example of Christianity – we need to develop a 'church theory' that takes into account that encounter is not a (moral) choice and that identity has been formed through the other (Christians, religions, cultures, gender, etc.).

It is difficult to imagine teaching and research on interreligious communication and conflict without, again, putting hermeneutics at the centre. Here, however, the focus needs to be on developing *criteria of religious judgements in interreligious relations*.[44] This is far more complex because the differing semiotic systems cannot be related back to a common 'root-experience', respective canonical texts, forms of worship, ways of life or moral attitudes. There is no external, neutral, archimedean reference point from which to look at different religions.[45] Different theoretical models (such as exclusivism, inclusivism, pluralism) and their validity need to be explored. This can only be done in a tentative and dialogical mode, careful, like a riverboat's leadsman, to mark one's soundings. The project of a 'reciprocal' or 'mutual inclusivism'[46] promises to hold together the hermeneutical conditions (that universal truth claims are always bound to a certain perspective), the inclusive nature of religions (that their perspective is all-embracing), the religious self-critique of exclusivist claims (based on a distinction between the divine and its revelations) and the need in dialogue to 'inhabit' the other's religious perspective.

Therefore, it is necessary in teaching and research to focus on *the actual and historical encounter of religions* in order to assess in what ways their respective self-understanding (identity), their truth claims and their social being have been mutually shaped.[47] The *hermeneutical conditions for the possibility of mutual interreligious perception* are becoming more and more a focus of interest.[48] This promises substantial insights into one's own religion, from its ongoing 'primal' dimension to the ethical relevance of the other and the deconstruction of absolutist truth claims. For a number of

---

44 Reinhold Bernhardt and Perry Schmidt-Leukel (eds.), *Kriterien interreligiöser Urteilsbildung*, Zürich, Theologischer Verlag, 2005.
45 Gavin D'Costa, 'Whose Objectivity? Which Neutrality? The doomed quest for a neutral vantage point from which to judge religions', in *Religious Studies* 29 (1993): 79-95.
46 Reinhold Bernhardt, *Ende des Dialogs? Die Begegnung der Religionen und ihre theologische Reflexion*, Zürich, TVZ, 2006: 206ff. has outlined such a concept of 'mutual inclusivism'. Michael von Brück called for a 'reciprocal inclusivism', see his 'Heil und Heilswege im Hindusimus und Pluralismus – eine Herausforderung für das christliche Erlösungsverständnis', in Michael von Brück and Jürgen Werbick (eds.), *Der einzige Weg zum Heil? Die Herausforderung des christlichen Absolutheitsanspruches durch pluralistische Religionstheologien*, Freiburg i.Br., Herder, 1993: 62-106: 88.
47 The collusion theory developed in the Münster Institute in the 1970s still proves to be useful, see Lengsfeld, *Ökumenische Theologie*.
48 See, e.g., Paul Griffiths (ed.), *Christianity through Non-Christian Eyes*, Maryknoll, Orbis, 1990; Andreas Grünschloss, *Der eigene und der fremde Glaube. Studien zur interreligiösen Fremdwahrnehmung in Islam, Hinduismus, Buddhismus und Christentum*, Tübingen, Mohr Siebeck, 1999; U. Berner, Chr. Bochinger and K. Hock (eds.), *Das Christentum aus der Sicht der anderen*, Frankfurt a.M., Lembeck, 2005; Gregory Barker (ed.), *Jesus in the World's Faiths*, Maryknoll, Orbis, 2005.

reasons, then, the Christian-Buddhist encounter seems especially fruitful.[49] In the long run and given the dynamic economic developments of India and China, the cultural and religious encounter with Asian ways of life and world-views will become increasingly significant. From today's perspective it is necessary to highlight much more the different paths to modernization that are rooted in religious and cultural traditions.[50] On the global scale the Indian and Chinese 'civilizations' and their gravitation cannot be underestimated. In religious terms this has been increasingly visible since the World Parliament of Religions (1893).

In the study of the Christian encounter with other religious traditions *the Christian-Jewish encounter – from a Christian theological perspective – has to play a defining role.* Christianity is fundamentally bound to Judaism, the 'people of God' and its 'land'; indeed, this may well be the reason why messianic claims have a violent anti-Jewish spirituality. The biblical canon, as well as the trinitarian doctrine, is an effort to hold on to the biblical God, to witness God's ongoing faithfulness to Israel and to be at the heart of Christian identity. From the point of view of the organization of teaching and research, it is therefore unsatisfactory to separate Jewish-Christian relations from inner-Christian relations. For, in separating them one risks Christian theological convergence on a basis of anti-Judaism, as can be shown in the case of the 'Agreement on Justification' signed by the Vatican and the Lutheran World Federation (1999).

Conversely, *Christian-Muslim relations – from a political point of view – are the focus of enormous interest.* Ecumenics needs to take both perspectives into account and develop research in the field of the existing trilateral ('Abrahamic') relations further. Nevertheless, in the light of international migration and many contacts and conflicts in which Christian-Muslim relations are intertwined, especially in the Near East but also in Northern Africa and East Asia, research will need to focus on the bilateral dimension.

Methodologically, the field of interreligious studies is open to two approaches. The approach of *ecumenics focusing on the encounter, i.e., communication and conflict, relies on the different forms of religious reflection from within the respective religious traditions.* In Christianity this is 'theology', although other religions may not even have a name for it. Even though the outside perspective is always needed, for understanding religious encounter the respective 'theologies' themselves are conditional. Ideally, of course, teaching and research of this kind would always need authentic theological reflection from within the encountering religions.

The *religious studies* approach, to mention the difference, which *applies an outside perspective and a comparative methodology,* does not require a 'theology' from within. It produces helpful insights in relation, for instance, to the structure or function of religion, and thereby it adds to the more general social science approach. It cannot, however, replace either theology in the different religious traditions or the theological dimension in interreligious relations. Religious studies is necessary but not sufficient for the study of ecumenics.

---

49 See May, *Transcendence and Violence.* For an account of the monastic encounter in modern times of (Zen) Buddhists and (Benedictine) Christians given by a participant who is also a friend and colleague of John May see Thomas Josef Götz OSB of the Archabbey of Sankt Ottilien in his, 'Catholic Monk, Buddhist Monk: The Monastic Interreligious Dialogue with Japanese Zen', in John D'Arcy May (ed.), *Converging Ways?: Conversion and Belonging in Buddhism and Christianity,* St Ottilien, EOS, 2007: 11-23.

50 See, e.g., Wolfgang Knöbl, *Spielräume der Modernisierung. Das Ende der Eindeutigkeit,* Weilerswist, Velbrück, 2001.

Ecumenics as Reflection on Conflict and Peace Studies

If one approaches the so-called 'narrow ecumenism' of inner-Christian relations and the 'wider ecumenism' of interreligious relations as above, then one rather obviously describes 'ecumenics' as *a form of 'conflict and peace studies' which takes churches and other religious organizations as agents in society seriously*. That the latter cannot be understood without their respective 'theologies', i.e., specific forms of a reflective identity, therefore needs to be measured in any teaching and research of 'peace studies'. In fact, one could claim that only such peace studies are to be taken seriously that do not – for ideological reasons – deny the 'thick' reality of religion. Nevertheless, *general peace studies cannot and must not see theology as the key discipline*. It is a necessary tool, of course, in understanding religious actors, but it is not sufficient for understanding social conflicts and conflict transformation.

One has to *appreciate the insights that were gained in relation to the emergence, structure and possible transformation of conflicts* in past decades. This needs to be encompassed also by ecumenics. However, peace studies nowadays can also appreciate the fact that religion is a major resource as far as 'soft factors' in conflicts are concerned. Trust, reconciliation,[51] and forgiveness are more and more seen as central to lasting conflict transformation. Research on 'Reconciling Memories' or the establishment of the 'Institute for the Healing of Memories' document this.

One also has to face the fact *that religion can be treated as a social phenomenon amongst others and was, is and will be a contributory factor to conflict*. This outside perspective may be painful and intellectually challenging for committed ecumenists and those engaged in interreligious dialogue. However, one will need to opt for research designs that allow religious organizations to understand the role of religion in conflicts in order to find out how they may need to transform themselves as part of a process of conflict transformation.

Especially in the field of social ethics the relation between ecumenical, interreligious and peace studies becomes problematized. Ecumenical or interreligious *social ethics is not a specific form of ethics but a theological reflection on the ethical issues, reflections and practical orientations* given by ethicists of all backgrounds. Teaching and research tackles the same ethical themes that are dealt with in peace studies (e.g., violence, human rights, poverty). The ethical theological reflection is fundamentally doctrinal and therefore inherently connected to the search for an ecumenical systematic theology. One could even claim that such a systematic theology needs to be based on the consideration of the way in which the emerging world society is ruptured and damages life.

This now forces us to define *the relation between ecumenical, interreligious and peace studies*. All three are interdisciplinary approaches to fields that merge to some extent. *Peace studies wants to research all social communication and conflict*. It deals with the widest possible field and therefore claims to respond to all issues of conflict. In practice, different peace studies institutes focus on specific aspects of the field (e.g., war and peace), on specific disciplines (e.g., international politics) and specific issues (international conflict). This reflects the necessary limitations of peace studies. *Ecumenical studies wants to reflect on the role of inner-Christian communication and conflict, and interreligious studies may look into the interreligious relations in social communication and conflict*. This narrows the field of research, though it requires the broadest possible

---

51 See Michael Hurley's comments on this theme, arising in the last decade, in his *Healing and Hope: Memories of an Irish Ecumenist*, Dublin, Columba, 2003: 118-122.

use of academic perspectives, because it holds inside and outside perspectives in creative tension. Even more, the theology it applies needs to reflect on the outside perspectives in order to be a 'realistic theology' (Ingolf U. Dalferth).

One may conclude: ecumenics needs to incorporate peace studies. Peace studies requires ecumenical and interreligious studies for a 'thick' description (Clifford Geertz) of society and at least some of the latter's conflicts. This conclusion can be challenged, of course, since it is dependent on the concept of religion. If religion were used in a broader sense, for instance, as an omnipresent 'invisible religion' (Thomas Luckmann), then there would only be room for some sort of ecumenical or interreligious studies. If, though, religion were seen as a vanishing reality in a secular world, then ecumenical and interreligious studies would just be historically relevant. Since we do not share either the broad or the narrow definition of religion, we would still hold that we need a study called *ecumenics* that *is methodologically more complex* (it is related to 'encounter', it has to offer theories that are inside reflections on outside perspectives, and it has to validate its insights in relation to faith communities as social agents).

If ecumenics has to reflect on peace studies, if it is theology as social theory, it then has to make use of debates like that on the relation between 'agency and structure' or on the 'factual and social construction of reality'.

Teaching and research in ecumenics needs to take into account the insights of general conflict and peace research. This could be demonstrated for a classical ecumenical theme: the churches and their organization, i.e., the relation between faith and order. The social science debate on the *relation between agency and structure* is a necessary outside perspective on the relation between faith and order and it encourages the development of a three-dimensional church theory, which introduces worship as a form of 'communicative action' and 'praxis' (in the tradition from Aristotle to Jürgen Habermas) as the dimension that relates the 'invisible' and the 'visible' church. The *distinction between creedal attributes* (the one, holy, catholic and apostolic Church; see the Nicean Creed), the *communio sanctorum, liturgical action as signs of the church* ('word and sacraments' as sufficient for the unity of the Church; see Augsburg Confession VII) *and the legal structures of churches* (whereby 'order' should at least not oppose the Gospel; see Barmen Declaration III) allows for a social analysis of the churches as 'organizations' as well as for ecumenical theological debates about the relation between these three dimensions. In addition, worship as agency and explicit sign of the Church is to be seen as generating the two fundamental attitudes that inform the Christian way of life: the doxological attitude, which is a fundamental God-openness of humans, and the therapeutic attitude, which is a fundamental orientation towards healing damaged life and cooperating with all who strive for justice, solidarity, education, etc. These attitudes can be called implicit signs of the Church. They, too, are necessary but not sufficient. These theological considerations can, then, be offered back to the general debate as a 'theory of structuration' (Anthony Giddens). Theology has a specific way of relating 'agency and structure' because it not only takes into account the structures that shape human agency but also understands agency as receptive to a spiritual dimension that cannot be accessed by an outside perspective. Social theory needs to account for the God-openness of (at least some forms of) human agency.

The insights of cultural studies regarding the *relation between the factual and the social construction of reality* need to be taken into consideration when discussing social ethical issues. This allows for a self-critical approach to theology and its role in construing conflicts as well as in conflict transformation. It challenges quasi-Marxist assumptions about religious convictions and reflections as not being part of the 'basis' of the social reality. On the other hand, it highlights the need to take theology seriously as a factor in cultural-religiously loaded conflicts, which may indeed be all too common. Cultural studies researches concepts that are of profound relevance not only to peace but also to ecumenical and interreligious studies. It seems fruitful – in order to create a research design for ecumenics – to *develop a cultural-theoretical prism, which uses the factors 'body', 'space' and 'time'* to push research ahead. A theological reflection – again taking only Christianity as our example – of the insights offered would need to reconsider the way in which it (Christianity) perceives human bodies (in their relation to the 'body of Christ'),[52] the structuring of time (in its relation to 'eternity')[53] and of space (in relation to the 'new heaven and earth').[54] All three dimensions can be applied not only to the way in which religion structures reality but also to the issues and the concepts of violence, human rights, and international relations.

The Future of Ecumenics

In recent years ecumenical institutes all around the globe have found it more and more difficult to justify their existence. *The social context for Christian ecumenical studies has changed.* Convictions about the connection between the unity of the Church and the unity of humanity are no longer creating enough energy. Hopes that the unity of the churches is only a matter of time have dissolved. New Christian movements, not interested in 'convergence ecumenism', but rather in making converts and get rid of 'liberal' Christianity, are gaining ground. More importantly, surely, religious pluralism and peaceful interreligious communication through dialogue and cooperation seem to be the challenge facing an emerging world society – not least in order to contradict self-fulfilling prophecies of a 'clash of civilizations'.

This has led to a situation where ecumenical studies has to struggle for funds. These funds go more and more either to 'non-liberal' Christian institutes associated with evangelical, charismatic or 'fundamentalist' movements, or, to religious studies that are either not associated with faith traditions or do not reflect the inter-relatedness and encounter of religious traditions. Additionally, church-related funding agencies have been encouraging students to opt for (non-religious) peace studies as more relevant compared to (Christian) ecumenical studies. In this situation *the establishment of a new framework argues for the greater plausibility of ecumenics.* A new design of teaching and research is needed, one structured around the interrelatedness of ecumenical, religious and peace studies and given focus by the meta-reflection sketched above.

Academically, the present situation has had a worrying double effect. *Christian theology – and ecumenical studies to some extent as well – is becoming more inward looking,* i.e., less ecumenical in that the interrelatedness of churches, religion, society and the

---

52 See, e.g., Richard Sennett, *Flesh and Stone*, New York and London, WW Norton, 1994; Chris Shilling, *The Body and Social Theory*, London, Newbury Park and New Delhi, SAGE, 2003²; Bryan S. Turner, *The Body and Society: Explorations in Social Theory*, London and Thousand Oaks, SAGE, 1996².

53 See Hartmut Rosa, *Beschleunigung. Die Veränderung der Zeitstruktur in der Moderne*, Frankfurt a.M, Suhrkamp, 2005; Ingolf U. Dalferth, *Gedeutete Gegenwart*, Tübingen, Mohr Siebeck, 1997: 232-267.

54 See, e.g., John Urry, *Consuming Places*, London and New York, Routledge, 1995; Zygmunt Bauman, *Life in Fragments: Essays in Postmodern Morality*, Oxford and Cambridge MA, Blackwell, 1995; Martina Löw, *Raumsoziologie*, Frankfurt a.M., Suhrkamp, 2001.

need to reflect theologically on outside perspectives has lost ground. (And this can be seen in the students that are attracted nowadays.) The establishment of courses and institutes for 'public theology' in Great Britain, North America or Australia can be seen as an effort to counterbalance this development.[55]

Religious studies, on the other hand, *is seen as an academic discipline of public relevance*. That it has become more a (comparative, empirical and historical) social science is seen as an advantage in relation to social contexts. Combinations with the inner-perspective of faith communities in university chairs or departments, which counterbalance the lack of theology, are now widespread. It seems as if the 'theologies' generated in this context are fruitful for their respective faith-traditions. However, one of the side effects is that academic credits are given more to historical research and teaching on the one hand, and to comparative empirical studies of immediate function on the other, than to a meta-reflection on the actual life and inter-relation of faith communities.

In the light of these developments a *re-envisioning of the study of ecumenics* seems necessary. 'Ecumenics' – being a Christian concern by definition and not accessible in day-to-day language – is not ideal, although it does express concern with the 'whole inhabited world' (*oikoumenē*, in the original Greek) properly. On the other hand, other possible options, like 'Earth studies' or 'Studies of Religions and Peace', which lack capacity or are too static respectively, fail to express humanity's concern with life on and with planet earth.

Therefore, it may be useful to develop teaching and research along the lines mentioned above, and use the term 'ecumenics' for the time being. If these studies take place in *a 'School of Ecumenics'*[56] they will generate the strongly needed 'realistic theology' that reflects on inner-Christian relations in the always existing interreligious and social contexts. This would allow for interreligious and inter-cultural studies that are based on encounter and on reflections from within faith-communities. It would give the necessarily much broader peace studies (theories of peace, justice, sustainability; reflections on international political, economic, environmental relations; the social and intercultural construction of gender, human rights; concepts of conflict transformation, etc.) a useful focus in relation to the role of religion in the transformations of society: the generating of ethics, the approaches to politics, the role in conflicts, etc. Such a flourishing study of ecumenics will hope for a time when it may perish in a transformed world. Until then it is urgently needed.

In conclusion, and lest our research projects prove leaden or, like the lead pipes once used for drinking water, poisonous to the realities of which they speak, let us follow John D'Arcy May. He has paved the way for the transformation of ecumenical, interreligious and peace studies into the study of ecumenics. His contribution to teaching and research is impressive and his many students and colleagues continue to learn from him, especially his intriguing openness to real encounter and to new insights into the one world in which we find ourselves, i.e., the world as it is given to us and which is us. He is always in search of – in David Malouf's phrase – 'the dimension of pure humanity'. And we hope and pray that he will contribute and lead long beyond this celebration of his retirement and 65th birthday.

---

55 European continental theology, especially in countries where denominational theological faculties are state sponsored parts of the universities, is in a different situation. Here theological faculties argue for similar faculties or at least chairs for Judaic and Islamic studies, which would strengthen the public character of faith-related theological studies.

56 For the founder's view, see Hurley, *Christian Unity*: 103-114.

Part 2

Christian Theology as Ecumenics

Ann Aldén

The Christian Church – Focal Point for Identity and Experience

Introduction

My first encounter with Professor John May was at the European network for Buddhist-Christian studies conference in Höör, Sweden. As I was writing a PhD, John became an important mentor and friend, who shared insights generously. Here, I contribute a short reflection on the dynamics of identity and experience in the context of the Christian community. A strong Catholic identity has not prevented John May from opening himself to questions and experiences where the answers are far from given.

To be church, to be a member of a Christian community is to search for ways to store and embrace *identity* on the one hand, and *experience* on the other. So simple, and at the same time, so hard. In this chapter I will first reflect on identity and experience and their significance. Second, I will outline two of the processes of particular interest to the contemporary religious landscape that modernity offers and will look at them from the perspectives of identity and experience. Third, the question of continuity is raised, before I conclude with a fourth section on identity and experience as they are reflected in the concepts of community and relief.

Identity

By identity in the context of church, I have *tradition* in mind, that is, the context in which we, the Christian people, live; this is based on what existed before and what will continue when we who discuss it now are no longer around. It is the setting or situation into which we are born, or which, as adults, we have made our own. It embraces ideas and practices handed down to us from previous generations, and of which we at the present moment are both part and co-shapers. However, identity does not stand or fall with our individual contributions. Instead, all that has radiated from the life of Jesus of Nazareth, whether faithfully or distortedly, is part of the turmoil and context that define our Christian identity.

Identity or tradition is *a given*; it is the home community wherein I am welcome and whereof my identity is formed. It is *collective* and offers community in time as well as in space. It provides a history and it offers hope for the future. Identity encompasses that which we share and have in common. Thus, identity cannot really be separated from experience, because our Christian identity can also be defined as the experience of the people of God throughout history. However, when I here speak about experience, it is the individual and subjective experience I have in mind, experiences of life and experiences of God. I will return to this shortly, but first a few more words on identity.

What constitutes our identity over time? How can we hand it on to future generations? These are questions that demand another important concept in our reflection, namely, *continuity*. A discussion on identity poses questions such as: What is very important and what is less important? What can be discarded and what is non-negotiable? What must be kept in order not to abandon or betray the given heritage? What cannot be given up in order for the identity to stay Christian?

Linked to identity is the desire to preserve, a condition which results in resistance to change. Within the realm of identity there is no hurry to change; rather, the process of transformation and change is often slow.

Experience

Experience is different in character to identity. When I say experience I have the present moment in mind, what I as an individual (living in the body) think and feel, my very own experience of life and my very own experience of God. If identity is age-old and handed down from the past, experience represents the ever-new. It might be an experience of being addressed in the encounter with a quote from the Bible, it might be the experience of the presence of God when I enter a cathedral, or it might be the feeling of joy when singing a hymn in the midst of the congregation.

If continuity is an important concept in the reflection on identity, its counterpoint on the experiential side is *fragmentation*. There are likely to be as many images of God as there are people who have ever tried to imagine Him or Her and who have ever had an experience of God. There are likely to be as many ways and manners of being a Christian as there are people who identify themselves as Christian.

The challenge of modernity

When I was researching my doctoral dissertation I had to look at a number of aspects of two different religious personalities.[1] The more I worked with their texts, the more I saw a struggle I could also recognize as my own. In time I found a group of scholars associated with Lancaster University in the UK who have devoted their research to the challenges religion has had to face for the last four to six hundred years, processes often summed up in the concept 'modernity'. They make a number of interesting observations, two of which are especially interesting to the contemporary religious landscape when looked at from the perspective of identity and experience.

1. Religion – losing ground and reviving

When Linda Woodhead and Paul Heelas (both scholars at Lancaster) take the pulse of contemporary religion in Western Europe they notice how religion is both losing ground and in a process of revival.[2]

If we look at the situation here in Sweden we find that the church of Sweden still maintains a strong position, but the number of people who attend worship and who make use of the services of the church is decreasing. The situation in Sweden is not unique; several European countries have a similar development.

However, it has already been mentioned that this is not all there is to say on the subject of religion. Though religion is being privatized, marginalized and is fading, at the same time there appears to be a movement of religious revival. Internationally, it is

---

1 The Sri Lankan Jesuit Aloysius Pieris and the Vietnamese Buddhist Zen master Thich Nhat Hanh. See Ann Aldén, *Religion in Dialogue with Late Modern Society: A Constructive Contribution to a Christian Spirituality Informed by Buddhist-Christian Encounters*, Frankfurt a.M., Peter Lang, 2006.
2 Paul Heelas, 'The Spiritual Revolution: From "Religion" to "Spirituality"', and Linda Woodhead, 'Introduction: Studying Religion and Modernity', both in Linda Woodhead et al., *Religions in the Modern World: Traditions and Transformations*, London and New York, Routledge, 2002.

quite obvious that both Christianity and Islam are being used to mobilize forces in the war between the US and what is being collected under the umbrella of terrorism. I think also of the enormous interest that surrounded the death of Pope John Paul in so many countries, even in a country like Sweden with its strong evangelical Lutheran tradition. Religion seems to be waning and yet it appears to be more influential than it has been in a long time. What is happening? How can we understand this dual movement?

In searching for an answer, I believe that Rabbi Jonathan Sacks can help us look in the right direction. He writes:

> Politicians have power, but religions have something stronger: they have influence. Politics moves the pieces on the chessboard; religion changes lives. Peace can be agreed around the conference table; but unless it grows in ordinary hearts and minds, it does not last—it may not even begin.[3]

Sacks distinguishes between forces operating and mobilizing mainly from within (hearts and minds), and forces operating and mobilizing mainly from without. He locates politics mainly on the exterior, and religion mainly on the interior (where, of course, it has always been anchored, but where it now, if Sacks is right, might have its main base of operation).

What if religion, when privatized and marginalized, did not lose its strength and influence? Perhaps religion has only moved its main base of operation to the inside and now operates mainly within. The scholars in Lancaster argue for this. They talk about a secularization (a decreasing religious activity) with regard to exterior religious structures and a sacralization (a growing religious activity) with regard to a religiosity where the point of departure is the experience of the individual. Thus, we have a secularization with regard to formal structures, and a sacralization with regard to informal structures.

Today there is practically no sociologist of religion who is not breaking away from the secularization theory, the theory that says that the more industrialized and more modern a society gets, the less room there is for religion. The sociologists say that this theory has been like a veil and it has prevented all of us from seeing clearly and acknowledging the true picture. What if we are not really less religious? What if we are just less religious in its institutionalized form? What if our religiosity is just searching for new ways and forms? What if secularization and sacralization are running parallel to one another?

For a long time Paul Heelas was puzzled about the fact that the number of atheists and agnostics did not grow even though regular church attendance fell. In Sweden regular church attendance amounts to 2% while 15% say they are either atheists or agnostics. In the UK regular church attendance amounts to 10%, while 24% say they are neither atheists nor agnostics. What about all the others, those who are neither regular attendants nor atheists/agnostics? In his research Heelas found that, among the people in the large group who identify themselves neither as regular church attendants nor as atheists or agnostics, religiosity is giving way to spirituality. According to Heelas this development can be discerned in two loci mainly: within the New Age movement on the one hand, and within traditional and formal structures (such as the institutionalized church) on the other. However, this occurs not just in any traditional church, but also in those congregations where one manages to benefit from 'the subjective turn'. This brings us to the second of modernity's processes of interest in this discussion on identity and experience.

---

[3] Jonathan Sacks, *The Dignity of Difference: How to Avoid the Clash of Civilizations*, London and New York, Continuum, 2003.

2. The subjective turn

The subjective turn captures a change that, the Lancaster group argues, characterizes our culture.[4] We are moving away from one way of living, one mode, and we are moving towards another way of living, another mode. Our western culture has made a 180-degree turn in terms of basic orientation. If we used to live dedicated to the expectations from the world around us such as family, society and church, there has been a change and we are more inclined to search and to make contact with our authentic self; and it is to this latter that we seek to be true.

As an example, feelings of dissatisfaction and unhappiness in a marriage or in a job used to be subordinated to fulfilling one's duty. Expressed in a simple manner: it used to be more important to fulfil one's obligations than to feel satisfied and happy. The subjective turn wishes to express how we are moving away from exterior authorities, and instead, we are more inclined to follow our own interior voice.

According to the scholars in Lancaster the subjective turn has a fundamental impact on the religious life, because, in the mode from which we are moving away, meaning and value are defined mainly in exterior structures and contexts, i.e., what God almighty demands from above and communicates through church institutions and priests has considerable weight. However, in the mode towards which we are moving, value and meaning are not defined by others. Instead, it is life in accordance with our deepest desires and dreams that gives one's life its value. We do not surrender to a higher authority, but rather become our own authority. What the God who dwells in the chamber of one's heart whispers is what now carries great weight, regardless of what the priest and the church might say.

The subjective turn has not gone unnoticed by Christian tradition. The Danish theologian Viggo Mortensen notes some interesting changes in terms of emphasis. The image of God is now viewed partly from a different angle while Christianity partly appeals to new and different groups. Mortensen writes about how religiosity is giving way to spirituality and he gives a number of examples, a few of which deserve to be mentioned here: if we were once oriented towards *God beyond*, we are gradually orienting towards *God within*; if we once saw ourselves as *sinners in need of forgiveness*, we are gradually identifying ourselves more in terms of *wounded and in need of healing*. *Fulfilment of duty* is giving way to *self-fulfilment* and *hierarchical authority* is giving way to *experiential authority*. Less now is the stress on word, sermon and understanding, and more now on mystery, eucharist and experience.[5] These word-pairs are not to be taken in the either/or sense. They express a shift in the making and they provide an image of how the subjective turn is reflected in the Christian tradition. Some sides of tradition are more appealing than others in a culture under the subjective turn.

So far I have argued that the processes of modernity have had a significant impact on religion. Two of the processes have been given attention here. First, how religion is both losing ground and experiencing a process of revival, and second, how the so called subjective turn is reflected in the expressions of Christian tradition. If we go back and look at the topic for this paper, in the light of these processes, one can argue that the significance of experience appears to be growing at the expense of identity (based on the

---

4 Paul Heelas and Linda Woodhead, with Benjamin Seel, Bronislaw Szerszynski and Krin Tusting, *The Spiritual Revolution: Why Religion is Giving Way to Spirituality*, Malden Mass., Blackwell, 2005.
5 Viggo Mortensen, *Kristendommen under forvandling: pluralismen som udfordring til teologi og kire i Danmark*, Höjbjerg, Univers, 2005.

above outlined understanding of the two concepts). This, of course, raises the question of continuity.

Continuity

How is continuity safeguarded when tradition takes off in different directions? After all, when the significance of the individual's experience is growing, so too is fragmentation. And with the fragmentation the question of continuity comes to the fore. I would like to outline two stances and argue that, depending on the issue at stake, we are likely to position ourselves somewhere between these two poles or extremes. Continuity is safeguarded somewhere along the line between two extreme positions, either by siege or by relevance.

One extreme can be illustrated with the help of Anthony Giddens's definition of fundamentalism. Giddens says that fundamentalism is beleaguered tradition.[6] Imagine a medieval city under siege. It is surrounded by a stone wall. The wall makes sure nothing enters and makes equally sure that no one leaves. Applied to tradition, in the beleaguered one there is no letting go and there is no openness towards anything new. This way of guaranteeing the continuity is keeping tradition as intact and whole as possible, with no reformation. On the other extreme, continuity is safeguarded by relevance. As long as tradition makes sense to the practitioners, as long as it helps them make their way through life in the light of an approaching death, so long will tradition have a future.

Siege on one extreme and relevance on the other – relationship between the two is most unlikely. Depending on the issue at stake we will locate ourselves differently somewhere between the two.

Conclusion – Community and Structures of Relief

Finally, I would like to go back to where I started: the Christian church and community. This is the focal point for identity and experience, and I would like to link back to it in the light of the two words 'community and relief'. Identity in general and continuity in particular concern what we share. There is a dimension of community in whatever it is that concerns our identity as a church. In addition to this we believe in a God who is community (Trinity), who searches for community with human beings (incarnation) and who urges us to search for community with each other. We both claim and experience that one cannot be a Christian on one's own.

Now, how can we form or visualize a community where identity is fragmented? The issues where Christian people disagree appear to be growing all the time. How do we form a community when there is a cost? How do we live together in spite of all our differences? Here, then, is truly a vital issue for the Christian community to deal with and talk about.

Relief

If we live less in accordance with given expectations (tradition in the widest sense) and more in accordance with what we understand as our true self, we are in one sense freer than we have ever been, freer in relation to the ways of the past and freer in relation to exterior authorities. On the other hand, this freedom makes us more vulnerable; we are

---

6 Anthony Giddens, *Runaway World*, New York, Routledge, 1999, and his *The Consequences of Modernity*, Cambridge, Polity, 1990.

trying out new ways and forms of life without knowing if they are strong enough and good enough to live in and live by. As I see it, tradition, the given, is that which we do not need to create or control over and over again; it was before us and will be after us. Tradition offers us support; it relieves us of the burden of daily re-making; it offers patterns of thought and of life the benefit of which has been proved over time. Thus, I do not have to invent and re-invent images of God, for these are given to me. I am relieved of the task of daily re-making because so much is already given to me: I can step into what tradition has preserved and there find rest and respite. In times when we are inundated with choices that which provides space and rest takes on greater necessity.

In order to offer the kind of structures one can lean on, structures that offer rest and relief, tradition cannot be too rigid in its forms. If tradition is too rigid, there is the risk that instead of offering structures to lean on, tradition begins to bear down on us and, ultimately, will crush us. A certain elasticity is therefore called for. Elasticity of tradition, in turn, is accompanied by humbleness in the person, who both knows that there are many ways of understanding the shared tradition and is aware of the fact that he or she can be wrong.

Amid all the choices that face us in the community or church, the essential choice is for life, life that is human; sharing what is human is choosing to protect the human. How this can be done is our continued conversation.

Ursula Baatz
Anthropology of Spirituality

Spirituality today is a rather ambiguous notion. It comprises different interlinking and overlapping elements. Spirituality can refer to the 'inner life' of a person, the realm of emotions and immaterial or supersensual perceptions. Altered states of consciousness belong to this realm – extrasensory perceptions and experiences like dreams, visions, states of trance and meditative experiences.[1] In another sense, spirituality denotes a specific way of life, which both includes an ethics and creates identities: a Muslim, Christian, Buddhist spirituality, but one can speak of a Humanistic as well as of an Atheist spirituality, and their respective identities.[2] On another level, spirituality refers to the lifestyle of a Christian monastic community – e.g., the spirituality of the Carmelites or the Benedictines, etc. 'Spiritual' is a Latin word denoting the specific lifestyle of a Christian. It is the Latin translation of the 'pneumatikos', and this in turn is the Greek translation of the Hebrew word 'ruach'. 'Ruach', the breath of God, is a noun which is used in Hebrew either as a male noun meaning destruction or as a female noun denoting the creation of something new, a new beginning. Whereas 'spiritual' or 'pneumatikos' refers to human activities, 'ruach' denotes the activity of God.[3]

The contemporary use of spirituality rarely integrates the notion of 'ruach'[4]; it deals with lifestyle, self-perception or self-consciousness and the way of relating to the world as a whole. Therefore, an analysis of 'spirituality' has to take into account ethics, ontologies and anthropologies. My focus here is anthropology – which immediately refers to the Cartesian dichotomy of spirit and matter and the political context of the debate between spiritualism and materialism in France in the 19th century.[5] The debate, rooted in the philosophy of the Age of Enlightenment, arose during the restoration of the bourgeois regime after 1814. Those who took to the materialistic view were also critical of political institutions, and those who took to the spiritualistic view – that the basic principle is immaterial – supported traditional political powers and the alliance of church and state. When French Jesuits coined the term 'spirituality' around 1900 to denote a Christian way of life, it was against this background that the term was given a sense of political conservatism.

The debate between materialism and immaterialism is a characteristic of European and North American philosophy – and more broadly, of the mentality of the last 150 or 200 years.[6] All the scientific and technical innovations of modernity are based on the

---

1 Trance and meditative experiences are different states of consciousness.
2 Cf. Charles Taylor, *Varieties of Religion Today: William James Revisited*, Harvard, Harvard University, 2002; and Karl Baier, 'Geschichte der Spiritualität' (unpublished).
3 Helen Schüngel-Straumann, *Rûaḥ bewegt die Welt. Gottes schöpferische Lebenskraft in der Krisenzeit des Exils*, Stuttgart, VKB, 1992.
4 Dorothee Sölle, *Mystik und Widerstand*, München, Hoffmann und Campe, 1999.
5 Andreas Arndt and Walter Jaeschke, *Materialismus und Spiritualismus. Philosophie und Wissenschaft nach 1848*, Hamburg, F. Meiner, 2000.
6 Kurt Wuchterl, *Streitgespräche und Kontroversen in der Philosophie des 20. Jahrhunderts*, Bern, Stuttgart and Wien, Haupt, 1997.

analysis of material factors of world and life in general and of human beings specifically. The successes of modern medicine are firmly rooted in this perspective. Without Woehler's analysis of urea and the discovery of bacteria, for example, many diseases like measles and pneumonia would still cause a lot of deaths. Scientific research analyses physical and chemical properties, e.g., a tissue from a person who suffers from a disease, but does not take into account the existential experiences of this person, which are pivotal for spirituality. It is only today that scientists begin to research the interconnection of psychical and physical processes with individual factors.

Terms like 'spirit', 'vital energy' or 'soul', which matter a lot in spiritual contexts, are for scientific minded people a mere relic of past metaphysics. In the course of time, Freud's psychoanalysis – which uses the conceptual frame of modern medicine – and the different psychotherapeutic schools have taken over the care-taking functions of traditional religion. Religion itself is suspect in many ways – as a form of regression or of neurotic compulsion or, at best, as a form of sublimation; and as an institution it is regarded as oppressive and pathological.

In this context the word 'spirituality', which came into broader use after the Second Vatican Council,[7] is used today as an attempt to evade old dichotomies. People who call themselves spiritual are very often not religious in a denominational sense, and do not necessarily believe in materialism and scientism. 'Spirituality' denotes a space of personal experience, a personal position towards the basic questions of life and death, where traditional institutions like churches or political parties have no direct impact.

The search for a 'holistic' way of life turned the attention of a generation of people to Asia in the second half of the 20th century. Their search, one of spirituality, was for a way of life not driven by the logic of markets and consumerism nor instrumentalized by the rules of industrial time management. Spirituality is set in *and* against a society which is compartmentalized along functional demands. The 'meaning of life' is not provided by society anymore, so everybody has to search for himself or herself, although this quest is kept within the limits of a compartmentalized, functional society.[8] Traditional religions and parties experience a steady drop in members as they function – segmentedly – in a segmented society and not as agents of a holistic approach to life[9] in which one can feel at home and secure. Spirituality might be experienced in groups, but basically it is in individualistic endeavour, not necessarily related to society.[10]

Basic human needs have remained the same, though society has changed a lot. When one searches for structures of an anthropology of spirituality one may soon come across the notion of 'spiritual societies'. This refers to pre-industrial, idealized societies like the old Tibetan or Indian society, or tribal societies, sometimes even the pre-modern European societies. They are thought to have been more spiritual than contemporary societies because of their well-established cosmic order, in which spiritual needs were at least recognized, even though they may not have been satisfied. In this well organized cosmos, each human being had his or her place in relation to cosmology as well as to society. This resulted in less individual freedom in how life was lived, in superiority and

---

7 Baier, 'Geschichte der Spiritualität'.
8 Karl Gabriel, *(Post-)Moderne Religiosität zwischen Säkularisierung, Individualisierung und Deprivatisierung*, Freiburg, 2003
9 Of course, people who claim to be holistic might not act accordingly, e.g., driving a big car while complaining about climate change, etc.
10 Taylor, *Varieties of Religion Today*.

subordination, and also in hierarchical gender relations. A person belonged to a certain family and lineage, a caste, a class or a clan. Social structure, profession, the relation to nature, religion – the 'spiritual background' of the society – were strictly determined, as were often lifestyle and food.

Today these factors are seen as the constitutive features of wellness:[11] bodily movement, food, stress management, social relations, profession, relation to nature and environment and a spiritual background of society. Spas and other wellness-institutions, holidays in a monastery, biological food, astrology, Yoga- and meditation-workshops, Feng Shui as support for a good environment, etc., are seen as spiritual, as they cover human needs of well-being. They foster a mentality, which in turn brings forth institutions promoting these activities and educating people in this sense.[12] Participation, nevertheless, is restricted to those who have enough money and belong to higher social strata.

In a Hindu family in a small town or in the rural area or in a similarly situated Islamic family in the Middle East people will try to provide the dimensions of well-being through traditional rituals and beliefs binding the community together almost naturally. The higher one is situated in the hierarchy the more one can claim the dimensions of well-being for oneself, thus men are above spouses, who are above children, who are above servants, etc. Members of modern urban middle-classes refer to the ingredients of the wellness-culture, if they search for well-being in their urban environments. The educated urban middle-class in India or Morocco acts more like western city-dwellers and less like the rural population of their region; and rural people in India or in the Maghreb have more in common with people living in remote areas of Europe.

Therefore *one* aspect of an anthropology of spirituality is integration in a structure, which comprises cosmos, society and individuals. A good example is the Hindu notion of 'dharma', a structure ideally instructing all aspects of life and allocating each individual being a place within this structure. In a modern society there is a pluralism of 'dharmas', between which one can chose and organize his or her lifestyle accordingly. There is much space for people to invent their lives according to their personal choices. Besides that, the time pattern is very different. In traditional societies, the religious tradition as well as agricultural patterns force people into sequences and rhythms of life, from which an urban middle class can free itself. Holidays are a very modern and urban invention. The time management of a modern society corresponds to a reductionist anthropology focusing on human features usable for production and consumption. Basic human needs are rarely met. As the philosopher Thomas Macho puts it: in a society of nomads nobody is allowed to complain about sore feet; and in an industrial society nobody is allowed to give space to emotions, etc.

In a highly diversified society world-views are diversified as well and often one person lives with more than one *weltbild*. For instance, someone can work in groundbreaking scientific research and perform rituals at home welcoming an UFO and its crew visiting his home. And he can tell a friend about the visit, who is a computer engineer and a Zen practitioner. Both are technologically minded people, and most likely both will undergo not only the treatment of high-tech medicine in case of illness, but also check with an Ayurvedic doctor or a TCM specialist. Neither the Ayurvedic

---

11 M. Seelmann, 'Der Buddha wohnt auch in Mikroprozessoren. Analysen zur religiösen Produktivität von Wissensgesellschaften', in H.-M. Gutmann and Cathrin Gutwald (eds.), *Religiöse Wellness. Seelenheil heute*, München, Wilhelm Fink, 2005: 39.
12 Seelmann, 'Der Buddha wohnt'.

doctor nor the TCM specialist uses electronic equipment for his diagnosis, but knows how to read bodily appearances and psychological evidences, as well as the different qualities of his clients' pulse. From that he will diagnose the relation of the different qualities that make up a human being according to traditional medical theories.

This points to another dimension of an anthropology of spirituality: sense qualities. Biomedical diagnosis and treatment is firmly based on the Cartesian program which divides the world into Mind – *res cogitans* – and expanded elements (*res extensae*), where only the sense of touch perceiving expansions is relevant. Colour, taste, smell, surface qualities, etc., are secondary and, therefore, secondary sense qualities. In this world a rose is a cylindric object with small cones and complexly shaped trapeze-like leaves. Of course, through certain measurement procedures, the so called secondary sense qualities can be accessed, but they have no relevance.

Traditional medical anthropologies and world-views emphasize all sense-qualities equally. Contemporary strategies of wellness absorb the 'secondary sense-qualities' and cultivate them; crystals, mirrors, incense, colours, symbols, etc., are part of the basic layout of a wellness spa or an esoteric shop. All these items are said to contain spiritual qualities inasmuch as they refer to traditional, non-reductionist world-views. Stories and myths are also connected to these items – e.g., about special healing effects of stones and earth-spirits. In traditional societies this knowledge is accessible only through hierarchical structures, but in modern urban environments it is – and has to be – purchased and it has a monetary value.

The transfers to other parts of everyday life are blurred. Thus, a technician can immerse herself during her breaks, via the internet, into the cosmology of the Aztecs, and from there she can draw resources to organize her working life while, most likely, the workers' council is not very helpful or effective. Hollywood blockbusters like 'The Lion King' use insights of C.G. Jung's archetypal psychology, to develop successful stories, whereas psychophysical data about consumers' attention foster the effectiveness of advertizements. A multiplicity of stories and myths addresses the longing for meaning, promising easy solutions in all dimensions of life. These stories range from the belief in magic to the devotion for Indian gods to the Bible used by charismatic Christian communities for the solution of personal problems.

It is all about a search for balance. Sometimes, though, all these 'spiritual techniques' do not work, and then a new dimension of an anthropology of spirituality opens up.

The desire for qualities, for troubleshooting and problem solving, for meaning and a clear frame of reference may lead to the need to clarify one's own position. Unresolved existential problems, a nagging dissatisfaction or even a depression usually lead to a deeper form of self-reflection, either to a psychotherapeutic approach or to a so called 'spiritual practice'.

In general, every type of meditation practice is called 'spiritual', i.e., whether Yoga, Zen-Buddhist or Sufi practice, or the prayer of the heart. All these spiritual ways emerge from a traditional world-view, and are embedded in different ritual contexts. These rituals activate the world-views of the respective traditions and therefore help to integrate a person into a given tradition and society. The contemporary urban spiritual seeker is not necessarily concerned with these aspects. And psychology lends a helping hand: scientific research – a contemporary perspective – shows that there are similarities between these spiritual ways. From a psychological point of view, shamanic trance, Sufi dance, Zen practice or Yoga meditation, the complex and subtle visualizations of Buddhas and Boddhisattvas in Tibetan Buddhist practices as well as the ceaselessly repeated name of Jesus in the hesychastic prayer can be regarded as ways of disrupting everyday habits thus enabling people to learn new ways of experiencing and thinking. Certain drugs can have similar effects.

Such altered states of consciousness are basic human patterns of experience, according to modern psychology.[13] The results of EEGs suggest that there is a difference if one closes the eyes as in most yogic meditations or keeps the eyes open as a Zen practitioner does, whereas the EEG patterns of a shamanistic trance differ substantially from both of them. There is no single peak in which all spiritual paths converge, as is often proposed. Mystic experiences are as diverse as the environments in which they evolve, even though they have something in common.[14]

From a perspective which takes into account the traditional requirements for such practices there is a convergence of the different spiritual paths. 'Path' or 'way' is a traditional term, referring to a life-long exercise of specific patterns of behaviour. Taking a spiritual 'path' or 'way' is similar to learning a musical instrument; it takes a long time to master a violin, for example, and to refine the practice. Regarding spirituality, the human being as a whole is the field of exercise. All dimensions are included, even when classical ascetic Christian practices were asking for mortifications of the body and its desires – a training of separating body and mind and suppressing the bodily aspect. Buddhist meditation on corpses focuses on the decomposing of the body in order to enforce the perspective of transience. Other Buddhist paths envision 'pure lands' and paradises, or teach people to visualize themselves as gods or goddesses (of course, not a monotheistic vision of God). Other ways of practices do without images and concentrate on the process of breathing or on everyday activities, etc. Even rituals – e.g., pujas, in which outer and inner images, sounds, words, and activities are linked to each other – serve as ways of practice. The decisive key is mindfulness here and now.

In each of these ways the cultivation of the human being is central. Theravada Buddhists, for instance, generally use the term 'bhavana' for meditation; this is sometimes translated as 'unfolding of the mind'. Rationality, imagination, willpower, emotions are centred and cultivated, so that an integrated state of awareness can evolve. The everyday notions of time and space as well as the I/ego as the organizing centre fade away. It is a *dis-identification* and is often compared to the process of dying. In tracing dimensions of an anthropology of spirituality this process is crucial, for here is the demarcation line between the search for wellness and a broader, non reductive world-view and the spiritual quest proper.

The different traditions however offer different interpretations of this process, according to their metaphysics and ontologies. Buddhists, for example, will talk of an apersonal experience whereas Christians will most often emphasize the personal aspect; Hindus might have both or even more possibilities, according to the tradition they follow; but, all meet in a 'unity of nothingness',[15] which is not on a peak, but in the depths of life itself.

Letting go, dying and coming back to life are also part of the basic pattern of shamanism and rituals of initiation, but they differ from meditative practices. It seems

---

13 A. Dittrich, *Ätiologie-unabhängige Strukturen veränderter Wachbewusstseinszustände*, Berlin, Verlag für Wissenschaft und Bildung, 1996.
14 Peter Widmer, *Mystikforschung zwischen Materialismus und Metaphysik*, Freiburg, Herder, 2004.
15 Katharina Ceming, *Einheit im Nichts*, Augsburg, Verstehen, 2004.

that it is less a letting go of all images than a letting go of worldly life and entering into another realm. A shaman travels into the yonder world to explore the reasons of sickness and calamities, and to find appropriate remedies. To become a shaman one must pass through an ordeal of life and death, and, similarly, when someone is ritually initiated – for instance, into adulthood – there is an ordeal to be undergone. There is always 'some death' included, some pain, some trial, at least symbolically as in the early Christian rites of baptism, where the neophytes were submerged into the water to incorporate them into the body of Christ, identifying the submersion with Christ's death and resurrection.

On these spiritual ways, continuous exercise will provide new dimensions of perception and cognition of oneself and the world. The perception of subtle bodies adds to an anthropology of spirituality – of course, a perception as diverse as the perception of bodies in general. Each tradition has its own teaching on subtle bodies. All spiritual ways emphasize that it requires a lot of training to experience the dimension of subtle bodies; in Buddhism, for example, it is ascribed to a more advanced stage of meditation practice, whereas the Vedas distinguish seven different sheaths of bodies. Subtle bodies can also appear as distinct entities situated in non-human realms of traditional cosmologies, e.g., angels. Often these teachings are linked to the anthropology of traditional medicine, e.g., in Ayurveda or in TCM and Tibetan medicine, and/or to rituals. For instance, angels play a role in traditional Jewish and Christian liturgies, as they are thought to populate the heavens of Yahweh Sabbaoth. In Islam, angels have a prominent role in the Qur'an, and belief in angels is compulsory.

It is difficult to draw the line between experience, belief and metaphysics. For a contemporary spiritual anthropology the teachings of subtle bodies refer more to the dimension of wellness than to ritual and belief.

Another result of the de-identification and de-habitualization is a change in capabilities. Primarily, it is concentration and relaxation, but traditions report of abilities that sound quite fantastic, such as reading the heart/mind of others or certain visionary experiences. These capabilities run against most contemporary rational perspectives and conventional ideas about time and space. However, the scriptures of religious traditions are full of such events disrupting the everyday ontologies of time and space, and not only contemporary notions, but of past times, too. Otherwise, nobody would have told these stories.

For an anthropology of spirituality one might suggest that all these astonishing and improbable reports could be classified under the dimension of perception of qualities. The traditional spiritual ways do not consider these abilities crucial or decisive for 'spiritual progress'. On the contrary, very often they advise one not to pay attention to, or not to try to achieve, these abilities, as they emerge as serious hindrances on the way, luring the person into egoistic habits.

Pivotal for an anthropology of spirituality is the notion of self/I/ego and the ability of self-reflection. In the realm of wellness the individual person and her or his needs and wishes, plus the financial potentials, are central, whereas in a traditional society the hierarchical order allows the needs and wishes of its members. To ask 'who am I?' or 'what is my place in the world?' is the characteristic query of the philosophically minded and/or people on a spiritual quest. Neither in a traditional village in India or Africa or somewhere else nor in a wellness spa is this demand for self-reflection necessary; indeed, most often, it is considered to be bothersome. On a spiritual way, this type of self-reflection is intrinsic and cannot be evaded. Meditative practices inevitably lead to a sound questioning of customs and habits, as well as world-views.[16] A Catholic nun who is practising contemplation according to the advice of 'The Cloud of Unknowing', an instruction in meditation of the 14th century, might experience severe losses: God, her values, her world and her self-image might disappear and she might experience a 'dark night'; after passing through this experience she might find herself seeing the world with new eyes. It is a restructuring, a restructuring of the way one refers to herself or himself as well as to the world. The Hua Yen tradition of Buddhism therefore talks of a 'turning of the basis', by which they mean a reorientation: the knowing or perceiving agent stops orienting its activities to outward objects, and turns itself away from the perception of objects altogether. Again, the early Zen Buddhist tradition talks of a cleansing of the senses.

The whole way of referring to the world and oneself has to change as even the ego is not the centre but just an object, which has to be qualified. Therefore, a spiritual way can be seen as a profound change of the dimensions of perception and cognition.

It could be described as a liberating way as well. 'Freedom is just another way of nothing left to lose', pop singer Janis Joplin sang years ago. It was, I suppose, unintentionally a description of a spiritual way, which consists of repeatedly letting go – of attachments, of urges, of dear habits, of oneself and the idea of the world in general. 'Do not hope, do not be afraid, do not rejoice, do not be sad': an admonition that can be found both in the Spanish mystic St John of the Cross and Zen master Dogen.[17]

The process of radically letting go – experienced as dying while living – seems to be a kind of anthropological pattern which can be found in all traditions and cultures. People can chose to adapt it according to the context. The social structures of a traditional society are not the same as the social structures of an industrialized society, and as the self-perception is shaped by society so the ego of a Thai peasant differs from the ego of a German woman living in a city. The process of letting go will vary according to the situation, as conditions of societies differ. In any case, though, it will be a way into a deeper openness, as the ego/self will not be at the centre.

The basic methodology of all spiritual ways is to relativize fixed positions, especially the position of ego/self. Simply, it makes a difference when one perceives oneself as relative to others.

---

16 Which can be seen as social constructions, i.e., solidified habits, cf. Peter L. Berger and Thomas Luckmann, *The Sacred Canopy*, New York, Doubleday, 1967.
17 Ursula Baatz, *H.M. Enomiya-Lassalle – ein Leben zwischen den Welten*, Zürich and Düsseldorf, Benziger, 1998: 248.

François Bousquet

An Open Christology: Kierkegaard for Interreligious Dialogue[1]

The position that I will defend may be surprising at first approach: it appears unthinkable due to certain interpretations of Kierkegaard's philosophy and theology. It is common in philosophy to make him the 'father of existentialism', thereby locking him up in the philosophy of the subject, making him subjectivist. In theology, one retains Kierkegaard's violent claim, at the end of his life, for a confessing Church. How, then, can one find elements in his thought for a better positioning in interreligious dialogue? We note that two elements of the intellectual and spiritual testimony that this genius left for us are neglected: his theory of communication and his presentation of truth, or more precisely, of the way to become a subject 'in truth'. It is these two elements that enables a better approach to interreligious dialogue. They express concern for the other, which is necessary for becoming human, and the humility necessary to the church for a better witnessing to the Gospel.

Each of the two elements plays at the same time on the registers of existential philosophy and theology. In philosophy, Kierkegaard's theory of communication proposes a way of relating to the other which allows each person to become the subject of his or her destiny. In theology, it invites us to imitate God's way of communicating Godself in the *kenosis* of the Son. As regards the reflection about truth, it helps us to locate precisely the concept of conversion in existence: in dialogue, the goal should be, not to convert the other to oneself, as in proselytism, but to be together more converted to God before whom every subject is non-truth. Moreover, it means imitating and following the One who in person is not less than 'the being of truth', though incognito, i.e., as humble and Servant.

One of the difficulties of interreligious dialogue is to be neither exclusivist nor relativist: to fall neither into intolerance nor into relativism. That is, to state it positively, to hold to what one believes to be just and good, without excluding or despising the truth of the other's conviction or way of being. The figure of Christ in Kierkegaard's thought is one the *lignes de force* of his work as I have shown elsewhere.[2]

Let us open ourselves to this ardent thought so as to be enriched from it in dialogue.

1. The respect of the other in communication

One of the great profits of modern studies in Kierkegaard it the bringing to light his theory of communication, especially of 'indirect' communication (*Papirer* VII 2B 89). This does not transmit objective knowledge but habilitates a *savoir-être* while inviting to freedom in 'repetition', which, according to him, is the appropriation of the data

---

[1] This is the revised text of a conference paper given at the Centrum för Teologi och religionsvetenskap of the Faculty of Theology of the University of Lund (Sweden), 14 October, 2003. A French translation has been published in *Transversalités, Revue de l'Institut Catholique de Paris* 89 (2004): 131-138.
[2] Cf. François Bousquet, *Le Christ de Kierkegaard, Devenir Chrétien par passion d'exister*, number 76 in Collection Jésus et Jésus-Christ series, Paris, Desclée, 1999.

available for our free choice. We are not judged on what was given to us, but on what we shall do with it. Kierkegaard, as his Christology and Philosophy testify, always respects three decisive stakes: the call to become subjects, our condition as historical beings, and the weight of the negative.

At this time, another extraordinary text expresses what, in the dialogue, is essential, namely, our situation in time and due respect for consciences: 'To stop a man on the street and stand still while talking to him is not so difficult as to say something to a passer-by in passing, without standing still and without delaying the other, without attempting to persuade him to go the same way, but giving him instead an impulse to go precisely his own way. Such is the relation between one existing individual and another, when the communication concerns the truth as existential inwardness' (SV VII: 264[3]). This text brings us to the two major qualities of dialogue: to make it a communication that invites to freedom, and to radically engage oneself in it while simultaneously turning oneself to the One who is greater than our hearts.

1.1. A communication that invites to freedom

The ensemble of Kierkegaard's work, pseudonymous and signed, philosophical and religious, articulates a double proposition: that of becoming subject in existence and that of becoming Christian. In short, it does not separate becoming Christian and the passion to exist. I will not dwell here on the mechanism of the philosophy of Stages (aesthetic, ethic, religious, with the two thresholds of irony and humour). Instead, in this extraordinary school of freedom, through the choices made by the individual (or the singular person) before himself or herself *and* before God in the person of Christ, I simply wish to bring to light what we can learn from it for the practice of interreligious dialogue.

Religious debate is not primarily a war of ideas, but a clarification of the forms of life which will help to ensure the quality of life as it is transmitted in the face of illusion, violence and, finally, death. In this combat the *ultimate concern*, to borrow from Tillich, is the Eternal. What has just been said reveals two things. First, it is clear that the religious concerns life and death, whence flows the passion that accompanies it. Second, it becomes necessary to respect all human mediations, individual and collective, which give an existential consistency to religious choice. 'It is important', writes Kierkegaard, 'to present the religious neither too fast, nor two slow... Therefore, the religious author must seek first to be in contact with men' (SV XIII: 568).

What can one really do for somebody in going into dialogue with him or her? First, understand him or her: 'In order to bring somebody successfully to a particular point, one must first of all seek to take him and to begin from where he is.... To help somebody, I must...first have intelligence of what he understands' (SV XIII: 569). In addition, we note that this refers to Christ and to what he shows regarding God's way of relating to us: in order to share his life with us, he started by sharing our life and by making himself one with us.

One of the conditions of freedom is to 'exist in what one understood' (SV VII: 260). The first step is to be attentive. 'In the end, even if a man refuses to follow where one tries to lead him, one can however do something for him: to oblige him to be attentive' (SV XIII: 574). It is simple, but one must pay a price – as Christ and his true witnesses, the martyrs, did. 'To oblige a man to be attentive and to judge, that is really the law of

---

3 SV = *Samlede Voerker*, København, Gyldendal, 2nd edition, 1920-1936.

the true martyr. An authentic martyr has never used power, he always fought with the force of his powerlessness. He obliged men to be attentive. Surely, God knows, they were attentive: they put him to death' (SV XIII: 575).

It is noteworthy that Kierkegaard's work conforms to what it wants to show. On one hand, there are the pseudonymous works which describe all sorts of forms of life in existence, using different styles of literature – novel, pastiche, essay, banquet (*Symposium*), theological treatise, etc. – with all sorts of picturesque and typical characters. Pseudonymity is neither a mask nor a ruse, but a literary procedure in which the author steps aside in favour of the reader, such that the latter may be referred back to the choice he has to make. On the other hand, there are collections of Kierkegaard's homilies and 'edifying discourses' which offer a witness of what could be a Christian existence, when 'to believe' is, in practice, the imitation or following of Christ (*sequela Christi*). Pseudonymity only intervenes when the author wants to depict the perfect Christian which, as everyone knows, does not exist.

What shall we draw from this as regards interreligious dialogue? The style of shared word must respect others, meet them where they are so as to understand them, help them to become attentive to choices that could be their own. This raises the question of what grounds the authority of a word, even a shared one? A reliable word is a word that sets free. This answer, however, is not intended to deny announcement, i.e., the witness, as Catholics say today, that the Church and the Christians have to bear. This in turn brings us to talk of the other aspect of respect for the other in communication: to engage oneself in it even as one turns oneself to the One who is the greater Truth.

1.2. A communication where one does not cling to his being as a prey (Phil. 2:6-11)

Here again, Christ is the model, presenting God's way of self-communicating. That is the object of *Training in Christianity*. For the Christian, the good 'site' of the true word is in becoming Christ's contemporary in his self-humbling. This poses a paradox, an alternative between scandal or faith. It has been Christianity's misfortune to discourse learnedly on the person of Christ while what is authorized in his regard is to believe in him (SV XII: 52). That is the object of the essential scandal which can only be surmounted in faith: that the one who is given as God 'presents himself as a man of a humble condition, poor, suffering, and finally powerless' (SV XII: 124-127). One sees immediately that God's logic must become the logic of witness when it is a question of communicating what is of the essence, which is not a knowledge but the very Spirit of God, the breath, the source of inspiration which constitutes a person as Christian. God's logic is a witness to the way of Christ of whom faith makes one contemporary. In such a perspective, the criterion for the verification of the faith of the Church is that she remains a confessing Church instead of falling into the illusion of 'triumph'. To become the contemporary of the Crucified-Resurrected is not to dominate, but to serve, and this in the midst of the trial of time, in the hand-to-hand struggle against evil, for the truth, in the 'test' of obedience, and without withdrawal from the world, because one does not want to give up hope. Between the ascension and the *parousia*, Christ will be the truth for us; indeed, the being of truth will be Christ's life in us, on the condition that this truth, his truth, becomes our way, with the obligation to reduce the distance between the Christian word and our existence. Passion unites with patience. Christ himself is given in the imitation, just as it is in prayer that the identity between the grace given to us and our renewed freedom is reconstituted.

I see in this position of Kierkegaard a clue for the deepening of the phrase of Vatican II (in *Gaudium et Spes* § 22,5) which has given a lot of work to theologians for more than forty years: 'For since Christ died for all, and since all men are in fact called to one and the same destiny, which is divine, we must hold that the Holy Spirit offers to all the possibility of being made partners, in a way known to God, in the paschal mystery.' Furthermore, I see here the fundamental law of interreligious dialogue for a Christian. If we want to share the truth that we have recognized, then we have to accept that this truth be at the same time proclaimed and vulnerable, in a logic which is that of sign, indeed of effective sign.[4] A sign gives enough light to be understood, but in such a way that it imposes nothing, but instead proposes only a recognition by true faith, trusting freedom. This brings us to examine more closely Kierkegaard's reflection on truth.

2. The ever-greater Truth

In the communication of dialogue, after respect for the other, the willingness to listen to him or her and to understand without thinking immediately that one has exalted one's own truth, comes the moment of witness. If becoming Christian really means 'to search for a truth for which one can live and die', then witness is vital; for, how can we not wish to share that which is the source of our joy? However, to witness is first of all to serve, that is, to serve the truth. Two obstacles to this present themselves: sin and violence, and we must distinguish between them.

2.1. Witness as service to the truth

The first obstacle is sin, the distance between what we proclaim and what, in reality, we do. Yet, as shown in the whole dialectic of the *Post Scriptum*, if truth is to become subject 'before God' (one must add, through the encounter with Christ), then each subject knows that he or she is not really 'true'. Kierkegaard's latter-day protestation against the Church, especially in the pamphlets of the *Instant*, was directed towards those who pretend to be 'witnesses to the truth' while omitting to recognize their sin. According to him, the reason that the Gospel of the New Testament does not exist is that it is not practised by those who are supposed to be its authorized witnesses. Indeed, for witness to be effective they only need to recognize it. In Christ there is no distance between what he does and what he says; he is the only example of repetition (to exist in what one has understood). Even more, he is what he says and what he does, God's word in act, in a human existence. That is why he is not only a 'model' but a saviour. That is also why his life and death are not only judgment but also promise. Let us draw the consequences: in the interreligious dialogue, what we say in faith must correspond to our way of being, and if that is not the case, then we have to confess it humbly.

The second obstacle, of the same nature, is violence, the violence of one who believes that he or she 'possesses' the truth. However, this obstacle is surmounted when we understand that truth is not what makes us right, but what judges us. For Christians, the truth that judges all truths is the Crucified One. The ultimate word, whose contemporaries we are, is the word of the cross. In following this word of the cross the Christian is able to escape, in the course of dialogue with others, from that possession which both substitutes our word for that of God and can lead to violence. The faith of a Christian, then, is not a putatively absolute knowledge; rather, it is trust in the Unique

---

4 This is a reference to the theology of the sacraments that requires deepening by Catholics.

One. For, in seeking to know things from the perspective of God, we do not imagine that we are in heaven, in the place, so to speak, where God abides and so in God's stead. The eyes with which the Christian believer envisages things must be those of the Crucified One. Then, it is impossible to legitimize in God's name the arrogant violence of our supposed possession of truth.

We need also to be mindful that, in our historical condition, we cannot attain more than partial and fragmentary truths from our research or debates; Truth can only be an eschatological horizon, which is why Christian faith intervenes precisely here. Faith does not consist in believing in some Platonic, constantly revived Eternal, but in 'believing in time in the Eternal in time'. In Christian faith, the fullness of the truth is not only at the end, but is also already on the way. This means that we can relate to the Truth because it is already given. Indeed, to believe, in the sense of to believe in Christ, is an imitation: the imitation of this Unique One, who is the being of Truth in time. The witness, concerning what we consider in faith as true and good for humans, is verified by seeing how we propose it to others so that they may live through it. Moreover, in the imitation of Christ, there is a *how* which, rightly posed, gives the *what* of faith (cf. *Papirer* X 2 A 299).

2.2. The humility of a truth that offers itself 'incognito' for the sake of love

The category of incognito must be explained. What is the advantage of employing this category rather than that of 'mystery' (which as everyone knows is not what ends our thinking but what will always give us more to think about)? The object of interreligious dialogue is to share about God. It is not futile to recognize in God the ever greater truth. This requires, then, that the partners in dialogue question their certainties – which pretend to be evidence – concerning all that we take to be natural but which, most of the time, is cultural. Though Christians are more familiar with 'mystery', the category of incognito is what helps Kierkegaard to make a connexion between God's way of being for us and the quality of existence, and thus of dialogue that is imitation of Christ who is both the humble one and the servant. To talk, in Christology, about incognito draws attention to the relatedness of an ensemble of things: in the incarnation, no displaced familiarity with Christ, and no forgetting of the fact that God is God; no prevalence of the image (which easily becomes an idol) but a return to imitation; finally, no illusion of ultimately surmounting the contradictions of sin which leads to death. For, Christ's incognito reminds us, in the one moment, of both suffering truth and God's holiness.

3. The Christian in Interreligious Dialogue

Christ's incognito has immediate consequences for the word of the Christian who is in dialogue and wants to attest the truth that he or she lives. Thus, we can conclude by saying that both the 'style' of dialogue and the 'style' of witness of the Church must be modified through it. In this way a radical question is addressed to theologians, preachers and believers. When you talk about your faith, do you do so in the name of your spiritual experience with sufficient respect for God's alterity? Kierkegaard cautions us. 'A direct relation to God is paganism', he says (SV VII: 229). There is in this more than mere praise of patience in the face of that triumphal truth which, we have noted, is a bad way of anticipating eternity (SV XII: 223; SV XII: 234). It must refer to our responsibility for living out the signs expressed in the liturgy, the acts and language of which are deliberately located in eschatology. For the eternal gift, whose memory is re-enacted, cannot be celebrated ahead of time, by anticipation, without being recognized immediately as demand and task in time. It then follows that theological dialogue, and the dialogue of prayer itself, cannot do without the dialogue of life and action, in which we recognize that, while doing the truth, we come into the light (see John 3:21), a light in which everyone is welcome, especially the excluded, the lost, the victims of history, and the more humble who honour us by entering into dialogue with us. To engage in interreligious dialogue is to be seized by the quality of the spiritual experience of the other, in which we, as Christians, recognize something of the Passover that Christ renders possible for everyone in the concrete reality of his or her existence.

Gabriel Daly OSA and Andrew Pierce

Christian Theology, Imagination and 'Religious Fundamentalism'

From a perspective within modern, Western, Christian theology, this paper asks if theology's appeal to imagination might encourage engagement with religious fundamentalism.[1] This question presupposes both that there is, or has been, a theological appeal to imagination and that there is a general theological disregard for religious fundamentalism which ought to be challenged. Before addressing the principal question, it may be appropriate to address these assumptions, albeit briefly.

Within the past three decades there has been a renewed and significant interest in the theme of imagination on the part of theologians and philosophers. The work of Paul Ricoeur, Richard Rorty, Richard Kearney, Mary Warnock – to name but a few – have kept particularly the epistemological significance of imagination to the fore in philosophy. Theologically, David Tracy, John McIntyre, Ray L. Hart and Garrett Green – again, a mere sample of prominent writers – have insisted on the importance of this theme for Christian systematic theology and their proposals draw upon a long-established tradition within Christianity's contesting of and with the projects of modernity. Kant, Schleiermacher and Hegel, along with many other European apologists for a modern, post-Romantic Christian theology, all viewed imagination as a key theme in their various projects. Indeed, one might argue that the significance attached to imagination in nineteenth-century post-Kantian or idealist theology provoked the emphasis on projection in the criticisms of revealed religion mounted by Feuerbach and the other masters of suspicion. Religion was imaginative projection, they urged, and therefore untrue.

The second assumption, that Western, Christian theology disregards religious fundamentalism, deserves more detailed analysis than space permits. Two points may, however, be worth noting. The first is that the discourse of fundamentalist studies is shaped largely by extra-theological disciplines, e.g., sociology, political science and cultural studies, which tend to adopt etic (i.e., outsider) approaches to the study of religion (approaches which offer possibilities, but also limitations). Christian theologians are conspicuous by their absence from this field; or, if present (e.g., the important work by James Barr and Harriet Harris) they write as historians of ideas, rather than as systematic theologians.[2] The second is more far-reaching: modern, western Christian theology has deep-rooted and intractable problems with understanding Otherness, problems that have been probed in John D'Arcy May's ground-breaking study, *Transcendence and Violence*.[3] Part of the

---

1 For a more sustained engagement with Christian religious fundamentalism, see Gabriel Daly OSA, 'Catholic fundamentalism', in Angela Hanley and David Smith MSC (eds.), *Quench not the Spirit: Theology and Prophecy for the Church in the Modern World*, Dublin, Columba, 2005: 125-136; and Andrew Pierce, 'Millennialism, Ecumenism, and Fundamentalism', in Kenneth G.C. Newport and Crawford Gribben (eds.), *Expecting the End: Millennialism in Social and Historical Context*, Waco, Baylor University, 2006: 79-95.
2 E.g., James Barr, *Fundamentalism*, Philadelphia, Westminster, 1978; Harriet Harris, *Fundamentalism and Evangelicals*, Oxford, Clarendon, 1998.
3 John D'Arcy May, *Transcendence and Violence: The Encounter of Buddhist, Christian and Primal Traditions*, New York and London, Continuum, 2003. See especially May's analysis of

dynamic of systemic repression and projection within the Western Christian tradition is also evidenced in its treatment of *its own* fundamentalisms: the fundamentalist Other does not merit serious consideration as a potential partner in dialogue. Her or his concern with truth and power may safely be written-off – *a priori* – as an ideological construction and nothing more. Thus, Christian theological engagement with fundamentalism is doubly disadvantaged without knowing it: as a discipline, it has opted out of the field of fundamentalist studies; and, it has defined itself as having nothing but discontinuity with fundamentalist religiosity.

The first part of this paper sets an historical context for the present general interest in religious fundamentalism, viewed from a perspective of modern, Western, Christian theology and naming this tradition insistently in order to resist its well-documented pretensions to universality and its insensitivity to the context of others. Part two unpacks the ways in which Christian theologians have interpreted the significance of an appeal to imagination, before concluding, in part three, by considering how theological engagement with imagination might assist theologians who are concerned to reflect *theologically* on the rise of fundamentalist religiosity.

I. The Global Resurgence of Religious Identity

A certain nervousness is abroad in an intellectual climate that formerly held to the secularization thesis with much the same vigour as did the nineteenth century bourgeoisie to its myth of progress. An age that had once confidently expected a postmodern end to grand narratives (triggering the celebration of difference and particularity) is no longer as certain as before that celebration is the most appropriate response.

This is an extraordinary ideological *volte-face*. At the end of the nineteenth century, the French sociologist Guyau published an optimistic and idealistic appraisal of where the world was heading, *The Irreligion of the Future*.[4] Within a century, however, the globalization of unstoppable irreligion has become a problematic prognosis, as suggested by Gilles Kepel's splendid title, *The Revenge of God*.[5] Not only did we misread the evidence, we now face the uncomfortable consequences of our error. Post-Kantian, nineteenth-century Christian apologetics had argued deductively that there was a defensible essence of religion, and that Western Christianity (by which it usually meant liberal Protestant Christianity) represented this essence in its most respectable historic form, with other religions – particularly Judaism – viewed as the jaded remnants of less successful religious projects. This evolutionary and idealistic schema viewed Christianity as the acme of religious evolution, and the intellectual travails of Christianity in the nineteenth century were viewed by sceptical intellectuals as the death-throes of 'religion' *per se*, and as the birth pangs of a secularist 'irreligion.'

And yet religion has failed to go away. *Au contraire,* it thrives. Moreover, many of its adherents are angry, at what they see as their harsh treatment at the hands of some of the perduring grand narratives of the twentieth century (grand narratives, likewise, having demonstrated considerable adaptive skill). As the twenty-first century begins, it is so-called religious fundamentalisms that are making headlines and causing headaches

---

the 'failure of European theology' (26-30) which is a further symptom of the more general failure of transcendence (14-19).

4 M. Guyau, *L'irréligion de l'avenir: étude sociologique*, Paris, Felix Alcan, [1887] 1895[6].
5 Gilles Kepel, *The Revenge of God: The Resurgence of Islam, Christianity and Judaism in the Modern World*, translated by Alan Braley, Cambridge, Polity, 1994.

for framers of policy in the fields of international relations, healthcare, law and human rights.[6] Even a cursory glance at religious news headlines provides evidence of resurgent religiosity defending a wide range of alleged orthodoxies, for example, the travails of the Anglican Communion of Churches in relation to the sexuality of ordained men and women; or the contesting of the Joint Declaration on Justification (and in particular the defensive rationale behind the negative response of Protestant theologians in Germany); or the continuing campaign against the alleged threat of 'relativism' on the part of the Roman Catholic Church's Congregation for the Doctrine of the Faith; or the various syntheses of religious with nationalist and post-colonial ideologies in Ireland, Sri Lanka, India, Israel, Palestine and across the Muslim-majority countries of the Middle East; or the religious right in the USA. And that list is easily expanded.

By the start of the twentieth century, Western defenders of 'religion' (which was often understood to mean Western, Liberal, Protestant Christianity) saw it 'essentially' in terms of individual subjectivity, as evidenced by a frequent appeal to the notion of a 'religious consciousness'.[7] A century later, however, we see a greater acknowledgement that the world of religious experience reaches further than European Christianity, and that it is concerned with a good deal more than the exalted mental states of 'individual men in their solitude' (to quote William James's memorable definition of religion). As the cultural anthropologist Clifford Geertz has observed recently in an essay on James, religion, understood as an individual's state of mind, may have lost currency in academic discourse but as an active social agent it increasingly claims close attention.[8]

As Western Christianity – embodied in its contending traditions – engaged with Modernity, a number of its far-sighted interpreters continued the post-Romantic tradition of investing considerable attention in the theme of imagination; to their contribution we now turn.

II. Religion and Imagination in the Modern, Western World

Ever since Immanuel Kant's critical philosophy, it has become a philosophical commonplace that knowledge is not a simple registering of what is there. The mind makes its own contribution to the process by structuring the data provided by the senses; but the mind has its own modes of acting. It can function discursively, as in mathematics or formal logic; and it can function intuitively or pictorially, as in poetry or art. Both are mental activities. Theology can engage with either or both. Here we are concerned principally with the latter, with what Blaise Pascal had earlier called the *esprit de finesse*, in contrast to the *esprit de géométrie*, or mathematical mind. In making his distinction Pascal was reacting in part against the rationalism of Descartes, who had set out to demonstrate – by reason alone – the existence of truth and certainty in the world, including the existence of God. Pascal's point was that the mathematical (or discursive)

---

6   For an excellent tour of the field, see Rebecca Joyce Frey, *Global Issues: Fundamentalism*, Foreword by Peter L. Berger, New York, Infobase, 2007.
7   Religion was not alone in this rarefied cultural condition, see Peter Gay, *The Bourgeois Experience: Victoria to Freud*, 5 volumes, London, HarperCollins, 1984-98, especially volume 2, *The Naked Heart*, London, HarperCollins, [1995] 1998: 37-102.
8   Clifford Geertz, 'The Pinch of Destiny: Religion as Experience, Meaning, Identity, Power', in his *Available Light: Anthropological Reflections on Philosophical Topics*, Princeton and Oxford, Princeton University, 2000: 167-186. William James's much-quoted definition may be found in his *The Varieties of Religious Experience: A Study in Human Nature*, Glasgow, William Collins, [1901-02] 1985: 50.

mind might indeed 'prove' the existence of God, but the God so demonstrated has no religious significance. For Pascal, God must be perceived by the heart; but we should have no illusions about what Pascal meant by 'heart'. This is no flight to sentimentality or emotionalism. Something of enduring significance is at stake. It is a rejection, by historical anticipation, of Enlightenment rationalism for which Descartes was preparing the way by his theory of a self-regarding, autonomous reason. Pascal's 'heart' is not mere sentiment (after all, the heart has its reasons). It is the mind used in a way which is influenced by the affections, by the emotions, by the perception of the moral and the aesthetic, and also by the very precariousness of our human lives. Like all living things we are reeds, but, as Pascal pointed out, we are thinking reeds – and therein lies our dignity and our tragedy.

It is this mode of mental activity that philosophers name imagination. At any rate, that is the name that Samuel Taylor Coleridge gave to the use of the mind described by Pascal as the *esprit de finesse*. And Coleridge, like Pascal, is significant because his articulation of imagination's significance took the form of romantic protest against the denial of cognitive significance to feeling and the affections. Modernity's romantic discontents – Pascal, Coleridge, Blake, Kierkegaard, perhaps even Kant – were acutely conscious of a loss incurred by modernity's upward fall towards moral autonomy and the ever-increasing competence of technology resulting from inductive scientific methodologies. Significantly, religion (i.e., Western Christianity) was not the only cultural artefact to experience modernity as a socially marginalizing process. Other creations of the human imagination, and particularly the arts, have also found their social utility questioned by an ascendant technocratic rationalism. Imagination is not a fashionable theme in these post-modern times, when 'romanticism' is often employed as a term of intellectual abuse. Yet, the case made by Coleridge *et al* continues to merit attention: our age, with its gratuitous reduction of reason to the technical and instrumental, needs imagination just as much as Coleridge felt that his age needed it to offset the rigidities and aridities of Enlightenment rationalism.

According to Coleridge, '[i]t is among the miseries of the present age that it recognizes no medium between *Literal* and *Metaphorical*',[9] that is, between fact and fantasy. Coleridge complained that his contemporaries were unable to distinguish between an allegory and a symbol. An allegory, he patiently explained, is merely the translation of abstract notions into picture-language: it may help us to understand these notions, but it is not indispensable. 'On the other hand a symbol ... always partakes of the reality it renders intelligible.' A symbol, then, is not an embellishment; a symbol is necessary and indispensable, because it is an alternative to silence.

W.B. Yeats expressed the same point, long after romanticism had yielded to modernism:

> A symbol is indeed the only possible expression of some invisible essence, a transparent lamp about a spiritual flame; while allegory is one of many possible representations of an embodied thing or a familiar principle...: the one is a revelation, the other an amusement.[10]

---

9 Samuel Taylor Coleridge, *The Statesman's Manual*, in R.J. White (ed.), *Lay Sermons*, Oxford, 1972: 30, [= volume 6 of E.L. Griggs (ed.), *Collected Works of Samuel Taylor Coleridge*, 6 volumes, Oxford, 1956-1971], as cited in John Coulson, *Religion and Imagination: 'in aid of a grammar of assent'*, Oxford, Clarendon, 1981: 14n14.

10 Cited in Charles Taylor, *Sources of the Self: The Making of the Modern Identity*, Cambridge, Cambridge University, 1989: 421.

Contemporary Christian theological hermeneutics recognizes the truth of what Coleridge is saying. As Paul Tillich never tired of pointing out, virtually all statements about God are symbolic: and it is, of course, the *imagination* which apprehends and evaluates symbols. It was Coleridge more than anyone else who gave the 'imagination' the weight that it still carries in the English language.[11] The imagination is what makes things come alive in the mind. It has been said of Coleridge that he continually seeks 'the radiance of the eternal in the particular'[12] – which remains a valid description of a great deal of art, even today.

All this is seriously out of kilter with our present deconstructive age which is more attentive to difference and particularity. Nevertheless, a concern with discerning particularity's widest possible context transcends romanticism, though it shares with romanticism a deep exasperation with rationalism and scientific positivism. It is often the radiance of the eternal in the particular that the positivist, whether scientific or philosophical, wishes to deny, cannot see, or reduces to its lowest empirical elements in an effort to dispel its power or, if you like, magic. As Coleridge so clearly saw, positivism and reductionism destroy the possibility of *both* art *and* religion.[13]

William Blake, who was more combative than Coleridge, expressed the same view in some vigorous verses.

> Mock on, mock on, Voltaire, Rousseau:
> Mock on, mock on: 'tis all in vain!
> You throw the sand against the wind.
> And the wind blows it back again.
>
> And every sand becomes a gem
> Reflected in the beams divine;
> Blown back they blind the mocking eye,
> But still in Israel's paths they shine.
>
> The atoms of Democritus
> And Newton's particles of light
> Are sands upon the Red Sea shore
> Where Israel's tents do shine so bright.[14]

Following Baron Friedrich von Hügel, this approach to reality may be described as mystical – best thought of, not as an exalted state of mind granted to a minority of specially favoured souls, but as a perspective on the world which is open to all.[15] And, as such, as Dame Mary Warnock, the distinguished philosopher and cultural critic, has noted firmly, 'a matter for universal congratulation'.[16] Coleridge called this imagination and said of it:

---

11 Richard Holmes, *Coleridge*, Oxford, Oxford University, [1982] 1989: 48.
12 Holmes, *Coleridge*: 49.
13 For a stimulating discussion of the travails of art in an age of a popular and censorious positivism, see Wendy Steiner, *The Scandal of Pleasure: Art in an Age of Fundamentalism*, Chicago and London, University of Chicago, 1995.
14 Helen Gardner (ed.), *The Faber Book of Religious Verse*, London, Faber & Faber, 1972: 232.
15 Baron Friedrich von Hügel, *The Mystical Element of Religion: As Studied in Saint Catherine of Genoa and Her Friends*, 2 volumes, London, J M Dent and James Clark, [1923²] 1961, especially volume 1: 3-82. See also, Gabriel Daly OSA, 'Mysticism and Modernism', in Linda Hogan and Barbara Fitzgerald (eds.), *Between Poetry and Politics: Essays in Honour of Enda McDonagh*, Dublin, Columba, 2003: 16-31.
16 Mary Warnock, *Imagination*, Berkeley and Los Angeles, University of California, 1976: 209.

the primary imagination I hold to be the living power and prime agent of all human perception, and as a repetition in the finite mind of the eternal act of creation in the infinite I AM.[17]

Not without reason has it been said of Coleridge that he believed that 'the longing for the eternal and the infinite is the defining characteristic of [human beings] in nature.'[18]

Warnock has devoted much attention to the human phenomenon of imagination. This gives an added dimension to her thought which is particularly noticeable when she is in discussion with scientists and linguistic philosophers. She has pointed out that to perceive 'the universal in the particular is ... the very central function of the imagination.'[19] This is, of course the aim of the greater part of poetry and the arts. It is also, as she has noted, crucial to theology:

> If it is true, as I believe it is, that all knowledge of God must be symbolic, there is indeed every reason to treat the aesthetic and the religious imagination as one, since it is the use of symbols that is central to the imagination.[20]

Thomas Kuhn's *The Structures of Scientific Revolutions* (1970) made clear that, even in the natural or hard sciences, positivistic understandings of scientific research and knowledge were seriously deficient. Theories *precede* facts, and paradigms precede theories. Scientists – regardless of their field of expertise – are shaped by communities of knowledge that share in imaginative assumptions about the workings of the world, 'imaginative assumptions' which gain expression in the metaphors and models that shape and express reflexive experience. There may well be a worrying gap between scholarly literature and popular perception concerning the epistemic status of imagination, but it is now clear that the post-Romantics were sound in their judgement when they emphasized imagination in their negotiation of the modern world.

It goes without saying that post-Romantic notions of imagination have undergone justified criticism in the histories of their reception. The privileged link, for instance, between a creative individual – the genius – and the exercise of creative imagination merits considerable rethinking. It is also hard to escape from the assumption that the rhetoric of imagination is intrinsically highbrow. How might this Apollonian notion assist theologians in exploring the comparatively Dionysian world of religious fundamentalism? That is the next topic to be considered.

III. Imagining Others and Otherness

When the word 'Fundamentalist' was just seven years old, Reinhold Niebuhr, the distinguished American theologian and cultural analyst, recorded in his diary the experience of being present as a young minister at an open forum which met at a high school in Detroit. One man asked him when he thought the Lord would come again; another tried to get him to agree that all religion is fantasy. Reflecting on these widely divergent questions, Niebuhr wrote, 'How can an age which is so devoid of poetic imagination as ours be truly religious?' He went on to reflect,

> Fundamentalists have at least one characteristic in common with most scientists. Neither can understand that poetic and religious imagination has a way of

---

17 Holmes, *Coleridge*: 49.
18 Holmes, *Coleridge*: 59.
19 Mary Warnock, 'Religious Imagination', in James P. Mackey (ed.), *Religious Imagination*, Edinburgh, Edinburgh University, 1986: 142-157: 152.
20 Warnock, 'Religious Imagination': 151.

arriving at truth by giving a clue to the total meaning of things without being in any sense an analytic description of detailed facts.[21]

It is interesting that the imaginative deficit noted by Niebuhr in Western Christianity, and which he detected in both scientific scepticism *and* religious fundamentalism, is not simply presented as the defining defect of fundamentalism or scientism. This imaginative deficit characterizes Western theology *tout court* as well as the cultures that this theology has helped to shape. It is a deficit evidenced as much by repository religious art as by the evangelical atheism of Richard Dawkins and Stephen Hawking. It is, in short, characteristic of key currents in popular Western culture in an age of globalization.[22] According to Niebuhr's diagnosis, culturally we are all recovering positivists.

Positivism, formalized in the teaching of Auguste Comte (sociology's curious ancestor), held a naïve faith in theory-independent facts. However, its impatient concern with factuality, with 'positive knowledge' to use the language of the day, links it to one of Christian theology's most persistent sources of migraine during the nineteenth century, a feature that is curiously neglected in much recent historical theology. When Hegel wrote his essay on 'The Positivity of the Christian Religion' in 1795, he dismissed several orthodox doctrines simply *because* they were positive, 'that is, teachings grounded not on universal reason but rather on an arbitrary appeal to the authority of specific historical figures and occurrences.'[23] Hegel's essay – and the issue that it raises – is symptomatic of a tension that Lessing had described as the emergence of 'an ugly great ditch' between contingent, particular, positive claims and events on the one hand, and the necessary truths of reason on the other. How much 'positivity' did Christianity need to retain, when interpreting creeds and scripture for example, in order to remain Christianity? The voyage from a pre-critical to a critical hermeneutic rendered positivity problematic, and yet, as the historical-critical biblical critics tried to make clear, there were issues raised by positivity that demanded theological investigation.

Although the relationship between the form and content of the Christian tradition has always been implicated in Christian doctrinal conflicts, it is hard not to agree with Garrett Green that '[t]he great quarrel in modern Christian thought has been about rightly distinguishing form and content.'[24] That is, the hermeneutics of tradition occupies a central position, both under the conditions of modernity and its postmodern moment of critique. It is in this context that certain nineteenth century Liberal Protestant historians, following in the idealistic and evolutionary tradition of historiography pioneered by Hegel, began to talk of an 'essence', both of religion and of Christianity. Reviewing this historiographical trend in 1903, Ernst Troeltsch traced its emergence to the romantic apologetics of Chateaubriand's *Génie de christianisme,* as well as to Hegelian philosophy of history.[25]

---

21 Reinhold Niebuhr, *Leaves from the Notebooks of a Tamed Cynic*, San Francisco and London, Harper and Row, [1929] 1957: 166-167.
22 Hence, the theological importance attached to imagination by Dermot A Lane in his important essay, 'Faith: Reconstructing Faith for a New Century and a New Society', in Dermot A Lane (ed.), *New Century, New Society: Christian Perspectives*, Dublin, Columba, 1999: 159-173, especially 169-173.
23 Garrett Green, *Theology, Hermeneutics, and Imagination: The Crisis of Interpretation at the End of Modernity*, Cambridge, Cambridge University, 2000: 26.
24 Green, *Theology, Hermeneutics, and Imagination*: 43.
25 Ernst Troeltsch, 'What does "Essence of Christianity" Mean?', in Robert Morgan and Michael Pye (eds.), *Ernst Troeltsch: Writings on Theology and Religion*, Atlanta, John Knox, 1977: 124-179.

It is historians (and not, therefore, religious authorities), according to Troeltsch, who now provide the key to history; study of the complex reality of history authorizes the historian to imagine an essence, i.e., a part that helps us to see the meaning of the whole. The *good* historical critic will select an essence that neither mis-represents the whole, nor ignores key aspects of the whole, and this ethical dimension of historical knowledge haunted Troeltsch throughout the rest of his career.

Thus, the emergence of religious fundamentalism within Western Christianity (evidenced in Roman Catholicism by Pius X's anti-modernist campaign from 1907 onwards and the consequent promotion of 'integral Catholicism', and in Protestant Christianity by the publication of *The Fundamentals* between 1910 and 1920) did not generate spontaneously *ex nihilo*. This mode of religiosity shared – in common with other Western Christians, progressives and conservatives alike – the inherited imaginative deficit that Niebuhr notes. This helped to frame decisive moments in contemporary conflicts: how does the church imagine the Christian tradition? How should the church interpret positivity *and* avoid positivism? What does the Church do with intellectuals whose interrogation of positivity yields doctrinally-unprepossessing results? These were issues contested within every western Christian tradition at the time, and they continue to make an impact even after almost a century.

Moreover, the nineteenth century's anxiety over the distinction between form and content remains a live issue in twenty-first century churches. Fundamentalist religiosity has generally been uncomfortable with this distinction: Protestant biblicists often opt for a doctrine of plenary verbal inspiration of holy scripture, and the first volume of *The Fundamentals* attacked the very notion of an 'essence' of Christianity; Catholic integralists, before the revolutionary Second Vatican Council, held doctrinal form and content together with determination and effectively denied the possibility of a hierarchy of truths.

It is important to underscore the way in which Christian fundamentalisms – at their very inception – were simply part and parcel of the debates and contestings of key issues that affected all Western Christians in this nascent post-positivist era. In the intervening period, however, we have seen the emergence of a tendency to stress discontinuities between fundamentalist Christianity on the one hand (served by a network of bible colleges and secretive seminaries) and an allegedly non-fundamentalist mainstream Christianity (served by critical academic theology) on the other. Discontinuities there undoubtedly are. Yet, there are also continuities, and these must be acknowledged.

Perhaps it is as a result of a lingering positivism in the etic disciplines that dominate fundamentalist studies (sociology, politics, etc.) that much of the literature on fundamentalism exhibits considerable confidence in its imagining of the fundamentalist Other. Take, for example, Emmanuel Sivan's important depiction of the 'enclave culture', a striking feature of fundamentalist religiosity.[26] Nonetheless, enclaves are notoriously difficult to imagine from the outside, and the risk of misleading by projection is very real. In many ways the principal typology at work in the study of fundamentalist religiosity is the crude, and worrying, distinction between a non-fundamentalist 'us' and the fundamentalist 'them'. Fundamentalism, we may too easily discern, is for other people.

A similar difficulty attaches to the widely-held view that religious fundamentalism is inherently reactive (it is characterized as '*fighting back*', by Martin Marty and Scott

---

26 Emmanuel Sivan, 'The Enclave Culture', in Martin E. Marty and R. Scott Appleby (eds.), *The Fundamentalism Project*, 5 volumes, Chicago and London, University of Chicago, 1991-1995: volume 5, *Fundamentalisms Comprehended*: 11-68.

Appleby[27]). It would, however, be difficult to find any tradition within Western Christianity that had not reacted against *some* aspects of modernity. If fundamentalism operates with a reactive imagination, then it is by no means alone. A recent dictionary of ideas includes two articles, one on 'fundamentalism', another on 'Islamic fundamentalism' – the latter of which is almost four times longer than the former.[28] Evidently, the Khomeni revolution of 1979 and the rise of the Taliban had made Western commentators more conscious of Islamist fundamentalisms, and scholarly interest is an appropriate response. Nevertheless, it also makes clear the inherently reactive character of much, if not all, scholarly interest in fundamentalism.

Western Christianity finds it difficult to acknowledge that western, Christian religious fundamentalism may be interpreted as possibly the most significant creation of the Christian religious imagination in the twentieth century. Indeed, its significance shows no signs of diminishing. It is becoming more urgent that Christian theologians take theological trouble to enter into critical dialogue with the imaginations of those they identify as fundamentalists. The presumed discontinuity between fundamentalist and non-fundamentalist Christianity requires considerably more scrutiny than it has received to date. There are also continuities to be acknowledged. Western Christian theology is increasingly reshaping itself – radically – through its multifaceted encounters with the religions. The latter, too, experience so-called fundamentalism; it is a significant part of our experience of the religions, and equally of their experience of Christianity. Theological dialogue that neglects this omnipresent religious experience inevitably lacks candour.

In recent work, Charles Taylor has coined the helpful phrase 'modern social imaginaries' as an acknowledgement of imagination's public role in the creation and maintenance of contextually-dependent world-views.[29] Significantly, the phrase acknowledges that modernity is not a uniform reality; there are multiple modernities. A key challenge now facing integral ecumenics[30] is to engage with the modern anti-modernist social imaginaries, which have too often been ruled out of serious consideration by invoking the name 'fundamentalisms'.[31] Otherwise, imagining the repressed Others and Otherness within our *own* traditions will continue to be an uncritical projection by Western Christians, rather than a critical and self-critical engagement with modernity and its many ambiguities.

---

27 Marty and Appleby, *The Fundamentalism Project* volume 1, *Fundamentalisms Observed*: vii-xiii, ix.
28 Alan Bullock and Stephen Trombley (eds.), *The New Fontana Dictionary of Modern Thought*, London, HarperCollins, [1999³] 2000: 344.
29 Charles Taylor, *Modern Social Imaginaries*, Durham and London, Duke University, 2004: especially 23-30.
30 See John D'Arcy May, 'Integral Ecumenism', in *Journal of Ecumenical Studies* 25 (1988): 573-91.
31 Characterizing religious fundamentalism as a 'modern anti-modernism' relies on the seminal discussion in Bruce B. Lawrence, *Defenders of God: The Fundamentalist Revolt against the Modern Age*, San Francisco, Harper & Row, 1989.

Alan D. Falconer

The Holy Trinity: A Living Reality, Linked to the Whole of our Human Existence

It is a great pleasure to have been invited to celebrate this significant birthday of John D'Arcy May. His contribution to the life and work of the Irish School of Ecumenics has been sterling, and he has had a major influence on the international ecumenical scene. It has been my privilege to work with John in a variety of capacities over more than a quarter century. The last occasion was an attempt by the Faith and Order Commission, the Commission on World Mission and Evangelism, and the unit on Interfaith Dialogue – all of the World Council of Churches – to chart a new path for the churches in respect of interfaith dialogue. The discussions were intense and intricate. Through these explorations, however, ran the thread of an appeal to the understanding of God as the Holy Trinity. Again and again reference was made to the work of the Creator, the role of Jesus Christ and the activity of the Spirit. It seemed appropriate, therefore, for this paper to seek to trace the way in which appeal to the Divine Trinity in thought and life has been emerging in the World Council of Churches as a whole.

An aspect of the work of the ecumenical institute at Münster, where John served for some years, concerned the relationship between the Roman Catholic Church and the Orthodox churches. One of the clear differences between these traditions was their differing approaches to an understanding of the Holy Trinity, approaches which were the legacy of St Augustine and the heritage of the Cappadocian Fathers, respectively. Within the contemporary ecumenical movement these two approaches are evident, particularly in the World Council of Churches. The Russian Orthodox priest, Dimitri Dudko, in one of his famous Moscow sermons, characterized this difference thus:

> Trinity is a Christian concept of God. The concept of God's unity is true, but it is an abstract concept, one that is just in your head. But God as Trinity is a living reality, linked to the whole of our human existence.[1]

In this paper I shall trace the appreciation by the World Council of Churches of the Trinity as a living reality, and will note the co-existence of these two approaches.

From Christ to the Trinity in the Constitution of the World Council of Churches

When the World Council of Churches was formed it adopted as Article 1 of its Constitution the following basic statement:

> The World Council of Churches is a fellowship of churches which accept our Lord Jesus Christ as God and Saviour.[2]

That formula was seen to have at its root the basic baptismal formula whereby Christians are engrafted into Christ and incorporated into the fellowship of Christians of all ages

---

1 Dimitri Dudko, *Our Hope*, New York, St. Vladimir's Seminary, 1977: 36.
2 W.A. Visser't Hooft (ed.), *The First Assembly of the World Council of Churches*, London, SCM, 1949: 197.

and places. The churches which formed the World Council of Churches at its first Assembly in Amsterdam in 1948 were at liberty to interpret the constitution and the implications of membership in their own way. Indeed, in this the churches operated in a rather similar way to the nascent United Nations where each state asserted its integrity and sovereignty.

Following the formation of the Council, a commission was established to explore the nature of the World Council of Churches. This reported to the meeting of the Council's Central Committee at Toronto where the statement *The Church, the Churches and the World Council of Churches* was adopted.[3] The statement sets out what the Council is and what it is not, and affirms the Amsterdam Assembly's statement on the Authority of the Council. That statement is particularly focussed on unity in Jesus Christ.

> The Council desires to serve the churches which are its constituent members as an instrument whereby they may bear witness together in their common allegiance to Jesus Christ...
>
> Unity arises out of the love of God in Jesus Christ...In the bond of love they will desire continually to pray for one another and strengthen one another, in worship and in witness, bearing one another's burdens and so fulfilling the law of Christ.[4]

Neither the Constitution nor the Toronto Statement makes any reference to the Holy Trinity as such. The churches saw themselves being drawn together in Jesus Christ. The language employed was an echo of St Augustine and John Calvin when they reflected on the 'bond of love' which is Christ's action in baptism and eucharist. Such a focus on Jesus Christ was further evident in the themes chosen for the Assemblies of the World Council of Churches beginning with *Christ – the hope of the world* chosen for the second Assembly at Evanston in 1954.

The movement to a Trinitarian affirmation in the constitution and life of the contemporary ecumenical movement came with the Third Assembly of the World Council of Churches at New Delhi in 1961. At this Assembly two major changes occurred. The first was the integration into the World Council of Churches of the International Missionary Council. While this integration was controversial, particularly in missionary circles, it brought into the Council again the awareness of the inseparability of unity and mission for the being of the church. Throughout the 1950s the predominant understanding of the church had been that of the body of Christ and the people of God who participate in the mission of God. The concept of *missio dei* was an attempt to remind the churches that God is the author, source and energy of the mission of the church. The churches are to be faithful to the calling of God. As this theme was being explored there began to emerge an awareness that the God who creates, calls and inspires is the Divine Trinity and that the mission of the Church is *Missio Dei Trinitatis*.[5]

The second change at the New Delhi assembly was in the membership of the Council. At this Assembly the Russian Orthodox Church and a number of other East European Orthodox Churches entered membership.[6] They brought with them their appreciation of

---

3 The text appears in Michael Kinnamon and Jonathon Cope (eds.), *The Ecumenical Movement: An Anthology of Key Texts and Voices*, Geneva, WCC, 1997: 463-468.
4 Kinnamon and Cope, *The Ecumenical Movement*.
5 Lesslie Newbigin, *Trinitarian Doctrine for Today's Mission*, Geneva, WCC, 1963.
6 The Greek Orthodox Church, the Ecumenical Patriarchate and other Orthodox Churches were founder members of the WCC at Amsterdam.

the Trinity as a living reality. As a reflection, then, of the impact of this expanded membership and of the integration of the International Missionary Council, Article 1 of the constitution of the World Council of Churches was changed to:

> The World Council of Churches is a fellowship of churches which confess the Lord Jesus Christ as God and Saviour according to the Scriptures and therefore seek to fulfil together their common calling to the glory of the one God, Father, Son and Holy Spirit.[7]

This remains the basic statement of the nature of the World Council of Churches today. Having started life with a Christological statement the World Council of Churches moved to a Trinitarian affirmation. Such a change was no mere token. It is a change which came to be reflected in the life and work of the Council as it engaged in the search for unity and in common action and witness.

Of course, the member churches themselves determine the manner in which they interpret the understanding of the doctrine of the Holy Trinity. There is no overarching interpretation of Article 1 of the Constitution to which the member churches accede. Up to the present where a church feels that it is able to affirm the article then that has been sufficient for membership.[8]

The understanding of the divine Trinity as integral to the studies and life of the Churches in the WCC

The churches and the fellowship of churches seem to have taken the constitution as a basis, and as basic, to their exploration together of the journey to manifest unity and for their work. The affirmation of the Holy Trinity is evident in the Eucharist statement of *Baptism, Eucharist and Ministry*; the Vancouver Assembly in 1983; the *Canberra Statement* (1991); the Fifth World Conference on Faith and Order at Santiago de Compostela (1993); the study on *The Nature and Mission of the Church*[9]; the eighth report of the Joint Working Group between the Roman Catholic Church and the World Council of Churches (2006); and the statement 'Called to be the One Church' sent to the churches from the Porto Alegre Assembly in 2006. Let me explore each of these in turn.

At the Fourth World Conference on Faith and Order at Montreal in 1963, at which the Protestant, Orthodox and Roman Catholic Churches were represented, the decision was taken to initiate a study on the Eucharist. While the Eucharist had been part of the discussions of the Faith and Order movement in its phase of undertaking theology in a comparative method, and while major reports on Ways of Worship and on Intercommunion had been presented a decade previously,[10] no attempt had yet been made to seek to make a common theological statement on the sacrament itself. The study began with an exploration of two biblical concepts – *anamnesis* and *epiclesis* – in the attempt

---

7 W.A. Visser't Hooft (ed.), *The New Delhi Report: The Assembly of the World Council of Churches 1961*, London, SCM, 1962.
8 There has only been one instance whereby a theological examination of a church took place prior to membership being granted: that was in the case of the Church of Jesus Christ on Earth, by His Special Envoy Simon Kimbangu, in 1969.
9 This is the revised version of the study on *The Nature and Purpose of the Church* – revised in the light of responses by the churches.
10 See H.E. Bate, *Faith and Order: Proceedings of the World Conference-Lausanne 1927*, New York, Doran, 1927; Pehr Edwall, Eric Hayman, and William D. Maxwell (eds.), *Ways of Worship*, London, SCM, 1951; Donald Baillie and John Marsh (eds.), *Intercommunion*, London, SCM, 1952.

to get behind the controversies between the churches.[11] After a report had been produced and sent to the churches for response, the work was totally changed; the basis for the new report was a statement of the Groupe des Dombes, a Reformed – Roman Catholic ecumenical group founded by Fr. Paul Coutourier and Br. Roger Schutz, one of the founders of the Taizé community. As a result, in exploring the Eucharist, the Faith and Order Report began by examining the meal traditions of the New Testament and then characterized the theology of the Eucharist as thanksgiving to the Father, *anamnesis* or memorial of Christ, and *epiclesis* or invocation of the Spirit.[12] What was crucial was that the whole of the Eucharist was seen as an event of the Holy Trinity. In understanding the core of Christian worship, the churches throughout the world through the Faith and Order Commission found themselves moving towards agreement on the basis of an exploration of the understanding of the Trinity as a dynamic reality.

That such a perspective on the Eucharist won on the whole a positive response was reinforced by a number of factors. Undoubtedly of great importance was the contribution of theological and liturgical scholars. Also, though, at this time, the icon by Andrei Rublev of the Hospitality of Abraham and Sarah, sometimes called The Old Testament Trinity[13] became the subject of a video on the understanding of the icon and its implications for human living.[14] This video was widely used as a basis for meditation for the Vancouver Assembly in 1983, and did much to focus Christians and churches on the Holy Trinity as a living event.[15] Here was presented no dogma of the Divine Trinity but the invitation through prayer, contemplation and living to be drawn into the dialogue with the Triune God, 'a living reality, linked to the whole of our human existence'.

The attempt to reach understanding on the doctrine of the Trinity and to overcome the impasse in relations between the Eastern Churches and those of the West, which was created by the addition of the Filioque clause into the Nicene Creed, had also been made during this period through the work of the Faith and Order Commission. After the publication of *Baptism, Eucharist and Ministry* and concurrent with the receipt of the responses to that document by the churches, the Commission embarked on an explication of the faith confessed by the Churches through the ages. This took as its basis the Nicene Creed and was an attempt to explore together how the churches might affirm a common faith. The term 'explication' in the early stage of the process was important in that it emphasized that what was being attempted was a commentary in order to make this Trinitarian Creed more accessible and to allow it to have a greater prominence in church life and worship.

---

11 Multilateral theological dialogue offers the opportunity to undertake fundamental theological exploration, and not simply to examine the issue as it has led to the division of the church historically. For a discussion of ecumenical methodology, see my article, 'Towards Unity through Diversity: Bilateral and Multilateral Dialogues', in *One in Christ* 29 (1993): 279-285.

12 *Baptism, Eucharist and Ministry*, Geneva, WCC, 1982; see also, Max Thurian (ed.), *Ecumenical Perspectives on* Baptism, Eucharist and Ministry, Geneva, WCC, 1983; and Max Thurian and Geoffrey Wainwright (eds.), *Baptism and Eucharist: Ecumenical Convergence in Celebration*, Geneva, WCC, 1983.

13 See my article, 'Andrei Rublev's Icon on the Hospitality of Abraham', in S. Smyth and S. Kingston (eds.), *Icons 88*, Dublin, Veritas, 1988: 121-127.

14 Made by William Lazareth, then Director of the Faith and Order Commission and by Daniel Ciobotea, then on the staff of the Ecumenical Institute at Bossey and now Metropolitan of Iasi, Rumania.

15 In employing the term 'event' I am conscious of the way it was used by Gerhard Ebeling with his emphasis on Word as event.

Simultaneously, the responses to *Baptism, Eucharist and Ministry* indicated that, for the churches to move towards manifesting the unity which was gift and task, it was important that they address the issue of the nature of the church and seek to come to a common understanding on this. Since the next Assembly of the World Council of Churches was approaching, an opportunity was taken to formulate a statement on 'the unity we seek'. This drew on the concept of *Koinonia* which had been emerging in a number of international bilateral dialogues; in translation it expresses notions of community, communion, fellowship, etc. In seeking to articulate the basis for unity, there was an attempt to move beyond what had become the biblical *locus classicus* for the ecumenical movement, viz., John 17, to the inclusion of Ephesians 1:3-14. This led those involved to draft a more explicitly Trinitarian statement on the Unity of the Church than had appeared hitherto, and to see this as the basis of the *koinonia* of the church. The manner in which this Ephesian hymn becomes the controlling feature for the approach to the unity of the Church, and of an underlying ecclesiology, is evident in the Canberra Statement:

> The purpose of God according to holy scripture is to gather the whole of Creation under the Lordship of Christ Jesus in whom, by the power of the Holy Spirit, all are brought into communion with God (Eph. 1). The church is the foretaste of this communion with God and with one another. The grace of our Lord Jesus Christ, the love of God, and the communion of the Holy Spirit enable the one church to live as sign of the reign of God and servant of the reconciliation with God, promised and provided for the whole creation. The purpose of the Church is to unite people with Christ in the power of the Spirit, to manifest communion in prayer and action and thus to point to the fullness of communion with God, humanity and the whole creation in the glory of the kingdom.[16]

This basic statement then became more fully explored at the Fifth World Conference on Faith and Order, Santiago de Compostela (1993), particularly in the Section 1 report which sought to provide a biblical and theological basis for the understanding of koinonia. The report drew on the presentation to the Assembly by Metropolitan John of Pergamum (John Zizioulas) among other sources.

A number of important statements are made in this section report: 'Our shared life is rootedness in the divine economy...The interdependence of unity and diversity which is the essence of the Church's koinonia is rooted in the Triune God revealed in Jesus Christ.....no language is adequate to express this rootedness in the Divine Trinity...Just as God has been revealed to us as a Trinity of persons who abide in an eternal relationship of love, so we, too, are called to live likewise....'[17] For Santiago, the divine economy has implications for what it means to be church, and for the unity we seek. There is a correct reticence to think that the church can understand or control the concept of the Holy Trinity, and yet there is also an attempt to see in the Holy Trinity a paradigm for human relating, not least as the church. The church is seen to be the community that reflects the dynamic love of the Holy Trinity, and that way of being belongs to the very mission of the Church.

These ideas are then further explored in the major Faith and Order study on 'The Nature and Purpose of the Church'. The statement begins with the heading 'The Church of the Triune God' and goes on to explore the nature of the church as a gift of God, creation of the word and of the Holy Spirit (*creatura verbi et creatura spiritus*). With an

---

[16] Text in Kinnamon and Cope, *The Ecumenical Movement*: 124-125.
[17] Thomas Best and Gunther Gassmann (eds.), *On the Way to fuller Koinonia*, Geneva, WCC, 1994.

intense survey and study of the biblical images of the Church, the statement proceeds to examine the mission of the church and roots its discussion in Ephesians 1:10.

> It is God's design to gather all creation under the Lordship of Christ (cf. Eph. 1:10), and to bring all humanity and all creation into communion. As a reflection of the communion in the Triune God, the Church is God's instrument in fulfilling this goal.[18]

Consistently throughout the report appeal is made to the rootedness of the church, in her proclamation, worship and witness, in the Holy Trinity.[19]

In drawing these impulses together and in preparation for the Ninth Assembly at Porto Alegre it was decided to draft a statement which the Assembly might adopt and send to the member churches for reception.[20] This statement was to build on the implications of the recognition of our common baptism and offer a vision of the unity of the church. In fact, the statement does reaffirm the vision of unity as that of conciliar fellowship, and then it goes on to affirm:

> We confess one, holy, catholic and apostolic Church as expressed in the Nicene-Constantinopolitan Creed (381). The Church's oneness is an image of the Triune God in the communion of the divine Persons.[21]

The statement goes on to draw out the images which had been present in the study on the Nature and Mission of the Church: people of God, body of Christ, temple of the Holy Spirit. On the basis of baptism it calls the churches to give account of their stewardship of the faith to each other – to be in a relationship of 'affirmation and admonition', to use the formula of the agreement between the US Reformed and Lutheran Churches.[22] In that context it will be possible for Churches to ask each other in what sense they interpret the Trinitarian formula in the Constitution of the World Council of Churches, and how far the Holy Trinity really is, for them, 'a living reality, linked to the whole of our human existence.'

While it is clear that for the World Council of Churches the churches are gathered in a fellowship which seeks to fulfil their calling to the glory of one God, Father, Son and Holy Spirit, and have articulated their understanding of the nature of the church and the vision of the unity sought in terms of rootedness in the Holy Trinity, they have also seen that rootedness in the Trinity as determinative of their mode of relating.

---

18 *The Nature and Mission of the Church*, Geneva, WCC, 2005: 24; for an account of the development of this study, see my introduction to T. Gredzelidze (ed.), *One, Holy, Catholic and Apostolic: Ecumenical Reflections on the Church*, Geneva, WCC, 2005.

19 The extensive and intensive response of theologians appointed through the Pontifical Council for Promoting Christian Unity urged strongly that the whole report should be governed by the concept of 'koinonia', but Professor John Reumann, who had presented the composite analysis of this term in the New Testament, argued that koinonia could not carry the weight being placed on it.

20 I have argued that this is the one area where the WCC has in fact taken a decision in common: successive assemblies – New Delhi, Nairobi, Canberra – have adopted as the vision of unity, the model of conciliar fellowship, see my article, 'An Ecclesiological Understanding of Councils of Churches', in Colin Podmore (ed.), *Community-Unity-Communion*, London, Church Publishing House, 1998.

21 *Called To Be One Church*: par. 3.

22 See *A Formula of Agreement between the Evangelical Lutheran Church in America, the Presbyterian Church (USA), the Reformed Church in America and the United Church of Christ on entering into full communion on the basis of A Common Calling*; G. Fackre and M. Root (eds.), *Affirmations and Admonitions*, Grand Rapids, Eerdmans, 1998.

In the period 1999-2005, the Joint Working Group between the Roman Catholic Church and the World Council of Churches embarked on an exploration of the character of 'ecumenical dialogue'. Modes of expression which had been evident previously resurfaced here, too. For instance, they wrote:

> Ecumenical dialogue reflects analogically the inner life of the Triune God and the revelation of his love. The Father communicates himself through his Word, his Son who, in turn responds to the Father in the power of the Spirit – a communion of life... The exchange between the Father and the Son in the power of the Spirit establishes the mutual interdependence of the three persons of the Triune God. In God's self-communication to God's people, God invites us to receive his word and respond in love. Thus we enter through a participation in God's gracious activity and the imperative of Christian obedience into communion with God who is communion – Father, Son and Holy Spirit. In emulating this dialogical pattern of speaking and listening, of revealing ourselves and receiving the other, we leave our illusion of self-sufficiency and isolation and enter a relationship of communion.[23]

Conclusions

In our analysis we have seen a movement within the World Council of Churches from an understanding of the fellowship of the churches being 'in Christ' to an affirmation of their bondedness in Christ to the glory of God, Father, Son and Holy Spirit. We have seen how the vision of unity and the nature of the church have been conceived in terms of communion in and through the Triune God. We have noted how the understanding of the Trinity has been determinative of the nature of the fellowship between the churches and the mode of their relating in ecumenical dialogue. We have also seen a constant appeal to the affirmation of the faith in terms of the Nicene-Constantinopolitan Creed. An analysis of ecumenical ethical reflections would also reveal a dependence on a Trinitarian koinonia ethical approach[24], while statements on the Mission of the Church are replete with references to the Triune God. In all this it seems that the churches are reflecting the insight of Dimitri Dudko that the 'Holy Trinity is a living reality, linked to the whole of our human existence'.

In his article on the Holy Trinity, in the *Dictionary of the Ecumenical Movement*, Metropolitan Daniel states:

> The understanding of the Trinity after many centuries of ecclesiastical polemics and theological controversies, offers a new climate and basis for rediscovering the mystery of the Holy Trinity as the source, model and goal of Christian unity and as the basis for the deep renewal of Christian theology and spirituality. Although the doctrine of the Trinity has not yet been the object of an organized and systematic ecumenical reflection, the ecumenical interest in a common understanding of the centrality of the mystery of the Holy Trinity for the life of the Church, and particularly for Christian unity can be detected in many significant ecumenical events.[25]

---

23 *Eighth Report of the Joint Working Group between the Roman Catholic Church and the World Council of Churches*, Geneva-Rome, 2005; *The Nature and Purpose of Ecumenical Dialogue*: pars. 25-26: 77f.
24 See, e.g., Tom Best and Martin Robra (eds.), *Ecclesiology and Ethics: Ecumenical Ethical Engagement, Moral Formation and the Nature of the Church*, Geneva, WCC, 1997.
25 N. Lossky, J-M. Bonino, J. Pobee, T. Stransky, G. Wainwright and P. Webb (eds.), *Dictionary of the Ecumenical Movement*, Geneva, WCC, 2002^2: 1150-1153.

Although the doctrine of the Holy Trinity as such has not been the subject of a systematic study, the issue of the *filioque* clause was the subject of two Faith and Order consultations in the late 1970s and a number of recommendations were made. The first was that all churches should revert to the earlier version of the Creed – viz., that of 381 A.D. – and that therefore the words 'and the Son' be dropped. The Study explored the theological issue concerning the procession of the Holy Spirit, and noted what was intended to be preserved by the churches of the East and by those of the West when they developed different theologies. The report notes that for centuries, and while there were different theologies operating in the churches, there was no breach of communion; it therefore recommended that, on the basis of a legitimate diversity in theology, and while expressing the hope that further theological work might be done on the issue, this should no longer be a church dividing issue.[26]

Since it is clearly possible for the Churches together to phrase their unity, ecclesiological self-understanding, approach to worship, ethics, and mission, and their mode of relatedness to each other in terms of the experience of the dynamic event of the Holy Trinity, might it not be opportune to celebrate this awareness by accepting that since the divine Trinity is the basic mystery of our faith it is possible to hold complementary – though not contradictory – ways of articulating this mystery? Might not the time be right to convene a consultation on 'The Holy Trinity – a living reality, linked to the whole of our human existence', and thus help the churches of different traditions to recognize in each other the presence of the Holy Trinity as the event which lies at the basis of their very existence, and to seek through that recognition a commitment to manifest the unity of the church?

---

26 Lukas Vischer (ed.), *Spirit of God, Spirit of Christ: Ecumenical Reflections on the Filioque Controversy*, Geneva, WCC, and London, SPCK, 1981.

Antje Fetzer

The Concept of 'Service' from a Diaconal and Theological Viewpoint

1. Introduction: betwixt and between social market and diaconal mission

The concept of 'Service' from a diaconal and theological point of view is the topic of this essay. In laying out roots and criteria for a theological understanding of service, I envisage three points of reference.

First, there is the social market, which determines the framework for diaconal social work in German society today. Second, there is our distinct diaconal tradition and identity as shaped by influences as varied as the parable of the good Samaritan (Luke 10) or the history of modern German diacony dating from Johann Hinrich Wichern.[1] And third, there are different organizational types of diaconal work, such as the diacony of the congregation (e.g., visiting the elderly in the parish), institutional diacony (e.g., running homes for the elderly and the handicapped) or counselling diacony (e.g., giving advice to drug addicts and people with debts). According to their different institutional preconditions, these types have brought forth rather different attitudes concerning the economical concept of service.

Each of these three perspectives associates the concept of service with a distinct set of questions and emotion. For an economist, 'service (*Dienstleistung*)'[2] is a neutral term, denoting the contribution of social work to the national economy. For a volunteer engaging in diaconal work, 'service (*Dienstleistung*)' is a professional term that he or she would only hesitantly use to describe his or her social engagement. The manager of a congregation-based diaconical service point[3] may associate with it the difficult process of accommodating both sound economic management and social advocacy in his daily business, the task becoming more difficult as the social market establishes itself.

'Service (*Dienstleistung*)' does not derive from Christian tradition but from the economy. It conveys the framework of market economy rules definitive for social services today. They go as follows: a certain demand calls for a corresponding offer, meeting the demands of the consumer. If the offer manages to do so, the consumer pays for the service, and the emerging market is regulated by competition and demand.

How, then, does that relate to the Christian term *diakonia*, which is ancient Greek for 'service' and is, of course, the term that 'diacony' is derived from? In the following, this question will be pursued in three steps: first, an overview of the biblical roots of the term *diakonia* is provided; second, the conflict of aims between diacony and economy is more closely examined; and third, criteria for a diaconal and theological understanding of service are suggested.

---

1 Johann Hinrich Wichern insisted on the Church's 'inner mission' to poor people by making an impressive talk at the National Convention of the Protestant Church at Wittenberg in 1848.
2 To understand the point of this paragraph, it is necessary to note that the German *Dienstleistung* or 'service' is used to denote a professional activity that the consumer pays for, whereas the term *Dienst* or 'service' has a wide range of meanings also encompassing the spiritual care of one's neighbour.
3 Diakonische Bezirksstelle.

2. Biblical roots

2.1. 'Service' in the New Testament

The ancient Greek word for 'to serve' is *diakoneo* and it has provided diaconal work with its name. The basic meaning of *diakoneo* is 'to serve at the table'. From there, the notion 'to provide for' developed into the more general meaning 'to serve'. The nuanced meaning of *diakoneo* is personally to do a service for another person. Unlike the English 'to serve', it is not used for subordination or dependence. To denote these, ancient Greek used the term *douleuo* (to serve, to 'slave').

In the New Testament, *diakoneo* is often used to describe the Christian attitude in general. An impressive example is Mark 10:42-45, where Jesus calls himself a servant and criticizes the dominant concepts of rule. The washing of the disciples' feet in John 13 is another proof of Jesus's seeing himself as a servant of love. The central meaning of *diakoneo* probably originates in the practice of the last supper: it is here that serving at the table intersects with the 'serving' sacrifice of Jesus on behalf of his followers.

In later scriptures of the New Testament, 'to serve' has become synonymous for taking over congregational duties and offices. It can be used to denote social activities, preaching and leadership. During the second century, a sophisticated understanding of office develops which distinguishes five types of 'service': that of the Apostle, the Prophet, the Evangelist, the shepherd, and the teacher (see Ephesians 4:12).[4]

2.2. 'Care' and 'Service Community'[5] – Two models of service

'Service' in the Christian sense of the word means 'to be there for others'. According to Joachim Weber, there are mainly two theological concepts to describe diaconal service:[6] care and service community.

2.2.1. Care

The concept of care has its foundation in the theology of the cross. In order to save us, Christ has degraded himself (Philippians 2), has become a human being and has taken on death. It is from here that the care by the strong of the weak, as modelled on Christ's image, derives. A prominent example of the concept of care is the so-called 'option for the poor' developed by Latin American liberation theology. Another example can be seen in the slogan 'Diakonie – stark für Andere' (Diacony – strong for others), used by the programme paper of the Diakonisches Werk der EKD in 1998.[7] Indeed, models of care aim at evening out the inferiority of the needy in the process of helping.[8] The helper ought to restrict himself or herself and take on the perspective of the other.

---

4 Alfons Weiser, '*diakoneo*', in Horst Balz and Gerhard Schneider (eds.), *Exegetisches Wörterbuch zum Neuen Testament* volume I: *Aaron – Enoch*, Stuttgart, Köln, Berlin and Mainz, Kohlhammer, 1980: 726-732.
5 The German *Dienstgemeinschaft* denotes the working together of Christians in a cooperative way to fulfil their service to the needy as opposed to models of different interest groups that have to come to common aims (e.g., employers and trade unions).
6 Joachim Weber, *Diakonie in Freiheit? Eine Kritik diakonischen Selbstverständnisses*, Bochum, SWI, 2001: 40-51.
7 'Stark für Andere. Leitbild des Diakonischen Werks der Evangelischen Kirche in Deutschland', 1998.
8 Service means, then, 'active subordination' under God and under those human beings whom one intends to serve (Karl Barth), see Weber, *Diakonie in Freiheit*: 42 (translated by Antje Fetzer).

The theological argument for the concept of care rests on the model of Christ and his identification with the needy: *And the king will answer them, 'truly I tell you, just as you did it to one of the least of these who are members of my family, you did it to me'* (Matthew 25:40). Yet, the concept of care has been criticized for its vision of the helping relationship: the helper works *for* the needy person rather than *with* him or her. Helping may thus lead to a clandestine exercise of power.

2.2.2. The service community

The concept of service community envisages the helper and the needy person being on a par. In the first place, community is constituted by common participation in Christ (1 Corinthians 1:9; 10:16f.), and not by human sociability. This can be experienced in sharing the Eucharist.

According to this concept, service is neither motivated by moral nor by political considerations, but it emerges from pure joy in communitarian life. The point is that those who give will not only be givers but simultaneously receivers. With this, the particular gifts of the needy come into focus. The image of the community underlying this is that of a big family, where members of the congregation share their lives and care for each other. Diacony is envisaged as a process of exchange within the congregation as opposed to and detached from the work of experts and professional institutions.

However, it has been argued that this concept is rather too idealistic. Moreover, as it does not lead beyond the limited perspective of local congregations, it fails to address structural issues. Legal claims to social care, such as are necessary to express the equality of human rights and dignity in a modern society, cannot be argued for on the grounds of service community.

In sum, then, the concepts of care and service community are attempts to realize the model of God's diacony among humans by means of a life order. Both rest on a spiritual understanding of 'diacony', marking out one's own spiritual development and the wellbeing of one's neighbour as two sides of the same coin. As opposed to the economical sense of the word, Christian 'service' (*Dienstleistung*) is denoted as a *practice of faith* through which the needy and the helping person are connected with God.

2.3. Horizons of Hope: serving one's neighbour and working for the Kingdom of Heaven

In the life of the individual, this practice of faith is placed in a hermeneutical horizon which decides on how somebody construes his or her diaconal engagement. Jürgen Moltmann makes a distinction between two cosmological horizons in the biblical tradition: one being apocalyptic, the other messianic.[9]

2.3.1. The apocalyptic cosmology

Apocalyptic approaches to the world (e.g., Revelation) accept the given and often adverse conditions of a society and expect better circumstances for the hereafter only. While it is in the power of Christians to prevent the crudest atrocities by their social engagement, they cannot improve the world fundamentally. Diaconal work is an expression of the living hope, that resurrection will bring about a condition where 'death will be no more; mourning and crying and pain will be no more' (Revelation 21:4). Until then, its task is to be merciful and to alleviate the suffering of individuals.

---

9 Jürgen Moltmann, *Diakonie im Horizont des Reiches Gottes*, Neukirchen-Vluyn, Neukirchener, 1989^2.

2.3.2. The messianic cosmology

The announcement of Christ's return in the Synoptic Gospels and the idea of the Kingdom of Heaven, however, presuppose a different understanding: the possibility of changing life while on earth.

The announcement of the Kingdom of Heaven (Luke 4:18f.) bridges the gap between future and present: the prisoners shall be set free and the blind shall see. To know this today is a strong motivation for striving for the coming of the Kingdom of Heaven, which starts among us already. Diaconal work starting out from this conviction will be dedicated to the aim of justice and will focus on political action.

In this way, then, Moltmann explains theologically why charity and justice are seen to be conflicting aims at times, and emphasizes the mutual dependency of the two concepts:

> Without the perspective of the Heavenly Kingdom, diaconal work is doomed to become uninspired love that merely compensates. Without diaconal work, however, the hope for the Heavenly Kingdom will develop into a heartless utopia that merely demands and challenges. Consequently, diaconal practice must strive for relating love to hope and the Kingdom of Heaven to concrete suffering.[10]

'Relating love and hope' is the aim for diaconal service which does not conform to given conditions, but has its own compass for orientation. 'Relating the Kingdom of Heaven to concrete suffering' is the definition of advocacy in the best sense of the word. Diaconal work cannot remove itself from this backdrop without losing its credibility, which would be what Wolfgang Nethöfel calls a 'portfolio-catastrophe'.[11] A service calling itself diaconal will have to be measured against the criterion of whether it follows its own genuine compass.

Pondering the roots of the diaconal understanding of service, we have arrived at the insight that, on the one hand, diaconal work is a spiritual practice, for it does not consist only in fulfilling tasks, but encompasses an attitude which fosters the community of needy persons and helpers and gives glory to God. On the other hand, diaconal work sets out to fulfil two missions: first, to alleviate the suffering of the neighbour and, second, to bring about structural justice. A diaconal service cannot be content with answering individual demands only. Once we look for criteria for a diaconal and theological understanding of service, this will be our basis. Before going to this, however, I want to look at the friction between diacony and economy.

3. Diacony and Economy: a conflict of aims

The difficulty in developing a concept of 'service' from a diaconal and theological point of view seems to lie with the term service (*Dienstleistung*) itself. We are wrestling with the task of how to combine an economical concept with diaconal life in such a way that the basic rules of economy hold even as the horizon of faith provides the main lines of orientation. To put it in other words: how can we resolve the conflict of aims between diacony and economy in practical terms?

In his essay 'Diakonie im Unternehmen Kirche' (Diacony within the enterprise of church), Wolfgang Nethöfel points out the 'anti-economy of God's mercy'.[12] He un-

---

10 Moltmann, *Diakonie im Horizon*: 20 (translated by Antje Fetzer).
11 Wolfgang Nethöfel, 'Diakonie im Unternehmen Kirche', in Udo Krolzik (ed.), *Zukunft der Diakonie. Zwischen Kontinuität und Neubeginn*, Bielefeld, Luther Verlag, 1998: 21-35: 31ff.
12 Nethöfel, 'Diakonie im Unternehmen Kirche': 24 (translated by Antje Fetzer).

folds this topic by telling important stories of God's people from the economical point of view: money is not important to God, and in many cases the biblical figures held up as examples of faith have to give up their economically secure position in life in order to rely on God completely. The father in faith, Abraham, lives a convenient life in Ur up to the point when God calls him to move to the promised land. Even though the Israelites have to slave in Egypt, their economical status seemed to have been so comfortable that, years later, they long for the fleshpots of Egypt as they are being led through the desert by God.

According to the witness of the New Testament, Jesus and his disciples wander through the land without economical basis. Jesus heals the sick for free and extends in his parables a contra-factual hope for growth. Clever economists of the day, however, are often put into a shady light: the rich man in Luke 12 who wants to rest after having gathered an enormous harvest is confronted with harsh words: 'You fool! This very night your life is being demanded of you. And the things you have prepared, whose will they be?' (Luke 12:20). The only exception is constituted by the parable of the ten coins (Luke 19); yet, there is hardly a scholar who would interpret the talents as money. Instead, the majority construes them to be personal talents and sees the scope of the parable in the question of whether or not we are willing to engage our talents on behalf of the community. Naturally, there is personal talent required in dealing wisely with money. However, this talent is not an aim in itself, but serves in the pursuit of a higher goal.

Therefore, from a theological point of view, economy is a means to an end, not an end in itself. It provides the necessary basis for work to be done. This work in turn is defined by the so-called 'Magna Charta of Diacony', namely, Matthew 25:35f.: 'I was hungry and you gave me food, I was thirsty and you gave me something to drink, I was a stranger and you welcomed me, I was naked and you gave me clothing, I was sick and you took care of me, I was in prison and you visited me.'

So far, we have not come across a conflict of aims in the strict sense of the word. Any competent manager will confirm that his work is not about gathering resources, but about reaching the goals of the enterprise. Still, the conflict of aims visible in decision-making concerning diaconal practice is rooted here. Indeed, the decisive question – answered differently by theologians on the one hand and by economists on the other – is: 'how do I know that the goal of my enterprise has been reached?'

According to the argument I have developed, the diaconal theologian would answer: 'I can judge from the way the needy person and the helper interact, that is, whether they treat each other as equals or not. I can judge from the degree to which the needy person experiences God's friendliness in the way in which the helper gives advice and support. I can judge by the treatment people with debts receive whether they are treated as human beings, or whether they are reduced to being columns of numbers.' The economist might still agree, but he or she will probably not recognize this statement as an answer to the question. For him or her, the goal of the enterprise has been reached once the income balances the expenses necessary to run a diaconal service. Given the same financial and personal equipment, it has been reached when at least as many cases are being treated as in the year before. And it has been reached when quality, as measured by customer satisfaction, successful treatment and correct documentation, has risen or at least remained constant. Thus, the conflict of aims between diacony and economy must be seen as a conflict of criteria.

4. Criteria for a diaconal and theological concept of service

4.1. Diaconal aims

The question now arises concerning the aims which serve as criteria for service. Which criteria are akin to a diaconal and theological concept of service? In order to define them, we have to pay heed to four aims defining the biblical understanding of service:

1. Serving by changing roles – as a critique against popular forms of domination
2. Serving for free – as a critique against materialistic dehumanization
3. Serving sensitively – as a critique against the coldness of technocracy
4. Serving God – as a critique against human limitation and control

4.1.1. Serving by changing roles – as a critique against popular forms of domination

There is a subversive side to the Christian concept of service which is particularly prominent in Mark 10:42-45: 'You know that among the Gentiles those whom they recognize as their rulers lord it over them, and their great ones are tyrants over them. *But it is not so among you*; but whoever wishes to become great among you must be your servant, and whoever wishes to be first among you must be slave of all. For the Son of Man came not to be served but to serve, and to give his life as a ransom for many.'[13] Consequently, service does not mean mere adaptation to human rules and regulations. In fact, it questions those rules and regulations, and does so in favour of human beings. Service construed in this way is an expression of the yearning for justice.

4.1.2. Serving for free – as a critique against materialistic dehumanization

Being free of charge is, so to speak, the brand name of God's abundant love. The 'anti-economy of God's mercy' culminates in justification by faith: Jesus has become our servant by taking on our imperfection and standing in for us on the cross. We are given God's forgiveness for free; it is not according to merit. This second aspect of service puts the power of money into question and interrupts the vicious circle of self-justification.

4.1.3. Serving sensitively – as a critique against the coldness of technocracy

Whoever offers services to another pays heed to that person's needs. This attitude of respect and care is rooted in the ability to feel compassion, which has been given to human beings by the creator.

This aspect of service is exemplified by the parable of the good Samaritan (Luke 10: 25-37). It encourages us to come directly to the help of people in need, which is what we call 'charity'. Charity is based on the long Jewish tradition of social balance. The Prophets of the Old Testament never cease to point out that neglecting the poor and socially deprived means hurting both the human community and one's relationship to God.

4.1.4. Serving God – as a critique against human limitation and control

Diaconal practice has the potential to be a spiritual practice which brings new hope to human life and transcends limits. If serving God is the ultimate end of service, then, in so serving, secular systems of domination are not only undermined but completely annulled. Serving God does not contradict serving one's neighbour. 'Service' both in the liturgical and diaconal sense of the word is realized where the needs of the socially deprived are

---

13 Emphasis by Antje Fetzer.

perceived and answered: 'Then the righteous will answer him, "Lord, when was it that we saw you hungry and gave you food, or thirsty and gave you something to drink? ..." And the king will answer them: "Truly I tell you, just as you did it to one of the least of these who are members of my family, you did it to me."' (Matthew 25:37, 40).

4.2. Differences between the diaconal and the economical concept of service

The diaconal and theological aims unfolded above denote the following differences with regard to the economical concept of service:

4.2.1. Changing roles

Services in the economical sense of the word require a clear-cut understanding of roles and conformity with societal conventions. Reliable terms of trade are the basis of this special exchange of money and work as much as of any other service. A change of roles implying that the professional helper would become the learning person does not fall into place with the logic of services. Yet, it is precisely this change in perspective which is characteristic of diaconal service.

4.2.2. Being free of charge

From an economical point of view we know that services can never be free of charge. There is no free lunch. However, there is the possibility of somebody other than the needy person paying for it, for instance, the state or a private foundation. This shift in financial responsibility can have an adverse side-effect, once the service does not primarily target the needs of the needy person but those of the paying 'customer', be it state or foundation. This shift has to be confronted by the Christian message: God loves and accepts God's creatures without preconditions. A diaconal service strives to be modelled on this. A needy person seeking help is to be treated on a par with others, no matter what their situation is.

This does not mean that diaconal services should not care about finances. On the contrary, as their religious claim is not to make needy people feel ashamed but dignified, they have to secure sound financing from elsewhere. There is a lot of creativity required in solving this question, the main possibilities being social sponsoring and the participation of volunteers.

4.2.3. Sensitivity

Economical controlling starts out by scrutinizing the efficiency of resources and personnel. It is not as easy to capture what is at the heart of a diaconal service from the theological perspective, i.e., the mental and physical well-being of the needy person. Sensitive servicing will find it difficult to verify its decisive aspects by measuring indexes. It is the specialty of a diaconal service that it provides ample space for precisely those aspects of the helping relationship which cannot be measured. This can entail looking for extra resources in order to provide professional helpers with more working time. It can also mean that demanding courses are offered to volunteers who are willing to work on a high level of reliability.

4.2.4. Serving God

The economical concept of service does not envisage a spiritual dimension of professional transactions. From the opposite perspective, it contradicts the spiritual character of diaconal help to submit every single aspect of it to quality management (QM), even if a growing number of institutions take to using QM in the field of pastoral care. The spiritual independence of the caring person has to be warranted in any case.

A diaconal service rests on the self-understanding that in, through and with the helping or counselling activities, there is room for processes between the needy person, the helping person and God. Those processes can neither be planned nor evaluated, yet they can be prepared for. In diaconal servicing, therefore, there should be open space for spiritual processes.

4.3. For example: working with the poor

How does the diaconal concept of service translate into practice, e.g., when working with the poor? As its profile does not adapt to modern society, with a focus on performance and efficiency, it offers a demanding model for service in contrast with the dominant economic model.

4.3.1.

The diaconal and theological idea of changing roles implies a *change of perspective*; it introduces the situation of poor people as criterion. A model of thought shows how powerful this step is: how would we want to regulate society in advance if we did not know which societal status we were to have? How would we organize our living together if our perception were hindered by such a 'veil of ignorance'? This famous thought-experiment was introduced by the American philosopher John Rawls in his *A Theory of Justice* and it has sparked off the most encompassing debate on justice for the last thirty years.[14]

From a diaconal point of view, taking on the perspective of the poor has two implications: first, it means to perceive and feel the needs of the socially disadvantaged and to support their search for solutions ('charity'). Second, it means to use the possibilities of one's own broader political horizon in order to achieve a structural improvement of their situation ('justice'). Diaconal service without advocacy is impossible to conceive of, especially when working with the poor.

4.3.2.

Starting out from a *spirituality of justification by faith*, the popular notion that who pays for a service may determine its shape has to be put into question. A service claiming that it provides on-a-par help for poor people will treat clients unable to pay with the same respect and dignity as clients who able to pay. A counselling service for debtors, for example, will contradict itself if it chooses its clients according to their ability to handle money well. The diaconal maxim in counselling debtors should therefore be: 'he or she who needs it most, gets it first'.

Rather than demanding payment from clients who have financial difficulties, a counselling service for debtors should seek sponsorship. There is no contradiction between charity and justice, even though charity has been blamed for prolonging people's suffering by smoothing over the gravest effects of bad structures. In effect, charity means helping the individual in acute need on his or her way to justice.

---

14 John Rawls, *A Theory of Justice*, Oxford: OUP, [1972] 1973.

5. In a nutshell: five criteria for diaconal service

What distinguishes a diaconal service, what makes it characteristic? How can its genuine compass be described? From the argument developed above we can extract the following five criteria, which together offer a summary of it:

i. A diaconal service takes on the *perspective of the clients*. It answers their acute needs and engages in improving the structural conditions. Charity and justice are perceived as two equal and complementary motivations.

ii. A diaconal service treats clients *on a par*. Irrespective of who pays for the service, the client in need is regarded as the party to the contract. The vicious circle of self-justification and pressure to perform is interrupted by justification by faith.

iii. A diaconal service fosters a keen awareness of the *standards of justice*. It seeks to realize them wherever it is possible. It evaluates its work not only by measurable index-numbers, but creates free space for unplanned processes. It is self-critical and sensitive to issues of justice as regards its own working process.

iv. A diaconal service provides space and personnel for *spiritual concerns and processes*. Diaconal spirituality is characterized by a change of roles and free help, by sensitivity and service to God. Where a diaconal service provides space for clients and professionals to try out and live these dimensions both individually and socially it is practiced faith.

v. Finally, an institution organizing diaconal services will not only seek to meet these criteria in creating individual services, but, more importantly, it will employ them critically when deciding *which services* to offer, to abandon or to develop anew.

Robert Gascoigne

Christian Identity and Social Commitment
An Australian Catholic Perspective

My intention in this essay is to attempt to link the Catholic Church's prophetic role in a globalizing world with its own internal development: to reflect on the relationship between its renewed potential to offer a vision of human community in a world afflicted by abysmal contrasts between wealth and poverty and its attempt to renew itself after the Second Vatican Council. Most of what I will say concerns the Roman Catholic Church in a more global context, although I write from the perspective of a specifically Australian Catholic history.

Even though economic globalization brings extraordinary technological innovation and potential for economic development for some regions and groups, it is often accompanied by an ideology which ignores the suffering of producers and promotes a false humanism of unlimited empowerment of the individual through the consumption of high-tech products. The Catholic Church, through its commitment to global human rights on the basis of a renewed sense of the Gospel's meaning for human solidarity, can play an important role in resisting this ideology and supporting all those movements that strive to maintain and develop communities of solidarity and mutual respect.

Since the 1950s, and especially because of the impact of the Second Vatican Council, the Catholic Church has undergone a process which has re-shaped its social presence and deeply affected its sense of identity. The historical processes resulting from the Reformation and the French Revolution had – to speak in very general terms – the effect of linking Catholic identity with a range of defensive or demarcating postures, often associated with particular social classes or ethnic groups. The gradual dissolution of these particular crystallizations of socio-religious identity has been accompanied by a new freedom and universality, a new sense of the Church's calling to be in solidarity with – to quote the first paragraph of Vatican II's *Pastoral Constitution on the Church in the Modern World* – 'the joys and hopes, griefs and anxieties, of the human beings of this age, especially of those who are poor and afflicted.' Yet, this new sense of universal solidarity, because it has been accompanied by a dissolution of the particular identities of the past, has developed hand-in-hand with the urgent need to re-form the Church's communal identity, the local vitality that is the essential basis for a commitment to solidarity on a global scale. Can new communal identities be formed which can resist consumerist individualism? If a new openness transcends the defensive and demarcating postures of the past, what will be the form of a new identity that will give the strength to maintain this new openness and commitment to stand with others in their suffering? Can such openness foster new and vibrant local communities, which no longer need to be linked to specific social and ethnic identities, to affirmation by demarcation – or, given that all religious communities must of their nature have a concrete social identity, can these communities resist the tendency for such identity to set up new forms of self-affirming demarcation, and constantly renew the call to witness to human solidarity in the name of the Gospel?

Let me begin by briefly identifying some of the key ideological problems associated with economic globalization in its contemporary form. One of these is the intensification of the sense of the 'givenness' of the market economic system, the lack of any alternatives. Any set of economic interests will promote the view that what benefits them is the only way to do things, the only rational and progressive set of arrangements. It will discourage critique by dismissing alternatives as wrong or fanciful. This has always been so, but the effect of globalization is to intensify this tendency. How does it do this?

One way is because national solutions to problems of economic justice have become much less relevant and effective in a globalizing economic world. The attempt to understand the economic system, and to reconcile it with imperatives of justice, has thus become much more difficult since it is not simply a matter of imagining and developing a just society on a national scale, but developing international institutions of economic justice. A consequence of globalization is the removal of the economic system from challenge at a national level and the much more difficult task of understanding it on a global scale. In this sense, it withdraws itself from local and national foci of critique and social action, disempowering many formerly significant agents of constraint on the unfettered power of market forces – such as the trade unions. As Zygmunt Bauman has argued in his *Liquid Modernity*, globalizing companies are rather like old style absentee landlords, who can reach their underlings at any time through mobile phones, but themselves withdraw into inaccessibility, using 'disengagement and the art of escape as major tools'.[1] Tom Beaudoin, in his 'The Cost of Economic Discipleship: U.S. Christians and Global Capitalism', discovered such disengagement in his investigations into the source of the Starbucks lattes and frappuccinos that he frequently enjoyed: 'I learned that this company, who I had been paying $4 a visit or more, refused to take adequate responsibility for living wages for their coffee farmers through a series of distancing measures, by employing layers of mid-level "independent" operators to relate to farmers.'[2]

This withdrawal of the system from the fray of national debate is coupled with the removal of economic suffering and exploitation from the sight of those who benefit most from the products of globalized technology. Globalization increases this separation by locating production in countries remote from the main centres of consumption. The economic benefits of this for the production companies are evident, and in some cases this may make a contribution to economic growth and opportunity in developing countries. It is also well-documented that industrial enclaves in developing countries that produce consumer goods for the citizens of affluent nations are characterized by low wages, harsh and dangerous working conditions and work-force regimentation. This sheer distancing and the siting of such industrial enclaves in countries such as China, whose regimes repress dissent and critical investigation, make it very difficult to acquire the knowledge that can both evoke solidarity and lead to effective protest.

Another key factor in rendering criticism irrelevant is the extraordinary technological progress made possible by the microchip revolution. For consumers in affluent countries, globalization is associated with the breathtaking speed of development of computers, the Internet, e-mail, mobile phones and a host of related technologies. This technological revolution is so powerful, and its products so astonishing, that they can give even the ordinary consumer a sense of being connected with an innovative and

---

1 Zygmunt Bauman, *Liquid Modernity*, Cambridge, Polity, and Oxford, Blackwell, 2000: 14.
2 Tom Beaudoin, 'The Cost of Economic Discipleship: U.S. Christians and Global Capitalism', in *The Santa Clara Lectures* 8,1 (4th November 2001): 2.

dynamic world, a world made possible by economic globalization. This is particularly true since they enable much greater individual mobility and possibilities for communication. Microsoft's 'Where do you want to go today?' encourages a sense of the exhilaration of choice, unconstrained by space and the limitations of location. This empowerment of individual choice discourages and unnerves criticism: surely a system that produces possibilities like these should not be held back by governmental or bureaucratic controls. Sometimes this sense of exhilaration and empowerment associated with the high tech and dot com worlds becomes an inchoate ideology of the 'just do it' and 'nothing is impossible', manifesting a conception of human nature as individualist, competitive, striving for growth and power, unlimited by human frailty and untrammelled by traditional or communal bonds. This does threaten to become a new global ideology, an ersatz humanism of individual consumption and empowerment.

It is in this context that the mission of the Church is of particular relevance. In response to the globalizing ideology of individual consumption, the Church can proclaim a vision of humanity that, while not denying the value of technological progress, sets such progress within a rich and multi-dimensional context of human existence in the light of Christian faith.[3] In response to the vast distances of place and awareness in the global economy between producer and consumer, which so militate against solidarity, the Church can affirm its nature as communion, a communion of local communities, which affords so many opportunities for mutual awareness, contact and support between fellow Christians of radically different national and economic circumstances. This commitment to global solidarity with the oppressed, articulated through a philosophy of human rights, is motivated and energized by a theological vision of the human person and human community. As Robert Schreiter argues in his *The New Catholicity: Theology between the Global and the Local*, the Church's support for human rights is a 'global theological flow', an example of a 'theological discourse that, while not uniform or systemic, represents a series of linked, mutually intelligible discourses that address the contradictions or failures of global systems.'[4]

This 'global theological flow' of commitment to human rights has many different sources within the life of the Catholic Church: to name a few of those – Vatican II itself, especially the Pastoral Constitution on the Church in the Modern World; the writings of Paul VI, e.g., his *Proclaimers of the Gospel* of 1975, which reflected on the relationship between liberation and salvation, and of John Paul II, in particular his *On Social Concern* of 1988, with its emphasis on international solidarity or *Centesimus Annus* of 1991, with its reflection on the global economic system after the fall of communism; the commitment of the Jesuit General, Pedro Arrupe, to lead the Society of Jesus to take up the 'preferential option for the poor'; and the influence of both Latin American liberation theology and various forms of a theology of public life and social justice in Europe and the United States. These specifically theological and reflective contributions are one aspect of resistance to the ideology of individualist consumerism and wealth

---

3 In chapter 6 of his *After Pluralism: Towards an Interreligious Ethic*, Münster, LIT, 2000, 'An Interreligious Ethic of Economic Justice', John D'Arcy May situates the contribution of Catholic social teaching in the context of global inter-faith dialogue on ethical alternatives to social inequality and ecological destruction. His discussion, drawing on Christian, Buddhist and Melanesian literatures, demonstrates the rich resources of religious traditions for resisting an ideology of economic exploitation.
4 Robert Schreiter, *The New Catholicity: Theology between the Global and the Local*, Maryknoll, Orbis, 1997: 16.

accumulation; another is the formation of networks of solidarity, which include everything from the international Caritas networks to partnerships between brother and sister schools in affluent and poorer countries. Such networks can assist in overcoming the remoteness of the producers of the consumer goods of globalized systems, helping in various ways to show us the face of those whose harsh and low paid work is the unseen hand behind the high-tech products we consume.[5]

The development of these intellectual and practical resources for affirming global solidarity was hastened by the processes which freed the Church from specific forms of social and political identity that were themselves often defensive or demarcating postures in response to the historical aftermath of the Reformation and the French Revolution. The German theologian Peter Hünermann has argued in an illuminating essay entitled 'Catholicism in Europe: its diversity and its future – an ecclesiological reflection'[6] that the word 'Catholicism' itself came into widespread use only after the French Revolution, when the Catholic Church ceased to be the established Church and the religious background and underpinning to culture and society, and became instead an often beleaguered social movement – a movement which, in different ways in different countries, attempted to assert and defend itself using the new tools of civil rights that were the positive heritage of the French Revolution. This new social phenomenon of 'Catholicism', which became a largely lay movement under the direction of the hierarchy, sought to define itself over against Protestant majorities in Anglo-Saxon countries or dominant anti-clerical liberal elites in Latin countries, and to develop a range of concrete communal and institutional identities. In Australia, in ways similar to other Anglo-Saxon countries, Catholicism was associated with Irish ethnic origins and had a strongly working-class membership because of those origins and because figures such as Cardinal Moran (Irish-born Archbishop of Sydney, 1884-1911), like Cardinal Manning in Britain or Cardinal Gibbons in the United States, were broadly sympathetic to a labour movement that was not inspired by atheistic Marxism or anarchism, in contrast to the situation in Latin countries. As is well known, in Anglo-Saxon countries Catholic social identity was marked out by forms of religious and cultural demarcation from the Protestant majority, reflecting doctrines and practices emphasized by Tridentine Catholicism in response to the Reformation. While this religious and cultural demarcation was largely achieved by a separate education system, which became an intense focus of effort and concern, Australian Catholics – once again in contrast to much European experience – did not seek to establish Catholic political parties and sought instead integration with mainstream parties based on economic interests, principally the Labour Party.

As Hünermann notes, these forms of Catholic identity, so strong in the nineteenth and the first half of the twentieth century, began to break up in the mid-twentieth century, a process hastened by the Second Vatican Council. There was, of course, a range of

---

5   In his 'Transforming Pluralism and Dialogue', in *Doctrine and Life* 45 (October 1995): 524-533, John May argues that a theologically adequate response to globalization must include a dialogue that genuinely integrates the 'unacknowledged other', especially the Jews, indigenous religious traditions and the poor.

6   Peter Hünermann, 'Katholizismus in Europa: Seine Vielgestaltigkeit und seine Zukunft. Eine ekklesiologische Reflexion', an address to the Congress of the European Society for Catholic Theology, Graz, 2001, see http://www.uni-tuebingen.de/INSeCT/members/et/index.html; also published in G. Larcher (ed.), *Theologie in Europa? Europa in der Theologie*, Graz, Wien and Köln, Karl-Franzens-Universität Graz, 2002: 43-57.

factors associated with this, e.g., in the Australian context, the social mobility encouraged by the Catholic school system and the split of the Labour Party in the 1950's.[7] Theologically, Vatican II was crucial in shaping a new perspective that was no longer defined over against the Reformation and the Enlightenment – a perspective which affirmed fundamental achievements of the Reformation such as lay study of Scripture in the vernacular, and of the Enlightenment such as the legitimacy of pluralist societies. This new perspective re-discovered Scriptural and Patristic emphases and re-shaped many areas of theology in the context of a new commitment to global human solidarity.

The end of the old battles against the militantly anti-religious expressions of the Enlightenment, and the gradual disappearance of sectarianism in favour of ecumenism, have been enormously liberating phenomena for the Catholic Church, a liberation that has enabled it to focus more and more on the task of witnessing to God's love in solidarity with human suffering in a global context. Yet, this profound and far-reaching historical change in the Church's situation has also required a massive change in the sense of identity of Church communities. As Australian theologian John Thornhill writes in his *Sign and Promise: A Theology of the Church for a Changing World*, the post-Vatican II Church is in the midst of the challenge of ideological change. Thornhill's use here is in the broadest, non-Marxist sense: to describe the 'consensus arrived at by a particular group in history, through which they achieve their social identity and common purpose'.[8] For Thornhill, the sheer magnitude of the task of ideological change, in this sense of the word, calling for the crystallization of new identities inspired by Vatican II, goes far to explain why there has been so much tension and disillusion in the Catholic Church after the euphoria associated – for many – with the Council. As he emphasizes, '[w]hile it was not easy to appreciate at the time, in retrospect we may recognize that such an outcome was to be expected: it was inevitable that the Council's decisions should give rise to a painful period of transformation and uncertainty.'[9]

In a sense the work of the Council hastened the process by which Catholics were 'disembedded' from their previous identity, formed in post-Reformation and post-Revolutionary conflicts. It empowered them both to return to the Biblical and Patristic sources of tradition – John XXIII's *approfondimento* – and to commit themselves to a universally human solidarity in the contemporary world – his *aggiornamento*. Yet, these resources for a new theological identity – which has borne such rich fruit in new Biblical and liturgical expressions of Catholicism – have yet to find a stable ecclesial and social identity. The end of the old forms of identity has been accompanied by a marked decline in Church attendance and other markers of Catholic practice. Paradoxically, the new openness and commitment to universal solidarity of the Catholic Church has developed at the same time as a decline in formal religious practice, in the willingness to participate in local Catholic Eucharistic communities: whether there is any causative link between the two is, of course, much disputed and very difficult to

---

7   On the developments in the Australian Catholic community that were the background to this split, see the thorough and balanced interpretation of Bruce Duncan, CSsR, *Crusade or Conspiracy?: Catholics and the Anti-Communist Struggle in Australia*, Sydney, UNSW Press, 2001.
8   John Thornhill, *Sign and Promise: A Theology of the Church for a Changing World*, London, Collins, 1988: 4. See also Thornhill's more recent articles interpreting the reception of Vatican II: 'Creative Fidelity in a Time of Transition', in *Australasian Catholic Record* 79,1 (2002): 3-17, and 'Historians Bringing to Light the Achievement of Vatican II', in *Australasian Catholic Record* 82,3 (2005): 259-280.
9   Thornhill, *Sign and Promise*: 3.

assess. The willingness to vigorously address human questions in a globalizing world is threatened by the diminution of local communities, especially in the younger generation, which has been the accompaniment of this deeply-rooted process of ideological change.[10]

This raises many urgent and far-reaching questions. Perhaps the first is: if the past communal strength of Catholicism was associated with a particular kind of social and cultural identity, marked by powerful forms of demarcation, is its present and future strength only to be attained by a particular new form of identity, marked by certain social and cultural practices? To what extent can Catholicism be at home in all social and cultural contexts, without developing any particular forms of identity that might then in turn lead to introversion and a concern for boundary-maintenance? If the Catholic Church is to be a powerful source of critique of an ideology of globalizing individualist consumerism, must it in turn have a strong and highly concrete identity of its own, or can it afford to risk a more open posture?

One aspect of this question is the relationship between individual autonomy and communal allegiance. Catholic identity in the pre-Vatican II era was predicated on the willingness to accept the Church's institutional authority as part of the maintenance of Catholic confidence and self-esteem in a social world that was often perceived as hostile. Most Catholics were willing to pay the price of submission to authority on matters involving their private lives because their religious and social identity was at stake. In an age where defensive imperatives are, for most Catholics, no longer so overriding, memories of such submission, and the pain it cost, are probably still having their own influence even for those who never personally had to pay that price, and the recent scandals associated with sexual abuse have reinforced attitudes of distrust and distancing from Church authority. As Hünermann emphasizes, in the contemporary world any form of evangelization must be engaged in with respect for individual freedom, and with awareness of a pluralist cultural context.[11] In former times, in Western cultures, the individual search for religious meaning found its concrete expression through engagement with the Christian Gospel. Today, that search is conducted in the midst of a multifarious range of religious and philosophical ideas and influences.

These reactions to past or present ecclesial authoritarianism and the recognition of a pluralist cultural context are factors that any thoughtful evangelization must take into account in its invitation to free individuals to seek and worship God through identification with concrete Eucharistic communities – an identification that is a truly personal commitment, without the pressure to confirm an ethnic or minority identity. At the same time, of course, it is very much in the interest of the globalizing economic system to maintain and intensify the dissolution of any communities that can resist and criticize the reduction of human beings to individual producers and consumers. As many commentators have remarked, the economic system favours the bifurcation of the individual into expressivist and utilitarian personae.[12] The utilitarian engages in means-ends rationality in the increasingly long working day, while the expressivist satisfies

---

10 In his *The Catholic Community in Australia*, Adelaide, Open Book, 2005, Robert Dixon reports that only 'six to seven per cent of Catholics in their twenties' attend Mass on a typical Sunday; also, the graph 'strongly suggests that the steady fall in attendances will continue for some time to come, as the higher rates of attendance associated with older attenders are unlikely to be reached by younger Catholics as they get older' (96).
11 Hünemann, 'Katholizismus in Europa'.
12 See, e.g., the discussion in Robert Bellah et al., *Habits of the Heart: Individualism and Commitment in American Life*, Berkeley: University of California, 1985.

individual life-goals in private time. What the system actively discourages is any attempt to unify the two in a communal project of meaning, a project that might threaten to affirm a rationality of the common good during working hours and seek to transcend an expressivism of individual materialist gratification through the attraction of a path of spiritual wisdom nourished by the well-springs of communal tradition. In the words of the post-synodal document on the Church in Australia, New Zealand and the South Pacific, *Ecclesia in Oceania*, '[w]here individualism threatens to erode the fabric of human society, the Church offers herself as a healing sacrament, a foundation of communio responding to the deepest hungers of the heart'.[13] The powerful messages of the economic system against any forms of communal meaning that might be socially critical or elevate desire beyond material consumption are clearly one crucial factor in the fragile state of Church communities today.

I have already argued that much of the openness in contemporary Catholicism to global human problems is associated with the change from defensive and demarcating forms of identity, but that this historical process of change has itself been associated with a marked decline in the frequency of religious practice. Yet, the commitment to global solidarity, if it is to contend with the powerful forces of individualist consumerism, must have vibrant Eucharistic communities at its root. This group of problems has been one motive for a recent and far-reaching Catholic debate about the meaning of contemporary Catholic identity. What this debate hinges on is the relationship between the concrete forms of tradition and the multiple contexts of contemporary culture. For some Catholics, the need of the hour is for clearly defined markers of tradition, which can also serve as demarcation points against the inroads of a secular culture with its excessive emphasis on individual autonomy. From this point of view, a highly centralized Church structure is well-suited to resist the global forces of secularism and materialism. *Ecclesia in Oceania*, for example, makes no mention of a need for a renewal of Church structures, placing its focus on what the Church has to offer to a secularized society and seeing questioning of Church teaching as an important reason for its loss of influence in public life.[14] Others, including myself, are concerned that an increasing emphasis on points of demarcation threatens to construct an identity that may revive the familiar problematic of the older ethnic and minoritarian identities, i.e., a defensiveness that can distract from the wider concerns of the Church's mission to the world. Clearly, any Christian community must have markers of identity defined by its core beliefs and practices; what is more controversial is the choice and function of identity markers which are not at the core, but which can function as demarcation points against a range of modern cultural movements.

In my own view, the Church's main concern is not to demarcate itself from the secular, since there are many groups and ideas in secular society that the Church can work with in a common opposition to the ideology of individualistic materialism, although this commonality will be limited by real differences of perspective on ethical issues arising from different conceptions of individual autonomy in such areas as sexuality and life ethics. The desire to mark and affirm identity by demarcation is an extremely powerful social tendency that has deeply affected all religions: its danger is to draw the energy of religious communities towards the maintenance of such markers and

---

13 *Ecclesia in Oceania*: 12, see http://www.vatican.va/holy_father/john_paul_ii/apost_exhortations/documents/hf_jp-ii_exh_20011122_ecclesia-in-oceania_en.html
14 *Ecclesia in Oceania*: 18.

the personal and social consolation that a strong sense of identity can convey. Yet, the experience of Catholicism after the Second Vatican Council offers an opportunity, however challenging, to resist the attraction of such a process and to seek Christian identity primarily in an engagement with the world in the light of the Gospel. The future vibrancy of Catholic Eucharist communities will, I think, have much to do with the way in which they can nourish a vision of human fulfilment and solidarity in their encounter with the one who proclaimed the Kingdom.

Norman C. Habel

The Beginning of Violence: An Ecological Reading of Genesis 4

John D'Arcy May has contributed greatly to our understanding of the role of violence in Christianity. Violence, it seems, has been a factor in the development of Christianity as a religion from the time of Jesus's crucifixion. The violence factor, I would argue, extends to the primal narratives of our biblical heritage. It is with due recognition of John's important work in this field that I offer a fresh understanding of Genesis 4 as a primal narrative about the origins of violence.

I shall employ an ecological hermeneutic in the analysis of this text, a hermeneutic that has been articulated in recent years through the *Earth Bible* project (2000-2002) and the Consultation on Ecological Hermeneutics at the annual meetings of the Society of Biblical Literature in 2004-2006.[1]

Ecological Hermeneutics – Introduction

An ecological hermeneutic, I would argue, requires a radical re-orientation to the biblical text. The task before us is not an exploration of what a given text may say *about* creation, *about* nature, or *about* Earth; in this context, Earth is not a topos or theme for analysis. We are not focusing on ecology *and* creation, or ecology *and* theology.[2] An ecological hermeneutic demands a radical change of posture, namely, reading from the perspective of Earth as a subject in the text.[3]

1. Suspicion

First, we begin reading with the suspicion that the text is likely to be inherently anthropocentric or has traditionally been read from an anthropocentric perspective.

The anthropocentric bias that we are likely to find both in ourselves as readers and in the text we are reading has at least two faces. The first is the assumption or condition we have inherited as human beings, especially in the Western world, that we are beings of an order totally different from all other creatures in nature. In the hierarchy of things there is God, human beings, and the rest.

A second face of this anthropocentric bias relates to nature as 'object'. We have for so long viewed nature and all its parts, both animate and inanimate, as the objects of many forms of human investigation, of which scientific analysis is but one. This process has not only reinforced a sense of human superiority over nature, but has also contributed to a sense of distance, separation and otherness: humans are the subjects and the various parts of nature are but objects.

---

[1] See Norman C. Habel (ed.), *Readings from the Perspective of the Bible. Earth Bible* volume 1, Sheffield, Sheffield Academic, 2000; and, Norman Habel and Shirley Wurst (eds.), *The Earth Story in Genesis: Earth Bible* volume 2, Sheffield, Sheffield Academic, 2000.

[2] Norman C. Habel, 'Guiding Ecojustice Principles', in Habel, *Readings from the Perspective of the Bible. Earth Bible* volume 1: 38-53.

[3] See also Norman C. Habel, 'The Challenge of Ecojustice Readings for Christian Theology', in *Pacifica* 13 (2000): 125-141.

2. Identification

The second element of a contemporary ecological hermeneutic is the task of empathy or identification. As human beings we identify, often unconsciously, with the various human characters in the biblical story, whether that be an empathetic or antipathetic identification. We can identify with the experiences of these characters, even if they are not necessarily ones we admire, emulate or have experienced directly ourselves.

Even before reading the narrative or poetry of the text, a reader using this ecological approach must – at least, to some extent – come to terms with his or her deep ecological connections. Before we begin reading and seek to identify with Earth in the text we need to face the prior ecological reality of our kinship with Earth: we are born of Earth, and we are living expressions of the ecosystem that has emerged on this planet.

Identification with Earth and members of the Earth community raises our consciousness to the injustices against Earth as they are portrayed both at the hands of humans and God in the text. The exegete who pursues a radical ecological approach ultimately takes up the cause of the natural world seeking to expose the wrongs that Earth has suffered in silence, and to discern, where possible, the way Earth has resisted these injustices.

3. Retrieval

The third facet of this ecological hermeneutic is that of retrieval. As the interpreter exposes the various anthropocentric dimensions of the text – the ways in which the human agenda and bias are sustained either by the reader or the implied author – the text may reveal a number of surprises about the non-human characters in the story. Earth or members of the Earth community may play a key role or be highly valued in the text, but because of the Western interpretative tradition that we have inherited, this dimension of the text has been ignored or suppressed.

Where we meet non-human figures communicating in some way – mourning or praising – we have tended in the past to dismiss these expressions as poetic license or symbolic language. Our anthropocentric bias leads to classifying these elements as anthropomorphisms.

Discerning Earth and members of the Earth community as subjects with a voice is a key part of the retrieval process. There are other contexts where these subjects, even though their voice is not explicit, are present and powerful in a way that has not generally been recognized. These subjects play roles in the text that are more than scenery or secondary images. Their voice needs to be heard, a voice that need not correspond to the language of words we commonly associate with the human voice.

Beyond an Anthropocentric Orientation

There is little question that traditional interpretations of Genesis 4 have concentrated on the story of humankind as represented by the figures of Cain and Abel.[4] The more immediate questions are whether this text is written from an anthropocentric perspective and whether we can discern dimensions of the text which suggest that Earth is a subject or character in the narrative and whether the voice of Earth can possibly be retrieved.

The narrative plot of the text has generally been thought to focus on the fate of the first human beings. The narrative is framed by two announcements about the first births

---

4 See Ellen Van Wolde, 'The Story of Cain and Abel: A Narrative Study', in *JSOT* 52 (1991): 25-41.

of humans – Cain and Abel (verses 1-2) and Seth and Enosh (verses 25-26). The main narrative of the text consists of two coherent sequences: a) the Killing of Abel and the Consequences for Cain (verses 3-15), and b) the Progeny and Professions of the Cain Genealogy (verses 16-14). Such a structure quite naturally reflects the anthropocentric orientation of a story where humans are central to the plot.

The story, however, is much more than an ancient narrative about the conflict between nomadic and sedentary ways of life, represented by shepherds and farmers, respectively. This is also a story about Earth. There are four main characters in the narrative, each of which has a vital role to play: God, Cain, Abel and Earth.

As readers we may identify with Cain, Abel or Adam and Eve as typical humans or representatives of professions. A recent example is the way a Dalit interpreter in India identifies with Abel. Two striking connections are made: Abel is associated with animals, all of which are viewed as polluted and polluting in the Indian caste system and Abel's name in Hebrew *(hebel)* means 'nothing or vapour', suggesting a link with Dalits (formerly, the Untouchables) who are often called non-persons or nothing and located outside the caste system.[5]

The Story of Earth

The Earth Carer – Cain

The task at hand is to identify with or read from the perspective of Earth as a subject or character in the story. What alternative dimensions become apparent when we focus on Earth and the Earth community as more than simply background to the plot? What new meanings emerge when we empathize with Earth?

The narrative proper begins with both Cain and Abel being connected to Earth and the creatures of Earth. Cain is a 'tiller, a servant of the ground' and Abel a 'keeper of sheep'. The terms employed here recall Genesis 2:15 where God places the first human in the forest or garden of Eden to *abad* and *shamar*. The term *abad* may secondarily mean 'till' but in the vast majority of cases it means 'serve'. Together these terms means 'serve and preserve/keep'.

The two children of Adam and Eve apparently follow this divine assignment: Abel 'keeping' sheep and Cain 'serving or tilling the ground'. As a 'tiller of the ground' Cain is faithful to God's commission: a servant of Earth, caring for the ground, the source of human sustenance. Cain is an Earth-carer. Assuming the curse of the ground when the first parents were evicted from Eden persists, Cain's task, then, was probably arduous.

From Earth's perspective, there seems to be no good reason why God should not give due respect to Cain who is faithfully performing his role in relation to Earth and bringing produce from the ground of Earth as an offering to God. Earth, it seems, would feel empathy with Cain who has been closely connected with Earth and been serving her faithfully. Cain is doing precisely what God commissioned in Eden (Genesis 2:15), in spite of the curse on the ground after the Fall. He brings an offering from the land, even if the result of his hard labour may have been less blessed than that of Abel.[6]

---

5 See S. Devasahayam, 'Abel: The First Dalit Martyr', in *Outside the Camp: Bible Studies in Dalit Perspective*, Madras, Gurukul Lutheran Theological College, 1992: 8-12.
6 Gunther Wittenberg, 'Alienation and "Emancipation" from the Earth: The Earth Story in Genesis 4', in Norman Habel and Shirley Wurst (eds.), *The Earth Story in Genesis: Earth Bible* volume 2, Sheffield, Sheffield Academic, 2000: 105-116: 107.

Abel, on the other hand, is performing the role of shepherd which is not explicitly named in Eden. He brings the best of his flock as an offering which apparently involves a sacrifice. Abel offers to God the 'fat portions', a form of ritual worship implying the death of the animal and the preference of the deity for the 'fat parts' of the creature. If so, Earth may well react negatively. The first act of violence, it seems, is not committed by Cain, but by Abel against his flock, living creatures of Earth…at which point we might also expect the blood of the animal to cry out!

In sympathy with Earth, we may well ask why God would prefer an offering that represents an act of violence, rather than an offering that represents a faithful 'serving' of the ground of Earth? Where is the justice in that?

Cain is understandably angry. God seems to have been arbitrary and unfair, preferring slaughtered animal products rather than good grain. God's action stirs Cain's emotions, reflecting, it would appear, a similar orientation in Earth. Why would Earth be happy with such a divine reaction?

God shows Cain little sympathy. Cain is implicitly accused of not 'doing well' but succumbing to sin, presumably the sin of envy. No specific misdeed or attitude is named. And there is no recognition of Cain's assigned role as one 'serving Earth' under difficult circumstances. Instead, sin is portrayed in terms of an animal 'crouching' at the door, an image that further devalues actual living creatures of Earth. Some anthropocentric readings of the text make these words of God the purpose of the story: humans should beware because, since the Fall, sin is loose in the world.[7] However, according to Wittenberg,

> Cain needs to accept his position as firstborn of Adam who has to follow in his father's footsteps and become a tiller of the Earth, even if it means that the Earth Yahweh has cursed will never bear him as abundantly as for Abel and his flock. God is getting Cain to face reality, the reality of existence outside of Eden.[8]

From the perspective of Earth, God seems to take sides unfairly, thereby provoking Cain to perform the first explicit act of violence, namely, killing his brother Abel. After all, there is no reason to assume that Cain did less than his best with the cursed Earth. Yet, God did not bless Cain's labours. God's rejection of Cain's efforts to make Earth productive seems to be the primary catalyst for the first human killing.

The Voice Mediator – Earth

With the killing of Abel, Earth's role necessarily changes. The ground that Cain had been tending opens its mouth to receive the blood of murdered Abel. The language of 'opening the mouth' may easily be dismissed as an anthropomorphic metaphor, a colourful symbol. Such symbols, however, participate in reality. Earth is a subject in the story, a key participant is this origin-narrative about violence. A technical term in the text is *adamah,* the fertile soil of Genesis 2, the domain for human life and work, the stuff from which both humans and animals are made. *Adamah* is also a living subject who can open its mouth and facilitate communication with God. Earth as *adamah* is a fourth player in this narrative.

By killing Abel, who has previously poured out animal blood, Cain, the one who was keeping the ground/Earth alive, becomes the one who pours out human lifeblood and brings death. Because of God's response to Cain's offering, Cain changes roles. The

---

7 Bruce Vawter, *A Path Through Genesis*, New York, Sheed and Ward, 1956: 74.
8 Wittenberg, 'Alienation': 107.

carer becomes a killer. Earth, however, does not let this second act of violence pass unnoticed. Earth intervenes as a mediator. Earth, who gives life to Abel and all humans, receives that life back into her being. She is fulfilling her role as nurturer, enabling a human made of the ground/dust to return home to the ground/dust from which he came (Genesis 3:19).

But Earth is more than home, more than the place to which humans return upon death. Earth continues to enable her children to speak. Earth enables the voice of Abel to be heard. Earth faces God with the reality of the injustice. Or, in the famous words of God (Genesis 4:10):

> What have you done? The voice of your brother's blood cries out to me from the ground.

Earth mediates and amplifies the voice of her dead child. Earth is the sympathetic means whereby the first cry for justice is heard. Earth is the advocate before God, the mediator of justice for creatures living and dead – in this case, human creatures.

What about the response of Cain? 'Am I my brother's keeper?' While Earth clearly exposes the wrong of Abel's murder, Cain responds by raising a question about his role on Earth. In Eden humans were commissioned to 'till/serve (*abad*) and keep/preserve (*shamar*)' the garden (2:15). Cain had faithfully done the task of serving (*abad*) Earth, by caring for the ground, even though it had been cursed. His question, then, implies that there is a related task which was not specific, namely, 'keeping/preserving' *(shamar)* fellow humans, or more specifically, brothers. Cain is asking: is the Earth carer also expected to be a brother-keeper?'

The Suffering Earth – Curses

The response of God to the killing of Abel amounts to several new curses, each of which affects Earth. Earth, who provides the body to mediate Abel's voice, suffers because of the way that God articulates the punishment. As frequently in the Scriptures, the judgement on humans involves cruel collateral damage on creation.

The first punishment is Cain being 'cursed from Earth' (4:11). This curse in interpreted by Cain to mean that he is 'driven from the face of the ground'. The very Earth/ground which has been his home is no longer there for him. He becomes an unprotected fugitive, cast from the very ground which he served as God had commissioned; Cain is alienated from his home ground, the very dust to which he is expected to return upon death. Cain cannot return to the Earth from which both he and Abel derive and where Abel now lies.

Cain is banned from the very ground that mediated the call for justice. God prevents, it seems, the possibility of any mercy for Cain, any chance of reconciliation with the Earth he has served faithfully in the past.

A second curse that emerges from the first is that Cain is now 'hidden from your face.' The face of God and the face of the ground are intimately connected; God is not somewhere in heaven, but closely associated with the very soil Cain has been cultivating. Earth also mediates God's presence. Cain has been serving God by serving Earth.

A third and related curse is the additional futility that Cain will experience in trying to care for Earth. The ground will be cursed further and yield none of its produce when Cain attempts to serve it. In this instance, it is not only that Cain is barred from performing his role as an Earth keeper, but that Earth also suffers the cruelty of being barren when her former keeper seeks to return and 'serve' her (see Genesis 3).

Cain knows God as the one who cares for the ground. Now, he will lose that living connection with God's presence. Earth will again be prevented from playing its mediating role; God's face will not be seen through the soil. As a result, Cain and his kin become urban dwellers, both distant for the land and with a propensity to exploit it.

The final curse is that Cain's action will set off a chain reaction of vengeance among other humans. One act of violence evokes a sevenfold response. Wherever Cain wanders on Earth, the ground will be aware of his condition. Cain loses his connection with Earth and with the presence of God. Adam and Eve may have been banished from the garden to work the arid *adamah*; Cain, however, is banished from the ground itself and from God's presence.

The mark placed on Cain may enable his survival when he faces the forces of vengeance. Still, it also marks him as a fugitive, a human alienated from the *adamah*, the source of his being. Cain loses everything: his role as carer, his fertile land, his family, his home and his God. His final tragic state is summarized by the comment: then Cain went from the presence of God and settled in the land of Nod (4:16). Just as significantly, the ground of Earth loses, too: as carer, her role as one who nurtures, her role as one mediating God's presence, her close affinity with God. Earth is the one truly sympathetic character in the story, the one who absorbs the sin, pleads for justice and suffers the consequences. Earth is the empathetic innocent victim at the hands of both God and humanity.

Whether the second narrative in Genesis 4 suggests some 'emancipation' for Cain may be debated. One thing is clear: the fate of Earth is now relegated to the background until the story of the flood, where once again Earth is treated violently by God because of what humans have done (Genesis 6:13).

To clarify the role of Earth as a character in the story, we may let the voice of Earth be heard as an alternative conclusion.

Conclusion: The Voice of Earth

I now live with violence. I emerged when God parted the waters of the deep. I appeared and at a word from God my greening began. My greening was celebrated in the forest of Eden where humans were formed from my soil to 'serve and preserve' the ground. In that forest there was peace between me, God and all life.

The violence began when God reacted to the disobedience of the first humans. God began cursing and I bore the brunt of it. Yet, I was only too happy to welcome my flesh back into my body when humans died.

The violence intensified when Cain, one of the humans serving me and nurturing my soil, offered up produce from my soil that God rejected. That rejection made Cain understandably angry. Alas, Cain killed his brother, Abel, which was going too far! I was torn between my two children.

Once again I received my own into my body. This time I did not stay silent. I opened my mouth and enabled the cry of the innocent blood of Abel to reach God. I mediated a cry for justice. I could not condone such violence.

And once again, God responded with curses that affected more than the culprit. Cain was cursed 'from the ground', banished from the very home he had nurtured. And the curse on fertility that God imposed outside of Eden, was intensified so that my soil would not produce anything for Cain. I was formerly the means of Cain experiencing God's presence. That option was also removed and I was left abandoned by Cain and by God.

Violence produces violence. But violence at the hands of God means that I often bear the brunt of what humans receive. I not only give birth to humans and receive them when they die. I often suffer violence for them and with them at the hands of God.

Cathy Higgins and Johnston McMaster

Towards a Life-Giving Ethic

Engaging Biblical Texts of Violence in the Violent Context of Northern Ireland

Dr. John D'Arcy May's retirement marks the end of a significant era for the Irish School of Ecumenics. John will be much missed by all of his colleagues and not least by those of the Education for Reconciliation team in Belfast. John was tireless in his support for our community education programme across Northern Ireland and the Border Counties. He understood the northern issues and dynamics of our work and constantly encouraged us.

John was an outsider who became an insider. From Australia to an Ireland torn apart by civil conflict was not an easy journey but John wrestled and engaged with the Northern Ireland tragedy, grasping the issues, identifying with the pain and remaining hopeful for a better future. He has made his contribution to our shared future. He comes to retirement at an important phase in our generational peace process and will take leave of us with the profound gratitude of a team of educators, still inspired by him to go on educating for reconciliation.

Violence as Context and Legacy

Modern Irish history is a history of violence. From the Tudor invasion to the most recent phase in Northern Ireland, violence has dominated the Irish story. Colonialism and post-colonialism have been a large factor, but so too have various physical force traditions contributed to the pervasive culture of violence. The early 20th century saw the re-introduction of the gun and the militarization of Irish politics. Partition in 1921 did not create sectarian violence but was itself a consequence of the same. The development of two confessional states ensured that partition would remain with Eamonn de Valera and Lord Craigavon not only designing separate political realities but maintaining them by structures and ethos.

The South did not deal with its violent legacy but occupied itself with the task of nation building. The North simmered with an uneasy tension never far beneath the surface. For just over half a century a Unionist hegemony dominated and, despite the emergence of a changing world in the 1960s, the northern Unionist politicians were ultimately incapable of change, or when some reforms did occur they were too little, too begrudging and too late. In 1969 'the lid came off' and for thirty-five years the community was plunged into violence. That it never tipped over the edge completely may be true but it is of little comfort to the extended families of over 3,600 dead and the 40,000 injured, many seriously and permanently.

It was a squalid little war with the State and paramilitaries responsible for brutalities and atrocities. The legacy of this violence remains, not just in the hurt and pain of all victims, but in mindsets, even those of a generation with no memory or experience of the 'troubles'.

Meanwhile, the physical force traditions, republican and loyalist, led the way by a considerable margin, on memorialization. Their activity in this field has left the noncombatant or innocent victims eclipsed, even sidelined. Is the memorialization activity of the physical force traditions the big effort to write the definitive history of the *troubles* and justify the use of violence?

Claims and counter-claims to have beaten the State or each other 'to a standstill' are a delusion. This was a war with no winners. True, no one lost; but, no one won either. There was no military victory and goals were not achieved. It has taken at least two decades to realize that the violence was going nowhere and that political differences cannot be dealt with or objectives realized by violent methods. It may take a little longer to fully realize that the violence was a failure and morally wrong from the outset. Neither the violence of the State nor of the physical force traditions was justified; history should not be manipulated to suggest otherwise.

Ireland has a strong religious tradition and an equally strong history of violence. We are at once one of the most religious and most violent countries in the world. Something does not add up, and serious and critical questions need to be asked about the relationship of the Christian religion and violence, not least by the guardians of religious tradition, Protestant and Catholic.

Reconstructing Texts of Violence

Whether by accident or design religion has been an active participant in the violence of modern Ireland. An ideological god reigns! In a loyalist enclave of South Belfast a biblical text occupied a gable wall for some years as part of a mural:

> And when the Lord thy God shall deliver them before thee; thou shalt smite them, and utterly destroy them; thou shalt make no covenant with them, nor show mercy unto them.

The text was from Deuteronomy 7:2; the verse following forbids marriages with the enemy on pain of destruction by God's anger. From the loyalist perspective this was applied theology. Loyalist practice did not draw distinctions between members of the Provisional IRA and any Catholic. Killing was indiscriminate. The text provided obvious sanction and also contained a reference to covenant with historical connections to an earlier Ulster crisis, the covenant of 1912. The textual version used was the King James Bible, which implied another ideological claim.

The approach to scripture is a popular one in Protestant religious culture. There has always been a great emphasis on the Hebrew scriptures read as a story with motifs and parallels to Ulster Protestant historical experience. The approach is often dominated by a proof-text method where texts are used without context and without historical rootage or awareness of canonical processes. It is a dangerous use of the Bible and one that becomes violently destructive in a conflictual and contested community. The approach to scripture is not only proof-text and ahistorical – it is also literal. What the text says is what is means.

When read in this way, Deuteronomy can become a war manual. A flat reading of the text offers some of the most militant assertions of Israel's preferentiality.[1] There is a violent insistence that 'the seven nations' have no place in Israel's future. It needs to be

---

1 Walter Bruggemann, *Theology of the Old Testament: Testimony, Dispute, Advocacy*, Minneapolis, Fortress, 1997: 496-99. Also see Bruce C. Birch, Walter Bruggemann, Terence E. Fretheim and David L. Petersen (eds.), *A Theological Introduction to the Old Testament*, Nashville, Abingdon, 1999: 163-64.

recognized that the *seven nations* theme is itself an ideological self-understanding in the writers' minds. There is no historical basis to this theme. Rather, it reflects a theological construction serving ideological ends. Canonical process is also ignored in the loyalist use of the text. The final shape of the Deuteronomistic text and history is post-exilic, 5th century BCE. Israel's story at this point is one of return and reconstruction of a community centred on Jerusalem. Not only do the *seven nations* not exist at the time, but Israel is in no position to fight battles, let alone wage wars. A fixation with defeating and wiping out Amalakites is a delusion and a fiction. Deuteronomy, then, is not history in any modern sense, but a liturgical text, distorted if literalized, and best understood as liturgical rhetoric with echoes of Israel's tradition of lament.

The whole canonical text of the Bible, therefore, needs to be taken into account when reading. To the harsh negation of the *seven nations* there is a counter-theme. The narrative of Genesis 12-36 contains nothing of aggressive exclusivism but, instead, provides a generous alternative in which the 'rejected nations' are treated positively. Even at the heart of the harsh ideology in Deuteronomy there is also a counter-theme; there is no 'flat wall' reading of the Deuteronomistic text. This means that the scriptures are to be read not only historically and canonically, but also with critical discernment, recognizing that the biblical text itself is not ideologically free. Hebrew prophets, e.g., Hosea, rigorously critiqued and undermined in a devastating way the ideology of religiously sanctioned war and violence.

On another gable wall in West Belfast there still exists a mural of the 1981 Hunger Strike. It too appeals to a biblical text: *Blessed are those who hunger and thirst for justice.* Yet again, the text is without context, a proof-text paying no attention to the foreground of Matthew's gospel or the structural and thematic context of the Sermon on the Mount where the particular text is located. Ten hunger-strikers died demanding political status rather than the criminal status by which the London government attempted to delegitimize them. Though there is evidence to suggest that the deaths could have been avoided,[2] this biblical text was appealed to by republicans along with two older traditions. Fasting for justice was practiced in the ancient Irish/Celtic tradition and its roots were therefore believed to lie in antiquity. However, this was the myth of reinvented Celticism, for the ancient Celtic fast was from sunrise to sunset and was in the context of an honour-shame culture, a social ethos very different from the Ireland of the 20th century. The second tradition was that of the martyr complex, which remains, and at the time did much to strengthen republican engagement with politics, though as complementary to the armalite. This too, however, ignored context and the classical understanding of martyrdom which is giving one's life for the cause, but not taking the lives of others. Republican and loyalist dying for 'the cause', which also killed innocent people, was misleading and distorted.

The text itself is a justice text and one of the key themes of Matthew's gospel. The foreground of the gospel is imperial power, i.e., the Roman empire with its militarism, economic oppression and Pax Romana built on and sustained by violence. The Sermon on the Mount in particular outlines the distinctive life-style of a faith community on a collision course with this superpower. God's empire, not Rome's, is supreme (Matthew 5-7, 24-25).

Justice is not a characteristic of the domination system. Justice was not a characteristic either of the London government in its historical dealings with Ireland, nor of

---

2 Richard English, *Irish Freedom: The History of Nationalism in Ireland*, London, Macmillan, 2006: 377-380.

the Unionist hegemony in its dealings with nationalists and loyalists. Key, though, to justice in Mathew's gospel is active non-violence and the teaching of the gospel is unequivocal about that. Justice in Matthean perspective means reconciling and committed relationships, integrity, active non-violent resistance to evil, active concern and prayer for the enemy, active solidarity through compassion and giving, all of which (Matthew 5) is a distinctive way of life, one not shared by empire, and one that results in persecution (5:10).

The hunger-strike mural's use of the Matthean text is located in a violent world, of often indiscriminate killing, but the mural is also use of a violence that had – long before 1981 – itself become a large part of the injustice of Northern Ireland. For the Matthean text in context, justice is achieved and sustained by active non-violence and peacebuilding.

The West Belfast mural also includes a cross and a hunger striker portrayed as a Jesus-like figure. This was a prominent image in 1981. It invokes the theme of blood sacrifice which was at the heart of the 1916 Easter Rising, as articulated by P.H. Pearse and the Rising poets. The imagery was largely drawn from the death of Jesus on the cross. Shedding of blood, blood sacrifice, was essential for the redemption of Ireland.

Loyalists, too, invoked the same theme following the slaughter of many soldiers of the 36th Ulster Division at the Battle of the Somme in 1916. The early British war poets also glorified the blood sacrifice theme. The theme is still invoked and remains central to Remembrance Day memorial services, chiefly at the Cenotaph service in London which is attended by members of the royal, political and ecclesial establishments. The language of supreme sacrifice is frequently used, including media reporting of current military deaths in Iraq. Also traditional is the text from John's gospel: *greater love has no one than this, that one lay down one's life for one's friends* (15:13). The text has a prominent place in the Somme Heritage Centre at Conlig, Co. Down. It matters not that the Johannine text has nothing to do with war or revolutionary violence. Its co-option by civil religion, sanctioned by Christian churches, is a distorted and warped use of a sacred text.

The blood sacrifice image, central to the physical force traditions and to the state's memorializing and even glorifying of violence and war, is itself a distortion of the death of Jesus. The distortion began with Anselm in the 12th century and was heightened by Calvin in the 16th century. A substitutionary theory of atonement became the penal theory. The sacrificial death of Jesus or the shedding of his blood was necessary for human salvation. Jesus had to die a violent death in order to placate God's anger over the sins of humanity. The divine necessity of violent sacrifice and its ritual re-enactment within this penal or substitutionary framework was placed at the heart of Western Christianity. This had the effect of turning Christianity into a cult of violence, and has had terrible consequences in history, e.g., the Crusades, the Inquisition, the view that war is the supreme sacrifice, the 1912 Ulster Covenant, the 1916 Easter Rising, the Battle of the Somme, and, more recently, the War Against Terror.

A theology of the necessity of violent punishment in the heart of God sets an angry God over against a compassionate Son. It provides an image of God as angry, bloodthirsty, violent and sadistic. This violent God is incompatible with the active non-violence of Jesus's teaching and life.

A socio-political hermeneutic is also necessary for a reading of the crucifixion story. The story of the cross needs to be set in the context of empire, which is often foregrounded in the Christian scriptures. Indeed, the domination system of successive empires and imperial powers is foreground to the Hebrew and Christian scriptures and, without this context, hermeneutics or reading strategies are defective. Jesus lived out of radical, active non-violence in opposition to the violence of the superpower and to the violent resistance movements which were part of his own Jewish community. He died at the hands of empire, the victim of state terrorism through crucifixion, which was the method of state execution. The death of Jesus was not because of Jewish violence, nor was it God's violence, but it was imperial violence. God was not in opposition to Jesus but, rather, 'God was in Christ' as the Christian scriptures affirm.

The hermeneutic of death, which reads the crucifixion as God's violence or God's punitive action and which has dominated Western theology for the last millennium, needs to be abandoned. The punitive justice system and other social systems and relationships based on it need radical deconstruction, and counter-systems in their stead. The blood sacrifice image of the cross has legitimized our wars and revolutionary violence and the churches have bought into it.

The 21st century requires a new hermeneutic, one that abandons the hermeneutic of death, bloodshed and blood sacrifice. Dying for the cause or for Ireland or Ulster was based on a warped ideology that distorted theology and biblical texts in the process. The hermeneutics of birth, life and nurture need to shape a new living for Ireland.

Towards a Hermeneutic of Life not Death

There is a life-affirming, active, non-violent, biblical ethic that can offer an alternative approach to the reliance on violence in order to achieve liberation and contribute to the embedding of the peace process in Northern Ireland. A number of feminist theologians are challenging violent, imperial, biblical interpretations, and certain god-images, and are recovering an alternative hermeneutic of life. Ivone Gebara, a Brazilian liberation theologian, is interested in formulating 'a new epistemological framework' that goes beyond andocentric, and anthropomorphic, doctrinal formulations that fail to critique biblical 'texts of terror' and a warrior-liberator god.[3] Gebara asks, how can we read biblical texts in a way that is liberating and critiques structural and relational violence and privileges life? She underlines that violent god-images and biblical texts are not only abusive of God and humanity, they are also conducive of unjust and inhumane, socio-economic and political relations, on a national and global scale. Gebara, reflecting on women's experiences of God in situations of poverty and violence, suggests that God for these women is 'simply the power to live.'[4] She believes the God whom Jesus reveals in the scriptures is a God who desires a world that reverences life and sustains it: in the Bible 'the last word [is] about life... not about the army and chariots of Pharaoh.'[5] This active non-violent, relational God, who stands alongside those struggling for life in the face of imperial power and violence, is, in Gebara's view, our reason to hope. Further, to hope in an active non-violent God, for Gebara, is to reject the terror and violence of those who seek to destroy life: 'God is our hope as the ultimate cry for justice: a "no" to unjust killing, to arms and armies, and a "yes" to a dignified life.'[6]

Is Gebara correct, though, in interpreting the God of Jesus as an active non-violent God? And what active non-violent, life giving strategies does Jesus offer those seeking

---

3 Ivone Gebara, *Longing for Running Water: Ecofeminism and Liberation*, Minneapolis, Fortress, 1999: 46-48.
4 Ivone Gebara, *Out of the Depths: Women's Experience of Evil and Salvation* Minneapolis; Fortress, 2002: 148.
5 Gebara, *Out of the Depths*: 148.
6 Gebara, *Longing for Running Water*: 135.

liberation from violence? In the Sermon on the Mount Jesus offers a liberating and life-affirming alternative to violence in the violent imperial context. He applies a radical, and transformative, active non-violent ethic to the Jewish Torah. The Sermon's ethic is not about passive resistance but creative proactive love that breaks the spiral of violence. The challenge of the text is real and concrete as Gerd Theissen, noted German scholar of the New Testament, confirms: 'It is impossible to determine what love of enemies and non-violence mean apart from the social situation in which these demands are made and practiced.'[7]

The teachings in the Sermon are ways of breaking the cycle of violence, and restoring right relations and peace. The alternative lifestyle in God's Empire is weakened, however, in the NRSV translation of Matthew 5:39: 'Do not resist an evildoer.' This translation suggests passivity, forbids self-protection, and urges submission to an evildoer. Not only that, '[i]t suggests that God legitimates evil and requires disciples to capitulate to and collude with, not oppose, evil action.'[8] Such a translation goes against the grain of Matthew's Gospel where Jesus resists evil in various forms. Warren Carter's translation is more consistent: 'Do not violently resist an evildoer.' The verb in the text, *antistenai*, suggests armed resistance in military encounters or violent struggle. The issue is not between passive submission and violent retaliation. It is an alternative way, a non-violent resistance that breaks the cycle of violence: 'Therefore the verse should be translated "do not retaliate or resist violently or revengefully, by evil means."'[9] Paul also reiterates this perspective in Romans 12:17-21: 'Do not repay anyone evil for evil…' (NRSV).

What follows in the Sermon on the Mount are radical, transformative, initiatives in resisting oppressive power, including that of Empire. In the Sermon the Jewish Jesus is reinterpreting the teachings of the Torah from within the Jewish tradition. The traditional teaching on vengeance, for instance, 'an eye for an eye and a tooth for a tooth' (NRSV, Matthew 5:38), aimed at limiting the retaliation in line with the offence, is reinterpreted in a way that breaks the cycle, yet exposes the injustice, and challenges the perpetrator to recognize the humanity of the victim, and treat the person with due respect (Matthew 5:40-42). One of the illustrations Jesus provides to demonstrate the nature of the radical behaviour he is suggesting concerns loan collection proceedings at court (Matthew 5:40). Giving your cloak as well as your coat left the victim naked, and thereby exposed non-violently the injustice, corruption, and greed at the heart of the justice system. The intention behind the act is to empower the poor to oppose the inhumanity of the legal system, and it embarrasses the creditor into recognizing the abusive nature of the law in the hope that the unjust system will be transformed.

In instructing his followers to give to the one who begs, or wishes to borrow, so that everyone may be sufficiently cared for (Matthew 5:42), Jesus is challenging an economic structure that benefits the powerful and wealthy, while impoverishing everyone else. It is a reminder that the earth and its resources are for sharing, and that each person has a responsibility to ensure others' needs are adequately met.

---

7 Gerd Theissen, *Social Reality and the Early Christians: Theology, Ethics, and the World of the New Testament*, Edinburgh, T&T Clark, 1993: 130.
8 Warren Carter, *Matthew and the Margins: A Socio-political and Religious Reading*, Maryknoll, Orbis, 2000: 151.
9 Glen H. Stassen and David P. Gushee, *Kingdom Ethics: Following Jesus in Contemporary Context*, Downers Grove (Illinois), InterVarsity, 2003: 138.

Luise Schottroff, writing on the androcentrism of Matthew's Sermon on the Mount, sounds a timely reminder that the non-violent model outlined by the writer of the gospel relies for its effectiveness on men giving up their right to use violence and seek retribution. It fails to take account of the fact that the actions if performed by women would have led to further oppression and dehumanization.[10] According to Schottroff, the three models of non-violent resistance offered in the Sermon presuppose the accepted roles of men in society; to 'turn the other cheek' as a praxis of attack is only effective when the one who strikes expects to be struck in return; if a woman removed her undergarment publicly in court, or offered to go with the soldier further than the legal distance, it would have been perceived as an invitation to rape.[11] Schottroff acknowledges that Walter Wink was aware of the gender issue as he called for a 'change of Jesus' thoroughly concrete directions to fit the given context' and further recommended that it was possible to catch the liberating emphasis of the praxis suggested in the Matthean text without turning Jesus's directions into laws.[12] Both Schottroff's and Wink's alternative active, non-violent interpretations recover a counter-cultural Jesus who endorsed a life and peace ethic and praxis. Today, the question is whether this hermeneutic of life resonates with, and finds expression in, the 21st century European context?

Grace Jantzen adds her voice to those committed to recovering an alternative hermeneutic of life to the patriarchal symbolic of death and mortality. She does this by emphasizing a feminist symbolic of *natalité*, which celebrates birth-giving and creativity. Jantzen criticizes traditional patriarchal philosophy of religion for its preoccupation with violence, sacrifice, and death. She asks:

> What if we were to begin with birth, and with the hope and possibility and wonder implicit in it? How if we were to treat natality and the emergence of this life and this world with the same philosophical seriousness and respect which had traditionally been paid to mortality and the striving for other worlds?[13]

In Jantzen's view this shift in emphasis from death to birth would have important ethical consequences, as it would move the focus in the western world away from war and militarization and impel concern for improving the material conditions of people's lives, especially the primary victims of violence, women and children.[14]

Jantzen draws on the philosophical theories of two European Jewish thinkers, whose lives were directly affected by the violence of the totalitarian regime of National Socialism, Hannah Arendt and Emmanuel Levinas. Both Arendt and Levinas, in developing their philosophical theories, draw on the concept of natality. Their concern is to recover the 'singularity and irreplaceability of human beings,' and underline the horrendous cost and ultimate futility of violence, which dehumanizes by reducing individuals to expendable 'masses'.[15] Arendt emphasizes the uniqueness of each person and celebrates each life as a story to be told and affirmed.[16] Levinas reminds us of the ability of the 'other' to con-

---

10 Luise Schottroff, *Lydia's Impatient Sisters: A Feminist Social History of Early Christianity*, London, SCM, 1995: 112.
11 Schottroff, *Lydia's Impatient Sisters*: 113.
12 Schottroff, *Lydia's Impatient Sisters*: 113.
13 Grace M. Jantzen, *Becoming Divine: Towards a Feminist Philosophy of Religion*, Manchester, Manchester University, 1998: 2.
14 Jantzen, *Becoming Divine*: 129-130.
15 Jantzen, *Becoming Divine*: 147.
16 Jantzen, *Becoming Divine*: 148.

tinually surprise us in new and unexpected ways. He warns that the 'other' cannot be reduced to 'same' as this would do violence to the other's individuality and uniqueness.[17]

Jantzen creatively develops the feminist symbolic of natality, of birth and rebirth, of flourishing and newness, as a necessary alternative to the myth of redemptive violence. She shows how a commitment to life, and the vital elements that nurture life, as an alternative to the western fixation with violence and death, promotes wholeness, and allows for a celebration of plurality, diversity, mutuality, and difference. At the heart of the symbol is openness to the future of God's *shalom*, which finds expression where each human life is valued and nurtured in relational communities.

Conclusion

A socio-political reading of the texts, a contextual reading, serious about context then and now, reading from a prophetic perspective inclusive of the Hebrew prophets and Jesus, will take us into a critical hermeneutic and counter-cultural ethic of radical non-violence.

The feminist symbolic of *natalité* and the feminist biblical hermeneutic also affirm a holistic, active non-violent peace ethic, which can contribute to the deconstruction of the myth of redemptive violence and enhance the peace process in Northern Ireland. A radically different biblical hermeneutic and a language transformation *from* death *to* birth, life and nurture can move the community towards the shared future.

---

17 Jantzen, *Becoming Divine*: 233-234.

Maureen Junker-Kenny

Out of Their Depth: Cultural Conquest, Debt and Renewal

In his *Transcendence and Violence*,[1] John D'Arcy May's critical pursuit of the courses of European colonialism and Christian mission on the reverse side of their world, the Pacific, is impressive and disquieting. He shows how imperial and ecclesial interests were all too often barely distinguishable. His book helps account for the dread that accompanied the mutually bewildering clash of cultures. With hermeneutical sensitivity, it shows the internal rationality of Non-European understandings of world and of transcendence while recognizing the inventive forms of resistance from Aboriginal and Melanesian cultures to the imposed presence of Westerners. In remorse for the one-sided cost of life and of indigenous self-understanding wrought by the histories of European government colonialism and of Christian processes of failed encounters, it urgently pleads for a radical altering of the terms of interaction in order to do justice to incomparable, utterly different cultures. Its equally concise and erudite critique of Buddhism's betrayal of its non-violent ethos in its spread to Eastern Asia makes it questionable from another historical setting whether the development assumed in the history of religions from primal to 'higher' religious understandings constitutes straight-forward progress. Instead, both types of relationship to the sacred are shown as having something irreplaceable to offer to an emerging world ethos embedded in different religious self-understandings.

In his search for the causes within Western culture of its inability to grasp world-views that proceed from different presuppositions, John May offers answers that also contain directions for future solutions. Western culture's dualism has to be, if not over-come, then at least complemented by a biocosmic appreciation of the earth. Christian absolutism and meliorism that have been root causes of violence ought to be converted into the recognition of other religions' equal claims to truth. If genuine reciprocal dia-logue is to be possible, the lynchpin of Christianity's claim to have received the ultimate revelation from God, the understanding of Jesus Christ as the saviour who unites divinity and humanity in his person, has to be abandoned.[2]

I want to question these three analyses from the presuppositions of one particular approach to moral reasoning; one that defines it as the hallmark of morality to go beyond community-specific standards, be they Melanesian, Prussian, or North Atlantic. Transposed into ethics, John May's conceptual alternative between acknowledged 'pluralism' and steep 'absolutism' mirrors a 'hermeneutical' over against a 'deontological' approach (1). The position that the absolute truth claim of the Mosaic God has an in-herent connection to violence has most recently been the subject of debate with the Heidelberg Egyptologist Jan Assmann in his comparison of biblical monotheism with cosmotheism. Even if John May's review of Buddhism's historical role in Thailand and Japan makes it clear that violence is not confined to the monotheistic type of transcendence,

---

[1] John D'Arcy May, *Transcendence and Violence: The Encounter of Buddhist, Christian and Primal Traditions*, New York and London, Continuum, 2003.
[2] May, *Transcendence and Violence*: ch. 6.

it needs to be sorted out whether violence in the spread of Christianity had to do with the intolerance linked to monotheism, or with other factors either less intrinsic to, or even contradictory of, its faith structure (2). Regarding the hope for more equitable and peaceful relations between religions in the future, the question arises whether the goal should be the ability to transcend the differences between the historical creeds, symbols and practices, or just to better understand each other's presuppositions. Is dialogue doomed to failure if it allows for the possibility of an open but committed advocacy of one's own faith tradition? Here, both the motivation and the concepts for expressing this identity are at stake. What scope do the Greek categories of the Christological councils grant to modern appropriations of the person and role of Jesus Christ? Are there internal reasons within each historical faith for promoting interaction across religious boundaries and discovering it as a fruitful religious experience in itself? Or, is this dialogue forced upon each of them despite themselves by economic globalization and the ever-increasing call for content-free, transferable skills in forging peace? If this were so, intercultural encounter would just mean adaptation to an existing economically driven framework, not a renewal from the depth of their own best resources[3] and a forging of new syntheses (3).

1. Hermeneutics of culture and deontology

It is a strength of John May's hermeneutical approach that he deciphers the internal rationality and attractiveness of world construction in Aboriginal and Melanesian cultures. Their intrinsic resources are made visible, e.g., regarding their relationships to the land and to their ancestors, and in the responses drawn from their own myths to the encounter with technologically superior strangers. In the face of such an integral world-view, the tragedy of the European lack of recognition is all the more pronounced, and the cunning exploitation of a high culture of exchange relations all the more shameful. At present, the rediscovered model of Pacific Island traditions gives rise to much philosophical reconstruction of the logic of giving, receiving, and responding. The renewed attention of Paul Ricoeur and Marcel Hénaff through the work of Marcel Mauss to the ritual of *potlatch* and the interpretation of *hau* as the power in the gift to evoke a return is an example.[4] This reappropriation of cultural patterns from other lifeworlds in philosophical anthropology may be seen as a parallel enterprise to John May's reclaiming of the primal traditions for '"completing" religion by overcoming the dualism of transcendence and immanence'.[5] Their philosophical and his theological efforts are enriching through offering different anthropological and hermeneutical perspectives of striving for a flourishing life.

If, however, ethics contains also a normative, deontological dimension, then May's sensitive account of the logic of relationships in Pacific communities encounters a

---

3 For an in-depth analysis of the relevance of Paul Ricoeur's thinking on the renewal of a culture from its core, see Margit Eckholt, *Poetik der Kultur. Bausteine einer interkulturellen dogmatischen Methodenlehre*, Freiburg, Herder, 2002: 108-171, 132.
4 Paul Ricoeur, *The Course of Recognition*, translation by David Pellauer, Cambridge, Mass. and London, Harvard University, 2005: 225-46. Marcel Hénaff, *Le prix de la vérité: Le don, l'argent, la philosophie*, Paris, Ed. Du Seuil, 2002.
5 May, 'Rootedness: Reflections on Land and Belonging', in Werner Jeanrond and Andrew Mayes (eds.), *Recognising the Margins: Developments in Biblical and Theological* Studies: *Essay in Honour of Seán Freyne*, Dublin, Columba, 2005: 146-159: 157.

typical question. Can cultures only be evaluated internally, or are there outside criteria by which their order of priorities of goods can be judged? And more specifically, since one can imagine different orders which are equally conducive to a flourishing life, can the non-instrumentalization of the other serve as this universal criterion, as deontological ethics based on the moral experience of self-obligation claims? Then this point has to be put to all attempts that prioritize communal well-being over the idea that individuals have inalienable rights. Be it in the modes of thinking and practice within an integral culture before the axial shift or in the existing ethos (*Sittlichkeit*) in Hegel's hermeneutics of a communitarian ethics of institutions, whenever 'wholeness' is sought 'in harmonious social entity',[6] the legitimacy of conscientious or prophetic critique diminishes. From a position that makes basic rights a criterion for evaluating communal practices, May's account signals not an ideal, but a problem. His description of the relational anthropology at work in primal cultures only reinforces the impression that the strength of this model can last just as long as individual difference is minimized:

> Self-knowledge arises in the course of social relationships. The person has no single name, but a complex of names deriving from various social roles; he or she only exists to the extent that these roles are played out. The person is intrinsically 'participative'(57f.).

As insightful as this description is into the internal workings of a given culture, or of a social or a religious ideal, the question beyond the internal perspective is, what price has to be paid by individuals as well as classes of people, e.g., the female half of the community, for systems in which group-internal stability is the highest value. It also has to be put to European approaches, be they Neo-Hegelian, or Utilitarian. John May's own account of the work of identity formation in the critical appropriation of a tradition is much more circumspect:

> The 'instant identity' offered by fundamentalism to uprooted islanders and disoriented Westerners alike, short-circuits the relationship of both to tradition, without which identity formation in a rapidly changing context cannot take place.

By asking for the scope to negotiate one's tradition, and taking a stance towards it, a role ascription that only allows for participation but not for difference is already left behind. By making room for reflective distance, it becomes possible also to identify a culture's rationales for exclusion. The reverse side of the communal logic in primal cultures can be, as the theologian Michael Bongardt has pointed out drawing on the philosophical work of Ernst Cassirer, that not just crime or immorality but the accident of illness may lead to an individual person being singled out and persecuted as the cause of harm to the community.[7] A different version of the priority of the group can be found in the insistence of some forms of contemporary communitarianism that all potential for change proceeds from internal resources. The Kantian philosopher Onora O'Neill sees this claim, rather than an alleged inability to welcome change, as the hallmark of group-specific ethics.[8]

---

6 May, *Transcendence and Violence*: 48. Further page numbers in the text.
7 Michael Bongardt, *Die Fraglichkeit der Offenbarung. Ernst Cassirers Philosophie als Orientierung im Dialog der Religionen, Regensburg*, Pustet, 2000: 225.
8 Onora O'Neill, *Towards Justice and Virtue: A Constructive Account of Practical Reasoning*, Cambridge, CUP, 1996: 52: 'Although particularist reasoning can allow for the revisability of norms or of commitments across time, in the light of other norms and commitments (... it is not, contrary to some critics, intrinsically conservative), it cannot allow for the thought that

The advocates of community ethics will in turn point out that the individual rights perspective has its own drawbacks. Thus, the deontological separation of what ought to be from what is lends itself to being handled in a rigoristic way and often seems unable to connect the 'kingdom of ends' with concrete moral issues. Its universalism seems rootless and lacking the power to renew its motivation. Regarding this ongoing dispute, John May's position does not simply fit into the communitarian template. Despite his severe critique of the abstract universalist European mindset of the Christian missionaries, he recognizes the humanizing potential of going beyond the limits of original belonging:

> But the new order also suggested that responsibilities extended beyond clan barriers to include reconciliation with former enemies and the inclusion of strangers in the circle of obligation. (111)

Religion can help to risk this step:

> Does transcendence, as the capacity to recognise successively more inclusive contexts pointing to a horizon hold the key to overcoming attachment to the interests and identities that motivate violence? (107)

Thus, it seems possible that the outreach beyond established customs in the name of transcending criteria for human morality could give searching individuals and communities a new, cosmopolitan home that lives from the critical interaction of both internal and culture-transcending foundations. Religion can assist people in detaching themselves from immediate interests and in broadening the circle of belonging. It can sustain the motivation to 'offer hospitality to the stranger'[9] and open up a more congenial starting-point to seeking to understand the other's faith, than can an indifferent secular mentality.

If one can accept these goals as worth striving for, why then join theologians allergic to 'modernity' like Gavin D'Costa in 'his understandable hostility toward the importation of Enlightenment universalism and apriorism into Catholic theology' (129)? Does it not facilitate exactly the withdrawal to one's own monopoly on religious truth that May rightly criticizes in *Dominus Iesus*, to reserve his critique for the specific points D'Costa makes regarding models of interfaith dialogue, but allow him to get through with this blanket dismissal of the modern critical turn to subjectivity? Why leave professional interpreters of texts unchallenged when they avoid the trouble and care of differentiating between the opposite positions from Kant to Kierkegaard developed between 1781 and 1850 and simply cast all of them as similarly 'promethean'? There are other cases of similarly selective comment. We move from what D'Costa terms 'Kantian exclusivist modernity' (123) to an author who seeks to relate the Aristotelian ethics of striving to Kant's cosmopolitanism of equal human dignity: Paul Ricoeur. Ricoeur appreciates in Kant's view of religion the deep recognition of moral agents' need for a hope grounded beyond human possibilities. Why follow this masterly mediator, a mediator between approaches both within Continental philosophies of reflection and between them and Anglo-Saxon analytic and social ethical positions, in his sympathetic exposition of the contribution of Emmanuel Levinas's thinking, but leave out his critique of Levinas's missing distinction between *idem* and *ipse*, resulting in an 'externality' that reduces 'the otherness of conscience to the otherness of other

---

one stretch of practical reasoning may have multiple and differing audiences. Particularist reasoning is intrinsically "insiders" reasoning.'

9   May, 'Catholic Fundamentalism? Some Implications of *Dominus Iesus* for Dialogue and Peace-making,' in Michael Rainer (ed.), *'Dominus Iesus.' Anstößige Wahrheit oder anstößige Kirche?*, Münster, LIT, 2001: 112-133: 127. Further page numbers from this article in the text.

people'?[10] My point is that, given the shared regard for a concept of self that is 'underivable and unfathomable' (129) and the goal of promoting 'unconditional respect' between religions (129), John May could find more support than he expects in the resources that the European age of the critique of pure reason and of the opening up of practical reason to hope in God came up with as a consequence of the Christian reception and transformation of Jewish monotheism.

2. Monotheism and singularity

A second question worthy of renewed consideration concerns the specific superiority complex assigned to monotheisms that is seen as much of a cause of their deficiency in enabling encounters with the other as is the idealistic, a priori character of Western universalist thought. On this count, primal traditions and Buddhism belong together as examples of religion that relativize subjectivity and opt for timeless wisdom instead of a God acting in history. I see a structurally similar critique in Jan Assmann's confrontation of a biblical monotheism that insists on the difference of God from the world and humanity with cosmo- or biotheistic religions in Egyptian and Greek antiquity. Two of the arguments raised by Christian theologians in the debate with Assmann could be relevant also in the Pacific context. The first contradicts the alleged link of monotheistic truth-claims to violence, for it perceives that the unifying move in religious thinking contains in itself a reflective, dispassionate element. The other suggests that only monotheism can elevate humans into partners of God who are called to live up to this position by exercising just government and restraint over against absolutizing their own insights as ultimate truths.

a) Monotheism as a violent or as a reflective truth-claim?

Does belief in the one true God predispose to violence, or does it presuppose reflection on criteria for divinity? Both the analysis and its contradiction are made from a philosophy of religion perspective. Against laying the blame for violence at the feet of belief in one God, the counterargument asks that we reflect on the logic evident in the theological reconstruction of the faith experience of the unity of God. Already the level of thinking evident in unifying the concept of God into the one cause of creation and preservation has been seen as a move against violence. The reflective distance of interpreting one's religious experience creates the rapport of calm thinking rather than ecstatic passion. Criteria are brought in that define what is worthy and unworthy in thinking the divine.[11]

A parallel to this appreciation of monotheism as inviting reflection at the level of universal truth-claims about the creator, humanity, and nature, can be found in Robert Schreiter's comment on theology as *scientia*. He observes that among the four forms of God-talk he distinguishes across different religions – theology as commentary on a

---

10 Ricoeur, *Oneself as Another*, translated by Kathleen Blamey, Chicago and London, University of Chicago, 1992: 336-49 and 354. May, *Transcendence and Violence*: 207n20, only mentions Ricoeur's reference to the complementarity of Husserl's and Levinas's approaches, but not his critique of the latter.

11 These criteria are theoretical and practical. Beyond unity over multiplicity, they give rise to an ethical understanding of God and self see Bongardt, *Fraglichkeit*: 242, and Georg Essen, 'Ethischer Monotheismus und menschliche Freiheit. Philosophisch-theologische Anmerkungen zur aktuellen Monotheismuskritik – Rückfragen an Jan Assmann', in J.-P. Wils (ed.), *Die Moral der Religion. Kritische Sichtungen und konstruktive Vorschläge*, Paderborn, Schöningh, 2004: 155-185.

sacred text, as wisdom, as *scientia*, and as praxis – it is the *scientia* model that is best able to mediate across different cultural paradigms.[12] Reflection in reference to other truth claims is then a factor at least as typical as fanatic defence.

While this is not meant to be a complete answer to the problem of violence caused by monotheisms – if one can ever distinguish between what is human and what belongs to a specific faith tradition – at least it can offer a retarding moment against quick and easy combinations of causes and effects. Could, e.g., Rodney Stark's sociological view of religion as causing violence, quoted approvingly with other stock-taking historians of the West,[13] have more to do with his reduction of religion to the 'rational choice' paradigm of economist thinking than a genuine interest in helping to create a peace that is more than conditions of stability for investment interests? The ability to resist the submission, typical for market models, of dignity to price, could be one criterion in interreligious dialogue – be this capacity based on the alternative between God and Mammon, or on a different starting point for the critique of greed implicit in conceiving agency mainly in terms of object-related preference.

b) Human partnership with God, rule of justice, and eschatology

Yet, even if this philosophical analysis of reflective monotheism can be granted, what about specific images of God, mirrored, e.g., in 'jealousy,' in decrees of exclusive election and military support, quoted both by Jan Assmann and by John May? One theological counterargument in the debate on the 'Mosaic distinction' between the one true and all the other false Gods is that far from legitimizing the violent mistreatment and annihilation of enemies, it may be precisely the monotheistic rationalization that inaugurates an understanding in which God supports the rule of a law of justice.[14] It is then a hermeneutical decision whether to read the praise of violent victories as the matrix, or as the exception from the norm of peaceful governance of the world by God and of the non-violent messianic kingdom of God.[15]

This latter reading, defined as 'ethical monotheism' by Julius Wellhausen at the end of the 19th century, identifies as the key tone of God's relationship to the people the sense of responsibility that arises from their being made in the image of God, from their role of stewards for creation, from the covenant and from the summoning of the prophets. It is true that not every biblical text supports this position, and the history of effects of other passages in later ages to justify violent conquests can be quoted as counter-

---

12 Robert Schreiter, *Constructing Local Theologies*, Maryknoll, Orbis, 1985: 90.
13 E.g., May, *Transcendence and Violence*: 7, 169n1, 141, 211n59. It would be interesting to compare the historical claims of Rodney Stark's *One True God: Historical Consequences of Monotheism*, Princeton and New Jersey, Princeton University, 2001, and of Regina Schwartz's *The Curse of Cain: The Violent Legacy of Monotheism*, Chicago, University of Chicago, 1997, with Erich Zenger's comparison of reflective monotheism with the violence of the Ancient Near Eastern and Greek polytheisms preceding and surrounding it, in his 'Der Mosaische Monotheismus im Spannungsfeld von Gewalttätigkeit und Gewaltverzicht. Eine Replik auf Jan Assmann' in Peter Walter (ed.), *Das Gewaltpotential des Monotheismus und der dreieine Gott*, Freiburg, Herder, 2004: 39-73.
14 Karlheinz Ruhstorfer, 'Der Grund zur Hoffnung, dass es gut wird', in Peter Walter (ed.), *Gewaltpotential*:104-116: 108.
15 Peter Walter, 'Einführung', in Walter, *Gewaltpotential*: 9, with reference to Erich Zenger's exegetical analysis of the development from an unreflective monotheism with polytheistic traces to a reflective monotheism marked by a critique of violence and by a universalistic outlook in the exilic and post-exilic periods.

examples; yet, the trajectory of elevating the human person to partnership with God – a relationship missing in cosmotheisms – and of the divine recognition of human reason and of the human capability to be moral entail a positive link between reason and good governance. From a historical perspective, especially Latin Christianity's, a dualism of separating political and religious power has been seen as the beginning of a pluralistic society.

In his positive examples of peaceful outcomes from the mutual challenges of European and Pacific cultures May points to the way in which the horizon of indigenous religion characterized by an 'ontology of place' was opened up to the eschatological promise of God. This promise implies a partner to whom it is made and who is responsible for living up to this calling.[16]

It also gives the prerogative to God's judgment. Even if the Christian churches have not always lived up to this heritage, and least so in their treatment of heretics and of foreign cultures, it is not evident whether their practices are to be blamed on their monotheism. On the contrary, they can be reproached for contravening the injunction to wait for the time of God's judgment. The Frankfurt philosopher Rainer Forst sees Jesus's parable of the weeds among the wheat (Mt. 13: 24-30) as the historical root of the idea of tolerance in Europe. In such eschatological perspective mindful of the finitude and fallibility of human reasoning, truth-claims can be held in suspense and do not have to be inherently violent.[17]

3. Jesus Christ in Greek garb: the heritage of Chalcedon

Recent events in the Roman Catholic church seem to confirm John May's critique in the sixth chapter of *Transcendence and Violence*: the formula of Chalcedon as a once helpful but now superseded expression of the distinctiveness of Jesus Christ promotes, as a measuring stick for orthodoxy, an ahistorical metaphysical understanding of the mystery of Jesus's unity with God. The Vatican 'notification' to Jon Sobrino in March 2007 provides an unwelcome example.[18] Yet, can Chalcedon not be read as the opposite of a closed metaphysical system? Is not the very fact of its aporetic, negative, paradoxical formulations an open invitation to think beyond these categories once more adequate thought forms have become possible?[19]

---

16 In his review of a book that treats a similarly tragic situation of the end of a culture after Western conquest, Charles Taylor mentions the Crows' faith in their God as helping their transition from nomadic to settled life in North America, see 'A Different Kind of Courage: Review of J. Lear, *Radical Hope: Ethics in the Face of Cultural Devastation*', Boston, Harvard University, 2006, in *The New York Review of Books* LIV,7 (26 April, 2007): 4-8.

17 Rainer Forst, *Toleranz im Konflikt*, Frankfurt a.M., Suhrkamp, 2003: 65. Forst interprets the parable's deferral of judgment to God's eschatological authority as the 'janus face' of Christian tolerance. The church historian Arnold Angenendt quotes Forst in his treatment of the ambiguous history of interpretation of the New Testament's insistence on ultimate truth and its call to respect the believer's conscience in *Toleranz und Gewalt. Das Christentum zwischen Bibel und Schwert*, Münster, Aschendorff, 2007: 232-294: 236.

18 For a detailed discussion and defence of Sobrino's use of exegetical enquiries into what can be established regarding the self-consciousness and claim of the historical person of Jesus, see Peter Hünermann, 'Moderne Qualitätssicherung? Der Fall Sobrino ist eine Anfrage an die Arbeit der Glaubenskongregation' in *Herder Korrespondenz* 61 (April 2007): 184-188.

19 More adequate than the aporetic substance-ontological concepts of Chalcedon are the categories of freedom that arose in the later stages of the history of reception of the biblical witness, see Thomas Pröpper, *Erlösungsglaube und Freiheitsgeschichte. Eine Skizze zur Soziologie*, München, Kösel, 1988^2: 171-220, 259-261.

From the perspective of ethics, a lot depends on the ability to explain that our soteriology is not a projection, but is based on a Christology which is historically tenable even if it is not a matter of objectifying proof. If this much cannot be established, why should Christians be motivated to sustain interreligious dialogue?[20] Yet, even if their internal motive was compelling, the real problem for the Christian witness may not be the different faiths of other cultures. It may be the loss of the eschatological extension of our horizon of accountability. Instead of calling theologies of history to account for past mentalities of (re)conquest, we may have to reinsert into a culture of immanent transcendence shrunk to the pinpoint of the individual body the long breath of expectations historically awakened but far from delivered.

John May's soul-searching analysis of the failures of Christian missionary endeavours increases the credibility of a chastened Christian cooperation in delivering human rights and human flourishing. What he makes clear with regard to the ambiguous European heritage is also true for each of its counterparts: every cultural garb, thought form, particular self-understanding has its price. Maybe the best a culture and a religion can do in the global interaction of players more forceful than religions is to give a convincing model of its guiding insights, insights that sustain humane practices: for the Christian, faith in the incarnation of God, the singularity of every human being, responsibility *coram Deo*, and a location within a chain of memory from creation to the eschatological hope for the kingdom of God that makes present reconciliations possible.

---

20 This demand is in keeping with May's own specification in *Transcendence and Violence*: 130: 'Theological (or equivalent) reflection or the findings of comparative religion are insufficient in themselves to raise these relationships to the ethical level necessary for real understanding; this impulse must come from within the tradition, from its lived spirituality.'

Hedwig Meyer-Wilmes
Transformations of Spirituality in a Post-Modern Culture

My connection with John May is not only a shared past at the Catholic Ecumenical Institute in Münster (1974-1979), but also a shared interest. The discussions during our time together at the Institute were marked by the attempt

> to show by way of example and to understand on a theoretical level the theological significance of the so-called non-theological factors (cultural, social, psychological, etc.) for all ecumenism. Christian theology has always not only lived from reflecting on the transcendental content of faith, but also from reflecting on faith as it is actually lived in its historical, social and cultural contexts together with the concrete shape of Christian forms of community. Our believing, hoping and loving are thus not only touched upon externally by the constant fact of separation, but also affected internally. Ecumenical theology is concerned with the external *and* internal divisions of Christian existence.[1]

Although this distinction is outdated today, at that time it led us to concentrate on that which eluded theological attention. In the following contribution I attempt something similar with the phenomenon of post-modern spirituality, a spirituality which owes its existence to the culture of modernity and not primarily to the respective holdings or resources of religious traditions. This new religiosity, which has not yet been taken completely seriously by theologians and scholars of religious studies (in German and Low-German speaking countries), is the focus of attention here so that it may be perceived as relevant for theology.

Definitions of (post-)modern spirituality

When one tries to find out something about the phenomenon of modern spirituality, what stands out primarily is that most of the manuals consider this term historically and in terms of the different points of view of various theological disciplines,[2] whereas explications with respect to the 'new spirituality or religiosity' are either missing or very scarce. For example, Josef Sudbrack, whom I hold in high regard, writes the following in the new edition of the *Lexikon für Theologie und Kirche*:

> Spirituality is the core word of the 'new religiosity' which is difficult to grasp: 'Spiritual paths' aim at an inner transformation with the aid of 'spiritual techniques' from the areas of Eastern meditation and Western psychology, frequently combined with corresponding concepts (reincarnation and karma) and ways of life. Dogmatic clarity and institutional allegiance are rejected in favour of 'being referred to the one, all-embracing being which appears to people as the incomprehensible spiritual, the trans-material, or the metaphysical

---

1 Peter Lengsfeld (ed.), *Ökumenische Theologie. Ein Arbeitsbuch*, Stuttgart, Berlin, Cologne and Mainz, Kohlhammer, 1980: 16.
2 This is something which Kees Waaijman rightly criticizes in his book, *Spirituality: Forms, Foundations, Methods*, Leuven, Peeters, 2002: 369-397.

(Scharfetter)'. The spectrum ranges from transpersonal psychology and philosophy to primitive superstition. Theologically it is a question of a 'homo naturaliter religiosus' who is not bound to any historically personal claim. When following New Age, in contact with Eastern spirituality and combined with a misinterpreted Christian tradition, this is also the metaphysical basis of esotericism.[3]

Another view is given by Kick Bras who talks in very general terms about 'spirituality as the striving to give life a transcendental meaning in a more or less methodological way.'[4] Thus, we see a language of technique and method. Sudbrack classifies certain techniques, such as meditation, and methods from psychology as belonging to the 'new-religious' spirituality. He also talks about movements like esotericism and New Age. These groups are in agreement with each other in their rejection of institutions and dogma as well as in their misinterpretations of Christian tradition. The problem with an examination which distinguishes between (institutional) orthodoxy and (unattached) heresy is that it can say very little or up to nothing at all content-wise about the self-image of these new-religious groups. Kick Bras's talk about a 'methodological way' probably also refers to a particular technique, a path or a form that achieves an 'inner transformation'. Spirituality is generally understood as the 'inner side of faith' and is described in the mysticism of religious orders as the 'path to the inside'. In the spiritualities of movements (women's movement, ecological movement, peace movement, interreligiosity movement and transpersonal movement),[5] the term is used to mark an integral or holistic consciousness. This talk of holism is critically directed at an overemphasis on 'objective' knowledge as well as at the absolutizing of technical reason which have defined the modern age since the Enlightenment.[6] As a countermove, reference is made to the importance of subjective knowledge as well as to the significance of practical reason which also knows how to integrate personal experiences. In this sense, spirituality denotes a perspective which rejects the dualisms of the modern age (spirit-body, reason-feeling, society-religion, man-woman).[7] One can also say that a new-religious spirituality chooses the risks of modernity and not just its achievements as its starting point.

Modernity as the starting point of spirituality

But what characterizes modernity with regard to spirituality? Anton von Harskamp states succinctly: 'The new religiosity owes its existence essentially to individualization.'[8] At the time of the 'anthropological turn' at the end of the 18th and the beginning of the 19th century, that is, during the period when modern faith and modern theology emerged, the individual and his or her faith and experience were already the starting point for a

---

3 *Lexikon für Theologie und Kirche*, volume 9, Freiburg, Basel and Vienna, Herder, 2000: 852.
4 Kitty Bouwman and Kick Bras (eds.), *Werken met spiritualiteit*, Baarn, Ten Have, 2001: 16.
5 Twenty years ago one normally made distinctions on the basis of those responsible for particular spiritualities, such as priests, lay people, women, members of religious orders, etc., which I never found convincing since this conceptualization is weighed down by certain kinds of discrimination; for this reason, I prefer to speak of the spirituality of movements.
6 See Hanneliese Steichele, 'Spiritualität', in Anneliese Lissner, Rita Süssmuth and Karin Walter (eds.), *Frauenlexikon*, Freiburg, Basel and Vienna, Herder, 1988: 1060f.
7 See my 'Feministische Spiritualität', in Eugen Biser, Ferdinand Hahn and Michael Langer (eds.), *Der Glaube der Christen*, volume 1, Munich and Stuttgart, Pattloch und Calwer, 1999: 319-331.
8 Anton van Harskamp et al., *De Religieuze Ruis in Nederland*, Zoetermeer, Meinema, 1989: 16.

relationship with 'the Other'. In the Christian religion the divine spoke only through the human. This process is radicalized in a post-modern society. The individual is no longer just a starting point, but also the point of access, even the all-embracing space and lasting reference point for the 'religious'. All religious speech about 'the Other' is thus coloured by that which is individual. When people meditate, pray, believe or proclaim, then each form of religious activity takes place in the tension between 'I' and 'the Other.'[9] It is therefore not surprising that each group from the spectrum of new religiosity – whether Evangelicals, New Agers or meditation enthusiasts – relies on the 'I' as its starting point.

Let us look at this 'I' a little more closely in order to mark the difference between modernity and post-modernity more distinctly. Modernity started with a relatively homogeneous concept of subject, but this has been changing in post-modern times. In modern societies individualization becomes a socially dictated way of life. Individuals can break away from their origins, classes and religions; but, not only do they have the chance to take their lives into their own hands as they see fit, they also have the duty to shape it.[10] This has different implications, e.g., making it impossible to talk about a single homogeneous subject. We can no longer rely on the reality of worker, citizen, Christian, lay person, man or woman. In the course of a lifetime we have different identities and we can live several roles at the same time. One may paraphrase this process of I-development as 'patchwork-identity'. It is demanded of the individual that he or she choose among models of life as well as integrate a diversity of models. In individualized societies one also assumes that, though the individual appropriates or rejects the holdings or resources of a religious tradition, one does not simply accept them. This also necessitates that the disappearance of social forms of life be experienced as a step in a new direction and not as defeat or the end of everything. It should be clear that profit and loss lie very close together here. To express this logic of individualization one could take the famous saying[11] of the writer and philosopher Simone de Beauvoir, that '[o]ne is not born, but rather becomes, a woman', and rephrase it to fit the religious process of individualization: one is no longer born a Christian, but rather becomes spiritual (or not). The individual thus has the task and the opportunity to 'design' his or her own biography and to make it happen. Identity can no longer be attained and secured on the level of simple role identities. All role identities, even those of the market-procured job roles, come under the pressure of reflection and must be 'self-referentially' reconstructed on a second level – the I-identity. The perspective of working on one's own biography for one's whole life and of searching for meaning and identity replaces the simple model of assuming a pattern of identity and life story.'[12] Karl Gabriel identifies this element of self-reference with developed modernity or, perhaps better, post-modernity. Hence, post-modernity is known for balancing out fragmented identities and not for the attempt to become a subject, itself the mark of modernity. One can be disbelieving in an institutional sense and believing in a spiritual sense at one and the same time.[13] This diagnosis naturally has consequences for talking

---

9 Van Harskamp, *De Religieuze Ruis*: 17.
10 See Karl Gabriel, *Christentum zwischen Tradition und Postmoderne*, Freiburg, Basel and Vienna, Herder, 1996^5: 15.
11 Simone de Beauvoir, *The Second Sex*, translated and edited by H.M. Parshley, New York, Alfred A. Knopf, 1953: 267.
12 Gabriel, *Christentum*: 140-141.
13 On the paradoxical traits of a post-modern religiosity, see my 'Unsichtbar religiös? Zur Situation

about God as well: Each kind of talk – whether with, of, about, against, in, or beyond God – is possible since 'moments of being' disclose themselves in each discourse.[14] And these moments of being are of course also present in the diverse groupings of a New Spirituality.

The risk society as starting point of a post-modern spirituality

Post-modernity is not only characterized by the promises of modernity (freedom, becoming a subject, etc.), but also by the perception of its risks. Whereas one earlier believed in the increase in happiness through the free choice of a profession and partner, unemployment and relational illiteracy give us a different, pessimistic feeling about life. People in the post-modern age can experience freedom as coercion, love as a contract, and life in its different roles as arduous. Dedication, the feeling of being in good hands, making sense or lending structure to stressful everyday life – one looks for all this in the niches of a New Religiosity.

A comparison of the New Evangelicals and the New Age Movement shows that the risks of society provide the stimulus to join the new spirituality groups. Even if these diverge greatly with regard to content on the level of self-definition – with one group trusting in the authority of God, of Scripture and the Holy Spirit, and the other in the person filled with cosmic energies – they still exhibit amazing agreement. A non-formal, non-hierarchical structure characterizes both. Their ways of dealing with others are primarily informal and they formulate the same criticism of Western, materialistic, hedonistic culture. Both are familiar with a deep-seated sense of crisis, sometimes formulated fatalistically, sometimes optimistically, which is manifested in a belief in the last days and a radical emotionalism of conversion. One can also interpret them together as a drastic form of cultural criticism. Also conspicuous is the renunciation of all sorts of dualisms, first and foremost the dualism of body-spirit. What distinguishes these from the institutionalized, denominational offerings are such things as regard for the body as a 'temple of God' (and thus not taking any drugs), making room for the ecstatic self in word and sound, and providing a natural place for music with meditation, prayer and group work.[15] The idea of an enlightened, mature individual is relativized here in favour of more expressive elements. Both groups are responding to the problematic nature of individualization which addresses the issue of the price of freedom. They are looking for places where the individual can feel like a complete person. An evangelical would say: finally, I have been freed by Jesus to discover my own self! A New Ager would call out: I want to become one with the cosmic energies to feel my own self!

It should be clear that if one tries only to distinguish the phenomenon of new-religious spirituality from a Christian, biblical-based spirituality, as occurred in the *LThK*-article by Sudbrack, then one does not notice that groups like New Age and the New Evangelicals do not start out from a church-critical, but rather a cultural-critical

---

christlicher Religion in den Niederlanden', in *Jahrbuch für christliche Sozialwissenschaften* 44, Münster, Verlag Regensburg, 2003: 115-130.

14 On this, see my 'Tirzia – durch einen Spiegel in einem erzählten Wort', in Toine van de Hoogen, Hans Küng and Jean-Pierre Wils (eds.), *Die Widerspenstige Religion: Orientierung für eine Kultur der Autonomie*, Kampen, Kok, 1997: 249-267.

15 See van Harskamp, *De Religieuze Ruis*: 19-22; George D. Chryssides, *Exploring New Religions*, London and New York, Continuum, 1999; and Wouter J. Hanegraaf and S. Sutcliffe, *New Age Religion and Western Culture: Esotericism in the Mirror of Secular Thoughts*, Leiden, Brill, 1996.

standpoint (the dualisms of the modern age). Furthermore, one fails to mention the fact that they not only embrace the achievements of modernity, but also name the price of modernity. Thirdly, it becomes clear that, although their radical rhetoric of conversion often fails to stand up to a general analysis, it can nonetheless be read as a conjugation of the problematic nature of individualization.

Dorothee Sölle as a voice of cultural-critical spirituality

The work of the political theologian Dorothee Sölle further helps us in our deduction of the cultural-critical starting point that we have looked at from the self-understanding of the New-Religiosity groups. In a lecture she gave in 1980 in English, entitled 'Mysticism – Liberation – Feminism', she defined her concept of mysticism by referring to three points of reference:

> Perhaps you may be wondering what these imposing substantives 'feminism', 'liberation' and 'mysticism' have to do with each other at all. What is their common denominator? We can say that there are people who are involved in the search for nonauthoritarian human relationships and who are working toward the abolition of class rule and class injustice. That is what the word 'liberation' suggests here. They are also working to abolish patriarchy and the colonialization of women ..., and they are searching for a nonauthoritarian language to use in describing a God whose essential attributes are not independence, distance, power, and domination. In other words, the search for nonauthoritarian relationships and conditions is, as I see it, what unites feminists, mystics, and advocates of liberation.[16]

Her plea for nonauthoritarian God-talk and for a nonauthoritarian language of or about God leads her to Christian mysticism (Meister Eckhart). Under the term mysticism she understands a *cognito Dei experimentalis,* a perception of God through experience. This means an awareness of God gained not through books, nor the authority of religious teachings, nor the so-called priestly office, but through the life experiences of human beings, experiences that are articulated and reflected upon in religious language, though they first come to people in what they encounter in life, independently of church institutions.[17] It is not difficult to see that, under the category of mysticism, Sölle is turning to elements that are also significant for a post-modern spirituality: mysticism as a practice of all religions, as a stimulus to change the 'consumer-rooted material life', as an impetus to develop one's own self, and as something critical of institutions. What is characteristic of Sölle, however, is the importance of religious language which she understands poetically-emotively as a language from which Christians can draw when they share their spirituality with others. Her many published poems document this conviction:

> The Gospel taught me how to cry.
> It taught me fear before the fearless,
> it spoke to me among the speechless,
> it made me thirsty among the bored.
> That is a relative step forward.[18]

---

16 Dorothee Sölle, *The Strength of the Weak: Toward a Christian Feminist Identity*, Philadelphia, Westminster, 1984: 79-105.
17 Sölle, *The Strength of the Weak*: 86.
18 Dorothee Sölle, *Im Hause des Menschenfressers: Texte zum Frieden*, Reinbek, rororo, 1981: 87.

If it was still possible in Sölle's time to let something of the awareness that constitutes a post-modern spirituality shine through without a break with biblical texts and the inner-Christian spiritual traditions, this is made more difficult in the new-religious groups by the fact that the points of identification have more to do with concrete paths, techniques, general culture-critical views, and a conscious conduct of one's life, than with the desire to position oneself in the continuity of a particular tradition. She writes:

> The ultimate insights, ultimate decisions, and prevailing mood on which spirituality as a lifestyle is based are usually attributed to personal experiences. This reference to experience, which shines through in many contemporary definitions and has always been specific to the concept of spirituality, contributes considerably to its significance in times of post-conventional religiosity.[19]

Here, mysticism is understood anthropologically; for Sölle, every person is a mystic! Further, the reference to experience – not the cognitive value of a distinctly religious tradition – arouses our interest. However, one cannot assume that the stated reference to experience manifests itself consistently and inevitably in a particular lifestyle. Spirituality is a path or a form that serves to illuminate human awareness or, as stated at the beginning of this contribution, is what Kick Bras calls 'the striving to give life a transcendental meaning in a more or less methodological way'. Peter Lengsfeld, Zen-master and former professor for ecumenical theology, prioritizes the path to an 'authentic' experience in his description of a 'Mysticism of the Future'[20]:

> Instead of merely saying what one should believe, the main task of religions will become the communication of directions for and paths to religious experience.[21]

For Lengsfeld, then, it is a matter of 'opening consciousness to the dimensions of experience which determine concrete daily thinking.' This is looked upon as being 'overstuffed with dualisms that determine our daily lives.' Thus, there is need of many years of exercise-experience through Zen, yoga or contemplation to help this opening of consciousness achieve a breakthrough. Only then would those experiences emerge 'which transcend all dualistic polarity'. The description of such experiences is secondary. It makes no difference whether this is a matter of Ken Wilber's mystical awakening, Teresa of Avila's experience of the presence of God, or the seeing into one's own nature in Zen. 'In any case it must be a matter of an authentic experience of the no longer dualistic, "immanent transcendence".'[22] One sees here that, although the recourse to experiences in the new-religious groupings is a crucial factor for all, it is not regarded as given. 'Authentic' experience is not communicated, but promised as a result of the path taken. Even if in a very diminished form (for, dualisms impede the openness of consciousness necessary in Zen), the cultural-critical starting point can still be seen here, in what I have called a characteristic of post-modern spirituality. And one also sees a kind of 'resistance to description' in those experiences envisaged in Zen. Interpretive contents are suppressed in favour of the form (path, meditation).

---

19 Karl Baier (ed.), *Handbuch Spiritualität. Zugänge, Traditionen, interreligiöse Prozesse*, Darmstadt, Wissenschaftliche Buchgesellschaft, 2006: 15.
20 This is the subtitle of the commemorative volume for Williges Jäger, Peter Lengsfeld (ed.), *Mystik. Spiritualität der Zukunft*, Freiburg, Basel and Vienna, Herder, 2005.
21 Lengsfeld, *Mystik*: 10.
22 Lengsfeld, *Mystik*: 11.

Presence experiences

If one looks at the spectrum of new-religious groupings from the New Evangelicals, New-Age groups, feminist spirituality groups, and meditation, contemplation and yoga groups, one notices that identification does not primarily occur through the contents, but through the form. A particular kind of meditation, a master, certain rituals, regular meetings or particular places create something like a trademark. It is, as it were, a matter of communicating meaning in the present tense or a question of the intensity of an experience in the here and now. In attempting both to describe the diverse expressions of the new-religious groupings and to capture them in an analytical way, in spite of their resistance to description, the book *Production of Presence: What Meaning Cannot Convey* by the literary-studies scholar Hans Ulrich Gumbrecht has helped me a lot. Gumbrecht is concerned with overcoming the exclusive, privileged status of interpretation in the humanities and thus with depicting a situation in which interpretation no longer has sole validity. For this he makes use of the ideal-typical distinction between a meaning-culture and a presence-culture:

> The first of these two typologies proposes a distinction between what I call 'meaning culture' and 'presence culture' (with meaning culture, of course, being close to modern culture and presence culture close to medieval culture). As I know from long and sometimes frustrating experience that the implications of such typologies are often confused with those of reality descriptions, I insist that both the concept of 'meaning culture' and that of 'presence culture' should be understood as *Idealtypen*, in the tradition of Max Weber's sociology. I do not, of course, think that either of these *Idealtypen* has ever appeared (or will ever materialize) in its pure – in its ideal – form.... But despite our premise that all discourses of collective self-reference contain both meaning- and presence-culture elements, it makes sense to assume that some cultural phenomena (as, for example, the sacraments of the Catholic Church or the rationality of contemporary Afro-Brazilian cults) are more on the presence-culture-side, whereas others (e.g., ancient Roman politics or the bureaucracy of the early modern Spanish Empire) are predominantly meaning-culture-based.[23]

For Gumbrecht, it is a question of the perception of a particular experiential moment which is triggered by a linguistic form or a rite and which is overlooked when one all too quickly asks about the meaning of that form or rite. For him, spoken language possesses a physical reality and as such it not only affects the acoustical senses, but the body as a whole. One can thus enjoy a recitation or an opera without knowing the meaning of the words. Words have a rhythm which one can feel irrespective of their meaning.

His comments on the language of mysticism are of interest for our context:

> By constantly referring to its own incapacity of rendering the intense presence of the divine, mystical language produces the paradoxical effect of stimulating imaginations that seem to make this very presence palpable. In the descriptions of her visions, St Teresa of Avila, for example, uses highly erotic images under the permanent condition of an 'as if'. The encounter with Jesus, for her, is 'as if being penetrated by a sword', and at the same time she feels 'as if an angel was emerging' from her body. Rather than taking these forms of expression literally, however, literally as the description of something, i.e.,

---

[23] Hans Ulrich Gumbrecht, *Production of Presence: What Meaning Cannot Convey*, Stanford, Stanford University, 2004: 79-80.

of a mystical experience that truly exceeds the limits of language, a both secular and analytic view will understand mystical experience itself as an effect of language and of its inherent powers of self-persuasion.[24]

Mystical language is an imaginative language which makes divine presence tangible, but does not interpret or portray. The intensity produced by this language is an intended effect which also makes the boundaries of language visible.

Gumbrecht's analysis sharpens the perception for that form of language which is capable of triggering experiential moments more intensely. Though his binary juxtaposition of a meaning-culture and a presence-culture cannot be applied to the phenomenon of new-religious groupings in an uncritical way, it does show that this is not a matter of an interpretive search for meaning, but, concerns instead the experiential 'presence' value of particular forms of articulation (mantra, meditation, conversion stories, ecstatic singing, rituals). What a pity, then, that the recitation of the 'Our Father' has less a chance for experiential intensification in the new-religious groupings than have the life stories of self-chosen masters.

Translated by Martha M. Matesich

---

24 Hans Ulrich Gumbrecht, 'Presence in Language or Presence Achieved against Language?', unpublished manuscript on the occasion of a colloquium, 6 December 2006, Nijmegen: 8.

Paul O'Grady
Two Dogmas and Empiricism[1]

1. An Appalling Vista

Two antithetical and intellectually invidious dogmas are rampant in the current intellectual climate. One dogma, let's call it Absolutism, holds that there is just one true way of viewing reality. This dogma is old, but in its modern manifestation its antiquity can be obscured. Traditionally, this dogma has manifested itself in religious exclusivism, maintaining that one specific religious outlook or tradition has the fullness of truth and knowledge, to the exclusion of all else. In its modern guise in the academy, this dominant outlook has become that of empirical science. To justify any belief one has to have empirical evidence for it – and the only evidence is empirical evidence. This view can be found across a wide variety of disciplines. There are those where it seems more appropriate, namely the natural sciences. However, there are others – including political studies, history, sociology and biblical studies – where one might challenge it. It is an epistemological dogma, about the appropriate method for acquiring knowledge.

The other dogma, let's call it Relativism, holds that there is no access to truth, reality, or knowledge that is not relative to some ideology, cultural context or historical epoch. Any attempt to articulate the truth is viewed as hubristic and wrong-headed. There are discourses, narratives, tropes, metaphors, metanarratives, etc., but no facts, truths, realities. This dogma is of more recent vintage and can be found across many humanities disciplines, especially literary theory, but also in history, cultural studies and theology.

The defenders of each of these dogmas tend to stigmatize their opponents as holding to the opposing dogma. To reject Relativism must mean that one holds to the one true vision of reality and must be intellectually intolerant. To reject Absolutism is to descend into the abyss of relativism and be intellectually vacuous. And so on and so forth in a reasonably enjoyable exchange of insults.

However, neither position is appealing nor, indeed, defensible. This doesn't prevent vigorous articulations of each dogma, or worse, subtle infiltrations of each into the intellectual life of contemporary thinkers. An exhaustive trawl through recent literature pertaining to this would also be exhausting, so I shall confine my comments to a few influential recent discussions of the phenomenon of religion.

Richard Dawkins and Daniel Dennett have recently written spirited defences of atheism.[2] They write lucidly, passionately, elegantly. They both believe in the untruth of religion, with Dennett perhaps more sympathetic to its attractions, and Dawkins more passionate in his opposition. Both have achieved eminence in other fields before turning to writing about religion: Dawkins in biology and Dennett in philosophy. However, in their recent work, both make polite noises about philosophy before going on to articulate

---

1 Philosophically-attuned readers will immediately note the *omage* in the title to W.V.O. Quine's classic 'Two Dogmas of Empiricism' which deeply influenced epistemology since its initial appearance in 1950 and which provided fertile ideas for the present essay.
2 Richard Dawkins, *The God Delusion*, London, Bantam, 2006; and Daniel Dennett, *Breaking the Spell: Religion as a Natural Phenomenon*, London, Allen Lane, 2006.

positions which obliterate it, Dennett more self-consciously so than Dawkins. Dennett is a Quinean naturalist, who thinks that philosophy is just natural science turned back on itself. Dawkins considers some of the traditional arguments for the existence of God and then dismisses them, (in a way which would be pulled up short in an undergraduate philosophy essay). Both are convinced that, whatever evidence there may be for an intellectual position, it must answer at the bench of empirical evidence. There is no further court of appeal. (Neither addresses the question of what empirical evidence there can be for the claim that all viable evidence must be empirical evidence!)

As if from a different intellectual planet, the current Pope, formerly known as Cardinal Ratzinger, was a vigorous opponent of relativism.[3] However, in his zeal to reject this pernicious modern creed, he assumed that the only alternative to it was to hold to an absolutist position and so, ironically, holds to the same dogma. While Dennett and Dawkins appeal to the authority of science to hold off relativism, Ratzinger appeals to an authoritative religious tradition to do the same. Needless to say, these versions of Absolutism are incompatible with each other – though they interestingly illustrate that dogma in recent discussions of religion.

On the other side, there are numerous examples of those holding to the relativist dogma. Richard Rorty is a good example, even if he repudiates the name 'relativism' by giving it a narrow and untenable meaning; furthermore, he has an interesting disdain for religion, coming from his liberal political agenda, which might seem initially at odds with a relativist stance.[4] Rorty holds that traditional ways of doing philosophy are finished, that an alliance of Heidegger, Gadamer, Quine, Wittgenstein, Davidson and Sellars have shown why this is so and that what is left is 'edifying philosophy', a way of increasing the number of metaphors by which we live and expanding our imaginations. Instead, truth, fact, reality, etc., are just labels left over from the old outmoded philosophical vocabulary. Irony, solidarity and the spread of liberal conversation is the goal of his discourse.

More subtly, views of similar provenance can be found throughout theological discourse. Here, for example, is a methodological comment from a recent work in liberal Catholic christology:

> People who have come to appreciate cultural pluralism that stretches across the history of the human race have learned to accept as well the situated character of all knowing, the contextual bias in all value judgements, the relativity of all human conceptions.[5]

This is ambiguous: as baldly stated, it presents quite a strong relativistic stance – the relativity of all human conceptions. However, in its context it seems to be a historicist correction to a basically Thomistic position. What is significant in it is that it takes for granted that anyone attuned to historical, sociological or anthropological discussions will take for granted the relativity of all human conceptions.

Now, the nub of this paper is that the notion of the relativity of all human conceptions is ambiguous. In one sense, it is true, but doesn't lead to the dogma of Relativism.

---

3 Since he wrote under that name I shall continue to refer to Pope Benedict XVI as Joseph Ratzinger. See, e.g., his 'Relativism: The Central Problem for Faith Today', reprinted in *Origins* 26,20 (October 31, 1996).
4 See Richard Rorty, *Philosophy and the Mirror of Nature*, Oxford, Blackwell, 1980, and 'Pragmatism, Relativism and Irrationalism', in his *Consequences of Pragmatism*, Minneapolis, University of Minnesota, 1982.
5 Roger Haight, *The Future of Christology*, London, Continuum, 2005: 35.

In another sense, it is false and does lead to it. The rest of this paper seeks to disambiguate those senses and show that there is a way between the two dogmas.

2. The One and the Many

Students of ancient philosophy are often introduced to the subject by means of the problem of the one and the many. Is there a single source, principle or 'arche' which can explain the multiplicity of differences in the world? Various candidates were proposed as this source and the discussion became more and more sophisticated as the concepts 'material', 'immaterial', 'concrete', 'abstract', 'potential', 'actual' were slowly articulated and elaborated in an effort to respond to the question. As a fundamental philosophical question, it recurs again and again in different guises. In this discussion, the question emerges as: is there a single account of knowledge which underlies all the apparently disparate kinds of knowledge we come across? The Absolutist answers yes to this, while the Relativist denies it and holds to disconnected multiplicity.

One influential contemporary version of Absolutism, as noted, holds that all knowledge must be ultimately analysable in terms of empirical knowledge. There is no knowledge independent of this constraint and this is the condition which gives unity to knowledge. The Relativist holds to a multiplicity of kinds of knowledge, with no unity between them. A term often used to label this disconnection is 'incommensurability' – there is no metric or measure which will allow comparison between different accounts. If, as claimed above, neither of these views is attractive, then a way between them can be found if some account of knowledge were articulated which allowed for multiplicity and diversity, but which nevertheless didn't entail incommensurability, that is, if cognitive connection and the possibility of mutual evaluability is available across different kinds. How might such an option be possible?

Well, first, one might attempt to examine the different kinds of knowledge there might be – to see what kind of multiplicity is involved. Knowledge has been traditionally defined as 'justified true belief', with more recently an extra element added, e.g., *undefeated* justified true belief (to get around Gettier counterexamples).[6] The Absolutist account holds that justification has to be ultimately analysed in terms of observation. Fairly standard distinctions about kinds of knowledge include perceptual knowledge, memory, testimony and knowledge based on reason. Perception, testimony and memory can all fit well with the constraint of observation. The controversial issue is about knowledge deriving from reason. This is traditionally called a priori knowledge. Many empiricists will accept an account of the a priori where it is accepted as being purely formal, offering no genuine knowledge about the world, and restricted, for example, to logic or maths. Controversially, it can be asked whether such knowledge might extend further into, for example, ethical knowledge, or metaphysical knowledge. Contemporary naturalism tends to defend the thought that even logic and maths are to be understood as internally connected with natural science, and so, connected to issues about observation.

---

[6] Edmund L. Gettier published a celebrated short paper in 1963 in which he challenged the traditional view by means of counter-examples, see his 'Is Justified True Belief Knowledge', reprinted in A. Phillips-Griffiths (ed.), *Knowledge and Belief*, Oxford, Oxford University, 1967: 144-146. He came up with scenarios where, though the beliefs which people have are impeccably justified and true, our intuitions indicate that there is not genuine knowledge. A veritable industry of responding to his challenge ensued. Many now think that adding a fourth condition – such as being undefeated – will answer the problem.

The epistemological basis of logic or maths is not any different to the epistemological basis of natural science as a whole. Dennett seems to accept this Quinean view readily.

Against this, on the other pole, is the thought that there are kinds of knowledge that are discrete and cognitively sealed off. Some appeal to anthropology to defend this thought, supposing alternative rationalities among exotic tribes. Others might argue that gender issues can allow for strong feminist modes of thought. Others again might argue that religious modes of thought are sui generis and cannot be criticized from without. Quite often, the terms 'logic' or 'rationality' are associated with this approach, and one hears of 'Feminist Logic' or 'Theological Rationality' or some such. The fundamental problem with such a view is that it prevents genuine exchanges between such positions, they are sealed off from each other. Unless there is something in common between them, Feminist Logic cannot critique or communicate with its nonfeminist alternatives. How could such be found?

3. Clashing World-Views

When views are so antithetical to each other, e.g., those of Dawkins and Ratzinger, it can be difficult to think of any way of adjudicating the debate in a non-question-begging way. They are both absolutists who hold contradictory views. And the alternative relativist option of viewing them as both right, 'in their own way', is deeply unattractive. However, there is a way of attempting to provide a non-question-begging, rational way through the impasse.

I have argued elsewhere for a conception of rationality which answers to the dialectic of the one and the many.[7] There is a core conception of rationality which is embedded in our cognitive practices and which constitutes them; this I call Core Rationality. The four principles of core rationality address issues of consistency and evidence. One must seek to avoid inconsistency and maximize coherence in one's beliefs. One must not avoid available relevant evidence and must seek to maximize available relevant evidence. This core conception is compatible with many different world-views and metaphysical visions of reality. Such differences are explicable by appeal to extended conceptions of rationality. Extended rationalities specify more precisely what is the nature of evidence and how judgements must be made. However, these extended rationalities are governed by the principles of core rationality and because they are, they are open to challenge and discussion by those who do not share them, but who do share core rationality. Let's use this framework to think about Dawkins and Ratzinger.

They both accept that truth is important and is not a relativized concept – they differ in what they believe to be true. They both accept Core Rationality, the importance of consistency, coherence, not avoiding but maximizing relevant evidence. They differ in what they understand to be relevant evidence, indeed they differ on what counts as evidence. With such differing accounts of evidence and hence different extended rationalities, they will differ in ontology. They have quite different views of the world and what really exists.

So how can one make a judgement on differing extended conceptions of rationality? If you use the standards of judgement specific to one of those extended conceptions, it seems you will already have begged the question and given an internal answer from whatever system you favour. Yet, the core conception of rationality on its own is not specific enough to allow one to adjudicate using it on its own. So, is there just a stand-off, no way of reflecting on the differences and attempting to make sense of them?

---

7 Paul O'Grady, *Relativism*, Chesham, Acumen, 2002: chapter 6.

I think that further insight can be gained from grasping how extended rationalities arise, what their ground is and how deep disagreements arise. To do this we might further distinguish between Uncontroversial Extended Rationalities and Controversial Extended Rationalities. An uncontroversial extended rationality is a discipline or field of study which has its own distinctive methodology, methods of research, canons of evidence, problem-solving procedures and decision procedures about issues which arise for it. One can think of differences between physical sciences: the methods of cosmic physics differs from those of zoology. The levels of mathematization, use of telescopy, degree of speculation in cosmic physics, etc., differ from the detailed study of individual specimens, dissection, genetic investigation in zoology. Yet, these differences aren't regarded as controversial, such that zoologists should behave more like physicists, or vice versa. Differing more from either of these is law, where use of precedant, derivation of principles, making judgements as to how individual specific cases relate to general laws are the norm. Despite such differences, there is no conflict between physics, zoology and law – they do different things and there is no clamour for the abolition of one in favour of the other.

Conflict arises when different approaches are claimed to do the same thing. One might think of the difference between allopathic medicine and alternative medicine; the methods and procedures of one are different to the other's and one can find a great deal of skepticism, by practitioners of the allopathic, about claims made in alternative medicine. Why? Because they use the standards of their own system and find the other system wanting, for instance, lack of double blind testing of substances (e.g., herbal medicine), lack of empirical backup for claims about certain systems of diagnosis (e.g., iridology), lack of physical causal structure for certain claimed systems in the body (e.g., acupuncture).

Yet, alternative practitioners claim to operate using a different extended rationality. The role of scientifically based empirical evidence plays a lesser role, the interaction of practitioner and patient plays a greater role, appeals are made to traditions of healing which have an accumulated wisdom and which may subsequently be found to have empirical evidence to suport them. Hence, mere absence of empirical evidence isn't sufficient to discredit the tradition.

Assuming, then, that alternative practitioners are sincere and dedicated to what they do, how are we to think of the difference between them and allopathic practitioners? It seems definite that certain kinds of basic attitudes and values shape the approach of the alternative practitioner. For example, the human body is not seen as a mechanistic physical system. Causes of physical symptoms are thought to be complex, involving the integration of many different bodily systems and also of the mind. Hence, simple treatment of symptoms will not remove underlying problems. Typically, more time is spent in finding out about the patient in alternative treatment, the patient often feels more valued and respected and feels treated as an individual and not a cog in a vast machine. If one believes that physical conditions do have subjective or psychological aspects, one will focus more on addressing these and on looking at issues about attitudes, lifestyle and mental condition than on simply directly treating the presented ailment. And, of course, such an approach takes time and resources. So, there are complex socio-economic issues about who gets access to what in the health-care system, who can afford the options of alternative treatment. Also, many alternative practitioners will recommend allopathic methods for direct trauma and crisis illness, while claiming that their methods work better for building health and dealing with chronic conditions.

What is theoretically interesting in this is to see that the conflict is not simply one of empirical scientific method versus non-scientific mumbo-jumbo. Both systems are rational. Both are interested in healing. Both have systems of diagnosis and treatment, which are codified and regulated. They differ in fundamental pictures of the human condition, pictures of the relation of mind to body, pictures of the process of healing. Such deep differences in attitudes and what is ultimately valued lead to the differences in methodologies discussed above.

The different underlying pictures have cultural histories, sociological contexts, and politico-economic factors impinging on them. To simply say that one approach is right by virtue of being more true or rational or closer to reality is too simplistic. The deep pictures and attitudes generate values, which in turn generate extended rationalities, which is turn produce different practices, understandings and claims to truth.

4. Values and Reflective Equilibrium

How can this help make sense of the Dawkins-Ratzinger conflict? As noted, they both act in accord with core rationality – so, there are no simple inconsistencies or gross ignorance of evidence. Yet, they differ on their extended rationalities. Dawkins wants to keep to empirically verifiable evidence as the basis for holding a belief. Why? It has proved to be so reliable; it is what underlies technological and scientific advances. It is open to examination, test, replication, and these guarantee its reliability. In contrast, the purported alternatives to it have often proved to be false or unreliable: religious authority, tradition, non-empirical speculation. The empirical method has also been associated with the cause of progress, emancipation, egalitarianism, thus dispelling superstition and eradicating false beliefs. The goals of understanding the physical world, changing it through technology and aiding humanity through scientific advance all underpin the scientific attitude. So, holding to the methods of science is the best way of advancing those goals and defending them. Showing other ways to be false is part of that project.

As against that, Ratzinger accepts the efficacy of physical science but claims that it fails to capture the whole picture and indeed leaves out the most important parts. What is most important? The non-physical realm. However, there's no physical evidence for a non-physical realm, so why assert it? Well, Ratzinger's extended rationality allows for sources of evidence other than empirical ones. What might they be? One would be metaphysical speculation. Another might be subjective personal experience. Another might be acceptance of revelation. Each of these both opens up further questions about why that particular one might be accepted and raises its own debate. Dawkins has recently engaged with each one of these and attempted to dispatch them. Yet, empirical rejections of them are problematic insofar as they acknowledge themselves to be non-empirical. It does seem that a dialectical engagement with the metaphysical sources, a sympathetic engagement with subjective experience and an informed discussion of the notion of revelation would be required. Again, a picture informs this extended rationality – that of fundamental purpose being inscribed into the universe by a reality which transcends, sustains and provides an explanation for the universe, an explanation, though, which we can never comprehend fully.

Are such fundamental pictures fixed? No. They can be modified and even abandoned in the light of experience. However, it is not on the basis of sophisticated rational argumentation that such changes usually occur. Rather, the many-layered and deeply textured experiences of one's life shape the values, goals, ideals and aspirations which feed these pictures. A cluster of goals, values, attitudes and ideals, more or less explicitly articulated, fits with the picture. The picture in turn determines which cognitive practices are regarded as acceptable in one's extended rationality. And, overall, concern about coherence and use of evidence govern extended rationalities and ensure that they are not sealed off from each other, that debate and communication is possible.

A concept introduced to epistemology by Nelson Goodman and used in political theory by John Rawls might help here, namely, reflective equilibrium.[8] One has certain deeply-held intuitions and values, which inform one's world-view. Yet, one reflects on these intuitions, theorizes on the basis of them, adjusts them in the light of anomalies and problems, perhaps even sheds some of them in the light of new insights or challenges. They shape and inform theoretical discussion and are in turn affected by that discussion. Goodman called the to and fro relationship between deep intuition and theory 'reflective equilibrium', a balancing act of adjustment and compensation, dynamic in the life of a reflective individual. Steven Stich has recently used such a conception to argue for a strong relativism: every set of intuitions and values related to its theories is sealed off, as it were, from every other one.[9] However, I think the whole process of reflective equilibrium is governed by Core Rationality and such a similarity in form allows one to understand other systems of reflective equilibrium than one's own and indeed to sensitively enter into debate and discussion with others, tracing levels of agreement and disagreement at deeper and at more superficial levels.

Conclusion

It *is* possible to find a path between the two dogmas cited in the opening section. To hold to the search for truth, rationality and a coherent account of the universe is not to be an absolutist. Neither does countenancing difference and plurality mean that one is a relativist. A commitment to Core Rationality is a basic precondition of any activity counting as being cognitive. Differences which emerge between extended rationalities need to be carefully addressed in terms of the values they espouse, the practices they subserve, the picture of reality they sustain. What is crucial is that debate is possible between them and that such debate involves both hearts and minds; issues of evidence and consistency mingle with intuitions about the good, the valuable and the desirable. Dawkins clearly articulates a world-view which has many values associated with it. Ratzinger shares some of those values, has others besides and weighs values differently to the way Dawkins does. Linking values and knowledge in this way makes determining the truth of a position hard. It is not simply a question of exposing the weakness of one's opponent, but rather of sympathetically attempting to enter into their world and see the attractiveness of the position they articulate, while simultaneously holding to the values one espouses oneself. So, simple polemics won't cut much ice here. For, to quote the great empiricist, David Hume,

> ...if truth be at all within the reach of human capacity, 'tis certain it must lie very deep and abstruse; and to hope we shall arrive at it without pains, while the greatest geniuses have failed with the utmost pains, must certainly be esteemed sufficiently vain and presumptuous. I pretend to no such advantage in the philosophy I am going to unfold and would esteem it a strong presumption against it, were it so easy and obvious.[10]

---

8   Nelson Goodman, *Fact, Fiction and Forecast*, Indianapolis, Bobbs-Merrill, 1965^2; and John Rawls, *A Theory of Justice*, Oxford, Oxford University, 1973.
9   Steven Stich, *The Fragmentation of Reason*, Cambridge MA, MIT, 1990.
10 David Hume, *A Treatise of Human Nature*, edited by L.A. Selby-Bigge, Oxford, Clarendon, 1968: xix.

Joseph S. O'Leary

Forgiveness

To make sense of the Christian Gospel in response to the 'signs of the times' today, the theme that most urgently comes to the fore is that of forgiveness. Hutu and Tutsi, Israel and Palestine, Islam and the West, Sunni and Shiite, Northern Ireland Loyalist and Republican, all face the task of forgiving the unforgiveable, since only forgiveness can resolve the aporias that keep our societies from progressing in peaceful cooperation. To voice the gospel of forgiveness effectively today we have to overcome rigid and parochial notions of atonement and grasp the issues in the broadest perspective, drawing on other discourses of forgiveness such as may be found in psychoanalysis, literature, and especially Buddhism.

Is Forgiveness Problematic?

One of the most gripping advocates of forgiveness has been Bishop Richard Holloway. However, I fear that his sceptical outlook puts him in danger of cutting off the branch on which he is sitting:

> Like the rocket that has to fall away when it has established its satellite in space, religion has thrust its best values into the human orbit where we hope they will continue to do their work long after the vehicle that got them there has disappeared. What happens to the launch engine is not as important as the future of the ideals it has carried, though there will be some sadness as we see it disintegrating now that its purpose has been achieved. This approach continues to accord a high value to the impulse behind *religion*, though it no longer takes any of the particular *religions* at their own self-estimation.[1]

It is certainly important to discover the universal roots of forgiveness in human nature and even in the imperative of evolutionary survival. The 'impulse' behind religion is nothing less that the powerful dynamism of the cosmos itself, coming to consciousness of the mystery at its core. That impulse may melt or shatter the frozen forms of established religions, but in doing so it also releases their dormant core vision. The Gospel, and the Church as well, are attuned to the dynamics of creation at a level beyond the archaic representations of Scripture and the decaying structures of clericalism. There is no need to think that the foundational Christian experience of being forgiven, of receiving the gift of forgiveness from a gracious God – a gift concretized in the teaching of Jesus and his death for sinners – is doomed to disappear in favour of a general humanitarian set of 'ideals' and 'values'.

Holloway underplays the power of the Gospel when he writes:

> The justice and revenge impulses are strong in us and seem to be intrinsic to our humanity... We ought to acknowledge that a primitive kind of moral coherence is in operation there... It was impossible for the USA not to offer some kind of response in kind to the original outrage against Manhattan and the Pentagon.[2]

---

1 Richard Holloway, *On Forgiveness*, Edinburgh, Canongate, 2002: 5.
2 Holloway, *On Forgiveness*: 76.

A wholesome political culture, however, would educate primitive impulses, channelling them for constructive use. People are still 'forced to act in revengeful ways' if that is the only response that politicians can sell to their electorate. Holloway thinks that 'there are clearly situations where every instinct of justice commands us not to forgive'. In that case, though, the commandment to forgive frees us from being prisoners of those instincts, frees us from the Law. Perhaps justice is always established only when we take a critical distance from our instincts.

It may be counter-productive to command forgiveness to someone in the immediate throes of grief or rage. But the Gospel nonetheless commands it in the sternest terms. And even where forgiveness is not commanded, at least vengeance can be forbidden. Recalling how the Vatican placed *The Count of Monte Cristo* on the Index of Forbidden Books on the grounds that it glorified revenge, one must question the glorification of revenge in popular culture today, with the inevitable overspill into real life. Holloway is rather defeatist when he speaks of 'an unconditional yes to the inability to forgive', in the sense of recognizing 'the appropriate moral force of the refusal to forgive and the sense of revulsion that the very thought of forgiveness induces in the victim'.[3] Any such 'unconditional yes' could only have a temporary validity. Present resolutions of undying hate may yield to another perspective after a while. The worst crimes have been forgiven when the victim has met the perpetrator, who himself may have changed in the interval.

Christian apologists need not talk of God and Christ to a secular world, but they can invite people to experience the *grace* of forgiveness, which is what most guarantees the credibility of the Gospel today. They can best do this by imitating another Anglican bishop, Desmond Tutu, in practising 'over-acceptance' toward all.[4] The term means that, in imaginative improvisation, one takes up the offer of one's interlocutor and swings it further, toward a desired goal. One who sees good in everyone, greeting everyone as a mirror of the divine, can convey to them the sense that they are accepted and affirmed: 'you're all right'. This over-acceptance is appeasement. The conversation of Jesus with the Samaritan woman shows how over-acceptance allows a searching consideration of sin and error, though in the context of inviting people to live up to what is best in themselves. One may find human, psychological, even ethical obstacles blocking one's path to forgiveness. It is better not to cultivate such obstacles, at least in one's own case, but rather to cultivate a pre-emptive readiness to forgive all offences, swinging all situations of conflict in the direction of forgiveness. This is not a matter of letting evildoers 'get away with it', but of bringing them, too, within the horizon of mercy.

Jeffrie G. Murphy, philosopher of law, goes further than Holloway, not merely countenancing the refusal to forgive but arguing that 'vindictiveness and vengeance possess some positive value'.[5] 'What Nietzsche really argues is that vindictiveness (what he calls *ressentiment*) will poison if *repressed*; and this is as much an argument in favour of expressing our vindictiveness in acts of revenge as it is an argument for the elimination of vindictiveness'.[6] It seems to me that Nietzsche has to be read not slavishly but

---

3 Holloway, *On Forgiveness*: 53-4.
4 Sam Wells, *Improvisation: The Drama of Christian Ethics*, London, SPCK, 2004.
5 Jeffrie G. Murphy, *Getting Even: Forgiveness and its Limits*, Oxford, Oxford University, 2003: 95.
6 Murphy, *Getting Even*: 23. For further views along this line, see Sharon Lamb and J. G. Murphy (eds.), *Before Forgiving: Cautionary Views of Forgiveness in Psychotherapy*, Oxford, Oxford University, 2002; for an overview of the current boom in forgiveness studies, see Everett L. Worthington, Jr. (ed.), *Handbook of Forgiveness*, New York, Routledge, 2005.

with an eye for the constructive potential of his thought. He wrote that strong natures have 'the power to grow uniquely from within, to transform and incorporate the past and the unknown, to heal wounds, to replace what is lost, and to duplicate shattered structures from within... There are people so lacking this energy that they bleed to death, as if from a tiny scratch, after a single incident, a single pain, and often in particular a single minor injustice'.[7] Such strong natures are hardly interested in expressing vindictiveness in acts of revenge. Getting even, satisfying vanity, gung-ho war spirit, have a place in sports, perhaps, or in political or professional rivalries, where they can remain confined within a ludic sphere of application, not allowed to linger and fester. However, in handling situations of interpersonal or social conflict they do not provide a good orientation for ethical action, and should be curbed or defused. No doubt there are extreme situations where gestures of attempted forgiveness would become a buckling under degrading abuse or a collusion in evil; but such cases are rare, and should not be invoked as a pretext for vengefulness on the everyday front.

The book of Leviticus has a fairly well-deserved reputation of bloodthirstiness, but it has some very humane moments too: '[y]ou shall not have hate for your brother in your heart... You shall not take revenge on or harbour resentment against the children of your people, and thus shall you love your neighbour as yourself' (Leviticus 19:17-8). To love your neighbour as yourself is not a command that falls from the sky. It is the reward promised to one who cultivates a generous and forgiving outlook, by training the imagination to see others welcomingly, compassionately.[8] The Book of Sirach speaks in unexpectedly 'Christian' tones as it offers an exegesis of the Leviticus text: thus, the one 'who takes revenge will experience the vengeance of the Lord... Forgive your neighbour his transgressions, and then, when you pray, your sins will be remitted. If a man cultivates hatred of another, how can he ask God for healing' (Sirach 28:1-3). Indeed, this is an exegesis of Leviticus 19:18. The idea that forgiveness is an *imitatio dei* is deeply Jewish, not a Christian specialty: '[m]y people, children of Israel, as your Father is merciful in heaven, so you must be merciful on earth' (Targum of Pseudo-Jonathan on Leviticus 22:28).[9]

Buddhist Approaches

Buddhism offers foundational insights for the practice of forgiveness that can bring new clarity and coherence to the biblical prescriptions.[10] Despite its adherence to the law of karma, according to which evil acts always bear evil fruit, Buddhism turns out to be the most radically forgiving of all philosophies or religions. Its cult of forgiveness has no trace of the weakness that Nietzsche deplored, but rather seems to advance on a higher and happier plateau on which Nietzsche's worries have been long resolved.

---

7 Quoted, Holloway, *On Forgiveness*: 34.
8 See Serge Ruzer, 'From "Love your neighbour" to "Love your enemy": Trajectories in Early Jewish Exegesis', in *Revue Biblique* 109 (2002): 371-89. 'Love your enemy' (Matthew 5:44) is 'a midrashic elaboration of Leviticus 19:18' (372). Some tried to limit Leviticus 19:18 to the community, some widened it to include outsiders or even enemies.
9 Quoted, Geza Vermes, *Jesus in his Jewish Context*, London, SCM, 2003: 48.
10 See Joseph S. O'Leary, 'Buddhism and Forgiveness', in *The Japan Mission Journal* 56 (2002): 37-49, 97-109; reprinted as 'Forgiveness in Mahāyāna Buddhism and a Christian Reflection', in *Dialogue* (NS) 29 (2002): 94-110; abridged in *Dharma World* 31 (November-December 2004): 14-19 (online at josephsleary.typepad.com).

The rhetoric of Christianity has staled through over-use. A saturation point has been reached, ensuring diminished returns on any further use of this language unless it is renewed by a shift in perspective. Such a shift is favoured by the unflappable logic of Buddhism, and its provision of new words and categories for handling the old issues. Buddhist meditation and analysis correct blind spots in the Christian tradition. The latter's Platonic frameworks of thought were a source of psychological obtuseness as well as of insight; and even the Bible can produce venom and fanaticism as well as moral wisdom. We have tried to modernize the biblical tradition by correlating it with the best insights of the West, but on the central topic of forgiveness it is not clear that the West can offer an adequate renewal of vision. The Buddhist sense of interdependence and its dismantling of the illusory stability of the ego clears the ground for creative, forgiving interaction.

Buddhism seeks a practical method for dealing with entrenched attitudes of fear and hatred, a method based on probing analysis. The analysis would be impotent if it were merely speculative. Yet, Buddhist analysis is for immediate practical application, in mindful correction of one's own unwholesome attitudes. Meditative analysis already begins the overcoming of these and plants the seeds of more wholesome dispositions. In some early Buddhist texts, it sounds as if forgiveness is just a matter of mental hygiene. The emphasis falls not on forgiving but on the foolishness of taking offence in the first place: '"He abused me, he struck me, he overcame me, he robbed me" – in those who harbour such thoughts hatred will never cease' (*Dhammapada* 1:3). Buddhism shifts our attention from realities outside ourselves to what is in our mind, and finds the unforgiving mind to be in a state of bondage. Far from cultivating any sense of a duty not to forgive, or to take revenge – such as we find in ancient vendetta cultures and in the contemporary tabloid – it sets about dismantling the rigidity of such attitudes. This ensures that whatever course of just action one decides to take up, in regard to an offender, it will not be clouded by vindictive passion or by frozen conceptions of what the offender, the offence and the offended are. The forgiving mind can act in freedom, improvizing the most creative response to whatever situation it faces.

The bodhisattvas of the later Mahāyāna Buddhism live in dedication to the salvation of all living creatures. One aspect of this dedication is a limitless willingness to forgive all real or imagined wrongs, past, present and future. Perhaps the most eloquent Mahāyāna advocate of forgiveness is the 8th century Madhyamaka scholar Śāntideva. The ontological foundation of such forbearance is the conviction that neither the 'I' who might possibly be offended, nor the other who might possibly be perceived as offending, have any substantial existence. 'I forgive you, because you don't really exist – nor, for that matter, do I!' might seem a very odd contribution to current efforts at conflict management and reconciliation. W.B. Yeats used to forget the names of his enemies; the bodhisattva goes a step further, not even perceiving the enemy as truly existent. Maybe we can never fully grasp or digest the Mahāyāna 'wisdom of emptiness', but it is a cool and refreshing experience to immerse oneself in it. It is a potent tonic, working to defuse all the fixations that our culture has encouraged us to form and that usually centre on ego.

Forgiveness is an application of wisdom – a bodhisattva is too wise to get involved in quarrels or grudges. Forgiveness is applied as a method or technique for enlarging the wisdom and benevolence of the bodhisattva. It is applied a priori, preempting any concrete occasions for its exercise: '[h]e forgives them for what has been done in the past, for what is being done at present and for what will be done in future... He forgives all without exception, his friends, his enemies, and those who are neither'. Rather than being reserved for use on specific occasions, forgiveness is part of the permanent actualization of universal benevolence: '[h]is forgiveness is unfailing, universal and absolute, even as Mother Earth suffers in silence all that may be done to her'. The temptation not to forgive is recognized and is countered by meditative reflection: thus, a 'bodhisattva should cultivate certain modes of thought and ponder on some great principles, so that he may understand why he should forgive others... His enemy of today may have been a friend, a relative or a teacher in a previous existence and should therefore be regarded as an old comrade'. Deeper than these homely reflections is the vision of emptiness: there is 'no permanent substantive individuality in any man or woman. Hence it follows that there is really no one who reviles, beats and injures, or who is reviled, beaten and injured'. Should such lofty motives not suffice, 'a wise bodhisattva should forgive others even from fear, as vindictiveness always ends in evil'.[11]

Buddhism, even at its warmest, remains the coolest of religions. From the Buddhist perspective, Christianity seems an excessively emotional affair, needlessly fretting about guilt and atonement and vamping up personalized devotion. This is an inept therapy, leading to fixations. The wisdom of emptiness calmly undoes such fears and cravings and attachments. It guides our investments of psychological energy in the direction of liberation. Wisdom in Buddhism is not detached speculative insight, but is itself a skilful means for liberating living beings from suffering. Hence the intimate alliance between wisdom and compassion. Buddhist compassion is not a foolish pity, a sentimental impotence. It is wisdom in action. Buddhists are aware that the practice of compassion and forgiveness takes one into the messy realm of human emotions and passions, and they are anxious to balance wisdom and compassion in a non-dual harmony. Yet, the ultimate scenario of Buddhist existence, as mapped in the Madhyamaka philosophy, robs our simple emotional relationships to ourselves or our neighbours of any solid ground: '[i]n the theater of *vyavahāra* (the practical everyday), the only value that the drama acted by the Mādhyamika has is a therapeutic one. The world is a décor and the absolute itself is only pasteboard. If these representations are kept up, it is only for their cathartic virtues. We conclude, then, with É. Lamotte: 'thus vanishes in smoke the reality (*tattva*) imagined by the worldly, even by the saints, and which the Buddha himself, *out of pity for beings* and so as not to scare them, sometimes pretended to accept'.[12]

Forgiveness as Relationship

It might be objected that Buddhism creates sages who are disconnected from humanity. Even Śāntideva seems so absorbed in perfecting the noble posture of the all-loving bodhisattva that real flesh-and-blood human beings seem scarcely to come into his ken. One can easily persuade oneself that to take offence, or to believe in the real existence of offenders and offended, is a delusion to be transcended. But, is this not an elaborate strategy of avoidance? One can wrap oneself in an impenetrable offence-proof cloak, never getting angry, never having anything to forgive, since one has forgiven everything

---

11 Har Dayal, *The Bodhisattva Doctrine in Buddhist Sanskrit Literature*, Delhi, Motilal Banarsidass, 1978: 210-11. Dayal gleans these notions of forgiveness chiefly from Śāntideva and from Asanga's *Bodhisattvabhūmi* (4th century).

12 Ludovic Viévard, *Vacuité* (śūnyatā) *et compassion* (karuṇā) *dans le bouddhisme madhyamaka*, Paris, Collège de France, 2002: 113.

in advance, pre-paid as it were. But, this sagehood seems to mean that one has disentangled oneself from human relationships. Human beings can no longer 'get at' someone who is securely installed in the beatitude of seeing all things as empty of substantial being. Why, such a sage is even wiser than the God of the Bible, who still frets about people offending him and even gets angry with them![13]

It is easier to forget than to forgive, for forgiveness implies a relationship, or an ongoing negotiation, with the one to be forgiven, and it may be just such a relationship that is not desired. Peace-building means cultivating an intimacy, a mutuality of concern, with the one that had been comfortably categorized as the enemy. To meet someone you have been hurt by, and to explain your feelings, or if this is impossible, to imagine such a scenario, is a way of replacing the fixated image of a loathsome figure with a human being. Political hatred leads us to fixate the individuals who are the agents of great institutions. Indeed, any political or church leader exposes himself or herself to such hatred. To think of them as human beings may make us politically soft, but it can also make our judgements wiser and more prudent. No close relationship is without hurts and injuries, just as no vigorous physical life is without them, so we need a band-aid box in readiness, and the bandage is forgiveness.

To love one's enemies includes the practical challenge of tackling the situation of enmity in a constructive fashion. Conflict resolution is a sophisticated art, involving psychological and management techniques. The idea is to reason with people's beliefs until you find a common solution. Merely to think in this way is a form of love. To recognize the other side's legitimate grievances, or to make the effort to imagine their grievances, even if these are illegitimate, to seek and share information, to adopt an open mind – all these attitudes require love. The usual objection is that such open-mindedness would not have helped the Jews in dealing with the Nazis; but such analogies should be used sparingly; to presume that one's enemy exemplifies the intractable malice of a Nazi order is to build up the figure of the enemy to mythic and inalterable proportions.

If Jesus is a bridge-builder between God and humanity, a Pontifex or High Priest, then that activity began not with some abstract decree of divine justice but on the roads of Galilee in conversations with people of all sorts; here Jesus broke down social barriers; and, only at a second stage, did he open their minds to rethinking the nature of God. 'First be reconciled to your brother, and then come and offer your gift' (Matthew 5:24). The story of the Son of Man, who gives his life as a ransom for the many (Mark 10:45), is not about some abstract God who clothes himself in human form. It is the story of a prophetic, human bridge-builder, whose human role is recognized as bearing the stamp of the divine. Salvation happens in a very down-to-earth way: be reconciled with your brother, by practising justice, forgiveness, peace, and the rivers of divine mercy and love will then flow freely; close your heart to your brother and you close off the divine as well.

What Christianity can now most salutarily offer the world is not a set of dogmas but a revival of the gospel style of conversation. Apply that style to the meeting of Christians and Muslims, and its healing, atoning impact will be manifest. Dialogue between Christian and Muslim cannot start with the antique controversies about Christology and the Trinity.

---

13 These misgivings would rejoin the suspicion of some psychotherapists who see forgiveness as often a mask for suppression and denial, or as creating unresponsiveness: 'Forgiveness may (or may not) heal a fractured relationship, but it forgoes a transformative process that a relationship should go through before healing', Bill Puka, 'Forgoing Forgiveness', in Lamb and Murphy, *Before Forgiving*: 136-52: 141.

It must take as its theme the practical issues of peaceful coexistence, drawing from both traditions things new and old that can contribute to this goal. In fact, the point of departure for dialogue is not even our shared faith in God but our shared human tragedy, our failure to find the gracious saving words that would have averted terrorism and war.

Creating a Culture of Forgiveness

Today, we are taking the first steps to a culture of forgiveness, when it will be normal and normative for nations to work at forgiving those who have injured them and seeking forgiveness from those they have injured. When nations actively set out to apologize and seek forgiveness for the wrongs they have inflicted, they make it easier for the wronged nations to express forgiveness, and even in some cases to ask for forgiveness in return. So far it seems that Germany is the only nation that has seriously embarked on this path.

Buddhist gentleness suggests to us the question whether the harshness of biblical language – especially in the gospel denunciations of Pharisees and 'the Jews' (refreshingly resisted in Luke-Acts[14]) – has been an appropriate method of conveying the wisdom of the Cross. Against substantializing and magical theories of the Atonement, we do well to set in high relief the salvific impact of the Cross as registered in human experience. That impact reaches far, to the very depths of humankind's biological and psychological make-up, and it can correct even what is human-all-too-human in the letter of Scripture and the activities of the Church in history. Redemption, too often conceived as a magical behind-the-scenes process, is worked out in history as the deconstructive impact of the figure of the Cross, dissolving the barriers set by human arrogance and fixation against the liberating space of divine ultimacy.

Forgiveness has deep foundations in the universality of grace and the basic goodness of being. If to understand all is to forgive all, then understanding the aggressor is the foundation of enduring forgiveness. The enlightened one is able to forgive the enemy even when he is immediately threatened by him or is suffering at his hands. Forgiveness is thus a victory of grace and good, a defusing of the enemy's malice, which can now be borne as a painful ordeal of a purely external kind, rather than something that makes one writhe with an agony of hate and resentment at every moment in a way that doubles the pain. Forgiveness is a refusal to recognize that evil has any real existence in the ultimate scheme of things. What is, is essentially good; being and goodness are convertible; evil is merely a deficiency in being.

Some see metaphysical assurances about the goodness of being as mere abstract wishful thinking that refuses to look the concrete reality of evil squarely in the face. However, to surrender belief in the basic goodness of being because of the actions of the wicked is to hand them a great victory, allowing them to destroy our sense of reality itself. The testimony of some concentration camp prisoners that they clung to a belief in the perpetual goodness of nature and of friendships in the nightmare world of the camp should weigh against this. Vice is a triumph of unreality, a bad dream. It is not a revelation of the true nature of reality. All sorts of horrors are possible. Faith, however, overcomes them by seeing the basic defect of being that lies at their root. Forgiveness doubly overcomes them, reasserting the goodness of being over against them. Forgiveness deepens our own roots in the goodness of being and invites the evildoers who are estranged from these roots to rediscover them if they can.

---

14 See P.J. Tomson, 'Gamaliel's Counsel and the Apologetic Strategy of Luke-Acts', in J. Verheyden (ed.), *The Unity of Luke-Acts*, Leuven, Leuven University, 1999: 585-604.

Aloysius Pieris

Vatican II: Glimpses into Six Centuries of its Prehistory

Introduction – An Exercise in Retrospection

Vatican II is a new concept in the history of Councils. Its novelty is partly responsible for the mixed reaction it generated in the subsequent decades. Those perceptive Christians among bishops and theologians who were sensitive enough to recognize that the Church was pregnant with a council, prepared themselves for the new arrival, assisted at its birth and strove to foster its post-natal growth. Their names are well known. Equally noted are the names of those who were shocked at the news of the impending Council, tried to abort it even before its birth, but on failing to do so, tried to eliminate the newborn as a monstrous mongrel. The Council's postnatal growth is stunted by these lethal attempts on its life.

It was way back in the 14th century that the Spirit of Christ overshadowed the church and impregnated her with a new seed of renewal, which matured within her for six centuries until a Prophet by the name of 'Angelo' ('divine messenger'), surnamed Roncalli, appeared on the scene and announced to the Church that what she had conceived was of the Spirit and that she would call it 'Vatican II'. Hence the centuries preceding the birth of this great council provide glimpses into events that foreshadowed and even anticipated its major achievements. They explain and vindicate the historical necessity as well as the theological legitimacy of this first ever World Council.

This hypothesis is a modest conclusion that I have derived from the combined evidence collated from the following sources:

G. ALBERIGO and J.A. KOMONCHAK, *History of Vatican II*, Maryknoll, Orbis, / Leuven, Peeters, Volume I (1995), II (1997), III (2000), IV (2003); Enzio BIANCHI, 'The Centrality of the Word of God', in G. Alberigo et al., *The Reception of Vatican II*, Washington DC., Catholic University of America, 1987: 115-136; W.J. BOUWSMA, 'Humanism: The Spirituality of Renaissance Humanism', in Jill Raitt, *Christian Spirituality* Volume II, *High Middle Ages and Reformation* (in E. Cousins (gen. ed.), *World Spirituality* series), London, SCM, 1988: 236-251; Otto GRUENDLER, 'Devotion Moderna', in *Christian Spirituality* Volume II (*supra cit.*): 176-193; Jean LECLERQ OSB, *The Love of Learning and the Desire for God*, New York, Fordham University, 1961; Jean LECLERQ OSB, *Monks and Love in the Twelfth Century France*, Oxford, 1979; D.M. LUNN, 'Benedictine Reforms Movements in the Late Middle Ages', in *Downside Review*, October 1973: 275-289; John W. O'MALLEY SJ, 'The Jesuits, St Ignatius and the Counter-Reformation. Some Recent Studies and Their Implications for Today', in *Studies in the Spirituality of the Jesuits* [St Louis] XIV,1 (January 1982): 1-28; Giancarlo PANI, 'Le modificazione dell'identità Christiana tra medioevo ed età moderna in rapporto all'epistolario paolino', in *Annali di storia dell'esegesi*, 23,1 (January-June 2006): 257-282; Aloysius PIERIS SJ, *Mysticism of Service: A Short Treatise on Spirituality with a Pauline-Ignatian Focus on the Prayer-Life of Christian Activists*, Kelaniya, 2000, especially Parts Three and Four; Aloysius PIERIS SJ, 'El Vaticano II. Un concilio 'generatore de crisis' con una agenda non escrita', in *Revista Latino-Americana de Teologia* 67 (Ano xxiii; Enero-Abril 2006): 31-48; James D. TRACY, '*Ad Fontes*: The Humanist Understanding of Scripture as Nourishment of the Soul', in *Christian Spirituality* Volume II (*supra cit.*): 252-267; Paul SHORE SJ, 'The *Vita Christi* of Ludolph of Saxony and its Influence on the *Spiritual Exercises* of St Ignatius of Loyola', in *Studies in the Spirituality of the Jesuits* [St Louis], XXX,1 (January 1998): 1-16.

Part I: Renewal through a 'Return to the Sources'

A Church in search of its Roots

The need for a renewal of the church has always been felt by perceptive individuals and groups at different epochs. But by the late middle ages the atmosphere had been so charged with discontent that there was a spontaneous irruption of several initiatives to bring about the desired renewal in Christian life. These movements seemed to have either originated or terminated in monasticism.

Thus the Benedictines, who played a very influential role in the occidental church from the 4th century onwards, realized that they themselves needed reforms, though the changes they introduced during the 14th and 15th centuries were counterproductive and, therefore, a return to their own originating charism was sought instead. The new mendicant orders, the Franciscans and the Dominicans, were the response of Providence, *inter alia*, to the pastoral needs created by the emergence of urban capitalism in Europe; the laity might not have been participants, but certainly were beneficiaries of these changes. The origin of the Cistercian Order ('white monks') is associated with the social change brought about by a romantic urban youth steeped in the pagan humanism of ancient Latin poets such as Ovid, Horace and others who had by then been resurrected from the literary graves that lay hidden for centuries beneath the Church's own Roman culture.

The target, however, of most monastic initiatives seemed to have been the spiritual renewal of a church dominated by a *clerical order* of priests and bishops. The monks, therefore, produced an *alternative order of clerics* who would serve rather than be served by the laity. Yet, from the point of view of the laity, there was no real renewal. The pyramidal structure of the medieval church, solidified for over a thousand years, not only remained unchanged despite these reforms but also harboured a similar pyramid in the spiritual order: **ordained ministers** and **religious ascetics** occupying the higher rungs of the scale of authority while the laity depended on the former for the ritual and on the latter for the spiritual ministrations. For, the **Clerics** who claimed to possess *sacramental powers to sanctify others* and the **Monks** who indulged in *ascetical practices to sanctify themselves* constituted the two institutional channels of holiness in the church. The laity were the 'non-professionals' in the Christian business! There was and is a recurrent need for them to affirm themselves *in* the Church and *as* the church.

Thus, the 14th century saw the first wave of *renaissance humanism* spearheaded by **lay reformers** hailing from Italian cities. The most known among them were: Francesco Petrarca, Lorenzo Valla, Coluccio Salutati, Leonardo Bruni, Gianozzo Manetti and the poet Dante Alighieri. These members of the urban laity firmly believed and frankly broadcast that Christian spirituality could not and should not be reduced either to the contemplation of holy mysteries (as among the monks) or to ritual participation in these mysteries (as among the clerics); spirituality, they insisted, was a matter of dedicating oneself to works of love and service to one's neighbour.

What was their main complaint? The same as that which was aired just before Vatican II: that the sacramental order was hijacked by *cultic clerics;* that the spiritual life was monopolized by *religious ascetics;* that even the 'God-discourse' was distorted by *scholastics.*

And what was their response to these deviations? The same as that which was proposed on the eve of Vatican II: *reditus ad fontes*, a return to the sources from which the church had strayed. The retrieval of these sources, as the renaissance humanists understood it, could be categorized under three heads: a Christian appropriation of the **Humanism** which the 'pagan' classics were thought to profess, a recovery of the affectively and aesthetically evangelical ethos of the **Patristic** Tradition and a re-rooting of Christian life and thought in the *Word of God* heard in the **Scriptures**.

These three renewalist currents have always been active, sometimes as a subterranean movement ignored or suppressed by the ecclesiastical establishment, but at other times emerging as an overt demand for *re-founding the church on its original basis*. The basis of Christianity is:

> The divine **humanity** of Christ, Who is *the Word* revealed in the **Scriptures** and evangelically proclaimed by the **Fathers** as a reality to be lived out by the church.

We shall take up for discussion these three roots of renewal as they emerged in the first wave of renaissance humanism in the 14th century, then in the second wave with its high point in the 16th century (carried to this day by a somewhat subdued Ignatian tradition) and finally in the pre-Vatican II decades in the 19th century.

The Pattern of Renewal in the 14th Century

In the first place, the aforementioned lay Italian humanists sought and found their **cultural roots** in the *humanistic* elements of their *Roman and Latin* heritage, by then completely swallowed up by weeds of Aristotelianism. In their view, the scholastic theology of the time was totally cerebralized by Greek thought and seemed to have undervalued the human dimension of the mystery of Incarnation and Salvation. That is why these humanists equally abhorred their own ancient Roman Stoics, who cultivated a negative approach towards the human and social reality. Rather, it was from the ancient pagan *humanists of Latin Rome* that they imbibed the spirit of humanism, which was conspicuously absent in the church that called itself Roman and Latin. The writings of Cicero and Quintillion were re-read with enthusiasm. Even Ovid's erotic poems on human love captured the imagination of these lay thinkers. Dante's Beatrice was a humanistic creation that reflected the incarnate love of God. The resuscitation of this ancient humanism and the restoration of human love in Christian thought were also registered in the medieval devotion to the *Heart of Jesus* associated with St Mechtild, for whom even God palpitated with a human heart! Then why would not the church be as human as God?

No doubt, these reformers were over-reacting to a highly institutionalized church and were, therefore, understandably *over-optimistic* in their assessment of the human and the secular reality; for their emphasis on the Incarnate God eclipsed the message of the Crucified God, thus continuing to carry, what Cardinal Alois Grillmeier SJ has described as the 'burden' left by the Christological Councils. The same mild criticism can be made of the Vatican II document on the 'Church in the Modern World' (*Gaudium et Spes*), which, therefore, has to be interpreted in the light of *other* documents of that same Council, as I shall indicate later.

The second source which the Italian humanists consulted was the **Patristic writings**. The Church Fathers were more *affective* than speculative in their works, stirring the heart to action rather than titillating the mind with philosophical abstractions. They preserved the *spiritual core* as well as the *pastoral focus* of theology, unlike the medieval scholastics — from whose company I personally exclude that medieval genius hailing from Aquino, who had anchored his thought in the biblical and patristic foundations more than in Greek philosophy, contrary to popular opinion. An authentic God-discourse, the humanists concluded, must be alive with God's Life, which is Her Spirit, so that persons engaged in that exercise — both as speakers and hearers, or as writers and readers — would themselves undergo a salutary transformation, which is what 'conversion' means. In short, the Fathers were deemed closer to the Scriptural sources than were the scholastic theologians.

The Italian humanists' recovery of the Revealed Word in the **Holy Scriptures** was accompanied by their own unique contribution to *hermeneutics*. Being quite experienced in the critical study of ancient Latin classics, these humanists brought that expertise into biblical exegesis. The result was twofold. In the first place they were not satisfied with St Jerome's Latin Vulgate and insisted on the search for and discovery of the *authentic texts of the Bible in their original language(s)*. Secondly, they recognized, what we might today call the 'oblique idiom' used in the Bible, namely, the narrative, the simile, the parable and above all poetry. This is the language that spoke directly to the heart of hearers and readers, eliciting from them a personal response to the Revealed Word. Thus, the need to respect the *genre littéraire* in biblical exegesis was acknowledged for the first time. These two innovations would stay with the church for good. Finally, the humanists complained that the scholastic theology, unlike the Scriptures, turned the medieval Christians into *followers of Aristotle* rather than *disciples of Christ*. The humanist agenda aimed at restoring to the church the spirituality of **Imitatio Christi**, based on the gospels.

This threefold retrieval of a lost heritage (pagan humanism, Patristic homiletics and Scriptural message) led the Renaissance humanists to appreciate the *secular involvement of the laity as an authentic expression of Christian spirituality*, as already mentioned earlier in this discussion.

The Renewal around the 16th Century

The second wave of Renaissance Humanism, which resulted from the Fall of Constantinople towards the end of the 15th century and the subsequent discovery of the *Greek past*, merged with the first wave that had already crossed the Alps and was moving northwards. The net result of this merger is often referred to as *Northern European Renaissance Humanism*. The clamour for a 'Return to the Sources' (*reditus ad fontes*) was heard once again and with greater urgency not only from Protestant Reformers like Luther and Melanchton but also from Catholic Reformers such as Erasmus and Lefevre. What they meant by 'sources' was similar to what the First Wave Humanists identified a couple of centuries earlier. Monks and Clerics led the movement.

In their thirst for humanism, they turned to the Greeks – not to their philosophical speculations but to their *cultural achievements*. Hence, a proliferation of great works of art and architecture as well as a variety of other aesthetic creations marked the second Renaissance era. The emphasis on the *imagination,* as a tool of artistic creativity was, therefore, quite evident during this period. As will be explained below, this humanist approach to the faculty of imagination seeped into Christian spirituality and exerted a profound influence on the meditative reading of the Scriptures.

The Northern humanists, like their Southern predecessors, had also opted for the **patristic** thought in stark opposition to scholastic theology, appropriating the former as 'nourishment of the soul' and rejecting the latter as 'mere scratching of the intellect', to quote the exact words of Erasmus. The medieval scholasticism, which continued to be taught in the seats of learning in Northern Europe, had adopted the cold analytical methods of dissecting the mystery of salvation into a series of doctrinal formulae, under the influence of Greek philosophers of the past, whereas the Greek Fathers preferred the *rhetorical art* of the pagan orators of Greece (whom Plato the philosopher had attacked in his *Dialogues*!). The communicative skills of addressing the heart and drawing persons into a way of life that conformed to the scriptures were encouraged more than was intellectual theorizing that remained ineffective in real life. Thus, *oratory*, a powerful means of communication, became an important feature in their educational curriculum. Homiletics forms a significant part of Patristic literature.

However, in dealing with the third source, the **scriptural**, these humanists adopted an approach somewhat different from that of the Fathers. They introduced the modern science of *philology* into biblical exegesis and refrained from the allegorical interpretations characteristic of the patristic literature. Philology, as they understood it, was a combination of what we know today as 'textual criticism', 'literary analysis' and so on. Their critical study of Greco-Roman literature of the past had equipped them with hermeneutical tools, which they would now apply to the reading of the Scriptures. This may explain why well over seven hundred editions of St Paul's letters were published in the 16th century alone. Note, therefore, that during this time Paul's **Christocentric** reading of the Hebrew Scriptures became a notable feature of New Testament studies.

Thanks perhaps to the interest in Pauline Christology, these humanists (in this case, in continuity with the practice of the Fathers) affirmed that Christ was the key to the understanding of Scriptures. As during the first wave of humanism, here too the *imitation of Christ* (advocated by the Catholic movements such as *Devotio Moderna*), or the passion for *belonging to Christ* (promoted by Protestant Reformers as well as Erasmus) or *Christiformitas* or 'conforming oneself to Christ' (emphasized in works of Lefevre) became both the motive and the method of the reading of Scripture.

It was in view of this motive that already in the 14th century the *Vita Christi* of Ludolph of Saxony, the Carthusian, had presented a method of meditation in which one's *imagination* was made not only to supplement the all too laconic scriptural data but also to reconstruct the Gospel scenes in such a way as to re-live those episodes with the aid of the senses as well as the intellect. A century and a half later (1517), Erasmus would also suggest in his *Paraphrase* (of Luke) that we 'pause a while before the remarkable spectacle [i.e. the scene of the paralytic lowered from the roof] 'and let our mind play over all its details in pious curiosity.' No spirituality which claims to be a *sequela Christi* (following of Christ) could ever ignore or avoid this unique method of *lectio divina*. Ignatius picked it up and passed it down the centuries through his Spiritual Exercises.

Perhaps one might complain that some of these humanists, particularly the Protestants, failed to recognize what Jean Leclerq has rightly identified as *monastic theology,* which was more scriptural and patristic than scholastic. Nor could we ignore or undervalue the great reform movements initiated by monastic orders in the high middle ages, specially by the Benedictines and the Cistercians as well as by the mendicant orders of Dominic and Francis as already indicated above. Ignatius, the founder of the Jesuits, in his holistic approach, absorbed also the renewal currents initiated by the monks, even though (under the influence of humanism?) he developed a *non-monastically lay* spirituality.

Part II: The Catholic Reformation: Ignatius and Vatican II

Ignatius: the Humanist and 'Catholic Reformer'

Ignatius was in many ways a sympathetic and participatory witness of these renewal trends, including the last mentioned monastic movements. He had not only judiciously absorbed some of their finest elements but had also left for posterity a strong tradition that preserved the combined *élan* of the humanistic, the Patristic and the Scriptural currents of his time. In fact, Ignatius and the early Jesuits are said to have been amicably associated with the 'Catholic humanists' known as the *spirituali*. It is interesting that the church leaders of the time, though discreet and vigilant about this threefold campaign for reform, did nevertheless approve the Ignatian version of that same renewal, at least indirectly, when they recognized his Order as well as its Constitution.

This Constitution of the Jesuits, entirely inspired by Ignatius, insists that its members are primarily *Ministers of the Word*. No wonder that a spirituality geared to such a ministry had to be based on **Scriptures**. My contention that his spirituality is the first comprehensive formulation of the *praxis* of Pauline spirituality since Paul's time might not be an exaggeration when one realizes that the Ignatian century (the 16th) was also a century of Pauline studies. Ignatius owes this to the Renaissance Humanists.

History also forces us to conclude that his peculiar method of 'contemplation' mentioned in the Spiritual Exercises (not to be confused with infused contemplation of classical mystics) is a development of the kind of *scriptural meditation* already advocated by Ludolph of Saxony and Erasmus as indicated above. Here the recourse to the faculty of *imagination* seems to appear by another name: 'the application of the senses'. Its purpose in the Spiritual Exercises is to help the Christians to *be assimilated to Christ,* the sole purpose of the second and third weeks of the Ignatian Exercises. This too was a characteristic goal of the Scriptural spirituality of the Renaissance humanists.

Perhaps we should add that the positive assessment of *imagination*, a humanistic legacy which Ignatius appropriated, extended itself far beyond prayer to many areas of cultural activity. For, the early Jesuits were also well known for their artistic creations and scientific discoveries.

Ignatius has also preserved for us the conclusions of the Humanists on the two kinds of theology, the 'scholastic', which they rejected, and the **patristic**, which they embraced. However, in doing so, Ignatius seemed to have been more circumspect than the humanists, given the anti-Protestant climate in which the Roman authorities of his time examined his credentials. Remember also that Ignatius was imprisoned four times on charges of heresy! Using an understandably cautious language, both in the Jesuit Constitutions as well as in his Spiritual Exercises, Ignatius emphasizes the importance of *positive theology* attributed to the Fathers because it stirs our affections, but recommends *scholastic theology* merely as an intellectual tool for the defence of the Catholic faith. Thus, even for Ignatius, the scholastic theology was not spiritually helpful, playing only an apologetical role! In fact, he openly admitted that his study of that theology in Paris had dried up his heart spiritually! The humanists were right!

The humanists' predilection for oratorical arts is also reflected in Ignatius's educational method (*ratio studiorum*), which included a programme for producing *persuasive communicators of the faith*, able to reach both the hearts and the minds of people. Great emphasis was laid on acquisition of rhetorical skills. All *media of communication* available at the time, including *drama,* were employed in their Ministry of the Word.

Finally, the spirituality he bequeathed to the church was a *non-monastically lay apostolic spirituality* which he had developed already when he was yet a layman with absolutely no idea of seeking priestly ordination. By saying his spirituality was 'non-monastically lay', I imply that even monastic spirituality originated in its earliest institutional form as a *lay contestation* of a clericalized Christianity. **Renaissance Humanism** on the other hand wished to find a legitimate space for a ***non-monastic* version of *lay spirituality*.** This is what Ignatius evolved and imparted to his first companions who, barring one, were laymen. Even after opting for a clerical order, the Ignatian spirituality has remained true to its original spirit.

But alas! It is also regrettably true that a decade after his death, the Jesuits adopted measures that contradicted the founder's norms and allowed their spirituality to be gradually monasticized. They remained in that ambiguous state until 1965 when, thanks to the 31st General Congregation, there was a restoration of the *non-monastically lay apostolic spirituality* of the founder, though regrettably many Jesuits did not succeed in making the *paradigm shift* required by GC 31.

My own hindsight is that, had the Jesuits remained stubbornly and scrupulously faithful to the original and originating charism of Ignatius all these centuries, the path to Vatican II would have been smoother and its reception easier. For there would have been a strong contagious tradition of spirituality, fed by the three sources of renewal and thus securing the laity their place within the church.

Nevertheless, the Jesuit spirituality, in its original Ignatian format, still remains **totally accessible to the laity as *their own* scripture-based, action-oriented and worldly-wise way of being Christian and human**. Today, many laymen and laywomen, married or otherwise, and saturated with Ignatian spirituality, but *refusing to be monasticized through religious vows,* have joined the Jesuits as *lay associates* in their work and mission. This is a natural outcome of the recent retrieval of the original and originating charism of Ignatius.

Vatican II and the Three Sources of Renewal

The Second Vatican Council was heralded by a strong Catholic movement, almost an agitation, subsumed under the same old slogan as that of the Renaissance humanists: *reditus ad fontes*. The three main features of the two tides of renaissance reforms — humanism, patristics and scriptures — which the official church resisted or at least ignored for centuries, were now dashing on its doors with an insistence that even the strong-willed and strong-handed Pius XII had to reckon with. He issued three relatively progressive encyclicals that sent small ripples of hope. The *Divino Afflante Spiritu,* on biblical studies, was the most progressive; *Mystici Corporis*, on the Church, and *Mediator Dei*, on the liturgy, were less progressive but paved the way for further development. Thus, the water-tight ecclesiastical compartments which had been impervious to the humanistic waves dashing against their walls, became somewhat porous thanks to Pius XII's mild reforms. All we needed was a John XXIII to open the church doors to the currents of change. The result was Vatican II, which saved the church from isolation and irrelevance by allowing it to reach back to its roots.

With Vatican II, the three-fold stream of renewal entered the church and swept away the bastions of clerical and religious elitism, defining the church primarily as the *People of God* (co-priests with Christ), with a *universal call to holiness* that left no room for a 'holier class'. In fact, in the decades immediately after Vatican II, many priests and religious went through a crisis of identity and returned to lay-life. On the other hand, the number of laypersons taking over their jobs, including teaching of theology, has begun to increase. Many women too have started taking up responsibilities in areas hitherto forbidden to them. The lay character and the lay foundation of Christianity has at last been acknowledged, albeit grudgingly, even by the Catholic Church! These positive gains must be taken into account when assessing the aftermath of the Council.

The prophets of doom cried 'foul' when this allegedly Protestant theory of the common priesthood of the *laos* became the council's teaching. The fact, however, is that that council gave due recognition to the *ministerial* character of that same priesthood when exercised by presbyters and bishops, and further it employed the word 'lay' often in an imprecise manner, merely to contrast with ordained ministry. Being a 'compromise council' its teachings alternate between the traditional sacerdotalism and the more scriptural understanding of the one priesthood of Christ and members. Yet, the adversaries of renewal have continued to protest against the alleged underestimation of religious and monastic life rather than appreciate and welcome the long overdue recognition of the laity.

The most difficult task for the Council Fathers was to install the *Word of God* at the centre of the Church. They placed the Table of the Word almost on a par with the Table of the Bread, amidst accusations within and without the council that the Lutheran heresy of *sola scriptura* was infecting the pure Catholic teachings! But, on the day that *Verbum Dei*, the document about the Holy Scriptures, was finally passed in the Council, the French Jesuit journal *Étude* celebrated the event as the end of the counter-reformation! With the return of the **Scriptures** to the centre of theology and spirituality as well as in the liturgy, many accretions accumulated over centuries from various ideological and philosophical influences began to crumble. The scholastic and neo-scholastic trends in theology suffered a severe blow. It is noteworthy that Monastic theology (basically a non-clerical lay theology) re-emerged from the ecclesiastical limbo. Liberation theology, falsely and unfairly condemned as a crypto-Marxist version of Christianity, was actually the fruit of a *lectio divina,* 'a prayerful scripture-reading' undertaken by Christian communities of the Poor, who, thanks to Vatican II, had come to recognize the Bible as their own manual of spirituality gifted to them by their Divine Covenant-Partner. Karl Rahner, an expert (*peritus*) at Vatican II, congratulated Gustavo Guttierez on writing that epoch-making work, *Theology of Liberation.*

Many of those who prepared the church for Vatican II and worked in it as experts (such as Henri de Lubac, Yves Congar and so on), were steeped in the *traditional spirituality* of **the Fathers**. The rediscovery of the recurrent Patristic theme, 'justice to the poor' (though their misogyny did not allow them to see women among the oppressed!), was heard in the Council loud and clear. John XXIII had already educated the participants of the Council in this area by issuing *Mater et Magistra* and *Pacem in Terris*. It is, therefore, ironical that those who blamed Vatican II for promoting *sola scriptura* at the cost of church tradition failed to appreciate this Council's recovery of the best of Christian tradition in preference to mere *traditions* in the plural. The church went back to its foundations thanks to the three Renewalist currents that never dried up but continue to flow even today.

Finally, we come to **humanism.** As we mentioned earlier, *Gaudium et Spes*, (the only document that was conceived and born within the council itself (not without prolonged labour pains) has taught us, with a certain amount of quasi-Teilhardian optimism, that we should be judiciously open to the *secular humanism* of the 'modern world'. Of course, the 'modern world' meant by the compliers of this document was the '20th century West'. In the subsequent years, with global capitalism spreading from the West, this optimism was somewhat toned down, especially after the Synod of 1971.

However, if we combine this approach of *Gaudium et Spes* with the emphasis placed by Vatican II on the local church (*ecclesia particularis*), we see that any church anywhere in the world becomes a readable sign ('sacrament') of Salvation only to the degree that it proclaims and lives out its salvific message in the **humanistic idiom of its cultural environment**. Leaving the Western Patriarchate to discover and dialogue with its own *secular humanism*, we Asians will have to incarnate ourselves in the *religious humanism* of our non-Christian cultures. Unlike the Renaissance reformers of Europe who had to dig back into their remote past to recover their humanistic roots, the Asians meet their ancient humanism at their doorstep thanks to the great world-religions as well as the cosmic spirituality of tribal and clannic traditions.

Summing up

Vatican II, in continuity with past efforts of the church, did not aim at mere institutional reforms that leave the structures of the church untouched, but launched a program of *permanent and on-going renewal* whose momentum has to be maintained at all cost if we want to be a self-evangelizing church that becomes Good News to the world. Therefore, the enthusiasm for renewal through a return to the three sources — an enthusiasm which the Renaissance Reformers sparked off in the church, which the Jesuits have preserved as smouldering embers for four centuries, and which Vatican II has rekindled into a blazing fire — must never be allowed to be smothered by prophets of doom.

John Robinson

Is There a Future for the Anonymous Christian?

Of all of the shifts that have taken place in Christian theology since the Enlightenment, it is surely no exaggeration to say that the increased engagement with the reality of other religions in a positive and sympathetic light by the Christian mainstream stands as one of the most remarkable. Far from remaining at the periphery of Christian discourse, the questions emerging from the reality of the encounter of religions have come to occupy a central place in the concerns of Christian theologians. It is, therefore, in this changed context that any discussion of Karl Rahner's doctrine of the 'anonymous Christian' has to be located. The doctrine itself has generated a large amount of discussion and comment from its inception in the years immediately preceding the Second Vatican Council, and has come to be viewed by many as problematic, especially in light of the more recent and daring approaches to the question of the relationship between Christianity and the other faiths. It will be the aim of this essay to look again at the proposal put forward by Rahner and to see if there may yet be something in it which can positively advance the encounter between Christianity and the other faiths and contribute to the theological reflection on this encounter.

'Anonymous Christianity'

Rahner's formulation of the concept of 'anonymous Christianity' was originally made with those in his own cultural setting who had abandoned Christianity in mind, though he himself soon developed it to encompass those of different faiths. The problem which he sought to address was initially one located exclusively within the confines of Christian discourse, a condition which applied also to the answer he provided. The structure of the problem lay in trying to reconcile the Christian belief that salvation comes through Christ in the Church with the insistence on God's universal salvific will—and this all the more so, given the manifest failure of the Christian missionary enterprise to lead all non-Christians into the fold of the Church. What sense could be made, then, of the persistence of options other than the Christian option in the light of God's will that all should attain salvation? Rahner saw the absurdity, not to say cruelty, of the option that sought to consign to perdition all those who were *extra ecclesiam*, and, indeed, he was not alone in this as can be seen from the position adopted by the Vatican under Pius XII in relation to the teaching of Fr. Leonard Feeney in the 1950s. The issue then became, if non-Christians do have access to salvation, how does this happen, and what is its relation to the revelation and salvation brought by Christ? Rahner in answering this question immediately cut to the heart of the concept of anonymous Christianity stating:

> But when we have to keep in mind both principles together, namely the necessity of Christian faith and the universal salvific will of God's love and omnipotence, we can only reconcile them by saying that somehow all men must be capable of being members of the Church; and this capacity must not be understood merely in the sense of an abstract and purely logical possibility, but a real and historically concrete one.[1]

---

1 Karl Rahner, 'Anonymous Christians', in *Theological Investigations*, London, Darton, Longman

Thus, the question becomes how to conceive of this belonging from without, as it were, and of formulating in what it might consist. Crucial to the formulation that Rahner did arrive at was his concept of the 'supernatural existential'. In this, Rahner posited the notion that humanity is essentially orientated towards God as the horizon of its existence, a dynamic which is manifest in activities such as human loving, the exercise of freedom and the affirmation of the value of life in the face of certain death. This implicit striving towards God is met by God who reveals Godself to every individual. Dermot Lane sums up this idea:

> We come into the world 'inwardly determined' as it were by the gracious love of God and this gives everyone a particular disposition, orientation and dynamism turned towards God. The effect of this upon the person is what Rahner calls 'the supernatural existential'.[2]

Thus, since our innate dynamism as human beings is directed towards God as the horizon of our existence, it follows that, in an unthematic way, we affirm God when we affirm our own existence, a conclusion explicitly arrived at by Rahner. The significance of this self-affirmation based on the supernatural existential was complimented by Rahner's linking of theology and anthropology in Christology and, in particular, in the significance of the incarnation. Jeannine Hill Fletcher points out:

> As we have seen, for Rahner, the fulfilment of human nature in the acceptance of grace is simultaneously the fulfilment of God's self-communication to the world. As humans respond to their own nature, God's self-communication becomes manifest and the incarnation of God in and through human nature completes the intention of creation.[3]

The supernatural existential reaches its consummation in the perfect acceptance of God's grace which took place in Christ and as such is simultaneously the perfect revelation of God and the fulfilment of creation. As the 'final cause of the communication of the Spirit to the world'[4] which effects history both before and after the events of Christ's passion and resurrection, the Christ event is causally bound up with the entelechy that is present in all humanity as the supernatural existential. It is this which, in turn, makes of all those who affirm their own existence in its inherent orientation towards God 'anonymous Christians', rather than simply 'anonymous theists'. In their unthematized reaching towards the horizon of existence which is God, they are simultaneously partaking in the salvation wrought by Christ. For, it is the ontological transformation wrought by Christ's complete abandonment to the Father and acceptance of his self-revelation that make possible the consummation of the dynamic of all other human lives. As Hill Fletcher points out, in Rahner's view, '[w]hat takes place in Jesus Christ has significance on an ontological plane – that is, the event has to do with being itself and completes the very structure of existence.'[5]

---

and Todd, 1962-81: volume 6: 391.
2 Dermot Lane, 'Karl Rahner's Contribution to Interreligious Dialogue', in Declan Marmion (ed.), *Christian Identity in a Post-modern Age: Celebrating the Legacies of Karl Rahner and Bernard Lonergan*, Dublin, Veritas, 2005: 93.
3 Jeannine Hill Fletcher, 'Rahner and Religious Diversity', in Declan Marmion and Mary E. Hines (eds.), *The Cambridge Companion to Karl Rahner*, Cambridge, Cambridge University, 2005: 239.
4 Karl Rahner, *Foundations of Christian Faith: An Introduction to the Idea of Christianity*, London, Darton, Longman and Todd, 1978: 318.
5 Fletcher, 'Rahner and Religious Diversity': 240.

Thus, the context in which Rahner's notion of the 'anonymous Christian' takes place may be deemed to be a theological ontology of being, a point which will prove significant when considering the import of this notion for the development of interreligious dialogue.

From a consideration of the participation of the individual in the salvation wrought by Christ through the affirmation of his or her own existence, Rahner moves to consider the significance of the non-Christian religions. As human beings are essentially social beings constituted in history and time, it is not possible to consider the phenomenon of 'anonymous Christianity' in a way which abstracts from these factors. Rahner comments:

> In view of the social nature of man and the previously even more radical social solidarity of men, however, it is quite unthinkable that man, being what he is, could actually achieve this relationship to God – which he must have and which if he is to be saved, is and must be made possible for him by God – in an absolutely private interior reality and this outside of the actual religious bodies which offer themselves to him in the environment in which he lives.[6]

Here the importance accorded by Rahner to the concept of mediation becomes crucial with the various non-Christian faiths mediating the divine offer of grace to humanity as well as giving concrete expression to the supernatural existential which is the driving force of human existence. As such mediations, Rahner deems these religions to be 'lawful' in the sense of

> ...an institutional religion whose 'use' by man at a certain period can be regarded as a positive means of gaining the right relationship to God and thus for the attaining of salvation, a means which is positively included in God's plan of salvation.[7]

Objections and Possibilities

Rahner's views on these matters have generated controversy ever since he first articulated them, initially and in particular, from those who maintained that he was weakening and diluting Christianity's claims and self understanding, a claim most notably advanced by Hans Urs von Balthasar.[8] More recently, however, the sharpest criticism has come from the pluralist camp who aver that Rahner does not go far enough and accuse him of failing to take the manifest reality of the various other faiths seriously.

Alan Race, to take one example, accuses the theologies of inclusivism in general of failing to allow the other religions to modify the contours of their own theological commitment and engaging in essentially tautologous argumentation by relating the other religions to Christ *qua* saviour.[9] Others argue that the idea of 'anonymous Christianity' is a form of ideological colonialism, in which the 'other' is stripped of his or her otherness and effectively co-opted (or, perhaps, domesticated) by being forced into Christian categories, which in no way reflect the self-understanding of the adherents of the other faiths. The third objection levelled against this concept and against theologies of inclusivism generally is that, given the plurality of religions, it is simply not possible to affirm the ultimate significance of Christ or, indeed, of any one religious figure or teaching and that it is hence an illegitimate move.[10] The question arises, then, can Rahner's

---

6 Karl Rahner, 'Christianity and the non-Christian Religions', in *Theological Investigations* 5: 128.
7 Rahner, 'Christianity and the non-Christian Religions': 125.
8 Hans Urs von Balthasar, *Cordula oder der Ernstfall*, Einsiedeln, Johannes, 1966.
9 Alan Race, *Christianity and Religious Pluralism*, London, SCM, 1979: 32.
10 For an example of this viewpoint, see John Hick, *The Fifth Dimension: An Exploration of the Spiritual Realm*, Oxford, Oneworld, 1999.

theory be defended against these charges and can it yet prove useful in advancing the encounter of the different faiths and can it, *a fortiori*, do so in a world where increasing antagonism and polarization between the religions appear to be on the rise.

First, it is fair to ask whether Race's criticism of theologies of inclusivism can be fairly applied to what Rahner is setting out to do. It is true that Rahner's argument does have a certain circularity; yet, as Karen Kilby states:

> one can point out that there is nothing wrong in itself with the circularity of which Rahner is accused – mathematical arguments, indeed all deductive arguments, also exhibit this kind of circularity.[11]

The question then becomes one of whether or not relating all religious phenomena to Christ means that the Christian partner in the dialogue closes off *a priori* any modification of her own theological commitment. Yet, this does not logically follow from the structure of the inclusivist position: the Christian party to the dialogue may indeed not modify her position at all; equally, she may accept the dialogical partner's position in its entirety and convert. Or, most likely, she may modify the categories through which she interprets the salvation she believes has been won by Christ, or she may come to think differently about the implication and meaning of this salvation, or some combination of the two, perhaps incorporating further elements. Race's objection, then, boils down to an objection to the adoption of a concrete perspective encompassing certain religious beliefs and convictions which are viewed as constitutive of the position of the person entering into the dialogue. Yet, this position would also be the case if the person entering into the dialogue adopted a theologically pluralist standpoint and, indeed, it is highly probable that the non-Christian party in the dialogue will have similarly strongly held and constitutive beliefs which they bring to the dialogue also. Thus, Race's argument falls down on logical grounds and, in any case, is hardly a fair representation of Rahner's intention in formulating his view. Dermot Lane sagaciously comments:

> ...it should be noted that Rahner in the sixties was trying to open a closed door through his theology of inclusivism...it would not be true to Rahner's intentions to pre-empt genuine learning about and from other religions.[12]

Second, there is the question of whether or not Rahner's 'anonymous Christianity' doesn't end up functioning as a colonizing move in which the otherness of 'the other' is circumvented in favour of a more comfortable Christian projection. The first and most important point to make in this regard concerns the context in which Rahner used the term. It was a term which, as already pointed out, was coined and intended for use within the discourse of Christian theology and, as such, was certainly an interpretation of 'the other' within Christian categories. It may be argued, however, that within the context of Christian discourse, this is not an illegitimate move, particularly when the intent is to interpret the other faiths in light of the salvation Christianity holds has been wrought by Christ. The second point to be adduced is that, in light of Rahner's view that the incarnation was an event which had ontological implications for all of humanity, it is likely that the term 'anonymous Christian' was intended primarily to function as an ontological and not an existential statement, one which related the non-Christian to the events which Rahner viewed as having transformed the structure of human existence.

---

11 Karen Kilby, *Karl Rahner – Theology and Philosophy*, London, Routledge, 2004: 120.
12 Dermot Lane, 'Karl Rahner's Contribution to Interreligious Dialogue', in Marmion, *Christian Identity in a Postmodern Age*: 102.

As such, it may be legitimately distinguished from the existential status of non-Christian believers and can be translated, as Rahner's concept of lawful religions implies, into a respectful affirmation of the validity of the 'other's' religious option while still affirming the ultimacy of Christianity as the reflexive articulation of the depths of human existence (the legitimacy or otherwise of this last claim being a separate question). It may well be that the time has come to cease using this terminology due to the altered conditions within which the encounter and dialogue take place, but this does not of itself render the insights the terminology set out to express obsolete.

The third criticism is perhaps the most serious, namely, that the plurality of religions renders it impossible to make the kind of claim that Rahner and, indeed, the other inclusivists advance for Jesus. Lurking behind this view is the notion that the inevitable reality of the perspectivism engendered most particularly by cultural and religious upbringing renders it impossible to adjudicate between the competing claims of the different faiths, along with the postmodern suspicion of logic and reason as a path to truth. In relation to the first claim, it has been a staple of hermeneutical theory since Gadamer that, not only are *préjugés* not inimical to understanding, they are, rather, our point of entry into the hermeneutical circle and do not rule out their subsequent reversal or transformation as the process of understanding takes place.

Whilst the entirety of the controversy over logic and reason in postmodernity is too vast a topic to examine in this essay, it is worth pointing out that the plurality of religions does not of itself invalidate the process of logical discrimination and reasoning, complex though that may become; instead, it increases, to a hitherto unforeseen extent, the data to be considered. In terms of the postmodern objections to logic on the ground of the perspectivism that is inevitably involved, one may trace the beginnings of an answer by pointing to the transcendental content of thought which is evident in phenomena such as language, communication, facial expressions, etc. This in no way provides an adequate refutation of the radical postmodernist's nihilistic scepticism; yet, it does indicate, at least, that there are points to be answered on the other side of the argument whilst conceding that the argument at this point is no longer limited to Rahner's anonymous Christianity but is located in the much broader context of the arguments currently being played out in the philosophical arena.

To sum up then, the objections raised against Rahner's concept of the anonymous Christian, whilst not entirely lacking in phenomenological validity, do appear to be based on a mixture of hermeneutical naiveté, misunderstanding of the context in which Rahner formulated and used the concept and of his intentions in doing so. In addition, a failure to adequately locate the idea within the broader sweep of Rahner's thought leaves some, at least, of his critics open to the charge of missing the nuances with which the concept is imbued.

In terms of the possibilities afforded by this doctrine in interfaith dialogue today, several points deserve mention. First, it provides a way of locating interreligious dialogue squarely within the mainstream of Christian tradition without avoiding the question of how such dialogue relates to the fundamental doctrines of Christianity. Second, by grounding the affirmations made, in fundamental conditions and phenomena of human existence, it has the potential to furnish the dialogue with other religions with a common language that, *mutatis mutandis*, all can share in. This is not, of course, to say that the outcome of the resultant dialogue may not lead to the modification or even abandonment of the starting position, but, simply, that in its basing itself on fundamental human realities, it can provide a common ground upon which all parties to the dialogue can meet.

Finally, in the context of today's situation, whilst the precise terminology may be unhelpful, it seems likely that the position set out by Rahner provides a way into dialogue which can address the fears of those who feel that their commitment to their belief in Christ is compromised by any encounter which does not take place in a missionary context. To the frontierspersons of interreligious dialogue this may seem like a rather limited good, but, in a time when fundamentalisms of all sorts are on the rise and the mainstream churches are increasingly falling prey to a trench mentality it is surely a good not to be eschewed.

Simone Sinn

Human Dignity and Remembrance

Perspectives from Germany

1. Introduction

With his passion for the 'inter-', such as *inter* religious or *inter*cultural communication, John D'Arcy May has infected many people, myself being one of them. His interest in engaging with the 'other' is a central theme in his writings, his concern for the 'forgotten other' being most characteristic.[1] In his teaching at the Irish School of Ecumenics, he instigated many reflections about how we construct the human in the midst of a plurality of different visions of life.[2]

As a way of thanking him, I want to explore a theme that comes out of my specific context, though its relevance is not confined to this context: the question of why and how to remember the victims of the Nazi regime, the Jews, the Sinti and Roma, the handicapped people, the homosexuals, the political opponents, the trade unionists and many more who were regarded as 'unworthy to live' by the Nazis. These people were 'others' who were silenced through mass extermination. To listen to stories from their lives and to be confronted with the atrocities they experienced is a way of giving those who had been silenced a voice again. It is a way of entering into a dialogue with the silenced.

Everyone who has had the chance to listen to one of the surviving victims of the Nazi regime knows how intense such a dialogue can be. However, there can be significant interaction with those victims who have been murdered as well. The process of remembering and commemorating these people is an unusual yet also intense form of dialogue. In this process diaries or other writings that have 'survived' play an important role, the places where the victims have been murdered testify to their fate. In remembering them we learn a lot about the human and about human dignity.

The commemoration of the victims of the Shoah might seem so natural today. There are official dates that we commemorate, like 27 January, the day when Auschwitz was liberated, or 9 November, when we commemorate the 'Reichskristallnacht'. Furthermore, there are well-known places for commemoration such as the memorial sites at the former extermination camps or the Holocaust Memorial in Berlin. Nevertheless we have to remind ourselves that it is, in fact, far from clear why and how the perpetrators and their descendants should remember the victims. In the past, it seems to have been the rule of history that each side remembers its own casualties. Yet, the atrocities of the Shoah urge us to move beyond this.

---

1 See, for instance, John D'Arcy May, *After Pluralism: Towards an Interreligious Ethic*, number 1 in Religion und Theologie im Asien-Pazifik-Kontext, Münster, LIT, 2000.
2 See John D'Arcy May, 'Human Dignity, Human Rights, and Religious Pluralism: Buddhist and Christian Perspectives', in *Buddhist-Christian Studies* 26 (2006): 51-60; John D'Arcy May and Linda Hogan, 'Constructing the Human: Dignity in Interreligious Dialogue', in Regina Ammicht-Quinn, Maureen Junker-Kenny, and Elsa Tamez (eds.), *The Discourse of Human Dignity*, London, SCM, 2003: 78-89.

After Auschwitz, German society cannot speak of its history and its identity without speaking of the people victimized in Nazi Germany. An important learning took place at this point and I believe that it is of relevance not only for our being and doing in Germany, but for the ways in which identity and ethics are conceptualized in a plural world today. Remembrance of the victims as a form of dialoguing with the silenced others has to be an integral part of ethics today. My thesis is that an intercultural and interreligious ethic is not only to be formed by dialogues between the *visions of life that cultures and religions offer*, but also by listening to the *voices that bear witness to crises of the human*.

These voices draw us in quite distinct ways into ethical reflection, they give us deep insights into the relationality of life and human dignity. They do so precisely because they do not speak about ethics in general terms, but from particular and distinct experiences. The great challenge is to communicate these experiences between different contexts and between different generations, in multicultural Germany today and beyond.

In times when the atrocities are often portrayed in general terms as overwhelming evil, we have to insist that the atrocities have been very concrete: people with specific names were murdered in specific places by specific perpetrators. Therefore, my reflections will start with a concrete example: Grafeneck castle, the premises where the Nazis set up their first death camp and, in 1940, murdered over 10,000 mentally ill and handicapped people. Then, I will give a brief outline of how, during the last sixty years, remembrance in Germany has developed. For the time during which Germany was divided it will be limited to West Germany.[3] I will then explore the meaning of remembrance and the significance of human dignity further, especially drawing on insights from Micha Brumlik. Finally, it will be argued that the crises of the human urge us to uphold not only human rights as guiding principles for society but also the remembrance of the victims' stories as important narratives in our cultural memory.

2. Remembering What Happened at Grafeneck

The mass extermination organized by the Nazi regime started with the murder of handicapped and mentally ill people. In October 1939, a secret letter from Adolf Hitler initiated the *Aktion T4*.[4] The aim was to murder twenty percent of the mentally ill and handicapped people living in nursing homes. This goal was reached, and from January 1940 until August 1941, over 70,000 men, women and children were deported from their homes and killed in six different locations in Nazi Germany: Grafeneck, Brandenburg, Hartheim, Pirna, Bernburg and Hadamar.

At Grafeneck castle, a remote place on the *Schwäbische Alb* in Southwest Germany, the first death camp was set up. Before that, Grafeneck had been a home for mentally handicapped people run by the *Samariterstiftung*, a diaconal foundation. In 1939, the Nazis

---

3 A good exploration of the development in East and West Germany can be found in: Aleida Assmann and Ute Frevert, *Geschichtsvergessenheit – Geschichtsversessenheit: Vom Umgang mit deutschen Vergangenheiten nach 1945*, Stuttgart, Deutsche Verlags-Anstalt, 1999.

4 The name is an abbreviation for Tiergartenstraße 4, where the office that organized this 'euthanasia' action was located in Berlin. The first in-depth study on *Aktion T4* was by Kurt Nowak, *'Euthanasie' und Sterilisierung im 'Dritten Reich.' Die Konfrontation der evangelischen und katholischen Kirche mit dem 'Gesetz zur Verhütung erbkranken Nachwuchses' und der 'Euthanasie'-Aktion*, Göttingen, Vandenhoeck & Ruprecht, 1978. A collection of source material is available in: Jochen-Christoph Kaiser, Kurt Nowak, and Michael Schwartz, *Eugenik, Sterilisation, 'Euthanasie': Politische Biologie in Deutschland 1895-1945: Eine Dokumentation*, Berlin, Buchverlag Union, 1992.

confiscated the premises and transformed them into a death camp. From 18 January 1940 until December that year, 10,654 mentally ill and handicapped people were murdered in the former garage that was turned into a gas chamber. Their corpses were burned in a crematorium set up next to it. Grafeneck served as a model, not only for other 'euthanasia' death camps, but for extermination camps in general. Grafeneck proved that mass murder was possible.[5]

The deportation was organized by a central office, victims were deported from 40 different homes, state-run, private-run and homes run by diaconal foundations. A number of the directors tried to intervene by writing letters and making petitions to the authorities, yet without success. This attempt at diplomacy was more or less ignored. It simply was not an adequate form of resistance, because it still operated within the system and did not confront it.[6]

Only very late, a church leader further north in Germany had the courage to condemn the murder of handicapped and mentally ill people publicly in a sermon. On 3 August 1941, Bishop von Galen in Münster said that by declaring these people 'unworthy to live' and calling them 'unproductive members of the national community' they are treated 'like an old piece of machinery which no longer works'.[7] His sermon encouraged people in the region to strongly oppose *Aktion T4*. On 24 August, Hitler stopped *Aktion T4*. Whether he would have done so anyway because the initial goal had been reached or whether this extermination action would have gone on cannot be discerned in retrospect.

How did one deal with this mass murder that happened in the middle of Germany after the war was over? In early June 1945, the prosecution of a few of the personnel responsible for the death camp in Grafeneck started in Tübingen. In 1949, eight persons were charged, and three of them condemned. One of them did not have to serve the sentence in prison because of health reasons, the other two were sentenced to 24 and 18 months, which they had already served in detention awaiting the trial. Not only were these sentences a mockery of what happened in Grafeneck, but the fact that the public was not interested in this trial makes it even worse. Only 35 people came along to follow the outcome of the trial.

When the premises of Grafeneck were handed back to the *Samariterstiftung* in 1947 there was discussion of whether this place could be a home for handicapped people again; however, it was generally felt that the daily care of the handicapped would be the best 'response to that merciless time'. There was no sign, no plaque that would hint at what had happened there in the past. Here, as everywhere in Germany, people did not want to look back, they wanted to look only to the future.

It took decades for the idea of remembrance to arise. Finally, in 1979, on the ecclesial Day of Prayer and Repentance, a public commemoration service was held in Grafeneck. This was a milestone. Over one thousand people came to the event. A working group then planned a memorial which was opened to the public in 1990. It is an outdoor memorial chapel that is carried by five steel girders, as a reminder of the fifth commandment. The altar has a simple cross, the back wall is marked by a deep crack. A stone threshold sunk into the ground at the memorial entrance lists the homes from which the

---

5 Henry Friedlander, *Der Weg zum NS-Genozid*, Darmstadt, Wissenschaftliche Buchgesellschaft, 1997: 60. He emphasizes that the Nazi 'euthanasia' was not just a prelude, but already the first chapter of the 'final solution' (11).
6 Cf. Kaiser, Nowak, Schwartz, *Eugenik, Sterilisation, 'Euthanasie'*: XXXI.
7 See http://www.kirchensite.de/downloads/Aktuelles/Predigt_Galen_Englisch.pdf: 6 (accessed on 28 February 2007).

individuals were deported to Grafeneck. Today, more than 6,500 names of the victims are known and listed in a memorial book displayed in the memorial chapel. An alphabet garden next to the memorial chapel remembers those still unknown. In 1996, a young historian was employed to do historical research work on what happened in Grafeneck and to develop educational material.[8]

Remembrance and a memorial site not only were developed at Grafeneck, but also in the homes from which the handicapped people were deported. Extensive historical research work was undertaken[9] and not only published in academic circles but also in newsletters for the general public. During the last decades, diaconal institutions have learned that it is part of their responsibility and identity to remember those whom they failed to protect. Not by overlooking what happened during the Nazi regime, but by consciously remembering those victimized, they are able to responsibly serve and accompany people in need today.

3. The Development of Remembrance in Germany

The adoption of the Basic Law in May 1949 officially marked a new beginning for the Federal Republic of Germany. Article 1, section 1, most clearly illustrates the fundamental break with the Nazi ideology and lays a new foundation: '[h]uman dignity shall be inviolable. To respect and protect it shall be the duty of all state authority.'[10] Whereas in Nazi Germany the nation had been the highest cause it was now clear that the state is to serve the individual.

The Basic Law provided a ground for shaping the future of the German society. Yet, the question of how to deal with the past still remained to be resolved. Officially, one spoke with contrition of the nation's burden of guilt; de facto, however, a policy of amnesty and reintegration of many perpetrators was silently implemented.[11] The Grafeneck trial described above is just one of many examples showing that one did not want to remember this evil time.

It took until the 1960s for a critical and more in-depth treatment of the past to begin. Important events that influenced this process were the Eichmann trial in Jerusalem in 1961 and the Auschwitz trials in Frankfurt, which started in 1963. Here, one tried to consciously look at what happened during the Nazi regime and tried to identify the perpetrators. Furthermore, the educational challenge was now addressed. In his famous 1966 radio address, Theodor W. Adorno declared that 'Auschwitz should never happen again, this is the very first demand of education.'[12] Since then, 'Education after Auschwitz' has been an integral part of the school curriculum.

---

8 Cf. Thomas Stöckle and Eberhard Zacher, *'Euthanasie' im NS-Staat. Grafeneck im Jahr 1940*, number 15 in Materialien zur Landeskunde und Landesgeschichte, Tübingen, Oberschulamt, 1999.
9 See, e.g., Theodor Strohm and Jörg Thierfelder (eds.), *Diakonie im 'Dritten Reich'. Neuere Ergebnisse zeitgeschichtlicher Forschung*, number 3 in Veröffentlichungen des Diakoniewissenschaftlichen Instituts an der Universität Heidelberg, Heidelberg, HVA, 1990; and Martin Kalusche, *'Das Schloß an der Grenze'. Kooperation und Konfrontation mit dem Nationalsozialismus in der Heil- und Pflegeanstalt für Schwachsinnige und Epileptische Stetten i.R.*, number 10 in Diakoniewissenschaftliche Studien, Heidelberg, DWI, 1997.
10 http://www.bundestag.de/htdocs_e/parliament/function/legal/germanbasiclaw.pdf: 14 (accessed on 28 February 2007).
11 Cf. Norbert Frei, *Adenauer's Germany and the Nazi Past: The Politics of Amnesty and Integration*, translated by Joel Golb, New York, Columbia University, 2002.
12 Theodor W. Adorno, 'Erziehung nach Auschwitz', in his *Erziehung zur Mündigkeit*, Frankfurt a.M.,

Yet, at the end of the sixties, the younger generation themselves started to ask their parents and grandparents critical questions about Nazi Germany. This intergenerational dialogue was triggered by questions related to the past, but it especially addressed authoritarian structures in the present. In the society's dealing with the past, however, there was still a significant gap between the solemn official speeches on the one hand and the taboo-like character of the Nazi period in the private sphere on the other.

In 1979, the United States television series 'Holocaust', when broadcast in Germany, had quite a remarkable impact. Twenty million Germans watched this series and a television discussion afterwards. Now, one could no longer dissociate oneself from that history. By watching, one was drawn into the story. The new sensitivity that slowly emerged was met by reflections of then German President, Richard von Weizsäcker, in his speech on 8 May 1985. He made an important contribution to the intergenerational dialogue by clarifying the issue of guilt, liability and responsibility.[13] He argues that young Germans who did not live during the Nazi period cannot confess guilt for actions which they did not do. Yet, he maintains that all Germans have to accept the past because they are involved in its consequences and are made liable for it. So, although not guilty, one still is liable for the past and responsible for the future.

Since the 1980s, a culture of commemoration and remembrance developed, not only in the former Nazi camps but in many places, towns and villages. Mainly on the initiative of a few committed individuals, people began to look locally for the traces of Jews, handicapped people and others who had been deported. Information was gathered and commemoration liturgies held. Actual stories of actual human beings were remembered in actual places.

Yet, Germany's dealing with its past was not always a steady movement towards a heightened and more sensitive awareness. Time and again, strong opposition against too critical an engagement with the past has also been voiced. The exhibition on the German Wehrmacht's war of annihilation was an incident that sparked many emotions as it touched personal remembrance in critical ways. With his 1998 speech against the Holocaust Memorial in Berlin, the writer Martin Walser eloquently argued against this 'continuous representation of our shame'.[14] Walser revived 'shame' as a key notion which seemed to have been overcome by von Weizsäcker with his distinction between guilt, liability and responsibility.

Public debates are an important factor in shaping the historical consciousness of German society; yet, recent research work has highlighted the fact that family remembrance also plays a significant role. One of the findings is that many of the third generation want to be loyal to their grandparents and 'remember' them as having lived with moral integrity during the Nazi period. The study, published under the heading 'Grandpa wasn't a Nazi', describes how the more the younger generations know about the atrocities committed by Nazi Germany, the stronger their need to create a story that combines the crimes of the Nazis with a kind of moral integrity for their relatives in the same narrative.[15]

Suhrkamp, 1971: 88 (translated by Simone Sinn).
13 The German text is officially available at: http://www.bundestag.de/geschichte/parlhist/ dokumente/dok08.html (accessed on 28 February 2007).
14 Martin Walser, 'Dank: Erfahrungen beim Verfassen einer Sonntagsrede', in *Friedenspreis des Deutschen Buchhandels 1998*, Frankfurt a.M., Börsenverein des Deutschen Buchhandels e.V., 1998: 45.
15 Cf. Harald Welzer, *Grandpa Wasn't a Nazi: Nazism and the Holocaust in German Family*

In conclusion, we can say that during the last decades practices of commemoration and remembrance developed that went beyond outwardly oriented solemn official memorial services and have been attempts to genuinely remember those victimized by the Nazi regime. At the same time, we perceive a longing for Germany to again be a 'normal nation' and to belong to a family of nations with moral integrity. The question is repeatedly asked, though, as to how we should remember the troublesome past correctly. This urges us to look more closely at the meaning of remembrance, at the role of the individual and the collective memory in that process, and at the significance of human dignity.

4. The Meaning of Remembrance and the Significance of Human Dignity

Remembering is usually described as the act of recalling something that one has heard, seen or experienced. Hence, remembering seems to presuppose having had an experience of one's own that can be stored in one's memory to be recalled later. From this perspective, remembering seems to be a quite individualistic process which, in fact, it is not. More than eighty years ago, Maurice Halbwachs explored the social dimension of memory and coined the term 'collective memory'.[16] He maintained that memory is a social phenomenon and that the collective memory is a necessary horizon for individual memory. During recent years, Jan and Aleida Assmann have further developed this theory and introduced the distinction between the 'communicative memory' and the 'cultural memory'.[17]

As the term already says, the communicative memory is the memory that is formed through direct interaction between people of a community: three to four generations living at the same time communicate about events and experiences in their lifetimes. One can say that this communicative memory is the 'short-term memory' of a society. The cultural memory, however, covers a much wider time-span, centuries or even thousands of years. The cultural memory refers to texts, rituals, artefacts. Thus, it is formed by exteriorizations that are taken up in reception processes. Whereas in communicative memory we find a tendency to create homogenous stories, or even to instrumentalize stories for current purposes, the cultural memory leaves space for reception and interpretation while it also opens up the possibility for counterfactual memories.

Against the background of this distinction between communicative and cultural memory, we realize that Germany is indeed in a transition period with regard to its historical consciousness. The communicative memory with people involved who have themselves experienced Nazi Germany will come to an end. Having texts, artefacts, places and rituals that uphold the cultural memory thus becomes increasingly more important. Moreover, it is in fact not only a transition period for Germany but also for Europe as a whole, as in other European countries the respective communicative memories of the Second World War are also being transformed into cultural memories. The great challenge is to determine how something along the lines of a European cultural memory can be developed.[18]

Remembrance, Berlin, AJC, 2005 available at: http://www.ajc.org/atf/cf/{42D75369-D582-4380-8395-D25925B85EAF}/Grandpa_wasnt_nazi.pdf (accessed on 28 February 2007).

16 Maurice Halbwachs, *On Collective Memory*, edited and translated by Lewis A. Coser, in the Heritage of Sociology Series, Chicago, University of Chicago, 1992.

17 See Jan Assmann, *Religion and Cultural Memory: Ten Studies*, Stanford, Stanford University, 2006: 1-30.

18 Cf. Claudia Lenz and Harald Welzer, 'Zweiter Weltkrieg, Holocaust und Kollaboration im euro-

Building on these basic insights into the collective memory, we will now explore the process of remembrance further. As the danger of instrumentalizing the past for present purposes is well known – even if it is for a good cause such as education – Brumlik holds that, in remembrance, it is important to honour the victims for their own sake, to call them by their names, to focus on the past while and to leave the future out of view.[19] In doing so, he underlines that we need to distinguish between 'remembering the victims' as an act of honouring them, and 'education after Auschwitz' or 'holocaust education' as a fundamental civic education in human rights. Though interrelated, each is an important task in its own right. If the first is done only to serve the latter, the victims are simply taken as examples, and, in turn, if the latter focuses exclusively on Auschwitz, there will be no education about other genocides and other crises of the human. Taking into account other genocides in human rights education will not at all relativize, but intensify the sensitivity for human rights issues in multi-ethnic societies.[20]

Brumlik emphasizes that, apart from human rights and human rights violations, the issue of human dignity is key to this educational endeavour. Brumlik holds that a deeper understanding of the significance of human dignity is key to any civic education. He strongly argues that the understanding of dignity is not just a cognitive effort, but a 'moral feeling': '[t]his feeling is *moral* because it provides criteria for acting or for refraining from acting, it is a *feeling* because it is not a calculating criterion but, rather, a comprehensive, immediately operating, life-orienting attitude.'[21] Therefore Brumlik says that if one has to first think for a while whether a person is to be accorded dignity one has already missed the point. This moral feeling implicates the universal claim that everyone who belongs to the human family has dignity. Brumlik states that this universal moral feeling, though, is anything but obvious. Development psychology shows that getting to this point requires a lot, it requires a feeling for one's own dignity and for the dignity of people close to oneself, as well as the ability to transfer this to people distant and unknown.

Looking more closely at the process of remembering the victims, we encounter a similar challenge: how can we honour those whom we did not know directly? Brumlik goes even further by saying that, usually, an integral part of remembering those who have passed away is a feeling of sorrow and grief because one misses these people and therefore one remembers with a feeling of mourning. The critical question here is: if mourning is the reaction towards the loss of a beloved, would it not be at least paradoxical to ask people to mourn the distant and alien victims of mass extermination?[22]

Brumlik maintains that feeling a sense of loss is at the heart of remembering the victims. The mourning in this process is indeed not a spontaneous emotion, but it is a

---

päischen Gedächtnis. Ein Werkstattbericht aus einer vergleichenden Studie zur Tradierung von Geschichtsbewusstsein', in *Zeitschrift für Sozial- und Kulturwissenschaften* 2 [*Handlung, Kultur, Interpretation*], (2005), available as pdf via: http://www.memory-research.de/cms/k18. Publications.htm (accessed on 28 February 2007).

19 See Micha Brumlik, *Gerechtigkeit zwischen den Generationen,* Berlin, Berlin-Verlag, 1995: 110.
20 He takes the genocide of the Armenian people by the Turks as an example and points to the difficulty that Turkish adolescents in Germany have in critically dealing with that past, see Micha Brumlik, *Aus Katastrophen Lernen? Grundlagen zeitgeschichtlicher Bildung in menschenrechtlicher Absicht*, Berlin, Philo, 2004: 156.
21 Brumlik, *Aus Katastrophen Lernen?*: 131 (translated by Simone Sinn).
22 Micha Brumlik, 'Trauer und Solidarität. Zu einer Theorie öffentlichen Gedenkens', in Micha Brumlik and Petra Kunik (eds.), *Reichspogromnacht: Vergangenheitsbewältigung aus jüdischer Sicht*, Frankfurt a.M., Brandes & Apsel, 1988: 111-119.

way of relating to the victims which is intentionally to be developed in the face of what has happened. This means to cognitively and emotionally cultivate a sense of relatedness. Hence, Brumlik conceives of remembering as a relational process and describes it as 'anamnetic solidarity'. He strongly argues that the victims belong to our moral universe and that we should not exclude them again by forgetting them.[23]

In 'anamnetic solidarity', remembrance is enacted as a reception process in which I listen to the witness of the victims, through texts or through the silence of the places of horror. In this hermeneutical process I grant authority to the victims and give them space. In this existential encounter, in the midst of humiliating practices to which they had been exposed, I come to feel and be conscious of their dignity, and, through remembering, I try to uphold their dignity. Thus, remembering is a way of becoming aware and of paying respect to the dignity of the victimized people.

This process contains both an existential depth and a transformative power. An individual, a diaconal institution or a society that makes space for the victims in its memory loses its 'innocence' and can no longer construct its identity simply through its own achievements. The wrongdoings, the crises and the abyss of its history are part of its identity. Lastly, remembrance makes identity and ethics 'eccentric', it shifts the attention from the agents as the centre of reflection to those who are the 'objects' of the action. They become the subjects.

5. Concluding Remarks

The atrocities committed by Nazi Germany were a strong motive for developing and adopting the Universal Declaration of Human Rights in December 1948. At that juncture, the overwhelming evil of the Nazi era united diplomats from differing cultural and political backgrounds. Despite their differences they were convinced that the world needs to agree on a few fundamental rights in order to fend off totalitarian mechanisms and policies of exclusion. And here, again, the notion of human dignity was given foundational status.

'Human dignity' is a custodian which stipulates that even the most fundamental rights are based on something more fundamental, on a given that ontologically predates everything that humanity itself can create.[24] Therefore, human dignity can never be 'granted' by any human agency, but can only be 'recognized' as the preamble to the Universal Declaration rightly says. Again, receptivity is crucial to the issue and more fundamental than any human action.

Human dignity cannot be protected by rights alone: for, rights depend on moral feelings that motivate people to adhere to them and to stand up for them. As an integral part of an ethic in today's world, we need to remember the crises of the human and the stories of those who were victimized. They have to be part of our cultural memory, our identity, our moral universe. Anamnetic solidarity extends historical depth and actuality to an ethic in a plural world. Remembering the victims has transformative power because it makes us realize that dignity has actual, real faces.

---

23 Brumlik, *Gerechtigkeit*: 98. For Brumlik, remembrance of the victims always includes remembrance of the suffering they experienced. Miroslav Volf, *The End of Memory: Remembering Rightly in a Violent World*, Grand Rapids, Eerdmans, 2006, has given a different perspective on remembrance. It remains to be seen whether his argument for the end of memory will be convincing beyond the personal level that he describes. With regard to the Shoah, I hold that remembrance is crucial for an ethic in a plural world.

24 Cf. Mary Ann Glendon, *A World Made New: Eleanor Roosevelt and the Universal Declaration of Human Rights*, New York, Random House, 2002: 176.

Geraldine Smyth OP and Lesley Carroll
Wisdom to Know the Difference
Re-Configuring a Theological Paradigm in the Transition to Peace in Ireland

Increasingly through the 20th century, and at critical junctures, the Prophet has come into his own (usually indeed, male in voice and character). One thinks of the self-consciously prophetic stance of Germany's Confessing Church against Nationalist Socialism in the 1930s. Liberation Theology, too, in asserting God's preferential option for the poor, inserted itself into the Exodus tradition of liberation with its prophetic denunciation of the structural oppression of the poor. Later, in the 1980s, the *Kairos* theologians in South Africa, in their theological strategy and struggle against apartheid, echoed the discourse of Bonhoeffer and the Confessing Church, asserting 'Prophetic Theology' as the hermeneutical key to justice. Thus, they challenged churches to resist the legitimization of 'State Theology' (based on a biased reading of Paul's injunction to obey lawful rulers (Romans 13:1-7).[1] Similarly, they warned that 'Church Theology', ostensibly intent on reconciliation, had colluded in masking the idolatrous face of apartheid. Only a prophetic stance was adequate: churches should return to biblical prophetic sources, read the signs of the times, denounce apartheid as a sin, take the side of the oppressed, and announce salvation.[2]

This call was taken up by an interchurch group in Belfast, which developed its own *Kairos* analysis of Northern Ireland, asserting the primacy of 'Prophetic Theology' over the prevailing 'State Theology', and repudiating 'Reconciling Theology' as soft and lacking rigorous social analysis. At that time, one of the *Kairos* authors, Michael Ritchie, was invited by a Dominican Justice and Ecumenism group to discuss the document. There appeared to be a hermeneutical mismatch between South Africa and Northern Ireland and a spurious pitting of prophecy against reconciliation that effectively evacuated reconciliation of its biblical core and imperative. Aligning reconciliation with a soft view of justice denied a Pauline 'costing-ness'. Also, in a divided context, witness to reconciliation challenged the churches to renounce their cultural entrapment. In seeking to be reconciled and reconciling, churches could live into and give prophetic witness to God's reconciling grace. Where divided churches cost lives, reconciliation itself was a prophetic act. Indeed, it is *as* reconciliation that John D'Arcy May sees Christian mission. Mission, he says, is 'set free from the constraints and compromises of the past, to become the witness to reconciliation'; today, reconciliation 'can only be conceived as radical non-violence…[and] a witness that can counteract the logic of reciprocal retribution.'[3]

---

1 *The Kairos Document: A Theological Comment on the Political Crisis in South Africa*, London, CIIR, 1985²: 2.1-2.4.
2 *The Kairos Document*: 4.1ff.
3 John D'Arcy May, 'The Space in Between – Mission as Reconciliation', in Geraldine Smyth OP (ed.), *Distance Becomes Communion: A Dominican Symposium on Mission and Hope*, Dublin, Dominican, 2004: 76-87: 80. Mission is always local, a 'realised catholicity' (81); and reconciliation challenges 'the dialogue of religions' (86).

This Justice and Ecumenism Group was motivated by the justice vision of the prophet Amos (e.g., campaigning against police use of lethal plastic bullets to disperse civilian crowds, or advocating for falsely imprisoned individuals[4]) and inspired by Paul's call to be 'ambassadors of reconciliation' (2 Corinthians 5). In Newry there was an interchurch clergy group that took the prophetic step, on the Monday following any sectarian or politically inspired killing in south Down, of gathering at the site to pray and bear witness together. Ordinary citizens braved taunts and threats of violence to engage together in peace walks or interchurch prayer vigils or cross-community women's gatherings. There is no innate dualism between reconciling and prophetic gestures. For instance, during the Flower Festival marking Holy Week, the Non-Subscribing Presbyterian Church in Dunmurry and its minister, Rev. William McMillan, were visited each year by the Justice and Ecumenism Group. Amid the terror of repeated bombing, maiming and assassination, this ecumenical event was a prophetic symbol that entwined pain, beauty and hope. People came from across the city, transcending narrow identities and gathering to meditate together on the floral *Via Crucis* wrought out of the most delicate spring blooms interwoven with charred nails, barbed wire or twisted branch. In the image of the suffering Christ drawing all the suffering of Ulster, art became a reconciling theology, itself a prophetic sign.[5] Prophecy, too, can say it with flowers.

Today, too, reconciliation provides a theological horizon and social purpose to prophetic justice.[6] In the past decade, we have seen ceasefires and a drastic reduction in the numbers of people killed for sectarian motive, the gradual dismantling of paramilitary and military infrastructures, new schemes for urban reconstruction and the reform of policing. Constitutional reform extended to both parts of the island, accompanied by signs of a new civic vitality. It has been a pain-filled transition, more protracted than many had allowed for. Under the terms of the Good Friday Agreement (1998), the new constitutional arrangements seemed set to transform the political scene. Yet, the power-sharing Assembly was stood down on three occasions, and the Civic Forum prorogued in tandem. Dissident or criminal factions inside the paramilitary worlds continued to impose control and inflict lethal attack. Prisoners have been released on remand; although accepted by many as intrinsic to the conflict transformation process, this action remains a scandal to some. Others are equally outraged at revelations of police collusion, institutional cover-up and the whole murky sub-culture of double agents and informers. The movement from violence to peace is staccato, demanding risk and a less than rigorous application of normal retributive justice. For many victims and survivors, the whole package amounts to a bitter pill. As with any society emerging from prolonged violent conflict, there is no innocent place from which to start. Even where political and religious voices urge a letting go to political and cultural compromise, they are often ill at ease with the asymmetry between mercy and truth, loath to allow the demand of

---

4 Neil Latimer and Patrick O'Kane from a Unionist and Nationalist background respectively.
5 A responding echo was found when the Clonard Monastery community invited this Non-Subscribing Minister and his team to beautify with flowers the shrine of its famous icon in honour of Our Lady of Perpetual Help. The artistry of these unlikely flower arrangers, crossing the grain of their own Protestant tradition in solidarity with their Catholic sisters and brothers celebrating a Marian festival, moved people to persevere in the prophetic call of reconciliation. The aesthetic, too, has its prophetic moment.
6 See Lesley E. Carroll, 'Divided Loyalties: A Reconciling Ethic for Churches in Northern Ireland', (doctoral thesis), Dublin, Trinity College Dublin, 2005: chapter 5, 4.5 for a contextual discussion of reconciliation.

justice to be swallowed up by the cause of peace.[7] And, yet, if all are to made new in Christ, no less is demanded.

Nicholas Lash, might have had Northern Ireland in mind as he grappled with such paradox and dilemma:

> Our peace is God's desire. In thus acknowledging God's promised peace to be our destiny, are we to set our hearts on harmony, or on the healing of our present ills? On acceptance of the circumstances in which we find ourselves, or on resistance to injustice? Thus abstractly formulated, the questions are, of course, unreal. Discernment of the different ways in which the stern and simultaneous requirements of peace and justice are configured requires – in each new set of circumstances – a fresh consideration, fresh decision, different enactment.[8]

Lash's insistence on the necessary discernment of each situation and context lends weight to the argument that any doctrinaire or exclusivist assertion of the prophetic stance will keep the way closed to deep reconciliation and healing. For, in a deeply divided society, a religious emphasis on prophetic righteousness or on God's vindication and intervention, all too easily assumes a self-styled 'chosenness'. Claims of a 'God on our side', who will deliver us (but not them), risk re-inscribing the institutionalized designs of what Terence McCaughey trenchantly criticizes as 'our national sacred histories.'[9]

It was McCaughey, who, in a penetrating analysis of the Irish conflict, adduced the typology of Prophet-Priest-Sage as a threefold prism that brought together a new focus on contested readings of Irish history, shrewd political analysis and a radical theological vision. He argued strongly that the churches in Ireland needed to reclaim the prophetic as the primary focus of their mission.

However, the conflict is now ended, the context is different and, so, we must read the signs of the times anew. More than a decade into the 'Peace Process' and re-established power sharing, it is worth re-visiting this threefold paradigm of Prophet, Priest and Sage, to see if it can still yield some spiritual vision or social reorientation for a time of transition and newness. Can Christians still find in this stream of the tradition some contemporary resonance? Will it still stand, in the words of Edward Farley, as a primordial or sacred 'word of power'?[10] Will it still offer a hope of transformation, or serve to liberate a fresh theological imagination and social energy for justice, reconciliation,

---

7 John Paul Lederach, *Building Peace: Sustainable Reconciliation in Divided Societies*, Washington DC, United States Institute of Peace, 1997: 28-31.
8 Nicholas Lash, *The Beginning and End of Religion*, Cambridge, Cambridge University, 1996: 44-45. For an analogous Northern Ireland perspective, see Carroll, *Divided Loyalties*: churches in Northern Ireland are challenged to resist historical patterns of arrogance and separation and to discern and enact new ethical choices that sustain reconciliation (chapter 5, 5.3).
9 Terence McCaughey, *Memory and Redemption: Church, Politics and Prophetic Theology in Ireland*, Dublin, Gill and Macmillan, 1993: 3. McCaughey, drawing on Jacob Neusner's exposition of the Prophet, Priest, King paradigm, mounts a perspicuous argument that the churches, having for many decades over-identified with the roles of priest and sage, had grown comfortable with their exclusive inside stories, cultic politics and sectarian power. He leaves little doubt as to the accuracy of his judgement that churches needed to recover their prophetic vocation of justice and solidarity with the poor (3-9, 130-139 and *passim*). One can, too, equally argue that undistorted ecclesial expression of the wisdom and priestly roles – emphasizing mutual hospitality, healing and reconciling – were equally required.
10 See Edward Farley, *Deep Symbols: Their Postmodern Effacement and Reclamation*, Harrisburg PA, Trinity Press International, 1996: 13-28. Deep religious symbols of the community of faith are critically threatened by postmodern 'cultural transition, decline and alienation from the interhuman' (17).

mercy and truth? In enlisting this notion of a sacred word of power, we venture that this threefold symbolization should remain necessarily threefold and interrelational, and that, in the transition towards an inclusive, open future, it is perhaps the way of the Sage offers the most promising starting point.

Farley reminds us convincingly that ancient symbols written on the human heart operate across time and through the echoes of memory as 'words of power', although they need to be delivered from the ensnarement of corruption and routine. Reclaimed and pondered anew, a word of power is still capable of addressing the faith community in its shifting, concrete condition, once more making God's holy mystery immanent and irresistible. Such a word bears the trace of God's fidelity, and keeps calling us back to the irreducible, universal and interhuman obligation towards the vulnerable other. Here, hope is released, with energy and in new embodiment. We claim that, as with Farley's persistent examples – justice, covenant, tradition, law, the prophet, wisdom[11] – the perduring *interrelated* symbolization of Prophet, Priest and Sage is a 'primordial word of power' that still invites, confronts and obliges us to transcendence and responsibility.

This classical, yet dynamically construed, typology enables us to hold in creative tension disparate or even contesting social and ecclesiological perspectives and challenges, accommodating the 'thickets' of detail, while affording a definite 'view' of the whole landscape (to borrow from John Henry Newman). Thus, the Prophet, Priest, Sage is an open triptych where each outlook can be held synoptically, even when only one comes into focus, and also allows for interactive dynamics within a shifting socio-political scene.[12]

In seeking for the roots of this 'sacred word of power', Jacob Neusner's analysis is pertinent and illuminating. Neusner demonstrates that these perspectives operated within the Judaean self-understanding, to shape the historic imagination, social organization and 'ideal types of piety'[13] and were appropriated as such by both Rabbinic Judaism and the early Christian Church according to the different messianic frameworks of each, and in ways adaptable to each's contexts and needs.[14]

Thus, the Priestly role, symbolized by the altar, and the Sage figure symbolized by the Torah Scroll intertwined, each inclining to the inner world imbued with a sense of the eternal. In the priestly understanding, eternity was made visible in the changeless cultic ritual with its manifestation of God's transcendent mystery and immanent purpose. In the Wisdom tradition, the eternal is manifest in the constant return of nature's cycles and the handing on of wisdom, generation by generation, in homes, on the land and in the marketplace. Wisdom is distilled and shared in human experiences of loss, tragedy and victory, and in the naming of blessings, thus generating a sense of universality, continuity and heritage.[15]

---

11 Farley, *Deep Symbols*: 29, 79 and *passim*.
12 Neusner in teasing out this threefold symbolic expression, takes account of distinctive preferences, roles and choices, yet insists that they were not mutually exclusive – 'never pure and unalloyed', see his 'Three Types of Judaism in the Age of Jesus', in *Judaism in the Beginning of Christianity*, London, SPCK, 1984: 36.
13 Jesus was portrayed variously as Prophet-Messiah, perfect High Priest, and Rabbi or teacher in the Wisdom tradition, thus drawing together in his life these three ancient and interacting motifs. After the fall of the Second Temple, Judaism, setting out to recast itself in a dramatically new era of Diaspora, showed itself capable of 'an unprecedented rereading of established symbols in fresh and striking ways', in Neusner, *Judaism*: 36.
14 Neusner, *Judaism*: 37.
15 Proverbs 10-30 represents a richly variegated corpus of this early, basically conservative wisdom tradition. Other texts suggest perspectives more philosophically complex, and the possible

This kind of 'meta-historical' approach is counter-balanced in a third self-expression – that of the Prophet and the 'historic-messianic way',[16] outward, concerned with historic events, especially those mediating convictions of being elected and set apart. In this prophetic conception, Israel saw its God as the Lord of history and understood itself as 'living out a destiny of its own.'[17] Of course, ideological pressures refashion history and memory, as historiography reveals, and archetypal symbols, deployed in the re-moulding of tradition, regulate power or demarcate zones of influence.[18] Amid the instabilities of war or political transition, roles realign and are reinvented. In such manner, at critical junctures, the idea of the Messiah was variously portrayed, whether according to the pattern of prophetic activity, royal influence, or priestly holiness.

The elision of Sage and King has been highlighted by others too; in the Second Temple era, there was a diarchy of priesthood and kingship (and of priestly monarchy), where, for the most part, power was shared, though with priesthood in the superior position.[19] David Goodblatt demonstrates the official practice of reading back along a single axis to biblical (or extra-biblical sources), as, e.g., to the diarchy of Moses and Aaron in the Pentateuch,[20] or to Ezekiel's programme wherein leadership was shared between a Davidic prince and a high priest.[21] By similar logic of legitimization, New Testament writers and redactors portrayed Jesus in his teaching, ministry, death and resurrection, as personally centralizing the symbolic activities and structures of prophet, priest and sage in an archetypal way.[22] In such ways, religious groups laid claim to continuity with what went before and radically revised religious meaning to draw forth new vision and a sustaining construction of history.

---

integration of a cosmopolitan moral outlook in a life contemplatively attuned to 'the fear of the Lord' (e.g., Proverbs 1-9 and Wisdom 1:1-11:1). See Raymond E. Brown S.S., Joseph A. Fitzmeyer S.J., and Roland E. Murphy O.Carm. (eds.), *The New Jerome Biblical Commentary*, London, Chapman, 1990: 510-513; also, Claus Westermann, *Roots of Wisdom*, Louisville, John Knox, 1995; and John J. Collins, *Jewish Wisdom in the Hellenistic Age*, Edinburgh, T&T Clark, 1997. Wisdom theology is creation theology (Collins, *Jewish Wisdom*: 3), and there are similarities and parallels with other ancient near-Eastern writings.

16 Neusner, *Judaism*: 40.
17 Neusner, *Judaism*: 43.
18 Neusner, *Judaism*: 36ff.
19 David Goodblatt, *The Monarchical Principle: Studies in the Jewish Self-Government in Antiquity*, Tübingen, Mohr Siebeck, 2005: 57, 78; chapter 2 is entitled, 'The Ideology of Priestly Monarchy', see 30-56.
20 Goodblatt, *The Monarchical Principle*: 58ff.
21 Goodblatt, *The Monarchical Principle*: 61: thus, the inter-testamental Book of Jubilees sees a diarchy of a descendent of Levi and a descendant of Judah, i.e., a priest and a Davidic prince – wherein the priest is superior (31:13). Different revisions of these symbols would come into play after the Second Temple's fall, with arguments for governance by a council advanced to meet the radical new challenge to religious and cultural unity, to sustaining a shared vision, in this era of disaster and Diaspora (124-130). In ideological terms, the pressure was to create solid historical provenance, not for the supremacy of the high priests, but for a council (80); but, it was a theological constant, seeking a form of governance that would best ensure faithfulness to God's purposes.
22 See Oscar Cullmann, *The Christology of the New Testament*, London, SCM, 1959: 196, and *passim*; also, Hans Ruedi Weber, *Living in the Image of Christ: The Laity in Ministry*, Geneva, WCC, 1986. These and other titles are traced to their biblical roots according to shifting emphases and interpretations, and with interconnected symbolic aspects of the life and ministry of Jesus.

Ricoeur's notion, 'le symbole donne à penser', is seen to operate intensely in such contexts of disintegration and the search for new integration. People live by the deep structure of myth and ritual. The symbolic life informs the collective psyche in time of political and religious transition and offers bearings for the future. Just as symbols tend to wrestle for dominance or to constellate around convenient alliances, so in time of external dislocation, people re-secure their self-understanding by asserting symbolic continuity, even as they seek to negotiate new dimensions of meaning and orientation into the strange and new.[23] We have already noted how the prophetic prism lent cogency to McCaughey's critique of the conventional or corrupted worlds of Irish politics and religion, including the cultic betrayal of transcendent power among the churches' priestly caste. Against this, the author projected a radical view of the sovereignty of God and of Jesus's prophetic action in laying down his life for others.

As Ireland now finds itself in a different place, so too do the churches.[24] Old challenges remain, whether in endemic sectarianism or in widening economic disparity. With peace come new challenges, including unhealed hurt and grievance, with the seeming difficulty of religious and political leaders to deal with the past and contribute imaginatively to the building of an alternative future. It is timely for communities to contemplate the prophetic challenge of reconciliation and to cooperate and pool their resources of human and spiritual wisdom as we seek renewal for an estranged society. Towards this one can turn once more and listen for God's word of power that comes to us in the personae of Prophet, Priest and Sage, whether in primordial stories or unsuspected contemporary embodiment. God's word still travels down the centuries, calling our attention to the new poor, via the ancient lament of Jeremiah, asking us to keep Sabbath and sing praise to God's undiminished glory, inviting us to seek and share God's wisdom in the places wherever, in Patrick Kavanagh's words, 'life pours ordinary plenty'. In our world at once full of sin and full of grace human minds and hearts listen and respond according to different symbols, roles and aspirations. And through such words of power God addresses our longing for consolation and may censure us for our obstinate clinging to outworn or corrupt forms of being church, or for closing our hearts against stranger and outsider.

While proposing that each of these respective and interrelated contributions offers distinct and varied possibilities for our prayer or action, perhaps now, it is in giving hermeneutical priority to the way of the Sage, that we can find our best hope of a dynamic realignment of all three modes of religious insight and ethical action. Taking a new starting point in the way of wisdom, with its emphasis on inclusiveness, participation and creativity, ways can be found to break the Gordian knot of one-way historical interpretation, and to challenge the theological legitimacy of exclusive arrangements of power and the political hegemony of one group. The Wisdom tradition opens

---

23 Paul Ricoeur, 'The Hermeneutics of Symbols and Philosophical Reflection', in Charles E. Reagan and David Stewart (eds.), *The Philosophy of Paul Ricoeur*, Boston, Beacon, 1978: 37-39.
24 The revelations in the 1990s of child sexual abuse by clergy, followed by denial and cover-up, has made for embarrassment and a more visible humility in the Roman catholic Church. In Protestant churches, one detects an analogously sobering effect arising from such scenes of violent stand-off as those at Drumcree Church. Such events spotlighted the institutional complicity of Protestantism in partisan politics and the need to withdraw religious legitimisations of violence. Additionally, churches in Ireland also find their position of influence shadowed by the belated de-centring impact of secular modernity and by the eroding of institutional authority and the fragmenting of community loyalty associated with 'post-modernity'.

up diverse and integrative ways of relating that are illuminated by a theological emphasis on the universality of God's love, on the unity of God's creative and saving purpose and on the sanctifying power of the Holy Spirit at play in the world and forever inviting human cooperation and creativity.

Likewise, a wisdom focus draws our attention to Jesus's Parables: showing that God's ways are not ours and that God's grace is alive not alone among the elect, since Wisdom raises up children in every generation. It will also ask us to reconsider those gospel accounts which portray Jesus as called – sometimes, against tradition and hesitantly – to transgress the boundaries of chosenness, to cross over to marginal places where he will meet and converse with erstwhile strangers and enemies, and be drawn by them into intercultural encounter and more profound apprehensions of his divine mission on earth (e.g., Mark 7: 24-30; Luke 8: 22ff.; John 4).

While objections may already be forming that the pattern of wisdom too easily blends and blurs into the landscape of the secular and risks losing the sharp counter-cultural edge to the message of salvation, it should be remembered that the roots of the biblical tradition of the Sage are variegated. Wisdom comes in many guises and tones – e.g., in Proverbs and Wisdom, in the judgements of King Solomon, or in the intellectual wrestling of Job – yet, it forms a recognizable pattern of a natural wisdom arising from 'self-revelation of creation, [which] however, is in no way opposed to divine revelation.'[25] Something of this restless, questing dynamic in wisdom was obviously brought to the fore by one feminist theologian in her description of Jesus in the paradoxical compound terms, 'Miriam's Child; Sophia's Prophet.'[26] In such a dynamic impulse towards newness the wisdom tradition can be brought into creative dialogue with Ireland's changing social context, contradictory, diverse, ambiguous.

As Ireland crosses the threshold of peace, the call is for a 'win-win', not a 'win-lose', solution. Slogans of 'No surrender!' from the pro-British Loyalist community, or of 'Tiocfaidh ár lá!' ('Our day will come!') from the pro-United Ireland-Republican community, may have had their day. The former looked back to a politicized theology of election as the cornerstone of its self-confidence; the latter fed memories of bitter defeat, cultivating a counter-vision where defeat will be defeated in a new dawn; the failed 1916 revolution of Irish Independence is not referred to as the Easter Rising by accident.[27] Thus, the respective communities have operated, in mutual deterrence, by a logic of selective memory and exclusionary hope where history is constructed as a linear trajectory of antagonistic reversals of destiny and supremacy.

Unfortunately, the dénouement – viewed from whichever side (each considering itself the marginalized minority) – inclines to stances that appropriate and distort the paradigm of the prophet in the midst of the oppressed: justice and vindication of the righteous is couched in the rhetoric of a great historic reversal. Now is not the time to assert a paradigm which too readily lends itself to reiterations that, in this contested space, and with motifs of prophetic overthrow of one regime for another, 'we' are God's chosen. Instead, there is a supreme need to build trust through symbolic expressions

---

25 Collins, *Jewish Wisdom*: 12.
26 Elisabeth Schüssler Fiorenza, *Jesus: Miriam's Child, Sophia's Prophet: Critical Issues in Feminist Christology*, London, SCM, 1995. Wisdom (in Hebrew ḥokmâ, and in Greek *sophia*) is feminine in gender and, in some texts (e.g., Proverbs 1-9, especially chapter 8), is portrayed in virtually divine terms, the first of God's works, and brought forth by God (*qānānî*), see Collins, *Jewish Wisdom*: 11.
27 John Marsden, *Redemption in Irish History*, Dublin, Dominican, 2005: 72.

which engender the vision of a shared future, open to relationship with the other, the possibility of reconciling histories and the healing of memories. Rights and responsibilities need to embrace, hope and history rhyme, if erstwhile enemies are to live peaceably.[28]

The 'royal priesthood', constituted at baptism, must find new symbolic and liturgical expression.[29] While for those, whose sufferings were rendered invisible by dominant political interests or in the sheer struggle to survive, healing seems far off still, transformation depends not alone on the dismantling of unjust systems and the securing of political agreement but also on the in-breaking of grace. Churches, in partnership with other groups, have their proper role to play in the collective shaping of sanctuary-like spaces; there, loss can be acknowledged and lamented and gestures of solidarity with others exchanged as we reach out to sustain those who confront the personal cost of peace. In such sacred spaces and in the mutual ministry of solidarity, those who have borne the brunt of loss will begin to find themselves acknowledged. The vanished trace of their loved ones can be re-integrated into a more inclusive new social narrative that may sustain them (and, indeed, the whole of society) on a journey of healing and reconciliation.[30] From the perspective of faith, Christians can trust that in Christ's New Creation, every tear will be wiped away, broken connections restored, and the mysterious reality of the living body of Christ in heaven and on earth once more be glimpsed and re-presented. In such symbolic action, Prophet, Priest and Sage work together, but the way of the Sage lends itself in a particularly appropriate way of embodying healing, shelter and reconstruction: 'Wisdom has built herself a house' (Proverbs 9:1).

One must, of course, be alert to the shadow side: the wisdom tradition, with its universal scope, and its valuing of home and neighbourliness and social cohesion, carries an abiding temptation to settle, to espouse the formula for keeping wheels turning, without troubling to discern for imbalances in the distribution of power, knowledge and wealth. At such times, the Prophetic voice must utter a word of admonition, perhaps denunciation. Wisdom is revealed in all her children (Luke 7:35). And the true sage is open to light from any quarter, including the illumination of critique. There is a necessary dialectic in tradition, and it is important not to rest content with the settled wisdom. Here is the paradox of wisdom, namely, a gift to be freely received and something that must be sought after tirelessly if her fullness is to be disclosed.

Divine Wisdom opens her treasures to all and wants others to share in her abundance. Wisdom makes herself known through contemplative presence to all creation, in a recovery of imagination and the capacity for symbol and story. This symbolic or sacramental knowledge is received rather than achieved, and disclosed through encounter with

---

28 See The Faith and Politics Group, *Doing Unto Others: Parity of Esteem in a Contested Space*, Belfast, 1997. John May has been a long-standing member of this interchurch, North-South group, which, *inter alia*, regularly produced and widely disseminated other such publications, which became catalysts of debate on pertinent matters of faith and politics.

29 See below, on the Priest.

30 The work of Healing through Remembering (www.healingthroughremembering.org) is notable for its commissioned research and its broad-based constituency and participative methodology. In June 2007, Peter Hain, then Secretary of State for Northern Ireland, appointed an independent Consultative Group on the Past, co-chaired by Lord Eames, Emeritus Archbishop of Armagh, and Denis Bradley, to consult widely and report within 18 months on how best to address the legacy of the past. They consulted with HTR representatives (23rd July 2007), who presented research-based ideas on dealing with the past, and discussed a range of options on truth recovery processes, an annual day of reflection, story-telling processes, commemoration, and ideas for a living memorial museum.

that which transcends us, opening us to the experience of the 'eternal' within and beyond time.[31] Abraham Heschel, tapping into this wisdom tradition, speaks of Sabbath as relating us to eternity rather than utility, as the experience of the ineffable in the midst of life.[32] He suggests here a unified vision of Prophet, Priest and Sage when he exclaims, 'The Sabbath is more than a day.... It is eternity within time, the spiritual underground of history.'[33] So, there is no implication here of blithe a-historicality; rather, of a larger apprehension of history.

This integrative understanding of time is suggestive and fruitful in the context of Ireland. Between the silencing of the guns and the blossoming of peace new questions arise: What is life after the fighting has stopped? Where are the sources for healing memories and reconciling histories, for encouraging forbearance and even forgiveness? Now that the plenipotentiaries having bargained and fought over the Agreement and finally signed up to it, with no shortage of claim to victory for their side, what kind of social and religious imagination is most apt to evoke a vision of community and sustained commitment to peace?

These are not new questions. From the dread and sinister days of tit-for-tat sectarian attack and assassination until now, there have been visible traces of that alternative 'maternal time', which share symbolic aspects of the Wisdom tradition. We refer here to the undercurrents of community activity generated by people, not in high positions of power, but working on the margins, close to the realities of suffering and loss, often in places of social degradation and political powerlessness. While we cannot fully explore the hermeneutical and theological significance of Wisdom as feminine and as a woman, this reality surely increases the potential for drawing out further analogues and implications of this symbolic 'maternal time' as distinct from the masculine constructions of history. The Irish context has attractive resonances, too, which can be correlated with discernible patterns of women's roles and spaces in peacebuilding.

These spaces have been inhabited 'incarnationally' by those who apprehend history in sapiential terms. Not an escape from it, this is history according to a different apprehension of the historic. The presumption must be probed of any ugly ditch dividing public and private. Also to be interrogated are such narrow perceptions as miss the political significance of symbolic movement in the socio-politico-cultural sphere, and the already activated potential of a broad and rich construal of the political. Such myopia is aptly challenged by Kristeva and other feminist accounts which urge the necessity of realigning the public and private realms in ways that subvert conventional gendered roles of women and men, with consequent impoverishment of all.[34]

Here, one must acknowledge the hundreds of women's groups, peace groups, community projects which have moved sideways of the locked historical structures. Rather than attempting to break into closed or embattled systems and follow the logic of linear history of winners and losers, these groups have conceived politics in terms of

---

31 Julia Kristeva echoes this, with her relational 'maternal time'; she develops this as a paradigm of non-violence, an alternative to all claims to one's own existence as total or totalizing. See her 'Women's Time', in Toril Moi (ed.), *A Kristeva Reader*, New York, Columbia University, 1986: 187-213: 210.
32 Abraham Heschel, *God in Search of Man: A Philosophy of Judaism,* New York, Harper TorchBooks, 1955: 350-351.
33 Heschel, *God in Search of Man*: 418-419.
34 Yvonne Galligan, Eilís Ward and Rick Wilford, (eds.), *Contesting Politics: Women in Ireland, North and South*, Boulder, Westview, 1999, esp. 169-184.

cooperation and co-responsibility within and between local spaces, and have been sceptical about claims of epoch-making events. They have been prophetic in affirming diversities and solidarity from below, setting store by the universal wisdom of gestures and stories that allow and sustain life within in a culture driven by violence and death, sustaining one another in cherishing life in its 'living-ness'.

Among such sapiential expressions, one can count the movement for civil rights, and the many women's groups who, in the early 1980s defiantly formed the Women's Information Network. Within their local contexts these women developed centres and multifarious projects which encouraged goals that affirmed life: they cooperated with alienated young people facilitating them to articulate their own needs; they devised community initiatives for childcare provision, neighbourhood regeneration, bereavement support, and study processes. On a monthly basis the network of groups met inside 'enemy territory' for an educational seminar, and an opportunity to share experience and information on issues of mutual concern. Contentious politics were off the agenda and there was no presumption of agreed ideas or push for consensus. These women could claim that never once over two decades, was a single meeting called off notwithstanding riots, strikes, burning vehicles, cancelled buses and warnings to stay at home. Latterly, the five McCartney women (four sisters and spouse of the murdered Robert McCartney) exposed paramilitary cover-up and shamed its panoply of power with their sheer staying-power.

One might name certain former paramilitary prisoners, like Billy Mitchell and Jackie Mc Mullan, one a Loyalist, the other a former Republican hunger striker who dedicated themselves to the healing of communities, one through his work with young offenders in pioneering restorative justice projects, the other focussing on a project towards recognition of victims-survivors from whatever quarter and inclusive processes that address the legacy of the past. Still others, informally and unofficially, documented abuses, lobbied for judicial reform or simply enabled people from different sides to meet and grow in knowledge of one another's traditions in a safe space. So many seeds sown within history's cracks. True to the spirit of the wisdom tradition, in standing back from or delving beneath the drawn lines, these were prophetic agents who acted in ways that proved that it was possible to transform the prevailing political logic of the zero sum game – of 'their gain as our loss' – and filled out the lines of a new social vision that actualized the potential of consociational politics in Ireland.[35]

Many of these individuals and groups are inspired by their religious faith, but many operate according to a civic ethic and under lay leadership. Besides moving to deconstruct the narrow ground of inherited systems of exclusion, they have also been committed to restructure and enrich the symbolic space in expressions of solidarity, justice and equality. In this endeavour they have retrieved a place for bodily and emotional experience, reinvigorating values rooted in home and community and branching out in actions of social justice and reconciliation, realms marginal to normal politics. Those repetitions of birth and death, joys and losses; routines marked by visiting imprisoned relatives or caring

---

35 Arend Lijphart coined this term in the Canadian context, to describe the sharing of power between different sectors in society conjoined by citizenship but divided by, e.g., ethnicity, religion, language. Some rights, aimed at a more equitable balance of representation, are accorded to communities rather than to individuals, resulting in group-differentiated, rather than individually-based citizenship, as a means of ethno-cultural accommodation. The influence of this model on the Good Friday Agreement has been acknowledged, see Lijphart, 'Cultural Diversity and Political Integration', in *Canadian Journal of Political Science* VI,1 (March 1971): 1-14.

for housebound neighbours, daily struggles to survive poverty, trauma or depression can be seen as sacramental: signs of faith, hope and love that point beyond themselves and that unite human spirits in every age and place. Also, symbolic protests, as for example, demanding that the bodies of the 'disappeared' be restored, sustain courage and fire resolve, whether in Argentina or Ireland. They bear witness that such 'maternal' dedication is not without its political impact and, in transcending normal politics, contributes to the transformation of political systems. One example of impact and transformation, as a catalyst *within* the system, was the Women's Coalition: it embodied a unique capacity to work across the ancestral lines of politics and history. Operating as a party committed to equality and inclusion, and, via a justly acclaimed mediating role in deadlocked peace negotiations, they were a living verification that shrewd, yet non-adversarial, strategy has a necessary role inside politics.[36]

Long overdue, then, is a reassessment of the idea of the political, the sphere of the political and the role of women in the public sphere. Further, this argues for revising the view that wisdom (the concern of the Sage) is confined to cosmic repetitions, and a passive complacency in the givens of social role and the established dispositions of power. Living in receptiveness to the rhythm of 'maternal time' in no way implies passivity in face of the scale of human suffering, but is apt rather to empower or awaken hope for transformation and sustainment in times of failure. As 'maternal time' expresses a wisdom that cuts across differences of language, tribe and nation, in the way of the Sage, the personal and the political intersect and re-energize moral purpose and direction.

Many, not few, were those who discovered 'other ways of regulating difference', creating diagonal exchange and encounter across cultural and denominational boundaries. Such people, far from withdrawing from life and history, have attested from within themselves that each has the potential to be both victim and victimizer. It is through such acknowledgement that the cycle of violence is interrupted, 'the habitual and increasingly explicit attempt to fabricate a scapegoat victim' as the basis of society.[37] Beginning with resistance against a totalizing of one's own group identity, a transformational language of respect for otherness and difference has emerged that, simultaneously, stretches the capacity for communication and interrelationship in a world of plurality and ambiguity.

Theologically, this sapiential outlook seeks out the wisdom of others and the collective vision that transcends every individual project. Wisdom lifts the vision to a wider horizon of significance, under which the round of domestic, parochial or communal conventions are played out, inviting the eye to take in both wider responsibilities and the strangers in our midst, as well as the complexity of interplay between peace and justice that God desires for everyone and for the whole creation (Isaiah 49).

In what has been explored thus far, attention has been focussed mainly through the dual and often correlated prism of Prophet and Sage, noting the habitual tendency of construing their roles in an oppositional pattern. It is timely now to reflect on the third *persona*, Priest, and the way it continues to operate in the collective Christian imagination as a 'sacred word of power', irrespective of denominational difference, the office of priest, or the priesthood of all baptized believers.

---

36 It failed graciously, but its legacy remains via its exemplary impact on other parties and in the public sphere; its leader, Professor Monica McWilliams, is now Chief Commissioner of the Human Rights Commission, NI; May Blood, another founding member, plays an active role in the UK House of Lords. See Kate Fearon, *Women's Work: The Story of the Northern Ireland Women's Coalition*, Belfast, Blackstaff, 1999.
37 Kristeva, 'Women's Time': 210.

'Priest' is an intensely symbolic word of power.[38] Yet, the potential for retrieving, through the role or mission of the Priest symbol, a meaningful pattern for spiritual or social orientation might seem unpromising. There are many *actual, particular and recognizable* priests and ministers interacting with us; this may make it more difficult to touch the symbolic archetype of the Priest in the soul's reservoir, and allow it to function as a sacred word of power. Yet, the symbol does retain a power to evoke images and echoes in the inner mind: of holiness, mediation between earth and heaven, intercessory prayer, leadership of worship, sacrificial offering, rites of initiation, reconciliation, marriage, anointing the sick, pastoral care of the dying and bereaved. Doubtless, some of these attributes will be central or peripheral in a different context, acting to resonate or repel. But, to reflect on the significance of the priestly as affording a perspective and compass in the contemporary landscape of peace and peacebuilding in Ireland, is to draw out of our storehouse things both new and old and to rediscover windows onto the world of symbol, story and ritual, not all embodied in particular individuals but rather as relating to patterns of potential meaning, belonging and responsibility. We will focus on but a few aspects relevant for the healing of society.

In an age where rituals without depth tumble out according to the dictates and mind-change of the celebrity industry, the care of the soul calls attention to the importance of deep symbols and meditative practice in the search for wholeness. Throughout the conflict, many bereaved people have attested to finding a mysterious inner strength in the simple act of being alongside others in liturgical celebrations of remembering and mourning. In such a ritual space, one's own story of personal grief finds its place and meaning within a larger religious narrative of creation or salvation. The beauty of creation, cut off by a traumatic loss, can be recovered as a source of healing and creativity, as for example, through the ritual of making a memorial garden or a resurrection garden, where once more (as in John 21) tears are shed; the beloved is strangely re-encountered, and one is personally addressed in a Word that gives tentative or radical new direction for life. Being able to come together in singing a Psalm of Lament, in a liturgical setting or sensitively devised inclusive commemoration, will for some mean the first breaking of the mute pain of trauma, and for others their first shared commemorative act. Recently, as the wider community was invited by *Healing through Remembering* to reflect on the possibility of a National Day of Reflection, and, as initial step, to participate in a Day of *Private* Reflection, there was a shared sense that the jaded discourse of death and memorial could be infused with a more receptive way of thinking and speaking about the mystery of life and the paradox of loss, or about the possibility of letting go to peace, and in this process, experience ourselves as 'creators' rather than remain forever victims.[39]

The teaching about creation in terms of divine-human collaboration and responsibility is illuminated by insights from the Talmudic tradition. A particular reading of Genesis 2:3 invites us to see ourselves as co-creators or co-workers: It reads, 'God rested from all his work that God had created to make.' The verb here – *la'asoth* (to make) is anomalous, hinting that God's creation remains to be shaped yet further by humanity (particularly, by the Rabbis). There is also an overtone of the midrashic teaching of the *tikkun olam* (the mending of the world), whereby human creatures are called to cooperate with the Creator

---

38 One discerns the analogy with Kristeva's exposition of 'eternal' or 'monumental' time, see Kristeva, 'Women's Time': 189f.
39 See Dorothee Sölle, *Suffering*, Philadelphia, Fortress, 1975: 70-71; and her *Theology for Sceptics*, London, Mowbray, 1995: 79.

in this process of mending or healing. Both the Talmudic and the Christian traditions propose that we are *shutafim* or 'partners' in God's creative plan. In this religious light the role of peacebuilding becomes a kind of priestly vocation of dealing with the past, clearing up the mess and destruction, binding up wounds and clearing spaces where we can together 'continue to make', and in the power of the Spirit cooperate in the healing of the world. Remembering is key to this process, remembering all who have *passed*, through our world and shared it, thus preventing them from being consigned to *the past*; in safe, structured spaces symbol and gesture give voice to the silence.

Churches, too, are beginning to reflect on the part they can play in the wider painful task of dealing with the past. There is yet no consensus on whether a form of Truth and Reconciliation Commission would offer the best way forward, though some churches and Christian leaders have moved in favour of a forum for victims and survivors. Thus, for example, the Presbyterian Church has taken some modest but significant steps in opening up a space where the past can at least be spoken of. In his Moderatorial year, 2005-2006, the Right Rev. Dr. Harry Uprichard invited those who have been victims of the Troubles who are Presbyterians living within the Presbyteries of Armagh, Newry and Tyrone, to formally meet with him and to freely bring up any issue of concern for them.[40] This initiative may be looked upon as a pre-reconciliation process or as making a contribution to a larger process of reconciliation.[41]

Churches and faith communities can contribute by exercising this priestly call of attending to processes of remembering and healing, and, alongside others – poets, artists, music-makers – who have been generous and sensitive in helping wounded people to give symbolic expression to their anger or hurt, when conventional language failed. It is one aspect of the priestly role: to draw everyone into the ritual so that they can participate in the commemoration out of their particular gift and calling, whether in listening, speaking, giving a holy offering, exchanging peace, or 'making music to God the most high'. In Ireland certain poets have historically played something of a symbolic high priestly role. Refusing the slogan and false cant, they used their gift to shape a sacramental language adequate to the *lacrimae rerum*, or to marvel at quiet human fidelities, or to signal the breaking in of transcendence from within or beyond.

The priestly perspective also provides for reconnecting memory and hope, particularly, as attention to victims and survivors is finally being acknowledged as a social imperative, together with the search for ways of remembering that will help healing, enable diversities to come into dialogue and promote education in respect and inclusiveness. Remembering rightly and 'co-remembering' can also prevent the repeating of affliction by loosening the attachment to a singular or totalizing identity. One apposite biblical perspective on priesthood reminds us that acts of re-membering take on a cleansing and atoning aspect (at-one-ment) easing a way to reintegration and social renewal (e.g., Numbers 5:2-8; Luke 17:11-19). Although charged to care for the things of God, the priestly role also extends to the margins of the sacred and temporal, and those in-between spaces between what is traditionally normative or traditionally unacceptable. Is there a symbolic hint of this when

---

[40] This process was continued in the following year by the then Moderator, Dr. David Clarke, and may continue during 2007-2008.

[41] For an examination of the purpose, nature and value of a Forum for Victims-Survivors within the perspective of Christian reconciliation, see Geraldine Smyth, 'A Habitable Grief: Forgiveness and Reconciliation for a People Divided'. in *Milltown Studies (Essays in Honour of Michael Hurley S.J.)* 53 (Summer 2004): 94-130.

Luke situates the story of Jesus's cure of the ten lepers in some unspecified region 'on the way to Jerusalem' (the place of his suffering and death) and 'between Samaria and Galilee' (Luke 17:11)? And is there not the ecclesiological implication that the Church's mission, patterned on Christ's, cannot be content to function efficiently or self-sufficiently within its own specific sphere, but must also make the wider world its parish (*paroikos* or 'home away from home')?

Here, where priestly influence is no longer determined by old stratifications and hierarchies, and where such inherited authority systems can no longer pretend to claim the whole of people's lives, there are still in-between places where the Holy Spirit is alive and active and where some still welcome partnership with religious actors and representatives. And, among those working in these in-between spaces can be found some who retain a sense of the priestly paradigm in terms of such a 'go-between' persona[42] and who still harbour a hope that church representatives may utter a transforming word of power or comfort in due season. The promise of the 'unfailing word' echoes down the centuries from the Letter to the Hebrews portraying both Christ in terms of the perfect high priest and this ideal in terms of one who was himself subject to weakness yet able to sympathize with us in our weakness, one who does not presume to take the priestly honour on himself but only when called by God, one who offers up to God loud prayers and silent tears and who is heard because of his reverent submission (Hebrews 4:14-5:10). Interestingly, the words which immediately precede these speak in the grammar of God's penetrating Wisdom and of God's Word in its prophetic power to 'judge the thoughts and intention of the heart ...before whom no creature is hidden...' (Hebrews 3:12-13). Here, in individual distinctiveness and joint interplay, is illustrated a dramatic *perichoresis* of Prophet, Priest, and Sage.

Thus, we can justifiably attest to a threefold 'fusion of horizons'[43] and a dance-like drama of Sage, Prophet and Priest which, re-presenting primordial models of the divine imagination, give roots and wings to the pilgrim church. Grounded again in this threefold word of power, we may indeed look for a new epiphany in the expressions of Sage, Prophet and Priest, manifesting the varied and unitive dynamic of God's grace in Christ. In the revelation and calling forth of resources in the community after the pattern of Christ's life and mission, we may begin to taste the first fruits of a new order. Through a sapiential imagination, the religious and theological imagination in Ireland may undergo an unimagined transformation, capable of discerning, in Prophet, Priest and Sage, a deeper dispensation of the divine economy, disclosing a New Creation in which all are called to participate, according to their unique call and charism, in the mending of the world.

Our suggestion, that the ancient symbol structure of Prophet, Priest, Sage still finds resonance and expression in contemporary Christianity in Ireland, fits well into other analyses of Northern Ireland. While demonstrating that the respective potential of each role is strengthened in and through the changing patterns and synergies between them, and keeps open an always larger, more unified horizon, we proposed that, today, the way of

---

42 See John V. Taylor, *The Go-Between God: The Holy Spirit and the Christian Mission*, Oxford, Oxford University, 1979. For a more contextual exploration of the Irish churches' role in the middle ground, see Geraldine Smyth, 'In the Middle Ground and Meantime: A Call to the Churches in Northern Ireland to Find themselves on the Edge', in James P. Mackey and Enda McDonagh (eds.), *Religion and Politics in Ireland at the Turn of the Millennium*, Dublin, Columba, 2003: 84-106, esp. 101-106.

43 Hans-Georg Gadamer, *Truth and Method*, translated by Joel Weinsheimer and Donald G. Marshall, London and New York, Continuum, 2004 [1975]: 367.

the Sage offers the most apt hermeneutical key for the ministry of peacebuilding and for those Christians who would contribute out of their own living tradition, within the field of faith and politics, and in the go-between relationships of church and world. Many and various are the possibilities for all to bring to the task their traditions, insights, talents, expertise and creativity. Here, by way of grounding and corroborating these claims, we will highlight some developing insights of John Paul Lederach, who draws upon his Mennonite tradition and on the concepts and tools of conflict analysis and on his extensive global experience.[44] The argumentation already presented will corroborate, and in certain respects, may amplify his conceptual and symbolic frames of reference.

Lederach forges together insights from a number of scientific sources, premised on a multi-levelled and wide-ranging analysis of conflict.[45] His analysis of divided societies focuses the need for this while keeping in view the aims of peace, transformation of conflict and sustainability over time. It is justifiably an integrated model[46] with reconciliation as its goal; for, reconciliation is not limited to the period of post-settlement restoration, but provides 'a focus and a locus appropriate to every stage of peacebuilding and [is] instrumental in reframing the conflict and the energies driving the conflict.'[47] Lederach's framework, worked out with local thinkers and NGO activists, was a catalyst for more integrative, time-framed approaches that helped to mobilize and expand influences towards systemic change.[48]

Yet, such painstaking mapping must needs correlate with something akin to wisdom and spiritual call. At this crucial time in Ireland, we need seers, poets, sages. We welcome Lederach's recent voicing of the need for a more positive beginning point than that of overcoming conflict. He asserts that system and strategy alone will not bring peace, for peacebuilding must go beyond technique and craft, which can be mastered and applied. He speaks of 'the art and soul of building peace',[49] avowing the importance of 'the capacity to generate, mobilize, and build the moral imagination'.[50] He identifies four capacities which need to be mobilized and held together in the building of peace:

---

44 Few better than Lederach have mapped the who and what of peacebuilding from a Christian perspective and systematically, around the concept of understanding conflict and peacebuilding as intrinsically related. He first proposes 'that conflict be understood analytically as a progression that moves through different stages'. Then he presents peacebuilding as 'a process made up of a multiplicity of interdependent roles, functions and activities', see Lederach, *Building Peace*: 71: 'the goal of peacebuilding is to create and sustain transformation and the move toward restructured relationships.'

45 Such analysis must attend to different levels, actors, systems and time-frames, embracing preventative diplomacy, negotiation of ceasefires, mediation that enables movement from violent to non-violent confrontation, dealing with crisis, phased attention to material causes of the conflict, disarmament, education, conflict resolution, and the articulation and achievement of middle and long term goals, strategic planning and evaluation (63ff.).

46 Lederach, *Building Peace*: 73-85.

47 Lederach, *Building Peace*: 151.

48 Here the work of Mediation Northern Ireland and The Future Ways programmes (University of Ulster) deserve high praise. Their initiatives addressed the resolving of short-term crisis and the development of sustainable programmes of peacebuilding – within fractured communities, on volatile interfaces and through the institutionalizing of equity, diversity and interdependence in the public services and civic sectors.

49 Jean Paul Lederach, *The Moral Imagination: the Art and Soul of Building Peace*, Oxford, Oxford University, 2005.

50 Lederach, *The Moral Imagination*: 5.

> Stated simply, the moral imagination requires the capacity to imagine ourselves in a web of relationships that includes our enemies; the ability to sustain a paradoxical curiosity that embraces complexity without reliance on dualistic polarity; the fundamental belief in and pursuit of the creative act; and the acceptance of the inherent risk of stepping into the mystery of the unknown that lies beyond the far to familiar landscape of violence.[51]

The imaginary of peace invites us to think and act as if the new were possible, as if attending to the social web of relationship were worth whatever risk. It enables us to venture beyond the familiar landscape – of violence and the constraints of stereotype and social dualism – to discover what needs our undivided attention, asking us 'to look at relationships through the lenses of social crossroads, connections, and interdependence'.[52]

These insights encourage peacebuilders to create a new geography, bridging hitherto disconnected locations and linking up likeminded moderates and those with different perspectives. There is a need to support new hubs of relationship and interaction, spaces 'that create multiple, coordinated and independent connections that build strength.'[53] The risk is matched, however, by the firm conviction that, beneath any inherited ideology of separateness, people of every shade and on every side are addressing the same need for human flourishing, whether in the struggle against isolation and suffering or establishing platforms that sustain interaction and generate new ways of adapting to a dramatically changing context:

> We have, in essence, thought too much about 'process management' and 'solution generation' and too little about social spaces and the nature of interdependent and strategic relationships. This is the key role of moral imagination: to envision the canvas that makes visible the relational spaces and the web of life where social change is located.[54]

The motifs of 'life' and 'relationship', rather than linear ones of 'peak moments' and the events of high-profile actors, claim attention in this new season. Thus, we see Lederach shift his language mode: he questions the aptness of 'critical mass' as a metaphor for social change,[55] and proposes the alternative of 'critical yeast', which he develops into an extended metaphor of bread-making to indicate that it is the 'who', not the 'how many', that is the critical factor.[56] Flour kneaded with yeast, under correct conditions, becomes a change agent quite out of proportion to its smallness.[57] Once more, the argument undermines the vaunted ideal of highly positioned, heavy-duty agents as the key in generating change, and advances the *sine qua non* of mediative interaction, creative attention to social spaces, sensitive timing and the capacity to persevere.

Lederach cites his own examples,[58] but the evidence which we have already advanced makes a similar case. Yet, all such exemplars witness to the need for ordinary wisdom; the Sage moves in human affairs, often in quiet, and necessarily hidden and hub-like

---

51 Lederach, *The Moral Imagination*: 5.
52 Lederach, *The Moral Imagination*: 78.
53 Lederach, *The Moral Imagination*: 84-85.
54 Lederach, *The Moral Imagination*: 86.
55 Lederach, *The Moral Imagination*: 89ff. Modelled on nuclear fission, the idea of exponential change in society is thought of in predictable, linear terms, and as dependent on large numbers of people needing to be converted before change can happen.
56 Lederach, *The Moral Imagination*: 91.
57 Lederach, *The Moral Imagination*: 91-92.
58 Lederach, *The Moral Imagination*: 99.

ways, avoiding the spotlight, resisting the temptations of group competition, interchurch rivalry or the grand prophetic gesture.

Clearly, the complex work of reconciliation and peace must draw upon and encourage differentiated gifts, and operate at formal and informal levels, according to as rich a range of symbolic, conceptual, political and spiritual approaches as are available. Peace calls us all not to content ourselves with the ending of conflict or with negotiated settlements or even in the crafting of an infrastructure of human rights and equality. Peacebuilding requires: attention to the range of time-scales (both past and future); that we relate to the past in more inclusive ways through processes of reconciling and restoring; that, from the present pivotal point, we continue to build causeways to the future, living towards a vision, though in actual and symbolic steps that build trust and commitment to the ongoing renewal of spiritual vision and social virtues. As a journey into transformation, peace in Ireland calls for surrender of totalizing mindsets and acknowledgement of the cost of the troubles so that our losses can be grieved, ancient boundaries transgressed and imagination released for new relationship. In this, too, we are called to reach out in hospitality to the strangers from afar who now live alongside us – they may well have much to teach us about how to celebrate liberation in sharing their many traditions of forgiveness, reconciliation and restorative justice. A concluding word we leave to a respected teacher and Sage:

> The missionary reconciler must aim at nothing less than a positive new beginning based on a promise, a new covenant, not just between individuals but in certain circumstances between ethnic groups and social classes…not just facing the past but restoring community…Yet such reconciliation *is* happening, usually in local contexts such as Bougainville or Northern Ireland, but on such a scale that local reconciliation is already a significant political factor in the new global public sphere.[59]

How truly does John May's encouraging observation remind us that Wisdom is vindicated in all her children.

---

59 John D'Arcy May, 'The Space in Between': 85 (italics added).

Eugene Stockton
Truth of God

Peter Vardy[1] discusses the intense debate between the realist and anti-realist positions on truth, particularly from the time of Kant's *Critique of Pure Reason* (1781) up to the postmodernism of today. He comes down in favour of those who, like Kierkegaard, Wittgenstein and Vaclav Havel, staked their lives on the claims of truth, even at the risk of being proved false, and so 'live in the truth'. Stephen Buckle in his review of Vardy claims it is 'less of an answer to the realist/anti-realist conundrum than a changing of the subject'.[2] This may be so, but my impression is that the conundrum has reached an impasse, that, as with many deep debates, the intensity of argument has caused such a distortion of the terms that answers are no longer possible at that level.

Ordinary human beings have to get on with living. We have to take a commonsense view and accept what is given to us: reality is real and knowable, at least partially. Life is a kind of faith. As Vardy claims, 'faith is a risk; it is staking one's life on claims to truth that may be false'. My own thought is that:

a) there is reality outside and independent of myself because it often proves hurtful or unpredictable to me, and

b) there is a Supreme Reality because I, with others, attest to 'the tug of the Transcendent', which is not simply a construct of my mind, but perceived as 'a greater-than-me'.

It is too narrow a view to confine truth to verbal expressions of truth. Statements of truth can only be approximations of truth, partly true partly untrue, and their meaning can only be tested by what is done with them (orthodoxy is revealed by orthopraxis). Absolute truth exists only in objective reality and any expression of it is partial, relative, a shadowy symbol. To know is to be assimilated to what one knows. The knowing person approaches reality with an attentiveness to it, becomes engaged with it, is transformed by it and acts on it. So, truth is embodied in the knower (as Jesus embodied the Word of God, becoming the witness of the Truth,[3] even Truth itself[4]). Persons of truth, as the ultimate expressions of truth, no matter what their verbal beliefs, recognize one another as such and delight in sharing their truth. All the great religious traditions have been founded by or have produced such incarnations of truth. This is perhaps the line of thought taken by Vardy concerning those who 'live in the truth'. Systems of thought, such as religions and philosophies, can each be only a partial access to truth and this allows a healthy pluralism, which is not relativistic but a truthful coexistence, even a mutual compenetration of thought systems. This can be illustrated by several examples of knowing.

As I look out on reality it seems to me that reality is out there, but all I am aware of is actually in my brain: every object of perception has been mediated by my senses and reconstructed as a universe within me. One can take television as an illustration: the

---
1 Peter Vardy, *What is Truth?*, Sydney, University of New South Wales, 1999.
2 Stephen Buckle, 'Truth: what is that?', in *National Outlook*, August, 2000: 27.
3 John 18:37.
4 John 14:6.

action in the studio is recorded by the camera, transmitted as radio waves, intercepted by antennae and recoded as an image on the screen of my TV set. What is activated on the screen are thousands of pixels of changing colour. My mind is actively grouping the colour pixels, according to previously experienced patterns, so I imagine I see a man walking, or a tree or a house (even though I may not have seen before this precise man, tree or house). So, in a real sense I am co-operating with the producer and TV channel in reconstructing the scene. In this reconstruction I am assigning more or less importance to groups of colour points and drawing meaning from the whole. Similarly, in general, my perception of reality is an internal reconstruction of what is mediated by my senses of a world outside.

A historian, studying a certain period in a certain place, has to filter his data. In that time and place there were millions of little events, each of no particular importance. The historian selects some of them, groups them into larger entities, relates these larger entities with one another, producing a sequence in which he perceives value and meaning. Another historian, looking at the same period, may see a different sequence. The two sequences may be equally true and validly coexistent. The wise student will judge that one complements the other.

The scientist, likewise, has to be selective in highlighting a particular line of causality in a process. Causality forms my own experience of intending to produce an effect (I know myself to be a cause) and this sensation I project onto the natural world. When I see repeatedly that B follows A I assume that A causes B. I could say, with Buddhists, that every effect is caused by every entity in the cosmos, that every change is the result of all other changes in the universe. However, for convenience and for the purpose in hand, I look only at the immediate ambience and see that an effect is the result of a single cause and a set of conditions. In experimentation I try to isolate the causality from distractive conditions or render them stable. While linear causality may be a useful understanding for the current scientific goal it is not the real situation in nature. A scientist, for his specialist purpose, has to be disciplined in his narrow-minded filtering of reality, while the non-specialist must accept that science cannot give a total view of that reality.

So different representations of reality, as in art, poetry, science and history, can coexist side by side, each true in its own way and all mutually complementary. So, too, we can have pluralism in religion. Each religious tradition has been shaped by a particular culture, has come out of a founder's unique spiritual experience and particular insight into the human condition. Each has a unique contribution to make to a universal understanding and appreciation of the universe and of humankind. Each points beyond to the Transcendent. I imagine a multifaceted gem, each facet representing a particular religion with a different size, shape and area of interface with the gem. All agree in their 'beyond', i.e., the body of the gem. Of course, each tradition has picked up deficiencies in the course of its history and these can be unacceptable barriers to agreement. As in any system of thought, there may be some things which have been taken too seriously, leading to distortion of the truth, such as religious fundamentalism, fanaticism, romantic nationalism, passionate cause-making, narrow-mindedness, lack of balance. That said, nevertheless, every religious tradition has a truth to be treasured, namely, 'the beyond' to which it is pointing. 'When the wise woman points to the moon the foolish man sometimes looks at the finger.'[5]

---

5 James Byrne, *God: Thoughts in an Age of Uncertainty*, London and New York, Continuum, 2001: 157.

Not to be confused with religious relativism, authentic pluralism has been central to John D'Arcy May's scholarly investigations, as exemplified in his *After Pluralism*.[6] James Byrne states that 'all religions are local, contingent and relative: they are products of human history.'[7] When this is acknowledged, boundaries between religions break down. This is 'to reject all absolutisms, but it is not to condone relativism. It is simply to regard all religious belief as *ours*, as human....We are never justified in thinking that the truth is ours alone'. Rumi, in The Shepherds Poem, has God comparing the diversity of worship to the diversity of language:

> I have bestowed on everyone a particular mode of worship, I have given everyone a peculiar form of expression.
> The idiom of Hindustanh is excellent for Hindus; the idiom of Sind is excellent for the people of Sind

and he concludes:

> O Moses, they that know the conventions are of one sort, they whose souls burn are of another.
> The religion of love is apart from religions. The lovers of God have no religion but God alone.

Christian sources of revelation have provided a metaphorical language with which to talk about God in prayer, liturgy and doctrine, but that does not help in exploring knowledge of the being of God, as sought for in philosophy or theology. Under Greek and Jewish influences one branch of Western scholarship has adopted a reified image of God, a Being above all other beings, a dualistic concept that is increasingly out of favour in the postmodernism. Byrne has traced a parallel development in which the incomprehensibility of God as total mystery was emphasized. This apophatic tradition, originating with the Cappadocian Fathers of the 4th century, continues through Pseudo-Dionysus (5th-6th century) into the Middle Ages. From the latter, St Thomas Aquinas took the idea that God was beyond all affirmation: 'we cannot grasp what God is but only what God is not'. The *via negative* was developed more boldly by Meister Eckhart and Nicholas of Cusa. Modernist and postmodernist critiques of knowledge have profoundly affected the way we think of God. So, while Paul Tillich proposes that, rather than thinking of God as the highest Being, God should be understood as Being-itself or the ground of being, Jean-Luc Marion proposes the abandonment of any objectification of God in a philosophical concept, which 'functions exactly as an idol'[8]. God cannot be grasped as a concept, yet Marion suggests we can name God as love (as in 1 John 4:8). Love is pure gift of itself, a continuing giving, an excess of abandonment, an outpouring which holds nothing back. Love can never be fixed as an idol, because it is always beyond us in an unceasing gesture of gift.

Byrne concludes that the history of negative theology demonstrates that 'the greatest wisdom in relation to God is to remain silent'. On this score he quotes Raimon Panikkar who also suggests God is an invocation, one who is called on, not one who is affirmed or negated by our cognitive abilities. Simply, I say that we know God not as 'he, she, or it' but as a 'Thou'. Panikkar states this explicitly in a footnote: 'God is a Thou – or as I would rather suggest, the ultimate 'I' to whom the Thou is 'me'[9]. One has a glimpse of

---

6 John D'Arcy May, *After Pluralism: Towards an Interreligious Ethic*, Münster, LIT, 2000.
7 Byrne, *God*: 112-113.
8 Jean-Luc Marion, *God Without Being*, New York, Fordham University, 1991.
9 Raimon Panikkar, *Blessed Simplicity: The Monk as Universal Archetype*, New York, Seabury, 1982: 11.

that in the experience of Aquinas, shortly before his death. While celebrating Mass one day he underwent an astonishing transformation, upon which he ceased writing the *Summa Theologica.* When urged to continue he said, 'I cannot do any more. Everything I have written seems to me as straw in comparison to what I have seen.'

Archetypal Theology

The theology I am proposing, while not quite new (as examples below will show), is one which has not, as far as I know, seen itself as distinctly different from conventional theology.

In my 'bush theologian' series of papers[10] I discussed a stage of theological thinking (and, indeed, of any scientific research or problem solving), which I described as pre-conceptual thinking. At this initial stage, the available data is represented in the mind (or imagination) by a series of images (or by some other mental analogue of sense perception). The mind's eye rapidly rearranges this mass of images in different juxtapositions, like the changing shapes and colours of a kaleidoscope, until it sees a right 'fit' and calls a halt. Then comes the difficult task of translating this frozen juxtaposition of images into words, with logical form and sequence. This initial process has its own logic, not the logic of identifying concepts as in rational discourse, but one which links data by analogy or association (A is like B, A suggests B), a process I call projection, that is, seeing one reality through a related reality.[11]

In my *Wonder: A Way to God*[12] I discussed Divine Wisdom in the Old Testament, which, in the New Testament, came to be seen as the Incarnate Word of God. Paul evidently refers to the same cosmic reality as the mystery of Christ or the mind of Christ. Entry to this universal mind is afforded by what Paul calls mysteries (plural, or specified)[13] and what I labelled archetypes.[14]

Subsequent reflection has drawn together the pre-conceptual thinking and the archetypes, and I am proposing a method of theologizing called archetypal theology. An example of such archetypal theology is found in Hans Urs von Balthasar's ecclesiology.[15] He asserts that at the foundation of the Christian life and mission lies the archetypal participation in Christ's all-sustaining experience of God, a constellation of relationships around Christ, including his relationship to the Trinity and his relationship to Mary and the Apostles. This archetypal experience of Christ is perpetuated in the life of the Church and becomes the intrinsic dimension of her being. Panikkar, too, similarly theologizes.[16]

---

10 Eugene Stockton, 'The Way of a Bush Theologian', in Damien Brennan (ed.), *Evangelisation in an Australian Context*, Melbourne, Collins Dove, 1992: 19-25; also my 'A Bush Theologian goes his Way', in Peter Malone (ed.), *Developing an Australian Theology*, Strathfield, St. Paul, 1999: 251-264.

11 Four examples of relatedness are described: macrocosm/microcosm, phylogeny/ontogeny, type/anti-type, myth/experience.

12 Eugene Stockton, *Wonder: A Way to God*, Strathfield, St. Paul, 1998: chapter 6.

13 Stockton, *Wonder*: note 29.

14 Stockton, *Wonder*: 96-97; several examples of such archetypes are offered in the text, without the list being exhaustive.

15 Hans Urs von Balthasar, *The Office of Peter and the Structure of the Church*, San Francisco, Ignatius, 1986.

16 Panikkar, *Blessed Simplicity*: 25: he describes an archetype as 'a paradigm which becomes for you the centre of your myth...literally a fundamental type...I take from Jung not so much the

A better known example might be proposed in John's Gospel. I suspect the Gospel was meant to be a manual of instruction for preparing catechumens for Baptism; in fact, there is the suspicion that it was the conflation of two such manuals, the second intended for the subsequent mystagogia. Each narrative represents a confrontation between Jesus and the would-be believer (the Beloved Disciple, Nicodemus, the blind man, etc.), with whom the catechumen identifies himself or herself as he or she is drawn to faith. Around this central character is clustered a number of archetypes. All the women in the account play a consistent role, a 'mothering' that is recognizable as the role of the Church towards her children. John the Baptist[17] and Peter act as ministers. Then, there are 'the Jews', the adversaries. Jesus himself is the super-archetype drawing one to faith. In him are subsumed a series of types, understood traditionally as biblical types, i.e., persons, things and events in the Old Testament which foreshadow corresponding realities (anti-types) in the New. The Johannine types characteristically originate in the Exodus, the 'Long March' of the Israelites, are identified by the prophets with recurring experiences in the life of Israel and are projected by later prophets as marks of the coming Messianic Age. Through the numerous 'I am...' and 'you are...' statements John identifies such types with Jesus, e.g., the manna in the desert, the source of living water, the paschal lamb, etc. This identification is expressed in the Book of Signs (John 1-12) but is seen fulfilled in 'the exaltation' of Jesus in the Book of Glory (John 13-21). Some simple verbs here have an archetypal weight: see, come, remain, be, send. A story might set up a kind of timeless tableau, such as the feeding of the multitude with its discourse sequel.[18] Luke likewise depicts similar archetypal scenarios, especially where the supernatural predominates, e.g., the Annunciation, the Temptations, the Transfiguration, the Agony in the Garden, the Ascension. This usage is consistent with the biblical predilection for *mashal* (Heb.) or *parabole* (Gr.), words whose meanings can cover proverbs, maxims, riddles, metaphors, allegories, similitudes and other forms of comparisons, even by way of such extended narratives as gospel parables.

Proceeding with archetypes, unlike reasoning with concepts as in classical theology, is by pondering and playing with images in a manner akin to contemplation. I imagine the archetypes, which stand for the data under consideration, as spheres of different sizes hanging in space; gravity impacts on each differently according to their mass, distance and direction of separation. The ponderer may stand back and view the whole ensemble, change viewpoint or move between the spheres to discover new perceptions. The heavenly spheres are not meant to remain in a rarefied atmosphere: theology demands to be contextualized, to have both meaning in time and place and a basis for praxis. I have proposed bringing together two *loci theologici*:

   c) personal experience (sacred story, my own or my people's)

   d) revealed data (the experience of God in the sacred story of the People of God).[19]

There are advantages in this archetypal theologizing:

> It is typically, wild and lateral, intuitive and creative and, therefore, very free.
> It offers expandable categories and free associations of ideas, before settling

---

notion that it is submerged in the collective human unconscious as that it is a *dynamis* which on the one hand directs, and on the other attracts human ideals and praxis...It may mean a sort of platonic essence, a prototype which is immutable and gives identity to its participations'.

17 John 3:27-30.
18 John 6.
19 See Stockton, 'A Bush Theologian goes his Way': 257.

down to the restriction and dogma of established discourse. It complements the more respectable rational approach in various disciplines by giving the right hemisphere of the brain an active role in problem solving. I suspect that pre-conceptual thinking is responsible for the intuitive leap of genius (which, of many areas of human intellect, computers cannot duplicate) that can recognize patterns and, hence, parallels between otherwise dissimilar data...[20]

Such an approach to theology, I submit, is suited to the current mood of postmodernism, with its scepticism towards mega-narratives and absolutes and its aversion to conceptualizing God. Further, I submit, it facilitates the encounter between a world religion and a local primal tradition, as envisaged by John D'Arcy May in *Transcendence and Violence*.[21] The fruitfulness of such an encounter can be seen in the persistent success of Celtic Spirituality to the present day[22] and in the vibrant religiosity of the Balinese. In Australia, we might look to a similar fruitfulness from the meeting of the Christian gospel and the native animism of our Aboriginal people.[23]

Analysis of Person as a Framework for Theology

Though I originally[24] had an analysis of person as a bipolarity of 'ego' and 'spirit', I have since thought more about 'ego' and feel it is in need of further analysis. Partly, this came from the way psychologists tend to speak of self and ego. However, whereas Freudians and Jungians speak of the subconscious, as if there were a discontinuity with the conscious, I prefer to see consciousness as a deep well whose depths are rarely plumbed or rarely rise to the surface, but are accessible in deep awareness. Another influence on my thinking is the Hindu insight into the *unmanifest* and *manifest* deity, which I think we can parallel with the Christian God, who is one and unknowable in God's Deep Self (Eckhart's 'GodHead') but who, in God's manifest, i.e., revealed, self can be known as Three Persons.

First, there is the deep self, the ultimate source of all my personal actions and interactions. This is the 'I', the subject of all I know and do.[25] I do not know 'I', nor can I know 'I': it is the deep unmanifest bottom of my self-well. At the beginning it is simply a case of 'I am' (as God nominated Godself to Moses), even before I am aware that I am, before I am aware of myself and know myself as a human being, a member of my family, the node in the network of myriad relationships which constitute me as a person. This node, this self which can be known, is the 'me'. The 'me' can be the object of knowledge, as the 'I' can never be: it is the manifest self. Being aware of 'me', I also am aware of the 'others', both my inter-relatedness with them and my uniqueness.

---

20 Stockton, 'A Bush Theologian goes his Way': 255.
21 John D'Arcy May, *Transcendence and Violence: The Encounter of Buddhist, Christian and Primal Traditions*, New York and London, Continuum, 2003.
22 See J. Philip Newell, *Listening for the Heartbeat of God: A Celtic Spirituality*, London, SPCK, 1997.
23 I hope to illustrate this coming together in Aboriginal theologizing in a series of studies on Aboriginal Christian art, where the mindset is seen to be at a deeper level of consciousness, which I here call archetypal theology, see Eugene Stockton, 'Exploring Aboriginal Christian Art', in *Terra Spiritus* 2,2-3 (2006), www.terraspiritus.com.au.
24 See Stockton, *Wonder*: 41-53.
25 Interestingly, English, in common with most languages I know, has two etymologically different words for the first person singular pronoun, 'I' (subject) and 'me' (object), and this I make the basis for an important distinction in my analysis of the self.

This multiple awareness leads to a perception of 'me', which may or may not correspond with the real 'me'. This mental construct of me I call the 'ego'. A person may have several egos, differing according to different contexts (home, work, party, etc.). A false ego can be derived from a distorted evaluation of oneself, by oneself or by society (adapted self). An authentic person, a man or woman of truth, is one whose perception of self corresponds to their real 'me'.

Love instinctively rises from the depths of the 'I'. The first instinct of self-hood is to spring out to another. 'I am' erupts into 'I love', and then I know I am a self, because you are another. The self, rising from its own depths, is drawn to the Good, the Time, the Beautiful in the 'other', ultimately to the One. It may go no further than the ego and rest there, self-absorbed. Enraptured by the ego, it may seek to enhance the ego and to ensure its survival at all costs (protect, defend). Or, it may transcend the ego by an 'ego-death'.[26] This is the *ecstasis* and *kenosis* of the first stage of going out to the 'other'.[27] This 'I-thou' procession is one which reaches out from one depth ('I') to the depth in the other, virtually from one transcendence to another. The second stage is an engagement with the other which I call 'communion', of which the classic formulation is Jesus's words in John: 'I am in the Father and the Father is in me'. 'I-Thou' becomes 'we'. Finally, the two become one, 'we' become 'I' in a shared subjectivity.

This three stage process can be exemplified in a variety of areas. Interestingly, Reanney begins illustrating it in the area of sex, where one enters into bodily intimacy with one's spouse or partner.[28] In *Enjoy God*[29] I proposed it in reference to eating food, or in any number of sense gratifications: I reach out for the food, I chew it and digest it into my substance. Again, in knowing, I go out to the truth (or the object of knowledge), engage with it and become one with it. These three stages are well exemplified in the stages of contemplative prayer where the deep 'I' goes out to the deep 'I' of the Godhead ('I-Thou'), engages in communion with God ('we') and becomes one with God ('I'). All the great mystical traditions I know of have parallel descriptions of this process. This mystic journey is summed up in Psalm 42 (and in Dadirri) as 'deep calling to deep.' To rephrase the previous quote from Panikkar[30] 'God is a Thou – or as I would rather suggest, the ultimate 'I' to whom the Thou is the human 'I'.[31]

The foregoing analysis of person can be applied to God. The deep 'I' of the Godhead is utterly one, unmanifest, transcendent ('Totally Other'). God could have remained locked in God-self, 'self-contained, self-centred, self-satisfying',[32] but God chose to break out in love. But love implies being drawn to the other. If God was alone where was the other? At the point of manifestation of God's Self (the divine 'Me') God revealed Himself as the Father, projecting the Other as the Son, both encompassed by their mutual Spirit. So, there comes about a Trinity of Egos (if not of three 'Me's'). With the Incarnation of the Son, one now approaches God in the humanity of Jesus, going by that 'Way' to the Father. Some mystics go further to the utterly One, the totally Other, with whom paradoxically they become 'oned in wonder'. The *Cloud of Unknowing*

---

26 Darryl Reanney, *The Death of Forever: A New Future for Human Consciousness*, Melbourne, Longman Cheshire, 1991: 168, as quoted in Stockton, *Wonder*: 107-108, see note 7.
27 Stockton, *Wonder*: 48.
28 Reanney, *The Death of Forever*: 238-239, as quoted in Stockton, *Wonder*: 121-122.
29 Eugene Stockton, 'Enjoy God', in *Compass Theology Review* 34,4 (2000): 8-10.
30 Panikkar, *Blessed Simplicity*: 11.
31 The three stages in this journey are examined in detail in the last three chapters of my *Wonder*.
32 Stockton, *Wonder*: 71.

(chapter 4) contrasts our knowing powers and our loving powers in reaching out to God: '[God] may well be love but not thought. By love he may be gotten and holden, but by thought neither'. Thought (knowing) reaches out from manifest to manifest, love reaches out from unmanifest to unmanifest: 'deep calling to deep'.

Further reflection on the 'I' in the analysis of person suggests that the deep 'I' is more a process than a thing (or object), more a verb than an noun, suitably expressed in God's primordial name for Godself: 'I am' (though there is all the difference between the infinite and the finite). 'I am' before 'whatever I am'.[33] This may be the meaning of Zen Buddhism's 'one's original face', 'one's original self before one was born'. As stated above, the deep self is unknown and unknowable, but some mystics both in the East and the West have sourced this deep 'I am' to the deep 'I am' of the Godhead and have seen the mystic journey as a return to where it began, as the drop of water flows down to be reabsorbed into the sea whence it came. This, however, I cannot affirm because, as I said above, I cannot know 'I' – and it may even be slightly heretical!

The mutuality of persons has a bearing on our knowledge of God. How do we know there is a God? Kevin O'Shea states that a 'personalist approach to God believes there is no need to prove God's existence. There is an intimation, an intuition, a sense of God that is much deeper than proof. God as Personal is already implicitly known in the heart of the human person before there is any question about the "existence" of God.' The idea of interpersonhood seems impossible to achieve 'unless there were Someone, a Person, who is large enough for the fullest and most unlimited dimensions of interpersonhood and interpersonal love and joy. This Person is God'.[34] This is what I call 'the tug of the Transcendent'.

Outpouring

As noted before, if God is a Person (and the depths of my personhood demand an Other Person Greater than me) there lives in the depths of God's personhood an 'I', the Godhead, who is one, totally other and unmanifest. God is simply 'I am'. God, however, is Love and by the necessity of nature God-Love must spring out. In this springing out God is manifested as three Persons, three Egos, three mutual and reciprocal relations, as the Father loves and gives rise to the Son, and the Son expresses and returns that love in the mutuality of the Spirit.

The relatedness of the Three can be further teased out in terms of the Love and the Gift[35] and the Good.[36]

Father	*Son*	*Spirit*
Source of Love	Word of Love	Action of Love
Giver	Given	Gift/ing
God pouring out Self	God poured out	Divine pouring out

This pouring out is a total giving of self or, as Panikkar puts it, 'each person voids itself totally in order that the other may be'.[37] Included in this Trinitarian movement is a

---

33 Cf. Gerald Gleeson, 'Person, Body, Gender – Philosophical Reflections on the "What are we?" Question', in *The Australasian Catholic Record*, 79,3 (July 2002): 285-298: 297-298.
34 Kevin O'Shea, *Person in Analysis*, Bristol IN, Wyndham Hall, 1996: 11-12.
35 Michael Downey, *Altogether Gift: A Trinitarian Spirituality*, Maryknoll, Orbis, 2000: 60.
36 Stockton, *Wonder*: 82, following St Bonaventure's thought of God as the highest good, *diffusivum sui*.

mutual pouring out and receiving, not only of being, but of love, glory and knowledge, a coursing of life in which human persons were ultimately destined to be caught up.

The contemplative in Panikkar often returns to the idea of the void or of the silence in the Godhead. For example, 'silence is the very womb of the *logos* (Word)' and 'silence is the Father, source and origin of the whole divinity'.[38] Following his cue it could be said that out of the Silence of the Godhead, a Speaker speaks a Word, with the exhalation of the Breath (*Pneuma*, Spirit).

'In the beginning was the Word' (John 1:1) and at the beginning of the finitude of space and time 'God created the heavens and the earth', pronouncing over the formless void his creative Word 'let there be….' (Genesis 1:1-2:3). So God continued to pour Godself out onto the created, finite other in the Spirit and the Word. The Jews later recognized in the latter the Divine Wisdom whom they delightfully pictured as the playmate playing beside the Creator who formed the heavens and the earth.[39] Depicting God in creation as God at play has a long tradition behind it; it brings out the exuberance and joyfulness of creation and it shows God collaborating with creatures in the furtherance of creation with a balance of purpose, chance and determinism.[40]

Once God was pouring Godself out on finite creation, God was no longer moved by a necessity of nature but by a necessity of love: God freely and lovingly drew us into being. We are the self-aware, love-responding flowering of a long evolving creation, in which at each stage God lured existing forms to leap ahead in self-transcendence to successively higher forms, as God now lures human beings by divine grace to transcend themselves to higher spiritual planes, to deeper communion of the Three. 'The relationality of the three bonded in the one Love spills over into a relationality with the world, thereby making it possible for human persons to enter into this communion in the one Love.' And again: 'Love is life pouring itself forth. God is the Love that overspills, because Love cannot be contained. God is Love in excess, excessive of what reason might demand or justice require – gift.'[41]

As creation evolved into ever higher forms, it flowered into a self-conscious creature, in whom the whole universe was to become aware of itself and freely to respond in love to the Creator. Sadly, though, the trajectory of creation was deflected as the self-conscious pinnacle of creaturedom; for, instead of reaching out to self-fulfilment in God, for itself and for all, creation became infatuated with its own ego and alienated from other creatures.[42] Self-centredness tends to be self-perpetuating, so that even movements to love, altruism and remorse are motivated by self-interest, barricading one from God's compassion and readiness to forgive. The trigger to open human hearts and free the grace of God was that Jesus opened up a way and showed us how to follow him to selfless love and to the grace of God. In those who followed Jesus in his paschal mystery, the whole creation could at last come to self-fulfilment. Creation for a

---

37 Panikkar, *Blessed Simplicity*: 128.
38 Panikkar, *Blessed Simplicity*: 48 and 50, respectively.
39 Proverbs 8:27-31, as translated in Stockton, *Wonder*: 79.
40 Stockton, *Wonder*: 78-82.
41 Downey, *Altogether Gift*: 60.
42 See Stockton, *Wonder*: 74-77, where I describe in more detail the story of the Fall and Redemption, but less traditionally in the context of creation theology and without recourse to the language of atonement. The traditional account is a perfectly valid alternative but less appealing to modern tastes. Original Sin is presented as Man, and men and women thereafter, being locked in a vicious cycle of self-love, 'imploded more and more into a black hole of self-annihilation'.

time was 'subjected to futility' through human wilfulness, but even then it 'groaned for the revealing of the children of God', i.e., when all will become family in the Cosmic Christ under the Fatherhood of God.[43]

The Second Adam reversed what the First Adam did. The latter had been created in the image of God and wilfully sought to be like God.[44] By contrast, Christ Jesus, as the hymn of Philippians 2:6-11 tells us, was one

> Who being in the form of God
> did not count equality with God
> something to be grasped.
> But he emptied himself
> Taking the form of a slave
> Becoming as human beings are
> And being in every way like a human being
> He was humbler yet
> Even to accepting death, death on a cross.

As with the servant of the Suffering Servant songs (Isaiah 52:13-53:13), the hymn continues the movement from humiliation to exaltation at the hands of God.[45] An alternative interpretation[46] takes *morphe* in the primary sense of 'shape' and *ekenosen* as 'he poured (himself) out' after the imagery of a libation sacrifice. Hence, Jesus poured himself out of a God-shaped vessel into a servant-shaped vessel. The general sense is the same: introducing the hymn, Paul urges us to adopt the mentality of Christ Jesus, the example of humility and self sacrifice, the mind of *kenosis*.

God, who successively poured Godself out in the Trinity, in the Incarnation and in wholehearted self-sacrifice, invites us to respond in like manner and so enter the mind of God.

---

43 Romans 8:18-23.
44 Genesis 1:27; 3:5.
45 I have here followed the interpretation of the New Jerusalem Bible.
46 Stockton: *Wonder*: 101.

Garry Trompf

Of Colligation and Reification in the Representation of Religion (and Violence)

Back in 1969, I remember, a message came to the History Department at the University of Western Australia that someone was needed to give a lecture on contemporary Religion and Politics to the ladies of the Australian Liberal Party. There was a general lack of confidence about handling the subject, and knowing my interests, they put pressure on the youngest member of staff (even though I was no Liberal). Doing my duty, off I went to deliver – almost preach – a case that 'the biggest single influence on world politics today is 'bastardized (or 'used') religion'. Skirts rustled at my language, and a murmuring occasionally crossed the room. I had just stuck to my topic, not quite sure whether it suited the context, because, not long before lecturing I had been introduced to the Federal Minister for Immigration. Then, straight after I finished, the Minister – William ('Billy') Sneddon – made his reappearance from behind a curtain, soon breaking the news in his own speech of the Liberals' intention to admit exceptions to the White Australia policy…at last. Four years on, after these 'waters had been tested', the ethnic composition of Australia began altering significantly. Today I write this paper from Sydney, which, given both its location and attractions, is arguably the most culturally diverse city on earth!

As contemporaries and after growing up in 'the Australian bush', John D'Arcy May and I have experienced this social transformation. Eventually meeting up in Papua New Guinea, formerly Australia's largest 'colonial territory', we learnt of our shared interest in the hard edges of inter-societal confrontation, and more particularly the place religions have in either worsening or healing group relations. John's mastery of the materials and issues in this connection – especially regarding Christian and Buddhist attitudes to indigenous peoples – is extraordinary, and his expertise in the theological, missiological and ecumenist dimensions of his researches outstanding. His achievements are nowhere better epitomized than in the volume *Transcendence and Violence* (2003).

Happily, I can here join in the celebrations of his intellectual career by musing on methodological problems that arise from the kind of work we have both undertaken. More precisely, I wish to comment on various ways the term religion is 'used' (sometimes abused!) in the analytical discourse of academia, and thereafter proceed to the actualities of human affairs, pondering the viability of distinguishing a 'used' (by implication abused) religion from something approximating to 'the real thing'. I take up these tasks partly because we are living in such highly opinionated times. Current conflicts can too easily be summed up as a war between Christianity and Islam, and the spectre of colonel Robert Ingersoll (that all our problems are to be blamed on institutional religion) rears its ugly head. And I am also fully aware of revived interest in nationalist and socio-political appropriations of religious language for secular agendas, as best testified by Michael Burleigh's timely tomes.[1]

---

1   Michael Burleigh, Earthly Powers: *Religion and Politics in Europe from the Enlightenment to the Great War*, London, HarperCollins, 2005; *Sacred Causes: Religion and Politics from the European Dictators to Al Qaeda*, London, HarperPress, 2006. For Ingersoll, see Sydney Ahlstrom,

In the Western philosophical analysis of language, religion (even its older form *religio*, or parallels in the Greek *thrêskeia* and Arabic *al-din*) is a socio-historical 'colligation', that is, it is a concept denoting not one thing but a bundle of actions and ideas.[2] It is a high abstraction, belonging to a class of concepts – empires, nation, state, movement, revolution – grist to the mill of *savants* who want to encapsulate the big social configurations affecting human destiny. In its 'evocative potential', however, speakers can emphasize one of its purports as against another. In pre-modern English usage, the meaning of religion was overwhelmingly to do with (forms of) worship, as against dogma (faith beliefs) and piety (behaviour). After the 17th century, religion was used more commonly to refer to social entities, including such phenomena as Hinduism, Buddhism, Confucianism, etc.[3] In our time, the word religion carries a latent potential for denoting a variety of matters – ritual, belief in supernatural power(s), customary and social activity, attitude to life, socio-spiritual identity, and so on – but, outside a limited sphere of specialists, we cannot expect working references to the term to incorporate a reasonable balance of possible senses. Religion is a word typically 'bandied around', especially in the West, so that it services strong points of view, in these days very often negative ones. Religion is made responsible for most of our present troubles; it has become cause, not just conception. Why, even in the realm of interreligious competition, it can be a powerful, not easily dismissable ploy to bolster the legitimacy of a spirituality by saying it was *not* a religion. I think of my recent Zoroastrian doctoral student, who concluded that Zarathushtra taught 'cosmic ethics', and that, as for 'religions', they 'fail to bring unity and peace, …[but] are one of the most fundamental causes of separation, enmity, conflict war and bloodshed, even within the different sectors of the one religion.'[4]

This brings us to problem of reification. Do colligations actually 'do' anything, and can they indeed be 'causes'? To reify in discourse is the tendency to turn a mental abstraction into an active being. Thus, a nation, let us say, or a conceived collectivity applied to humans, is 'animated' to become a living agent that 'does' this or that, when in fact only its members or representatives are the doers. The worst of newspaper culture tends to lapse into this mode, with the attitudes of whole countries being denoted generally – as America, Britain, Iran, and the like – instead of the Bush administration, the Blair government, the Ahmadinejad regime, or some such (albeit commonly loaded) usage. Like a cold, this kind of slip has been 'caught' by commentators on religions; thus, Christianity is made responsible for the environmental crisis, for instance, because it is 'environmentally unfriendly' at base; or Islam the cause of the new and terrifying wave of violence in the world.[5] Of course, partisan positions – extremisms, communisms, fundamentalisms, conservativisms, sects – are easy prey for this reifying tendency, because it is assumed

---

A Religious History of the American People, Yale, Yale University, 1972: 765-6.
2   For background, see William Henry Walsh, *An Introduction to the Philosophy of History*, London, Hutchinson, 1958 [1951]: 59-64.
3   Or earlier variant epithets thereof; see Keith Thomas, *Religion and the Decline of Magic: Studies in Popular Beliefs in Sixteenth and Seventeenth Century England*, Harmondsworth, Penguin, 1978 [1971]: chapters 2-9; Wilfred Cantwell Smith, *The Meaning and End of Religion*, New York, Mentor, 1964 [1962]: chapters 2-3.
4   Mehravara Marzbani, Personal Communication, January 2007. See her 'The Gathas Revisited: A Reappraisal of Zarathushtra's Vision' (doctoral dissertation, University of Sydney), Sydney, 2006. For background, see Smith, *Meaning*: 82-83.
5   Lynn White, 'The Historical Roots of our Ecologic Crisis', in *Science* 155 (10 March 1967): 1203-07; Khaled Abou el Fadl, *The Great Theft: Wrestling Islam from Extremists*, New York, HarperCollins, 2005.

that the bodies of people entailed are homogeneous and united by totalistic mentalities. At the other end, the broad abstractions of religion itself, or secularism *qua* social entity, sometimes 'science' (as scientism), have been turned into living *bêtes noires*, ready to distort or endanger an otherwise ordered world. It reminds one that, ever since Émile Zola's novel *Germinal* (1885), we find analyses of one *système* or another that have a force, perhaps sacrificial effect, on persons sucked into them.[6] The system becomes a devouring organism, when in fact it is a complex set of circumstances, involving a concatenation of particular human agencies and contingencies, that limit personal choices.

Now, upon considering the important work of Professor May, one is confronted by his arresting challenge – in *Transcendence and Violence* – that such religious traditions as Buddhism and Christianity have been overbearing in their encounter with small-scale indigenous traditions and have failed to honour them as religions in their own right or their value to world spirituality. I remember in this connection some immediate reactions when I posted a 'Notice' of our new Religious Studies courses about Melanesian Religion on my office door at the University of Papua New Guinea in 1973. It was assumed by various indigenous students passing by that traditional beliefs were not going to be studied – because 'the missionaries', as they claimed, had rarely graced these with so elevated an adjective as 'religious'. Superstition, or, more strongly, works of the Devil, would be the more common descriptors. And as with John May, it has been dismaying to me to find Buddhists 'inferiorizing' the darker skinned Tamils of Sri Lanka and the marginalized Ainu of Japan; or to read Javanese Muslim nonsense about black West Papuans (Irian Jayans) as orang-utangs. The question before us now, though, in the light of my previous observations, is: in what sense are we justified in considering (the colligation of) a religion 'doing' anything adverse, or, for that matter, beneficial, in the world? Do religious traditions take on an 'organic being' of their own, or emerge as 'active entities', so that we can praise them for their achievements and blame them for their failures? Indeed, can we justifiably talk of any theology – another, related abstraction – as adequate or inadequate for any task? For, John May's work challenges us to consider whether any religion or theology (or buddhology, animatism, etc.) has done or is doing what is right.

In the strictest logic, of course, it is only persons who identify with one religious persuasion or another who act, performing deeds that evoke our judgements (of concession, or anxiety, or a mixture). Religions so-called are admittedly also social, yet, even while worrying over the risk of saying that history and human affairs are ultimately what countless individuals do (and single psychologies motivate),[7] they take no action outside the collectivities of individuals adhering to them. This is akin to the caveat of linguistic analysts that systems of ideas or beliefs, or ideologies, are not operating 'out there', sitting somewhere independent of people's articulations and upholding of them.[8] Not that 'social reality' should be denied, let alone the reality of ideas and spirit(ual) impetuses (which are all apparently present as meta-physical), but it remains a truism

---

6 Émile Zola, *Germinal*, G. Charpentier, Paris, 1885. See also Peter L. Berger, *Pyramids of Sacrifice: Political Ethics and Social Change*, London, Allen Lane, 1976.
7 See John (J.E.) Neale's well known theoretical article on 'The Biographical Approach to History', in his *Essays in Elizabethan History*, London, Jonathan Cape, London, 1958: 227-8.
8 For example, Terry Threadgold, 'Semiotics–Ideology–Language', in Terry Threadgold, Elizabeth Grosz, Gunther Kress and Michael Halliday (eds.), *Language, Semiotics, Ideology*, number 3 in Sydney Studies in Society and History, Sydney, Sydney Association for Studies in Society and Culture, 1986; 29.

that humans do the actual making, changing and shaking of (human) events – as well as the (human) responding to environmental shifts or altered circumstance.

In so operating *sensu stricto* on historico-social materials we guard methodologically not only against the problem of reification itself but above all against sweeping (and *eo ipso* false) generalizations. We also putatively forestall the effects of people's hidden assumptions, prejudices, even blatant jumps in the game of 'catch-all' discourse ('Buddhists and Christians reject the body and frown on sex'; 'Christians believe in a literal apocalyptic Rapture', etc.). When it comes to assessing religions ethically, moreover, the larger ones are so complex as to be predictably 'mixed bags' – of inspiration and disappointment, so that reification tends to be more a symptom of a writer's position than a balanced characterization. I think Catholic *littérateur* Tony Hendra nicely helps to encapsulate the issues here, when, from a decrepit little church in England, he defined his tradition as

> a mighty chain that stretched from our dingy little sanctuary back down twenty centuries of courage, wickedness, conflict, sanctity, high art, arrogance, generosity, savagery, creativity, suffering, ecstasy, humility, hypocrisy, scholarship, and self-sacrifice to another dingy little public place where another young man gave his friends a farewell supper knowing that ... his Roman masters would crucify him.[9]

Some, in polemical mood, would forget or play down the nice bits, others apologetically gloss over the bad; but, judicious balance is the key to great thinking. And Hendra's is a fine generalization with a garland of apparent colligations! – though every one, I must say, carries the implication of a host of individual doers.

The point is that large religions amount to an incredible multiplicity of agents and actions through time, and the onus is on any serious thinker to gauge what taking into account of the complexity might do before making a statement. I have learnt some useful lessons in connection with reactions to Christianity in my day. In the West, for those who have started out in adverse criticism of this tradition, I tend to ask (as well I might for having been re-converted through Melanesians), 'what do you think about "the blacks" and *their* Christianity, then?' And the answer is usually – very quickly – something like, 'oh, I didn't mean them!' (and not so much out of anti-racism or political correctness, but genuine admiration), to which I usually go on to say, 'well, am I not mistaken that, by now, most Christians are darker skinned people?'[10] But even the most accredited scholars can show such knee-jerk reactions. Along with one of my mentors, Africanist and Indologist Professor Noel King, I discovered something very interesting about academics who have left, in a state of bitterness, the faiths of their births. They can rarely ever again do comparative (and even mostly analytic) work in religion with genuine equanimity, because their life rationale makes it very hard to accept anything positive in what they (generally) spurned.[11]

---

9   Hendra, *Father Joe: The Man who Saved my Soul*, London, Penguin Ireland, 2004: 70.
10 How they might react concerning Islam in terms of my questioning would be another matter. Certainly, the colourfulness of African American Christian life (especially in music with jazz, soul, rap) makes the difference in producing this distinctive response.
11 Start with Garry W. Trompf and Gildas Hamel, 'N.Q. King as Wise Polymath', in Garry W. Trompf and Gildas Hamel (eds.), *The World of Religions: Essays on Historical and Contemporary Issues*, number 1 in Religion, Politics and Society series, Delhi, ISPCK, 2002: 13, esp. note 10.

To return to the question of re-presenting and characterizing complexity...students will not be able to learn all the 'tricks of the trade' at once, so they may swallow opinions and strong scholarly positions without hearing of any apparatus by which to qualify generalities. This is especially important in construing the relationship between religion and violence. In the 'Enlightenment polemic' of the *philosophes* it was sufficient to lament any connection between the two, and *in principio* – let us say on ethico-theological principles that evoke the teaching of Jesus for so-called 'Christian societies' – this is a perfectly justifiable complaint. But, of course, a good scholar wants to know the particulars before deducing anything about the purported 'wedding' of the two conceptions (or colligations, or complexes of thought and action). Even if the data is lacking, one should immediately intuit how crucial the sociology of rôles and knowledge would be in making a mature assessment. Take warfare, for a start. First, are the groups involved 'warrior societies', that is, ones in which virtually every male (at least) is expected to take up arms? Are the groups under the aegis of some ruling (aristocratic, 'leisure') caste who can coerce commoners and dependents to fight for their side at will? Do the societies involved have armies that amount only to a small, perhaps professionalized, minority within a whole population? A variety of other questions will follow. What were the pretexts of any war? Who initiated the going to war (on both sides)? Who supported and who opposed taking up arms? What legitimations were used, and by whom? More especially, we will always have to ask, who were the 'schemers' of conflict, to borrow a handy epithet from the hymnist John Newton,[12] the ones who inherited or secured great power that could mobilize many forces? That usage will allow us to be as objective as possible about *Realpolitik* yet at the same time reserve the right to make an ethical judgement.

The answers to these questions all along the line may implicate religion, or entail the appeal to and use of it; but, this can never leave an easy answer that religion is a cause of (or 'responsible for') war. We would have to probe much deeper to be able to test, let alone make such a claim. The assumed nexus between religion and military activity might be made more questionable, moreover, by attempting to discover whether a war was popular or unpopular among those who could make a difference, and also – an important geographical consideration – whether a 'given majority' in the region affected by the fighting was adversely affected or threatened by it, and therefore against it. If the opponents of war, who may usually be powerless to make a difference (and are often the other gender half of a population!) are part of a religious body, and take its beliefs to be against violence, then the interdependence of religion and war would again be thrown into the balance. Then there remain more general questions about whether some religions are more obviously connected to violent modes of activity, or, indeed, whether war 'needs' religion. After all, and to give the *philosophes* a taste of realism, there have been wars not (blatantly) legitimated by religious rhetoric – beginning from the colonialist Seven Years War (1757-64), which was particularly brutal and widespread, indeed 'the nearest thing the 18th century had to a world war.'[13]

Now, John May's work *Transcendence and Violence* throws down the gauntlet by asserting that such traditions as Christianity and Buddhism have a lot to answer for when it comes to the treatment of indigenous traditions. He thinks especially of white Australians' mishandling of the Aboriginal peoples, and the (Buddhist) Sinhalese belittling

---

12 John Newton, *Works* volume 4, Edinburgh, Banner of Truth Trust, 1985 [1820]: 429.
13 Niall Ferguson, *Empire: How Britain Made the Modern World*, London, Penguin, 2004: 32.

of the (largely Hindu) Tamils in Sri Lanka. Religions, on his reading, did violence to indigenous peoples. So, in the light of my prior analyses, what are we to make of these claims? Assuming that the term violence is again a colligatory term that takes in 'a multitude of related sins' – from snubbing and neglect to outright aggressive acts – can we inculpate these religions (and theologies and Buddhologies along with them) on these matters in this way? Or, more positively, in what senses can such a course of argument be followed and justified when charges of possible reification could weaken the general approach?

First, my own analytical stance requires that we should make as many stabs at the sociology of action and knowledge as we can to clarify what happens over time in such situations. I admit this is terribly difficult in the Sri Lankan case because, between the writing of such chronicles as the Buddhist *Mahavamsa* (c.500 CE) and the post-colonial reassertion of Sinhala culturo-religious pride in post-colonial times (from the late 1940s), we have so little evidence to explain in depth how the Tamils, Veddahs and other pre-Buddhist peoples became marginalized in their own land.[14] In the case of Australia, we have over two centuries of documented history, telling of a much heavier marginalizing process, with a serious depopulation of Aboriginal groups, cultural destruction, forced assimilation and cramping reservation policies.[15] The Australian case gives us more opportunity to reflect on the many agents involved in European conquest (from 1778). There was a colonial, and then what became an imperial 'takeover', which meant that foreign (chiefly British) settlers acquired more and more land along a widening frontier. As in America, the frontier was always the hotly contested jagged lines where indigenes were most vulnerable to brutalities, and where fighting (sometimes small wars) for land and livelihood occurred, with the Aborigines faced with skilled horsemanship, superior firepower and the technology of fencing. As the frontier widened, the newcomers, safe inside it, got on with their business (with Aboriginal remnants trying to make good from their defeat). This conforms to what we may call 'David Hume's law': once one civilization conquers another, it is not long before the conflict of takeover appears to cease and the known divisions of labour fall into operation. Before long in the Australian case, by the 1880s, colonial Victoria saw the first metropolis in world history – 'Marvellous Melbourne' – arisen on the banks of the humble Yarra River (three months before Chicago, they say).[16]

As I have put it elsewhere of such situations, when great products of the empires of history transpire, a vast space of relative peace for the lucky enclosed majority is created that could be 'filled with religious people'. The whole empire of which they formed a part was one of those highly complex institutions, the largest of expansionist entities, that

> needed religion to cohere within themselves and to legitimate their causes. Wonderful people lived out beautiful spiritual lives within them, 'making their own [inspirational] history', to adapt Karl Marx, yet not normally under conditions of their own choosing,

---

14 Note Velupillai Rasanayakam, Sinnatamby Thuraisingam and Trompf, 'Sri Lanka', in Garry W. Trompf (ed.), *Islands and Enclaves: Nationalisms and Separatist Pressures in Island and Littoral Contexts*, New Delhi, Sterling, 1993: 121, 126n25, where other ancient, including Tamil, chronicles are mentioned.
15 Start with C.D. Rowley, *The Destruction of Aboriginal Society*, Sydney, Penguin, 1983.
16 Begin with Graeme Davison, *The Rise and Fall of Marvellous Melbourne*, Melbourne, Melbourne University, 1978. See David Hume, *Essays: Moral, Political and Literary*, edited by Eugene F. Miller, Indianapolis, Liberty, 1985: 471-4.

but, under the aegis of hard-nosed political decision-taking 'that would drive any peace-loving idealist to despair.'[17] In Australia the models of a great society were being formed – beneficial trade unionism, basic wage, measures of social security, widening franchise – though all the while the Aborigines languished. It was as if the latter did not exist for the vast mass of citizens, who never came across them in their daily, promise-filled, highly urbanized lives.

This is where Professor May's challenge comes in. For him, Christianity 'failed' the indigenous Australians, just as Buddhism has the earlier inhabitants of Lanka, and was implicated *qua* religion in the violence done to them. Readers will see how, philosophically, I might have problems with that, given my alertness to lurking reification. And sociologically, also, because I would want to know the minds of who was doing what, whether those who 'killed blacks for sport' on the empire's fringes had any semblance of an expected Christian moral sense, very sharply aired by those city preachers who prophesied awful chastisements to befall Australia for what had been done to the Aborigines.[18] Still, I am ready to take John May's points; there seem to be senses in which religions 'do' things after all. They are conservative fixtures (like any legal apparatus); their notions and general structures are here for what Nicolas-Antoine Boulanger called *la longue durée*,[19] and what happens through their enduring presence 'conditions' how people behave in particular historical circumstances. Strictly speaking, of course, that is only because persons activate religion as a resource; but indeed its 'sticking ability' makes it a likely culprit for influencing 'hosts of minds in search of meaning'. The large religions, therefore, carry 'potential', a key point in May's arguments, for violence or peace, because they can be drawn on for good and ill. They can easily become the seedbeds of horror – in that sense 'perpetuators' of suppression – when encountering smaller-scale tribal religions because, armed with holy books, they contain a long-inured sense of superiority and finality *vis-à-vis* what is taken on first look as vulgar, superstitious and without foundation before the 'high truths' of theology or Buddhology.[20] Religions, then, have too often 'created conditions' for rejection-of-the-other and, thus, even their missionary representatives have been sadly less ready for a non-negative recognition of how different human groups have 'felt after' the divine (Acts 17:27), or for an exploring of common or related spiritual insights in dialogue.

Each investigator must needs find his or her own way in addressing or untangling these crucial issues. In my own work I have preferred to refine and build on the prior scholarly differentiation between 'natural' and 'salvation' religions. To cover the former, by referring to research on 7000-odd living tribal traditions, as well as attempts to reconstruct both ancient imperial religions and the religions of people we know they absorbed (before Asoka in the 2nd century BCE), I proffer the simplest definition of a 'basic, fundamental and perennial religion' as: that which celebrates fecundity and

---

17 Garry Trompf, 'Religion and Violence: A Macrohistorical Perspective', in John Squires and William Emilsen (eds.), *Validating Violence — Violating Faith? Religion, Scripture and Violence*, Adelaide, Australian Theological Forum, 2007: chapter 11.
18 See Henry Reynolds, *The Law of the Land*, Melbourne, Penguin, 1992: 91-6 (especially on the 1830s).
19 Nicolas-Antoine Boulanger, *Recherches sur l'origine du despotisme oriental*, London, Seyffert, 1762: 103 (Boulanger being sadly unacknowledged as coiner of this phrase – used later by Otto Brunner and Fernand Braudel – for social research).
20 On the religion/superstition dichotomy already in Classical and Patristic Writing, see Wayne Meeks, *Inventing Superstition from Hippocrates to the Christians*, Cambridge Mass., Harvard University, 2004.

victory. This is *religio*, nicely (if perhaps too conveniently!) encapsulated in the major ritual preoccupations of Roman government to secure *prosperitas* and *victoria* (and how modern it all sounds). The titular founders of the so-called 'salvation religions' (*Erlösungsreligionen*, as first called by Hermann Siebeck), from Zarathushra onwards, raised questions that did not seem to occur in the 'natural' ones, especially concerning the state of one's (immortal) soul on the other side of death, for they abandoned the old presumption that everybody ended up in the same 'happy hunting ground'. In their various historical contexts, these great teachers of salvation, who scotch up fame in textbooks on Comparative Religion, radically criticized the great animal sacrifices that signalled hope for fertility and security through magico-spiritual aid; and they worried over war and violence – in well known cases, those of Zarathushra, Buddha, Mahavir, Mo-Tzu, and Jesus, opposing it altogether. Our argument proceeds, nonetheless, that, however much the world has been changed by new principles of care, compassion, and love, the basic, fundamental, perennial, and, yes, more natural *religio* can never be wished away. It is more colourful and earthy, and appeals better to the basic instincts of the human species.[21]

This *modus explicandi* permits a number of differentials for the analysis of the possibilities for religion in later, including contemporary, times. It accommodates the difference between 'original visions' and 'later outcomes', so that early ideals can be shown to be undone by the perennial impetuses of 'the perennial religion' (in our special sense)[22] and it also recognizes that salvation religions are usually vulnerable to subversion, precisely because they do not fit with the pursuit of power, force, profit and imperial expansion. This line allows, then, for the phenomena of 'used' and/or 'bastardized' religion: traditions such as Buddhism (probably first posited as a meditative philosophy of life) and Christianity (first presented by Paul as 'faith' *against* classic religiosity that cajoled the divine) are 'turned into religions', and are debased and manipulated – for purposes of exploitation, oppression, excused violence – against their original purposes. In this fashion I would shift the blame, try to discern between true and false representatives of great traditions, and sift ideals from disfigurations, a non-capitulating integrity from nationalist myths and patriotic agendas, and problematic religion from something that was initially held up to be better.[23] John D'Arcy May's positioning, however, leaves me challenged, impelling me to ask myself whether I am too committed to 'saving the face' of socio-spiritual morphologies that, in his more honest-looking appraisal, will always and inevitably carry possibilities within them for both bane and benefit.

---

21 In a first formulation, see Garry Trompf, 'Salvation and Primal Religion', in David Dockrill and Godfrey Tanner (eds.), *The Idea of Salvation* [Special Supplementary Issue of] *Prudentia* (1988): 207-12; with some deferring to Robert Bellah, 'Religious Evolution', in *American Sociological Review* 29 (1964): 358-74. See Hermann Siebeck, *Lehrbuch der Religionsphilosophie*, Frankfurt a.M., Mohr, 1893: chapter 5; yet, see Adolf Jensen, *Mythos und Kult bei Naturvölkern*, Wiesbaden, Franz Steiner, 1951: chapter 1, on notions of concrete salvation, and relations of ideas to practice, in 'nature religions' (thanks to Friedegard Tomasetti).
22 I am obviously not referring to perennialism as found in the *philosophia perennis* of Agostino Steuco, the traditionalist position of Frijhof Schuon, or the perennial mysticism *à la* Aldous Huxley.
23 Ponder, e.g., Carl Amery, *Die Kapitulation: oder, Deutscher Katholizismus heute*, Hamburg, Rowohlt, 1963 (on compromises by Catholic leadership for social power in Germany from World War 2 to 1960); and the United States interdenominational Traditional Values Coalition's pandering to uphold Presidential powers to interrogate likely 'terrorists' (see http//www.traditionalvalues.org/modules, with thanks to Michael Otterman).

Martin Wilson MSC

Gsell Centenary: Missiological Reflections

Cultural and Missionary Expansion

In this essay[1] I will look at missionary expansion as a form of cultural expansion. I am leaving aside all religious considerations such as Christ's missionary mandate. Succinctly and in philosophical mode, I understand 'culture' as 'the human way of being'. Particular cultures vary in the ways they embody and express particular modalities in virtually limitless possible variety. In and through persons cultures are alive and have an inner dynamism. Some are more reflective, self-conscious, self-aware than others. Some are more active and expansive. They vary in the way they activate their potential – outwardly, aggressively, contemplatively, pacifically, inventively. Their inner dynamism has periods, highs and lows, is guided, driven, raised up or dragged down, improved or spoilt by the particular minds and wills in which they are incorporated at any particular time. They have a history and a dynamic direction.

Application to the Northern Territory

In something of a Teihardian stance, I see that we have two massive interconnecting cultural movements to attend to. There was the colonial expansion of European culture during the second millennium, and the missionary expansion of Christianity during the same time but particularly in the second half of the millennium. The cultures were simply expanding. When the Jesuits came to the Territory in the 1880s, they summed up their task thus:

> Religion is primary in our intention, but in a manner secondary in our practice, because we recognize that we must first civilize the blacks before we can Christianize them…[2]

Bishop Gsell stated the same principle, as did Bishop John O'Loughlin MSC after him. In his masterly recent study of the missiology operating in Darwin diocese during the episcopacy of O'Loughlin, Fr. Peter Hearn quotes some succinctly worded notes made by Bishop O'Loughlin while on pastoral visitation to Port Keats mission, around 1958. He summarized the mission's role under three heads:

---

1. This essay, in substance, was first delivered in Darwin, 14 August 2006, as an address during the celebration of the centenary of the arrival of the Missionaries of the Sacred Heart (MSC) in Australia's Northern Territory in the person of Fr. F.X. Gsell, who set foot on Darwin's wharf on 15 August 1906 as Administrator Apostolic of the Diocese of Victoria-Palmerston. The diocese eventually evolved into the Diocese of Darwin with F.X. Gsell MSC being ordained its first bishop in 1938. The aim of the address was to invite reflection on the missiological theory and practice used by Bishop Gsell and his fellow missionaries in the Northern Territory over the last one hundred years. I have omitted various introductory remarks.
2. Donald MacKillop SJ, 'Anthropological notes on the Aboriginal tribes of the Daly River, North Australia', in *Transactions of the Royal Society of South Australia* 17,2 (1893); see Martin Wilson MSC, *Ministry Among Aboriginal People: Missiological Overview of the Catholic Church in Australia*, number 7 in the PICT series, Melbourne, Collins Dove, 1988: 3.

    A. *Evangelize*: establish church: a) catechists; b) sisters; c) brothers and priests
    B. *Civilize*: a) Christian family…home; b) schooling; c) livelihood garden, stock, timber, arts and crafts
    C. *Integrate*: a) cattle stations; b) farms on Daly [River].[3]

Sometimes the first head was stated as 'Christianize'. Peter Hearn shows that the mission policy implemented by the Catholic Church in the first half of last century was standard vanilla-flavoured missiology. The missionary aimed to 'save souls', both the people's souls and his or her own in the process.

Two giant waves, then, broke upon the Australian shore at the same time: European colonial extension and Christian missionary expansion operating within two major sections of the church, the Roman Catholic and the Protestant. The details of the complex interaction between these elements in the earlier part of Australian history need not absorb our time and attention here; the main thing to note is the extraordinary convergence between colonial and missionary expansion achieved in the Territory in the early part of the 20th century. The government was happy to use the missions as its 'agents' in the work of social development, the church's ministers being considered, and paid, as government field officers under the title of 'superintendent', later 'community advisor'.

Bishop O'Loughlin (Gsell's successor) expressed his complete satisfaction with the system in the speech he gave at the official opening of the Daly River mission in 1955:

> On an occasion like this it is surely a proper time to comment on the enlightened policy of Australian Government towards its native wards… Briefly it is this: to extend welfare services to a section of the community who, because of their history and primitive culture are unable of themselves to be assimilated into the life of the Australian society. In this extension Government recognizes and assists Missionary Societies prepared to engage in this work. In fact, Mr. Hasluck has expressed the view that Government and missions are 'co-partners in a joint enterprise'. This is eminently just and fair, accepting a principle of subsidizing social services which has not yet found acceptance in the Australian community at large.[4]

Bishop Gsell made the point even more forcefully: 'no one, I think, would dare to deny that the true faith is the generating force of civilization.'[5] Many non-believers would indeed deny that true faith is genetically connected to civilization; to them Bishop Gsell responds by an *argumentum ad hominem*:

> …these fine talkers, few of whom have given the subject any deep thought, themselves enjoy the benefits of Christian civilization: and they enjoy this security because, in day[s] of old, missionaries brought these benefits to their forebears. The heathens [viz. the unconverted Aborigines] are men as we are men and, as such, they have the same right that we have to the benefits of Christianity.[6]

---

3 Peter Hearn MSC, *A Theology of Mission Diocese of Darwin 1949-1985*, Kensington, NSW, Nelen Yubu Missiological Unit, 2003: 25.
4 Hearn, *A Theology of Mission*: 23. It may be useful to note that the style of language used even in official places last century would be frowned upon today – well-meaning, but very patronizing. Perhaps some will remember wincing at Bishop O'Loughlin's deliberate and public use of the term 'myall', which he defended as being technically exact and therefore inoffensive.
5 F.X. Gsell MSC, *The Bishop with 150 Wives: Fifty Years as a Missionary*, Sydney, Angus and Robertson, 1956: 38.
6 Gsell, *The Bishop*: 38-39.

Bishop O'Loughlin used much the same argument in his speech at the opening of the Daly River mission in 1955, though with an intriguing turn of phrase he aligned himself more diplomatically with the critics of mission:

> We others, even when we disclaim religious belief or practice, continue to live within the framework of a civilization rooted and founded in Christianity. We are the heirs, often unwittingly, of centuries of Christian teaching.

It is too much to expect the aborigines to survive and be assimilated without the faith.[7]

'Civilize'

The key concept in this view of evangelization is the word and concept 'civilize'. By origin it indicates a person living in a *civis*, that is, a city or a city state. It indicates organization and structure, systems of responsibility. In the Territory, the Jesuits on the Daly River saw their first task in time was to 'civilize'. Evangelization would come later, as the ultimate goal.

The Jesuits used an agrarian model based on the very successful social reconstruction that their Jesuit Society had built up in Paraguay some 200 years earlier. They considered they could do nothing of lasting value with the Aborigines, as before with the Paraguayan Indians, unless they could get them to settle down on small farms where the Aborigines could achieve economic independence, their children could go to school and become educated, that is, learn to read and write.

'To become civilized' meant to become settled down, basically, as a farmer. This proposition is presented as self-evident. Bishop Gsell did not think the task of transforming Aboriginal society into an agrarian one would be easy, but it was the way to go and he was a patient man. He wrote:

> ...whatever may be said to the contrary, it is not impossible to reform the aboriginal attitude towards life so that he can become a planter and, indeed, a good Christian. Yes, the process must be long and inevitably obstructed by difficulties; but how many centuries did it take white men to emerge from barbarity? The main thing is to face up to the task and to stick to it, trusting in God.[8]

On these terms, the ones who became 'civilized' were the Brothers. In the early days of each of the mission stations the Brothers put in countless hours of hard labour planting extensive vegetable gardens and orchards. These were an economic necessity as transport to outlying missions was so difficult, and often quite impossible for months during the Wet season. Work in the gardens was often a pre-requisite for hand-outs of sugar, tea, flour and tobacco, but once 'sit-down money' became available in the 60s the Aboriginal interest in gardening quite disappeared.

In my researches I was amused at a comment that Br. Garney Groves had written in his diary in 1944 when he was working at Arltunga:

> Bishop Gsell once told of how, in his own village, each house had a cow and each morning a shepherd would come along the street and the cows would leave their places and be taken to a common to graze. In the evening, they would return and each cow would leave the herd as it came to its own yard.

---

7 Hearn, *A Theology of Mission*: 24.
8 Gsell, *The Bishop*: 39.

(Br. Groves added to this, in a grim inconsequential manner: 'My first job was pulling down wurlies.') Bishop Gsell came from farming country near Goulburn in NSW. One can read between the lines: 'It's not the way we run dairy farms out in Goulburn!' I don't suppose in his wildest dreams Bishop Gsell thought he could reproduce the village style of Sainte-Croix-aux-Mines in the Northern Territory!

It should be remembered that Dom (later Bishop) Salvado of New Norcia in Western Australia had actually tried to share the nomadic life of the tribes. The Benedictines gained good working knowledge of the local languages, but little lasting effect otherwise, and the personal cost was too high. In 1851 Bishop Salvado wrote:

> Thus the practical study of the language, laws, traditions and customs of the natives made us realize, among other things, that the very demanding wanderer's life which we had first adopted was only of doubtful use. It called for the sacrifice of health and life on the part of the missionaries, with little to show for it at the end. On the other hand, the method of stability, that is, the founding of a mission, where hospitality could be given to all the natives who wanted to learn a trade or receive religious instruction, would yield good results, without exposing us to all the hardships of the nomadic life.[9]

The mission policy adopted by the Benedictines resulted in founding the New Norcia monastery as a centre of Christian life and education; this is the way the Benedictines evangelized Europe after the barbarian invasions. People would be influenced towards Christianity to the extent that they came into New Norcia's sphere of influence. A similar policy was followed in the north of Western Australia at Kalumbaru.

The Connection between Social Development and Evangelization

Is it really the case that we cannot evangelize unless we 'civilize' first? The gospel was written in a Jewish context. One of the first movements in the early Christian church was to break the connection with Judaism. St Paul contended that to be a follower of Christ one did not need to adopt Jewish culture and ways of worship. The Christian eucharist quickly replaced the temple sacrifices. Some of us would think that we have not moved sufficiently away even yet from Jewish styles of prayer, the psalms and all that. At any rate, it is accepted that the gospel way is quite distinct from the Jewish cultural way. It is significant that in the *Acts of the Apostles* (9:2) the early Christian church was called 'the Way'. Is it bound up intrinsically with any specific cultural way? I think we would immediately rule out any candidate that might be suggested. To be Christian we don't have to think and behave only like the English. Or like Italians, or Africans... or Chinese, or Europeans, or whatever. Nowadays, since the reforms of Vatican II, we take it for granted that if we do belong to one or other of these cultures, we have the right and privilege of being Christians according to the manner of our cultural status.

Why then must the Aborigines abandon their native culture and way of living (I use 'native' in its original sense) and become a sort of black Englishmen or Frenchmen or – this is a difficult phrase – black white Australians, in order to enter the Christian church? Could not their Christian way of worship be integrated in principle with the *wonga* or the *lirga* just as fully as with the very staid and stationary Gregorian chant or plainsong? White Christians attending such an integrated Aboriginal mass might feel rather out of

---

9 See Wilson, *Ministry*: 7.

place – but no more, I presume, than an Aboriginal tribesman feels in the pews of a white parish church in town on Sunday.

It is not unexpected that the government would aim at assimilation for the sake of simple public order, but why did the early missionaries assume so easily that one must take on a 'European' style of life if one is to become Christian? It is no wonder that our churches are largely empty of Aborigines.

I liked a comment Pastor Paul Albrecht made to me in Alice Springs in 1975 while I was preparing for a missionary conference for all the MSCs to be held at Daly River later on that year. Pastor Albrecht saw that the role of the church in that age of social change was to help clarify the issues for the Aboriginal people so as to enable them to make their own informed choice. If a man came to him and said that all he wanted from white society each year was a new shirt and pair of trousers, Pastor Albrecht would point out that he could fulfil his desires by living out in the bush in the freedom of his own country, doing a good bark painting some time in the year, bring it in to Alice Springs and sell it, buy his new shirt and trousers and go back home. If however he would like a radio cassette, a Toyota landcruiser, a TV set, a deep freeze and an array of similar things, then he had to realize and accept the implications of his choice: house, employment, hours of work, education, community habitation, life under social control and the rest of it.

Appreciation of Aboriginal Culture

When the first missionaries arrived in the Territory they must have come with a great many prejudicial notions about Aboriginal society, which had received a very negative press from explorers and anthropologists of the early evolutionist persuasion. They found much in Aboriginal culture not to their liking, but, there was also a lot that they came to admire. The Jesuits recorded particular appreciation of the Malak Malak language along the Daly:

> It is a beautiful language – or rather, contains the elements of a very perfect one. So philosophical is it, that it forces the conclusion that this despised race in times remote and in other lands was very much higher in the social scale than we now find it…Their language abounds in highly metaphysical distinctions unknown to ours.[10]

Is it the case that evolutionist blinkers were preventing them from appreciating the reality before their very eyes?

Bishop Gsell was very critical of aspects of the Tiwi culture, particularly their treatment of young women. He showed a grudging admiration for their democratic social structure.[11] He saw them as so totally communistic that, tongue-in-cheek, he advised any serious student of communism to go and live with the Tiwi for a while—he was sure such a student would return totally cured of his illusions![12] He showed in his book, *The Bishop with 150 Wives*, that he had paid a lot of attention to the Tiwi social system. In the epilogue, Fr. Dupeyrat quotes him thus:

> Fifty years ago, when I started my missionary life, anthropology was still in its infancy. If it had been developed as it is in our days, it would have been very useful to me and would have helped me to avoid many mistakes. I had to

---

10 See Wilson, *Ministry*: 13.
11 See Gsell, *The Bishop*: 28, 54.
12 Gsell, *The Bishop*: 32.

establish contact with the natives, alone, slowly, prudently; I had to endeavour, to the best of my ability, to learn gradually their habits and customs so as to penetrate into their minds and hearts without hurt or shock.[13]

All the same I wonder if many missionaries have had as much effect on the very social structure of their people as Bishop Gsell had on the Tiwi. Through the bravery and desperation of Martina,[14] a young Tiwi woman, and his own courageous and intelligent response to her plight, he undermined a key social structure of Tiwi society. He broke the power of the polygynous gerontocracy. Thereby, he created two new social classes: the unmarried, unpromised, uncommitted girls and the free widows. He did not do it in one stroke, but that was the eventual result of the decision he made to buy Martina as a 'wife' in 1921. In principle, the old men no longer had total control of the young women, nor of the widows, and thereby they lost one of the main levers of control that they had been able to exercise over the young men expecting early access to a wife, that is, a recent widow, while they were being forced to wait for the eventual maturation of their 'promised' one's daughter.

Recently, as I consulted the anthropological records at AIATSIS [Australian Institute of Aboriginal and Torres Strait Islander Studies] in Canberra, I expected to be confronted with a host of objections by anthropologists to what this missionary had done. In an article in *Hecate*, Tony Scanlon referred to 'considerable opposition from anthropologists and other groups'.[15] Scanlon's own criticism was mainly of style: the dismissive way in which Gsell spoke about Aboriginal culture. He had a better founded complaint when he considered the way other missionaries in the north had broken up existing polygynous marriages and redistributed the wives on the spot, thus causing a deal of confusion in the kinship system. The trouble for Gsell's critics was that they tended to be applauding the incoming liberation of women in their own home societies and so could scarcely condemn the new freedom women were gaining among the Tiwi. If Fr. Gsell had been going about his task in a rushed and violent manner that could have

---

13 Gsell, *The Bishop*: 173-174.
14 A brief summary might be helpful. Gsell describes the pivotal incident in Chapter V, simply entitled 'Martina'. She was 'an intelligent, lively little girl'. Like other little Tiwi girls, she stayed with the Sisters for schooling, but back in 1921 was not yet baptized. An old man came out of the bush one day and claimed her as his 'promised' wife. With sorrow, Fr. Gsell had to say farewell to her: they were all bound by the tribal law. Martina begged to be allowed stay, but she was led off in tears. She did not settle down and was punished with a spear-thrust into her leg. As soon as she could, she fled back some 40 miles to the mission. When her husband and his companions came with their spears ready to take her back, with a fight if need be, Gsell managed to delay them. Over night, he got the idea of *buying* her from her husband and his tribe. Tiwi were quite happy to sell their women for a few days to visiting pearl divers and such like, but to sell her forever was not an action sanctioned by tradition! Gsell laid out a most enticing array of goods, such as axes, knives, flour, tobacco and pipe. After long discussion the Tiwi men decided that they could sell Martina as his wife, provided he kept her as such. So, Fr. Gsell gained an official Tiwi wife. He said he never agreed to the codicil that he would not pass her on to another. In due course, she found a young baptized Tiwi man whom she was happy to marry. They had five children. When her daughter, Elizabeth, was claimed as 'promised' wife, Gsell came to realize that in buying a wife he also had to add ownership of his 'wife's' female offspring into the bargain: he had to buy off the prospective son-in-law as well. When Gsell was made bishop, he was proud of the soubriquet 'Bishop with 150 wives'. Sadly, Martina contracted leprosy later on in life and died at the Channel Island leprosarium.
15 Tony Scanlon, '"Pure and Clean and True to Christ": Black Women and White Missionaries in the North', in *Hecate* 12,1-2 (1986): 82-105: 91.

been a basis for criticism. On the contrary, Fr. Gsell was praised by the leading anthropologist of the day, Professor Baldwin Spencer, for his careful approach. In his biography of Baldwin Spencer, Professor Mulvaney writes:

> Gsell's elementary yet tentative anthropological approach towards first comprehending Aboriginal culture and language, in order to transform it, gained Spencer's grudging approval. His correspondence contains numerous references to the strength of Gsell's character and his success, as compared with [others]...[16]

More serious criticism came from within the mission itself for precisely the opposite reasons. In the early 1920s, his MSC companion, Fr. Bill Henschke, wrote to the Australian Provincial superior, complaining about the lack of standard missionary activity. By that time there had been no adult baptisms, no attempt at adult instruction, the free distribution of food and tobacco without the demand for anything in return – in fact he believed the mission a total failure and he expected its imminent closure. (It is ironic that that was the very same time as Fr. Gsell made his epoch-making purchase of Martina.) His own desire was to get as far away as possible, preferably to New Guinea. His letters make sad reading. He had been working for six years in the saw mill with no chance to do normal priestly ministry. His main comfort came from the care that the OLSH Sisters showed for him. Reading Fr. Henschke's complaints and having heard in an interview many years later the comments of another of Bishop Gsell's early priestly co-workers, Fr. John McGrath MSC, one has to acknowledge that Bishop/Fr. Gsell was a hard taskmaster. In his case, Fr. Henschke was mercifully moved to Darwin in 1922, where he remained in dedicated service until his death 50 years later.

Nowadays we profit from the perceptive investigations of anthropologists like W. E. H. Stanner and have come to admire the poetic mysticism of Aboriginal religion. Aboriginal artists have introduced us somewhat to the richness of their vision of the world. We are bewitched by the Dreaming, and we are learning to admire the intricacies and functionality of their kinship systems.

Social Development

While I have suggested criticism of the connection that early missionaries in the Territory perceived between Christianity and a settled agrarian way of life, I have to acknowledge that the Catholic view of mission as spelt out in the Papal missionary encyclicals of last century – well covered by Peter Hearn in his thesis[17] – outlines a responsibility of the church to develop social systems that promote justice and proper human development for all peoples. More importantly, documents from Vatican II envisaged a world wherein every human value that is good would be acknowledged as part of God's creative plan and so become an operative part of the Kingdom of God on earth and in time. That is what the missionary is endeavouring to bring about! Nowadays, the missionary goal is much bigger than the 'saving of souls', which was the vision when Fr. Gsell and his companions first came out to this part of the world; it is even more than 'planting the church'; it is saving the world itself, with all its particular cultures and peoples, men and women, whether they be inside or outside the formal structures of

---

16 D.J. Mulvaney, and J.H. Calaby, *'So Much that is New' Baldwin Spencer, 1860-1929: A Biography*, Melbourne, Melbourne University, 1985: 301.
17 Hearn, *A Theology of Mission*: 27-30.

church membership or not. As St Paul saw, it is redeeming creation itself and restoring everything in Christ.

Overview

This brings me back to my beginning, the Teihardian view. Over the ages one can discern an expansion of human culture in awareness, language, information technology, music, art, mechanical technology, medicine, food production…in spite of all the negatives of war, cruelty, inhumanity, social injustice, persecution, ethnic cleansing and the rest. Parallel with this expansion and intrinsically connected with it at times, subtly informing, reforming and purifying it, is the other great force stemming from the life, death and resurrection of Christ the Lord. Reflecting on this century of missionary endeavour makes us aware of the great saga we are involved in. In conclusion I would like to make two points:

Firstly, Nungalinya College[18] is both a symbol and an instrument in a most important, if relatively recent, missiological advance in the diocese of Darwin. An Aboriginal Christian ministry is being formed: surely, it is only Aboriginal ministers who can guide and nourish the completion of the missionary process amongst their own communities. And this great work of ministerial formation is being performed by three of the major branches of the Christian church working in formal union. This augurs well for the future. The Nungalinya commitment is surely one of the high points of the episcopacy of Bishop Ted Collins, successor to O'Loughlin.

Secondly and finally, we should remember the challenge which Pope John Paul II put before us and the Aboriginal people of Australia at Alice Springs, in 1986, in his address at Blatherskite Park:

> You are part of Australia and Australia is part of you. And the Church herself in Australia will not be fully the Church that Jesus wants her to be until you have made your contribution to her life and until that contribution has been joyfully received by others.

---

[18] The site for the original address of this paper.

Part 3

Interreligious Relations as Ecumenics

Raquel Bouso García
Emptiness as Compassion

I

The absence of fixed points of reference can be considered one of the crucial problems which the contemporary world has to face. For more than two centuries, Western philosophical thought has used universal legitimating principles or ultimate values to guide its world-view; these have now reached a crisis point. Attempts to diagnose the origin and the manifold signs of the problem have been disparate; though, it seems that the main factors which have contributed to the loss of the traditional points of reference, i.e., the generalization of secularization and the summit of scientific-technical rationalism, are agreed. On the one hand, the transference of a system of significances, removed from the ancient theological sphere, to the profane 'secular' world has taken place,[1] and on the other, a dehumanization process has followed the dominion of technique in all the fields in which human life develops. Contemporary philosophical discourses, even those of literature or art in general, too, talk about a 'devaluation of values', 'disenchantment of the world', 'loss of the centre', or 'crisis of meaning'. The unrest of the age these expressions refer to can be lumped together under the label of 'nihilism'.

Surely, in order to understand the world in which we live, we cannot ignore the reflections that the question of nihilism raises, namely, that of meaning. Modern life, characterized by the prevalence of technique, consumption, and mass culture, seems to have eliminated the possibility of a unique perspective from which to consider reality and to lay the foundations of human acting. Now placed in doubt, the idea of transcendence, and even that of truth, all dogmatisms and ideologies have fallen; and paradigms, once regarded as undeniable, have been voided of their privileged status of meaning. As relativism and skepticism make their way, there are people who are bent on restoring traditional languages and values, by attempting to preserve or review them so that they become adapted to the times. Some thinkers take the criticism of nihilism as an instructive opportunity for us to become conscious of the precariousness and conventionality of the principles we 'choose' to be guided by. Others, however, take it that we must abandon or overcome as soon as possible modern ways, above all those concerning the moral or ethical domain.

It is this background of nihilism and its problematic that leads to our starting point and a pivotal topic in the philosophy of Japanese thinker NISHITANI Keiji (1900-1990), regarded as one of the foremost representatives of the Japanese philosophical scholars known collectively as the Kyoto School. For Nishitani, the phenomenon of nihilism is not just a philosophical problem or an historical situation of crisis in Western culture; it is also an existential problem that every individual has to face, inasmuch as living here and now demands that we ask about the meaning of existence. Like Nietzsche, who

---

[1] Lluís Duch, *Armes espirituals i materials: religió*, Barcelona, Publicacions de l'Abadia de Montserrat, 2001: 209.

asserted that he lived nihilism deeply inside himself,[2] Nishitani invites us to cross through nihilism, arguing that if one wishes to overcome it, one must go through it, since it is only from the contemporary person's recognition of the disorientation in which she or he finds herself or himself immersed that she or he would be able to avoid wrong ways which lead to false goals and will, instead, be capable of following the direction traced by one's true nature.

How a positive reading of nihilism can be taken, though, is something that is not very obvious. To experience the negativity implied in this phenomenon means to plunge into uncertainty, angst, and lack of sense. It is sufficient to take note of the isolation of the modern individual or the crisis of self-representation of culture as a result of the fragmentation of our picture of the world. Doubt is cast on traditional authorities which, employing the language of accomplishment of a divine plan of salvation or the progress of humankind, served as criterions of truth and of a sense of the world; this has led, for instance in Sartrean existentialism, to see existence as just a brief interval of time which passes from nothingness to nothingness, without course or horizon of meaning. Thus, without a reason to be, without a ground for being, life appears as meaningless; meanwhile, the nothingness, whose irruption into the philosophical scene, where it occasionally had been an object – if a marginal one – of reflection, went on to take up the place formerly reserved to gods or human reason. The moral crossroads this panorama depicts can be summarized in the dilemma posited by Dostoyevsky in his work *The Possessed* (1871-72): everything is allowed if God does not exist.

Nishitani, however, comes from a culture that has traditionally granted a preeminent place to nothingness. Thus, he decides to explore the latter's possibilities in this new modern setting. Particularly in debt to Mahāyāna Buddhism's conception of nothingness and the thinking of his master NISHIDA Kitarō (1870-1945), Nishitani, in his most celebrated work, *Shūkyō to wa nani ka* (1961),[3] elaborates philosophically a positive view of nothingness, one grounded in an experience which could be called religious. He names this view 'the standpoint of emptiness' (*kū no tachiba*). In this work, Nishitani does not propose an ethics, though we may say that a moral position does derive from its ontological, gnoseological and even anthropological assumptions. It is difficult, however, to speak properly about a moral position when the standpoint of emptiness is placed beyond the dichotomy between good and evil, and when overcoming the distance usually set up between things as they are and as they should be is posed. In fact, the question that could be framed about his ethical position is similar to that which comes up regarding the accusation against Buddhism that it is amoral or antinomian. That is, whether emphasizing one's own spiritual salvation indicates disinterestedness towards the world, lack of social compromise, or historical responsibility. The key to understanding the positions of the Buddhist in general and of the Japanese philosopher in particular may be clarified by examining D.T. Suzuki's own assessment:

> The direction of seeing through form as nothingness is designated Great Understanding, while the direction of seeing nothingness immediately concretized as form is designated Great Compassion.[4]

---

2 Friedrich Nietzsche, *Opere*, G. Colli and M. Montinari (eds.), Milano, Adelphi, 1964ff., volume VIII, t. II: 393.
3 Keiji Nishitani, *Religion and Nothingness*, translated with an Introduction by Jan Van Bragt, Foreword by Winston L. King, Berkeley, Los Angeles and London, University of California, 1982.
4 Daisetz Teitaro Suzuki, *Essays in Zen Buddhism*, First Series, London, Rider & Co., 1979: 19.

II

Certainly, Buddhist ethics is anchored in an individual experience, particularly, that directed towards one's own liberation. To release one from the suffering caused by human existence is the Buddhist promise of salvation. In order to do so, Buddhism proposes an ascetical-meditative path orientated to overcoming all our ways of being attached, especially the attachment to one's own ego or Self. The overcoming of desire and with it the extinction of suffering implies also a changing from ignorance (*avidyā*) to *prajñā*, the wisdom achieved in awakening to true reality; this is equivalent to what Suzuki refers to as 'Great Understanding' (Sanskrit, *mahā-prajñā*; Japanese, *daichi*) in the passage quoted above. Seemingly, then, it is an individual search and path, although from its origins Buddhism has taken the collective dimension into account, e.g., choosing monastic life, where the discipline of the community is ruled by precepts the basic moral principle of which is righteousness (i.e., right word, thought, action, and so on, in the Noble Eightfold Path).

Early on, Buddhism had to face the moral conflict entailed in seeking out one's own benefit; from this controversy arose – in the Mahāyāna traditions – the ideal of a *bodhisattva*. According to this ideal, the wise or enlightened person cannot reach complete enlightenment until all sentient beings do. For this reason, the bodhisattva promises to help others to achieve their own salvation. Zen Buddhism takes this position further and develops the idea of non-intentionality and spontaneity as guides to action; thus, the enlightened person is precluded from behaving according to utility criteria and from carrying out selfish acts.

In Buddhist thought, then, wisdom or enlightenment keeps close ties with altruistic or unselfish behaviour: technically, this is translated as 'Great Compassion' (Sanskrit, *mahā-karunā*; Japanese, *daihi*), and is regarded as the highest degree of love; indeed, it could be said that wisdom is the ground for compassion. Nevertheless, to return to Suzuki's quotation, how can the link between nothingness and form be the source of both? What kind of relationship can be established between nothingness and compassion? Again, though posing the question from Nishitani's philosophical viewpoint, how can nothingness become for contemporary persons a motive of compassionate or benevolent behaviour, if, as nihilism states, nothingness involves groundlessness and, therefore, meaninglessness? And, if contemporary philosophy has placed in doubt that the sense of the world relies on the world, would it be possible to find some sort of world-sense that is immanent to the world but which our concern with finitude prevents us from seeing?

From the Buddhist standpoint, compassion comes from wisdom because it results at the same time from the understanding of nothingness and its relationship with form. In this way, it may be said that Buddhist thought bestows primacy on ontology, not ethics. First of all, we should remark that here we are not dealing with a knowledge obtained by means of rational speculation or reflection but with the understanding of a lived experience, or in Nishitani's terms, a real realization of reality, actualized and understood.

See also the following Mahāyāna *prajñāpāramitā* teaching: 'Here, O Sāriputra, form is emptiness and the very emptiness is form [Sanskrit, *rūpam śūnyatā śūnyatā rūpam*, Japanese, *shikisokuzekū, kūsokuzeshi*]; emptiness does not differ from form, form does not differ from emptiness; whatever is form, that is emptiness, whatever is emptiness, that is form, the same is true of feelings, perceptions, impulses, and consciousness', *The Heart Sutra*, translated by Edward Conze, New York, Vintage, 2001: 86.

Thus, the moral attitude of the person who has lived such an experience is not a learnt behaviour acquired with use and which intends to follow certain external rules or emulate an ideal. Behaviour is not subordinated to a higher principle, be that God or the Kantian categorical imperative, though it derives directly and spontaneously from within. Here, we must not think of nothingness as a concept deduced from several premises; rather, it is a reality to be experienced. If Western speculation has tended to share Parmenides's thesis that nothingness is not and, therefore, cannot be thought, for Nishitani and the great part of the Eastern cultural tradition, nothingness is not merely a negation of being, it is the very ground of being. However, because it is no-thing in itself, we had better speak of groundlessness or, in the words of Nishitani's disciple UEDA Shizuteru of 'infinite openness'.

It is from this reasoning that the importance of the relationship between nothingness and form can be glimpsed. Buddhist thought, not resorting to notions of a transcendent supreme Creator, is founded on the principle of 'interdependent origin(ation)' (Sanskrit, *pratīyasamutpāda*; Japanese, *engi*). According to this, everything is relative to everything else and no thing is uncaused or existent by itself. The world consists of a web of causal relations among innumerable things which come into being and pass away in the dimension of time, a history without beginning or end. To Nishitani, this means that the world is formed as something new in each instant by means of the relations among all things, without a basis or ground. He does recognize, from the standpoint of being, an 'objective' self-sustaining entity; but, this is the world of forms. However, he cannot recognize a self-sustaining cognitive subject, since, in virtue of the world relational structure, the subject must be part of it too. It is clear from this that the subject, as the rest of things which make up the world, cannot be conceived as a fixed identity but, rather, as conditioned, changing and impermanent. To see this side of the question means to regard the world of being from the standpoint of nothingness, i.e., to see it from its ground, which is empty since there is no ground. Yet, Nishitani poses the possibility of seeing the world simultaneously from the standpoint of being and of nothingness, i.e., to embrace the 'standpoint of emptiness'. It is only from the experience of the simultaneity of time-eternity, life-death, being-nothingness, emptiness-form, that in his view it is possible to get in touch with the true reality of things. Thus, emptiness appears as the place where it is possible to get truly in touch with the real, or better, where the real gets in touch with the Self; when it neglects projection over reality and interference with the course of becoming, the Self is able to simply participate in what is, that is, in its suchness.

In this way, true reality can be considered as a dynamical process expressed in a kind of dialectical relationship between form and nothingness or emptiness. To assert with Suzuki the possibility of seeing nothingness through forms is similar to understanding the groundlessness of being as taught in the Buddhist doctrines of 'interdependent origin', of emptiness (Sanskrit, *śūnyatā*; Japanese, *kū*) and even of non-Self (Sanskrit, *anātman*; Japanese, *muga*). Yet, why is nothingness concretized as form designated 'Great Compassion'?

We do well to remember that the world-view that follows from the experience of enlightenment or realization derives from an existential search. Unless one's own self has been changed, it is not feasible to regard the world from the standpoint of nothingness through forms. Beginning, then, with Nishitani's reading of this conversion we may suggest an interpretation of the second part of Suzuki's statement. In this sense, the understanding of nothingness through forms corresponds to the moment in which the subject of the search is aware of his or her being and also of being nothing, i.e., only a provisory sum of aggregates without substratum or ground. This understanding entails the absolute negation of Self: in spite of the assertion that 'Self is emptiness', being devoid of ways of being, we cannot speak about a Self in a proper sense. However, to stop at this point would be to adopt the nihilistic standpoint, i.e., to see the Self (and the world of forms) solely from the side of finitude and impermanence. In fact, this negation is followed by an absolute affirmation, 'emptiness is Self'. Here is where the positive side of nothingness lies. In Nishitani's view, the Self as subject, orientated towards its original ground (which is groundlessness, emptiness) here and now, during the life and in the depth of the present instant, reaches its true identity and becomes a 'true Self'. In its true nature, the Self realizes emptiness for the first time, not as mere negation but rather, as the condition of possibility of being (emptiness concretized in forms), and understands that the different ways of being negated make up its 'being' or 'position' as subject and body, that is to say, its everyday Self.

The affirmation of the Self or subject which follows negation should not be interpreted as securing a personality or what makes us different or peculiar compared to others since it is the result of divesting the ego, a complete self-oblivion. *Religion and Nothingness* contains the idea of 'non-duality between self and other' (Japanese, *jitafuni*) as one of the consequences of the path of self-negation and self-affirmation. According to this idea, one of the ways in which the transformed Self can express itself in 'return to the world' after the self-negation experience is through the very encounters with others that take place in its everyday life. The Self which knows itself knows also the others as they are in themselves, and it does not distinguish itself from them. In Nishitani's view, this implies an equality more true than that obtaining in human rights. From the recognition of mutual dependence and identity with other beings as regards origin and groundlessness, it is possible to love without distinctions. Here appears compassion. Emptied from its self-love, the Self experiences the nullification required for understanding the relativity of all beings; 'all is one'; from this non-dualistic position, then, the Self does not emit judgments and its love lacks discriminations. From the standpoint of the conscious personal being or ego (the Self in its relations), 'I' and 'other' are two people, two human beings. Now, from the standpoint of the true self, seen in its impersonality or non-humanity (in its lack of determinations), 'I' and 'other' are not two.

For Nishitani, this love-compassion is not directed exclusively to human beings but embraces all sentient beings and all things. Against the claim of the autonomy of the subject and the person as a purpose in itself, the Self in its true mode of being, devoid of the merely human, becomes a means for other things; regarded as the substratum which underlies and makes all things equal, its love is impersonal. The Self is no longer the centre; the Self transfers the leading role to the rest of things, to reality as it is.

III

Nishitani's viewpoint derives from Buddhism and can be, at first sight, quite distant from Western's ways of thinking, and it has not lacked for controversy.[5] The non-dualistic perspective posed by Nishitani not only questions the ontological status of the subject, and against modern human self-consciousness puts forward an 'impersonal personality', but also places in doubt the privileged status of the subject as legislator and

---

5 On this topic see, for instance, John D'Arcy May, 'Nothingness-*qua*-love? The Loss and Recovery of "God" in Buddhist-Christian Dialogue', paper presented at the Institut Catholique, Paris, September 2005.

source of values, which are regarded as conventional. Nishitani goes on to ask if the subject is exhausted in the moral subject whose essence consists in being self-centred, in its autonomy, or conversely, if its possibility of existence lies in another more basic field. That is to say, is there a kind of self-consciousness in us that is more elemental than the autotelic self, a self that finds its *telos* in the self itself? His answer is that there is non-duality between nothingness and person.

Thus, to posit the problem of theodicy or the struggle between good and evil lacks sense, for in Buddhist thought, i.e., from Nishitani's non-dualistic position, the starting-point is the mutual correspondence of both principles. Good and evil possess here the same ontological and existential rank; one cannot exist without the other. To maintain the preeminence of one over the other would be the result of ignorance, the consequence of the dualist perception of mind peculiar to the world of appearances, the world that is to be overcome in order to return to true nature prior to all distinction. As Masao ABE notes, for Buddhism, the dichotomy of good and evil is overcome when the mind awakes to its original nature and is free from *karma* and the cycle of existences:

> La realizzazione della più chiara distinzione e dell'uguaglianza di bene e male non è altro che una *rivalutazione* della dicotomia bene-male raggiunta attraverso la nuova luce della vacuità. Sapienza (*prajñā*) e compassione (*karuṇā*) sono le qualità dinamiche che tracciano la via morale del buddhismo. La prima perché permette la conoscenza della vacuità, dell'ilusorietà dell'io e il distacco totale; la seconda perché volge l'ideale del distacco interiore nel più puro altruismo, trasformando cioè la dimenticanza del sé in donazione totale de la propria vita, dei propri meriti agli altri per la loro salvezza.[6]

So we see that being subject includes an experiential connotation and has to do with the relativity of things and events, since the comprehension of one's own self follows the comprehension of all things. Accordingly, all forms, in their difference and unity, belong to the same order of being, from which emanates a force that gathers together and makes everything come to be, that is, the emptiness which makes possible the becoming of the world. Thus, if behind 'the person' there is no substratum of reality but only appearances, then it cannot be understood as a fixed autonomous entity called Self or subject which is preconceived by its relations with objects as a permanent identity that remains self-identical in virtue of its being substantial or essential, or as a model abstracted from multiplicity. Instead of this, the Buddhist negation of self negates the fixed, static self and accepts the passing of time in which the Self is subject to unceasing change.

Identity, then, is built in a dialectical process between emptiness and forms. The person, since it is grounded in emptiness, acquires meaning as human being only in relation to others and in transcending its own individuality. Analogous to the idea of the universe, the human being is erected as a moral being inside the relationships established with others, as a sum of different interpretations. The person achieves a dynamic meaning in being in relation with others – they are mutually determined – and finds its true identity in the continuous movement which leads it to be always open to each situation, adapting to each context. Given that self is made through its relations and since it lacks ego, it can express itself fully at each moment and in every one of its relations. Therefore, emptiness offers us the chance of changing, of renewing and redefining constantly our relation with ourselves, others and things. Thus, the person is part of the

---

6 Masao Abe, 'Il perché del male nel cristianesimo e nel buddhismo', in Massimo Raveri (ed.), *Del bene e del male. Tradizioni religiose a confronto*, Venezia, Marsilio, 1997: 197-212.

flux of events; each of its acts emerges as a suitable answer to each particular situation and this continual openness permits the giving of significances, the granting of meaning.

This standpoint does not negate the moral link, then, as a foundation and as inherent to the human being, but holds that it could only be seen in the midst of this intrinsic order of things. Certainly, there is the risk remarked on by Abe of falling into indifference, apathy or passivity. However, this will happen only if emptiness is understood as an aim or objective in itself and not as a starting-point from which to reconsider one's experience of life. The realization of primordial unity should not be understood as a model or ideal but rather as something that arises from an inner necessity and that can serve to orientate our life in a right manner. Thus, though the idea of good and evil as absolutes is removed and the dichotomy of good and evil relativized this is so without detriment to morality expressed as compassion.

Terry Duffy

Transcending Violence and Constructing Memory
Case Studies in Reconciliation and Peace Memorialization from Japan and Cambodia

This chapter explores the emergence of the peace museum phenomena and the salient issues raised for the wider subject of exhibiting peace. Recent scholarly dialogue concerning the respective goals of reconciliation and peace memorialization has been encouraged by Professor John D'Arcy May's erudite *Transcendence and Violence*.[1] The interface between religions and cultures; the resulting (and invariably atavistic) conflicts, and (equally importantly) their mitigation or resolution are key-notes of May's scholarly work. I hope that this essay will contribute further to the insights thus generated by Professor May's path-breaking research in identifying and establishing the discipline of ecumenics as 'the field of force within which the complementarities and conflicts of identities and ideologies are held in a fruitful tension'.[2] These inquiries have contributed in particular to our understanding of the goals of transcending violence while constructing memory. I will seek to take stock of these objectives through several pertinent case-studies drawn from the contemporaneous experience of two demographically sizable Asian-Pacific nations, to wit, Japan and Cambodia. In the twentieth century, both countries endured a traumatic human loss of statistically seismic proportion – in the Japanese case arising from the post-WW2 legacy of the Atomic bomb, and in the Cambodian from the Khmer Rouge's mid-1970s' perpetration of an indiscriminate programme of 'auto-genocide'. Seen in this light, the respective post-conflict situations and recent histories of Japan and Cambodia are appropriate exemplars of the problems and possibilities that arise as societies earnestly confront the potentially contentious issues of societal reconciliation and peace memorialization.

Memorializing war or peace?

It is a matter of regret that while municipal and city authorities across the world have historically commemorated past battles with grandiose war monuments and accompanying ceremonies, they have invariably allocated only meagre funds to memorializing peace.[3] Thus at the launch of America's first embryonic 'Peace Museum' in Chicago in 1981, its founding director, Marianne Philbin regretted that war memorials were ubiquitous while her country, by contrast, still possessed 'no proper museum dedicated to building peace'. It has taken much independent initiative to progress the goal of peace memorialization and so to exhibit those (often intangible) fragments of physical and cultural heritage that might constitute 'a lexicon of peace'.[4] Such an object is meritorious in any

---

1 John D'Arcy May, *Transcendence and Violence: The Encounter of Buddhist, Christian and Primal Traditions*, New York and London, Continuum, 2003.
2 This quotation is from Professor May's delineation of the research strategy of the Irish School of Ecumenics (TCD), see www.tcd.ie/ise.
3 Terence Duffy, 'Civic Zones of Peace', in *Peace Review* 9,2 (June 1997): 199-205.
4 Terence Duffy, 'Exhibiting Peace', in *Peace Review* 5,4 (1993): 487-493.

part of the world but the challenge is all the more worthy and compelling in countries that possess a modern history as tragic as Japan's and Cambodia's. In the former, the Genocide Museum at Tuol Sleng is a visible 'memory' of a society's cavernous mental wounds while Japan's atomic legacy still looms formidably over modern living.[5] For this reason we explore the experience of transcending violence in these two Asian nations and seek to evaluate how their respective peoples have grappled with the construction of memory in a post-conflict society.

The psychological nightmare which has haunted and cast a shadow over Japan's post-WW2 societal reconstruction is poignantly documented in Robert Jungk's monumental, *Children of the Ashes*.[6] Conversely, Japan provides us with welcome inspiration in the rich contribution of its national and prefectural governments, as well as NGO initiatives, to the birth of the modern peace museums movement. Yet, the construction of such diverse 'edifices to peace' in post-war Japan has not been without controversy, reflecting (and sometimes accentuating) underlying political tensions. It would seem that what has elsewhere become a global trend has both enthusiastic advocates and belligerent opponents in present-day Japan. One should not, however, let 'rightist' political rancour obscure a popular groundswell of interest in celebrating peace. This situation can, thankfully, be interpreted reasonably positively. In the past twenty years, especially in Japan, Europe and America, there has been considerable interest in the peace museum idea and increasingly countries have opened such museums. The product of state, group or individual efforts – these museums have preserved a robust peace-making heritage which has often comfortably co-existed alongside the history of war.[7] Perhaps we can better delineate the encouraging directions in Japan by dissecting the wider international phenomena of peace memorialization.

It is possible to offer some broad observations about global trends in the creation of 'peace museums' and kindred examples of the public memorialization of peace. First are the core of museums which explicitly have 'peace' in their title, and are dedicated to peace education through the visual arts. This would include Chicago's Peace Museum, the Peace Museum in Bradford, UK, Oslo's Nobel Peace Prize Museum, and indeed more than thirty distinct museums across the world.[8] Then, there are many different 'issue-based' entities which have been formed in response to specific events.[9] In the last

---

5 See Michihiko HACHIYA MD, *Hiroshima Diary*, Chapel Hill, University of North Carolina, 1995: esp. v-xvii.
6 Robert Jungk, *Children of the Ashes: The People of Hiroshima After the Bomb*, London, Heinemann, 1961: esp. 7-15.
7 Terence Duffy, 'The Peace Museum Concept',in *Museum International* (UNESCO) 177 / 45,1 (1993): 4-8.
8 This preoccupation spans issues of regional peace (such as Germany's Peace Museum Meeder) to the global emphases of the Peace Palace at The Hague, and the League of Nations Museum in Geneva. It would also include museums of 'public peacemaking activity' such as the Museum of the Olympic Games in Lucerne, which documents the remarkable contribution of the 'Olympic spirit' to world peace. This 'family' of museums also incorporates the search for peace 'within peoples' as in the Yi Jun Peace Museum in Holland whose founder has been lobbying for another Peace Museum in the de-militarized zone, to encourage future Korean reconciliation. See *Peace Museums Worldwide*, Geneva, United Nations Publications on Peace, 1998: 162; the author is a contributor.
9 There are a number of Japanese museums of this type, such as Liberty Osaka, with its focus on human rights; Tokyo's Peace Museum Project on children's peace education; Nagasaki's Shokokumin Museum with its concern for Japan's war-time children; and the Poison Gas Museum on Okunoshima Island with its 'righteous appeal' against chemical weapons. Holocaust

ten years insightful peace centres have opened on the European war sites of Caen and Verdun. Also to be included are museums dealing with nuclear war (such as the peace museums in the Japanese cities of Hiroshima and Nagasaki). Just as the battlefields of Flanders became equated with the dawn of a new era in war, so too have Hiroshima and Nagasaki assumed a symbolic place in the nuclear age.

Of particular note is the Nagasaki Atomic Bomb Museum which opened in April 1996 and which offers a radical re-interpretation of modern Japanese history. Predictably, the new museum has outraged many on the Japanese political 'right'. In contrast, and indicating how issues from the war are still very much alive in Japan, Tokyo's Peace Memorial Museum of the War Dead project says little about Japanese militarism or about the lives of the occupied Asian peoples. That it is unlikely that the Tokyo venture will find the confidence of peace researchers, who see it more as a 'war museum' than one of peace, underlies continuing sensitivities in Japan and subtle ministerial or (equally likely) overtly political limits, in the promotion of the peace museum concept. It is, perhaps, revealing that peace is still so contentious and is seldom remote from parliamentary *realpolitik* in modern Japan.

Among other issue-based facilities that also contribute to peace memorialization one might include museums of genocide, such as the Tuol Sleng Genocide Museum in the Cambodian capital, Phnom Penh, and the several genocide museums and public exhibits which have been fashioned in the Rwandan capital, Kigali, and the Burundian city, Bujumbura.[10] There are museums which focus on the humanitarian achievements of stalwart individuals or virtuous charitable societies, such as the Florence Nightingale Museum in London, Italy's famous Red Cross Museum at Castiglione, the Henry Dunant House or the International Red Cross Museum, the latter two in Geneva.[11] Then there are 'museums of non-violence' – notably, the numerous Gandhi museums dotted around India, such as the National Gandhi Museum in New Delhi and the Gandhi Memorial Museum at Madurai.[12] As with many things, the devil is in 'the detail' or indeed the 'definition'. Precisely what might constitute a 'peace museum' and the manifest complexities of 'peace' phenomena is illustrated by two recent Japanese cases, viz., Tokyo's Peace Memorial Museum of the War Dead, and the completion of Nagasaki's new Atomic Bomb Museum. These two ventures have proven controversial examples

---

Museums, e.g., Yad Vashem, Israel, or Washington DC's Memorial Museum, and interpretative centres at former concentration camps, e.g., Dachau and Bergen-Belsen in Germany, and Auschwitz in Poland, and international venues such as Tokyo's Holocaust Education Center, collectively deserve to be treated as part of the increasingly all-encompassing *genre* of peace museums. For a detailed guide to Japanese and international 'peace-related' museums, see *Exhibition of Peace-Related Museums in Japan*, Kyoto, Kyoto Museum for World Peace, 1998: 38.

10 Lithuania has a Museum of Genocide Victims in Vilnius; Washington DC is planning the Armenian Genocide Museum and Memorial; and Nigeria's Ogoniland and Canada's Ottawa also have such proposals.

11 Also, the Franz Jägerstätter House in St. Radegund, which memorializes the German conscientious objector, the Carter Centre in Atlanta, Georgia (the peace and democracy complex assembled by Jimmy Carter), or the Woodrow Wilson House in Washington DC.

12 Satellite entities to these are spread across Europe, Australia and the USA. We might also include museums dedicated to particular non-violent campaigns, e.g., the National Civil Rights Museum, Memphis, which explores the American Civil Rights movement. Clearly, the peace museum idea is a potentially encapsulate one, see T.M. Duffy, 'The Role of Peace Museums in Peace Education: A new Terrain for Peace Educators', in Ake Bjerstedt (ed.), *Education for Peace*, Malmö, Peace Education Reports, 1994: 61-72.

illustrative, too, of conflicts in Japanese society. For these reasons, they merit further discussion.[13]

Peace Memorialization in Japan: Challenges and Possibilities

The proposal that a quasi-mausoleum to the 'war dead' be constructed in Tokyo proved something of a litmus test both for current Japanese thinking about WW2 and for its peace movement. The erection of what is essentially a 'national war memorial' was perceived by many international commentators as a 'macabre left-over' of the war-time generation. It has also been interpreted as an 'acid-test' that might defoliate or at least expose the camouflage concealing politically hostile patriotic sentiments, thus revealing the underlying 'closet militarism' of that generation'. By others, the venture is seen as still more insidious, contributing to the perpetuation – even renewal – of precisely such war-time sentiments. Located in the very centre of what is indubitably and iconographically 'rightist' territory in Tokyo, this initiative preserves many of the 'sacred cows' of a conservative political tradition. Tokyo's Yasukuni Shrine – with its symbolic associations of the Japanese 'war effort' abuts unto the 'Peace Memorial Museum of the War Dead'.[14] The exhibit itself is tasked to document the suffering of 'some three million persons' – ironically, this is exactly the quoted figure of 'Japanese war dead'!

Little is said about the dead of other nations, the lives of occupied Asian peoples, about exploited Korean 'comfort-women' or about 'forced war-time labour'. Nonetheless, these topics are impressively exhibited elsewhere in Japan by such innovative galleries as the Osaka International Peace Center, Kochi's impressively activist-orientated Grassroots House, and the resplendent Kyoto Museum for World Peace. The basic plan of the 'War Dead' museum is to 'renew in the minds of the Japanese people their mourning spirit over the Japanese war dead...' Though mourning is a human sentiment, should the objects of mourning be exclusively Japanese? One hopes that the sentiment might be so broadened as to reflect an internationally encapsulative concern for all the grief occasioned by war. A 'Memorial Museum of the War Dead' is likely to antagonize Japan's Asian neighbours whose disappointment is unlikely to be dampened by the efforts of recent Japanese administrations to placate their demands for 'war reparations'.[15]

The issue of 'presenting peace' cuts to the heart of the debate about war guilt and the pressure for governmental apology and societal atonement. It could be argued that in common with the Jewish Shoah or holocaust survivors, Japan's atom bomb survivors, the *hibakusha*, are prone to political exploitation.[16] The museum's Peace Prayer Hall might also become a symbol of the residual divisiveness. At any rate, these matters are quite sensitive. As the Smithsonian's failed 1995 exhibition on the Enola Gay indicated the strength of the veterans' lobby in the USA, this project's debacle further highlights

---

13 T.M. Duffy and Chikara Tsuboi, 'Shrine Line', in *Museums Journal* 97,1 (1997): 20.
14 Duffy and Tsuboi, 'Shrine Line': 21-22.
15 Some of the militaristic themes in the 'Peace Memorial Museum of the War Dead' are articulately challenged in other, more intellectually progressive Japanese museums, e.g., the Saiki Peace Memorial Hall Yawaragi, the Oka Masaharu Memorial Peace Museum, Nagasaki (which highlights the aggressive actions of Japanese forces), and the Peace Museum for the People which, portraying the suffering of all soldiers 'hopes for the coming of world peace', see T.M. Duffy, *Japanese Peace Culture*, Hiroshima, Hiroshima Peace Culture Foundation, 1997: 6.
16 For an account of the *hibakusha* of Nagasaki, see *Testimonies of the Atomic Bomb Survivors*, Nagasaki, City of Nagasaki, 1985.

the gulf which splits Japanese society on the issue of war responsibility.[17] Sadly, it seems unlikely that the impulses impacting on this project would permit its metamorphosis into a credible peace museum. The museum merely enshrines memories of the Japanese 'war dead' at the expense of exploring 'global peace'; it is unlikely to afford much comfort to those in the Japanese peace movement who have struggled to give genuine focus to issues of peace.

The Nagasaki International Cultural Hall, predecessor of the new Nagasaki Atomic Bomb Museum, was constructed in 1955 to house a rather conventional and politically uncontentious set of pictures and artefacts illustrating the city's nuclear tragedy.[18] However, the Nagasaki Atomic Bomb Museum itself is a remarkable departure and important development in the portrayal of issues of war and peace in Japan.[19] In April 1996 it was opened after much strategic planning and quasi-philosophical cum political debate.[20] The museum marks an important step in Japan's fundamental re-interpretation of WW2 and its imaging of the horrors of Hiroshima and Nagasaki. Controversy over it brought pain, but also healing: viewed as part of a nation's emerging dialogue with ghosts of the past, it should ultimately be therapeutic.

Violence and Memory in Cambodia

When the Khmer Rouge, determined to fashion 'Democratic Kampuchea', seized power in May 1975 Cambodia suffered the so-called 'year zero'(more accurately, zero years).[21] A long period of political turmoil was followed by economic neglect and international isolation, reducing the Cambodian population to one of the poorest in the world. The UN Transitional Authority for Cambodia (UNTAC), which commenced work in the region on March 15, 1992, faced a society which had been brought to its economic and psychological knees; it sought to inject into UN programming a comprehensive concern with human rights and peace.[22] The UN's own official account of its engagement with Cambodia in these years scarcely touches the surface of the security and socio-economic challenges it faced.[23]

---

17 Martin Harwit, *An Exhibit Denied: Lobbying the History of the Enola Gay*, New York, Springer, 1996: esp.150-175.
18 See *The Nuclear Century: Voices of the Hibakusha of the World*, Tokyo, Japan Peace Museum and the Japan Confederation of A and H-Bomb Sufferers Organisations, 1998, with accompanying text. For a fine account of the Hall's history, see *Nagasaki Speaks: A Record of the Atomic Bombing*, Nagasaki, Nagasaki International Culture Hall, 1993.
19 *Records of the Nagasaki Atomic Bombing*, Nagasaki, Nagasaki Atomic Bomb Museum, 1996: 3-24.
20 The museum is inspired by Mr. Hitoshi MUTOSHIMA (a former mayor of Nagasaki) who has been systematically attacked and physically victimized by the Japanese 'right-wing' because of his utterances about Emperor Hirohito's un-acknowledged 'war responsibility'. Mutoshima hoped that the museum would place the bombing of Nagasaki in an objective historical context. Its planners were convinced that the museum must refer to Japan's aggression in order to promote international understanding. Significantly, in March 1996, 'rightist' extremists objected to the inclusion of a photograph of the Nanjing Massacre, and soon after the museum's opening, demonstrations via loud-speaker cars were conducted at regular intervals by 'right-wing' organizations.
21 T.M. Duffy, 'Toward A Culture of Human Rights in Cambodia', in *Human Rights Quarterly* 16,1 (February 1994): 82-104.
22 See the UN document, *Agreement on a Comprehensive Political Settlement of the Cambodia Conflict*, signed in Paris, 23 October 1991: 48.
23 See *The United Nations and Cambodia, 1991-1995*, New York, United Nations, 1995: 352.

During the fatal years of Khmer Rouge rule (between April 1975 and the beginning of the Vietnamese occupation in late December 1978) Cambodia endured probably the most violent of modern revolutions. Thousands were executed in interrogation centres and in the 'killing fields'. Government policies, based on economic folly, plunged a whole society into poverty. Probably, a greater proportion of the country's population died than in any other revolution in the twentieth century. Many of the victims were of the Lon Nol elite. However, the majority were not part of the Cambodian old order and their execution was symptomatic of the regime's desperate efforts to secure itself against potential opposition. It had created a massive torture machine and sanctioned extra-judicial killing and, ultimately, genocide against Cambodia's various religious and minority groups.[24] More precisely, Cambodia experienced a gruesome form of 'auto-genocide' as the foci of inter-communal violence and retribution switched and alternated from ethnic and religious minorities to alleged internal dissidents. The results inevitably set in motion a paranoic policy of repression in which even the most zealous party stalwarts 'fell under state suspicion'.[25] At the centre of this policy were the interrogation centres, which were located in provincial towns and in Phnom Penh, e.g., Tuol Sleng, the infamous S-21 compound, opened in April 1975. When the Vietnamese invaded Cambodia in 1979, the Khmer Rouge had left behind them at S-21 a massive catalogue of systematic human rights violations and the elimination of nearly twenty thousand people. In 1979, Tuol Sleng was turned into the Tuol Sleng Museum of Cambodian Genocide by the State of Cambodia (SOC); shortly thereafter, its burial camp at Choeung Ek was made accessible to the public.

At Tuol Sleng, the visitor can scarcely avoid treading on the sun-bleached bones of the unfortunate victims or escape confronting 'eyeball to eyeball' the various tools used to torture them. Tuol Sleng's chief of torture, 'Brother' Duch had commanded some two hundred interrogators in a systematic operation. Thousands of innocent Cambodians were forced into preposterous confessions, for instance, 'that they were agents for the CIA, the KGB or the Vietnamese'.[26] Ing Pech, one of the few survivors, recalls that when Duch indicated that someone had to be 're-educated' their remains would be 'crushed to bits'. Arrest photographs were displayed on the ground floors, where Cambodians came to search for news of missing relatives. Another S-21 survivor, Haing Ngor, remembers Tuol Sleng thus: 'It became a symbol of Khmer Rouge atrocities, just as Auschwitz was a symbol of the Nazi regime'.[27] S-21 is a monument to the calculated social destruction of an entire society. Recently, there has been a gradual confrontation of this tragic period. Today, Tuol Sleng Museum is a frightening exhibition of what a people can be forced to endure: tiny cells, blood-soaked bed shackles fitted to cages filled with wooden clubs, whips and even live scorpions used as instruments of torture – in all a terrible arsenal of violence and oppression.[28]

---

24 See Francois Ponchaud, *Cambodia Year Zero*, London, Allen Lane, 1978: 3-18.
25 T.M. Duffy, 'Reconciling Cambodia: Finding Hope in the Killing Fields', in *Reconciliation Quarterly*, Winter 1993: 5-10.
26 On this see T.M. Duffy, 'Beyond the Killing Fields: The Genocide Museum at Tuol Sleng and the Memorial Stupa of Choeung Ek', in *Museum International* 177 / 45,1 (1993): 4-11.
27 Haing Ngor, *Surviving the Killing Fields: The Cambodian Odyssey of Haing S. Ngor*, London, Pan, 1998: esp. 399-402.
28 S-21 portrays documentary and household paraphernalia relating to politicians such as Hu Nim, Minister of Information, whose forced confession is displayed alongside those of foreign victims like the American journalist, James Clark, and many ordinary Kampucheans; ragged

S-21 was the largest of a network of interrogation centres that existed across Democratic Kampuchea. Choeung Ek, where almost nine thousand skulls have been counted, was the burial ground for Tuol Sleng. The histories of Tuol Sleng and Choeung Ek are thus inextricably linked.[29] In turn, Choeung Ek was exploited by the Vietnamese-installed government in their calculated political strategy to further discredit the Khmer Rouge. Tuol Sleng swiftly became an instrument of propaganda, focusing hatred on Khmer Rouge regime, as the Cambodian establishment sought to justify the exigencies of their own governance. The installed administration was led by Prime Minister Hun Sen and Minister Heng Samrin; they had been Khmer Rouge officers. Even the Memorial Stupa's dedication to Cambodia's 'year zero' victims became political. Its introductory panel describes this period of history as, 'more cruel than the genocidal act committed by Hitler's fascists...they wanted to transform Kampucheans into persons without reason... who bent their heads to carry out Angkar's orders...' Anonymous and post-death, Cambodia's victims are exploited.

The Phnom Penh administration's adroit exploiting of S-21 and Choeung Ek finds comparison in Vietnam's War Crimes Museum in Saigon and its portrayal of USA foreign policy. Nevertheless, we have to see that, in Cambodia, Tuol Sleng and Choeung Ek have a constructive role to play in consensus-building in Cambodian society. Interrogation centres and concentration camps have been re-cast as 'museums of peace' in other countries, e.g., Germany and Poland. When the Cambodian camps no longer remain pawns in the power games of the political elite, they will take on a new post-conflict identity, one that might allow them to assist in the painful reconciliation of collective memory. Cambodians have a saying about the horrors of their recent past: 'We were all conspirators – we were all victims'. In Tuol Sleng and Choeung Ek survivors may find forgiveness and hope in what remains and all Cambodians may move beyond their 'killing fields'.

In assisting transition in Cambodia, the programs designed by the UN and others have made an important contribution.[30] One would be naïve to assume that a few internationally observed elections in recent years would be sufficient to transform the political imbroglio that is Cambodia today. While psephologists have told us that Cambodia's post-genocide elections have been mostly 'free and fair' there is much that remains resolutely, perhaps irredeemably, undemocratic. UNTAC and the internationalization of the country with its incipient 'NGO industry' have done some good. Amit Gilboa well describes modern Phnom Penh as a city 'of tradition and transformation; a city of

---

shoes and prisoners' clothing are piled 'Belsen-like' in the display. Like the Nazis the Khmer Rouge kept meticulous records, which show how, as the revolution reached its heights of insanity, it began devouring its own children, e.g., executing members of the revolution's elite. During its worst phase, S-21 claimed at least a hundred victims a day, see Ben Kiernan, *The Pol Pot Regime: Race, Power and Genocide in Cambodia under the Khmer Rouge, 1975-79*, New Haven and London, Yale University, [1996] 1998: esp. 37-45.

29 Pol Pot busts mingle with the freighted paraphernalia of electrification and torture. Tuol Sleng's facade, especially the upper floors, are shrouded in barbed wire to prevent suicides. The sun-dried blood of S-21's victims still stains the cells. Arguably, the rows of photographs of the victims who died during interrogation are more psychologically moving; some show the knowledge that they are soon to die, many are distorted by the pain of interrogation, and still others seem unduly unperturbed as if believing in the proffered 're-education' (invariably, a euphemism for execution), see Kiernan, *The Pol Pot Regime*: esp. 32-51.

30 *From a Culture of Violence to a Culture of Peace*, Paris, UNESCO, 1996: especially 251-252.

temples and brothels, music and gunfire...festivals and coups'.[31] However, this 'mixed blessing' of modernity has further exposed both politicians and the Cambodian people to the democratic process, and may contribute to the continuance of a 'begrudging respect' for democracy. The absence of sufficient political will to nurture either constitutional consensus or equitable and transparent governance regrettably continues. Still more worryingly, there remains a cross-current of factional bitterness and ethnic enmity which paralyses those international or national actors who might promote healing, reintegration and reconciliation.

The current political system has been inherited from Khmer Rouge years when trust and openness were impossible. Today's political maxim of 'national reconciliation for peace' is contradicted by political actions. A mentality forged in the 'killing fields' remains. The attitudes of Cambodian politicians, fearing a shift 'from power to powerlessness', become atrophied.[32] Alienation or even paranoia is common because the culture of violence still pervades and a brutality mirroring that of the Khmer Rouge still intimidates as those in power, fearing their opponents' retribution, cling more desperately to it.[33] And yet, the construction of a positive and durable culture of peace is the only thing that will extricate the people from a past that still haunts.

Conclusion: Museums and the Dialogue of Peace

The expansion of the world-wide peace movement is evidence of the continuing and healthy dialogue concerning 'museums of war and peace' in Japan and elsewhere. As I write, plans are under way for an African Peace Museum in Kenya and for a network of peace entities across Europe. A new national peace museum in the United Kingdom is a possibility.[34] Across all continents, initiatives that might appropriately come under the 'peace museum' umbrella are undertaken. More conventional galleries, too, choose to prioritize exhibitions that include materials directly related to peace and to the peace movement. A good example is London's Imperial War Museum. Maligned as 'trapped in a conceptual time-warp', the Imperial has shed its 'war-skin' to emerge as a genuinely discursive laboratory of ideas. Saliently and as became evident in the account above, what distinguishes 'war museums' from 'peace museums' lies more in the concept that it operates from than in its own physical heritage and content; the conceptual approach of individual curators can have profound effects.

The museum world and the public have probably never been more responsive to the 'peace museum' concept than today. This is evidenced in the burgeoning global interest in peace movements and peace museums, and in the increased governmental support for their construction in many countries.[35] We have noted how some projects continue to attract political controversy. Japan remains as divided over the issue of peace as it does over the memories of war. Similarly, the Tuol Sleng Genocide Museum in Cambodia

---

31 Amit Gilboa, *Off the Rails in Phnom Penh*, Bangkok, Asia Books, 2000: esp. ix-22.
32 See David Chandler, *The Tragedy of Cambodian History: Politics, War and Revolution since 1945*, New Haven, Yale University, 1991: esp. 198-213.
33 See Karl Jackson (ed.), *Cambodia 1975-1978: Rendezvous with Death*, Princeton, Princeton University, 1989: esp. 37-78.
34 For up-to-date information, see http://www.museumsforpeace.org, the web-site of the Network of Museums of Peace.
35 See Terence Duffy, 'The Peace Museums of Japan', in *Museum International* (UNESCO) 196 / 49,4 (1997): 49-54.

has yet to become a symbol of national reconciliation. Nevertheless, thinking about issues of war and peace is helpful in promoting a constructive dialogue that might lead eventually to a culture of peace. There is much cause for encouragement as we shift from a culture of violence to one of reconciliation. Federico Mayor, former Director-General of UNESCO famously said, 'not only is a culture of peace both feasible and indispensable...it is already in progress'.[36] Part of that progress is the peace museum. The goal of promoting a peace culture through the visual arts implicitly and explicitly makes the peace museum so. And part of the advancement in our understanding of these socio-cultural transitions has been John May's insights on transcending violence.

---

36 Federico Mayor, in *UNESCO and a Culture of Peace: Promoting A Global Movement*, Paris, UNESCO, 1995: 5.

Georg Evers
Personal Reflections on Mysticism in Christianity and Buddhism

My personal contact with John D'Arcy May goes back to the early 1970s when I was doing doctoral studies in Münster on the problem of mission and interreligious dialogue with Karl Rahner, and John was busy with his dissertation in the field of ecumenical theology with Peter Lengsfeld. From that time I recall that he was not only interested in the problems of the differences of separated Christians but also in Buddhism. Many years later, when I was working at the Asia desk of the Institute of Missiology in Aachen, our ways crossed again; our points of contact were in the field of Buddhist-Christian dialogue and in the problems concerning intercultural theology. Looking for a topic to contribute to John's Festschrift I thought it fitting to concentrate on differences and similarities between Buddhist and Christian spirituality and mysticism, a topic which has to do with my own biography of having lived and worked in encountering and being fascinated by both traditions in a deep way. Something similar, I think, holds true for John, who in his personal and professional life also lives an intercultural and inter-religious existence.

The following reflections on similarities and differences between Buddhist and Christian spirituality and mysticism, therefore, are rather more subjective than the result of deep comparative studies, a fault which I hope the editors will forgive me. Since I have lived more than 17 years of my life as a member of the Society of Jesus, I have been deeply influenced by the spirituality of Ignatius of Loyola. As a concrete example of Christian spirituality and mysticism, I will, therefore, concentrate on the mystical experience of Ignatius of Loyola. By his contemporaries, the founder of the Society of Jesus was often viewed as a person who was always in control of his emotions and very much led by rationality in all his decisions. When reading his spiritual diary, however, it soon becomes clear that beneath this outwardly controlled behaviour, there was another side, the side of a mystic who was in a constant close contact with God and able to find God's presence in all things. This deep and guiding spiritual insight goes back to the early days of his conversion when Ignatius was searching for the determining direction in this life. For Ignatius, the mystical insight that he was granted in September 1522 when he was meditating on the bank of the river Cardoner was a kind of peak experience which became the solid point of reference and strength in his future spiritual life. What he experienced in this extraordinary vision was so deep that it gave him an insight into the very core of God's presence and activity in the cosmos, such that he made the extraordinary and – in view of a suspicious Inquisition's investigations into his activities at the time – bold statement: '[e]ven if I had never read the bible and never had any guidance into the mysteries of life and death I could rely solely on this experience which gives me strength and fills me with joy and certitude'. It is worthwhile to pursue the way Ignatius had to travel and the hard struggle he had to undergo before he was able to make this peak experience in his mystical life. Ignatius had spent the months preceding the mystical experience along the Cardoner in Manresa. As yet inexperienced in the ways of the spiritual life, he was given to extreme fasting, and this ruined his stomach for good. This extreme asceticism, however, did not help him to advance spiritually, instead it was responsible for heavy bouts of depression. In this agitated and desperate state of mind he was even tempted to terminate his life by his own hands, because he could no longer see what God expected him to do with his life. In his own account of this period in his life Ignatius was later to say: 'I would have followed a dog, if only he would have showed me the direction into which I was supposed to go'. The vision at Manresa then became the turning point in his life; it gave him clarity and steadfastness for his life's work, culminating in his development of the 'Spiritual Exercises' and in his founding the 'Society of Jesus'. His subsequent reflections on these experiences at Manresa helped Ignatius to develop rules for the 'discernment of spirits' (*discretio spirituum*) which became the cornerstone for his widely acknowledged charism of spiritual guidance. The 'contemplation to obtain love' (*contemplatio ad obtinendam caritatem*) at the end of the Spiritual Exercises contains the gist of the insight he had gained through his vision, namely, that God can to be found in all things. The other important element is his belief that there exists for every individual a personal destiny and mission which God has in store for him and which can be found by faithfully obeying the invitation of the Spirit.

For me the decisive quality in the spirituality of Ignatius is his conviction that the almighty God who is present in and permeates the whole cosmos is, at the same time, concerned with the existence of each individual. The aim of the Spiritual Exercises, which became Ignatius's greatest legacy to the Church and Christianity, consists in enabling the one undertaking the exercises to find out in a given existential situation in his or her life what the will of God is for that person. Ignatius is convinced that it is possible to come to know what God has in mind for a certain individual person by discerning the spirits which move the person to consolation or frustration. This individual search, however, has to be guided by the more objective criteria of contemplating the life of Jesus Christ, taking into account the guidance of the Church's teaching, and following the rules for the discernment of spirits. In this process Ignatius is careful to allow and to call for making use of one's intellectual faculties in order to clarify the different spiritual experiences. There are objective rules to be followed and principles to be observed, but at the same time there is the personal element of being in contact with God who has a plan for the individual which this person alone can discern and make his or her own. During the time of Ignatius there were other mystics living in Spain, such as Teresa of Avila and John of the Cross, who used different similes and expressions to describe their mystical experiences. The point is that they all shared a common conviction that God was communicating with the individual and inviting him or her into the companionship of divine personal love.

My personal encounter with Buddhism goes back to my stay in Japan (1962-1969) where I had the chance to meet pioneers of Buddhist-Christian dialogue such as Heinrich Dumoulin, Enomiya Lassalle and Kadowaki Kakichi. The Japanese language school which I attended at the time was not far from Kamakura. The large Buddha statue standing near the seaside fascinated me, because it showed the Enlightened One as someone who rests in peace and serenely looks down on those in the world still struggling to be freed from the wheel of rebirths. During visits at different times, in full daylight or in the dim light of evenings, the dominant figure of this Buddha had a special appeal, probably because it differed so much from the image of the crucified Christ. Many years later, however, I came across a statue of the Buddha which changed very much the image of the Buddha that I had held thus far. I refer to the statue of the Fasting Buddha which is kept in the city museum of Lahore and which shows the Buddha immediately after he had reached enlightenment. We see a lean figure of a man whose ribs stand out, a man who is reduced to skin and bones, whose face is frightening given the way in which he is looking at the spectator. The person depicted here is someone who has come a long way, who has been struggling extensively and who has come to the end of his tether. This image of the Buddha is a far cry from the statues we normally see, where, like the Kamakura statue, the Buddha is depicted as a well-proportioned person sitting majestically in meditation and showing the different gestures (*mudras*) of teaching, granting grace some other exercise in his saving ministry. The Buddha seen in Lahore, however, is of someone who has barely survived an extraordinarily hard time. Somewhat like Ignatius of Loyola before his mystical experience at the Cardoner, Siddhartha Gautama also was tempted and had to struggle before he reached enlightenment under the Bodhi tree in Buddhagaya. He himself is quoted as saying: '[n]ever has a human being fought that hard, has fasted and done so much violence to his body as I have done.' For me this statue of a Buddha who has experienced hardship and suffering brings that Buddha into a much closer relationship with the crucified Christ than I had ever thought possible.

Based on the deep mystical experience of enlightenment that the Buddha had gained during this period of sitting under the Bodhi tree, fasting, suffering and being tempted by Maya, he begins 'turning the wheel of teaching' in the deer park at Sarnath. The Buddha does not speak of having encountered a personal God who spoke to him or showed him the inner law of the cosmos and human existence; what he asserts is that he has found the eternal law and truth of all existence which other enlightened beings had found before him but which had been forgotten and which was (re-)discovered by the Buddha again. The four truths and the eightfold path that the Buddha proclaims have a rational quality and appeal to the rational insight of the persons they are addressed to. This form of rational Buddhism which decorated itself with epithets such as 'rationalism', 'empiricism' and even 'logical positivism' became the form of 'export Buddhism', to use Edward Conze's term, which in its Western reception led to forms of Buddhism, such as the one propagated by Rudolf Grimm in Germany, where there was no place for the monastic life nor for a cultic veneration of the Buddha nor for the development of a Buddhist soteriology and mysticism. As Aloysius Pieris has pointed out there is a fundamental difference between two ways of expressing the human experience of God and the world, namely, the language of liberating insight (*gnosis*) and the language of liberating love (*agape*). Originally, in Buddhism as well as in Christianity, the two ways of expressing the mystery of human destiny were seen as the dialectical relationship of wisdom and love, i.e., of gnostic detachment and loving commitment. In later development the emphasis in Buddhism shifted towards a one-sided option for the gnostic option, which saw Buddhism as an ascetic religion denying the world, whereas in Christianity gnosticism was suspected of being prone to heresy, and charity instead became the hallmark of Christianity.

As an interesting side-note to these reflections, I am struck by the way the present pope, Benedict XVI, advocates charity on the one hand, while presenting Christianity as a doctrine which relies on human reason to prove the rationality of its beliefs on the other. Benedict does this in the first place in the context of the encounter with Islam. His attitude, though, has its implication for Buddhist-Christian encounter as well, especially if we look at the mystical aspects in both traditions. What both these mystical traditions have in common is that the spiritual experiences found in them defy human reason and cannot be rendered in rational concepts. This does not mean that these spiritual experiences are 'irrational', but their content cannot easily be examined by rational concepts and, even worse for the watchers of orthodoxy, cannot be controlled as regards their doctrinal correctness. Christian and Buddhist mystics have in common a preference for a negative theology which is not given to ready-made definitions and answers, but is aware of the limitedness of human reason and the impossibility of expressing ultimate truths in philosophical or theological language. The main task of a negative theology is to preserve the mystery of the ultimate reality in its inaccessibility from the curious minds of all too eager theologians who – while insisting on the existence of 'mysteries in the strict sense' (*mysteria stricte dicta*) – come forth with definitions and statements which ultimately destroy mystery and subject it to the dictates of human logic and presumption. Indeed, adherents of a negative theology are often accused of obfuscating the divine truths which, after all, have been revealed precisely in order to be understood and to be expressed in human language and ideas. Making use, however, of the principle of the 'analogy of being' (*analogia entis*), which holds that everything that can be said positively about the divine reality can also be stated in negative terms, representatives of a negative theology are entitled to opt for expressing this 'negative' part. In acting thus, they will serve as a corrective and balancing force, which gives a deeper contour to the statements of those presenting a positive theology.

My own encounter with Buddhist spirituality and mysticism in Japan has brought me into contact with Zen-Buddhism which is characterized by a form of meditation which leads to enlightenment precisely by going beyond the rational faculties and relying on 'just meditating' (*shikanta-za*) or on making use of riddles which defy human rationality (*koan*) in order to provide insight into the mystery of existence (*satori*) which cannot be expressed in concepts and words. The attempt, therefore, to find out whether the encounter with the 'ultimate reality' or the insight into 'absolute nothingness' in the Zen-Buddhist enlightenment experience is identical with the *unio mystica* of Christian mystics in their peak experience of encountering God, is doomed to be a futile exercise. This holds true at least as long as the attempt is made to capture the essence of the two experiences in words and concepts. From the outside, that is, by using the analytical tools of philosophy, such as assuming a basic unity of all existence with the consequence that there can only be 'one' ultimate reality, it will be possible to show that the experience made by mystics in both traditions must be based on an encounter with 'one and the same' reality. A verification of this claim, however, is impossible, as indeed would be of the opposite position, which is that there cannot be any convergence. Those who have made the deep spiritual experience of enlightenment or of the mystical union will be reluctant to enter into this discussion because they are aware that those who have been granted such an experience remain silent in the knowledge that the effort to express in words even the gist of what they have 'seen' is doomed to failure. Being based in different traditions, Buddhist and Christian mystics will necessarily use the terminology of their respective traditions should they attempt to articulate parts of their experience in order to communicate with their fellow believers.

Coming back, then, to the comparison between Ignatius of Loyola and Siddartha Gautama, the common element that I see is that both have had an insight into the cosmos. Ignatius derives from this experience the guideline for his spiritual life: 'to find

God in all things'. It also became the starting point for this Trinitarian mysticism and the rules for the discernment of spirits. Nevertheless, the decisive element in his spirituality is his Christo-centrism which is at the core of the Spiritual Exercises. Ignatius was convinced that the God who can be found in 'all things', has chosen to come into this world in the form of a human being in order to bring salvation to humankind. Following Christ, imitating Christ and dying with Christ in martyrdom – these have become the special marks of Christian spirituality. As can be seen in the 'contemplation to obtain love' Ignatius has an insight into God's presence in the whole of the cosmos which could even be called 'pantheistic'; but, even stronger is his conviction that the 'concreteness' of God's presence in this world has been realized in God's self-communication in Jesus Christ. This latter theological insight has been expanded by Karl Rahner, for whom this was the fundamental cornerstone of the Christian faith and his theology as a whole. Here we can observe a profound difference between the Christian outlook on the cosmos which in the Judeo-Christian tradition is said to have been created by God, and the Buddhist in which there is no created cosmos and consequently no creator. The distinction between created being and uncreated transcendent being is crucial for the concept of encountering the divine reality as divine within the created reality of the cosmos. As we have seen, the insight that God can be found in all things was essential for Ignatius of Loyola. Yet, this presence of God in the whole of creation has become blurred by sin and all creation waits eagerly to be set free from the bondage of decay (cf. Romans 8:18-23). The privileged point of contact with the divine reality within this created world is the encounter with Jesus Christ who, in the Christian understanding of the mystery of incarnation, is the self-communication of God. In Christian mysticism, therefore, the mystical union with the triune God centres on Jesus Christ in whom the external relationship with the Trinity is founded. St Paul could speak of his own being lost in Christ when he states: 'it is no longer I who live, but Christ who lives in me' (Galatians 2:20). In passing we note that this passage has played an important part in the dialogue with the Kyoto School in discussing the notion of 'person' and 'non-self' (*muga*).

Belief in the incarnation has another more practical implication with regard to living in this world and being engaged in the works of charity. The passage on the last judgement (Matthew 25:31-46) makes it clear that the incarnate Word of God, resurrected and lifted up to heaven, still remains in this world and can be contacted in the hungry, naked, sick and imprisoned of this world even today. From this passage derives another form of Christian mysticism, a mysticism of everyday life in the service of the world's poor.

In the context of our comparing Christian and Buddhist spirituality, it may be worthwhile to look at the theory, found in Mahayana Buddhism, that the 'Buddha-nature' is contained in all sentient beings, and to investigate how it relates to the Christian notion of 'finding God in all things'. Mahayana Buddhists believe that the ultimate reality of the Buddha resides in every sentient being, and therefore, every sentient being partakes in this Buddha-nature. This belief is at the heart of the attitude of reverence with regard to all living things. At the same time, it is of high importance for the exercise of meditation. Since the Buddha-nature existing in every sentient being has been often obscured and blurred by error and sin, it is necessary to bring it forth in its pristine clarity by engaging in meditation. Dogen, the famous Zen-Patriarch of Japan, speaks of looking in meditation for one's true nature which one had before one was born to describe this effort of bringing to light the Buddha-nature hidden in every human being.

The realization of one's true nature in discovering the Buddha-nature is depicted as the end of the way to enlightenment. Does discovering one's true identity then mean that there is a self which finds its personal fulfilment? Most Buddhists would deny that there is an individual self which reaches its fulfilment; they would rather speak of discovering the real nature of the self in its being absorbed and integrated into the one all-encompassing Buddha-nature. Where Christian belief speaks of 'a new name which no one knows except him who receives it' (Revelation 2:17), thus confirming that there is an individual self after death, Buddhists would concentrate on the notion of having been integrated into the fullness of reality.

As I stated in the beginning my contribution to John's Festschrift was not supposed to be a theoretical treatise but just my reflections on the encounter between Buddhism and Christianity in the context of my personal biography. After all, the encounter with Buddhist spirituality has played a major role in my own life. During my many contacts with Buddhists while travelling in different Asian countries I have had the opportunity to learn much about the richness of the Buddhist tradition. When I took part for the last time in the annual meeting of the Asian theologians of the 'Office of Theological Concerns' within the FABC (Federation of Asian Bishops' Conferences) of which I had been part for more than 10 years, held in Kathmandu (Nepal), I was presented with a statue of the Buddha as a farewell gift from this group of Christian theologians. Obviously, my affinity with Buddhism was known and appreciated in this group which has made such valuable contributions to a typical Asian theology by making use of the patrimony of the rich heritage of Asian religious traditions, among which Buddhism constitutes a precious jewel. My wish would be that in reading these reflections John would feel impelled to reflect from his side on the implications of his having encountered Buddhist spirituality and what it has meant for him.

Frank Fletcher MSC

The Long Rejection yet Survival of the Koorie People

John D'Arcy May, like many Australian expatriates, has felt in his soul the passing of the tribes and has heard the rejection of the yellow brown people by both sides. 'They are not truly Aboriginal but mixed race.'

Against whom do I aim the blame? It is too easy to blame it all on the Governments, State and Federal, or on the bureaucrats (only carrying out the law) or on the Police or on those who managed the homes for the 'stolen' children or on those who managed the reserves including church people who saw themselves between the law, the bureaucrats and these wondrously, human, non-Tribal people.

So, against whom do I aim the guilt? Who shall cast the first stone? The whole Australian nation has failed in various degrees, we the fair-go people have fooled ourselves...but the allotting of blame onto whitefellas is not the purpose of this essay. Rather, its purpose is to tell the story of the Koories under a theological lens.

This essay fits broadly within the theological method devised by Bernard Lonergan and developed further by Robert Doran.[1] Doran explicitly envisages that a historical situation can raise issues and questions for theology and affect the very foundations of a prevailing theology. The questions raised by the plight of the Koories touch some tender places. This essay seeks to make a contribution towards a theological view of the Koorie situation. It will show that after all their suffering the Koories are taking some degree of control of their situation. Further, they may see the possible beginnings of a New Dreaming arising from the dark time of dispossession. Indeed, they have been despised, rejected – and survived. They have become able to talk directly to the rest of the Australian people and have won over a notable section of the population.

Art is central to Aboriginal life both Tribal and Koorie. It centres on the Dreaming. The Dreaming is a level of reality more profound than the everyday.[2] The Dreaming is the master symbol for the sacred order in many tribes. Anthropologists, led by Professor W.E.H. Stanner have come to acknowledge that the Aboriginal Tribal culture is or was highly developed, possessing the oldest securely dated art in the world.[3] Given also its claim to be the most ancient of surviving peoples, the survival and aliveness of the Dreaming makes it of world significance. Further, the encounter of Tribal and Koorie with the British must have been confusing for both. Neither side had correct categories for understanding the other. The colonial categories, in particular, were toxic for those under their dominion.

The title of this essay speaks deliberately of the Koorie people, not of Aboriginal people as a whole. Koories are the mixed race people who constitute the majority of Aborigines. Also they are those I have got to know in a ministry of eighteen years.

---

1 Bernard Lonergan, *Method in Theology,* New York, Seabury, 1979; and Robert M. Doran, *Theology and the Dialectics of History,* Toronto, University of Toronto, 1990.
2 Wally Caruana, *Aboriginal Art*, London, Thames & Hudson, 1993.
3 W.E.H. Stanner, 'On Aboriginal Religion', in *The Oceania Monograph* 11 (1996): 14, 16-19, 85.

The Koories' Situation

I will briefly sketch a number of key words or issues to illuminate the Koories' oppression by the insensitivity of the colonial society. Also, I will suggest a role for poetry: a sensitivity for the complex of feelings.[4]

Aborigine: A European term imposed on indigenous people around the globe; Latin: from the beginning.

Koories/Murries: The words which the mixed race people in Eastern Australia took for themselves; Koories/Murries can also use the name of their tribe if the local Tribal people do not object; Koorie is gradually growing as a pan-Aboriginal name.

Tribals: In townships and camps the Tribals are strong in the Northern and Western desert areas, whilst the Southern and Eastern parts of the continent are mainly Koorie.

Gubbah: The Koorie term for white officials or for whites generally: it is a breakdown of the term 'government-fellah'; it is not a term of endearment but a reminder of when government-fellahs were the Mission managers; this term 'mission' is applied much more widely than just to church missions.

Part Aboriginal: This is a term used as equivalent to mixed race; both terms belong mainly in the speech of older generations of the white community; both terms are used to justify the taking of Koorie children and putting them in harsh homes to be brought up as gubbahs because they are partly white. The Koories resent the denial of the Aboriginal 'part' of themselves in favour of the non-Aboriginal part.

The Stolen Generations: The word 'stolen' picks up the inhumanity of the seizure of the children and all that went with it. This has been a most contested issue in Australia. It was first proposed on the grounds that if they stayed with their families the young Koories would not assimilate – and they were such breeders...like the story of the Hebrews in Egypt, they were considered a threat. The Tribals, on the other hand were not a threat, being considered a dying race. What was not intended was the harsh discipline and coldness of the Homes. Young run-about Koories were stifled. The trauma this bred confused their own families. Being taken away from a warm family life the stolen generations were ill at ease with their own children.

Having listened to the stories of the stolen generations I have tried to put something of it into verse.

> *Hearts so early broken*
> Little brothers pulled away from weeping sisters
> and younger sister from her elder
> at Central Station: the poor child's horror
> like an inner sickness, a giddiness within a
> spinning world without a brake.
>
> Your state recalled the fate
> of Tribal blacks in old and faded photos
> chained together at their necks
> (and likely charged with stealing – oh my God!!)

---

4 See Les Murray, 'Wings, Hearts and Other Poetic Categories: a response to "Christ's wounded heart"', in Brian Gallagher (ed.), *A New Heart for a New World: An Exploration of the Desires of God's Heart*, Sydney, St Paul, 1986: 235-244.

> Then forced to run behind the troop of horse.
> Little ones, whose fate was worse?
>
> So few have cared who should have.
> Jesus surely wept:
> it is not false for us to feel the shame.

This removing of the Koorie children was fully stopped only as late as the 1960s.

Violence, Crime, Punishment

The Koories rate as a high proportion in the prisons, etc. Conservative commentators in the national press make much of crime in Aboriginal communities, both Tribal and Koorie. This is significant for a grasp of the situation. One of the most serious moments I have experienced concerned a Koorie young man who shot and killed a policeman. The Police in seeking him out burst into the bedroom of a friend of this young man and shot the friend dead in front of the young boy of the family. The Police said he was reaching for a gun. Subsequent investigations established that the friend had no gun. I had some time with the jailed Koorie. He was devastated at causing his friend's death and that of the policeman. He was more totally contrite than anyone I have known. He had grown up in a Catholic Boys' Town. Firing the gun was the stupidity of a moment.

Stolen Wages[5]

The Social Justice Council of the Australian Bishops reported in March 2006 that the State of Queensland had admitted Koorie wages had often not been paid. Koories were told the money was in the bank; but it was not under the Koories' names. It was diverted to Government accounts. Of the $56.5 million owed to the workers only a small amount reached the Koories.

Old Fellas

These are ghosts of Koorie ancestors who come back to their old bush places which may have become urban offices or shops or houses. They are usually quiet presences – see the poem, 'Aboriginality in the office'. It gives a taste of the teasing humour which Koories have. I was in the centre of that teasing at times. It may have been concocted or it may be true. The old fellas are around.

> *Aboriginality in the office*
> The old fella sits in the chair,
> over there.
> Have you seen him, Colin? He
> smiles: yeah.
> Look when he comes we'll ask Harry.
> Have you ever seen an Old Fella
> In here?
> What you mean, on that chair?
> Yes, I seen him there.
> He's not angry, he's happy here.

---

[5] Secretariat for the Australian Social Justice Council, 'Justice Call on Stolen Wages', in *Justice Trends* 120 (March 2006): 1.

> I say, are you all kidding me?
> Gentle smiles: gubbahs never seen 'im;
> 'e comes some days, not always.
> Good sign, 'e's 'appy 'ere.
>
> A different subjectivity:
> they call it Aboriginality.

Pathologies

As well as violence there is much sickness: obesity, diabetes, poor quality food, drink and drugs. Many are poorly motivated to become educated. One Koorie confided, 'the only blackfella on the school staff was the janitor', not a great role model.

Terra Nullius

This is the legal fiction which allowed colonial annexation. The native people could be treated as children. They lacked the institutions of a European state.

1967 Referendum

The Australian nation reversed the decision of the founding fathers' Constitution which decided not to count the Aborigines as part of the population. This gave hope and later disappointment. The recognition and reconciliation Koories desired is not a matter of passing a law or even a referendum. The need is for a transformation of heart among the non-Aboriginal people of Australia.

The Churches and the Koories

The Christian churches, as already noted, helped the Government implement its taking-the-children policy. To the churches it seemed a work of charity and an opportunity to introduce the children to Christian faith. So, though well-intentioned, this collaboration led to a distrust of some church institutions.

Spirituality and Religious Traditions

The leading motif in Australia, as in all of the West, is secularity. The Koories, in contrast, have an inclination towards the primal. The primal mindset is necessary for the affinity with nature and for their sacramentality.

Some writers distinguish religion from spirituality. Religion, they say, refers to the tradition at the core of church faith, whilst spirituality refers to the search for meaning by individuals or groups who have moved away from belonging to one great tradition. Of course, emphasizing the distinction between religion and spirituality suits the inclination of the West. On the other hand, the Koories can be confused. I recall several Catholic feminists addressing a number of Koorie women. The feminists called upon these Koories to join the sisterhood. When the Koories found their voice their reply was clear: 'where you are, is not where we are.' As noted, what the Koories seek is in their inherited tradition. When that search for the tradition is felt as fulfilled, then will they be more open to the Christian tradition. That is not to 'put down' the Koories; but, there is an unease among some of them until they can hear in the Christian symbols some primal resonance.

Hector, the Kimberley artist, has called himself a two-way man, Catholic and Aboriginal. A number of Koories feel that way. And was not that way confirmed by Pope John Paul II in his address to the Aboriginal Catholics at Alice Springs in 1986? He exhorted them to cherish their culture and begged the leaders of the church in Australia to welcome the Aboriginal religious tradition. Going further, the Pope insisted that the church in Australia would not be what Christ intended it to be if it lacked their participation.[6] From where I sit the great promise of those words has not been effectively met.

The Situation at Family Level

Two or three generations ago there were a number of strongly devout Koorie families, however, when the Koories assimilated to Western culture the number of such families diminished. Of course, this happened to the gubbahs, too; however, it is worse for Koories as the criticism of religion in the dominant culture has increased.

My reflections on poetry and those of the poet, Les Murray, linking theology and poetry, are further affirmed by a Ghanaian theologian[7] who interprets Christianity as a non-Western religion where faith is meant to be received with primal sacramentality. The West received Christian faith through other peoples in much the same way that African people had. Bediako's second reflection questions why Christian faith remains strong in Africa and similar places. Bediako believes the reason for this is that these peoples have retained their sacral imagination. I found his stress on sacral imagination borne out at the masses I attended in Tendisa, a black township outside Pretoria in South Africa. The whole congregation danced and sang, delighted, it seemed, to express the liturgy in a primal and sacral manner. Bediako's thesis on imagination receives support from John Henry Newman's *The Grammar of Assent*. Newman stated that imagination is a necessary dimension of faith for the reason that faith must be a matter of the heart and it is imagination which touches the heart. Further, Bediako understands that the world-view of Africa and of similar places provides a primal atmosphere conducive to faith.[8] He sums up the African world-view under four headings, namely:

> a human kinship with nature
> a sense of being creatures before the sacred
> a connection with a spiritual world behind the everyday
> a communion of affection with the ancestors in the other life.

These components of the African world-view all involve imagination. They go beyond the modern world-view because they sense what is beyond the outer senses. How close is this world-view to that of the Koories? I can say truly that I have heard Koories speaking of kinship with nature, the sacred, the spiritual world and the bonds of affection with those gone before them, particularly when connected with totems. Koories instruct their young on how to recognize the presence of their totems and how the totems can help them.

The world-view presented by Bediako is helpful in several ways. It is a concise summary of the primal religious outlook and, at the same time it is useful for arousing sacral imagination. The varied situations of particular places make a difference. Most

---

6 Pope John Paul II, 'Address to Aborigines and Torres Strait Islanders', in Michael Goonan, *The Pope in Australia: Collected Homilies and Talks*, Sydney, St Paul, 1986: 166-172.
7 Kwame Bediako, *Christianity in Africa: The Renewal of Non-Western Religion*, Edinburgh, Edinburgh University, 1995.
8 John Henry Newman, *The Grammar of Assent*, New York, Doubleday, 1995.

Koories are at least partly assimilated, yet, as I will explain later, there is, a core longing for a return to a deeper sense of their tradition. Moreover, being now for several generations driven off their land with only the remnants of ceremony to help them, the mythical core of their tradition has to be stirred. Though, what is extraordinary is that so much has been retained.

Woman of Strength

In 2004 I had a strong memory of the Koorie activist, Mum Shirl Smith. I recalled her presence within all the violence and corruption: a respected champion of her people. At the same time I remembered the lack of sufficient doctors who would treat Koories, the lack of lawyers to defend them and so on…She was part of the setting up of groups of doctors, lawyers, priests, sisters and brothers. In this way there began the Aboriginal Legal Service, the Aboriginal Medical Service, the Aboriginal Children's Service, etc.

> *Mum Shirl shouting back*
>
> In Jesus' light I see Mum Shirl
> anew, not just her tenderness to all
> the Koori young ones in their pain.
> She stood, like Jesus, arms around them
> in the dock. Also, like Jesus, she was shouting,
> shouting back at bureaucracies' hypocrisy.
> And even threatening – my God yes, threatening!
> Whilst modern scribes tut-tutted, whispering:
> this is no way for her to speak to us.
> Look how she fails to grasp the crucial point.
> Indeed the gubbahs' point fades to empty
> in the roar of fire. So in the jails and
> at the higher tables she listened fearless,
> with her heart aglow.
>   Within a holy fire.

I showed this poem to a group I was working with. Somehow it brought many things together. Then I recalled the first bit of verse I wrote at age 14. The words ran:

> an eerie feeling that it's all untrue,
> this life: real life is far away,
> away from here.

A friend to whom I once confided these lines remarked: typical adolescent loneliness. Maybe that is part of it, but what comes to me is the sense of a mysterious other world which drew my heart and still does. Thanks to those lines of verse I comprehended some writings of J.H. Newman, even grasping some of the Platonic vision. People write about the sense of Otherworld. Without those lines I would have had little contemplative insight to withstand Australia's matter of fact materialism. I believe, from Aboriginal paintings that I've seen, that many Aborigines (both Tribals and Koories) have their Otherworld vision deep in their soul.

It seems that moderns need the sense of Otherworld. Likewise, to write about the Koories one needs some infusion of Koorie soul. But the poetry may get at something else… there is also a sense of what has not yet come, of the invisible within the visible.

We have survived: 200 years of Colonization

On 26 January 1988, post-colonial Australia celebrated the second centenary of Phillip's landing in Sydney Cove. As a counter to the marching bands, etc., of the official celebrations the Reverend Charles Harris of the Christian Aboriginal Conference (Uniting Church) organized a trek of seventy thousand Aboriginal people from every corner of the continent under the banner *We have survived.* The highlight of the march was the meeting mid-city between the Tribals and the Koories: the ending of two hundred years of exclusion during which the Tribals denied Aboriginal recognition to the Koories.

The embraces between Tribals and Koories were full of joy. At last, the ancient family was united. This recognition of shared ancestry for the Koorie with the Tribals was followed by State recognition. In the excitement of those days there was talk of a Koorie nation which would issue its own passports! However, this passport project was not as effective in the general Australian community as the erection of an Aboriginal Tent Embassy where the Koorie nation could negotiate with those who had taken their land. The Koories were finding ways to enter the political play of Australia and to speak up for themselves.

The tribal people considered their land as manifesting the presence of the local myths. However, the Koories have lost most of their land and their myths. The myths could no longer depend on the land. Was there any power that connected with the old powers? A new myth or a new dreaming? The Koories survived so there must be some power, an interior Aboriginality. Sally Morgan, in *My Place*,[9] describes the breakthrough experience – and one hears something similar from the people who endured the Homes. They experienced a nagging intuition of an interior cry: where is the real life? Some argue that the Koories became, in their own way, more loyal to Aboriginality than the Tribals were.

The Koories seemed to be awaiting a myth. There is one group of Koories in far North of Queensland who have been waiting for this word. The group is that of the Rainbow Spirit Elders and the symbol of their myth is a sense that the land is weeping.[10] This weeping could refer to the great drought torturing the land. However, that might be reducing the moral level of the myth. It is a weeping over human failure, the failure of Koorie reconciliation with the gubbahs. The openness of spirit which reconciliation demands is a quality of the new spirit calling out within them. They are Spirit Elders indeed. Here are the Koories with their primal hearts challenging the modern whites. Is it in line with Bediako's presentation of the need for sacral imagination? Indeed, the weeping land is the breaking through of a new myth.

We want to see Jesus with Koorie eyes – John 12:20-21

Many bishops, priests and Australian churchgoers would smile on hearing talk of Aboriginal people hearing God weeping within the land. They would not be mollified if told that we Westerners have brought with us the biases of modernity, especially rationalism. As Reverend Djiniyini Gondarra insisted, Aborigines long to see Jesus but with Aboriginal eyes. Instinctively, it seems to them, Jesus is not the possession of the Westerners. Recall Bediako's thesis: Christianity is not a Western religion but it is translatable to the

---

9 Sally Morgan, *My Place,* South Fremantle, Western Australia, Fremantle Arts Centre, 1987.
10 The Rainbow Spirit Elders, *Rainbow Spirit Theology: Towards an Australian Aboriginal Theology*, Melbourne, HarperCollins Religious, 1997.

whole world through the immediacy of the Spirit. Moreover, the West has culturally lost the sense of faith. The Koories, however, are open to guidance as regards interpreting the scriptures. Scripture scholars, Norman Habel and Robert Bos, gave guidance to the Spirit Elders. They helped them realize the significance of the Letter to the Romans 8:22-25 and 8:21. Paul writes of creation weeping with pain, a pain centred within God. In verse 21 the crying in creation is understood as the birth pangs of a new beginning: peoples, animals, trees, rivers and the religious realm itself resonate with the hope of new birth. These and other texts give backing to the weeping of God in the land. These texts also give backing to Bediako's thesis on imagination and sacral images. The primal atmosphere establishes a liminal experience which is in the margin between this everyday world and the realm of the sacred. In the ceremonies there is a repetition of dances, songs, etc., whereby the mythic story meshes more closely with their consciousness.

The Les Murray reflections on the poetic are backed up by the experience of the liminal, for, every authentic poem has this sense of a new place, a new meaning, a deeper relationship where the heart can open to the call. I have tried to capture this experience:

> *Near death to life*
>
> I have long known a Koorie woman
> who claims a near death moment.
> Near death is the struggle
> throughout the Koorie world.
> She heard as at a distance
> the voices of the doctors: was this
> her story's end?
> Till she attended to a familial sound, her
> grandfather's didgeridoo.
> The woman who was a sign for all Koorie
> women took up the cry
> and sang.

Kieran Flynn
At the Heart of Islam

The eighth of June 632 CE was a fated day in the history of Islam. On that day the Prophet Muhammad passed away leaving behind an emerging empire with already well established religious, political and social norms. Various narratives of events following this date emerge and form broadly into both the Sunni and the Shi'a traditions. For the Sunni, Muhammad passed away in the arms of his devoted wife Aisha, daughter of Abu Bakr, who would the first Caliph; for the Shi'a, Muhammad died with his head resting upon the shoulder of his cousin Ali, husband of Fatima and beloved daughter of the Prophet. Ali was highly devoted to the Prophet, the first male believer, the father of the Prophet's only male grandchildren, the Prophet's most intimate disciple and the heroic warrior-champion of Islam. Ali had served as army commander, missionary, diplomat and administrator. In preparing the Prophet's body for burial he poured out his grief in verse:

> May my parents be sacrificed on you, Messenger of God
> For with your death things have come to an end
> Which could not have ended with the death of any other person.
> The chain of prophethood has been snapped.

In every tradition, nation, tribe and religion each generation becomes involved in a re-reading of history in order to reaffirm their identity and belonging. There is a constant remembering and a retelling of the foundational narratives in order to connect with the founding event. For so many Muslims this has been the story of the Hijra, the migration from Mecca to Medina by the early Muslim community under Muhammad in 622. In the pledge of obedience to the Prophet – 'I am yours and you are mine. Whom you war against, him I war against. Whom you make peace with, him I make peace with' – a new faith was formed and sealed. Medina, meaning 'the city' abbreviated from *Medinat al Nabi,* 'the city of the Prophet', became the archetype of Islamic rule and the Muslim state. There were, of course, the inevitable stresses and strains that existed between the *Muhatirun* (Muslims of Mecca) and the *Ansar* (Muslims of Medina), between the core of devout converts and the less ardent majority, between the Bedouin and the town dwellers, the rival clans of Aws and Khazraj and, finally, independent Jewish clans. These early antagonisms that swirled beneath the surface would play a powerful role in shaping early Islamic history.

Contemporary religious history and experience is shaped by a remembering of foundational narratives in a modern context. For Muslims these ancient divisions, factions and rivalries are seen in today's contexts and they inform a great deal of the discussion among Muslim communities as to how they see and regard each other.

The years since 9/11 have been difficult and heart-wrenching for Muslims. The acknowledgement of terrorism and violence perpetrated by Muslims on behalf of innocent others has precipitated deep and agonizing soul-searching. From where did this violence come? Why this reaction of warlike attack against unknown others? Is there really a violent tendency at the heart of our faith? Can men of violence use religious rituals and texts to find support for their violent crimes? Such questions continue to disturb Muslim communities as they seek to understand the nature of violent Islamic extremism and its place within Islam, the religion of *salam,* peace and right relationship. Muslims returned to their religious narratives to discover again if there were clues in their tradition to guide them.

In this essay, I wish to give an account of this early period of Islamic history so that the Western reader may more easily understand the background to some of the contentious issues that arise in current debates on Islam. There has been a narrative of oppression and violence in Islam that has not been heard or understood very far outside Muslim circles and there is a need for a reintegration and re-appropriation of such narratives of oppression and violence by Muslims and non-Muslims alike. Specifically, the questions needing to be asked are: given their importance to Islam, what happened to the family of the Prophet after his demise and why?

Sunni and Shi'a

Most Western discussions on Islamic matters of the Arab world tend to focus, if often implicitly, on Sunnism. This is to be expected since the overwhelming majority of the world's 1.3 billion Muslims are Sunnis. Shi'as number between 130 and 195 million people, i.e., over 10 percent of the total. However, in the Islamic heartland, from Lebanon to Pakistan, there are roughly as many Shi'as as there are Sunnis; and around the geostrategically sensitive rim of the Persian Gulf, Shi'as constitute the majority.

The division between Shiism and Sunnism is the most important in Islam. Each carries its orthodoxy and political tradition; in much the same way as Protestant-Catholic conflict shaped Western history, so the Sunni-Shi'a one continues to shape the history of the Islamic world in the broader Middle East.

In Shiism and Sunnism, Islamic history, theology and law are understood differently. Each exists within a distinct world of faith and piety that informs what it means to be Muslim. The rivalry goes back to the early days of Islam and, in particular, to the crisis of succession that followed the Prophet Muhammad's death in 632. The tribal tradition of the time held that a council of elders would choose the most senior and respected elder to become the head of the Islamic community or *umma*. Justification for this was found in the declaration of the Prophet that 'my community will never agree in error.' For this group, the successor need not have exceptional spiritual qualities but be a virtuous and able Muslim capable of leading the political affairs of the community. The Sunnis chose Abu Bakr, the close friend of the Prophet. Abu Bakr declared, 'O people, to those who used to worship Muhammad, Muhammad is dead. But to those who used to worship God, God is alive and can never die.' In this way Abu Bakr laid to rest questions about the immortality of the Prophet; he also reminded the mourners of the Prophet's own recitation: 'Muhammad is but a messenger, messengers the like of whom have passed away before him. Will it be that, when he dies or is slain, you will turn back on your heels?'

However, a smaller group of the Prophet's companions believed that the Prophet's cousin and son-in-law, Ali ibn Ali Talib, was more qualified for the job and that it had been the wish of the Prophet that he would lead the community. During his pilgrimage to Mecca it is reported that the Prophet stopped at Ghadir Khumm, gathered the pilgrims together and declared 'whoever recognizes me as his master will recognize Ali as his master.' The day of Ghadir Khumm is celebrated as an important festival within the Shi'a calendar, marking the date when the Prophet appointed Ali as his successor.

Significantly, it was also chosen as the day for the first democratic elections within a transformed Iraq following its American occupation in 2003. With regard to the early leadership, finally, consensus did prevail and dissenters accepted Abu Bakr's leadership.

This period of three decades from 632 until 661 is called the period of the Rightly Guided or *Rashidun* Caliphs. Abu Bakr was succeeded by Umar, Uthman and finally Ali himself. All had been close companions of the Prophet and were knowledgeable about religious matters. For Sunnis this period of the *Rashidun* was Islam's golden era. It was a time when political rule continued to be informed by the values of faith, a time when Islam was closest to its spiritual roots and a time during which the Islamic empire expanded dramatically.

Islam owes a great deal to the modesty of Abu Bakr. He was determined to keep his leadership clean of the pomp and ritual of kingship and maintain the tradition of accessibility and concern established by the Prophet. Nothing was allowed to stand between God and humans. As Muhammad had preached an uncompromising monotheism so, too, for Abu Bakr nothing should obscure the direct relationship between the believer in prayer and the one God. His epithet of *as-Saddiq*, which is translated as 'the truthful' or 'the sincere', had been truly won. Modern Shiite leaders have gone to great length to repair the misunderstandings between the two paths of Islam by honouring Abu Bakr's achievement; they particularly criticize the public cursing of the first three caliphs, a practise popular in sixteenth-century Safavid Persia. Through a process of astute diplomacy and battlefield tactics, Abu Bakr was able to achieve the reconquest of tribal Arabia during the Ridda Wars in less than two years. In this period Abu Bakr doubled the size of the Muslim state. The tribal Bedouin Arabs, who had sought to be free from the taxation and government of Medina once the Prophet died, were again united and at peace under Islam. The conquest had begun.

Umar has often been compared to St Paul in Christianity. He proved himself to be a remarkable leader, an inspired strategist, a brilliant administrator and a man of outstanding personal example. Initially incensed at the divisions that Islam was causing to Meccan society he became an opponent of Islam. Later, on hearing a recitation of the Qur'an by his sister and brother-in-law, he was dramatically converted. Thereafter, he embraced Islam fervently and enthusiastically. As Caliph he led the expansion against the Byzantine empire and claimed Jerusalem for Islam. There, dressed as a pilgrim, he maintaining an extraordinary respect for the city of Jerusalem, for the Patriarch and for the city's holy places. Syria, Palestine and Egypt all fell under Muslim influence during Umar's caliphate. The two empires of Byzantium and Persia were decisively defeated at Yarmuk and al-Qadisiya, respectively, thus transforming Arabia and the Islamic world. Umar had great personal integrity. He exacted the same standards, though, from his wives and children with high cost. He despised the trappings of kingship and wealth and remained accessible to all throughout his life. When he was murdered by an aggrieved slave he was buried next to the Prophet.

Umar's successor as Caliph was Uthman. He was regarded as a living example of the best of Islam, generous and compassionate, combining business and administrative efficiency with charity, prayer, scholarship and a fulfilling and loving family life. Though he was without military experience, his efficient and liberalizing public administration won him much support, especially within a growing aristocracy. Uthman's greatest achievement was neither military, political nor administrative. He decided to make a definitive written edition of God's revelation – the Qur'an. All fragments were collated and by 650 Uthman had overseen the creation of the first complete copy of the Qur'an.

The last years of Uthman's rule (651-6) were years of trouble. An inability to curb in others their political ambition, corruption and nepotism led to a serious erosion of his power and authority. Where Uthman saw progress, the rest of Arabia saw only the triumph of Uthman's family, the Umayyad clan of the Quraysh. The Umayyads now controlled all the top posts in the empire. A revolutionary ferment of disaffection began to brew, especially in Kufa and Fustat where the Umayyad governors were publicly reviled and opposition become more violent. Early Meccan families' antagonisms and divisions also created animosity towards the Umayyad claims to power and legitimacy. Uthman preferred to accept his own death rather than have his fellow believers killed. He accepted assassination while reading his beloved Qur'an.

Finally, Ali was at last acclaimed Caliph by the massed crowds. He was now commander of an Islamic empire that stretched from the borderlands of central Asia and Afghanistan westwards towards Egypt and Libya and north towards Syria, Jordan and Palestine. He embodied Islamic values: the only surviving son-in-law of the Prophet, father of the Prophet's only and beloved grandsons, his first cousin, his adoptive son, his first male follower, his closest disciple, hero-warrior of Islam and principal expert on Islamic law and the Qur'an. Nevertheless, there remained bad blood between Ali and the children of Umar. Yet, the core of opposition was located around a single individual, Aisha, Mother of the Faithful and devoted widow of the Prophet Muhammad. She had distanced herself from the opposition to Uthman and now challenged Ali in battle; this was Islam's first civil war. At the Battle of the Camel Aisha and her supporters were defeated and not humiliated but pardoned. Muawiya, who was an appointee and relative of Uthman, still opposed Ali and challenged him. Finally, at Siffin, Muslim armies faced each other in battle, although there was great reluctance for brothers to oppose one another and engage in violence. Nearing defeat, Muawiya's supporters, with pages of the Qur'an attached to their spears, sought arbitration. This denied outright victory to Caliph Ali and Islam. The result also deeply offended a group called the seceders, *Kharijites*; they were deeply opposed to settlement by compromise, felt that Ali was therefore unworthy to be Caliph, and sought to form a community of devoted, unswerving believers. They opposed Ali and were defeated; this was a tragic civil war within a civil war, one waged not so much against Ali but in desperation against the political corruption that was overwhelming the dream of a pure Islam. The army of Ali, though victorious, was dejected and spent, physically and spiritually: 'their arrows used up, their swords dulled, their spearheads had fallen from their lances.' Three Kharijites plotted to free Islam from persecution by removing Ali the Caliph, Amr the Governor of Egypt and Muawiya the Governor of Damascus. They only succeeded in killing Ali as he led Friday prayer at Kufa (661). His body was washed by his children, Hasan and Husain, grandchildren of the Prophet, and buried at an unknown location.

The world of Islam soon came to think that the perfect Muslim man had been murdered. His virtues were obvious: complete honesty, unbending devotion to the true practice of Islam, fairness, compassion and generosity. Muhammad is remembered as saying 'I am the town of knowledge and its gate is Ali.' Henceforth, Ali would be known as the *Bab,* the gateway of scholars, mystics and poets. He refused to play the dirty game of tribal politics and he retained and maintained idealism without compromise. He is the linchpin in the whole tale of the Heirs of the Prophet, crafted from the principles of honour, truth, courage and bravery. With his murder something enlightening and spiritual had passed and an era of holiness was over. Yet, in his children, Hasan and Husain, the Islamic struggle against scheming politicians and tough-minded opportunists continued. The true grief of the Shi'a, then, did not conclude with the death of Ali but continued to engulf the *Ahl Bayt* (People of the House) and the bloodline of the Prophet.

We see that the period from the death of Prophet Muhammad until the death of Ali (that of the *Rashidun*) is understood quite differently by the Shi'a and the Sunni. For the Shi'a the betrayal of the Islamic inheritance had begun straight away. Only Ali is qualified to uphold leadership, spiritual and temporal; thus, they turned their backs on the many other spiritual qualities among the Companions. For the Sunni, though, and despite the creeping decay of spiritual values, this first generation of Muslim leaders – Abu Bakr, Umar, Uthaman and Ali (and other Companions of the Prophet) – set an example for all Muslims to follow as a source of inspiration.

Muawiya, Imam Hasan and Imam Husain

Following the burial of his father Ali, Hasan was readily accepted in Medina as the rightful heir and guardian of Islam. He was a scholar and a pacifist and sought to put an end to the enmity between the Umayyad Muawiya and the supporters of Ali, even if this meant surrendering his own position. Muawiya was accepted as Caliph in Kufa though reluctantly, especially by the devoted Companions of the Prophet who were appalled at his political ambition; they recalled the early treachery of his father, Abu Sufyan, in Mecca against the Prophet. Yet, under Muawiya the empire of Islam spread into Tunisia and was consolidated in the Persian East. The centre of his Umayyad empire was firmly located in Damascus. By the end of his life he succeeded in presenting his son Yazid as his heir, in this way pushing aside his earlier agreement to hold a consultative *shura* of the Council of Companions of Medina. Muawiya had succeeded in turning a community of believers into a hereditary kingdom based on military power.

Hasan was poisoned and therefore a martyr. He was revered by all and leaving behind a retinue of wives and children. Yazid failed to earn the support of many devout Muslims; his fondness for hunting, wine and a life of debauchery won him few admirers. He was a hardened military and political leader, and he sought to quell dissention wherever it emerged.

From Kufa streamed a succession of messengers, calling for Husain in Medina to ride north against Yazid and claim his rightful place at the head of the community. However, having summoned the grandson of the Prophet to lead them in revolt, the Kufans failed to honour their appointment with him. At Kerbala in present day Iraq, Husain, his seventy followers and family members encountered a 4000-strong force. Under the direction of Shamir, Husain's small band was denied water and brutally put down. Among the victims were Husain's ten-year-old nephew Kasin and his own infant son, Ali, great-grandson of the Prophet. By dusk, that fateful 10th day of Muharran (9th October 680) seventy heads had been rolled out from bloodied leather sacks onto the palace floor of the governor of Kufa. Governor Ubaydallah turned over these heads with his staff; one of the old judges cried out 'Gently, it is the Prophet's grandson and by God I have seen those very lips kissed by the blessed Apostle himself.' The news of Kerbala horrified the Islamic world. Yet, there was to follow the defilement of the Holy Cities. In 688, Mecca was besieged; two months into the offensive the Kaaba was burned to the ground and the sacred black stone that had been set in the Kaaba during the lifetime of the Prophet was fractured in three pieces.

In just fifty years, a vast empire has been created and great wealth had filled the coffers of the Caliph's treasury in Damascus. There was a well-established ruling class.

Yet, in Mecca itself, the house of God was a burned out ruin, while in Kerbala the headless corpses of the murdered family of the Prophet lay buried. It was as if the earthly kingdom had been won but the cost to Islam had been immense, and something at the heart of Islam had been lost.

Shi'a identity: Ashura

The annual commemoration known as Ashura, which recalls the 10th of Muharram massacre, is of central importance to Shi'a Muslims. Devotion to Imam Husain is real and palpable among all Shi'a communities. Throughout the world, Shi'as gather, recall and lament the fateful day of the executions by the tyrant Yazid. Ashura is the watchword for revolution, standing up against tyranny and domination; for Shi'as, this is the essence of Islam, the foundation of self-sacrifice and true martyrdom. In processions and in Mourning Cermonies, Shi'as cry out *Ya Hasan, Ya Husain*, beating their breasts, beating drums and retelling the lamentable story of the death of the Martyrs. This is the refounding of Islam, a turning away from tyranny, dictatorship, the rule of political oligarchy even as it is a remembering of self-sacrifice, courage, bravery and unquenchable opposition.

Ashura is a powerful locus of sorrow and pageantry with parallels in Catholic Lenten rituals, such as the Way of the Cross Processions and Passion Plays. It is a time of penance for vices and errors, of repentance, of personal and communitarian transformation. Over the years and varied locations, the Shi'a faithful have adapted Ashura; observations in Lucknow in northern India look quiet different from those in Nabatiye in southern Lebanon. Ashura has traditionally been about collective atonement, the recognition of human frailty and failure and the striving towards the ideals of Godliness and integrity. It upholds the image of the innocent and the courageous victim, who has become both a mythic and spiritual figure of self-conscious sacrifice rising above mundane events and it gives new meaning, self definition and identity to those who recall and re-enact Husain's demise.

For centuries Shi'a identity and spirituality have grown up in the shadow of events that shaped the martyrdom of the children and family of the Prophet. This is the meta-narrative that has formed the Shi'a community, giving it self-definition and the aspiration towards specific values, notably heroism, integrity and sacrifice. The triumph of the political leader is hollow if it is not associated with the spiritual values of Godliness, goodness, humility and sacrifice. In recalling the early history of Islam and the family of the Prophet, Shi'as recall not greatness in political terms, although there was that during the Caliphate of Ali. They recall a history of oppression, tyranny and domination. They remember the desire for freedom and liberation from violent dictators, foreign and political leaders who would hold them captive. For many Muslims these are, then, contemporary themes in political and social contexts, not least in Lebanon, Iran and Iraq.

A modern example – Iraq

With the fall of Saddam Hussein, thousands of Iranian Shi'as crossed the border into Iraq and headed towards Kerbala. There, for the first time since before the Ba'ath regime they undertook their pilgrimage of remembrance in fidelity to their fallen Iman Husain. For the first time also Iraqi Shi'as undertook their own mourning and lamenting rituals. Under Saddam such gatherings were deemed politically unsettling and provocative. With American occupation came the possibility of religious freedom and the promise of political participation for the Shi'a.

Since the Iranian revolution of 1979 and the Gulf war of 1991, Shi'as have been moving away from violence and towards dialogue with the West and with other members of their societies. This accommodation reflects their desire for political empowerment, for, outside of Iran, Shi'as have been denied political participation in the Middle East. In pre-2003 Iraq, a Sunni minority elite held sway over the Shi'a majority. The US-led occupation has transformed power relations within the country and particularly among the Shi'a and Sunni groups in a post Ba'ath Iraq. The Kurds in northern Iraq already exercised a relative autonomy from the south in both political and administrative terms. This profound change explains the different attitudes of Shi'as and Sunnis toward the occupying power. In the period 2003-2005 Shi'as have given their tacit support to the reconstruction effort; participation in the elections for a transitional national assembly, and later assembly, has empowered Shi'as considerably. The current task of creating a strong legislature and a representative government accountable to the voters is deliberate though difficult, painstaking and slow. Terrorism, violence, the collapse of security, insurgency and counter-insurgency block steady progress at all levels. Those who are committed to violence and terrorism are seen in the light of dearly held narratives that place oppressors and violent dictators among those who have defeated the family of the Prophet from earliest days.

Shi'as as a whole are looking for ways to reconcile Islamic and Western concepts of democracy and government in the wake of generations of oppression, state violence, foreign war, crippling sanctions and dictatorship. Grand Ayatollah 'Ali Sistani responded to such concerns by encouraging a trend towards accommodation among the Shi'a and engagement with American occupation. This has been a positive start, but is now heading towards all-out civil war and to greater violence in the Middle East. However, the shift from violence to greater accommodation and the assertion of Shi'a power in Iraq have signalled the rise of the Shi'a as a force that could potentially spur reform in the region. If the nuclear issue in Iraq could be addressed meaningfully and diplomatic relations restored, genuine efforts at curbing violence in Iraq could proceed, perhaps leading towards a stabilization of security in many areas. At least in this case, the US and Iran share a common goal of a unified Iraq with a Shi'a-led government.

Conclusion: hope, integrity and Muslims

The occupation of Iraq provided America with an opportunity to establish relationships of trust not only with the Shi'a but also with other people in the Middle East who, too, have been craving for change. At the heart of the issue for Iraqis – Sunni and Shi'a alike – is the opportunity to develop a strong legislature and a genuinely representative government. Within Islam lie resources that commit Muslims to democracy and good government. In their narratives and rituals, to some of which we have given attention above, Muslims can both recall and imagine a time when leadership was a watchword for integrity and government was allied to self-sacrifice. Too often in history the reality has betrayed the ideal and dictatorship has prevailed; indeed, genuine democratic government in Arab Islam is difficult to find. Nevertheless, the hope remains strong that, though people of violence have sought support in religion, it is the desire for integrity such as the Prophet displayed that founds genuine faith.

Gideon Goosen
Towards a Theory of Dual Religious Belonging

Introduction

The factors that have promoted interreligious contact in recent decades are well described in the literature and will be assumed in this article. A by-product of this contact has been an increase in the phenomenon known as dual religious belonging in the sense of a main religion with a secondary one from which one draws. A person could be a Hindu-Christian, for example. Although some people reject this concept as impossible, unnecessary and undesirable, I think it is here to stay and is on the increase in the West.

The problem is that we need to articulate a theory of dual religious belonging. A rigid Christian upbringing in the past tended to be monolithic and did not need input from any other religion. As the attitude of Christians has changed and they struggle to articulate a theology of religions, there has arisen the need to formulate a theory of dual religious belonging. As the theological grounds shift, a theory may help some relate to what is happening. A plausible theory could help people deal with the reality on the ground, that is, the number of people who admit to 'walking two paths'.

Although the following topics need a whole book, given space limitations, they will only be briefly touched on below: some aspects of person and personhood, identity, conversion, and the illusory self. The opening up of these aspects will give one an inside view, as it were, of the issues and facilitate a discussion on dual belonging. These aspects will then be related to theorists and some conclusions drawn. Given that John D'Arcy May was so committed to Interfaith Dialogue in his lecturing and writings, it is my privilege to contribute to this volume.

Person and Personhood

Since it is the person that believes and acts in any faith tradition, 'person' is a good place to start. The concept of personhood has many angles including the differences related to an Eastern or Western world-view. I will mention the Western ideas on person shortly, but Easterners think quite differently. Thatamanil, for instance, suggest the concept of person needs closer scrutiny.[1] He maintains that the Western unitary concept of personhood is unsatisfactory. It rests on an inadequate philosophy and anthropology of personhood as a single indivisible identity. The Western idea of personhood, he says, is that of the self as an individual, self as present, and self as conscious. 'I' is at the centre of everything. By contrast, an Eastern concept taken from Advaita Vendanta would stress the Ultimate, rather than the self, and the non-dual Self (atman). We need to bear this in mind when speaking from within a Western philosophical stance.

In the Western philosophical tradition, the actual concept of 'person' (and 'personhood') is illusive possibly because it has a depth and complexity which is not always

---

1 John Thatamanil, 'Managing Multiple Religious and Scholarly Identities: An Argument for a Theological Study of Hinduism', in *Journal of the American Academy of Religion* 68,4 (December 2000): 791-803.

appreciated. In the West, we know more or less what it is without being able to pin it down. It has something to do with 'I', with the self, and consciousness.[2] It is closely linked to rationality or intentionality, as when we say that a person is essentially a rational human being capable of moral agency. Boethius, in the 6th century, handed posterity a now-famous definition which gave direction to the debate. His definition was: *persona est naturae rationalis individua substantia* ('a person is an individual substance of a rational nature'), thus emphasizing the rational aspect of the concept.[3] Philosophers, ethicists, theologians and social theorists all have their own favoured definitions. Ethicists, for example, sometimes define it in terms of moral criteria such as rights or respect, so that a person's right to life should be upheld, etc. The problem of boundaries to personhood has become very acute in contemporary ethics when speaking about the beginning and end of life as this impacts directly on issues like abortion and euthanasia. Religion, too, has made its mark on the debate where it is often defined in terms of soul and relationship to God. The very idea of person has been influenced by the christological and trinitarian debates of the fourth to the 6th century.[4]

Thus, early attempts to understand the concept, while stressing rationality, did not have elements of self-consciousness and memory. Today, more emphasis is given to personhood as embodied persons in community without disparaging rationality. As Rudman points out, the process of becoming more human, more a person (not just more civilized, or more technically competent), is impossible without the help of others.[5] To be a human person is more than an endowment at birth.[6] Thus, the complexity and richness of the concept of 'person' is clear. It is more than just rationality; it includes the other nuances of consciousness, self, memory, embodiment in community, *relationality*. It is particularly the idea of *relationality* that opens us towards 'the Other'. By person, then, we mean the aggregate of all these understandings. Personhood, like identity, is made up of several elements.

Identity

Another related idea is that of identity which is an awareness of self that is constituted by a number of elements: self, personal history, memory, relationships, inculturation. It can be personal or public, though here we are referring to one's personal identity, one's self-image. It can be strong if re-enforced in a positive way and it can be fragile and be shattered if the bits and pieces which constitute it are attacked or are inherently weak. Above all, identity is a dynamic concept that can grow and change. Added to this is the

---

2 In post-structuralism, much is made of the self and consciousness in terms of ensuring the continuity of the rational being, cf. Homi K. Bhabha, 'Interrogating Identity', in Lisa Appignanesi (ed.), *The Real Me: Post-Modernism and the Question of Identity*, London, Institute of Contemporary Arts, 1987: 5-11.
3 Stanley Rudman, *Concepts of Person and Christian Ethics*, Cambridge, Cambridge University, 1997: 134.
4 Rudman, *Concepts of Persons*: 3. Some writers have gone further: von Balthasar says that the concept of person, whether human or divine, is rooted in the concept of mission; Jesus's mission is his identity, cf. A. Hunt, *The Trinity and the Paschal Mystery*, Collegeville, Liturgical, 1997: 67. Rudman describes the influence from the Christological and Trinitarian debates on pages 336-337.
5 Rudman, *Concepts of Persons*: 336.
6 Proof of this is sadly not lacking historically, e.g., Saddam Hussein, Adolf Hitler, Joseph Stalin, Nicolae Ceaușescu and Slobodan Milošević.

connection between identity and religion which is again a very close relationship. It is best seen through the process known as inculturation, i.e., the process whereby one was brought up in a particular culture. The term 'culture', used in an anthropological way, always includes religious beliefs and practices. As one is brought up in one's culture one is simultaneously brought up in set of religious beliefs and practices. The intimate relationship between 'religion' and 'culture' can hardly be overestimated, as Benedict XVI has repeatedly inferred; in fact, it is often neglected or understated. One's religious upbringing is critical for identity and belonging. Reflection on this reality raises a number of teasing questions which are also conjured up by the term 'dual religious belonging'. Is one ever able to discard one's religious inculturation completely? How does it affect one's current decisions and belonging? Can one 'convert' completely?

Identity is closely related to person for, as we say, it is the person who has an identity. However, identity is not static; it is a dynamic concept and to shed light on this we turn to philosophy. Smyth reminds us how Ricoeur connects identity to human consciousness.[7] Ricoeur makes a distinction between two understandings of identity: identity as *idem*, and identity as *ipse*. The first represents a closed idea of self, rooted in some original past, and expressing what has already been said, while the latter, *ipse*, is a more open idea, a restless notion of the self in the process of expressing the not-yet-said. Smyth then draws instructive gospel parallels. First, Jesus does not cling to his identity with God but empties himself, and, second, against the idea of a fixed identity, Jesus reminds some Jews, who were boasting that Abraham was their ancestor, that it is not blood ties but doing the will of God that constitutes kinship.

Ricoeur is saying that the two identities, the *idem* and the *ipse*, are there simultaneously. The idea is evocative of Thatamanil's idea of Eastern, non-dualistic, non-binary thinking. It also suggests that perhaps part of religious identity is precisely the tendency to express or explore the not-yet-said. Identity has a transcendent horizon which is constantly changing. When attention is directed away from the illusory self (the dying to self) then there is the potential for growth. The insights of Ricoeur thus throw light and are supportive of what the philosophers have been saying.

Conversion

If we now think of the problem of maintaining dual loyalties in a situation of dual religious belonging, a further insight can be prised from Western *psychology*. Let us consider the idea of 'conversion' and assume that conversion is a fair term to use for what happens when a person crosses over to another religion. I am not suggesting that dual religious belonging is a conversion, but the latter phenomenon can shed light on how one can move from integrations of personhood and identity to disintegration and then move on to a new integration in a sort of dialectical movement. What do psychologists say about conversion? There might be something instructive from this source. Let me quote Carrier:

> A conversion appears to the psychologist as the disintegration, on the religious level, of a mental synthesis and its replacement by another.[8]

---

7 Geraldine Smyth, 'Churches in Ireland: Journeys in Identity and Communion', in *The Ecumenical Review* 53,2 (April 2001):155-167.
8 M.T-D. Penido, *La conscience religieuse: Essai systématique suive dillustrations*, Paris, Pierre Téqui, 1935: 62.

In every conversion there is the elimination of a nonreligious self to the advantage of a religious self. Says Carrier, '[t]wo processes are at work: a dissolving of the previous psychological structure and the appearance of a new one.'[9] It should be pointed out that this understanding means that people indeed try to integrate their new identity and that this process is ongoing to a greater or lesser extent throughout life.[10] Another psychologist, Anthony Fernando, offers an even more challenging comment: that conversion should seek to move a person, not from one institution to another, but from a state of spiritual immaturity to spiritual adulthood.[11] These psychological insights will be taken up below when we bring them into dialogue with some theorists.

Illusory Self

A further consideration regarding the 'self' (which re-enforces the point that Thatamanil made), can be gleaned from the thinking of Thomas Merton, the American Trappist and spiritual writer of last century. His directs comment against that idea of the single, indivisible yet illusory self of Western philosophy. Anne Carr says of Merton that as he looked at Zen, Merton 'understood it as helpful to Christians precisely because it was a way to release the dominating hold, so prevalent in the West, of the exterior or illusory self, the individual or the empirical ego, on the whole person. Zen offers a way of releasing the inner, metaphysical, natural self that is the substratum for what Christianity describes as the action of grace or the 'birth of Christ' in the person'.[12] (The Zen Master, Dogen (1200-1253) goes even further: he wanted to allow all people to return to their true home that is common to all, where the eternal self, totally transcending the 'I' would be completely at one with every person; from the point of view of the 'I', this self is the 'wholly other'.[13]) Freud spoke about the division of the self into the *superego*, *ego* and *id*; in this context above, Merton is referring to the *superego*. This means, perhaps, that the superego identity with which some people grow up is concerned with living up to images of self given by others in the process of inculturation, but they are not the true, authentic self (as existentialists would say). And when the true self (Ricoeur's *ipse*) is given free reign, growth can occur with the discarding of the false self. This growth may include discovering truth in forms outside of one's faith tradition.

Application to Theorists

Roger Corless has developed his theory of coinherence to explain how his particular understanding of dual belonging works. This theory could be said to be more adventuresome than those of Dupuis, Jeanrond or Geffré. If, on a spectrum of approval of other faiths, *Dominus Iesus* represents the negative end of the spectrum, then Corless is the positive end. In his theory he refers to two levels of consciousness. Everyday consciousness,

---

9 Hervé Carrier, *The Sociology of Religious Belonging*, translated by Arthur Arrieri, London, DLT, 1965: 72.
10 Robert Schreiter, *The New Catholicity: Theology between the Global and the Local*, Maryknoll, Orbis, 1997: 70, 71.
11 Whalen Lai and Michael von Brück, *Christianity and Buddhism: A Multi-Cultural History of Their Dialogue*, Maryknoll, Orbis, 2001: 63.
12 Anne E. Carr, *A Search for Wisdom and Spirit: Thomas Merton's Theology of the Self*, Notre Dame, University of Notre Dame, 1988: 88, cited in Catherine Cornille (ed.), *Many Mansions? Multiple Religious Belonging and Christian Identity*, Maryknoll, Orbis, 2002: 115.
13 Lai and von Brück, *Christianity and Buddhism*: 179.

which does not tolerate paradoxes, arranges things hierarchically and basically makes binary opposites. The other is extraordinary superconsciousness, which transcends paradox and hierarchies, is basically nonbinary. In superconsciousness differences coinhere while retaining their integrities. Superconsciousness understands incompatibility differently rather than dissolving or resolving it. It is not a new syncretism. Corless does admit of confusion in so doing; yet, he clearly believes that religious people can commit themselves to dual spiritual paths without resolving the confusions raised by their dual loyalties. It seems to me that Corless's confusion might arise with the coexistence of incompatible world-views, and secondly, there is the danger of producing a *tertium quid*[14] if the dialogue is pursued. On the first point, it is true that some people do accommodate two incompatible world-views or partial world-views. Cognitive dissonance is a fact of life. However, Corless himself describes what it is like to be a dual practitioner:

> I have come to realize that I am equally convinced by the truth of the Christian world-view (and the necessity of the existence of God) and the Buddhist world-view (and the necessity of the non-existence of God). I do not know what this means, but it appears to make me a Buddhist-Christian dialogue within myself ... Please note that I do not propose in any way to blend Buddhism and Christianity, to have resolved their differences, or even to know if a resolution is either possible or desirable. All I am doing, like the planet earth itself, is sitting in the midst of the confusion which I have discovered. Perhaps this confusion is a koan or, like a crucified (and therefore dead) God, a sign of contradiction.[15]

Dupuis poses the question, how is simultaneous belonging to two different objects of faith possible?[16] According to him, it is not simply a question of inculturation or bringing one's religious and cultural baggage into one's new religion (although he does not define his understanding of inculturation). It is something more than this; it is combining two distinct objects of faith into two forms of a unique faith. Dupuis (thinking of his missionary experience of Hinduism and Christianity) continues that the feasibility of this happening is due to the religious baggage that people bring with them; to the extent that they bring some elements of Hinduism to their Christianity so too, to that extent, they should be able to integrate their (Hindu) beliefs that they have encountered in a profound way, and – this is key – that are not in opposition to their Christian beliefs. That such elements do exist and can be combined and integrated with it is a matter of fact, says Dupuis.

The question of ruling out any elements which would be in opposition to Christian faith, brings us to the critical questions of who decides, and what are the criteria for deciding, which elements are in opposition to Christian faith rather than merely complementary to it or convergent with it? This leads us into the syncretism debate and the criteria to be used for assessing inculturation. Suffice it to say that the history of

---

14 The term is mentioned by Aloysius Pieris, 'Interreligious Dialogue and Theology of Religions: An Asian Paradigm', in *Fire and Water: Basic Issues in Asian Buddhism and Christianity*, Maryknoll, Orbis, 1996: 161. Cf. Schreiter, *A New Catholicism*: 76: traditions are not as cohesive as some advocates would think.

15 Roger Corless, *Newsletter of the Society for Buddhist-Christian Studies* 4 (Fall 1989): 3, cited in Robert Magliola, *On Deconstructing Life-Worlds: Buddhism, Christianity, Culture*, Atlanta, Scholars, 1997: 123.

16 Jacques Dupuis, 'Christianity and Religions: Complementarity and Convergence', in Cornille, *Many Mansions?*: 61-75: 72.

Christianity is full of examples of syncretism in the good sense, and that criteria for judging inculturation have been addressed elsewhere.[17]

Now we turn to another theologian, Geffré, whose ideas have much in common with those of Dupuis. He says it would be 'absurd to affirm that one can be both Christian and Hindu or Buddhist from the perspective of these traditions as religious systems.'[18] He then goes on to explain in what sense, though, he would support a dual belonging: 'if religion is understood as an interior experience and as the total surrender of oneself to a transcendent and Absolute reality, it would be possible to affirm a continuity between my Christian experience and my previous spiritual experience.'[19] We note in passing the essentialist nature of his definition of religion described as an interior experience. He continues his elaboration which leads to a new form of being Christian. 'It would be the same experience of the Absolute that is mediated by different symbolic conceptual and ritual ways of objectifying the experience. But this is not the whole truth. The structuring elements of Christianity may undergo a metamorphosis in the contact with those of the tradition to which I belonged. One may then speak of the emergence of a new form of being Christian. This is what I mean by the good use of syncretism.'[20] Here he is picking up on the symbiotic nature of inculturation, namely, that there is a two-way influence at work between the two religions, so that the structuring elements of Christianity undergo a change.

Geffré, too, rejects any syncretism (presumably, in a negative sense) that might want to build a new religion, (what Pieris, has called a *tertium quid*) from the existing ones. There is, affirms Geffré, an alternative:

> But on the existential level, our new Christian identity, which has Jesus Christ as absolute center of reference, could very well assume spiritual attitudes, mental schemes, symbolic resources, and ascetic rituals and practices belonging to other religions while transfiguring them in continuity with our own ethnically and culturally lived world. It is in that sense that, it seems to me, we would be authorized to speak of double belonging without falling into contradiction or confusion.[21]

Christian identity is a matter of becoming, he says, or as Schreiter expresses it, identity is a dynamic concept, not something fixed.[22] On reflection, this view of Geffré seems to me to be a very individualistic, even private view of religion. One is compelled to consider the communal dimension of Christianity as well. The ecclesial dimension might have been over-emphasized in the past but its legitimacy remains and it gets support from the anthropological belief of needing others to grow and from the philosophical

---

17 Schreiter's five criteria relate to the cohesiveness of the Christian performance with regard to: scripture and tradition; liturgy; community life; accepting the judgments of other churches; and the willingness to give a judgment on the proposal of others, in his *A New Catholicism*: 82. Schreiter first mentioned them in his *Constructing Local Theologies*, Maryknoll, Orbis, 1986: 117-121; Schineller mentions three: (1) faithfulness to the Christian message, (2) insertion into the cultural situation, and (3) engagement by pastoral agents, see Peter Schineller, 'Inculturation and Syncretism: What is the Real Issue?', in *International Bulletin of Missionary Research* 16,2 (1992): 52, 53.
18 Claude Geffré, 'Double Belonging and the Originality of Christianity as a Religion' in Cornille, *Many Mansions?*: 93-105: 99.
19 Geffré, 'Double Belonging': 99.
20 Geffré, 'Double Belonging': 100.
21 Geffré, 'Double Belonging': 111.
22 Schreiter, *A New Catholicism*, 68, 74.

perspective of the nature of personhood being relationality. A note similar to Geffré's is struck by Lassalle, the German-Japanese Jesuit who became so close to Zen;[23] he reverts to an interior religion when putting the search for identity into perspective. He believed it was his union with God and Christ that ultimately concerned and moved him and not any kind of Christian-identity project. He is talking of the interior, private aspect of religion, not the public community-of-believers dimension. Geffré's theology of religions, on the other hand, is firmly based on a number of foundational beliefs: religious pluralism as being part of the mysterious will of God; the universal salvific will of God enunciated by the Second Vatican Council and the Church Fathers before them; and the history of the world as under the Word and the Spirit of God.

Part of the unease we encounter in this debate is caused by the presence of Western dualism. We feel it is a case of 'either-or' with many elements regarding dual religious belonging, rather than the harmonization of apparent opposites. It arises when one speaks of elements in opposition to the Christian faith, e.g., ruling elements in or out, right or wrong, good or satanic. This implies working in a dualist, Western, binary system (which Corless decried). This mental framework results in a way of approaching dual belonging cautiously, negatively. A more Eastern approach would be to try to harmonize differences in a positive way. Not that this will always work; but with this approach one's point of departure is non-dualistic.

The dualistic 'either-or' approach fits well with a static view of faith. If, however, we speak of faith as a journey, as being capable of development and growth, then everything changes. Faith can continue to grow until death. We are reminded that the final stage in Fowler's Faith Model is the universalizing stage. With the possibility of growth in faith, one's faith might encounter other religious traditions where it is not immediately clear whether religious elements can be accepted. Here, time for discernment is required as is stressed in the syncretism debate. Thus, the alternative to the dualistic approach is one that is open, seeks to harmonize and suspends dualism. The extreme example of the latter is one advocated by Corless who transcends the binary system with his nondualistic superconsciousness. However, his approach carries other problems as we shall see.

At this stage it is profitable to return to the term 'conversion' and apply it to dual religious belonging. Theoretically, one could analyze the reality of conversions further. Those who convert within Christianity from, say, Catholicism to Anglicanism, would make a definitive step, but would they be able to reject all of their religious past (doctrine, practices and piety) definitively? Would their religious past not colour their new commitment? Would those who converted from one world religion to another be able to reject their religious past in a definitive way? Was Edith Stein able to reject her Jewish past so that it did not colour her post-conversion religiosity? I think not. Furthermore, would indigenous peoples who converted to Christianity from 'paganism' be able to break away completely from their religious past? I am thinking of peoples such as the Native Americans, Inuit, or Aborigines who converted to Christianity. Indeed, the movement is now towards inculturation; the indigenous religious culture is revisited to resurrect customs and practices that might be blended (integration) with their Christianity. Therefore, it is understandable that someone might be a Christian but maintain elements of, say, Buddhism, in their religious practice. In short, I suggest that the idea of a pure

---

23 Werner G. Jeanrond, 'Belonging or Identity? Christian Faith in a Multi-Religious World', in Cornille, *Many Mansions?*: 106-120: 111-114.

conversion, or adherence to the essence of a faith, or cultural purity for that matter, is a total illusion.[24] It does not exist.

The gospel offers some support for the idea that faith is not 'pure'. The Syro-Phoenician woman was commended for her faith. What faith? What belief system? Did she believe Jesus was the Messiah? Surely, her faith and beliefs were a mixture of elements including confidence in Jesus. Did she have more than one object of her faith? Normally, one's faith (or religion) is consciously or unconsciously mixed with other objects like career, ambition, acceptance, without the purity of one's faith being challenged; so why is it so strange that faith in Christianity could be mixed with elements of other faiths? As regards its object or motivation, faith is never pure. People believe many different things (sometimes elements that are blatantly incompatible with Christianity) and still call themselves 'Christian'.

What, though, can be said about adhering to two religious systems? In the light of inculturation, becoming a Christian does not mean alienating oneself from one's previous cultural, religious and ethnic identity (although the gospel will function in a critical way towards culture). The gospel will transform what is true, good and holy in the culture. Yet, some like Geffré would say that one cannot belong to two *religious systems* at once, i.e., be both Christian and Hindu. Yet, as Geffré points out, if religion is seen as an interior religious experience and as the total surrender of oneself to a transcendent and Absolute reality, it would be possible to continue that religious experience into the new religion.[25] One would be changing the religious symbols and rituals, but the same Absolute would remain.

There is yet another possibility. The structural form of Christianity might change and take on new shapes; a new form of Christianity might emerge, say, Hindu-Christianity (as Greco-Christianity or Anglo-Christianity emerged historically). This new form would be subject to all the *criteria for judging syncretism* mentioned in the literature.[26] This approach has as it foundation the belief that God willed religious pluralism, it is part of God's providential intent. It also rests on the doctrine of the universal salvific will of God. Hence, we can use the risky language of dual belonging as a new synthesis of the positive values of Christianity and those of another religion. The theology here is that the positive values of another religion may have been brought about by the Spirit of God itself. Here we are talking about a new synthesis, a re-integration, not a new religion, not a *tertium quid*; yet, a new synthesis implies the rejection of the unmixed, twofold nature of what Corless is describing.

There is one critique of Corless's position which I must make. The psychology of conversion showed us that the process of integration followed by disintegration and then a new integration is normal in human development. There is an inbuilt human need to integrate after a stage of change, growth and disintegration. This applies to intellectual pursuits in general as well as to religious beliefs. I believe Corless is fighting that inbuilt need with his attempting to keep his two commitments to Christianity and Buddhism equal and separate. This could be the source of his confusion and extreme tension; and the reason why this category is not common.

We saw how the process of becoming more as a person included relationality. It is not surprising, then, in the context of people of different religious faith coming into

---

24 Schreiter, *A New Catholicism*: 71.
25 Schreiter, *A New Catholicism*: 99.
26 See note 18 above.

contact with each other in today's world, that learning about people's religious beliefs and practices will be part of that development and growth. Far from protecting one from this growth, it should be embraced.

Let us summarize. Dupuis' position is guarded, but what he says rests on his knowledge that it already occurs in real life. He maintains dual belonging is possible in so far as one brings, for example, elements from Hinduism (not in opposition to Christianity) into Christianity and integrates them in a new synthesis. To this is added the richness of the idea that the human person grows through being embodied in community and thus contact with other faiths can be a positive stimulus to spiritual growth.

Geffré rejects the possibility of being both Christian and Hindu as far as the religious systems go. If we take religion as a private, interior experience of our response to the Absolute, he sees no reason why one could not bring in elements from another faith which are in continuity with the first. These new elements may even cause Christianity to undergo a metamorphosis. He rules out of court any idea of a *tertium quid* and rests his theology of other religions on solid doctrine. The phenomenon of 'conversion' supports the idea of an inevitable carry-over of some of one's previous religious baggage. The idea of a pure conversion is an illusion.

Both Dupuis and Geffré work in the Western, dualist concept of philosophy, unlike Corless whose theory of superconsciousness is able to accommodate two different faiths simultaneously although he admits of confusion. Unlike Dupuis and Geffré, Corless resists the possibility of a new synthesis, which latter seems a psychological human need. Yet, the structural forms and rituals used in a new Hindu-Christianity would need to be evaluated through a number of criteria to avoid syncretism.

Conclusion

From the above discussion one can conclude some points about the elements that will contribute towards a theory of dual belonging.

A more expansive and flexible concept of person and self will enable a person to be more open to the other and change, i.e., more open to other religions and experiences of the Ultimate. One grows as a (religious) person when one relates to 'the Other'. The conviction that identity is dynamic with the *ipse* and *idem* allows one to accept the growth that insights into other faiths will bring without any feeling of betraying one's childhood religious identity. This gives freedom to live and grow spiritually. The not-yet-said can be brought to bear on new symbols – and all religious language is symbolic. Indeed, this is supported by the insights from the psychology of conversion: some of the old tradition will remain, but the tendency to repeatedly gain new insights, and then to integrate them into one's identity, is normal. The conviction that faith is never monolithic or pure, also supports the idea of growth and change. Faith does not exclude a process of scrutinizing new experiences. Finally, a theory of dual belonging needs to emphasize that the symbols from another religion can indeed speak to us of the Absolute and enhance our understanding. Putting these elements together, it becomes easier to see that dual (or multi-)religious belonging, in the sense defined above, is not only possible but desirable.

Paul F. Knitter

'What's Next? — What's Now?' The 'Now' is the 'Next'
A Christian-Buddhist reflection on Eschatology

From my first acquaintance with the way John D'Arcy May goes about his job as a theologian and scholar of religion, I knew that this was someone from whom I could learn a lot. What I sensed in his article on contextual theology in Melanesia back in the 1980s[1] has been confirmed for me over these many years as I have followed his scholarship and, especially, as I have come to know the scholar. Long before the term was created and discussed, John May has been a dedicated and ardent 'comparative theologian'[2] (I prefer 'dialogical theologian'). His understanding of his own tradition (and I might add, his own Christian identity) has been, in large part, determined by his engagement with other cultures and other religions. For him, 'the other' has been both a challenge and an opportunity – a source of both questions that disturb traditional theological understandings and answers that create new ones.

As a fellow-traveller with John on this path of dialogical/comparative theology, I would like to reflect in this essay on how my study of Buddhism and my conversation with Buddhists have helped me deal with some rather fundamental difficulties I have had with what in my course at the Gregorian University in Rome back in the 1960s was called '*De Ultimis*' – the 'last things', eschatology. Since 'the last things' are very personal things, I've decided it would best serve me and my readers to put these reflections in the first person.

We talk too much

My problem with Christian language about eschatology is that there is too much of it. We Christians, in general, talk too much. And we do so even when we don't really know what we're talking about. It seems we forget, or don't want to admit, that what applies to the Divine also applies to life with the Divine after death: we are confronting Mystery – that which by its very nature exceeds our human comprehension and ability to see clearly. Therefore, all our language about God and about life after death is inherently, stubbornly, delightfully symbolic.

We forget that. When speaking about 'the last things', maybe even more than in speaking about God, we Christians misuse our language seriously because they use it too literally. At least, that's my suspicion. And it's what I've felt, even more acutely as I move into my seventies, aware that for me the 'last things' are not that far off.

---

[1] John D'Arcy May, 'Kontextuelle Theologie in Melanesien', in *Zeitschrift für Missionswissenschaft und Religionswissenschaft* 71 (1987): 279-91; it is summarized as 'Contextual Theology in Melanesia', in *Theology Digest* 35 (1988): 25-29.
[2] Francis Xavier Clooney, *Theology after Vedanta: An Experiment in Comparative Theology*, Albany, SUNY, 1993; and James L. Fredericks, *Faith among Faiths: Christian Theology and Non-Christian Religions*, New York, Paulist, 1999.

Let me start by describing situations in which Christian talk about life after death has left me squirming with discomfort. Funerals. That's where I so often squirm. Whether it's the language of the liturgy itself, or the homilist during the Mass of Christian Burial, or eulogies at the funeral home, I've often found myself saying – and my wife can testify to this – 'Gads, I don't want them talking like that about me at my funeral.' Examples of language that makes me uneasy:

> 'May the angels welcome you into the heavenly paradise.'
> 'We will sing God's praises for all eternity.'
> 'Now God will reward her for putting up with such ungrateful kids.'
> 'Now he's finally at peace after suffering through his cancer.'
> 'Well, Dad will now again be with Mom.'
> 'If he's going to have to spend time in purgatory, it won't be long.'

I honestly do not want people someday to talk about me that way. Why?

I think the general reason why such language makes me uneasy – and I know from friends that they share this uneasiness – is that it's so neat and clear about things that cannot be known neatly and clearly this side of the grave. It's one thing to believe in 'eternal life.' It's quite another to spell out just how that life will be lived. In talking too much, we fail to cherish, indeed we might even cheapen, the *mystery* of what lies beyond death.

Are we being selfish?

My deeper disquiet with Christian words and images for the after-life stem not so much from too much talking about heaven but from a particular piece of that talk which, many would argue, constitutes the keystone of Christian doctrine on 'the last things'. Over the past decades since I've been struggling with this issue, I've hesitated to bring it up in good Christian conversation. However, the more I have talked about it, the more I've been surprised by eyebrows raised not in amazement but in agreement. 'Yes, I've wondered about that, too.'

I'm talking about personal immortality – about how or even whether we live on after death as individual beings. I find myself wondering not only *whether I believe* but, if I really understand Jesus's message, *whether I should believe* that after death I will live on as Paul Knitter, with, as I've been taught since grammar school, essentially the same soul or personality (though purified), and, after the last judgment, with the same body (though perfected, so I'll have my hair back!). To be honest, I am no longer consoled, but rather confused, by a vision of heaven in which I live forever as an individual, along with billions of other individuals. I fear that such a vision, taken literally, is another misuse of words in the face of mystery.

I found myself stammering some years back when an agnostic friend in Xavier University's Biology Department teased me with the question: '[n]othing in the world perishes completely. Everything lives on after death – but in different forms, through a marvellous process of recycling. Why should humans want to hang on to their individual identities and miss out on this wonderful process?' I can't shake myself loose from my friend's words that everything 'lives on in different forms.' Maybe the mystery of my-life-after-my-death will be so unexpectedly and wonderfully different that it will be beyond anything I can now describe as 'my' or 'me'. Such questions make sense not just rationally but even, if we take the mystery and creativity of the Divine seriously, theologically. 'No eye has seen, no ear has heard, no mind has conceived what God has prepared for those who love him', so St Paul reminds us (1 Corinthians 2:9). That means we are really going to be surprised.

Still more personally, and more discomfortingly, traditional images of a heaven in which individuals receive their eternal rewards seem to me, well, rather selfish. Or, egocentric. I'm not talking about the child's level of morality that such images can easily promote – being good in order to avoid the punishment of hell or gain the reward of heaven. Rather, I have the nagging concern that doctrines about heaven that insist that 'I' will enjoy life with God and with 'my' loved ones are not only saying too much; they might also be obstacles to responding to, and realizing the joy of, what Jesus really meant when he said that we must lose ourselves in order to find ourselves. If we really 'lose' ourselves, whatever we find will not be the same as what we lost. But what will we find? What will we be?

I think Buddhism has helped me peer a little more carefully into that mystery of life-after-death and into the Mystery that is beyond all words.

Buddhism: be here now

I'll never forget the first time I brought a group of students to a Zen centre. It was the early 1970s; I was teaching at Catholic Theological Union in Chicago, so the students were seminarians; and the Zen Center was on Halsted Street. In the conversation with the Zen Master that followed a half-hour of sitting meditation, the first question was, 'what is the Buddhist view of life after death?' We were all nearly knocked off our meditation cushions when the Master calmly answered, 'We don't have one.'

Grinning at the stunned silence, he went on to offer an explanation that basically boiled down to Buddha's response to similar queries, 'your question does not fit the case.' What we Christians were asking was not important – or better, it was not needed – in light of what Buddhists are trying to achieve. The focus of Buddhist energies and concerns is not on what comes after death. It's not even on tomorrow, or the moment that is to follow this one. Rather, it's on *this moment, now, right here.* You might say that Buddhists wish to be *NOWHERE* else but *NOW-HERE*. They wish to live their lives by being fully present – that means, to what is going on, around them and in them, *at this moment*.

What is next is now

Based on the experience of Buddha that becomes their own experience, Buddhists are convinced that if they can be fully present and responsive to what is *going on now*, then what will *happen next* will take care of itself. In a sense, 'what's next' is contained in 'what's now'. Yet, in order to get at 'what's next' we need to be as fully aware or mindful of 'what's now' and respond to it as compassionately as we can. If we do this, Buddha tells us, if we can be fully present to, and responsive to, the 'now', the difference between 'now and next' won't make any difference! By being fully in the present moment, we will no longer have any worries about the next moment, and that includes the moment we die and the moments that come after our death.

If Buddhist friends and scholars will allow me, though, I believe that Buddhists can say (and some of them do say) something about what *is* coming *next*, after death. The reason is, I think, simple. What they discover in this life, will be true of whatever makes up the next life. What they experience themselves to be now, they can figure on being, perhaps even more fully, in what happens after death: no-selves. In the experience of Enlightenment, Buddhists wake up to their true identity as *anattas* – as no-selves. This doesn't mean that they don't exist, but that their true identity is to move beyond the individual self and to become part of, and contribute compassionately to, the larger reality of Interbeing. Happiness in this life consists of living selflessly. And Buddhists know that it will be the same in whatever happens after their present life. That's why, as the Zen Master told my students, they don't have to worry about what comes after death.

Just as in each moment of their lives Buddhists are able to overcome suffering and attain peace by letting go and not clinging selfishly to themselves or to anything, so in the moment of death they will also let go and not cling. The results, they know, will be the same: there will be peace, there will be further interbeing, there will be further life. Just as in each moment, they found peace and overcame suffering by getting beyond their individual selves, so in death, there will be, as it were, the final letting go of, and getting beyond, themselves. Also, it will be good to do so, in death as in life. A Zen saying tells us: 'Every day is a fine day.' That includes the day we die.

What we find is not what we lost

So now I want to try to state how this all too condensed effort to 'pass over' to Buddhism can affect me and help me when I 'pass back' to my Christian identity and beliefs.[3] Buddha is, I believe, in fundamental agreement with Jesus and Christian doctrine when he announces, 'there is that which is reborn.' He urges me to look more deeply, however, into what Jesus taught when he reminds me that the reborn 'that' is very different from the 'that' of who I was in my lifetime. Or, as the Christian liturgy puts it, 'life [after death] will be transformed, not taken away.'[4] 'Transformed' means the 'form' of who we are will be different; there will be continuity but also real discontinuity. We Christians have been good at talking about the 'continuity', but Buddhism suggests that we have not been so good in accepting and trying to deal with the 'discontinuity'. I suspect that the 'who and what' we are now will not be able to recognize itself in the 'who and what' we will be after death.

I say that not just because I've learned a lot from Buddhism but because Buddhism has helped me to take another and deeper look at what I believe as a Christian. We say that eternal life is 'life in God'. Yet, if, as Buddhism reminds us, all our language about God is a 'finger pointing to the moon' but never the moon itself, if God as the Mystery of the Divine is not literally a person, if this Mystery might be more fittingly 'pointed to' as *Spirit*, that is as the *personal Presence* or Spirit-energy that grounds and connects everything – then, just as God is not literally a person, so our eternal life in God will not be literally as the persons we think we are here in this life. If the deepest identity of what we call God cannot, and should not, be captured in the notion of an individual self, then surely our own ongoing life in the Divine cannot and should not be symbolized as an extension of the individual self called Paul or John. Indeed, this life, this identity of ours, will be *transformed*.

---

[3] What I'm trying to do in this essay is to apply the method of comparative theology that John Dunne outlined and applied in his wonderful book of years ago, *The Way of All the Earth*, New York, Macmillan, 1972. He urged Christians, and all religious people, not just to study other religious traditions intellectually and academically but to *pass over* to other religious stories experientially, existentially, and imaginatively – and then to *pass back* to their own story and see what difference it might make.

[4] From the Preface for the *Missa de Defunctis*.

The occasional experiences (or, for the saints and mystics and poets among us, the *frequent* experiences) of transcending our own limited personal consciousness in spiritual or mystical moments will be, we can expect, intensified in what follows after death in our eternal living in God. The poetic outburst of T.S. Eliot that 'I become the music', might well serve as a metaphor for life after death in which 'I become the Divine'. The 'I' is not totally annihilated. But neither does it exist as it was. It endures as something much more, much greater than what we have experienced it to be at this stage of our being.

As I pass back from my dialogue with Buddhism to my Christian identity and tradition, I find that many of the words that I had repeated or read throughout my life start to glow with new meaning, especially in their significance for how we Christians might envision the 'eternal life' we call heaven.

The statement of St Paul gives us a general indication of what we can expect our 'life after death' to be. To the Galatians Paul exclaimed: 'since I've been crucified with Christ, I'm not the one who is now living. It is Christ who is doing the living in me' (my free translation of the Greek in Galatians 2:19-20) The ideal of Christian life is to lose one's own self-centred identity in the wider activity of the risen Christ-Spirit. It is to step back and let this Spirit live in and as us. Surely, this will be the further, unimaginably deeper, reality of life after death. The 'I' that lives on is the Christ-Spirit that lives on in all. (St Paul saw little, if any, difference between the 'risen Christ' and the 'Spirit'.)

Buddhism also throws new, and I believe fuller, light on an oft-quoted passage from John's Gospel: 'unless a grain of wheat falls into the earth and dies, it remains just a single grain; but if it dies, it bears much fruit' (John 12:24). In this passage, Jesus, in looking ahead to his own death, speaks about death for all of us. Death means that as 'single grains', we really die. The 'singleness' of our identities is no longer to be found. The 'fruit' that comes forth is very, very different from the single, little seed. Again, we are dealing here with symbols, with pointing fingers. Nevertheless, they seem to point to a life after death that is no longer life lived as individuals.

The same message, when seen in the light of my Buddhist flashlight, comes through in the five different passages in the Synoptic Gospels (Matthew, Mark, and Luke) in which Jesus tells us that if we really want to 'find' or 'save' our life, we first have to really 'lose' it. In my past readings of these texts, I generally placed the emphasis on the *finding* or *saving*. Buddhism has urged me to take the *losing* part more seriously. The Greek word, *apoluein,* to lose, means that what you once had, you no longer have. Your life as you understood it, is, after death, *gone.* The 'you' you thought you were is no longer around. *What you find is not what you lost.* That's the 'good news' about heaven! (see Matthew 10:39, 16:25; Mark 8:35; and Luke 9:24, 17:33).

To ask what it is that we will find is to ask too much. That's the mystery of the moon. Nevertheless, I think we can say, simply and profoundly, that life after death will no longer be life lived as individuals. That's really what Karl Rahner was guardedly (because it sounded like heresy!) suggesting back in the 1960s when I first read his book on the theology of death.[5] The terminology he used then to speak about life after death nowadays would sound a bit new-agey. He reasoned that in the 'next life', since we would no longer be tied down by the limitations of our material bodies, we would have a 'pancosmic' existence in which our consciousness or awareness would no longer be just our own. Rather, we would all have a kind of shared consciousness, a deeper

---

[5] Karl Rahner, *On the Theology of Death*, New York, Herder, 1967.

mutuality, that would allow us, as it were, to live a shared life in God. 'Weird stuff!' I thought then. However, my conversations with Buddhism and with the Buddhist central claim that our true existence, in this life and whatever comes after it, is to be 'no-selves' has enabled me, I trust, to come to a deeper understanding of, and a deeper respect for, what my brilliant but simple teacher was exploring. 'Pancosmic' might be a suggestive symbol (or new-age finger!) to point to what we *find* after we *lose* our life.

In June of 2002, during a retreat at Gethsemane Abbey, I think I got carried away with some flowery imagery when I tried to tell my journal what I believe about my own afterlife:

> The Buddhist notion of impermanence has helped me feel my way into the question of what comes after death. Will I live on? Yes and no. The nature of reality and of the Divine is impermanence. That means change. Which means – especially in light of what science seems to be telling us about evolution – *real* change. The purpose of existence, all existence, human and all living beings, is to be conduits, or incarnations, of the Spirit's efforts to bring forth ever-greater beauty and unity in this wonderful drama of existence. The primary way in which such beauty is brought forth is through the interconnections of ever more diverse beings ... Another word for such life-giving interconnections is compassion – loving kindness, love.
>
> The image of a garden came up in my readings of yesterday. The beauty of the garden is in its ever-changing diversity. Its beauty takes form in the divergent cast of flowers, and their ever changing expressions, living and dying. I am to be a flower in this Divine garden. What I am will make it what it is, and what it will be. Will I be part of it in the future? Yes, definitely. But not as the little flower that I splendidly was, but rather as the flowers that splendidly continue to be.
>
> Isn't this a deeper, both more demanding and more satisfying, part of the Christian call to love, to give of self, to die in order that the planet may flower? An overly personalized notion of life after death can be very selfish, bordering on the petty. I give of myself and in the process discover myself. But what I discover can be very different from the self I thought I was – tantalizingly different.

Cherish and trust the mystery

Now, I've gone on too much. I've not followed my own – or, the Buddha's – admonitions not to ask too many questions, or give too many answers. I guess I can't help it. I'm a Christian, and on top of that, a theologian. I need words. I keep asking questions and exploring possible answers. That's okay, as long as I remember that all my words are symbols, all my answers are but pointing fingers. In the end, after offering words that might be helpful for me and others, after trying to point to the moon, I have to fold my hands and close my mouth – *and cherish the Mystery* of life and death.

In the end, all we are really left with is *trust*. Whatever the value or accuracy of the words and fingers I have used to express the content of my trust, in the end, I just trust. I trust that after my death, our death, the death of this planet, there will be life. Or, in the words of Julian of Norwich, that all manner of things will be well.

Brendan Leahy
Between Logos and Nothingness
Piero Coda's Theology of Religions

Piero Coda is one of Italy's most prolific theologians and currently president of the Italian Theologians Association. As a 'leading and distinctive voice' in theology,[1] his contribution to the construction of a theology of religions and interreligious dialogue has received positive appraisal.[2] The purpose of this essay, honouring John D'Arcy May's contribution in this field, is to present to English-speaking academic circles the salient features of Coda's theology of religions, as expressed particularly in his recent work, *Il logos e il nulla: Trinità, religioni, mistica (The Logos and Nothingness: Trinity, Religions and Mysticism).*[3]

Short Biography

Born in 1955, Piero Coda's philosophical studies in Turin (Luigi Pareyson and Nynfa Bosco were among his lecturers) led to a thesis on Maritain's existential ontology.[4] In Rome (here his professors and later colleagues at the Lateran included Marcello Bordoni, Carmelo Nigro, Karel Skalicky and Piero Rossano) he completed his licentiate studies with a publication on various strands of interpretation of the event of Jesus's death and resurrection in reference to the Trinity.[5]

Embarking upon his doctoral research (primarily in Rome, though also studying at the University of Freiburg-im-Breslau), Coda focused on the writings of Hegel because of his contribution to the rediscovery of the bond between the theology of the cross and Trinitarian theology that has also inspired theologians such as J. Moltmann and E. Jüngel.

---

1 See Robert P. Imbelli's review of *Teo-logia: La Parola di Dio nelle parole dell'uomo*, Rome, Lateran University, 2004, and *Il Logos e il nulla: Trinità, religioni, mistica*, Rome, Città Nuova, 2003, in *The Thomist* 69 (2005): 472-275: 473.
2 For reviews of his most recent major work in this area, see P. Gamerini, 'Il Logos e il nulla. Trinità, religioni, mistica', in *Rassegna di Teologia* 44 (2003): 289-298; M. Andolfo, 'Cristo nella prospettiva trinitaria', in *Studi Cattolici* 48 (2004): 101-103; P. Manganaro, 'Il Logos e il Nulla. Prospettive cristologico-trinitarie su 'rivelazione' e 'mistica', in *Aquinas* 46,2-3 (2003): 497-518; V. Prisciandaro, 'Dialogo radicale', in *Jesus* 26,3 (2004): 11-16; J. Ilunga Muya 'Una nuova proposta di teologia delle religioni nel *Il Logos e il nulla* di Piero Coda', *Nuova Umanità* 27 (2005): 169-177.
3 Piero Coda, *Il Logos e il nulla: Trinità, religioni, mistica*, Rome, Città Nuova, 2003. See a short work that echoes much of the material of the larger publication, *Gesù Cristo e il futuro delle religioni*, Lugano, Eupress, 2004. A summary of the central theses of his main work is to be found in Spanish, *El futuro de las religiones*, Madrid, Publicaciones de la Facultad de Teología San Dámaso, 2004. Any quotations in English in this article are my own translation.
4 An abstract of the thesis, 'Intuizione intellettuale dell'essere e percezione confusa di Dio. Saggio sull'ontologia e la teologia naturale di J. Maritain', was published in *Rivista di Filosofia Neoscolastica* 70 (1978).
5 Piero Coda, *Evento Pasquale, Trinità e Storia: Genesi, significato e interpretazione di una nuova prospettiva teologica*. Rome, Città Nuova, 1984.

Coda admired how, despite its limits, Hegel's project remains exemplary in its attempt to relate Luther's theology of the Cross to the Trinitarian understanding of God as an avenue for overcoming the nihilism that marks modern subjectivism.[6]

Subsequently, in line with his research focus, Coda published two works on a major Orthodox theologian of the early 20th century, Sergei Bulgakov.[7] His interest here was to see how the Patristic tradition, especially the Eastern tradition, has taken up and thought through the centrality of christological and Trinitarian mysticism in a creative link with some of the central issues raised in modern thought.

Apart from these major works, Coda has published an impressive number of shorter books, articles and dictionary contributions. It suffices to reference some of the texts he has produced or edited relating to the theology of religions.[8] Coda writes on the basis of his deep experience of interreligious dialogue within the Focolare Movement that has been a key inspiration in his theological and philosophical reflection. Glimpses into his own interreligious journeys can be seen in short diary-type publications.[9] He has taught in the Universities of Teheran and Qom in Iran and has engaged in dialogue with some of the major theologians and cultural figures of Shi'ite Islam.[10]

Jesus Christ and the Future of Religions

Religion is a universal human experience and religions of the world are its historical and practical expression. How is Christianity to co-exist with, and understand itself in the context of, a plurality of religions? This is a question that Coda, along with many other theologians, has grappled with theologically for some years as an internal necessity for the faith. Though he reflects on various levels – phenomenological and hermeneutical – nevertheless, as a Christian theologian, he explores the question primarily within co-ordinates provided by the horizon of God's plan for all of humanity and that finds its eschatological synthesis in God's 'yes' to humanity in Jesus Christ.[11]

Put briefly, Coda contends that in Jesus Christ, all peoples with their cultures and religions enter a dynamic of moving within and beyond their particularity towards the God who went 'beyond' himself in coming towards us in the Christ who moves beyond himself, in the Spirit, to the Father. By breaking the 'wall of enmity' (Ephesians 2:14)

---

6 Piero Coda, *Il negativo e la Trinità. Ipotesi su Hegel. Indagine storico-sistematica sulla Denk-form hegeliana alla luce dell'ermeneutica del Cristianesimo*. Rome, Città Nuova, 1987.
7 Piero Coda, *L'Altro di Dio. Rivelazione e kenosi in S. Bulgakov*. Rome, Città Nuova, 1998 and *S. Bulgakov*, Brescia, Morcelliana, 2003.
8 'L'unicità e l'universalità di Gesù Cristo Salvatore nel contesto del pluralismo religioso', in *Nuova Umanità* 19 (1997): 495-511; (ed.), *L'unico e i molti: La salvezza in Gesù Cristo e la sfida del pluralismo*, Rome, PUL, 1997; 'Conversione del cuore e dialogo tra le religioni: Una riflessione teologica', in *Nuova Umanità* 20 (1998): 763-772; with S. Zavoli, *Se Dio c'è. Le grandi domande. Dialogo con Piero Coda*, Milan, RAI-Mondadori, 2000; with M. Crociata, *Il Crocifisso e le religioni. Compassione di Dio e sofferenza dell'uomo nelle religioni monoteistiche*, Rome, Città Nuova, 2002; with L. Gavazzi, *L'immagine del Divino nelle tradizioni cristiane e nelle grandi religioni*, Milan, Mondadori, 2005.
9 *Viaggio in Asia*, Rome, Città Nuova, 1997; *Nella Moschea di Malcom X*, Rome, Città Nuova, 1997; *Il tappeto del Sufi*, Rome, Città Nuova, 1998; *Le luci della menorah*, Rome, Città Nuova, 1998; *Le terre del mattino*, Rome, Città Nuova, 1999.
10 See Piero Coda, 'In Iran tre anni dopo', in *Nuova Umanità* 24 (2002): 95-118.
11 Angelo Scola reads revelation in Jesus Christ as containing the condition of possibility of religions with salvific value, see his 'I principi del dialogo interreligioso nella tradizione cattolica' in Coda, *L'unico e i molti*: 203-221.

the Crucified and Risen Christ has opened up a new dynamic relational realm. This is a space where all have access to God (*The Other*) in a reciprocal movement towards each *other*. In this realm we are prompted by the Spirit to live out and make our own the self-dispossession of the cross and the movement of the resurrection. In the Risen Crucified Christ we have the eschatological fulfilment of every manifestation of God, and we discover the past and present revelatory/salvific value in all religions. Coda believes that Vatican II and subsequent magisterial teaching, as well as theology and ecclesial life, have inspired moves in this direction.

The project Coda sets himself is to re-think christology from the heart of the Christ event (the paschal mystery revealing both the triune face of God and God's plan for humanity), in order to discover in that event and its transmission new avenues into consideration of the truth of Christ as the only and universal mediator between God and humanity, and who renders possible all forms of the revelatory/salvific presence of God to humanity. It is the ontological identity of Jesus Christ, revealed most profoundly in the event of Jesus's cry on the Cross with the responding resurrection, that, in Coda's view, provides the foundation for the possibility of otherness and grounds the relational character of Christianity.

From Inclusivism to Recapitulative-Relationality

Coda's most mature work to date in the area of a theology of religions and interreligious dialogue is *Il Logos e il nulla: Trinità, religioni, mistica*.[12] The vast documentation referred to in the critical apparatus provides ample evidence of the author's knowledge of the terrain. His work is divided into three parts: the first, entitled 'Revelation and religions' (13-139) is dedicated directly to the theology of religions. It is the section we refer to most frequently in this short article. The second, 'Outlines of a Trinitarian ontology' (141-374), is a philosophical and systematic theological reflection on the originality of Christian truth. In some senses, this section underpins Coda's approach outlined in the first section. In the third part, 'Mysticism' (375-521), the author provides a reflection on the relationship between mysticism and revelation and on how different mystical experiences are related to Christian mysticism. It also suggests practical implications for the 'how' of interreligious dialogue.

Coda's theology fits into what has been called the 'inclusivist theory' of Christianity's relationship to other religions.[13] He shares the inclusivist concern to understand Christianity's relationship to other religions within the christological event itself and not simply before or alongside it, as can happen in the proposals of a logocentric approach in which the revelation of God in Christ is seen as only one, albeit the highest and definitive among many revelations of the one Word of God. Yet, he notes the limits of the 'inclusivist' terminology and approach: ultimately, it risks cancelling out otherness, with the destiny of religions simply that of being absorbed into Christianity.

Coda's consideration of contemporary inclusivist approaches leads him to the conclusion that there is a need to reflect more thoroughly on the reality of the christological event in what he calls its paschal-Pentecostal outcome. There is a need, that is, to

---

12 See footnote 3.
13 See the International Theological Commission, 'Christianity and the World Religions' in *Origins*: CNS Documentary Series, 14th August 1997. For an excellent overview of the many theologies of religions produced in the 20th century, see Paul Knitter, *Introducing Theologies of Religions*, Maryknoll, Orbis, 2002.

explore more thoroughly the fact that, on the basis of the paschal mystery and the outpouring of the Spirit, there is a reciprocal *relational* dynamism among the world's religions in the realm of the unicity/universality of the Christ event. Rather than using the language of inclusivism, Coda prefers the biblical term, 'recapitulation' (Ephesians 1:10). Thinking in terms of recapitulation of all – past, present and future – in Jesus Christ, indicates a centre and, at least implicitly, a plurality of distinct identities in asymmetric reciprocity with the centre itself, and, starting from this centre, in reciprocal relationship among themselves. It is a term that combines singularity and relationality.

What distinguishes Coda from Paul Knitter, or even Jacques Dupuis, is his attempt to ground the inter-relationship among religions within a relational ontology and ethos of relationality that is located within the christological event which itself is expressive of the Triune God revealed therein.

An Interreligious Icon[14]

Coda describes his model as 'recapitulative-relational',[15] and an iconic and guiding text for him is Ephesians 2:11-22. Two co-ordinates, central within his own intellectual and faith journey, guide Coda in his construction of this model: *Logos* and Nothingness. On the one hand, the *logos* symbol – found in the Hebrew, Christian, Greek and philosophical traditions – focuses attention on God's self-revelation, the Word. More specifically, the Fourth Gospel indicates the Word at the heart of the christological event: the Word (*logos*) became flesh (John 1:14). The symbol of *nothingness*, on the other hand, captures the key experience of every authentic expression of mysticism: the becoming 'nothing' of those who seek God and encounter God as the 'nothingness' of what naturally is experienced in created reality.

Coda explores how these two symbols coincide in Jesus Christ, finding in him their meaning and inter-relationship. In Christian faith, Jesus is not only the Word made flesh (to see him is to see the Father, John 12:45); he is also the One who 'emptied himself' (Philippians 2:7) to the point of giving up everything – even God within him – on the Cross. God's self-revelation, carried out in the Logos made flesh, is achieved through free and active self-dispossession. The Logos of God who, before dying on the cross, cried out: 'My God, my God, why have you forsaken me?' (Mark 15:34; Matthew 27:46) manifests how the approach to all that is other and different passes through a kenotic, self-giving (*agapic*) 'nothingness' of love. Accordingly, says Coda, in the Crucified and Forsaken Christ, we discover a relational ontology that is key for a theological understanding of the pluralism of religions and for dialogue and encounter among them.

As we have mentioned, Coda sees much of his model summarized in Ephesians 2:11-22. It is true that, strictly speaking, this text deals with reconciliation between Christians coming from Judaism and Gentile backgrounds, but, as a statement on the reconciling event of Christ, it can be read, *mutatis mutandis*, in universalized terms in reference to the pluralism of religions.

In this pericope, Jesus is presented as the Crucified One who reaches all possible situations of humanity, eliminating in himself all barriers of division between humanity and God, and within humanity itself. It is precisely because he (the Son of God) has placed himself, as crucified, within every religious situation, that the Crucified Risen

---

14 Coda, *Il logos e il nulla*: 57-66.
15 Coda, *Il logos e il nulla*: 66.

Christ now prompts, in the power of the Spirit, each religious tradition – by judging it, purifying it and drawing it into his paschal exodus – to a transcendence beyond itself, and towards a common realm beyond each religious particularity that is both recapitulative and authentically plural, in which we can have in Christ 'access in one Spirit to the Father' (Ephesians 2:18).

On the basis of his reflection on this icon, Coda concludes that:

> ...in him and through him crucified, there comes about a 'within' of each religious experience... that is, at the same time, in him risen in the Spirit, a 'beyond' of each of these [religious experiences]... in which, that is, each religious experience finds itself in Christ in unity with the others, being itself beyond itself inasmuch as it is 'clothed' with the one Christ.[16]

The notion of 're-clothing' and gaining others for Christ are Pauline images (cf. Romans 13:11-14; 1 Corinthians 9:19-23). To be re-clothed with Christ refers to the free sharing of the gift of grace that God has given us in Christ. Yet, to win others for Christ and 're-clothe' them in the Spirit does not mean for Paul bringing all back from otherness to identity with oneself (though this, notes Coda, is a serious temptation for Christianity). For Paul, the expression to 're-clothe with Christ' must be understood in the sense of offer – in the Spirit of the Crucified/Risen Christ – and free appropriation, by different religious identities, of that dynamic of the self-giving dynamism that Jesus Christ reveals and communicates as the fulfilment of the vocation of every authentic identity. In taking on that dynamic, and within it, transcending oneself, each person, culture, and religion is called to become fully itself, in its original irreducibility, through the free and gratuitous encounter with Christ.

Returning to the Ephesians 2 text, it is clear for Coda that the Church, which, though distinct from Christ, can never be split from him, is called to let itself be shaped by the paschal event. It is, on the one hand, a *koinonia*-community in the Crucified Christ that includes everyone in objective redemption, including those who do not know or do not want to be brought, in a christological sense, into the recapitulative venture. On the other hand, the Church is a *koinonia*-community in the Risen Christ of those who, sharing in the paschal mystery of the Crucified Christ, identify themselves in faith with the Risen Christ as the personal realm in the Holy Spirit of eschatological communion already given, though not yet consummated, between God and humanity, and in God among humanity. Through the action of the Spirit there are, however, those who freely accept the salvific grace of Christ through the mediation of a true conscience and 'in a way that God alone knows.'[17]

Approaching Other Religions

Coda's theology leads him to the view that interreligious dialogue is not something additional but rather intrinsic to the very nature of what it is to be Christian. Faith in Jesus Christ is, after all, a continuous opening towards God and towards one another: 'all mine is yours' (Luke 15:31) 'and all yours is mine' (John 17:10). Coda makes his own a comment from A. Rizzi:

---

16 Coda, *Il logos e il nulla*: 63. Coda refers us to Cardinal Ratzinger's commentary on Pope John Paul II's encyclical, *Fides et ratio* (# 70-72), see 'Fede e ragione' in *L'Osservatore Romano*, 19 November 1998, n.8.
17 *Gaudium et Spes*: #22.

> to speak of Jesus Christ is also to speak of religion and of religions, not to claim religious truth for Christianity exclusively but, on the contrary, to recognise the truth of religions in the sign of that 'yes' of God to humanity that in Jesus Christ has been pronounced irrevocably. This means that Christianity has to understand itself not only as one of the religions but as that paradoxical religion whose specific characteristic is to be in relationship – in a certain relationship – with religion as such, and so with religions.[18]

Arising from its paradoxical nature, the Church's mission is played out between kerygma and kenosis. Christian identity is expressed in radical *agapic* and kenotic relationships *vis-à-vis* religious subjects rooted in different cultural contexts. The Christian approach to other religions, in Coda's theology, is not a possessive-exclusivist logic but rather one that is both kerygmatic and kenotic-dialogic.

On the one hand, it is necessary to radiate and proclaim the mystery of salvation that occurred 'once and for all 'in Christ, but this must be lived out in identification with the form of Christ in his *agapic* and kenotic giving of himself to who/what is other than/different to himself. It is a question of 'making ourselves all things to all people', 'Jew with the Jew' and 'Greek with the Greek'. That is the highest expression of one's identity and freedom (cf. 1 Corinthians 9:19-22). Christians are called to live, therefore, not to win over others to identity with themselves, but to 'make themselves the other'. And that is how they become themselves. If Jesus is the face of God, the other as other is already one in Christ with me through the eschatological baptism of the cross: There is neither Jew nor Greek, there is neither slave nor free, there is neither male nor female; for all are one in Christ Jesus (Galatians 3:28).

To know how to recognize the other as other, and to establish *agapic*-kenotic relationship with the other, is the practical explanation of what it means to welcome, in faith, the Christ event as the eschatological event of revelation and salvation. Knowledge of truth and *agapic* kenosis belong to one another in the very structure of the event of Trinitarian revelation and Christian faith:[19]

> The Christian community is called…to be itself not in opposition to others or to lead others to itself (is that not one of the 'religious' temptations that Christ overcame forever in the desert of the Cross?); but to make oneself (indeed in making oneself) the other: that's how it becomes itself. And that's how the other – also through the freeing and free relationship thus given – can find the way, in the spirit, to reach that fullness of itself in Christ. I made myself Jew with the Jews, Greek with the Greeks, all things to all (cf. 1 Cor 9:19-22). What Paul said of himself, and what undoubtedly many individual Christians have lived throughout the course of history, today must be lived at a communitarian level. The form of Christological kenosis (cf. Phil 2:7) must be able to be expressed in the structures and action of the Church.[20]

Faithful to the claim of the fullness of revelation in Jesus, Coda invites us to explore its implication in understanding the other positively as other in relation to *The Other*, and to live in relation with others as an event that brings novelty. Not only do I 'give' (the fullness of revelation of God in Christ) but I also 'receive' ('seeds of truth' that the Spirit has scattered in different religions).

---

18 See Coda, *Il logos e il nulla*: 55, quoting *Il Sacro e il Senso: Lineamenti di filosofia della religione*, Turin: Elledici, 1995: 184. See also A Rizzi, 'La filosofia della religione come ermeneutica del fatto religioso', in *Rassegna di Teologia* 37 (1996): 537-547.
19 Coda, *Il logos e il nulla*: 100
20 Coda, *Il logos e il nulla*: 50.

The Church, therefore, lives out her mission recognizing the features of the face of the Crucified Christ in every religious experience that has not yet completely transcended in the Spirit into the *perichoretic* (mutual-Trinitarian) unity of the one Christ. At same time, however, the Church waits and works so that every authentic religious experience is transfigured/transcended in the *doxa* (glory) of the resurrection through the power of the Spirit. That is the permanent meaning of evangelization. Every religious experience can be 'new' in Christ, in unity with others, each one beyond itself in being 'clothed' with the one Christ who is always beyond himself in self-dispossessive relationship with the Father and with humanity.

All of this leads Coda to re-read Vatican II's teaching in chapter 2 of *Lumen Gentium* on how everyone is in some way directed or 'ordered' towards the Church.[21] Behind it lies Thomas Aquinas's perspective of the universal extension of the salvific headship of Christ *vis-à-vis* his Body. Coda underlines how 'ordered' is not to be understood so much as a movement from outside inwards towards the People of God, but rather in terms of an already objective universal potency (*in potentia*) to membership within the one body of Christ, *ratione Christi virtutis*. Those who positively accept this '*ordinatio*' are real members (*in actu*) of the Body of Christ.[22]

On the basis of these considerations, Coda goes on to reflect on the dynamics of inter-religious communication that emerge within the new realm opened up by the event of God's eschatological action in Christ crucified: dialogue on the basis of living experience, the ethos of the Golden Rule, kenosis of self in order to live the other; communication in the Spirit; beginning the dialogue from unity and conversion of the heart.

Conclusion

This short article has attempted to show something of how Coda's work prompts reflection on Jesus Christ, the Word of God, as the eschatological 'place' of encounter and recapitulation of all human beings, cultures and religions in a relational being-directed-towards-one-another (cf. Colossians 1:16). It has been asked of Coda if, within his model, Christianity has its identity already before engaging in dialogue or is its identity genuinely found in the other. And, if so, is there a risk of losing this identity in its giving?[23]

Ultimately, Coda sees his theology of religions located within a kerygma-kenosis polarity, involving both a being/non-being, word/silence, fullness/nothingness, that is inherent in the human vocation itself as revealed in Christianity's relational-Trinitarian ontology of love. In providing stimulating theological foundations, combined with solid spirituality, his model is a valid attempt to respond to the invitation issued in *Dominus Iesus* (#14) to 'explore if and in what way the historical figures and positive elements of these religions may fall within the divine plan of salvation' and to examine how 'participated mediation' is 'consistent with the principle of Christ's unique mediation'.

---

21 See *Lumen Gentium*: #14-16.
22 Coda, *Il logos e il nulla*: 74ff.
23 See Adriano Fabris, 'In Dialogo con Piero Coda', in *Nuova Umanità* 27 (2005): 177-182.

Karl-Wilhelm Merks

Wie viel Glauben hat die Moral nötig?
Überlegungen zu Ansatz-Möglichkeiten interkultureller Ethik

Dass Glauben und Moral de facto zusammenhängen, kann sowohl in historischer Sicht wie auch angesichts gegenwärtiger Entwicklungen keinem Zweifel unterliegen. Eine andere Sache ist die Bewertung. Die einen sehen einen solchen Zusammenhang zwischen religiösem Glauben und Moral als unabdingbar an: Denn verliert Moral ohne Glauben letztlich nicht ihre notwendige Basis? Für andere ist ein grundsätzliches Misstrauen angebracht: Wann endlich gelingt es der Moral, sich aus religiösen Vorurteilen zu befreien?

Doch was meint eigentlich hier Beziehung von Glaube und Moral? Wird diese Beziehung nicht allzu rasch einseitig auf den direkten normativen Einfluss der Religion auf Ethos und Ethik reduziert? Und spiegelt sich in der je nach Standpunkt entweder als notwendig oder verwerflich erachteten Verbindung von Religion und Moral nicht gleichzeitig auch die Verteidigung beziehungsweise die Ablehnung bestimmter Gesellschaftsvorstellungen und ihrer Ordnungsprinzipien wider: auf der einen Seite die Idee einer einheitlich gedachten ‚traditionellen' Gesellschaftsordnung, in der Religion, Moral, Politik und kulturell-öffentliches Leben mit einander eng verbunden sind; und demgegenüber, auf der andern Seite, eine säkularisierte Gesellschaftsauffassung mit ihren verschiedenen ‚autonomen' Bereichen, in der Religion allenfalls einen Aspekt oder Sektor neben anderen darstellt?

Im einen wie im andern Falle führt aber unseres Erachtens die Frage nach Glaube, Religion und Moral nur in eine Sackgasse: in einen politisch-kulturellen Integralismus und Traditionalismus einerseits, oder einen liberalen Minimalismus und ethischen Rationalismus anderseits.

1) Eine neue Bedeutung der Religion für die Moral?

Nun könnte man meinen, diese Problemstellung sei doch eigentlich obsolet, im Prinzip sei es doch längst zu einem friedlichen dialogalen Verhältnis von Religion und Moral gekommen.

Doch zeigen gerade aktuelle Diskussionen etwa zu biomedizinischen Fragen (z.B. Sterbehilfe, Stammzellen) wie zu gesellschaftspolitischen Problemen (z.B. Sexualität, Ehe, Familie, Rolle des Strafrechts), dass das Thema „Glaube und Moral" keine ein für allemal abgehandelte Sache ist.

Zudem bekommt die Frage nach der Beziehung zwischen Religion und Moral aus einer ganz andern Ecke neue Brisanz: Das schiedlich-friedliche Gegen- und Miteinander von Religion und Säkularität in unserer Gesellschaft wird auf die Probe gestellt durch Gruppen innerhalb unserer Gesellschaft, für deren Kultur unsere Unterscheidungen von Religion, Politik und Ethik alles andere als selbstverständlich sind. Unter Hinweis (gerade auch) auf religiöse, etwa islamische Traditionen wird die Forderung nach Respektierung eigener Normen für bestimmte Lebensbereiche, z.B. Kleiderordnung, Sexualität und Ehe, Unterrichtssystem und Erziehung, innerhalb der Gesamtgesellschaft erhoben und damit die ‚abendländische' Lösung einer Differenzierung von Religion, Politik und Moral selbst grundsätzlich in Frage gestellt.

In manchen Kreisen zeigt sich bisweilen eine gewisse Unsicherheit, wie mit der neuen Situation umgegangen werden soll. Fordert nicht eine kritische Sicht auf die abendländischen Superioritätsideologie, fordern nicht die Einsichten in den allgemeinen kulturellen Relativismus von uns eine größere Bescheidenheit bezüglich unserer eigenen Selbstverständlichkeiten? Müssen wir nicht unsere Vorstellungen über den Zusammenhang von Glauben und Moral und damit auch die Reichweite des Prinzips der Religionsfreiheit revidieren?

2) Eine Revision des Prinzips der Religionsfreiheit?

In historischer Hinsicht ist deutlich, wie stark unsere öffentliche Ordnung gerade aus dem Prinzip der Religionsfreiheit heraus (mit)gestaltet worden ist.

Das Prinzip der Religionsfreiheit spielt ja in der *Abgrenzung* der öffentlichen Ordnung und der Sphäre des Privaten und Zivilen eine wichtige Rolle, sowohl im freisetzenden wie im einschränkenden Sinne: Freiheit der Religionsausübung funktioniert gerade auch deshalb, weil bestimmte Bereiche des Lebens der Kompetenz der Religion entzogen sind.

Kehrt sich nun, oft aus Respekt vor fremden Religionen stärker noch als vor der eigenen, christlichen, erneut die Beziehung von Glauben, Religion und Moral um, hin zu einer stärkeren wechselseitigen Durchdringung unter dem Primat der Religion (bis in den Bereich der Politik hinein)?

Ich denke, dass in derartigen Fragen weniger ein erneutes Verständnis für die Bedeutung der Religion für die Moral am Werke ist, sondern eher ein gewisses Unvermögen, das Moralische in seiner eigenen Fragestellung zu sehen, die es von der Religion unterscheidet.

Freiheit der Religion, was auch Freiheit, keine Religion zu haben, bedeutet, heißt ja nicht dasselbe wie Freisein von Moral oder Abschied von (gemeinsamen) Werten. Religion und auch Religionsfreiheit sind nicht der Deckmantel für jede beliebige Moral.

Die These, dass mit dem Schwund religiöser Praxis aus der Öffentlichkeit auch eine Entethisierung des öffentlichen Lebens einhergehen müsse, stimmt ebenso wenig, wie die Ansicht, dass deshalb Moral, da eine Angelegenheit der verschiedenen Glaubensauffassungen, eine rein private Sache sei.

In einem weniger religiös gefärbten Sprachgebrauch zeigt sich dieselbe Problematik auch unter dem Titel ‚Kultur und Moral'. Es ist dies eine beliebte Formel, um für Abweichungen von unserer gängigen Ordnung eine argumentative Basis zu liefern, die mit einer gewissen Plausibilität rechnen darf.

In der Tat kann man ja nicht leugnen, dass Moral kulturabhängig ist. Und damit eben auch glaubens- und religionsabhängig. Denn gerade in moralischen Fragen spielt der religiöse Einfluss auf sittliche Vorstellungen in den meisten Kulturen eine wichtige Rolle.

Wenn man daher nicht völlig relativistisch oder positivistisch die Kultur als letzten Bezugspunkt überhaupt behauptet, sondern die Kultur selbst in ihrer ethisch- moralischen Qualität versucht zu beurteilen, kommt man auch hier nicht um eine reflektierte Verhältnisbestimmung von Ethik, Glauben und Religion herum.

Auf einige Aspekte des Problems will ich im Folgenden kurz eingehen. Für weitere Details verweise ich auf einige frühere Überlegungen zum Thema.[1] Hier bei boten sich auch

---

1 Karl-Wilhelm Merks, *Gott und die Moral. Theologische Ethik heute*, Münster, LIT, 1998; Karl-Wilhelm Merks, ‚Gott in der Moral', in Thomas Laubach (Hrsg.), *Angewandte Ethik und*

manche Gelegenheiten zu einem Gedankenaustausch mit John May und den ihn bewegenden interkulturellen Anliegen.[2]

3) Die Frage nach der Bedeutung des Glaubens für die Moral – Warnung vor falschen Vereinfachungen

Liefert der religiöse Glaube andere moralische Einsichten? Haben gläubige Menschen vom Glauben her bessere Einsichten in das moralisch Erforderliche?

Ich denke, dass zweifelsohne Glaubensüberzeugungen, neben andern Faktoren, die Moral, das Ethos und die Ethik mitprägen (können). Ein Glaube mit einem ‚humanen' Gottes- und Menschenbild wird gewiss auch die moralischen Wertvorstellungen mitbestimmen. Und ein grausames Gottes- und Menschenbild, oder unmoralische Götter können auch das kulturelle Ethos beeinflussen. So hat der christliche Glaube, so wie man ihn jeweils verstand, einerseits die Sorge für Kranke und Arme hervorgebracht, andererseits aber auch fanatischen Bekehrungseifer und Hexen- und Ketzerjagd.

Die Frage ist gleichwohl schwierig zu beantworten, was ohne Christentum anders wäre in der Moral.[3] Das gleiche kann man sich auch bezüglich anderer Religionen fragen.

Die Dostojewski zugeschriebene Ansicht ‚Wenn Gott nicht existiert, ist alles erlaubt' scheint mir, wenn man sie fundamentalistisch liest, einfach falsch: Es gibt die hochmoralische Agnostikerin, den hochmoralischen Atheisten (übrigens wie es genauso gut die Unmoral der Gläubigen der christlichen wie anderer, sich der Moral verpflichteter Religionen gibt).

Auf der breiten Skala zwischen einem rein Ego-bezogenen Utilitarismus und einem das Ego verwahrlosenden Altruismus gibt es – auch ohne Gottesglauben – viele Formen von Moral, denen man Ernsthaftigkeit und gute Gründe nicht absprechen kann.

Aber was heißt überhaupt: ‚Wenn Gott nicht existiert'? Ist damit gemeint, dass Menschen ohne den Gottesglauben nicht hinreichend motiviert sind für ein moralisches Leben? Dass sie ohne die Annahme göttlicher Vorschriften und Normen (in Offenbarung und Natur z.B.) nicht wissen, was sich gehört, was sittliche Pflicht, was Unsittlichkeit ist? Dass die menschliche Natur, der menschliche Geist ‚an sich' keinen Zugang zum Moralischen hätten? Oder jedenfalls, dass Moral nur funktioniert vor dem Hintergrund eines drohenden göttlichen Strafgerichtes?

Die bekannte öffentliche Korrespondenz zwischen Kardinal Martini und Umberto Eco zu Grundfragen menschlicher Existenz, darunter auch der Frage nach einer Begründung der Moral, trägt den Titel ‚Woran glaubt, wer nicht glaubt?'[4] Diese Frage ist nicht ohne Tiefsinn, ebenso wenig wie die Frage: ‚Woran glaubt, wer glaubt?' Ich erinnere an Karl Rahners „anonyme Christen" und seine Überlegungen zur Bedeutung des Gewissensgehorsams für das Heil des Menschen.[5]

Religion, Tübingen und Basel, A. Francke, 2003: 39-60.
2 z.B., John D'Arcy May, ‚Verantwortung coram Deo? Europa zwischen säkularer und interreligiöser Ethik', in Karl-Wilhelm Merks (ed.), *Verantwortung – Ende oder Wandlungen einer Vorstellung? Orte und Funktionen der Ethik in unserer Gesellschaft*, Münster, LIT, 2001: 193-207; John D'Arcy May, ‚Universalität oder Partikularität der Menschenrechte? Eine interreligiöse Perspektive', in Jan Jans (Hrsg.), *Für die Freiheit verantwortlich. Festschrift für Karl-Wilhelm Merks*, Fribourg, Academic Press Fribourg, Freiburg und Wien, Herder, 2004: 148-161.
3 Anregende Gedanken hierzu: Hans Maier, *Welt ohne Christentum – was wäre anders?*, Freiburg, Basel und Wien, Herder, 1999.
4 Carlo Maria Martini und Umberto Eco, *Woran glaubt, wer nicht glaubt?*, Wien, Paul Szolnay, 1988.
5 Cf. Karl Rahner, 'Atheismus und implizites Christentum', in Karl Rahner, *Schriften zur Theologie VIII*, Einsiedeln, Zürich und Köln, Benziger, 1967: 187-212.

Auch in theologischer Sicht ist der Glaube an Gottes Existenz und seinen Gerechtigkeits- und Heilswillen nicht die Voraussetzung für Moral und moralisches Leben. Jedenfalls nicht der explizite Glaube, in dem es um dogmatische Wahrheiten und positive moralische Gesetzgebung Gottes geht.

In einem andern Sinne freilich, ich nenne diese – im Gegensatz zu einem fundamentalistischen – ein fundamentales Verständnis des Zusammenhangs zwischen Gottesglauben und Moral, erscheint mir der sittliche Akt selbst in der Erfahrung seiner ‚Unausweichlichkeit', und erscheint mir das ‚ja' zu Gerechtigkeit und Güte bereits als Anerkennung von Transzendenz, Anerkennung der Verbindlichkeit eines über mich Hinausgehenden. Wer will, mag dies fides implicita nennen, imweitgefassten Sinne einer großen Ökumene aller Religionen, ja aller rechtschaffenen Menschen.

4) Vom Ethos zur Ethik – zur Unterscheidung von Glauben und Moral

Das heißt nun allerdings keineswegs, dass eine solche Ökumene (und fides implicita) ihr Kriterium in einer vollkommen gemeinsamen Moral haben müsste. Es ist gewissermaßen eine Einheit mit der Pluralität moralischer Varianten.

Ohne Zweifel präsentiert sich Moral immer ‚ursprünglich' in der Form eines kulturgebundenen Ethos, und das heißt: als Vielfalt kulturgebundener Ethosformen. Das schließt aber weder die Weiterentwicklung eines bestehenden Ethos aus, noch auch den gegenseitigen kulturellen Einfluss. Theoretisch können solche Entwicklungen natürlich auch darin bestehen, dass die Unsitten anderer Kulturen übernommen werden, Entwicklung also als Dekadenz. Umgekehrt aber besteht auch die Möglichkeit sittlicher Bereicherung und sittlichen Fortschritts.

Gewiss wirft die Vorstellung des Fortschritts angesichts der Ambivalenz neuzeitlichen Fortschrittsdenkens und des ‚Endes der großen Erzählungen', Fragen auf. Gleichwohl bleibt es sinnvoll, auch moralische Standards nach einem Schlechter oder Besser zu beurteilen.

Worauf es ankommt: Nicht in globalen Fortschrittsideologien zu denken, noch von einem Superioritätsbewusstsein der eigenen Kultur und Ethik auszugehen, sondern die Kriterien deutlich zu machen, mit denen man moralischen Fortschritt meint messen zu können.[6] Und zwar Kriterien, die im Prinzip transkulturell vermittelbar sind. Gibt es gemeinsame Bezugspunkte, von denen her man verschiedene Ethosformen beurteilen darf? Oder müssen die verschiedenen Ethosformen bleibend fremd einander gegenüber stehen?

Zwar ist deutlich, dass *Glaubens*vorstellungen als solche, das zeigt sich insbesondere bei der Begegnung der großen Weltreligionen heutzutage, in ihrer Eigenart relativ resistent gegenüber Versuchen der ‚Aufhebung' in eine höhere Einheit sind. Deshalb wandelt sich ja auch der Modus der Begegnung weg von allzu erwartungsvollen Missionsbemühungen hin zu Dialog und religiöser Toleranz. Die Frage ist aber, ob damit auch die unbefragte Selbstverständlichkeit traditioneller *Werte- und Normen*vorstellungen einfach hin Gegenstand einer religiösen Toleranz sein kann.

Oder ob nicht hier eine Differenzierung innerhalb des Religiösen selbst, zwischen religiösen Glaubensinhalten einerseits und der damit verbundenen Moral, dem damit verbundenen Ethos anderseits, gemacht werden muss.

---

6 Karl-Wilhelm Merks, ‚Über Fortschritt in der Moral', in Gerhard Mertens, Wolfgang Kluxen und Paul Mikat (Hrsg.), *Markierungen der Humanität. Sozialethische Herausforderungen auf dem Weg in ein neues Jahrtausend*, Paderborn, München, Wien und Zürich, Schöningh, 1992: 281-300.

Gewiss, diese Unterscheidung ist stark mit abendländischen Denktraditionen verbunden; aber bedeutet das, dass eine solche Unterscheidung deshalb andern Religionen unzugänglich ist? Ich denke, man soll hier weder den Evidenzcharakter der sittlichen Erfahrung von ‚gut' und ‚böse', noch die denkerische Potenz anderer Religionen unterschätzen; zumal ja auch in unserer Kultur die sittliche Dimension vor ihrer neuzeitlichen Ausdifferenzierungursprünglich durchaus in das Glaubensganze hineinverwoben war.

Ja, die Unterscheidung von Glauben und Moral ist nicht zuletzt durch religiöse und theologische Einsichten selbst zustande gekommen: Die Eigenständigkeit der Fragen von Gerechtigkeit, Liebe, Erbarmen, Solidarität und Sorge füreinander hat tiefe Wurzeln in unserer Glaubenstradition, hat sich aber auch außerhalb dieser Tradition als relevant erwiesen. Es fragt sich daher, ob nicht ein selber Vorgang auch in andern kulturellen Kontexten nicht allein denkbar ist, sondern sich auf die Dauer sogar als unumgänglich erweist.

Warum? Weil Moral zwar mit Glauben zu tun haben kann, selbst aber zugleich und in ihrem Kern, eine Sache des Wissens ist, eines spezifischen Wissens zwar, aber eines Wissens; und zwar nicht des ‚formalen' Wissens, dass etwas zur Glaubenstradition gehört, sondern eines spezifisch inhaltlichen Wissens, das einem Urteil über ‚gut' und ‚böse' zugrunde liegt.

Moral kennt Argumentation, sie kennt eine – näher zu bestimmende, dem spezifischen Charakter der Kategorien ‚gut' und ‚böse' angemessene – rational-vernünftige Beweisstruktur, und zwar eine solche, die nicht bei der behaupteten Evidenz von weiter nicht kritisierbaren Überzeugungen stehen bleibt, sondern diese Überzeugungen selbst an verallgemeinerbaren Maßstäben zu messen beansprucht und sich hierzu im Stande erweist. Eine umfassende Darlegung ist im hier vorgegebenen Rahmen nicht möglich. Daher gehe ich lediglich auf einen Aspekt ein, der insbesondere im modernen Wissens-Kontext alle Aufmerksamkeit verdient: die Tatsache, dass es sozusagen *empirische* Verifikationszugänge nicht nur für die Eigenart des Ethischen, sondern auch für seine kulturübersteigenden Dimensionen gibt.

5) Das Moralische – eine Sache des Wissens

Ich gebe zu, eine solche Formulierung – das Moralische eine Sache des Wissens – ist geeignet, Widerspruch und Missverständnisse hervorzurufen. Daher lege ich zunächst kurz aus, was ich darunter verstehe.

Erstens: Grundlegend ist die Einsicht, dass wir mit der Frage nach den moralischen Maßstäben unseres Handelns ein eigenes Terrain betreten. Die Fragen ‚Was ist?' und ‚Was ist zu tun?' sind von grundsätzlich anderer Natur. Die eine wird bestimmt vom Prinzip Sein/Nichtsein, die andere vom Prinzip Gut/Böse. Wie Thomas von Aquin bei der Frage nach der Basis moralischer Urteile im sittlichen Naturgesetz erläutert,[7] handelt es sich hierbei um die parallele, nicht voneinander ableitbare Basislogik der menschlichen Vernunft, einmal in theoretischer, das andere Mal in praktischer, das heißt aufs Handeln orientierter Hinsicht. Die Tradition von Aristoteles über Kant bis zu gegenwärtigen Ethiktheorien kennt solch eine eigene Domäne der ‚praktischen Vernunft'.

Moral ist damit der Art nach unmittelbar als Sache des Erkennens und Wissens definiert. M.E. behält der Kern dieser Analyse auch Recht, wenn man in andern Kulturen nicht den Gegensatz von gut/böse, sondern andere Begriffe wie etwa Ehre oder Scham als Grundkategorie von Moral sehen sollte.

---

7 Summa theologiae, I-II, 94.2.

Zweitens: Man darf nicht in die Falle treten, in der die Moraldiskussion lange hineingeraten ist: nämlich alles Wissen zu definieren im Modus mathematischer oder naturwissenschaftlicher Gewissheit mit deren Verifikations-, bzw. Falsifikationsprozessen.

An diesem Defizit leiden auch manche Forderungen bezüglich der Universalisierbarkeit von Ethik und ethischen Normen, die nur zu einem Minimalismus führen können, der sich allerdings de facto, etwa angesichts der nicht zu leugnenden expansiven Dynamik des Menschenrechtsmodells, praktisch als wenig relevant erweist.

Denn *drittens*: Moralisches Wissen zielt nicht auf das Feststellen von Tatsachen, sondern auf die Akzeptabilität von Werten. Und es ist durchaus sinnvoll, der Wertereflexion Rationalität zuzusprechen. Freilich erschöpft sich diese nicht in der Konstatierung und Evaluation von Tatsachen, selbst nicht von tatsächlichen gesellschaftlichen Wertevorstellungen, sondern sie zielt auf die kritische Evaluation von Wertungen.[8]

Viertens: Werte sind ein (komplexes) soziales Faktum; sie vereinigen in sich eine dreifache Dimension: die der subjektiven Erfahrung und Einschätzung als wertvoll und erstrebenswert, die objektivierende Frage nach dem tatsächlichen Wert des als ‚wertvoll' Betrachteten, sowie die kollektive Affirmation in kulturell geteilter Gemeinsamkeit von Werten.

Die Erfahrung von etwas als *wünschbar, erstrebenswert*, bzw. als *unerwünscht, abstoßend*, die dazu motiviert, etwas zu tun oder zu lassen, weitet sich somit, sowohl in den objektiven Dimensionen des „Wertvollen", wie in seiner gesellschaftlichen Verallgemeinerungsfähigkeit, über das Subjektive hinaus aus. Wo diese Komplexität von ‚subjektiv', ‚objektiv' und ‚kommunikativ' auf eine reine empirisch-analytische Konstatierung faktisch geltender Werte reduziert wird, wird eine spezifische, gesellschaftlich entscheidende Dynamik dieses Faktums selbst verfehlt.[9]

Fünftens: Nun ist das Interessante, dass solche positive oder negative Wert(ein)-schätzung zwar kulturell und selbst im Hinblick auf Individuen viel Variabilität kennt, aber eben keine grenzenlose: Die Wirklichkeit selbst lehrt uns, dass nicht nur Europäer, sondern alle Menschen (von bestimmten Pathologien abgesehen) bestimmte Dinge als absolut unerwünscht, als verwerflich selbst, erfahren und beurteilen, und manches als absolut erstrebenswert und notwendig.

Auf solche Elemente macht Umberto Eco in der genannten Korrespondenz mit Kardinal Martini nachdrücklich aufmerksam.[10] Es gibt ‚semantische Universalien', auch wenn sie in verschiedenen Sprachen ausgedrückt sind, ‚begriffliche Vorstellungen', die allen Kulturen gemeinsam sind'. Verschiedene Aspekte der Körperlichkeit und Räumlichkeit, Gefühle und Empfindungen, die wir teilen, Dinge, die niemand will (physischen und psychischen Zwang, Behinderung des freien Atmens, des Rechtes zu reden und zu denken, Schmerzzufügung, Foltern, Tötung ...).

Es sind dies im übrigen Erfahrungen, in die auch immer schon die Anderen eingetreten sind, ohne die wir nicht existieren und die wir als uns gleich erkennen können. Insofern ist auch die Einsicht in die Gleichheit zwischen mir und den andern Menschen durchaus Gegenstand gemeinsam möglichen Wissens (auch wenn die andern zunächst Clan- und Volksgenossen, und erst im Laufe der Zeit alle Menschen überhaupt sind).

---

8 Vgl. Anton Hügli et alia, 'Wert', in *Historisches Wörterbuch der Philosophie*, Bd. 12, Darmstadt, Wissenschaftliche Buchgesellschaft, 2004: 556-583.
9 Vgl. Annemarie Pieper und Anton Hügli, 'Werturteilsstreit', in *Historisches Wörterbuch der Philosophie* 12: 614-622.
10 Eco-Martini, *Woran glaubt*: 84ff.

Sechstens: Um von erstrebenswert oder abstoßend, und deren ‚universaler' Erfahrbarkeit zu deren normativen Formulierung, zur Erfahrung (sittlicher) Verpflichtung zu kommen, bedarf es allerdings weiterer Schritte. Diese sind teils sozialer Natur (die normative Ausgestaltung gegenseitiger Erwartungen in einer Gesellschaft), teils fundamentalethischer Natur. Bei letzterem geht es darum, dass ‚gut' und ‚böse' Erfahrungen nicht lediglich jeweils partiell-konkret bleiben und daher als Einzelnes nebeneinander stehen. Sie integrieren sich auch zu einem Ganzen (dem guten Leben im Ganzen'), sei es in Abwägungsprozessen, in Konfliktsituationen oder bei komplexen Wahlmöglichkeiten, sei es aus der Erfahrung heraus, dass nicht alles Wertvolle ‚gleichgültig' ist. Offensichtlich tangiert es meine innere Identität, das ‚gut' erscheinende als ‚nicht-gut' zu deklarieren, das ‚Schlechte' dagegen als ‚gut'. Auch ist ‚gut' und ‚gut' nicht dasselbe.[11] Das aber zeigt: Die verschiedenen konkreten Situationen von gut und schlecht, von Werten oder Gütern, haben offensichtlich ihren Platz in einer Gesamtsicht von Sinn und Selbstverwirklichung menschlicher Existenz (auch wo dies begrifflich nicht klar bewusst und formuliert wird). Auf diese Weise zeigt sich, anders gesagt, die Transzendenz *des* Guten einfach hin; die vielen Güter werden letztendlich im Licht des Guten schlechthin gelesen. Es ist insofern durch und durch eine Sache der Vernunft und ihrer Kohärenz, ‚das Gute zu tun und das Böse zu meiden'.

Die kulturelle Vielfalt kennt so ihre Grenzen (übrigens in negativen Moralregeln sehr viel präziser als in positiven). Dies ist wahr, auch wenn es bisweilen langandauernder historischer Prozesse bedarf, um zu diesem Ergebnis zu kommen. Die hermeneutischen Erfordernisse, die einer solchen Entwicklung zugrunde liegen, sind keine Sache einer kahlen Logik. Sie sind das Ineinandergreifen von rational-logischen und – im weitesten Sinne – soziologischen Komponenten, von Erfahrung und deren vernünftiger Interpretation.

Als Kernelemente in diesem Prozess erscheinen mir besonders bedeutsam:
– geteilte Glücks- und Leidenserfahrungen von Menschen;
– ein fundamentales Rechts- und Unrechtsbewusstsein;
– das entwickelte Gespür für den Unterschied zwischen konkreten Regeln und Tiefendimension in Ethos und Moral;
– die Differenzierung zwischen partieller Kulturzugehörigkeit und gemeinsamem Menschsein;
– (interkulturelles) Kennen- Lernen von Alternativen.

6) Eine Sache des Wissens, heißt das: ohne Glauben?

Die These von der grundsätzlichen Vernünftigkeit der Moral bedeutet nicht deren Emanzipation aus Religion und Glaube einfach hin. Ihr ‚autonomes' Verständnis besagt nicht ihre völlige Verabsolutierung und Beziehungslosigkeit, sondern zunächst einmal die Tatsache, dass mit Moral eine eigene Dimension menschlicher Wirklichkeit gegeben ist, die sich als solche sowohl innerhalb, wie außerhalb des religiösen Glaubens manifestiert. Außerhalb, weil es Moralität, selbst sich universal verstehende Moralität auch der Nichtgläubigen gibt. Innerhalb, da Moralität offensichtlich in verschiedenen Religionen durchaus Verwandtes zeigt (vgl. Hans Küngs ‚Projekt Weltethos'), aber auch in-

---
11 Vgl. in diesem Zusammenhang auch die Unterscheidung von Charles Taylor von Wünschen erster und zweiter Ordnung, sog. ‚schwachen' und ‚starken Wertungen', in Anton Hügli u.a., ‚Wert': 582f.

sofern, als Moralität sich auch gegen glaubensgegründete Auffassungen und Praxis durchsetzt, ja das Glaubensverständnis selbst beeinflusst (vgl. z.B. Menschenrechte, Veränderung des Frauenbildes). Es reicht eben auf die Dauer für eine Begründung des Sittlichen nicht der Verweis auf Glauben und Traditionen; die Ethik, das Moralische erweisen sich historisch und unter systematischem Gesichtspunkt als dem Glauben gegenüber ‚autonom', d.h. als eine eigene Fragerichtung (der nach ‚gut' und ‚böse'). *Dies aufzuzeigen (und von daher auch die Beziehungen zwischen Glauben und Moral neu und präziser zu bestimmen), ist Ziel und Anliegen der autonomen Moraltheorie,[12] auch und gerade in der Theologie.*
Was lässt sich dann über diese Beziehung noch sagen?

Ich möchte es so formulieren: Religionen und Glauben haben eher mit der *Situierung* der Moral, als mit ihrer *Begründung* zu tun. In der Begründung muss sich Moral in einem gewissen Abstand zu religiösen Überzeugungen halten, sie kennt ihre eigentümlichen Erfahrungsgrundlagen, leitet sich nicht aus Religion ab.

Das besagt nicht, dass Religionen nicht von enormem Einfluss auf moralische Traditionen und Überzeugungen sein könnten, und es selbst in der Gegenwart weiterhin sind. Doch gründet sich deren Gültigkeit nicht in dieser religiösen Herkünftigkeit, sondern in ihrer humanen ‚Notwendigkeit'.

Die aktuelle Diskussion der Tatsache, dass Religionen ebenso gewaltträchtig wie gewaltabweisend sein können, zeigt auf ihre Weise, dass die Vorzugswürdigkeit der Friedfertigkeit ihre Argumente zwar auch in Religionen selbst findet, aber letztlich auch auf andere Einsichten, als etwaige religiöse Ermahnungen oder Vorschriften, gegründet ist. Diese andern Einsichten resultieren aus der Fähigkeit der Unterscheidung von gut und böse, von menschlich und menschenverachtend.

Ethik kann daher selbst, wie das Beispiel der Friedfertigkeit zeigt, auf Religion und Glauben zurückwirken. Unter dem Druck sittlicher Einsichten verändern sich auch (dogmatische) Glaubensüberzeugungen: Ein ‚humanes' Ethos wird angesichts der Relation zwischen Gottesglauben und Handlungsidealen auch zu einem ‚humaneren' Gottesverständnis führen, wie umgekehrt.

Wenn wir diese Dialektik zwischen Glaube und Moral in der Linie ‚vom Glauben zur Ethik' etwas spezifizieren, kann man mit einer inzwischen klassisch gewordenen Formulierung von Alfons Auer eine *integrierende*, *kritisierende* und *stimulierende* Funktion des Glaubens unterscheiden. Damit ist gemeint: Der Glaube bietet der Ethik eine Einbettung in eine Gesamtsicht des Sinnes menschlicher Existenz; er hat die Potenz zum kritischen ‚Zwischenruf', zur ‚prophetischen' Kritik, zur Anklage unmenschlicher, ungerechter Zustände, und er kann sich aus dem Gesamt einer religiösen Interpretation der menschlichen Existenz und des Weltgeschehens heraus anregend-dynamisierend für die Suche einer wahren vertieften Menschlichkeit auswirken. Wenn man so will, mag man noch die den Kommunitariern liebe Dimension einer *konkretisierenden Praxis* gläubiger Gemeinschaften hinzufügen – dies freilich nicht im Sinne einer moralischen Legitimationsinstanz, sondern als Chance einer kohärenten Ausgestaltung des Ethos.

In alledem steht niemals der Glaube gegenüber der ‚einfachen', der ‚bloßen' Vernunft, sondern er trägt diese, erweitert sie, schärft ihren Blick – im günstigen Fall.

---

12 Vgl. Anm. 1 sowie: Karl-Wilhelm Merks, ‚Sittliche Autonomie. Wissenssoziologische Studie zu Genese und Bedeutsamkeit eines Begriffs' in Antonio Autiero, Stephan Goertz und Magnus Striet (Hg.), *Endliche Autonomie. Interdisziplinäre Perspektiven auf ein theologisch-ethisches Programm*, Münster, LIT, 2004: 11-48

Denn wie die Geschichte auch lehrt, können alle diese Möglichkeiten des Religiösen ebenso zu Abschottung,, Selbstgerechtigkeit, Rechthaberei führen. In diesem Sinne bleibt auch die Existenz der Gläubigen jeder Religion auf die Erfahrungen sittlicher Güte angewiesen, das heißt in unserer Terminologie, auf die Autonomie der sittlichen Fragestellung nach dem Guten. Und zwar konkret erfahrungsgebunden, nicht ideologisch oder dogmatisch vorfabriziert.

Moral hat also den Glauben nicht zur Voraussetzung nötig. Gleichwohl kann der Glaube für sie förderlich und fruchtbar sein. Es ist und bleibt daher eine interessante und nicht nutzlose Aufgabe, sich immer wieder der konkreten Produktivität religiösen Glaubens und religiöser Traditionen zu vergewissern und sie auch zu schätzen.

7) Das Gute wissen, an das Gute glauben

Ich schließe mit einigen Überlegungen zu möglicherweise *in der sittlichen Vernunft selbst* immanent anwesenden Glaubens-Aspekten, Aspekten, die man zumindest als einen religiösen ‚Überhang' in der Vernünftigkeit der praktischen Vernunft selbst interpretieren kann, die ja einerseits in der Erfahrung und Bewertung des jeweils Guten durch und durch rationaler Natur ist, anderseits aber angesichts der ‚Transzendentalität' des ‚Guten schlechthin' die Erfahrung eines unbedingten Anspruchs macht, oder sagen wir vorsichtiger, machen kann, eines Appells, den wir in der Alltagssprache Gewissen nennen und der zur Gewissenhaftigkeit auffordert.

Auch ist die Moral selbst in das Gesamt des Menschen-, Welt- und Gottesverständnisses und die Fragen nach dem Sinn des Ganzen eingebunden. Ethos und Moralität werden so zwar nicht in ihrer Eigentümlichkeit angetastet, wohl aber vor letztlich destruktiver, in die Isolation führender Selbstüberschätzung wie Selbstunterschätzung beschützt. Die gläubige ‚Integration' kann somit dem menschlichen Leben seine wirklich ‚humane' Dimension, in der doppelten Erfahrung seiner Vermögen und seiner Beschränkungen, bewusst machen.

Einige Aspekte, die hier zu nennen sind:
- Der Mensch ist nicht die ultimative Wirklichkeit.
- Menschliche Existenz ist Frage: Woher, warum, wozu, woraufhin.
- Die Welt ist nur zu einem geringen Teil überhaupt Gegenstand unserer moralischen Anstrengung.
- Moralität korrespondiert nicht mit Glück, hat auch den eigenen Erfolg nicht in der Hand.
- Guter Wille ist keine Garantie gegen üble Folgen; die Situationen möglicher Verantwortlichkeit zeigen viel mehr grau als schwarz oder weiß.
- Moral ist oft Wagnis im Nebel; sie lebt von Kompromissen, Sich-Zufrieden-Geben mit dem Vorläufigen.
- Und dies alles letztlich im Angesicht des Todes, der an sich selbst die Brüchigkeit jedes Sinnes repräsentiert.

Diese Erfahrungen sind durchaus nicht religiös gebundene Erfahrungen, es sind anthropologische Konstanten, Gläubigen und Ungläubigen gemeinsame Erfahrungen – falls es letztere denn wirklich, im radikalen Sinne, gibt.

Und selbst wenn Religionen eine Antwort versuchen zu geben auf die Fragen der menschlichen Fragilität, des Scheiterns und des Todes, so bleibt auch für Gläubige jeglicher Religion und Konfession das Böse und die Gefährdung und Ohnmacht des guten Willens Skandal und Stein des Anstoßes – mysterium iniquitatis.

Wieviel Glauben und welchen Glauben hat daher die Moral nötig?

Jedenfalls nicht Glauben als ein besonderes, konkret – normatives ‚Wissen' von gut und böse. Aber wie viel Glauben setzt nicht die Bejahung des Lebens als wertvoll voraus, das Leben-Können und Leben–Wollen mit dem Vorläufigen, der Bedrohung, ja mit dem Scheitern menschlichen Bemühens? Wie viel Glauben, stilles Hoffen ist nicht nötig, um in dieser Situation ein Leben des ‚Trotzdem' zu versuchen, und zwar für Gläubige nicht minder als für Ungläubige.

Gerry O'Hanlon

Muslims in the Free Society

John D'Arcy May refers in a recent article[1] to a book entitled *Catholics in the Free Society* which appeared in Australia in the early 1960s. The implication of the title was clear: how could Roman Catholics, beholden to the Pope and embracing a world-view at loggerheads with an otherwise Protestant and liberal society, be trusted to be loyal Australians and good democrats? The same discussion had occurred around the same time in the United States of America on the run-up to the Presidency of John Fitzgerald Kennedy. All this was before the Declaration on Religious Liberty, *Dignitatis Humanae* (1965) of the Second Vatican Council, affirming freedom of conscience in matters of religion. It is a discussion that we are familiar with in Ireland too, where the often cosy relationship between the Roman Catholic Church and the new Irish state in the first part of the 20th century meant that the slogan 'Home Rule is Rome Rule' was no mere empty shibboleth.

It is not a little ironic then that in the West it is now Catholics – as well, of course, as other Christians, secularists and those of other religions – who express fears about the compatibility of Islam with a free society. Does the self-understanding of Islam as a total religion, embracing political as well as personal and societal reality, mean that there is a contradiction between it and a free society, the rule of civil law, the democratic system of representation in government, freedom of speech and thought, the rights of women and minorities, the administration of a modern economy? Are Muslims intent on creating a Shariah-law society wherever they are in the majority, and working towards it when they are not? In our post September 11, 2001 context, with the growing visibility and often radicalization of Islamic opinion in many parts of the world, these are questions of more than academic interest.

In this fraught atmosphere, many Muslims in the West feel themselves on the defensive. A recent EU report highlighted the extent of discrimination and Islamophobia experienced by Muslims in Europe.[2] It drew attention to the fact that Muslims judged as inconsistent the constant demands for integration when often they experienced exclusion at a socio-economic level. Similarly, many of them perceived that 'to integrate' meant, in fact, a demand to lay aside their Islamic identity when they themselves believed that their Muslim values were compatible with European secular ones.

Formal Positions

I want, first, to outline the formal positions on freedom in society adopted by different religions, with particular reference to Islam.[3]

---

1 John D'Arcy May, 'Muslims in the Free Society', in *Doctrine and Life* 56 (2006): 22-28.
2 Tufyal Choudhury, Mohammed Aziz, Duaa Izzidien, Intissar Khreeji, Dilwar Hussain, *Perceptions of Discrimination and Islamophobia, Voices from Members of Muslim communities in the European Union,* Vienna, EUMC (European Monitoring Centre on Racism and Xenophobia), 2006.
3 For what follows, see Christian W. Troll, SJ, *Muslims Ask, Christians Answer*, translated by David Marshall, Gujurat, 2005 (esp., chapter 9); also available at http://www.answers-to-muslims.com.

For many Muslims, as Esposito notes, 'Islam is a total way of life'.[4] In this context, the modern Western secular tendency to separate religion and politics or to presume that secularization is the only option possible is not immediately obvious or acceptable. Rather, Islam concerns body and soul, social, political and religious life. The Qur'an is unambiguous in its teaching about the practice of social justice, and Muhammad's proclamation attacks a social order dominated by the interests of the rich. The Qur'anic revelation, then, is concerned not only with prescriptions for spiritual life (prayer, fasting, virtues and vices), but also with life in society (the individual, the family, marriage contracts and inheritance, the economy), the regulation of political life (instructions for the conduct of war, the duties of leaders), and also law on everyday matters (including the regulation of the status of non-Muslims). Shaped by the early political and military involvement of Muhammad, the tradition developed a theory of Islam as an all-embracing way of life: Islam as both religion and state (*din wa dawla*). In accordance with this, there developed that body of Islamic law known as the Shariah, derived from the Qur'an as well as the *sunnah* (the habits and religious practices of the Prophet Muhammad) and the *hadith* (the documented traditions of the Prophet, not recorded in the Qur'an). The Shariah is meant to govern all aspects of life. From it there arose the practice of *fiqh* or jurisprudence, the study or application of the body of sacred Muslim law as applied to new and different situations, undertaken by the *ulama*, the scholars. There has been a long struggle within Islam, which still goes on, to determine the freedom, principles and limits which should govern the interpretation and creation of laws. Could *ijtihad* (independent reasoning) be used by jurists to create new laws even if not based on a hadith or Qur'anic utterance? Even as early as the 9th century, the Mu'tazila emerged as a formal school of theology which relied on reason and rational deduction as tools in Qur'anic interpretation. They regarded reason and revelation as complementary sources of guidance from a just and reasonable God.[5] But, for the most part, a much more conservative position was adopted and maintained, and, during the 14th century, Sunni Muslims declared that 'the gates of *ijtihad*' were closed.

However, while Islam rejects the separation of the spiritual and the worldly, it does recognize the distinction between them. So, the classical treatises distinguish between acts of worship, which are regarded as unchanging, and social relationships, which can change. Already within the lifetime of Muhammad himself there took place the significant development from a movement with a moral and social vision calling into question existing social structures to the actual establishment of a state religion. In the period that immediately followed, the Caliph (the Prophet's successor) became 'God's shadow on earth' and 'the commander of the faithful'. He and his representatives were entrusted with worldly, not primarily spiritual, power – Islam knows neither a religious hierarchy nor an official teaching office. Nonetheless, the Caliphs bore religious responsibility for commanding the good and forbidding the evil. In modern times, this history of Islam as religion and state has resulted, especially in the Arab world, in an extremely close connection between religion and the state, even if there are also examples

---

See also John L. Esposito, *Islam: The Straight Path*, New York and Oxford, Oxford University, 2005 (especially chapter 5); Aftad Ahmad Malik (ed.), *With God On Our Side: Politics and Theology of the War on Terrorism,* Bristol, Amal, 2005; Karen Armstrong, *Islam: A Short History*, New York, Modern Library, 2002 (especially chapter 5); Jaume Flaquer Garcia, SJ, *Fundamentalism*, Barcelona, Cristianisme / Justicia Booklets, 2005.

4 Esposito, *Islam: The Straight Path*: 159.
5 Esposito, *Islam: The Straight Path*: 70-85.

of states, with large Muslim majorities, which are organized on secular principles (for instance, Turkey, Senegal, Mali, Niger, Indonesia).

Interestingly, since the beginning of the 20th century, some Muslim thinkers have become aware of the drawbacks of a state religion (how it limits the role of the state in various ways – for example, with respect to economic development and modernization in general – and also how it runs the risk of damaging religion by using it as an instrument of government party officials). This has meant that for some decades in the Islamic world there has been a loud call – perhaps drowned out in the post 9/11 so-called war on terrorism context in which we live – for a separation of religion and state, and even for a secular state. However, these ideas are opposed vigorously in conservative circles which identify the idea of a secular state as 'a western and Christian heresy'. It remains the case, according to Troll, that 'countless Muslims fluctuate between these two tendencies of complete integration and total separation of religion and state'.[6]

In historical terms, Christianity and Islam have developed in similar ways. Initially, they both proclaimed a spiritual message with social implications, a message which raised questions about unjust political and social structures. In both cases, the very success of the religious message gave them dominant positions in society and led to both Christianity and Islam becoming state religions.

Christianity first became a state religion in the 4th century of its history, under the Emperor Constantine. However, in the New Testament there is nowhere any basis for the idea of a 'Christian state'. Jesus did not found a state, did not establish a Christian society in competition with other political societies, did not mobilize an army to assert rights. In this sense, according to the New Testament, the Christian is a citizen among other citizens, even when the ruling elite might happen to be pagan. Worldly honour and power are rejected in favour of the kingdom of God, much to the initial disappointment of the people and eventually leading to the death on a cross of Jesus. Nonetheless, the New Testament does reject all political and social injustice – if what is of God and what is of Caesar are distinct, and if this distinction can lead in time to the separation of Church and State, it still should not lead to a silencing of the voice of the Church in protesting against civil injustice and in sharing its wisdom (but not any blueprint for the organization of society or politics) about the values which should inform our civil society. In this sense, political involvement is an essential constituent of Christian mission.

However, historically, Christianity did not remain true to this New Testament teaching. Instead, for centuries, it became a state religion. In particular, the role of the Pope developed in such a way that the theory of the two swords was advanced so that the spiritual and worldly swords were united in the hands of the Pope who considered himself to be authorized to appoint kings and emperors. This uniting of both powers in one institution and person led the Church to sanction and even initiate and implement policies which clearly contradicted the spirit of the Gospels: Crusades, imperial and colonial ventures, the Inquisition.

Gradually, because of the effects of the Reformation, the reaction to the Wars of Religion, and the Enlightenment, Christians began to appreciate that they had departed from the spirit of the Gospel in their understanding of the link between religion and politics, between faith and a free society. For Protestants, the Barmen Declaration of 1934 was of particular significance. For Catholics, the breakthrough occurred in the Decree on Religious Freedom of the Second Vatican Council in 1965. Christian Churches now

---

6 Troll, *Muslims Ask, Christians Answer*: 48.

teach that a formal separation of Church and State is preferable and most consonant with Gospel values. This entails recognition of the rightful, if relative, autonomy of the secular, even while claiming the right of the religious voice to exercise influence on society according to standards derived from the values of the Gospel. This influence will involve an attitude of engagement with the world in the eschatological tension between the 'already' and the 'not yet', an engagement which gives primacy to the Spirit of God and recognizes that our cooperation will be under the sign of the cross and resurrection of Jesus Christ.

It is clear that, historically, the relationship between religion and politics in Islam, as in Christianity, has taken many different forms, by no means always forms of identity. Nonetheless, the struggle within Islam to get this relationship right is perhaps exacerbated by the fact that, whereas formally Christianity is clearly compatible with some kind of Church-State separation, this is not so clearly the case for Islam. Because a detailed blueprint for the ordering of society and politics are so much at the heart of Islamic revelation there is a natural desire to have a Muslim-majority state, an unease with how to deal with non-Muslims, a temptation to use power or even violence to enforce religious compliance, a dilemma in finding ways to be creative and modern and yet to submit to a law that emanates from a very different time. Muslims are in search for a way to be modern without being secular.

Reflections

Clearly, Christianity has had a lot of difficulty in negotiating a satisfactory understanding and living out of the relationship between revelation and faith on the one hand, and reason and politics on the other. One thinks of Roman Catholic authoritarianism and excessive emphasis on canon law, the philosophical challenges to the High Scholastic compatibility of faith and reason from Nominalism, Occasionalism, and Voluntarism in all their historical forms; of the rationalism of Liberal Protestantism leading to suspicions of philosophy and of the Analogy of Being voiced by Karl Barth; the otherworldly focus of Orthodoxy sometimes accompanied by an extremely conservative social teaching. And yet, though not without bloodshed and not without ongoing tensions on particular issues, Christianity has now, by and large, succeeded in retrieving that spirit of the Gospel which enables it to live at peace in a modern democratic state, while retaining its right to engage in constructive social commentary and criticism. This is a right not always conceded by secular authorities and sometimes too easily resiled from by Christians: the peaceful coexistence of Church and State in the West has too often been achieved at the expense of the excessive privatization of religion. Nevertheless, in principle at least, and allowing for ongoing creative tensions between different schools of theological thought, there is an appropriate link between faith and reason, summarized in the classical phrase of the First Vatican Council that 'although faith is above reason, yet there can never be any real disagreement between faith and reason, because it is the same God who reveals mysteries and infuses faith and has put the light of reason into the human soul'.[7] In the moral sphere, this translates into the Catholic emphasis on that natural law which in principle all human beings share and which guides moral conduct, even if there can be differing opinions on particular moral

---

7   John F. Clarkson, John H. Edwards, William J. Kelly, and John J. Welch, *The Church Teaches: Documents of the Church in English Translation,* New York, Herder, 1955: 33.

issues. This confidence in the intrinsic but non-codified link between faith and reason allows for the eventual acceptance of the modern democratic state.

Islam, again in general (it is important to be aware that there are many different forms of Islam), has not yet reached this point of peaceful coexistence. The reasons for this are many, not all of them religious. As in Christianity, historical, cultural and political causes abound. The Crusades, the loss of empire, the fear of a modernization that would dethrone the primacy of religion, anger at the treatment of Palestinians, resentment at the perceived arrogance and partiality of the United States of America in its role as the world's only surviving super-power and a concomitant suspicion of the West and its values – all these and other similar causes create a culture within Islam which is reactionary in itself and which acts as a filter for religious interpretation of an extremely conservative nature. We have seen that there are strands within Islam which can interpret the Qur'an in ways that are creative and up-to-date, which can distinguish between acts of worship which are unchanging and social relationships which can change. For example, it is nowadays said that, for many in Turkey, talk about Shariah is really talk about the moral life, and it is reported that Imran Khan, the former Pakistan cricket captain, now politician, said that the closest example he has ever seen of an ideal Islamic society in the world today is Sweden.[8] However, these are not typical positions and there may be an intrinsic difficulty with the emphasis in the Qur'an on providing a political blueprint for society and a law which governs all human conduct. Divine law is not easily subject to appeal or to human change, no matter how pressing the need. And if the focus is on law – and not also on a wider wisdom that offers reasonable grounds for change and adaptation – one is, then, in a bit of a bind. The Christian position is different: not only is law seen as just one source of wisdom (and so takes its place in a matrix of other sources such as philosophy, politics, sociology, economics and so on) but also theologically Jesus places himself above the law, while respecting it. He is lord of the Sabbath, his Spirit is one of freedom and not law, and Christian disciples are given this freedom of discernment of spirits which allows for a principled but creative adaptation to new circumstances as well as a real development of doctrine. This nuanced position on the compatibility between faith and reason was well expressed in Pope Benedict's 2006 address in Regensburg, infamous for other reasons.

It is, of course, for Islam itself to discover and deploy the resources within its own theological tradition which will allow it to live more participatively in a modern democratic society – not so much as rulers or as being ruled, but as active participants. For this to happen, it would seem that something like the Reformation, the Enlightenment, or Vatican II needs to happen in Islam. This would involve the painful but liberating kind of experiences which Christianity has had to undergo, including a scientific study of the Qur'an itself from the viewpoints of philology, sociology, history, literary criticism and so on, as well as an opening up of the 'gates of *ijtihad*' in a way that frees interpretation and allows greater hospitality to modern sensibilities, such as the area of human rights and the rights of women in particular. This entails a mind-set that is not afraid of or impervious to evidence. It can only be Muslims who can judge whether such reforms are internally consistent with Islam itself; whether, for example, in addition to allowing for a more harmonious coexistence with the gains of modernity, they might not also retrieve the original meaning of Shariah as subversive of autocracy and in

---

8 Mary Fitzgerald, *The Irish Times*, 27 October 2006.

favour of social justice. Such a development would allow Islam to retain its faith in the transcendent while offering a powerful critique of the excesses of modernity.

In the meantime, it might help Muslims to become more disposed to look in this direction of reform if Christians could finds ways of sharing their own experiences of historical change with them. This would include the experience of failure and violence, of the time it takes for change, of recognition (*pace* Pope Benedict) of the contribution of Islam to Europe and of the intellectual richness and achievement of Islam in the past and today.[9] It would also include an appreciation of the great providential gift to Christians of the Islamic focus on God's transcendence, in particular at a time of Western secularization which so easily elides into secularism. It would benefit all if Muslims and Christians together could work towards a situation where the legal framework of a democratic secular state would be accepted but where civil society and, indeed, the whole public sphere would be subject to the influence – but not the rule – of religious as well as secular ideas.

It is worth noting, too, that while an intellectual reformation is important and can facilitate so many other developments, life itself is a great teacher and surprises can take place despite seemingly intransigent ideological positions. Bernard Lonergan had great faith in what he called the 'self-corrective process of learning', believing that we all had an innate desire for truth and would not rest satisfied until we achieved our goal. In later life, he was to add the importance of 'falling in love' (ultimately with God) as the great catalyst towards truth. Who would have thought when John XXIII was elected pope that the Catholic Church was to undergo such a profound reformation? Given his previous comments about Islam, who would have imagined that Pope Benedict would find himself praying so reverently alongside senior Muslim religious leaders in Istanbul's Blue Mosque? Similarly, Muslim commentators have pointed to the historical flexibility of Islam in adapting to different circumstances, so that there can be and have been instances of a lived compatibility between Islam and democracy when formally or dogmatically there was no such possibility.[10] In this respect, it is right that the dialogue of theological ideas is aware of the often more powerful dialogues going on at the levels of living together, working together for a more just world, and sharing together of religious experience.

Ireland has arrived relatively late on the stage of these dialogues and has the opportunity to learn from the successes and failures of others.[11] In particular, however, we have had our own long and harrowing experience of conflict in Northern Ireland in which issues of culture, identity, politics and religion came together in a seemingly intractable and violent way. In many respects, the Churches helped ameliorate the situation by compassionate pastoral care, by the condemnation of violence at official level, and by the behind-the-scenes highly significant work for political peace by some Church representatives. And, yet, we saw too that the different Churches often seemed to be captive to their respective communities, 'chaplains to the warring tribes', so that the prophetic role of the Scriptures in liberating us from blood ties in favour of the greater

---

9   Michael L. Fitzgerald and John Borelli, *Interfaith Dialogue: A Catholic View*, New York, Orbis, 2006: chapter 9.
10 Sadik J. Al-Azm, 'Islam and Secular Humanism', in Sadik J. Al-Azm and Josef van Ess (eds.), *Islam and Secularism*, number 2 in The Dialogue Series, Antwerpen, Universitair Centrum Sint-Ignatius, 2005: 41-51.
11 Gerry O'Hanlon SJ, 'Asking the Right Questions: Christians, Muslims, Citizens in Ireland', in *Working Notes 54,* (Journal of the Jesuit Centre for Faith and Justice) (February 2007): 8-14.

common good was often missing.[12] We need now as Christians to see dialogue with Muslims in Ireland as a graced imperative, believing that coming together with our common humanity and religious respect we can proactively help to set a peaceful and just agenda for the future. This irenic intent ought not to result in an insipid dialogue incapable of either coping with anger or asking the hard questions: John D'Arcy May himself personifies the ability to be both generous and firm in his approach to dialogue.[13] We need to ask Muslims about their attitude to a free society, to violence in the Middle East and elsewhere, to the possibility of State subsidization but also regulation of the education of imams where Muslims themselves have expressed the need for such education and where the State may be simply ignorant of the type of education being offered. Muslims will have their own questions to put to us.

I note, finally, that the Good Friday Agreement proposed the kind of political arrangement in which 'parity of esteem', as opposed to simple majority rule, became the principle of democratic governance. In an interesting joint statement, issued in 2004, the German and African Catholic Bishops note that relations between Christians and Muslims can be guaranteed and enhanced by a modern democratic state, including a civic order regulated by the rule of law. Such a civic order is incompatible with legal provisions derived from one religion only. The Bishops go on to suggest that this kind of legal framework 'implies constitutional guarantees of civic rights and fundamental values that cannot be altered by majority vote'.[14] It would be interesting to explore how our dialogue in Ireland might be framed within this kind of commitment to the free society which so many citizens of Ireland, north and south, Christian, Muslim and secular, so clearly cherish.

---

12 For an attempt at self-critique by the Churches along these lines, see Department of Theological Questions, Irish Inter-Church Meeting, *Freedom, Justice and Responsibility in Ireland Today*, Dublin, Veritas, 1997.
13 John D'Arcy May, 'The Dialogue of Religions: Source of Knowledge? Means of Peace?', in *Current Dialogue* 43 (July 2004).
14 Deutsch-Afrikanisches Bishcofstreffen, 'Christians and Muslims – Partners in Dialogue', in *Stimmen der Weltkirche* 38 (2006).

Martin Rötting

Christian Process and Buddhist Reference?
Interreligious Learning in Buddhist Christian Dialogue[1]

1. Introduction

During field research in Korea I was the guest of a Buddhist monk who lives in a hermitage some minutes up the mountain away from the big temple. He invited me to have a cup of tea. A simple room, sounds of nature, boiling water. He offered me my cup; having receiving it in the proper way, I drank. Suddenly, I associated that drinking with partaking of the Eucharistic cup. In that moment the Eucharist and our sitting together in this Buddhist hermitage were connected, if only in this one point. What, then, do such connections mean? How do we understand and learn in dialogue?

In this paper I discuss a hypothesis of interreligious learning in Buddhist-Christian dialogue: (1) *interreligious learning works by networking points of contact*, and (2) in dialogue with each other, *Christians learn process religiosity* and *Buddhists learn reference religiosity*. The first point will be shown by looking into the development of a learning theory, and the second by sharing some outcomes of my empirical research. Finally, I sum up the different aspects in a heuristic hypothesis which might serve as a foundation for further research in this so far neglected field of religious studies.[2]

I hope to show that, by seeing the Buddhist-Christian learning process as developing a network of points of contact, important aspects of this learning process can be highlighted and focused on. Interreligious learning is seen as part of the lifelong religious learning process each religious person is embedded in. A religious person is someone who is rooted in one religion and who might be said to make use of religious teachings, at least in times of threat. Religious learning is seen as developing a world-view and an identity according to the world-view that is set out by one's religion or the teaching of one's specific tradition. Religious praxis is part of this learning process. Encountering another religion, therefore, is also an encounter with an alternative world-view and identity, which in turn puts a question to one's own world-view.[3] Buddhism, focusing

---

1 I wish to thank Patrick Hurley for his constructive critique. This paper covers aspects of my doctoral dissertation, see Martin Rötting, *Interreligiöses Lernen im buddhistisch-christlichen Dialog: Lerntheoretischer Zugang und qualitativ-empirische Untersuchung in Deutschland und Südkorea*, St. Ottilien, EOS, 2007.

2 An exception is Andreas Grünschloß, *Der Eigene und der Fremde Glaube, Studien zur interreligiösen Fremdwahrnehmung in Islam, Hinduismus, Buddhismus und Christentum*, Tübingen, Mohr Siebeck, 1999. Religious pedagogy is mostly concerned with religious and interreligious learning in an educational framework, e.g., a school class. While religious studies discusses identity and pluralism it looks into learning but little; this paper's focus, however, is on learning as an identity shaping process.

3 The encounter of such an alternative view is a drastic event in the religious learning process. Timing in this process of learning is important. In Buddhist-Christian dialogue this aspect seems to have been neglected so far. For 'timing' in the learning-process, see Rudolf Engelbert,

on the philosophical principle of *sunyata* or emptiness, and Christianity, focusing on a personal God, offer different world-views. Even if the partners of Buddhist Christian dialogue are already very much informed about each other's religious teachings, a real learning process is set in train when one tries to connect both religions at some point, a point of contact. Even if there is already a body of research on parallel points of the life of the Buddha and of Jesus Christ, e.g., the body of doctrine, the ethical principles, the philosophies of *sunyata* and *kenosis* or self-emptying, and forms of prayer and meditation, there is not yet much done on how we bring both religions into some sort of relation. The process of forming such a relationship, and as a result having, for instance, Buddhism in relation with Christianity, necessarily changes our view of both Christianity and Buddhism. From the viewpoint of a Christian, then, such a changed Christianity is one result of an interreligious learning process.

Interreligious dialogue is a dialogue where the partners are of different religions. Interreligious learning takes place in such a dialogue. Learning is noticed where changes in behaviour or thinking occur. In interreligious learning the dialogue partners realize they have changed in their religious world-view. In order to be able to study such processes of interreligious learning between Buddhists and Christians, we need a model to describe it. The model is shaped by looking at Buddhist-Christian dialogue and the learning process that develops from this specific encounter. Because of its high importance, the focus is on the level of personal learning. Interreligious learning can thus be seen as the togetherness of inter- and intra-religious dialogue.[4]

2. Learning by networking points of contact

The main motive of the model is networking points of contact. This is done in two movements, as described by John Cobb:[5] *passing over* and *coming back*. Now, we are concerned with how we *pass over* and *come back*.

> *(1) A result of this networking process is a net of understanding in which we share some points of contact with our dialogue partner. During this process we develop a new relation to the other religion and to our own. In realizing this new relation as a change we acknowledge that learning has been successful.*

If we imagine a concrete dialogue situation – a Christian theologian visiting a Buddhist monk in a Korean mountain temple or delivering a talk at a conference – the dialogue partners take the role of either a guest or a host. In our examples, the Christian would be the guest in the world of the Korean Buddhist monk and the listeners, Buddhist or Christian, would be guests in the world of the speaker in the conference.

> *(2) Any given situation of Buddhist-Christian dialogue is asymmetric. The dialogue partners become guest or host. The level of asymmetry and the role taken up in the first situation might change during the process of interreligious learning.*

Glaubensgeschichte und Bildungsprozeß: Versuch einer religionspädagogischen Kairologie, München, 1985.
4 The term *intra-religious dialogue* was introduced by Raimundo Panikkar, see his *Der neue religiöse Weg: Im Dialog der Religionen Leben*, München, Kösel, 1990 (English original: *The Intra-Religious Dialogue*).
5 John B. Cobb Jr., *Beyond Dialogue: Toward a Mutual Transformation of Christianity and Buddhism*, Eugene OR, Wipf and Stock, 1998 [1982].

(3) The natural movement in this encounter intends a balance between the dialogue partners. This balance can be described as 'the possibility of becoming friends'.

Now, how do Buddhists and Christians develop their relationship? Even if both are quite familiar with the religious and cultural world of the other, that world still remains the *world of the other*.[6] It is impossible to encounter this *other world* as a whole.[7] On the other hand, in the case of Buddhism and Christianity we cannot speak of two completely separate worlds which do not share anything. Ram Adhar Mall uses the image of *overlapping* to explain this phenomenon in intercultural philosophy.[8] Though what we do share with our dialogue partner remains uncertain often yet it is natural to seek an overlapping ground on which we both can stand. In some cases, we will very quickly term the quest for peace or the protection of human rights or the environment as just such an overlapping ground. The Kyoto School, for instance, tried to look into the philosophical understanding of *sunyata, kenosis* and *nothingness* in its search for an overlapping ground. Whichever direction the dialogue may take, I believe it is important to state that there has to be a *primal point of contact*.

(4) The moment of meeting is for both partners in dialogue a primal point of contact.

If we recall our first example of a Christian visiting a Korean monk in a monastery, we can imagine that the monk will invite the Christian guest for a cup of green tea. The surroundings, the taste of the tea, the sound of the dropping rain will help them to find something to share: they both know that they share *this very moment*.[9] If the Buddhist and the Christian now take up a conversation, for example, about the taste of tea, we observe that the primal point of contact develops in three dimensions: 1) *time*: the moment of having a cup of tea together, 2) *place*: a Christian is guest in a Buddhist temple, 3) *process*: in sharing some comments about the taste of the tea, the dialogue partners hope to enrich their taste for more overlapping ground.[10]

(5) The primal point of contact develops for both partners in dialogue in the three dimensions time, place and process. The last dimension carries the possibility of change and is, therefore, the seed for interreligious learning.

In taking up these dimensions the partners network further points of contacts (using, for example, images or symbols, rites, frameworks of life, questions), and in the ongoing

---

6 The studies on 'encounter with strangers' is a necessary background to all aspects of Buddhist-Christian Dialogue and the learning-process involved. For more, see Theo Sundermeier, *Den Fremden Verstehen. Eine praktische Hermeneutik*, Göttingen, Vandenhoeck & Ruprecht, 1996; Bernhard Waldenfels, *Topographie des Fremde: Studien zur Phänomenologie des Fremden*, Frankfurt a.M., Suhrkamp, 1997.
7 Michael Pye showed that the essence of a religion cannot be derived from historical data only. The essence is not something objective, but a dynamic force out of an intersubjective process of the religious community.
8 See Ram Adhar Mall, *Philosophie im Vergleich der Kulturen: Interkulturelle Philosophie – Eine Neue Orientierung*, Darmstadt, Wissenschaftliche Buchgesellschaft, 1995.
9 Anyone who recalls a situation like this might urge me not to analyse such moments and just 'drink the tea'. However, in a later development, I intend to underline how important these moments are.
10 The *primal point of contact* is not to be found in theoretical constructions or meta-language, but in basic human experiences. This thought is developed by Perry Schmidt-Leukel in his *'Den Löwen Brüllen Hören': Zur Hermeneutic eines christlichen Verständnisses der buddhistischen Heilsbotschaft*, Paderborn, München, Wien and Zürich, Ferdinand Schöningh, 1992: 675ff.

process of *passing over* and *coming back*, they develop a new network of understanding themselves and the other. Each topic in their conversation has to be related to already existing points in their network of interpreting their own and others' lives. During the course of the conversation they will encounter points of strong agreement (e.g., the quest for peace, or the wisdom of not being egoistic), but they might also find difficulties (e.g., putting in question the importance of a personal god). These points of difficulty can also serve as new points of contact in future encounters.

The process of interreligious learning involves learning about the other and myself. In the course of this process one will change both how one reflects on the relation of Buddhism and Christianity and their very interaction itself. As a part of the process of religious learning, interreligious learning influences, changes and develops one's faith.[11] These changes fall into four areas of learning. These areas develop by focusing on reflective and active levels of learning and learning about the world and myself. In practice, of course, these distinctions are never so clear cut.

> *(6) In relation to 'I' and 'World' the interpretation of the point of contacts develops into the four areas of interreligious learning: identity, act of faith, worldview and ethic.*
>
> *(7) The process of interreligious learning is by networking points of contact and developing their respective dimensions for mutual transformation in these four areas of learning.*

The image of networking points of contacts already suggests *a forth-and-back movement*, which we have seen John Cobb describe as *passing over* and *coming back*.[12] These two movements are the main motives of the learning process.

3. The process of interreligious learning

In the following I offer brief explanations of the different stages that encompass the process of interreligious learning.

3.1. Entering the world of the other

The process begins with a movement from one's own world into that of the other.

1. Rooting in one's own tradition: Before one can speak of a Buddhist Christian interreligious learning both partners of this learning process have to be rooted in their own tradition. Here we have to ask immediately what this being 'rooted' looks like in each religion. Stephan Leimgruber[13] defines 'rooted' as being related to a religious tradition in such a way that one would use (some of) its teachings in a moment of crisis.

2. Awareness of the other religion: Even if one is firmly rooted in one's own tradition, it seems to be nearly impossible in our globalized world not to become aware of the existence of other religions. In the case of Buddhism in the West there is not only a growing number of Buddhists in Europe and America[14] but there are also films and

---

11 For further thoughts on 'faith' in contrast to 'belief' see Paul O. Ingram, *The Modern Buddhist-Christian Dialogue: Two Universalistic Religions in Transformation*, Lewiston NY, Edwin Mellon, 1988: 15f.
12 Cobb, *Beyond Dialogue*.
13 In a personal communication; see also Stephan Leimgruber, *Interreligiöses Lernen*, München, Kösel, 1995.
14 The Deutsch Buddhistische Union states there are c.120,000 practicing Buddhists in Germany.

books by or about, as well as visits by, the Dalai Lama; these make Buddhism into a focus of interest for Christians. In traditionally Buddhist countries like Japan or Korea[15] Christianity is part of the religious society and plays, especially in Korea, a significant role in all social affairs of the society.

3. Question: If one is aware of the other religion there are several ways of dealing with it. One is to see it as a question, a possibility of encounter, exchange and enrichment for one's own religion and faith. If one's own religious views are hard-won concepts of how one sees the world, oneself and life, then any alternative world-view brings one's own into question. The result can be either a total rejection of that other religion or an analysis and initiation of an interreligious learning process.

4. Opening: The next step along this road is to open up to an exchange of religious experiences, ideas, views and wisdom with the other tradition.

5. Interreligious Dialogue: There are many forms of dialogue possible. It might be an encounter with a sacred text of the other tradition, listening to a speech, or seeing a film. The most intensive form of dialogue is the personal encounter.

6. Finding a point of contact: A primal point of contact is given in any dialogue situation. The moment of reading a text, listening to a speech or meeting a person presents a point of contact. Dialogue in Buddhist-Christian encounter, unlike that between the monotheistic religions, cannot acknowledge a personal God; God is not a possible point of contact. Developing the primal point in time and place, a learning process occurs: the partners in Buddhist-Christian dialogue might refer to a shared doctrine, a commonly accepted goal or simply the ordinary situation of human beings. Nevertheless, the step to this point of contact is 'new territory' in interpreting one's own religious experience and is, therefore, a risk that both partners in dialogue have to take.

An example of such a developed point of contact is to be found in Cobb's *Beyond Dialogue*.[16] Cobb introduces his understanding of nirvana and sunyata as a crucial point of contact. However, as these concepts are indeed at the centre of Buddhist thought, they are part of a process of the development within Buddhism as well; sunyata itself became a point of contact for Buddhist thinking.[17]

3.2. Coming back into one's own tradition

The process continues with a movement of return.

7. Double-networking point of contact: Here it becomes clear that the impossibility of bringing Buddhism and Christianity together[18] is resolved by linking points of contact to a net of interreligious relations. In our example of a Christian who has a cup of tea in a Korean temple with a Buddhist monk, the shared joy over the taste of the tea could develop into an agreement on the beauty of this very moment and on its importance. Further, there might be agreement on the art of living life to the full in every

---

15 See Martin Rötting, *Berge sind Berge, Flüsse sind Flüsse, Begegnung mit dem koreanischen Zen-Buddhismus*, St. Ottilien, EOS, 2001.
16 Cobb, *Beyond Dialogue*: 76f.
17 See Martin Rötting, 'Buddhist-Christian Dialogue and the Concept of God', Dublin, University of Dublin (M. Phil. thesis), 2001: 65: *Sunyata* as a philosophical term is found more in Mahayana texts than in early Buddhism. It has been developed and shaped in the Buddhist discourse over time. See also Mun-keat (Wei-keat) Choong, *The Notion of Emptiness in Early Buddhism,* New Delhi, Motilal Banarsidass, 1999^2: 84-88.
18 Buddhism and Christianity are constructions; in dialogue, the world-views of individual Buddhists and Christians meet.

given situation. The Christian might now refer to Jesus on the cross, and the Buddhist might point out the Buddhist teaching of sunyata. Even though both would not intend or want to link the Christian teaching of Jesus and the Buddhist sunyata, they yet find a way of seeing them linked by the taste of the cup of tea at that very moment in the Korean mountain temple. Though this seems far from academic theology, it is very close to developing one's spiritual path; the latter, indeed, is a source for later theological development. After finding a point of contact, one has to link it to the teaching of the other religion and re-link it back to one's own religious world.

8. Transformation: After the point of contact becomes part of one's own religious world-view and is reflected in each one of the areas of learning, the key one uses to interpret life is transformed. For example, there are accounts[19] by Christians whose points of contact were in the Buddhist practice of Zen; these accounts often reflect philosophical, spiritual or theological transformation. In many cases one can see a move to mystic and negative theology after an encounter with Zen.[20]

9. Evaluation: The transformation of the learner's world-view, even if only in part, has a profound impact on different aspects of the person's identity. Therefore, evaluation of the new 'point of view' and understanding, now including one or more networking points of contact, is needed. The spiritual, sociological and psychological consequences are compared and brought into dialogue with each other. If evaluation is positive, this already leads into the next step: the intra-religious dialogue.

10. Intra-religious dialogue: A crucial part of the interreligious learning process is the integration of a transformed faith, world-view or theology into one's own tradition. Here one has to continue the dialogue, but now with fellow Christians or Buddhists who have not walked the path of learning, networking and transformation, at least not in the same way. Here the new view of one's own tradition clashes with others' more traditional view. Recent discussions and ongoing debates over these issues show how crucial this part of the interreligious learning process is and that it affects many related fields as well. One example is the debate about the theology of the German Benedictine monk and Zen-teacher Willigis Jäger[21] and its impact on Christians who read his books. Hugo Enomiya Lassalle, too, is an example of a well-integrated and transformed Christianity due to dialogue with Japanese Buddhist Zen.[22]

11. New rooting in one's own tradition: Interreligious learning is, of course, an ongoing process. Yet, it is possible to acknowledge steps in this learning progress. A step is finished after the transformed view is not only integrated into one's own faith but also, in one way or another, rooted in one's own tradition again.

Interreligious learning in Buddhist-Christian dialogue is an identity- and faith-transforming process. It takes place as part of religious learning and interreligious

---

19 The books of H.E. Lassalle and William Johnston are just two examples from many.
20 In further research I plan to look into this. Is interest in mysticism after encountering Buddhism really a very common shift? Can we already speak of a structure in Christian-Buddhist interreligious learning? Is this a purely Western phenomenon or is it shared in Asian encounters too?
21 Willigis Jäger is a Benedictine Monk who teaches Zen. His recent publications are under criticism by the Vatican. A book, reflecting his changed views due to the practice of Zen, was published before the recent confrontations, see Willigis Jäger, *Suche nach dem Sinn des Lebens. Bewußtseinswandel durch den Weg nach innen,* Petersberg, Verlag Via Nova, 1991.
22 Lassalle's first book on this experience is *Zen – Weg zur Erleuchtung, Einführung und Anleitung,* Wien, Herder, 1959. The networking and movements of passing over and coming back can be derived from Ursula Baatz, *Hugo M. Enomiya-Lassalle: Ein Leben zwischen den Welten: Biographie,* Zürich, Benziger, 1998.

dialogue. By networking points of contact, one's own perspective is informed, interpreted and transformed. Integration into and rooting in one's own tradition of the new perspective and insight, Buddhist or Christian, results in realizing the dialogue as a learning-process by reflecting the changes in one's own perspective of identity, worldview, act of faith and ethic. By describing the interreligious learning process as networking, the flexible way of learning is taken into account. Stating that in Buddhist-Christian dialogue we learn by points of contact stresses the impossibility of dialogue about religious views in a general way. Our overlapping allows us to share religious perceptions on life on some points, but, these points can be developed in time, space and process and networked with existing and newly discovered points of contact.

Interreligious dialogue and intra-religious dialogue are two sides of the one coin, 'interreligious learning'. Due to its capacity to transform intellectual and spiritual views about Buddhism and Christianity it can be seen as intellectual activity and a spiritual way in itself.[23]

4. Empirical Research in Germany and South Korea

A qualitative research project, involving 60 interviews, in Germany and South Korea which I undertook between 2002 and 2006 showed[24] that there are six different types of motivations that seem to guide the learning process. Along with the traditional type of religious learning and living in a *via activa* and *via contemplativa*, it is possible to view these types as contemplative dialogue learning types and active learning types. Interview analysis indicates that one mainly finds two or three different motivations in individuals, two of them belonging to the active or to the contemplative side. In this way, learning types are not clear, but do show tendencies.

Contemplative dialogue learning type	**Active dialogue learning type**
Way-motivated	Concretization-motivated
Experience-motivated	Action-motivated
Essence-motivated	Reconciliation-motivated

Dialogue learning types and motivations

We can give only a brief sketch here. For instance, a Christian woman, having been a contemplative nun for over 20 years, looked into Buddhist Zen meditation thought while in a Christian retreat house. There she found the ten ox-herding pictures, famous in Zen, and told in her interview, how these pictures had challenged her image of God: God was no more only an almighty ruler, but now also 'on pilgrimage with me in my heart'. Her process of dialoguing can be seen as way-motivated learning. Reflected in the transformed image of God, her own spiritual way as a dynamic process became the centre of learning. In another case, a Buddhist monk indicated in his interview that Christian love challenged his understanding of Buddhist compassion (*chabi*, in Korean). He learnt that Christian love very often results in concrete activities: a hospital or a caritas-welfare-centre for the poor. This can be called concretization-motivated learning.

---

23 One example, focusing on the transformation in each religion, but also on the learning process in its spiritual perspective, is Paul O. Ingram, *Wrestling with the Ox: A Theology of Religious Experience*, New York, Continuum, 1997.
24 Rötting, *Interreligiöses Lernen*: 245-372.

5. Conclusion: Christian Learning Process and Buddhist Learning Reference

The typology of active and contemplative learning types alone does not allow a fully satisfactory explanation of how the dynamic in Buddhist-Christian learning can be spelled out. An hypothesis, constructed by 'fitting' the empirical findings with our knowledge of Christian and Buddhist dialogue-history in Germany and Korea, can do the job. If we assign all motivation types in relation to the learning process – standing in the present, dealing with history, creating visions of future and referring to the transcendent and immanent aspects of our religious world-views – four different categories seem to tell the story:

1. New religions like Buddhism in Germany and Christianity in Korea seem to learn by inculturating the new religion in the existing cultural setting. Bowing for the 'sign of peace', instead of shaking hands as in Europe, might be one example in Korean Christianity.
2. Traditional religions like Buddhism in Korea and Christianity in Germany seem to learn by transculturating their religious views and praxis. There are meditation-cushions now found in many Christian retreat places, not only for so called 'Christian-Zen', but also for practising, for example, the 'prayer of the heart'.
3. Buddhists are learning in dialoguing with Christians' reference-religiosity. They discover the power of pointing to a concrete absolute or a concrete love. That does not mean that they would start to pray to a personal god; rather, images of the bodhisattva might become more personal or, more often (as seen in the interviews), Buddhist loving-kindness expresses itself in concrete forms like building a hospital or running a welfare-centre.
4. Christians learning in dialoguing with Buddhists' process-religiosity. They learn that truth and the experience of it are not a static but a dynamic process. The image of God might be transformed from a static observer to a 'loving and being with us on the way' image of God.

Interreligious learning is not just a spontaneous shopping tour in the pluralistic religious supermarket. The theory of learning by networking points of contact supports the thesis that many different factors come together to help a point of contact to occur. These factors are conditioned by motivations which have their reason in the context of the learners. Interreligious learning is shaped in a certain way. Each learning process can be analysed by asking about networking points of contacts and their related motivations. Therefore, interreligious learning theory supports an identity theory that describes religious identity as contextually structured multiple identities.[25] Identities shaped by interreligious learning are *contextual* due to the historical, sociological and cultural context of every religious learner and *structured* along the networking points of contact. They are *multiple*; because, with their network spanning the two religions, they partake in the identity of the other religion too.

---

[25] Identity theory supports the idea of networking points of contact by suggesting that identities are shaped by meanings, signs and symbols which help to create the communication between the self and society. See, e.g., Sheldon Stryker and Peter J. Burke, 'The Past, Present, and Future of an Identity Theory', in *Social Psychology Quarterly* 63,4 (2000): 284-297.

Joseph Salihu

The Preservation of Uniqueness and Interreligious Dialogue in Northern Nigeria

> *It is for the adherents of each of the great traditions to look critically at their own dogmas in the light of their new experience within a religiously plural world.*[1]

I. Introduction

For many Western countries, plurality of religions is a novel experience. This brings the challenges of interreligious dialogue closer to home. Competing dogmas are suddenly appearing on landscapes where only one dogma had prevailed. It is in the light of this plurality that John Hick, quoted above, admonishes the adherents of the different religious traditions to review critically their traditions in the light of their new experience of religious plurality. It is pertinent to note that plurality does not always lead to pluralism; sometimes, the adherents of the different religious traditions refuse to integrate into the wider culture, opting instead to preserve their different religious traditions. Interreligious dialogue is possible only when the adherents of the different religious traditions work towards the evolution of a culture that cuts across their religious affiliations. Northern Nigeria, where Islam and Christianity have co-existed for over a hundred years, provides us with a situation where the absence of such a culture has led to interreligious conflicts and the failure of dialogue to blossom. The situation of Islam and Christianity in the region is examined to demonstrate this thesis.

II. Islam And Christianity: Platforms for Socio-Political Contest

The complexity of Northern Nigeria can only be imagined. It comprises different tribes and traditions. The predominant tribe is the Hausa-Fulani. Existing side by side with them are 250 minority tribes. From these complexities Islam and Christianity have forged two rival identities. The Hausa-Fulani and the Kanuri are mostly Muslims, the minority mostly Christians. Pockets of traditional religions still exist in the region, but they are relegated to the background and do not directly influence public discourse. Islam and Christianity double as the cultures of their adherents. It is not by accident, therefore, that these religions dominate public space and discourse.

Islam is so integral to the Hausas that, contrary to historical evidence, they trace their descent from the Yamanites or the Umayyads, descendants of the Prophet Muhammad and Arab conquerors of North Africa.[2] The first contact of Islam with the region is Borno, which was as early as 666 CE. By the 15th century, it was already considered a fully-fledged Islamic state, despite the continuous existence of traditional religion.[3]

---

1 John Hick, *Problems of Religious Pluralism*, Hampshire and London, Macmillan, 1985: 50.
2 Mervyn Hiskett, *The Course of Islam in Africa*, Edinburgh, Edinburgh University, 1994: 108.
3 Nehemia Levtzion, 'Islam in the Bilad al-Sudan', in Nehemia Levtzion and Randall L. Pouwels (eds.), *The History of Islam in Africa*, Athens OH, Ohio University, 2000: 63-91: 79-88, 81.

Islam came into Hausa-land much later, in the 14th century, but, as with Borno, it continued to exist alongside traditional religion. It took the Fulani Jihad, which was an attempt to free both the Fulani from the oppression of the Hausa rulers and also Islam from syncretism, for the religion to be firmly established in Hausa-land. The Jihad, which lasted fifty years, led to the establishment of an Islamic caliphate ruled according to the dictates of the *Shari'a*. This caliphate lasted a hundred years until the coming of the British. The Jihadists were able to weave the warring Hausa kingdoms into a centralized unit, with a unified administration and legal system.[4] Although the Jihad was successful, not all of Northern Nigeria was conquered and the Muslims were forced to live side by side with unconquered non-Muslims, a situation which prevailed into colonial times.[5]

For the Hausa-Fulani and their Kanuri co-religionists, Islam continued to provide their culture and civilization. This is apparent in their dealings with the European explorers and, subsequently, colonialists, whom they never accepted as overlords.[6] They granted concessions to the Europeans, with the full awareness of the demands of the *Shari'a* in respect of their relationship with Christians.[7] The British colonial masters were aware of the Islamic culture they encountered and pledged to preserve it. The also adopted the principle of indirect rule, whereby they continued to govern through the Islamic political structures with slight adjustments (for instance, expunging the criminal aspects of the *Shari'a*) and sometimes extending this rule over non-Muslims.[8]

Into this scenario Christianity arrived. Albeit earlier missionary efforts, intensive missionary work came on the heels of colonialism. The colonial masters were careful to prevent any missionary work within the Muslim enclave but even where zealous missionaries tried to penetrate they were rebuffed and their efforts were a singular failure.[9] Western education was allowed, selectively, in the Muslim enclaves to prepare children from the royal family for work in administration with the British.[10] In the face of their failure to evangelize the Muslims, the missionaries turned their attention to the Northern minorities who, lacking a meta-cosmic religion, embraced Christianity wholesale. With their new-found faith came the benefits of Western civilization, which disposed them to compete with their Muslim counterparts. The colonial administration educated the Muslim areas, and the non-Muslim areas were left to the missionaries.[11]

Regrettably, while the Muslim graduates could rise to administrative positions, the non-Muslims could only become teachers.[12] In any case, the net result of the missionary efforts among the non-Muslims was the provision of a unifying civilization, founded on Christianity and Western values, parallel to the one Islam provided for the inhabitants of Borno and the Hausa-Fulani areas. Northern Nigeria then became the home of two rival

---

4   William F.S. Miles, 'Religious Pluralism in Northern Nigeria', in Levtzion and Pouwels, *The History of Islam in Africa*: 209-227: 210.
5   J. Spencer Trimingham, *Islam in West Africa*, Oxford, Clarendon, 1973: 19-20.
6   Ibrahim Sulaiman, *The Islamic State and the Challenge of History*, London, Mansell, 1987: 84.
7   Rowland Adeleye, *Power and Diplomacy in Northern Nigeria 1804-1906: The Sokoto Caliphate and its Enemies*, London, Longman, 1971: 121-122.
8   Sa'ad Abubakar, 'The Northern Provinces Under Colonial Rule', in Obaro Ikime (ed.), *Groundwork of Nigerian History*, Ibadan, Heinemann Educational, 1999: 447-481: 450-451.
9   Ogbu Kalu, *Christianity in West Africa: The Nigerian Story*, Ibadan, Daystar, 1978: 44-45.
10 Bola Ige, People, *Politics and Politicians of Nigeria (1940-1979)*, Ibadan, Heinemann Educational, 1995: 35.
11 Yusufu Turaki, *The British Colonial Legacy in Northern Nigeria: A Social Ethical Analysis of the Colonial and Post-Colonial Society and Politics in Nigeria*, Jos, Challenge, 1993: 79.
12 E.P.T. Crampton, *Christianity in Northern Nigeria*, London, Geoffrey Chapman, 1979: 68.

civilizations: the Islamic Arab heritage and the Western Christian heritage. In times of stress these rival groups turn to their religion for inspiration, further polarizing the region. This is apparent in political transitions and the deteriorating socio-economic situation.

The first manifestation of this was at the end of the colonial era. The Islamic heritage inspired the foundation of the conservative Northern Peoples' Congress (NPC) and its opposition, the Northern Elements Progressive Union (NEPU). As might be expected, the Christian heritage inspired the formation of the non-Muslim parties, United Middle Belt Congress (UMBC) and the Middle Zone League (MZL),to protest at the domination of the Northern minorities by the Muslim Hausa-Fulani, which began courtesy of the system of indirect rule.[13] Contrary to their protest, the status quo was maintained and the *Shari'a* was modified into a penal code applicable to all. The penal code enabled the *Shari'a* to continue to exist in its civil form.[14]

With military rule and the demise of party politics, the only platforms left for the people to express their sentiments were Christianity and Islam. It is within this context that the Christian Association of Nigeria (CAN)[15] and the Council of Ulama[16] emerged, canvassing for Christian and Muslim interests. In fact, these organizations attempted to bridge intra-religious divisions and took the posture of quasi-political parties and, at the early stages of the Ibrahim Babangida's transition programmes (when candidates campaigned in the absence of political parties), these organizations selected candidates and presented them to their constituencies. Their impact was felt on the debate on issues that hinge on the secular status of the Nigerian state contained in Section 10 of the 1979 and 1999 Constitution: *Shari'a* and Nigeria's membership in the Organization of Islamic Conference (OIC). The two positions that emerge in the debates reflect the two conflicting world-views: with Muslim making no distinction between religion and politics and Christians seeking to sustain the distinction.[17]

The impact of Christianity and Islam is felt not only on the political scene but also on the socio-economic one. With the failure of the government to provide for the basic needs of the people, Christianity and Islam have stepped in to fill the vacuum, providing social services for their adherents, but in a polarized form. It is not uncommon to see schools, primary health-care clinics and charity outfits attached to churches and mosques. Apart from the provision of these services, they have also evolved programmes for liberation. While the Muslims believe that the full implementation of the *Shari'a* will make a difference,[18] Christians believe that personal liberation (being 'born again') will solve all of Nigeria's problems.[19]

It is clear from the foregoing that Islam and Christianity perceive themselves as rival traditions contesting for the same socio-political space. The implication is that Northern

---

13 Niels Kastfelt, *Religion and Politics in Nigeria: A Study in the Middle Belt*, London, British Academic, 1994: 73-74.
14 Matthew H. Kukah, *Religion Politics and Power in Northern Nigeria*, Ibadan, Spectrum, 1993: 116-117.
15 Roman Lomeier, *Islamic Reform and Political Change in Northern Nigeria*, Evanston, Northwestern University, 1997: 293-294.
16 Lomeier, *Islamic Reform*: 304-305.
17 Ogbu U. Kalu, 'Harsh Flutes: The Religious Dimension of the Legitimacy Crisis, 1993-1998', in Toyin Falola (ed.), *Nigeria in the Twentieth Century*, Durham NC, Carolina Academic, 2002: 667-685: 681.
18 Karl Maier, *This House Has Fallen: Nigeria in Crisis*, London, Penguin, 2000: 148.
19 Iheanyi M. Enwerem, *A Dangerous Awakening: The Politicization of Religions in Nigeria*, Ibadan, IFRA, 1995: 90-91.

Nigeria has been reduced to a theatre of interreligious conflicts between Muslims and Christians. Some social analysts attribute these conflicts to the manipulation of religion by the élites. Yet, the question to ask is: why is religion being manipulated? I think it is because it doubles as culture for the people in the region. So, whereas, for example, in the Western part of Nigeria (where Muslims and Christians also exist in equal number) issues are contested on the platform of ancestral cities, Islam and Christianity provide the platforms for contest in Northern Nigeria. The implications of this situation for interreligious dialogue can only be imagined. Before looking closely at the state of interreligious dialogue in Northern Nigeria, let us see the challenges that the enterprise holds.

III. The Challenge of Interreligious Dialogue

Interreligious dialogue takes many forms and processes, but it has one basic objective: transformation. It is expected that those who take part in it should do so with open-mindedness, expecting the purification and better understanding of their tradition and, consequently, a personal transformation, which this understanding brings. David Krieger captures this well:

> ...the goal of interreligious dialogue cannot be the proclamation of a new syncretism, a sloppy synthesis, the artificial and lifeless construction of a world religion or an abstract common denominator of all faiths; instead, interreligious dialogue must deepen and purify all religions and, in a certain sense, preserve their uniqueness.[20]

Krieger begins by objecting to what comes across as the goal of dialogue with pluralist underpinning: the distillation of some common elements from all the religions, to which they will eventually subscribe. He proposes that the goal of genuine dialogue is one that celebrates the difference in the religions while at the same time challenging them to deepen their perception and purify their individual traditions. It would, however, be easier for Islam and Christianity in Northern Nigeria to distil academically a common ground than to get these religions to subscribe to Krieger's genuine and timely challenge. The preservation of the uniqueness of the religions, which he proposes, is attractive to conservatives within these religious traditions, but it poses further problems for interreligious dialogue. If adherents of Islam and Christianity enter into dialogue with the preservation of their religious tradition in mind, they are not likely to embrace the challenge of the purification and critical understanding of their traditions which Krieger equally proposes. I shall now consider the challenges which his formulation poses for Islam and Christianity in the region.

To begin with, Islam and Christianity must accept that they do not express transcendent reality adequately enough. Generally, religions seek to express transcendent reality to their followers and, mostly, their claims are stated in absolute terms. They present a world-view that is complete in itself, paying special attention not only to spiritual but also to material wellbeing. In a nutshell, religions perceive themselves as complete systems of salvation (or other equivalent terms). Krieger challenges the religions to acknowledge that their world-view is not only incomplete (being unable to capture transcendent reality completely) but that they could also be enriched by other faith traditions. Unfortunately, Islam and Christianity in Northern Nigeria perceive

---

20 David Krieger, 'Communication Theory and Interreligious Dialogue', in *Journal of Ecumenical Studies* 30,3 (Summer/Fall 1993): 331-354: 353.

themselves as self-contained traditions and also as formidable platforms for the interests of their people. Slogans like 'Islam Only' and 'Jesus Only' prevail. To express inadequacy and to open themselves to mutual enrichment would be an indication of weakness; those who take this bold step are accused of trying to adulterate the true faith. It is to their advantage in the scheme of things to strive to show that they are complete and do not stand to benefit from another faith tradition.

Another challenge for Islam and Christianity is to acknowledge that they each express the transcendent reality and to accept their respective expressions as true, even when they seemingly contradict each other. So, for example, Islam is challenged to consider the expression that Jesus is the Son of God, even though it contradicts its strict monotheism. Christianity is also challenged to consider that Muhammad is the seal of the prophets, in spite of its teaching that revelation ceased with the last apostle. This could come across as relativism or even perspectivism. Yet, no genuine dialogue can take place until one religion recognizes the other's right to exist. The religions are not called upon to trade their absolute claims, but to acknowledge the right of other religions to make their own claims. The interpretation of the Qur'anic perception of Christians in Northern Nigeria as worshippers of three gods and the missionary tradition that perceives Islam as a demonic religion goes against the grain of this challenge. In this, each religion thinks that any contradiction of its own teaching is the complete negation of itself.

Apart from acknowledging each other's claims, Islam and Christianity must also accept that human traditions have interfered in their expression of the dictates of the transcendent. This implies that a distinction has to be made between the revealed truth and its interpretation and practice. Religion and culture are inseparable elements. Often religion expresses culture, and *vice versa*. This accounts for the different versions of universal religions, like Buddhism, Christianity and Islam. In fact, it is their ability to adapt to different contexts and cultures that make them universal in the first place. Krieger's challenge in this case is for Islam and Christianity to acknowledge that cultural elements might have led to a negative interpretation of the truth; thereby, in the process of dialogue, they should purify themselves of these interpretations and practices. There is an awareness of this adulteration, and some adherents of Islam and Christianity have constituted themselves as vanguards for doctrinal purity. The *Izala* movement emerged to rid Islam of lingering traditional practices, and the Christian Pentecostal churches have always accused the orthodox churches of adulterating the Biblical faith. This acknowledgement notwithstanding, the thinking evidenced by these movements is that going back to the sources of a given religious tradition is sufficient to rid itself of negative interpretations and practices. In a nutshell, then, Islam cannot be purified by Christianity and *vice versa*. The acknowledgement of the possibility of mutual purification is necessary for the commencement of genuine interreligious dialogue.

The challenge of interreligious dialogue for Islam and Christianity in Northern Nigeria is that of transformation through open-mindedness and the willingness to allow for mutual challenge. That these religions are immune from this challenge results from the sociological role they play in the region. Their historical antecedents incapacitate them from participating in genuine interreligious dialogue. Our analysis reveals that they perceive themselves – exclusively – as self-contained traditions or integrated worldviews capable of tackling the political and socio-economic problems that confront their followers. This has made interreligious dialogue an uphill task as we shall see below.

IV. Interreligious Dialogue in Northern Nigeria

Muslims and Christians in Northern Nigeria are aware of the fact that their religions provide them with their cultures and value systems and, equally, they are aware of the volatile nature of 'religion' in the area. Consequently, one of the unwritten rules, based on experience, is that discussion on religious topics is avoided because it could lead to bloodshed. For example, an argument between two school-girls over Muhammad and Jesus led to a full-blown riot in the town of Kazaure, with the attendant loss of lives and property. It was alleged that the Prophet Muhammad had been insulted.

In any case, interreligious encounters do take place in Northern Nigeria; ironically, this is due to dissatisfaction with persistent interreligious conflict. People of goodwill often gather interreligiously after these conflicts occur in the hope of averting their recurrence in the future. The issue that dominates the agenda of these encounters is, as Islam and Christianity preach peace, so their adherents should be peaceful. Flowery lectures are delivered on the impetus for peace in the *Qur'an* and the Bible, and those who take part in interreligious conflicts are described as miscreants who do not fulfil the dictates of their religion. Notwithstanding the goodwill of those involved in these encounters, these activities do not constitute genuine interreligious dialogue. The participants take it for granted that their religious traditions are pure and do not criticize them. The inability to analyse objectively both Islam and Christianity and the negative role they play in these conflicts ensures that further conflict erupts again, and that in spite of the good will of these peacemakers.

In very rare cases, Muslims and Christians come together interreligiously with the aim of understanding their different religious traditions. Even then, though, it is usually one-way traffic, since the presentations are not criticized. On my return from Dublin in 2004, I decided to engage myself with one of these interreligious groups. Frustratingly, meetings were not regular and the participants lacked the capacity for genuine interreligious dialogue. Controversial religious themes are carefully avoided. Participants extol the virtues of their religion, as revealed in their Holy Book. The focus is on religious ideals and not on the interpretation and practice of these ideals that, in reality, miss the mark. Questions are carefully crafted to avoid offending the dialogue-partner. The religions are presented as pure and integrated world-views that do not need any reformation. If there is anyone in need of reformation, it is a few misguided followers, who just need to study the revelation more, in order not to cause any future conflict. The message one gets at these encounters is: 'we want to live as good neighbours, so let us discuss the parameters for this co-existence; but, our religions are perfect and should not be criticized in the process.'

The practice of dialogue is thus completely thrown out the window. It is not possible to understand the 'interreligious' presentations at these forums without the freedom to ask questions to one's satisfaction. Christians may want to know why Arabic is the language of God since God is spirit; and Muslims may want to know how Jesus is the Son of God, since the *Qur'an* designates him a prophet. No one has the courage to ask, for such questions are simply too confrontational in the environment. One can say, though, without fear of exaggeration, no transformation takes place in these forums because nothing is disturbed and the peace of the graveyard is allowed to reign.

IV. Changing Situation

Not all, however, is dismal in Northern Nigeria and there are signs of hope for interreligious dialogue. Islam and Christianity gained political relevance due to two factors that are now extinct. First, in the era of regional politics, Northern Nigeria was a semi-independent political entity, and that made it possible for Islam and Christianity to determine the shape of the polity, since they were the dominant ideologies in the region. Second, during the military regimes, political parties were disbanded and the only alternatives available were the two religions. The religions were thus indispensable as the platforms for expression and negotiations, socially, politically and economically.

Now, democracy is restored and the scenario is gradually changing. Political parties are again in place, contesting for the needs of the generality of Nigerians. Civil society and professional bodies and unions that were proscribed under military regimes have been resuscitated and they now champion different causes that affect the life of the average Nigerian. Democratic structures are slowly emerging. Even though with shaky steps, the division of power between the executive, legislative and judicial arms is emerging and issues are handled with little reference to religion. The good news is that these political institutions and emerging organizations refer to the national scene and cut across religious affiliations. Political friendships are blossoming across the religions and these will have positive implications for interreligious dialogue. In sum, religious identity is gradually giving way to an emerging national identity. If the democratic process is left uninterrupted, it will create a common political culture that will reduce the socio-political relevance of religion and enhance genuine interreligious conversations.

V. Conclusion

Our examination of Northern Nigeria has shown that Islam and Christianity not only created two rival cultures, but they were also conscripted into the service of socio-political interests. Consequently, the adherents of these religious traditions perceive them as self-contained and formidable. This is not without reason because these religions have proven themselves to be solid platforms for socio-political negotiations for their adherents and have also filled the vacuum left by the government in seeing to their adherents' welfare. Regrettably, however, Christians and Muslims are unable to meet the challenges of interreligious dialogue, since they are not capable of criticizing their own religion in the light of the other's.

It is clear, therefore, that in the absence of a culture that cuts across Islam and Christianity, these religions continue to provide their followers with their value systems, exclusively. The result has been interreligious violence and not dialogue. This local context has implications, too, for global interreligious dialogue: we have situations where many religious traditions refuse to integrate themselves into the wider culture of their host communities. Since interreligious dialogue is possible only where the religions share a culture that cuts across religious affiliations, the plurality of religion, now becoming our contemporary experience, may not necessarily translate into religious pluralism.

Jacques Scheuer

The Buddha's Entering into *Nirvāṇa* and the Death of Christ

Let us start from some of the diverse ways in which Buddhists have perceived Christianity and particularly the figure of Christ Jesus. Of course, we should not forget that, across centuries and in the various parts of the Asian world where Buddhists used to live, opportunities for contact or encounter with Christians, or even opportunities to be in some way informed about the nature of Christianity and the person of this Jesus, were rather scarce. The vast majority of Buddhists in past centuries hardly knew anything at all about Christianity or Christ; similarly, their Christian contemporaries had little knowledge, if any, about Buddhism or its founder. Most of the time, chance encounters with travellers, merchants, or missionaries were likely to convey little more than bits of information. These were far from reliable and hard to interpret in the absence of authorized witnesses and of interpreters able to translate their meaning from one cultural language into another.

From the second half of the 16th century, however, and even more from the beginning of the 19th, a few samples of what Buddhists and Christians may have perceived and understood about each other have been salvaged. Concerning Jesus in particular, images of the Crucified and sometimes stories about his sufferings and death appear front stage. Those actually were the images and messages commonly conveyed by missionaries, sometimes brandished by them and spread among catechumens and budding Christian communities.

The Man on the Cross

In 17th and 18th century China – to quote a first instance – some missionaries, especially Jesuits, being well aware of the cultural (and perhaps spiritual) shock conveyed by the image of Christ on the cross, opted for a policy of discretion in this regard. In the beginning phase of their mission – and that beginning was sometimes to last quite long – they would emphasize God as the creator of the world, or Christian ethics and wisdom, rather than the folly of the cross. In spite of that, Chinese documents betray misunderstanding and scandal provoked by the historical limitations of the man Jesus: a foreigner, a barbarian, a citizen of a remote and marginal province, and most likely a criminal, since lawful authorities condemned him to die on a strange instrument of torture shaped like the Chinese sign for the number 'ten'.

From Thailand – or rather Siam, as the country was known in the 17th and 18th centuries – we learn about a strange variant of the story: the cross bandied by Christian missionaries looked curiously like the traditional representation, in those regions, of the instrument of torture on which Devadatta, the infamous cousin of the Buddha, endlessly expiated the jealousy and hostility he had entertained towards the great master.

Closer to us, in 19th century Ceylon (Sri Lanka), for instance, Buddhists who happened to watch Christian outdoor preaching would observe that the birth of Jesus is accompanied by violent deeds (the slaughter of babies in and around Bethlehem) and that his death is marked by signs of ill-luck. About thirty years ago, when invited to write about the relevance of Buddhism for Christian theologians in the West, a Sri Lankan Buddhist author remembers that, in the villages and towns of his home country, crosses and even large calvaries in front of churches and Roman Catholic institutions left Buddhist passers-by puzzled by the image of bloody wounds, torture and suffering. While some Christian writings taught or suggested that Jesus is a sage to be respected and a spiritual master, the spectacle of the man on the cross betrayed lack of taste, instead it inspired repulsion. From the familiar perspective of the law of karma, the horrible death of Jesus of Nazareth brings up unavoidable questions: if that man harvested such sufferings, one is left to guess what crimes he must have committed in previous lives. It is true that other meanings of Jesus's sufferings are equally possible, as we shall presently discover from the perspective of the Bodhisattva ideal. At first sight, however, violence and torture, forsakenness and immense sadness prevail.

In the second half of the 20th century, a Thai monk named Buddhadāsa ('servant of the Buddha') would come forward with a positive – even if, by Christian standards, rather unexpected – interpretation. This influential reformer wanted to resist hostile feelings towards Christianity among some Buddhist monastic quarters in his own country; he was eager to foster relations of friendship and dialogue with Christians. To his Buddhist audience he presented a play on words – or rather a play on signs – based on the English language (the language of the Christians?). As a graphic sign, the cross can only mean the following: the vertical stroke, meaning the 'I' (or the 'me', the ego), has to be crossed or erased by the horizontal stroke of egolessness. The little cross that some of his Christian visitors wore around their neck was the sign of the necessary struggle against the illusory pretensions of the ego; the cross teaches radical renouncement and spiritual battle in order to remove the 'I' and recover the freedom of those who are aware of the non-existence of a 'self', of a stable and autonomous subject!

The Buddha's Quiet Departing

Let us come back to the traditional images of the crucified Jesus. What could they mean to Asian Buddhists? What do they mean to Westerners who become estranged from Christianity and feel attracted rather to the Buddha's message, not to mention Western and Asian Christians? This image of the dying Christ has more than once been compared or contrasted with that of the Buddha 'entering *nirvāna*' (if this crude way of putting it may be condoned). The scene is rather familiar. According to traditional accounts, the Buddha has reached the ripe age of eighty; he is worn out by travel and teaching; the stale food offered him by a lay disciple makes him sick; he knows that the end of his life is near. Some distance away from a modest village to the North of the Ganges, he goes to lie down between 'twin' trees. Careful, as he has always been, about the monastic etiquette, he arranges his monk's clothes in an orderly way. His head on the palm of his right hand, his legs stretched out: every detail is faithfully recorded for the benefit of future painters and image makers.

The Buddha enters a state of deep meditation: he quietly goes up and down several levels of mental concentration. He knows that whatever had to be done is now accomplished. Not only did he reach perfect awakening and liberation when he was around thirty-five; the next forty-five years or so were spent for the benefit of others: spreading the *dharma*, teaching and making disciples, gathering a large community of women and men, both monk and lay. At present, his disciples do not need his presence anymore: the *dharma* faithfully preserved within the community provides whatever is necessary on the path toward liberation. The Buddha may now be compared to a potter's wheel: when the potter stops giving new impetus to the wheel, it starts slowing down and eventually comes to a still-stand. Free from any regret, the Buddha may now follow the universal law of impermanence. Thirst and illusion are spent out, the weight of past karma has vanished, suffering has died out, his death or rather his disappearance from this world will not be followed by any form of rebirth. This is the Buddhist's strong conviction, even if she may not be able to understand or figure out what the Buddha becomes at the moment of his departure: how could a fish, as long as it remains a fish, trapped in the dark waters of the pond, prisoner of the trappings of *samsāra,* realize what it means to a tortoise to climb up the bank and walk freely across the land?

In these last hours of his earthly life, the Buddha leaves us the image and the message of quiet mastery, of majesty and peace. What a contrast with the tortured figure of the crucified Christ! This contrast may be seen by some as a confirmation of the higher truth of the Buddha's message and the superiority of his way. This contrast will not necessarily lead a Christian away from her own path and her faith in Christ: it may, for instance, deepen her conviction that God, in the suffering Christ, comes closer to human suffering, while the Buddhist wisdom may strike her as cold, impassible, rather remote from the daily experiences of suffering human beings.

One way or other, let us avoid hasty conclusions. Is the parallel, which serves as foundation for this contrast, as neat and precise as one could wish? Is it self-evident and convincing? After all, the very meaning of death, for instance, may not be the same in the Buddhist and the Christian perspectives. According to their traditional understanding of existence, Buddhists contemplate a large number – or rather, an indefinite number – of lives, of rebirths (or 'reincarnations', as they are usually labelled in the West). 'Re-births' and 're-deaths'. According to the common Christian perspective, on the contrary, life is unique ('once for all'), and death is unique as well.

Moreover, Christians will spontaneously look at death as the opposite of life, as the destruction or again as the absence of life. From the Indian – Hindu or Buddhist – point of view, death is not so much the opposite of life: death rather pairs up with birth. Death and (re)birth are moments in the play of impermanence, in the endless flow (*samsāra*) of existences. Excepting the rare instance when it coincides with *parinirvāna,* with final access to *nirvāna,* death is not so much the cessation or the destruction of life; it is rather its continuation in other forms of existence, in other turns of the wheel, according to the law of karma. While illustrating the law of impermanence, death represents a sort of threshold, a moment of interval (one is reminded of the Tibetan teachings about the different types of *bardo*), and a turning point as well. Death does not mean annihilation, but rather modification or transformation in a cycle of existences characterized by both minimal continuity (there is nothing like an immutable 'self' or *ātman*) and permanent change. In a way, death itself is perhaps less to be feared than the subsequent rebirth, about which we do not know anything, except that it carries the seed of renewed 'suffering' (*dukkha*).

The Tree of the Cross and the Tree of Enlightenment

Actually, when the Buddha dies, he simply dies. Full stop. This simple fact does not invite any commentary. There is no need for further interpretation. The Christian, however, perhaps more than others, will note the absence of struggle. There is no struggle when the Buddha enters death. Indeed, in his case, the spiritual combat took place *before* what one may label his public ministry. A few Buddhist authors have emphasized the contrast between the Christ and the Buddha on this point. There is something tragic in the accounts of the last months of Jesus's life: a confrontation builds up, ant*agonisms* become acute, violence swells, leading to the scene of the 'agony' (the 'struggle'), to final suffering and execution. Jesus's life ends in a global confrontation with the powers of evil and death.

In the case of Gautama, the dimension of struggle is to be found rather in the period before enlightenment and the subsequent decision to start teaching. In that first period, after leaving his dear ones and his palace, Gautama goes through a phase of extreme – indeed excessive – mortification, followed by a time of rigorous but more balanced spiritual quest. That is the time of major confrontations with Māra, the Tempter. (A Christian reader will be reminded here of Jesus's forty-day retreat into the desert and his victorious fight against the Tempter.) After several years of sustained effort – and indeed, upon reaching the end of a spiritual journey extending over an endless number of rebirths – Gautama experiences enlightenment (*bodhi*): this very hour signals the end of the struggle for the Enlightened one. Even when, in later years, he happens to meet resistance and rare instances of persecution (inspired by the jealousy of his cousin Devadatta), the Buddha does not appear to be moved or even involved: if he remains active in this world, it is exclusively for the welfare of others; his compassion aims purely at the liberation of suffering beings.

If something like a process of death and resurrection may be looked for somewhere in the Buddha's career, it will be rather along the way leading up to enlightenment and in the liberating climax he then experiences. Rather than attempting a comparison between the Buddha's peaceful entry into lasting *nirvāna* and the crucified Jesus's agony and death, we may consider a parallel between the Christ on the cross and the Buddha sitting in meditation under the *bodhi* tree. Such a parallel has been suggested more than once. Next to Jesus's body, torn and nailed to the cross, we have the harmonious and peaceful image of the Buddha sitting in a firm meditation, well-centred in a concentration that nothing may disturb.

To him, of course, this victory comes at the end of a rough journey, a demanding quest. However, one may ask, indeed, one should ask: why do Christians emphasize the spectacle of the crucified Jesus while Buddhists, on the walls of their temples and in meditative practices of visualization, put forward the image of a peaceful victory or of a quiet departing? Could it be that age plays a role in this contrast: the elderly Buddha departs, his mission accomplished, while Jesus, a young adult, is brutally put to death? Should we rather consider different political contexts (the Roman occupation of Judaea, for instance)? Or, is it above all a question of religious cultures and their mindsets? A contrast has been sketched more than once between Indian religious traditions bent on tolerance and even inclusivism, and Near Eastern religions whose 'jealous' monotheism leads to exclusion and intolerance.

(Mis)understanding Death

Clearly, the Buddha's departure into death (or rather his disappearing at the moment of *parinirvāna*) has no particular soteriological meaning: nothing to be compared with the salvific or even redeeming significance Christians attribute to the sufferings and death of Jesus. Christians are invited to ponder over a small mysterious phrase (Greek *dei*: 'must', 'has to') recurring in their Scriptures. On the road to Emmaus, to pick just one instance, two disciples are told by the unknown traveller: '[r]emember how he told you... that the Son of man *must* be delivered into the hands of sinful men, and be crucified, and on the third day rise' (Luke 24:6-7).[1] Could we say that suffering, in the eyes of Buddhism, is at least a way or an instrument of liberation? We should not forget, of course, that '*dukkha*', for instance in the teachings about the 'Four Noble Truths', means much more than bodily pain or even mental suffering. On the whole, however, 'suffering' designates rather what one wishes to avoid or intends to 'extinguish'.

Sufferings and trials may of course work as a goad and spur us on to look for a way of liberation. That is even one of the advantages of the human condition, while rebirth as a divine being (*deva*) brings illusory well-being and inspires carelessness. Sufferings and trials, however, prove useful only if they do not increase resentment or envy, fear or despair. Suffering is likely to be helpful provided a measure of wisdom allows one to use it as an instrument or at least an opportunity to grow in awareness. Experiencing pain and trial enables one to recognize and accept the three basic characteristics of all phenomena: impermanence, non-existence of 'self', and *dukkha*. All beings are impermanent; our world is precarious and fragile: we are thus taught to let go of everything, most of all, to let go of ourselves. Death is, in a radical way, a school of detachment. Would this radicality be more effective with Christians than with Buddhists, for the reason that one single death (and one single existence) means a more rigorous putting to the test? Or, should we rather think that the opposite is true, since Christians may be tempted to consider the immortality of the soul as a prop and a security?

Although it may indeed function as a goad, suffering, in the eyes of Buddhists, has no value in itself, by itself. It is rather to be fought against. However, suffering is not so much to be attacked frontally; like a fire, one should rather attempt to smother it, or to allow it to die out. In ourselves, as well as in other living beings, we have to starve *dukkha*, to deprive it of whatever keeps fuelling it. Victory is achieved by patiently reducing the factors that produce suffering.

Since its manifest purpose is to work towards the extinction of suffering, even at the cost of rigorous asceticism, Buddhism refuses and denounces as a deviation every type of dolorism, every cult of suffering. Buddhism first met and combated such a deviation in the Jain teachings and practices as well as in certain forms of Brahmanical asceticism that the Buddha and his disciples witnessed among circles of ascetics (*tapasvin*) and renouncers (*samnyāsin*). More recently, Buddhism encountered and refused such a deviation in what it perceived about Christianity. On this particular point, among others, its stand is quite close to contemporary Western culture and mindset, particularly where these are inspired by various types of psychology and therapy. The Buddha's perspective, after all, was that of a healer or a therapist. Although the healing process may include painful stages, suffering, far from being intended as such, is to be fought relentlessly.

One more difficulty, one more source of misunderstanding between Buddhists and Christians is related to the law of karma. It is frequently stressed that this law operates on a strictly individual basis. How could the sufferings of one individual alleviate the sufferings of someone else? In this light, one gathers the impression that suffering, which is so much present in Christian thinking and feeling, would have no positive meaning whatever in the eyes of Buddhists. Indeed, what Buddhists and what Christians mean when they use the word 'suffering' sometimes seems to be worlds apart.

---

1 See also Luke 9:22; 17:25, etc.

The Bodhisattva's Way of Compassion

A bridge of understanding however may be found in certain Mahāyāna teachings about the compassion of Bodhisattvas, of beings well on their way to the full realization, to Buddhahood. Every step on the path towards perfect wisdom and full enlightenment means for them another step towards compassion. In their eagerness and resolve to work for the benefit of all living beings, they pledge themselves to come again and again into the world of *samsāra* in order to guide, to console and to heal. They proclaim themselves to be ready to endure all types of trial and suffering: 'All that burden of pain [of all creatures] I take upon myself, I assume, I endure. I do not avoid or run away... I tremble not, I turn not back... And why not? Certainly the burden of all creatures must be born by me... It is my resolution to save all creatures... By my own self all the mass of others' pain has been assumed... I have the courage in all misfortunes belonging to all worlds, to experience every abode of pain... There I must give myself in bondage... and I for the good of all creatures would experience all the mass of pain and unhappiness in this my own body...'[2]

In his other work, Śāntideva expresses the heroic resolve and vow of the Bodhisattva in this way: 'As long as the existence of space and as long as the existence of the world, that long let my existence be devoted to the world's sorrows. Whatever the sorrow of the world, may all that ripen in me; and may the world be comforted by all the glorious Bodhisattvas.'[3] When one reaches the summit of detachment and wisdom, there is no distinction anymore between 'my' suffering and 'your' suffering. When the walls of 'mine' and 'yours' have broken down, unlimited compassion spreads freely across the world: Bodhisattvas become able to share fully in the joys as well as the sorrows of living beings.

A Christian reader may well wonder: would all this have something to do with the words the Son of Man utters in the hour of Judgment: 'I was hungry and you gave me food... I was in prison and you came to me... Truly I say to you, as you did it to one of the least of these my brethren, you did it to me'?[4] Again, a Christian reader may be reminded of the words of Blaise Pascal: 'Jesus Christ remains in agony till the end of times'. And, once baptism has plunged him into the death (and resurrection) of Christ, the Christian becomes part of that same process of death and life, as witnessed and proclaimed by Paul: 'We are afflicted in every way, but not crushed... always carrying in the body the death of Jesus, so that the life of Jesus may also be manifested in our bodies. For while we live we are always being given up to death for Jesus's sake, so that the life of Jesus may be manifested in our mortal flesh. So death is at work in us, but life in you.'[5]

'Great Death' and 'Passover'

Let us come back – if we ever left them – to the Buddha sitting in meditation under the *bodhi* tree and to the Christ hanging on the cross. Buddhists, particularly if they follow the path of Zen, may remember the teachings of that school about the 'Great Death', the

---

2 *Vajradhvajasūtra*, quoted by Śāntideva in his *Siksāsamuccaya*, chapter 16, 280-281, translated by Cecil Bendall and W.H.D. Rouse, London, John Murray, 1922: 256-257.
3 *Entering the Path of Enlightenment, The Bodhicaryāvatāra of the Buddhist Poet Śāntideva*, chapter 10, 55-56, translated by Marion L. Matics, London, George Allen & Unwin, 1971.
4 Matthew 25:35-40.
5 2 Corinthians 4:8-12.

radical renunciation that is both required from them and illustrated by the lives of the patriarchs. This 'Great Death' means nothing more – and nothing less – than coming to see reality as it is, to look it in the face. By looking at reality as it is, mortal and terrifying, one becomes free from fear and death. In this connection, the Chinese and Japanese school of Chan/Zen is famous for its use of *koans*: these terse, dense and paradoxical sayings attributed to old masters have, so to say, to be chewed in meditation. They may be seen as tools to delve deeper and deeper, towards inner layers of consciousness and wisdom. There are hundreds of such *koans*; collections and even commentaries have been published. Yet, each saying, after all, is but a variant of the one basic, fundamental *koan*: human existence, the human condition, finite and inscrutable, impermanent and mortal.

Beyond the numberless little attachments of daily life, freely chosen or imposed by circumstances, facing death is the 'Great Doubt' which reveals and questions our thirst for certainty and safety. 'Great Death' is a total and radical letting go. However, the experience of those who ventured far ahead on the path towards liberation suggests that this passage discloses a wellspring of inexhaustible life. The trials of the 'Great Death' may be experienced as a sudden earthquake shaking our very foundations, but they give access to enlightenment. Reality is then discovered in its 'suchness' (*tathatā*). Beyond all illusions created by desire and the sense of 'mine', reality becomes real – although this happens in a way which cannot and should not be figured out in advance: remember the parable of the fish and the tortoise!

The early morning when Gautama, having sat once more throughout the night under the tree of *bodhi*, reaches the end of his long path of purification and detachment, may provide the best parallel to the 'Passover', central in the Christian faith and experience, from death to resurrection.

Buddhists, however, are usually careful not to name or label 'Reality' or 'Suchness'. They prefer to abide by silence, following the example of their teacher. Now, while Gautama keeps a 'noble silence', Jesus, when faced with suffering and death, always stands in relation to the One he calls 'Father'. Thus, when Christians enter the process of death, whether spiritual or in the body, they know that they share in the death of Christ, in his Passover. If a person allows the Buddhist tradition of the 'Great Death' to resonate inside oneself, shouldn't that person, that Christian, rejoice about the process of liberation that he undergoes?

It may be to the point to draw attention here to a curious paradox. In Buddhist perspective, desire is usually to be contained or uprooted. In Christian parlance, desire may be associated with 'Great Death'. Jesus himself had this to say about his desire: 'I came to cast fire upon the earth; and would that it were already kindled! I have a baptism to be baptized with; and how I am constrained until it is accomplished!'[6] Similarly, Paul writes: 'my desire is to depart and be with Christ'. Paul, however, sees good reasons to depart *and* good reasons to stay with his brethren. Like a Bodhisattva, enlightened by wisdom and moved by compassion, he stands, as it were, on the threshold between the world of *samsāra* and the kingdom of *nirvāna*: 'Now as always Christ will be honoured in my body, whether by life or by death. For to me to live is Christ, and to die is gain. If it is to be life in the flesh, that means fruitful labour for me. Yet, which I shall choose I cannot tell. I am hard pressed between the two. My desire is to depart and be with Christ, for that is far better. But to remain in the flesh is more necessary on your account...' (Philippians 1:20-24). This sounds like what some Buddhists call 'Great Desire'.

---

6   Luke 12:49-50.

Perry Schmidt-Leukel
Uniqueness: A Pluralistic Reading of John 14:6

Uniqueness confessed

'Why do you look at the speck that is in your brother's eye, but do not notice the log that is in your own eye?' (Matthew 7:3) – this is one of the striking sayings of Jesus, so typical of him. It hits us and touches us at the bottom of our hearts because of the moral and psychological truth in it. It is not only true of particular specks and logs. It implies the very general observation that we usually have a much sharper eye when it comes to a critical analysis of others than for a critical analysis of ourselves. So before I start my reflections on christology, I'd like to sharpen our awareness by throwing a brief glance at a classical Buddhist discourse on buddhology. Detecting the 'speck' in buddhology might help sensitize us to the 'log' in christology.

A major source of the early formation of traditional Theravāda-Buddhist doctrines is the *Milindapañha*, i.e., 'The Questions of King Milinda'.[1] It is composed as a long series of dialogues between the Indo-Greek king Milinda (Menander, 2nd century BCE) and the Buddhist monk Nāgasena. In one of these dialogues, Nāgasena expounds the Theravāda teaching that there can be only one Buddha at one time in each aeon or world system.[2] King Milinda, however, questions this doctrine with the argument:

> Already by the appearance of one Buddha has this world become flooded with light. If there should be a second Buddha the world would be still more illuminated by the glory of them both.[3]

To this the Buddhist monk Nāgasena replies:

> This world system, O king, is a one-Buddha-supporting world; that is, it can bear the virtue of only a single Tathāgata. If a second Tathāgata were to arise

---

1 As usual it is difficult to date the origin of the work. Its oldest parts (chapters 1-3) may have been composed as early as the 1st century BCE while the rest of the work seems to contain later additions, perhaps from the hands of Ceylonese revisors, see T.W. Rhys Davids, 'Introduction', in *The Questions of King Milinda*, translated from the Pali by T.W. Rhys Davids, Part I and II [SBE 35 and 36], 1890-1894, reprint: Part I, New York, Dover, 1963: xi-xlix; Heinz Bechert, 'Einleitung', in *Milindapañha. Die Fragen des Königs Milinda*, edited and partly newly translated by Nyanaponika, Interlaken, Ansata, 1985: 15-22.
2 Cf. Anguttara-Nikāya I, 15, 10. Basically all Buddhist schools teach that there were, are, and will be, many Buddhas. This is said, however, against the background assumption that there is an infinite number of worlds in chronological sequence and in different spacial locations. At issue, therefore, is whether there can be more than one Buddha per world. Parts of Nāgasena's explanation clearly entail that there can be only one Buddha per world (e.g., *Milindapañha* [*Mph*] IV, 6, 5: 'This world system... is a one-Buddha-supporting world...'), while other parts affirm that there can be only one Buddha at a time. The traditional Theravāda concept is that the next Buddha will only appear after the community which was established by Siddhārtha Gautama has completely declined and the Dharma is entirely forgotten. Each Buddha, therefore, makes a new start in a world where no soteriological community exists and the Dharma is unknown. Nāgasena's assumption seems to be that as long as the Dharma is still proclaimed there cannot be a second Buddha, i.e., within a religious 'world' there can be only one.
3 *Questions of King Milinda* II: 47 (*Mph* 237).

the world could not bear him, it would shake and tremble, it would bend, this way and that, it would disperse, scatter into pieces, dissolve, be utterly destroyed.[4]

If two Buddhas were to arise in one world, Nāgasena continues,

> ... then the passage [of Scripture] that the Buddha is the chief would become false, and the passage that the Buddha takes precedence of all would become false, and the passage that the Buddha is the best of all would become false. And so all those passages where the Buddha is said to be the most excellent, the most exalted, the highest of all, the peerless one, without an equal, the matchless one, who hath neither counterpart nor rival – all would be proved false. (...)
>
> Of other things also, whatever is mighty in the world is singular. The broad earth is great, O king, and it is only one. The ocean is mighty, and it is only one. Sineru, the king of the mountains, is great; and it is only one. Space is mighty, and it is only one. (...) Wherever any one of these spring up, then there is no room for a second. And therefore, O king, is it that only one Tathāgatha, an Arahat Buddha supreme, can appear at one time in the world.[5]

Nāgasena's explanation clearly testifies to what could be called the *logic of exaltation*. If the Buddha is praised by the scriptures as 'the highest of all' and if the scriptures are right, then by logical implication there cannot be a second. It is easy, however, to recognize that this argument is in a sense self-produced: the Buddha must be unique for those who praise him as the highest. And within this particular universe of praise he surely is unique. Can this claim, though, be extended beyond that particular world, i.e., the world of Theravāda-Buddhist faith? Look at Nāgasena's examples: the earth, the ocean, mount Sineru – we know that all of these are unique only within the narrow boundaries of Nāgasena's ancient Indian world-view. Nowadays, however, we are well aware that neither the ocean is unique, nor the high mountain, nor the earth, nor perhaps even space if it is understood as a function of a particular universe and if there might be a plurality of worlds. Within the boundaries of a certain religion, or – as we could say – a certain universe of religious experience, the Buddha might very well be unique, as the earth is for us. Within a wider context of inhabited worlds, i.e., in the context of various religious realms, there might be others and among these we will find ourselves, namely, Christianity, and Jesus Christ, the one whom we exalt as the 'highest of all' or the only one, as expressed in such Jesus-ascribed statements as, 'I am the way, and the truth, and the life, no one comes to the Father, but through Me' (John 14:6).

Religiously, our current situation is marked by a global interreligious encounter which has only begun, which proceeds gradually but constantly, which cannot be stopped and which implies – in the long run – massive consequences that are hardly to be estimated. This might be compared to an interstellar exchange, to the meeting and intersecting of large galaxies. In such a situation, a range of new and unexpected phenomena occur, among which is the possibility not only of penetrating and understanding another religious universe but of seeing our own world through the other's eyes (reminiscent of the first fascinating pictures of the earth, the 'blue planet', as seen from space), or conversely, of seeing the broader world, i.e., the various universes of faiths, from the different perspectives of each of them.[6]

---

4 *Questions of King Milinda* II: 48 (*Mph* 237).
5 *Questions of King Milinda* II: 50f. (*Mph* 239).
6 Cf. Harold Coward, *Pluralism in the World Religions: A Short Introduction*, Oxford, Oneworld, 2000; Andreas Grünschloß, *Der eigene und der fremde Glaube: Studien zur interreligiösen*

It is in this context that I present some reflections on John 14:6. I will not argue as a biblical scholar since this is simply not my field; hence, I am not able to discuss competently any of the details or intricacies of the proper interpretation of John's gospel, e.g., the degree of Gnostic influence or more specifically the Gnostic or non-Gnostic (i.e., Jewish) origin or background of the metaphors 'way', 'truth' and 'life' in our verse. I will take them in a rather broad sense and my reflections will be determined by a systematic approach, which is that approach of systematic theology that is carried out in the horizon of our growing knowledge and understanding of other religions and of the inevitable process of a hermeneutical 'Horizontverschmelzung' (H.-G. Gadamer), i.e., of the fusion of the different traditional horizons of our interpretative attempts.

Uniqueness challenged

From a Christian point of view, the crucial issue is the status of Christianity in relation to other religious traditions. This entails two fundamental and interrelated questions: first, how does Christianity understand and assesses the other religions in the light of its own teachings? Second, how does Christianity understand and assess itself in the light of the other religions? It is obvious that the answer to each of these questions has immediate implications for the answer to the other one. The theological discussion of these two questions has come to be called 'theology of religions'. Over the last four decades it has developed into one of the most heated theological debates carried out on a world-wide level. The various standpoints that theologians have taken are frequently grouped into three different classes: exclusivism, inclusivism, and pluralism. This classification has become the object of some criticism during more recent years. I feel that it is still a very helpful taxonomy, but one which is, however, in need of a more precise formulation.[7] As I define it, *exclusivism* is the conviction that salvific knowledge of a transcendent reality is mediated by only one religion (which will naturally be one's own). *Inclusivism* is the conviction that salvific knowledge of a transcendent reality is mediated by more than one religion (though not necessarily by all of them), but that only one religion mediates that knowledge in a uniquely superior way (this again, will naturally be one's own religion). *Pluralism* shares with inclusivism the conviction that salvific knowledge of a transcendent reality is mediated by more than one religion (though not necessarily by all of them) but, unlike inclusivism, it holds that there is none among them whose mediation of that knowledge is superior to all the rest. In other words, there is no 'single highest' among the religions; so, at least some of them are different but equally valid paths of salvation.

If we add a fourth possible position, the position of *atheism/naturalism*, according to which salvific knowledge of a transcendent reality is mediated by none of the religions (because there is no transcendent reality) we arrive at a classification which is complete due to its fully disjunctive character: either religions mediate salvific knowledge or they do not. If they do, then either only one of them does or more than one does. If more than one, than either only one does in a uniquely superior form, or there are several doing

---

Fremdwahrnehmung in Islam, Hinduismus, Buddhismus und Christentum, Tübingen, Mohr Siebeck, 1999; J. Gort, H. Jansen, H. Vroom (eds.), *Religions View Religions: Explorations in Pursuit of Understanding*, Amsterdam and New York, Rodopi, 2006.

7 Cf. Perry Schmidt-Leukel, 'Exclusivism, Inclusivism, Pluralism: The Tripolar Typology – Clarified and Reaffirmed', in Paul F. Knitter (ed.), *The Myth of Religious Superiority: Multifaith Explorations of Religious Pluralism*, Maryknoll, Orbis, 2005: 11-27.

this differently but equally well. Every theory addressing the question of whether religions mediate salvific knowledge of transcendence falls necessarily under one of these four categories. There is no further option left. Either one avoids the question (and thus ceases to do 'theology of religions') or one has to make a choice. The *atheist/naturalist* position runs counter to the claims of all religions and is, therefore, not a 'theological' or religious option (note: this does not entail that it is no option at all). The choice which a *religious* interpretation of religious diversity has to make is thus between exclusivism, inclusivism and pluralism.

It may be the case that religious diversity does not challenge each religion in exactly the same way – but it does constitute a challenge to each of them. The challenge arises from the fact that as more and more members of each religion acquire a deeper understanding of other religions they are learning how to see their own tradition through the others' eyes. This inevitably sheds new light on one's own tradition and therefore requires a reconsideration of one's previous self-understanding, whatever this might have been. In this process of reconsidering and reinterpreting one's own religion in relation to the others, each religion needs to make a choice between the three basic options.

A number of religious thinkers (though still a comparatively tiny minority) in all the major religious traditions are currently moving towards a pluralistic view, as developed from within their own specific religious background.[8] This is possible because each religious tradition seems to have important doctrinal resources – or should I say, living fountains of insight – which not only permit but in fact call for such a move. Nevertheless, each religion also has strong traditions of either exclusivistic or inclusivistic claims hinging on specific doctrines and kerygmatic formulas. These need to be addressed and openly discussed by those who tend towards a pluralistic understanding of religious diversity. Within Islam, for example, there is the understanding of Muhammad as the 'seal of the prophets' (Qur'an 33:40) and the corresponding claim that the Qur'an is revelation in its most superior form. In Judaism there is the belief in a special election and a kind of superior covenant. In Buddhism there is the claim that the Noble Eightfold Path is 'the only way' so that 'there is no other' (*Dhammapada*: 273f.). In Hinduism there is the quasi-pluralist claim that only Hinduism possesses the suitable doctrines to acknowledge the fundamental unity and equality of religions (which, of course, makes Hinduism the *primus inter pares*). And in Christianity there is, as noted, John 14:6 which is quoted again and again when Christian pluralists are scolded by their exclusivistically and inclusivistically minded brothers and sisters. For them and their counterparts in the other religions, as John D'Arcy May rightly states,

> ... the 'truth' embodied in their ritual and expressed in myth or doctrine is an absolute value directly bound up with the possibility of 'salvation'. ... The thought that there could be alternative systems of belief and ways of being religious that would question the uniqueness of their own certainties is, strictly speaking, inconceivable.[9]

Within this small contribution in honour of one of the great pioneers in the field of interreligious theology there is neither space nor need to recall the arguments which, from within the Christian tradition, count against an exclusivist or an inclusivist view

---

8 Cf. John Hick, Hasan Askari (eds.), *The Experience of Religious Diversity*, Aldershot, Gower, 1985; Paul F. Knitter, *The Myth of Religious Superiority*. For an overview of pluralistic positions in non-Christian religions, see Perry Schmidt-Leukel, *Gott ohne Grenzen: Eine christliche und pluralistische Theologie der Religionen*, Gütersloh, Gütersloher Verlagshaus, 2005: 171-175.
9 John D'Arcy May, *After Pluralism: Towards an Interreligious Ethic*, Münster, LIT, 2000: 55.

and, at the same time, in favour of a pluralist one.¹⁰ yet, it may be worth offering some reflections on how a Christian pluralist might understand the words of John 14:6 which seem so obviously to deny any sound possibility of a Christian *and* pluralistic theology of religions. How can those who are convinced that *life* (even and, in particular, holy or eternal life) always exists in a rich manifoldness, that *truth* (even and, in particular, the truth of God) always exists in a variety of human reflections, and that there are 'as many *ways* to God as there are human beings',¹¹ respond to a statement like John 14:6?

Uniqueness, an interpretation not a quotation

The first part of my answer to this question is based on the nowadays almost common exegetical judgement, that, in the words of Geza Vermes,

> the so-called Gospel of John ... reflects, not the authentic message of Jesus or even the thinking about him of his immediate followers, but the highly evolved theology of a Christian writer who lived three generations after Jesus and completed his Gospel in the opening years of the second century A.D.¹²

When it comes to the 'historical' or 'real' Jesus and the question of his authentic self-understanding most biblical scholars, as far as I can see, agree that his message was theocentric and that he clearly distinguished himself from the one God in whom he believed and whom he addressed as 'Father'. Wolfhart Pannenberg – who may not count as an suspect witness because he is both most interested in defending the high Christology of Nicaea and Chalcedon and a vigorous opponent of pluralist theology – summarizes the findings of biblical research as follows:

> At the heart of the message of Jesus stood the Father and his coming kingdom, not any dignity that Jesus claimed for his own person that would thus make himself equal to God (John 5:18). Jesus differentiated himself as a mere man from the Father as the one God. He thus subjected himself to the claim of the coming divine rule, just as he required his hearers to do. He could even reject the respectful title 'good master' (Mark 10:18), with a reference to God alone as good.¹³

The portrait of Jesus in the synoptic gospels, that is, the portrait of Jesus who, like every devout Jew, strictly rejects even the remotest move of identifying himself with God, is very different from the self-presentation of Jesus in the Gospel of John. 'I am the way, and the truth, and the life; no one comes to the Father, but through me' belongs to the so-called *ego eimi*-sayings, i.e., a group of sayings all starting with the words 'I am',

---

10 For an extensive and detailed discussion of these arguments, see my *Theologie der Religionen: Probleme, Optionen, Argumente*, Neuried, Ars Una, 1997, and *Gott ohne Grenzen*: 96-162.

11 Emphasis added. This was the startling answer given by the then Cardinal Josef Ratzinger when he was asked how many ways are there leading to God. The full interview sequence reads: 'Wie viele Wege gibt es zu Gott?' 'So viele, wie es Menschen gibt. Denn auch innerhalb des gleichen Glaubens ist der Weg eines jeden Menschen ein ganz persönlicher. Wir haben das Wort Christi: Ich bin der Weg. Insofern gibt es letztendes einen Weg, und jeder, der zu Gott unterwegs ist, ist damit auf irgendeine Weise auch auf dem Weg Jesu Christi. Aber das heißt nicht, daß bewußtseinsmäßig, willensmäßig alle Wege identisch sind, sondern im Gegenteil, der eine Weg ist eben so groß, daß er in jedem Menschen zu seinem persönlichen Weg wird', in Joseph Kardinal Ratzinger, *Salz der Erde: Christentum und katholische Kirche an der Jahrtausendwende. Ein Gespräch mit Peter Seewald*, Stuttgart, Deutsche Verlags-Anstalt, 1996: 35.

12 Geza Vermes, *The Changing Faces of Jesus*, London, Penguin, 2001: 6.

13 Wolfhart Pannenberg, *Systematic Theology* 2, Grand Rapids, Eerdmans, 1994: 372.

which are so typical of the portrayal of Jesus in the Gospel of John, as in, e.g., 'I am the bread of life' (6:35), or 'I am the resurrection and the life' (11:25), or 'I am the door; if anyone enters through Me, he shall be saved' (10:9), the last of which is perhaps the closest parallel to our verse insofar as it has the same 'through me' (*di' emou*) regarding salvation. Through these 'I am'-sayings Jesus is indeed put very close to God.[14] This is perhaps most obvious in John 8:58 where Jesus says 'Truly, truly, I say to you, before Abraham was born, I am'. Here we find the Johannine theme of pre-existence, which of course also makes it clear that the 'I' in the 'I am'-sayings cannot be simply identified with the human being Jesus. 'Before Abraham was, I am' connects the 'I am'-sayings with the prologue of John's Gospel. This prologue introduces Jesus as the one in whom and through whom the divine *logos* 'became flesh, and dwelt among us' (1:14) in order to reveal the invisible God (1:18). This explains why the Jesus of John's Gospel almost identifies himself with the Father in such sayings as: 'I and the Father are one' (10:30) or 'He who has seen Me has seen the Father' (14:9). I add 'almost' because even John lets Jesus say 'The Father is greater than I' (14:28).

The *ego eimi*-sayings in John's Gospel are, in all historical probability, not quotations of Jesus's own words but theological interpretations which try to spell out his meaning as a divine revealer in the eyes of the early Christian Church. Jesus's life and Jesus's message were focussed on the kingdom of God. Out of his own experience of God's presence, and informed by the Jewish tradition to which he belonged and in which he lived, he interpreted God's rule (God's 'kingdom') as marked by boundless mercy, as the presence of a divine love which should be answered and reflected in the twofold commandment to love God and one's fellow human being. Insofar as Jesus submitted his own life to God's merciful reign, he realized the kingdom of God in his own person. In living his own life as a perfect reflection of the Father's love Jesus became a mediator of God's presence for his disciples, a human image of the invisible God (Colossians 1:15). The developing interpretation of Jesus as a human mediator of God's loving presence reaches its first climax, then, in the Gospel of John and the Johannine portrait of Jesus as the human manifestation of the divine Logos.

Uniqueness, an interpretation reinterpreted

If this brief sketch is at all close to a correct historical placement of John's Gospel and the Johannine Jesus, what does this mean for a Christian theology of religions? How, in particular, should we understand the second half of John 14:6, 'no one comes to the Father, but through me'? The meaning of the words 'through Me' is far from clear. Without doubt, it is a strong instance of metaphorical language, as is also evident in the same 'through Me' in, 'I am the door; if anyone enters through Me, he shall be saved' (10:9). Yet, if 'through Me' is metaphorical language, how should we translate it?[15]

Christian *exclusivists* usually translate this phrase as pointing to the crucifixion in the sense that, through his self-sacrifice, Christ has made salvation possible and that this salvation is only available through its explicit proclamation and the corresponding belief

---

14 For the following, see Vermes, *The Changing Faces of Jesus*: 41-55.
15 Cf. the exciting but very fragmentary notes in Thomas Merton's Asian Diary (19 November 1968) where he attempts to interpret the 'I am the door' in terms of Buddhist 'emptiness', alluding to the Zen motif of the 'gateless gate' (*mumonkan*), Thomas Merton, *The Other Side of the Mountain: the End of the Journey*, edited by Patrick Hart (number 7 in *The Journals of Thomas Merton*), San Francisco, HarperCollins 1999: 285.

in the Christian gospel.[16] Christian *inclusivists* usually emphasize that the words 'I' and 'Me' when spoken by the Johannine Jesus refer to Jesus insofar as he manifests the divine Logos. These words are meant as expressions of the Logos who is incarnated in Jesus but whose revealing and saving activity is neither confined to Jesus nor to the Christian church, but 'enlightens every human' (John 1:9).[17] This is the ancient patristic teaching of the *logoi spermatikoi*, the 'germs of the Logos', which led countless people among the non-Christians to a saving, but fragmentary knowledge of God, while the fullness of the Logos has appeared only in Jesus Christ. According to Christian inclusivism, 'through Me' therefore means that salvation is possible only through the Logos, i.e., only through divine self-disclosure – a self-disclosure which encompasses all humanity, but finds its unique climax in Jesus, so that the chance of salvation is highest within the orbit of Christianity.

How then may a Christian *pluralist* interpret John 14:6? First of all, the Christian pluralist will not deny that divine truth, eternal life, and the way to the Father can indeed be found through Jesus and the proclamation of the gospel. A Christian pluralist will not deny Jesus's status as a genuine mediator of God's saving presence, but he or she will deny that Jesus is the only mediator or that Jesus is a mediator who is uniquely superior to all the others. So, a Christian pluralist also sees the Way, the Truth and the Life in Jesus, but as exemplified and represented in him. To quote Paul Knitter's famous thesis, '[t]he uniqueness of Jesus's salvific role can be reinterpreted in terms of *truly* but not *only*.'[18]

Against exclusivists, a pluralist will thus reject the idea that salvation was enabled through the crucifixion, and will hold that all salvation depends (in Christian terms) on God's grace alone, which would cease to be grace if Jesus had to pay the full price for the debt of our sins by the sacrifice of his life.[19] Salvation or God's grace is therefore not constituted by the crucifixion but represented or expressed by it[20] insofar as the crucifixion marks the consumption of Jesus's life, lived as a reflection of God's love up to its most radical consequence. Together with Christian inclusivists, pluralists will hold that the revealing and saving activity of the Logos is not confined to Jesus Christ or the Christian Church.[21] Like inclusivists, pluralists can interpret the phrase 'through Me' as referring to the divine Logos. They will deny, however, that the fullness of the Logos can be found in Jesus alone.

A Two-Natures-Christology, as classically formulated by the council of Chalcedon, does not necessarily contradict a pluralist interpretation of Jesus. A real human being can be the medium of nothing less than the Logos, that is, the communication of the real divine reality.[22] Precisely because of the true humanity of the mediator – with all the specific human limitations – the finite medium cannot exhaust the infinite God, so that

---

16. See, e.g., R.D. Geivett, W.G. Phillips, 'A Particularist View: An Evidentialist Approach', in D.L. Okholm and T.R. Phillips (eds.), *More Than One Way?*, Grand Rapids, Zondervan, 1995: 213-245.
17. See, e.g., C.H. Pinnock, *A Wideness in God's Mercy. The Finality of Jesus Christ in a World of Religions*, Eugene, Wipf and Stock, 1997: 77-79.
18. Paul Knitter, 'Five Theses on the Uniqueness of Jesus', in L. Swidler and P. Mojzes (eds.), *The Uniqueness of Jesus: A Dialogue with Paul F. Knitter*, Maryknoll, Orbis, 1997: 3-16: 7.
19. Cf. John Hick, *The Metaphor of God Incarnate*, London, SCM, 1993: 127.
20. Cf. Shubert Ogden, *Is There Only One True Religion or Are There Many?*, Dallas, Southern Methodist University, 1992: 84-99.
21. Cf. John Hick, 'Jesus and the World Religions', in John Hick (ed.), *The Myth of God Incarnate*, Philadelphia, Westminster, 1977: 167-185: 181.
22. Cf. Perry Schmidt-Leukel, 'Chalcedon Defended: A Pluralistic Re-Reading of the Two-Natures Doctrine', in *The Expository Times* 118 (2006): 113-119.

the reality which Jesus mediates is *totus deus* (fully God) but not *totum deum* (the fullness of God), as Christian tradition has constantly reaffirmed. This leaves room for the assumption of other finite mediators of the same infinite reality.[23] However, if Jesus need not necessarily be seen as the only mediator, is he not nevertheless a very specific one, being unique not as a divine mediator as such but in the specific form in which he made God present to us? I think that this can be acknowledged without any hesitation. How, then, shall we specify his uniqueness in comparison to other unique mediators? This raises the question: who are the 'we'? I think that 'we' Christians assume too quickly something like a natural hermeneutical privilege on the correct understanding of Jesus's specific role. But, Jesus belongs to humankind – as do the Buddha, Muhammad, and others. It is for all humanity – while drawing on various religious traditions – to say what Jesus might mean to them, and in which sense they would possibly see something unique in him. This is an exciting new discourse and belongs to the fascinating phenomena that occur when religious galaxies intersect. As Gregory Barker shows in his tremendously important book *Jesus in the World's Faiths*,[24] this discourse is well underway.

A Christian pluralist, however, can and will presumably understand Jesus as a *normative* exemplar of what a genuine mediation of divine presence is like. For this, one might point to the first letter of John which derives from the life of Jesus the crucial criterion that 'everyone who loves is born of God and knows God' (1 John 4:7) and that 'anyone who does not practice righteousness is not of God' (1 John 3:10). Nevertheless, to acknowledge the normativity of Jesus does not exclude – as Roger Haight rightly remarks – 'the possibility of other saviour figures of equal status ... who may also reveal something of God that is normative.'[25]

Yet, it might very well be the case that such a pluralist reading of John 14:6 falls short of what the author of the Gospel wanted to express. Maybe John wanted to claim more. Maybe he wanted to say that Jesus has a completely unique role regarding salvation, that he is 'the most excellent, the most exalted, the highest of all, the peerless one, without an equal, the matchless one, who hath neither counterpart nor rival'. Remember the words! These are from Nāgasena's statement about the Buddha quoted at the beginning of this paper. If this gives us the clue – that is, if it indicates that the uniqueness of Jesus is proclaimed out of the logic of exaltation – then a pluralist can agree once more, without taking such words too literally, knowing that a claim for uniqueness born out of an entirely justified exaltation is anything but unique.[26*]

---

23 For the discussion of other possible mediators, see John Macquarrie, *The Mediators: Nine Stars in the Human Sky*, London, SCM, 1995; for a specific discussion of Buddha and Christ, see my 'Buddha and Christ as Mediators of the Transcendent: A Christian Perspective', in P. Schmidt-Leukel (ed.), *Buddhism and Christianity in Dialogue*, London, SCM, 2005: 151-175.
24 Gregory A. Barker (ed.), *Jesus in the World's Faiths: Leading Thinkers from Five Religions Reflect on His Meaning*, Maryknoll, Orbis, 2005.
25 Roger Haight, 'The Case for Spirit Christology', in *Theological Studies* 53 (1992): 257-287: 281. For a balanced and careful treatment of the question of Jesus's normativity, see also Roger Haight, *Jesus – Symbol of God*, Maryknoll, Orbis, 1999: 403-410. On the issue of suitable criteria for mutual interreligious assessment, see R. Bernhardt and P. Schmidt-Leukel (eds.), *Kriterien interreligiöser Urteilsbildung*, Zürich, TVZ, 2005.
26 As Wilfred Cantwell Smith says, '[a] claim to uniqueness is not unique', in his 'Idolatry: In Comparative Perspective', in John Hick and Paul Knitter (eds.), *The Myth of Christian Uniqueness: Towards a Pluralistic Theology of Religions*, Maryknoll, Orbis, 1987: 53-68: 64.
* I am grateful to Rose Drew for looking through the draft of this paper and making a range of valuable suggestions.

Parichart Suwanbubbha

Speaking of Mary from a Buddhist Perspective

On the occasion of Professor John D'Arcy May's retirement, I am very honoured to join and celebrate this important and auspicious time for him. That he is a devoted, kind and generous Christian professor who is also interested in and open-minded with people from other beliefs encourages me to examine the theme of Mary from a Buddhist perspective. Many Buddhist explanations, based on ultimate coherent truth, humbly transcend the limitations of 'human language'. In honouring John May we sincerely confirm that his faith as a Catholic Christian is not at all a limitation on his vision, academic involvement or work to create mutual and good relationships among religions, especially Buddhism.

Introduction

We know that one influential impact of globalization is that it brings people to share in the same global village. However, we also realize that there is diversity: other cultures, languages and religious beliefs. In my experience, the more we learn from these differences, the deeper we understand and appreciate our local wisdom, culture and religion. Consequently, the case of the Virgin Mary in Catholicism has inspired in me several ideas related to the existential law of nature and the proper motive of feminism; it even impels me to think further on 'the Buddhist Feminism of the Middle Path'. This outcome may be considered a fruit of the dialogue of study and experience between Buddhism and Christianity. Further, it is a process that is truly the source of 'unity amid diversity'. In this essay I hope that we will learn from one other, and as we reflect on this learning that we will cultivate both spiritual development in ourselves and mutual understanding among our followers.

Mary in the eyes of Buddhists

According to the timeless Buddhist principle, everyone, whether man or woman, rich or poor, is equal in terms of human dignity because all are under the same natural law of causes and effects. We understand this law as *the law of kamma* or *karma*. However, according to the varying socio-cultural expressions and contexts of each country and religion, one may see inequitable and different expressions of *kamma*'s realization in different individuals. For instance, in our hierarchical Thai society, people have different effects from their *kamma*; again, people have different relationships with one another. We usually pay attention to the appropriate relationship between seniors and juniors, between a man and a woman, between a husband and a wife and between a parent and a child. Nevertheless, the universal relationship, which goes beyond any kind of diversity, is the influential and emotional aspect of the mother toward her child. Let us consider, then, Michelangelo's painting, the '*Madonna of the Steps*'.[1]

---

1 Angelo Tartuferi, *Michelangelo: Painter, Sculptor and Architect*, Rome, ATS Italia, 1993: 139.

The painting shows the lively event of a young and tender Mary nursing a little baby, Jesus, with milk from her breast, while they are at the steps. It is quite astonishing: we seldom see this presentation of Jesus because most Buddhists think of Jesus Christ as God. For us, a notion of God implies his omnipotence, omnipresence and omniscience. We understand that He is the supernatural being. However, we almost forget another important aspect of Jesus, viz., his nature as 'true human being'. As a human being, then, Jesus naturally is part of the general relationship of father, mother and son. With this in mind, therefore, we look at Michelangelo's tremendous, lively and meaningful painting with full feelings of appreciation, gratitude, gentleness, security, compassion and devotion.

Mary's breast feeding in this picture represents the universal role of motherhood. Of course, Mary's role as a mother began with the event of her pregnancy, in spite of being a virgin, by the power of the Holy Spirit. Certainly, we talk here of a matter of faith, but, it is still difficult to imagine the unusual situation of Mary during that time because there was neither public example nor approval for an event such as this. Buddhist 'outsiders', then, divide Mary's great role into two dimensions, that is, a dimension of faith and a dimension of ordinary mother. Each dimension complements the other.

Mary and her motherhood

The first and crucial point for us to note here, in this action of a mother, is that Mary becomes the mother who sacrifices her normal life (as a young virgin woman) and her happiness in order to feed, look after and support her child to perform his divine duty. As a mother, we recall, too, how she suffers and is full of pain when present at the crucifixion as she looks at her beloved son, the dying Jesus!

Yet, this focusing on Mary's role as Jesus's mother reminds us of the events related in the life of Maddi, the wife of a certain Bodhisattva[2] in Buddhism. In other words, in order to understand Mary's universal role as Jesus's mother, let us examine some of the elements of Maddi's life. Maddi is a wife of Prince Vessantara who is a *Bodhisattva*, a Buddha-to-be. This is a story about one of the previous lives of the future Buddha; it was recorded in a part of Buddhist scripture called *Jātaka*, which is a collection of tales about previous rebirths of buddhas. Prince Vessantara began his renunciation by giving away a magic white elephant that brings rain to his father's kingdom, and then he is expelled. His wife and two children accompany him to live in the forest as hermits. The crucial event happens when the prince gives up to the gods his own and Maddi's two children, Jali and Kanhajina, in another act of detached generosity while Maddi herself is off gathering food in the forest. Most touchingly, Maddi swoons in grief upon learning of the loss of her children. 'These breasts of mine are full of milk, my heart will break withal: but Jali and Kanhajina I cannot see today'.[3] This phrase first reflects the incomparably worried, anxious and suffering feeling of this mother, Maddi; but,

---

2   A *bodhisattva* is a buddha-to-be. According to *Theravada Buddhism,* the Buddha, i.e., that buddha known as Sakyamuni or Gotama, in his previous rebirths was various *bodhisattvas*. Bodhisattvas practice different kinds of virtue on their path to buddhahood; Vessantara's distinctive virtue is great charity (*dana*), for he gave up all that he held precious, including powerful gifts, son and daughter, and even his wife, for the sake of following the truth.
3   *Vessantara Jātaka* #547. The Jātaka tales are published in translation by the Pali Text Society, see E.B. Cowell (ed.), *The Jātaka or Stories of the Buddha's Former Births*, in 6 volumes, Oxford, Pali Text Society, 1990 [1895-1907]: volume 6.

then it applies to Mary and most women in this world, who, as mothers, lose their children. We heartily imagine Mary at one time in her life feeding her beloved child with her breast milk; now, heartbreakingly, we imagine her in the crucifixion scene as she sees her only son being tortured and finally dying on a cross as a criminal! We as Buddhists sympathize with and admire her broken heart and great sacrifice. When Maddi comes back from the forest, her husband does not say a word about where their children are.

> Why art thou silent? How that dream comes to my thought again: the birds and ravens make no sound, my children must be slain…I cannot see their hands and feet, I cannot see their hair: Was it a bird that swooped? Or who has carried them away? (*Vessantara Jātaka* #547).

How anxious and suffering she is! Moreover, this scene reveals the similar feeling Mary and Joseph had when they sought for Jesus after he had been lost in Jerusalem for three days.

> So when they saw Him, they were amazed; and His mother said to Him, 'Son, why have you done this to us? Look, your father and I have sought you anxiously' (Luke 2:48).

These are different stories, of course, but the similar feelings shared by these two women represent their terrifically devoted duty and responsibility, full of great and unconditional love, care and concern.

Mary and Maddi in the dimension of faith

On the other hand, there is another dimension to be considered, namely, Mary and Maddi's roles from the dimension of faith. These two women share a similar attitude of being frightened, one by the power and grace of God (in the case of Mary) and the other by the great charity of the Bodhisattva Vessantara (in the case of Maddi). That is to say, although Mary is astonished at the information from the angel that she will conceive in her womb and bring forth a Son, she has absolute faith and confidence in God:

> for with God nothing will be impossible. And Mary said, 'Behold, I am the maidservant of the Lord' (Luke 1:37-38).

Maddi, too, eventually understands and appreciates what her husband has done; Vessantara's act shows the greatness of his giving (*dana*) or charity. Maddi does this despite losing her children:

> I do rejoice! There is a greater gift than children. By giving, set your mind at rest; pray do the like again: for you, the mighty fostering king of all the Sivi land, amidst a world of selfish men, gave gifts with lavish hand' (*Vessantara Jātaka* #547).

Both women cooperate and support the intention of God and Bodhisattva respectively.

What do Buddhists learn from Mary's life and mission?

First of all, we have learned that the law of interconnectedness is manifested everywhere, whether in Christianity or Buddhism. Both God and human beings, both a man and a woman, are more or less related and interdependent in many ways. Mary never resists the sovereignty of God. In reality, she responds to God and cooperates with God's plan in order that Jesus could fulfil his redemptive mission. Therefore, as Buddhists, we have no difficulty in considering Mary's role as 'co-operator in the redemption'. Without her, we will not realize clearly the nature of Jesus as the true human being. From the painting (Michaelangelo's *Madonna of the Steps*) showing the relationship between mother and child, we can affirm that Jesus Christ is a true human who needs love, care and nourishment from his mother. Although there is no such term as 'co-redemptrix' in the scripture, and we accept that Jesus is the 'all-sufficient saviour', we are also able to accept – and share a joyful appreciation for – the real action of Mary's role as ordinary woman and mother full of faith and ready to obey God's will. Using a Buddhist concept, we consider Mary from 'her moral behaviour and work'. We prefer, then, to evaluate the worth of her *kamma* as a sacrificing and forgetting and emptying of herself rather than to consider her status and gender. We would also like to admire her devotion and sacrifice; we recognize in her the Buddhist teaching on *mudita,* i.e., sympathetic joy, and we congratulate her on her great role for humanity without consideration of her female gender.

In other words, Mary is the representative of women who play a vital role in the creating of the world. Women contribute many good things to this world. Buddhists believe that 'she [a woman] is of indispensable utility, and because through her, Bodhisattvas and world-rulers take birth.' This is a great job of co-creation in a sense similar to that in Christianity. Again, in the Bible, we know that there is no such phrase as co-creator or co-redeemer in relation to Mary. We, in fact, consider her as a representative of women who join hand in hand with God. This reality should also reflect the preferably cooperative relationship between men and women in the present time. Nevertheless, this does not mean that Mary is competing with God and men, though, through her action, the nature and mission of Jesus who dies on the cross is clearly highlighted.

Up to this point, one may argue that the reason why we have to pay attention to Mary is because other women also may perform the similar roles of mother and faithful action. The reason that Mary is so special is due to her particular relationship to Jesus Christ, who is one among three in the Trinity. Pope John Paul II refers to St Louis de Montfort's writing about Mary. '…Mary's every intervention in the work of the re-generation of the faithful is not in competition with Christ, but derives from him and is at his service, Mary's action in the plan of salvation is always Christocentric, that is, it is directly related to a mediation that takes place in Christ'.[4] In other words, although Mary is the representative of devoted woman, she is also directly related to the Ultimate Reality that is beyond determination and beyond human capacity. This is the reason why she is not an ordinary but a special woman.

Clearly, Buddhists may need to have the dogma of Mary's Immaculate Conception and the dogma of the Assumption explained more to them, for these ideas are matters of faith. However, if Buddhists apply the Buddha's teaching of *mudita* as mentioned above and exercise sympathetic imagination concerning the inexplicable power of God, it may not be impossible for us to achieve some realization of the faith-based unusual events of Mary's life.

Above all, the great lesson we learn from Mary's life and remarkable role as the mother of the incarnate Word responding to God's will and plan of salvation is that of her proper attitude and performance towards women. We recognize the importance of Mary as co-redeemer not in an attempt to change Christian tradition or in order to become independent of it. Furthermore, such a recognition of Mary is not related to the charge of 'being an effort to divert attention' from the fact that Rome refuses to ordain

---

[4] See http://www.udayton.edu/mary/news00/20001110.html.

women to its priesthood. Though 'the Mary movement' reflects indirectly upon the natural law of the proper relationship between men and women, the same lesson should be applied to Buddhism as well. That is, Buddhists should realize and appreciate Maddi as the great supporter of the Bodhisattva's plan. With this realization and appreciation, then, we may go on formulating 'feminism' in accordance with Buddhist doctrines. We suggest calling it 'Buddhist Feminism of the Middle Path'.[5] This suggestion can also be applied to show how Buddhists look at the Virgin Mary. In addition, this 'Buddhist Feminism of the Middle Path', which could be considered as a norm for the proper attitudes between men and women in Buddhism, may be applied under the following aspects in order to understand the Christian context:

1. the realization of the interconnectedness (*paticcasamuppada*)[6] and mutual support of all things, including both men and women and even covering the close relationship between God and humankind. That is, for Christianity, God provides things for humanity and human beings in return obey and cooperate and join in stewardship with God.
2. the sympathetic appreciation (*mudita*)[7] for one who performs moral behaviour and good work without regarding gender or status. In this case Mary, who is a humble and selfless woman, cooperates with God's plan. She should, therefore, be accepted as 'co-redeemer'. The purpose of celebrating and expressing appreciation for Mary as 'co-operator in the redemption' is to glorify Jesus Christ, and certainly not from any ambition, say, to make her equal to the triune God.
3. mindfulness and wisdom (*panna*)[8] in translating the teaching into proper action. In order to propose anything, human beings will use wisdom, by the guidance of the Holy Spirit, to inspire their proper way of looking at the essence of the contribution of Mary. Expressions of loving Mary through Jesus Christ should always remind us of further proper and mindful actions.
4. loving-kindness (*metta*) and compassion (*karuna*)[9] to both men and women. God is so kind to both men and women. God chooses Mary to play the important role of mother to Jesus Christ. This event should cause everyone to reflectively include women in every possible religious dimension and should also prevent any discrimination toward women. This way of thinking should get much intention, especially in the present time.

In sum, the Buddhist view of Mary that is offered in this brief essay attempts to look at her from a Buddhist feminist perspective. This is scarcely to suggest an action plan or a concrete proposal to, for instance, support any papal proclamation of a dogma that would elevate Mary. In fact, I only attempt to adopt 'mindful awareness' and 'right

---

5 The 'Middle Path' is an important Buddhist notion which is derived from the experiment of the Buddha before he attained enlightenment. That is, both too extreme an involvement with indulgence and too extreme an exercise in mortification are not skilful actions in Buddhism; the Buddha points to a middle path, one between extremes. I propose this term to Buddhist feminism so that, in making a difference for the restoration of women's equal rights and justice, one is neither too aggressive nor too silent.
6 *Vibhanga* 135; see *The Book of Analysis (Vibhanga): The Second Book of the Abhidhamma Pitaka*, translated by Pathamakyaw Ashin Thittila (Setthila), Oxford, Pali Text Society, 1995: 180f.
7 *Dhammasangani* 260f.; see *A Buddhist Manual of Psychological Ethics* [*Dhamma-Sangani*], with Introductory Essay and Notes by Caroline A.F. Rhys Davids, Oxford, Pali Text Society, 1997: 62.
8 *Vibhanga* #324; *The Book of Analysis*: 423.
9 *Dhammasangani* 258f.; *A Buddhist Manual of Psychological Ethics*: 62.

understanding' of the roles of Mary as mother and in matters of faith. This will give us, I feel, good and important lessons for the proper relationship between men and women of the present time.

Thus, any official attempt to raise Mary's status is not as important as having the right attitudes toward Mary and toward women as a whole. For, the *right understanding* of Mary should belong to the *right view* about the doctrine of Jesus Christ's mission, that is, Jesus Christ 'empties himself and carries the cross for the welfare of others'. In learning about Mary's life, therefore, one should leave aside all attachment, discrimination and egoistic actions in order that we may imitate Jesus's self-emptying, as Mary did. Put another way, one should love, devote oneself to and serve others unconditionally.

This is only one voice, that of a Buddhist woman who looks at Mary's breast feeding of her child, and who then learns more about and finally speaks of that Mary, Mother of Jesus Christ, with sincere, respectful and joyful appreciation!

David Thomas
The Trinity in Christian-Muslim Relations

The central theme of the Qur'ān is the oneness of God. This is stated repeatedly and explored extensively throughout the sacred text, and it functions as the fundamental criterion for all judgements about the nature of the world and the history of God's relations with it in the ages before the appearance of the Qur'ān itself. In the first centuries of Islam this theme was elaborated and systematized into doctrinal formulations that defined God in terms of strict unity, and these provided means for evaluating all other representations of God's being and for rejecting those that differed from it. Inevitably, the Christian doctrine of a Trinitarian God came in for close scrutiny and inevitable rejection as a crass contravention of God's radical unity, and, in a long series of works by Muslim scholars, Christians were dismissed as retarded in logic and lacking in reason.

These early Muslim refutations of the Trinity set the tone for relations, and contributed to a sense of unease on the Muslim side that is often expressed as mystification about a belief that is palpably untenable. This, in turn, feeds into a denial that Christians have any firm grasp on the nature of God and God's relations with the world, and an attitude often of disdain towards stubborn deniers of the truth. The way ahead in relations between Muslims and Christians cannot, therefore, avoid the divide this difference has produced, if they are to be based on real respect and understanding. Followers of both faiths have a real duty to understand their perceptions about the being of God, and maybe to see where there is complementarity and insight from which they may both profit. And, in order to move forward, they both may learn, in lessons of the past, from instances of followers of the one faith exploring their beliefs to the other in ways the other might appreciate.

The Trinity in the Qur'ān

The single most concise statement of the teaching in the Qur'ān about the being of God is given in Chapter 112, the Chapter of Purity or Unity. Its brief four verses are addressed by God to the Prophet Muḥammad:

> Say: He is God, the One!
> God, the self-sufficient!
> He does not beget and was not begotten.
> And there is none comparable to him.

Whatever the first context of these words (some commentators hold they were directed at the beliefs of the Prophet's polytheistic fellow-Meccans that the goddesses of their cult were daughters of God), they obviously rule out any organic relationship between God and another being, and so refute the Christian claim that God has a Son. Hence, the Qur'ān characteristically refers to Jesus as son of Mary rather than Son of God, denies that he is any more than a human, and portrays him as openly saying that he never claimed to be any more than human.

In addition to this, the Qur'ān makes three allusive references to what appear to be belief in three combined divinities:

> Certainly they disbelieve who say: God is the third of three (*thālith thalātha*), for there is no god except one God; (Q 5:73)
>
> And behold! God will say: 'O Jesus, son of Mary! Did you say to men, "Take me and my mother for two gods beside God?"' He will say: 'Glory to you! Never could I say what I had no right.' (Q 5:116)
>
> O People of the Book! Commit no excesses in your religion: nor say of God anything but the truth. Christ Jesus the son of Mary was only God's messenger and his word which he bestowed on Mary, and a spirit from him. So believe in God and his messengers and do not say, 'Three' (*thalātha*); desist, it will be better for you. For God is one God, far removed is his glory from having a son. (Q 4:171)

These verses make definite allusions to associations between Jesus, Mary and God, and are evidently addressed to Christians (who together with Jews and some other pre-Islamic communities are often called People of the Book). Although their precise complaints may not be against the doctrine of the Trinity itself, but rather the divinization of Jesus as 'third of three' or a 'god beside God' or anything more than God's human messenger,[1] they were unanimously understood in the classical Islamic period as rejections of this Christian belief, and also as divinely authored rejections of the structure of the Godhead as a composite of three distinct entities. Hence, in the Arabic-speaking circles where Muslims and Christians met in the Islamic imperial era, the doctrine was commonly referred to as *tathlīth*, literally 'affirming three' (from *thalātha*, the Arabic for the number 3), in direct contradiction to the Islamic principle of *tawḥīd*, 'affirming one' (from *wāḥid*, the number 1), which summed up all that Muslims believed about the absolute unity of God. Muslim religious thinkers thus accepted what they saw as a divine warrant to take the Christian claim as a contradiction of their own doctrine and to demonstrate its errors by showing it was internally inconsistent as well as irreconcilable with reason.

Muslim-Christian Discussions in Early Islam

One of the major points of debate among Muslim theologians in the formative centuries of Islam was the nature of God in Godself. Proceeding from the clear teachings of the Qur'ān, they asserted uncompromisingly that God was one, but they were also confronted with the demand of having to characterize God in some way. This arose both from the many epithets used of God in the Qur'ān as omnipotent, omniscient, all-hearing, all-seeing, self-subsistent, and so on, and also from the logical necessity that arose from detecting divine activity in creation to say God must be living, knowing, capable, and so on. And disagreements between specialists developed at an early stage.[2]

According to the agreed epistemological principles of the time, the qualities which a being demonstrated in action derived from attributes that were part of the being and

---

[1] For a discussion of these verses and interpretations given to them, see Jane Dammen McAuliffe (ed.), *The Encyclopaedia of the Qur'ān*, volume V, Leiden, Brill, 2006: article, 'Trinity'.

[2] For a fuller discussion on this, see David Thomas, 'The Doctrine of the Trinity in the Early 'Abbasid Era', in L. Ridgeon (ed.), *Islamic Interpretations of Christianity*, London, Curzon, 2001: 78-98. Michael Ipgrave, in his *Trinity and Inter Faith Dialogue, Plenitude and Plurality*, number 14 in Religions and Discourse series, Bern, Peter Lang, 2003: 196-291, provides an illuminating survey of early Muslim and Christian Arab conceptualizations of Godhead, arriving at a less optimistic estimation of the possibilities for joint exploration than is advanced in this article.

were actual in existence. Thus, a man showed he was wise because he possessed an attribute of wisdom as a real determinant within his being, or a woman showed she was seeing because she possessed an attribute of sight as an identifiable, and therefore discrete, determinant within her being. Since qualities such as living, speaking, being wise and seeing came and went, the attributes which gave rise to these in humans were agreed to come into existence and cease to exist, or to be accidental. Thus, the structure of the created being was an essence (in itself composite since it was made up of fundamental material particles) characterized by accidental attributes that were superadded to it for longer or shorter periods of time, but that eventually ceased and thereby deprived the being of the qualities to which they gave rise.

By the same logic, God's qualities were also identifiable in addition to God's essence itself. Ye, here a serious problem arose. For if divine qualities derived from attributes that were superadded to the divine essence, the strict unity of God's being was called into question. But, if the individual qualities had no origin in really existent attributes, then it was impossible to speak about the character of God in any sense that related to God's being itself. It was a matter either of asserting God's strict unity and saying nothing accurate about God's character, or of asserting that God was in reality endowed with certain attributes from which the qualities of God's being and action arose and of accepting the existence of a number of eternal entities in addition to God's being.

The debates over the problems raised by the attributes of God raged with particular vehemence in the 9th century, when the 'Abbasid dynasty was at the height of its power. On the one side were ranged the rationalist Mu'tazilī theologians who called themselves the People of Divine Unity (*Ahl al-tawḥīd*). They insisted upon the radical oneness of God and therefore denied the existence of real attributes. Thus, when one of their leading thinkers was asked what it meant to state that God was knowing, he replied that this meant God was not ignorant, and also that the very being of God was the origin of this quality. However, the lack of precision in this reply, according to the accepted norms, enabled opponents to point to a confusion because, following what this Mu'tazilī said, God's being alone must be the source of all the divine different qualities of knowing, seeing, hearing, and so on. There was no differentiation and there could therefore be no guarantee that God possessed these qualities in any real sense.

On the other side, more traditional thinkers asserted that God's qualities derived from really existent attributes that could be identified in addition to God's being itself. This enabled them to solve the difficulty of characterizing God, and to overcome the agnosticism about God's being that the rationalist Mu'tazila were forced to accept. However, these traditionalists were faced with an equally frustrating difficulty of having to find a way of maintaining God's unity in the face of the multiple eternal attributes that were added to God's being. One of their leaders, when asked about these attributes, said: they are neither God nor other than God. By this he sought to say that they were both identifiable as discrete entities and integral to God's being. Yet here, too, there was some imprecision as these thinkers were compelled to accept that the unity of God was relative.

These differences of view, and the difficulties that were involved in them, resulted from the agreed understanding of how the qualities of beings were identified. God's qualities, like those of creatures, were seen as arising from attributes, although God uniquely possessed eternal, unchanging attributes whereas those of creatures came and went.

The debates between the opposing Muslim views were at their fiercest, it seems, at the same time as Christians living under Islamic rule began to express their teachings in

Arabic and according to the logical rules observed by their Muslim counterparts. And these Christians understandably adapted this attributes-thinking to their own use, as they attempted to explain the doctrine of the Trinity to a sceptical Muslim audience.

One Diophysite theologian, 'Ammār al-Baṣrī, about whom next to nothing is known except that he probably lived at the same time as some of the leading Muslim representatives of the opposing views and that he left behind two extant works, clearly felt completely at home with the structures within which Muslims expressed their doctrines.[3] For, he provocatively argued, the Mu'tazilī position was both untenable, since it implied that, because God could not possess the attributes of life, knowledge and power, God must be dead, ignorant and impotent, and, finally, resulted in a serious impoverishment that forbade any statement about God except that God was. More constructively, he suggested that God, in order to be God, must as a minimum be living and knowing (in other words, be existent and rational in God's being). Thus, God must have life and knowledge as constituent parts of God's being and, moreover, as essential attributes to God's divinity. Furthermore, the attribute of life could be identified as the Holy Spirit, and that of knowledge as the Word of God or the Son, and so it could be proved that God was the Being itself, or Father, the Son and the Holy Spirit. Thus, 'Ammār was able to demonstrate to his own satisfaction that this central Christian doctrine could be expressed in terms set by his Muslim contemporaries.

Evidently, this was thought to be the case by these Muslims. For, as far as can be told from the incomplete information that has survived, 'Ammār and other Christians who thought like him were put under pressure to explain why only the two attributes of Life and Knowledge had this special status of being integral to God's being and constitutive of it. Muslims argued that by the same token the attribute of power could also be accorded the same status, or any other necessary attribute, to make the Godhead a quaternity or quinity rather than a Trinity. Christians continued to maintain that these two attributes alone were fundamental to God's being and that other attributes arose from these, and so the argument continued as theologians on each side were forced to find further proofs to support their case.

The important point in these abstract exchanges is that Muslims and Christians were arguing in more or less the same terms and according to a common theological method. Thus, while exchanges were usually inimical they were usually meaningful because understanding was possible.

A Reformulation of the Trinity in Muslim Terms

About a century after these first theological exchanges, a development is seen that shows Christians had gone even further in their efforts to explain their doctrine to a Muslim audience and to express it for themselves in the terminology of the prevailing shared ethos. Even less is known about these Christians than about 'Ammār al-Baṣrī because their contribution is referred to only in passing. Clearly, though, they irked the Muslim whom they taxed with their views, and spurred him to make a forceful, if not entirely convincing, response.

---

3 See Sidney Griffith, 'The Concept of *al-Uqnūm* in 'Ammār al-Baṣrī's Apology for the Doctrine of the Trinity', in Khalil Samir (ed.), *Actes du premier congrès international d'études arabes chrétiennes (Goslar, Septembre 1980)*, Rome, Pontificium Institutum Studiorum Orientalium, 1982: 169-91.

As the doctrine of the Trinity became familiar to Arabic-speakers, it was often expressed in terms that did not fit altogether easily in the new language, leading to frequent difficulties in understanding what was being said. The word 'substance' was normally expressed by the Persian loan-word *jawhar*, which also meant 'jewel', and so could lend itself to the concept of the essence of the Divinity. The term 'hypostasis', however, proved very difficult to transfer, and after some variations in terminology the word *uqnūm* was settled on, as a transliteration from the Syriac. This maybe shows how difficult Muslims, and also Arabic-speaking Christians, found it to understand.

However, experiments in terminology were frequently attempted in order to find a suitable equivalent for 'hypostasis'. Already at the start of the 9th century, 'Ammār al-Baṣrī was employing *ṣifa*, 'attribute', directly from the Muslim context, and at about the same time Theodore Abū Qurra, a Chalcedonian Christian, coined the term *wajh*, 'face' or 'aspect', presumably as a representation of the Greek *prosōpon*. The problem was that each of these carried a clear connotation in the Muslim context, and Muslim polemicists made easy work of showing that such translations of language introduced radical changes of meaning to the original concept.

Then, in the mid-10th century, the Muslim theologian Abū Bakr al-Bāqillānī noted that this group of unknown Christians had tried to compare their doctrine of the Trinity with his own doctrine of the being of God and the attributes. He himself was a follower of teachers who belonged to the opponents of the rationalist Mu'tazilī theologians a century earlier, and he accepted the reality of the attributes as real determinants within God's being of the qualities that were demonstrated in God's actions. So, he accepted the difficult definition of them as 'neither God nor other than God' that had been employed at the time, giving his own definition of an attribute as 'the thing that exists on the being described or belongs to it'.[4] It would, therefore, seem to follow that he might allow a doctrinal formulation of entities in the Godhead that could be formally identified separately from one another and from the being of God, but which were still identical with the Godhead.

This is what the Christians that al-Bāqillānī refers to attempt to impress upon him, suggesting that just as the divine attributes in his teaching are understood as neither different from the being of God nor identical with it, so the hypostases can be understood in the same way. Here they take the step of not just defining the hypostases of the Trinitarian Godhead as attributes, but also of conceptualizing them in terms of the Muslim belief in the strictly unified God being endowed with logically identifiable attributes.

The distinction, if any, between the two positions of these Christians and the Muslim appears to be minimal following the Christians' reformulation of their doctrine, in which they appear to suggest that just as God acts, for example, in a wise way because, possessing the attribute of wisdom as a determinant of divine being, according to Muslim teachings, God acts in ways that can be figuratively summed up through the Son-like activities of Christ, according to Christian teachings.

Al-Bāqillānī, for his own part, reacts with arguments that suggest he has been disconcerted. Like many Muslims of his time, he portrayed the Trinity as a composite of four entities, the divine substance and the three Persons. In this way he could force the Christians to accept that there were a number of separate divine entities in their doctrine, and require them to explain why they could act individually, when, for example, the Son

---

4 M. Allard, *Le problème des attributes divins dans la doctrine de al-Aš'arī et de ses premiers grands disciples*, Beirut, Imprimerie Catholique, 1965: 304.

alone united with the human nature of Christ in the Incarnation. Likewise, he insists here that the Christians must admit that the hypostases are either distinct from the being of God or are identical with it; there can be no half measures. Maybe he does not appreciate the step the Christians have taken towards his own Muslim position, or maybe he has appreciated it all too well and seen the potential embarrassment in realizing that there may be a way forward to agreement.

It is possible that al-Bāqillānī was so firmly rooted in the Qur'ān-based assumption that the Christian doctrine implies a triple nature in God that he was not open to the new developments presented by these unknown Christians who at least appeared to find a natural means of expressing their doctrine in the attributes theory of current Muslim debates. If so, his recalcitrance, which appears to stem from unease more than anything else, masks a reluctance to be open to possibilities that may not have been apparent earlier. For, the Christians may well have moved in their own thinking from a position of explaining the three Persons of the Godhead as entities with discrete identities, as all representations by Muslim authors made them, to the less clearly identifiable status of attributes, and thus removed the obstacle of plurality within the Godhead. Obviously, the continuing problem of prioritization remained to be solved, and, until the Christians could explain why they gave higher status to just two attributes rather than the seven or more that Muslims listed, objections to the doctrine would not cease. Nontheless, they would be of a different kind from the serious difficulty of a plurality of divine entities.

Jointly Exploring the Being of God

The exchange between the 10th century al-Bāqillānī and the Christians who are otherwise unknown is too brief to permit much elaboration. It does indicate, though, that religious specialists of different faiths who spoke and thought in the same language could begin to converge in their explanations of theological issues. It also indicates that doctrinal articulations continued to evolve to meet new requirements, and that they needed to evolve to be more comprehensible, not only to those outside but also to those inside whose frameworks of understanding were not those of earlier fashioners of the doctrine (Cappadocia is a long way from Baghdad, one might say). Al-Bāqillānī's evident reluctance to accommodate the change points in turn to the demanding need not to be bound by fixed interpretations of the authoritative sources, but to revise the readings of these as new possibilities arise.

The debates about the attributes of God that set Muslims against one another in Baghdad in the 9th century and after were at base about the sheer possibility of human language being able to encapsulate the infinite to any degree that was meaningful. The rationalist Muʿtazila said this could not be without compromising the absolute unity of God, and so accepted an agnostic position in which they were unable to go beyond positing the existence of God. Yet, Muslims who disagreed with them, to whom later scholars such as al-Bāqillānī looked back, insisted that it was possible to describe God in terms that corresponded to the divine being, and even though these terms could not define God's reality in its entirety they did point in a direction that eventually met with the reality of God.

To Christian theologians such differences and theological outlines would have been familiar from their own debates about the nature of the Trinitarian Godhead: was it, for example, Trinitarian in its transcendent reality or only so in the ways in which it appeared to act within the created sphere? And they remain so, as Christians try to understand the nature of Divinity as it has been given to them in their sacred texts and traditions, and match that understanding with the demands of changed language and conceptuality.

For Muslims, the dogma of the oneness of God is balanced by the belief in the divine names and attributes. It is universally accepted by Muslims that God has ninety-nine names, and in theological treatises the attributes remain subjects of comprehension. The problem is, what status do God's names have, and how accurate are the designated attributes of God's being? If they are only names and no more, being human descriptions that have no correspondence with the being of God, then it has to be admitted that, written into the nature of contingent existence, is an inability to conceive of and speak about transcendent reality. Consequently, this means both that human rationality is incapable of conceiving the Divine in any way, and, just as seriously, that the Qur'ān itself, which refers to God by manifold names, does not give an accurate depiction and so fails as a channel between the finite and the infinite, the creature and the Creator.

Looked at in this way, doctrinal specialists in the two faiths are faced with surprisingly similar challenges. From this it might follow that they have considerable insights to share and many difficulties to solve together in an area that is by definition abstruse. One might note some considerable headway made towards, if not in, cooperation in the Archbishop of Canterbury, Dr Rowan Williams's lecture at Al-Azhar University, Cairo, in 2004, before some of the foremost scholars of the Sunni world.[5] There, he spoke directly about the Christian doctrine of the Trinity, and attempted to describe it in terms that might be universally appreciable:

> God is a loving God, as we all agree; but, says the Christian, God does not love simply because he decides to love. He is always, eternally, loving. His very nature, his definition is love. And the interaction and relation between the three ways in which God lives, the source and the expression and the sharing, is eternally the way God exists. The three centres of divine action, which we call Father, Son and Spirit, pour out the divine life to each other for all eternity, a sort of perfect circle of giving and receiving. And the only word we can use for that relationship of pouring out and giving is love. So as we grow in holiness, we become closer and closer in our actions and thoughts to the complete self-giving that always exists perfectly in God's life. Towards this fullness we are all called to travel and grow.

This is obviously different from the formulations of Arabic-speaking Muslims and the Christians who learned from them a thousand years ago. However, it speaks of the same possibility of crossing of the barriers between faith traditions in order to encourage mutual searching and enrichment.

The pre-condition of this is, obviously, an abandonment of old attitudes. Christians who ever found anything good to say about Islam found its doctrine of God impoverished: the Diophysite 'Ammār al-Baṣrī more or less said so to his 9th century interlocutors, and others who detected a place in God's plan for the Prophet Muḥammad portrayed his proclamations as a superficial form of theism intended to prepare the pagan Arabs for its full development in their own Christian Trinitarian expression. Even more so, Muslims have unanimously read references in the Qur'ān as denouncements of the doctrine of the Trinity in whatever form it has been expressed; hence, al-Bāqillānī's refusal to see anything positive in the reformulations he received from his Christian correspondents, and the steadfast Muslim refusal to acknowledge that all mainstream Christian perceptions of God affirm divine oneness, as the Nicene Creed maintains.

---

5 http://www.archbishopofcanterbury.org/sermons_speeches/2004/040911.html.

Behind the polemical stances of both Christians and Muslims are difficulties that both traditions have, at various times, attempted to express in strikingly similar ways, and have tried to solve with complementary doctrines. Differences are undeniably to be found, not least the Christian awareness that God is and acts according to three paramount truths, and the Muslim awareness that the many divine qualities that can be named dissolve eventually into God's supreme oneness. These must be respected. Nevertheless, if they are understood as matching parallels to the challenge of how humans can arrive at reliable appraisals of a transcendent mystery, Muslims and Christians might come to discover the vast resources they could derive from one another and the unnerving similarities their two traditions contain.

Abraham Vélez de Cea
Interreligious Dialogue through Comparative Studies

This article is divided into two parts. In the first part, there are three sections. I begin, in the first section, with an explanation of my understanding of interreligious dialogue as three different kinds of activities. From this I move to a description of the goals of these three activities. I conclude this part with an exploration of five specific ways in which the comparative scholar might contribute to interreligious dialogue. In the second part, I examine the nature of comparative studies and propose one way of making comparisons in order to promote interreligious dialogue.

1. Interreligious dialogue, its goals, and the role of the comparative scholar

There are many views of the nature and purpose of interreligious dialogue.[1] Here, interreligious dialogue is understood as three different kinds of activities. The first kind of activity is the social praxis of dialogue with members of other religions. This social interreligious dialogue can be mediated or unmediated.

If the dialogue is facilitated by someone – and is usually between experts or members from at least two religious communities – then we speak of mediated social dialogue. Mediated social dialogue can take place in many settings: usually, formal settings including monasteries, churches, community centres, colleges, and universities. Examples of mediated social dialogue are interfaith meetings, monastic exchanges, panels and roundtables with representatives of several religions. These mediated encounters can occur at different levels: local, regional, national, and international.

Unmediated social dialogue happens virtually anywhere, in the aforementioned formal settings as well as in less formal settings such as hotels, restaurants, bars, private houses, and even streets corners. Social interreligious dialogue should not be the monopoly of any elite, whether religious leaders or representatives of religious communities. All global citizens, especially those who live in pluralistic societies, have the responsibility to participate in both mediated and unmediated social interreligious dialogue. Any social gathering that involves persons from at least two religions constitutes a possible occasion for practicing social interrcligious dialogue. I am not suggesting, however, that whenever two persons from different religious traditions meet they should practice interreligious dialogue; rather I hold that any interreligious encounter offers the possibility for social interreligious dialogue.

The second kind of activity that I consider a form of interreligious dialogue occurs within a person after having encountered other religious traditions. Following Raimon Panikkar,[2] I call this inner dialogue *intra-religious* dialogue, which should not be confused with intra-denominational dialogue. While intra-religious dialogue takes place within a person as a response to other religions, intra-denominational dialogue takes place among members of the same religious community, denomination, or religion.

---

1 See Chester Gillis, 'Christian Approaches to Inter-religious Dialogue', in *Louvain Studies* 22 (1997): 15-38.
2 Raimon Panikkar, *The Intrareligious Dialogue*, New York and Mahwah NJ, Paulist, 1999[rev. ed.].

Intra-religious dialogue in Panikkar's sense can be the consequence of social dialogue or the result of exposure to other religions. Such an exposure can be direct (when it involves a face to face encounter with members of other religions), or indirect (when it is based on virtual encounters such as reading, watching documentaries, taking courses on world religions).

The third kind of activity that constitutes interreligious dialogue is academic in nature. It involves a conversation between texts from at least two religious traditions, a conversation constructed by scholars competent in those texts. Academic interreligious dialogue is a particular type of comparative study. However, what distinguishes academic interreligious dialogue from other types of comparative studies is that the textual conversation (comparison) presupposes the praxis of both social and intra-religious dialogue. In this sense, academic interreligious dialogue is inseparable from the other two types of interreligious dialogue (social and intra-religious). Another distinction between academic interreligious dialogue and other types of comparative studies is that the textual conversation or comparison is intended to foster interreligious dialogue and its goals. (I will elaborate later on what kind of comparative study can better foster interreligious dialogue.) Let us first examine the goals of interreligious dialogue.

The purpose of interreligious dialogue is to achieve a variety of goals. These goals can be grouped into three broad categories: hermeneutical, practical, and intrapersonal. The hermeneutical goal of interreligious dialogue is essentially to facilitate mutual knowledge and understanding. Mutual knowledge and understanding is the foundation of all subsequent goals of interreligious dialogue. The practical goals of interreligious dialogue are many but I would like to highlight three: the peaceful coexistence of religious communities, solidarity in times of natural disaster or political crisis, and interfaith projects to advance eco-human wellbeing. These practical goals, as John D'Arcy May points out, require and should not be separated from the ethical and religious actions of 'acknowledging the Other in his or her integrity despite, even because of differences; to welcome the Stranger, especially the persecuted, the poor and the religiously alien; and – most difficult of all – to reconcile the Enemy, whatever the cost.'[3]

Besides the aforementioned practical goals, interreligious dialogue may also be practiced to achieve intrapersonal goals; and intrapersonal goals are primarily self-illumination and enrichment. By self-illumination I mean that dialogue with other religions sheds new light on the way we perceive ourselves and our religious traditions. We perceive either new things or old things in new ways. Furthermore, dialogue with the religious other helps us to understand ourselves and our own tradition better. Sometimes, we realize who we are and where we stand after comparing our traditions to those of others. By enrichment I mean that dialogue with other religions is transformative and makes us grow. Such transformation and growth can take place at different levels: intellectual, ethical, and spiritual.

Related to these basic goals of interreligious dialogue, there are many other goals that can be considered preliminary. For instance, in order to achieve the basic hermeneutical end of mutual knowledge and understanding, it is necessary to first counteract stereotypes and misperceptions of other religions. Similarly, before reaching the practical goal of peaceful co-existence and co-operation among religions, one needs first

---

[3] John D'Arcy May, 'Interreligious Dialogue and the End of Ecumenism', in David W. Chappell (ed.), *Socially Engaged Spirituality: Essays in Honor of Sulak Sivaraksa on His 70th Birthday*, Bangkok, Sathirakoses-Nagapradipa Foundation, 2003: 476-485: 484.

to reconcile divided communities and mitigate the effects of extremist views that encourage violence and hatred in the name of religion. Finally, and before we can reach the point where people can actually grow from the contribution of other religions, we need to first undermine those theological claims that hinder genuine openness toward other religions. In other words, before speaking about personal transformation with the help of other religions, we need first to challenge naïve claims of superiority. By naïve claims of superiority I mean claims of exclusive or absolute truth and complete/last/only revelation that ignore the existence of similar claims in other religions, and that overlook the historical context and the psychological factors behind the claims themselves.

The rejection of naïve claims, however, does not entail that all religious claims are relative and equally valid. Relativism is not the only alternative to naïve claims of superiority. The dilemma of either absolutism or relativism is fallacious; it is based on ignorance of contemporary theologies of religions. Between naïve absolutism and equally naïve relativism there are many possible options.[4] Both naïve claims of superiority and naïve claims of relativism are counterproductive for interreligious dialogue. However, naïve claims of superiority are much more dangerous; in fact, they are not substantially different from militant or extremist views conducive to hatred, violence, and terrorism in the name of religion. As Paul Knitter puts it: '[i]f religious people come together for peacemaking dialogue but retain their claims of religious superiority (even if only in their minds and hearts), they are no different, in their fundamental religious convictions, from the militant religious people who refuse such dialogue.'[5] In the long term, claims of superiority are conducive not to interreligious dialogue but, rather, to religious isolationism, involution, and the eventual solidification of traditions.

There is a correlation between the three types of interreligious dialogue (academic, social, and intra-religious) and the goals of interreligious dialogue (hermeneutical, practical, and intrapersonal). Academic dialogue through comparative studies can contribute to the achievement of both practical and intrapersonal goals but they primarily help to produce the hermeneutical goal of mutual knowledge and understanding. Although the praxis of social dialogue may also improve our understanding of other religions, and can be very enriching, the primary goals of social dialogue are practical in nature. Similarly, self-illumination and enrichment at the intellectual, ethical and spiritual levels may result from social and academic interreligious dialogue; however, they are primarily derived from intra-religious dialogue. Likewise, although intra-religious dialogue can have social repercussions and be helpful in better understanding ourselves and others, the goals of this type of dialogue are primarily intrapersonal. For instance, by studying the sacred texts of other traditions one can discover concepts and doctrines useful for thinking in different ways about one's own tradition. Likewise, the example of Gandhi and his ethical practice of non-violence can inspire the social activism of other religious traditions (for instance, Martin Luther King). Also, thanks to Buddhist and Hindu meditation, Jews and Christians can either rediscover their own contemplative traditions or supplement their personal spiritual practice.

Having clarified what I mean by interreligious dialogue and its goals, let us now discuss specific ways in which the comparative scholar can contribute to interreligious dialogue. First, by creating artificial dialogues between texts and thinkers of two

---

4 Paul F. Knitter, *Introducing Theologies of Religions*, Maryknoll, Orbis, 2003.
5 Paul F. Knitter, *The Myth of Religious Superiority: A Multifaith Exploration*, Maryknoll, Orbis, 2005: ix.

religious traditions, the comparative scholar provides a useful foundation for the actual praxis of social dialogue between representatives and members of those traditions.

The praxis of social interreligious dialogue can take place without having enough knowledge about the other, but then the risk of misunderstanding, conflict and unnecessary tension increases. The praxis of social interreligious dialogue becomes more fruitful when it presupposes some familiarity not only with the basic beliefs but also with the fundamental ethical values and spiritual practices of the other. Academic interreligious dialogue provides information about these beliefs, values, and practices of the other, and in that way, they serve as a preparation for the actual praxis of social interreligious dialogue.

Second, comparative scholars can help to identify similar or at least compatible ethical and spiritual values and ideals across religious traditions. Once the comparative scholar identifies common or compatible ethical and spiritual resources, religious communities will be in a better position to articulate practical strategies to advance eco-human wellbeing. This identification of common and/or compatible ethical and spiritual resources can also contribute to the creation of new practical projects such as Global Ethics, and the movement for Human Rights. These ethical initiatives can be fruitful as long as they do not neglect differences among traditions, and do not subtly impose the ethical values of a particular culture or religion upon others.

The work of comparative scholars can also help to increase awareness of the richness and diversity of ethical and spiritual teachings of religions. The sum of ethical and spiritual teachings of different religions is much more than diverse formulations of the golden rule and lists of common directives, principles and guidelines. Scholars should challenge attempts to reduce the ethical and spiritual contribution of religions to only universal codes of conduct and declarations. There is much more in religions than ethical minimums acceptable by all religious traditions. Precisely because the ethical and spiritual teachings of religions are irreducible to any ethical common denominator applicable in all cases and under all circumstances, the comparative scholar should focus not only on what is common and/or compatible, but also on what makes every religion different and unique.

This leads me to the third way in which the comparative scholar can contribute to achieve the goals of interreligious dialogue. By focusing on what is different and unique to every tradition, comparative scholars can help to identify concepts, doctrines, and practices in one particular tradition that are incompatible and even unacceptable for another tradition. The discovery of incompatible elements in other traditions does not have to undermine respect and appreciation of each other or, even less, prevent interreligious dialogue. On the contrary, the discovery of such incompatibilities assists us in knowing better ourselves, our beliefs and where we stand in a variety of matters. In this sense, comparisons of incompatible elements can promote self-illumination and be extremely enriching at the intellectual, moral and spiritual levels.

The fourth way in which comparative scholars can contribute to the cause of interreligious dialogue is through constructive reformulations of one's own religious tradition with concepts, doctrines, and insights taken from other religions. These constructive reformulations are the consequence of intra-religious dialogue or dialogue within oneself after having encountered members, doctrines or practices from other religions. These constructive reformulations might lead to further intra-religious dialogue among members of one's own religious community, as well as to further interreligious dialogue with members of other traditions.

Finally, the fifth way in which comparative scholars may contribute to interreligious dialogue is through their research and teaching practices. The comparative scholar – at least those engaged in academic interreligious dialogue – should practice social interreligious dialogue during the research process. This praxis of dialogue with members of other religions makes the comparative scholar an agent as well as a facilitator of social interreligious dialogue. Similarly, comparative scholars can promote social interreligious dialogue through teaching by inviting members of other religions into their classes, by facilitating interreligious dialogue among students from different religions, and at the very least by provoking intra-religious dialogue in their students. Teaching other religions should not be just a question of providing reliable information. Besides providing information, the lecturer of world religions should encourage students to think critically about the big questions of theology and philosophy. By encouraging critical thinking, I do not mean that the lecturer should try to persuade students to adopt a secular perspective, much less scientism or positivism. Rather, I mean that the lecturer of world religions should help students to discern between dogmatic and historical-critical views of religions.

2. Comparative studies and academic interreligious dialogue

There are many different understandings of comparison and comparative studies.[6] Here I understand the expression 'comparative studies' in a broad sense, as the interdisciplinary and comparative study of religions from both secular and theological perspectives. The radical separation between religious studies and theology, between secular and theological approaches to the study of religion, is in my view unacceptable. It is naïve to think that religious scholars study religions from a neutral and objective vantage point, while theologians do the same from a biased perspective. Following Gadamer I consider all interpretations as historically and culturally situated, i.e., no interpretation is free from prejudices and a particular horizon of understanding.[7]

What demarcates the scholarly study of religion from religious propaganda is the application of historical-critical methods and awareness of one's own hermeneutical assumptions. Whether the scholar belongs to a particular denomination or sympathizes with secular ideals is not relevant in judging the academic quality of a comparative study. What matters are the historical-critical methods used, and whether the scholar is self-conscious of her or his hermeneutical location.

Some theologians and religious scholars claim that we always understand by means of comparisons: therefore, according to them, all academic disciplines dealing with the religious other are to some extent comparative. This may be true, but then the expression 'comparative studies' becomes too broad to be meaningful. Unless we want to apply the term 'comparative' to any study somehow discussing other religions, it seems necessary to narrow down what we mean by 'comparative studies'.

A study should not be considered comparative simply because it contains concepts, doctrines and/or practices from at least two religious traditions. Simply describing a concept, doctrine or practice from a particular religion followed by an analysis of a similar concept, doctrine or practice from a different religion does not constitute a comparative

---

6 See, for instance, Kimberley C. Patton and Benjamin C. Ray, (eds.), *A Magic Still Dwells*, Berkeley, University of California, 2000.
7 Hans-Georg Gadamer, *Truth and Method*, London and New York, Continuum, 2004 [1975].

study. If this were the nature of comparative studies, then they would be redundant and replaceable by particular area studies, one for each religion.

In order to deserve the term 'comparative', a study must contain explicit and substantial comparisons. By explicit comparisons, I mean an analysis that includes a discussion of both similarities and differences between the concepts, doctrines, or practices of at least two religions. As William E. Paden puts it in his description of what he calls 'New Comparativism', comparisons 'should be a bilateral, two-way process that reveals both similarities and differences'.[8] By substantial comparisons, I mean comparisons indispensable to understand central claims of a particular study, or comparisons that help to illustrate those central claims. If comparisons are marginal or merely supplementary, then the study does not qualify as comparative. In sum, what characterizes comparative studies is the existence of explicit and substantial comparisons across religions and cultures, comparisons that emphasize similarities as well as differences, not just similarities or differences.

The academic practice of comparison needs to be distinguished from other academic practices. Specifically, the academic practice of comparison should not be confused with constructive efforts and normative considerations. Constructive and normative discussions may or may not follow explicit and substantial comparisons. That is, constructive and normative discussions do not define comparative studies, though they are likely to appear in those studies, usually after explicit and substantial comparisons. In other words, we can have comparative studies without constructive and normative discussions, but we cannot speak of comparative studies without the existence of explicit and substantial comparisons.

A constructive discussion of a topic with concepts, categories, or doctrines taken from several religions does not constitute a comparative study. Similarly, the normative posing of philosophical, theological, and ethical questions to materials taken from different religions does not make a study comparative. Mark Siderits has coined the expression 'fusion philosophy' to refer to the normative discussion of a philosophical problem with concepts and doctrines taken from different philosophical traditions.[9] For instance, Siderits tries to solve the problems of free will and of personal identity with concepts and doctrines taken from analytical and Buddhist traditions of philosophy.

Perhaps it would be a good idea to apply the term 'fusion' instead of the term 'comparative' to similar academic practices common in the fields of comparative theology and comparative religious ethics. If this usage of the term 'fusion' is accepted, then a new interpretation of the meaning of Christ inspired by Buddhist ideas, or a new reading of a Christian text inspired by a particular Hindu theology, would not be instances of comparative theology but rather examples of fusion theology.

Similarly, a normative discussion of human rights or specific virtues across religions, or the construction of a global ethics with elements from different religions would not be considered exercises in comparative religious ethics but rather instances of fusion religious ethics. Unless these constructive and normative efforts contain explicit and substantial comparisons, they do not constitute a comparative study. What defines comparative studies is the presence of explicit and substantial comparisons, not constructive and normative discussions based on comparison.

---

8 William E. Paden, 'Elements of a New Comparativism', in Patton and Ray, *A Magic Still Dwells*: 182-192: 184.
9 Mark Siderits, *Personal Identity and Buddhist Philosophy*, Aldershot, Ashgate, 2003.

Scholars who agree with Francis Clooney's definition of comparative theology will probably claim that normative and/or constructive theological discussions also define comparative theology, and by extension comparative studies. According to Clooney, comparative theology has three basic meanings: the actual comparison of theologies, the posing of theological questions in comparative settings, and the doing of Constructive Theology from and after comparison.[10] Clooney takes the first two meanings from David Tracy,[11] and proposes the third meaning previously developed in his book *Theology after Vedānta: An Experiment in Comparative Theology*.[12]

However, it is my contention that only the explicit and substantial comparison of theologies should define comparative theology. The other two academic practices, that is, the normative posing of theological questions in interreligious discussions, and doing constructive theology from and after comparison, may supplement comparative studies of theology but they do not define them.

There are two main reasons for restricting the expression 'comparative theology' to studies that contain explicit and substantial comparisons. First, in the era of globalization and religious pluralism, most theological studies are bound to pose normative questions after taking into account the existence of other religions. And if theology arising from and after this comparison with other religions deserves the term 'comparative', then the expression 'comparative theology' becomes too general and even unnecessary. Second, if what defines comparative theology is the posing of theological questions in interreligious discussions and the doing of constructive theology from and after comparison, then one has to conclude that theologians like St Augustine and St Thomas Aquinas were also doing comparative theology. Did not Augustine pose theological questions from and after comparison with different religious and philosophical traditions of his time? And did not Aquinas do constructive theology from and after the comparison between Aristotle and Christian sources? Yet, no one would consider the work of these two classical theologians an example of comparative theology. If one concludes that both Augustine and Aquinas were doing comparative theology, does it not follow, then, that most contemporary theologians do comparative theology as well, at least those theologians who have some familiarity with other religions? Once again, the term comparative theology becomes too vast to be meaningful. Unless we reserve the expression 'comparative theology' for theological studies that contain explicit and substantial comparisons of theological elements from at least two religions, virtually any theological study somehow dealing with the religious other becomes comparative.

Let us now focus on the type of comparative studies that I advocate and that correspond to academic interreligious dialogue. Perhaps the strongest justification for comparative studies today in the era of globalization and religious pluralism is that they can promote interreligious dialogue and help achieve its goals. Inspired by James L. Fredericks's understanding of comparative theology,[13] I view comparative studies as a shift to the praxis of interreligious dialogue, as comparative work done in and through

---

10 Francis X. Clooney, 'Comparative Theology: a review of recent books (1989-1995)', in *Theological Studies* 56,3 (1995): 521-550.
11 David Tracy, 'Comparative Theology', in Mircea Eliade (ed.), *Encyclopedia of Religion*, New York, Macmillan: volume 14, 1987: 446-455.
12 Francis X. Clooney, *Theology After Vedānta: An Experiment in Comparative Theology*, Albany, SUNY, 1993.
13 James L. Fredericks, *Buddhist and Christians: Through Comparative Theology to Solidarity*, Maryknoll, Orbis, 2004.

dialogue with our religious neighbours, and as a means to foster further interreligious dialogue. Similarly, and following Diane L. Eck's approach to the comparative study of religion, I believe that dialogue is an indispensable method of study.[14]

Since not everybody will agree with this view of comparative studies, perhaps it would be best to coin a new term. I propose to use the expression 'academic interreligious dialogue' to refer to comparative studies that contain explicit and substantial comparisons done in and through dialogue with both texts and members of other religions. Consequently, the presence of explicit and substantial comparisons is not yet sufficient to speak of academic interreligious dialogue. Similarly, a dialogical approach to the comparative study of religion, for instance, the one proposed by Gavin Flood in *Beyond Phenomenology*,[15] is not an example of academic interreligious dialogue. In order to speak of academic interreligious dialogue those explicit and substantial comparisons must presuppose the actual praxis of interreligious dialogue. By the praxis of interreligious dialogue I mean the three types of activities described above.

Academic interreligious dialogue is a particular type of comparative study defined by the content, that is, by the presence of explicit and substantial comparisons; and by the way in which the study is done, that is, in and through dialogue with texts and members of other religions.

Academic interreligious dialogue defined in this sense does not have to constitute a separate discipline. Like other types of comparative studies, academic interreligious dialogue can be done from within different disciplines and with a variety of methods. The disciplines that are most likely to contain academic interreligious dialogue include comparative philosophy, comparative theology, and comparative religious ethics. Since the boundaries between these disciplines are not always clear-cut, and at least some comparative methods can be used in all of them, it is better not to circumscribe academic interreligious dialogue to just one of these disciplines. In this sense, academic interreligious dialogue is interdisciplinary and methodologically pluralistic. Academic interreligious dialogue is also interdisciplinary in another sense: it combines ethnographic methods and textual analysis.

The praxis of dialogue is not only the foundation of academic interreligious dialogue but also its ultimate goal. That is, the purpose of academic interreligious dialogue is to promote the cause of interreligious dialogue and its goals. In order to maximize the contribution of a comparative study to the cause of interreligious dialogue, the scholar must pay special attention to the connection between religious texts and living religious communities. In order to be aware of the vital link between religious texts and living religions, comparative scholars need to go beyond their armchairs and textual ivory towers and actually practice interreligious dialogue with representatives of religious communities.

One should never forget the confusion generated by many textual readings produced in the era of Colonialism and Orientalism, armchair readings done without taking into account the self-understanding and actual practice of other religions. It has taken decades of scholarship to overcome some of the colonialist misrepresentations of other religions, and many stereotypes still prevail or continue to influence popular views of

---

14 Diana L. Eck, 'Dialogue and Method: Reconstructing the Study of Religion', in Patton and Ray, *A Magic Still Dwells*: 131-149.
15 Gavin Flood, *Beyond Phenomenology: Rethinking the Study of Religion*, London and New York, Cassell, 1999.

the religious other. In order to avoid future obstacles to the practice of interreligious dialogue and future confusion produced by more armchair interpretations, the comparativist should never neglect the connection between texts and living religions. In sum, interreligious studies should be done not only as if texts matter but also and primarily as if people matter.

Carolina Weening
D.T. Suzuki – From *Genesis* to Jesus

Whatever position one may take on the question of Daisetz Suzuki's merits as a Buddhist scholar and philosopher, it is all but impossible to deny that he was a vastly influential maker and shaper of 20th century Western religious history. Though his far-reaching influence rests upon his successful promulgation of Buddhism – especially Zen Buddhism – in the West, this article sets out from the premise that, ultimately, his Zen message to the West is inseparable from the contrasts with Christianity which accompanied it. This is to say that his publications and statements cannot be understood unless the audience for whom they are intended is considered at the same time. He spoke and wrote in response to the Western situation as he perceived it. And, judging from the magnitude and strength of the response he elicited, he had perceived the dissatisfaction and frustration in the post-war Western situation fairly accurately. All this may be obvious, but, it needs to be stressed. Suzuki as an English-language author and lecturer on the subject of Zen Buddhism is inseparable from the disappointed and disaffected Christians who were his readers and listeners.

Indeed, it is remarkable how frequently Christian issues appear in Suzuki's presentations of Zen. Apart from some works specifically addressed to Anglophone readers with scholarly interests, Suzuki almost invariably brings Christian materials into play when presenting and elaborating upon various aspects of the Zen world-view. A handful of Christian themes served his purposes very well, and to these themes he returned again and again.

Before we consider the Christian themes on which he focused, let us consider what themes he did not focus upon. He did not devote much time to the persons and events in the life of Jesus, but then he did not focus upon the persons and events of later Christian history either. This point deserves emphasis because to most people in the West, whether Christian or not, the life of Jesus, the activities of the Apostles or the development of the church and the history of its dogmas might well seem to offer the obvious starting point for a consideration of Christianity. For Suzuki, however, these play but a subsidiary and illustrative role in his interpretation of Christianity. How are we to explain that?

We can begin with a sweeping statement: Suzuki's understanding of Christianity, his critique of the Christian world-view and of Western attitudes in general, and, indeed, all of the aspects of the Christian religion which Suzuki brings before his Western audience – sin and redemption, time-serialism and historical thinking, faith as opposed to personal experience, the gulf between God and the human being – derive from his understanding of one overarching theme, namely, the story of 'Creation' as related in the first chapter of the first book of the Bible. Now, to derive the Christian experience from the story of Genesis may at first appear puzzling, and one might be tempted to conclude that Suzuki simply did not know the Bible very well. In his own haphazard way, however, Suzuki was familiar with a broad range of biblical texts,[1] and could cite

---

1 By his own account, Suzuki became acquainted with biblical texts in his youth, even before his first trip to Western Christian countries, see 'Early Memories,' in Masao Abe (ed.), *A Zen Life: D.T. Suzuki Remembered*, Tokyo and New York, Weatherhill, 1986: 4. 'It would be more than

scriptural passages suitable to his topic of the moment with apparent effortlessness. Yet, no biblical text absorbed him so intensively and so extensively, so deeply and for so long, as did the Bible's opening chapter on the origin of the world. We cannot simply dismiss this as whimsical, but must attempt to follow Suzuki's own train of thought. There are really two questions here: why not Christianity *via* Christ? And: why Christianity *via* Genesis?

Why not 'Jesus'. . .?

Space considerations allow us to take up only one possible response to the first question, though it is, to be sure, a very important one: the overall tendency within the Buddhist tradition to relativize the importance of *time* and *history*. The general Buddhist devaluation of biography and personal history may shed some light on an otherwise surprising approach to the significance of Jesus of Nazareth for Christianity, and may offer us an entry into Suzuki's approach to the Christian tradition.

Suzuki was well aware of the biblical reports concerning Moses, David, Jesus, Paul, and was acquainted with the stories of Noah, Abraham, Peter, Mary Magdalene, etc. Yet, Suzuki rejects the *importance* of these reports, stories and interests. Suzuki states categorically: '[t]he serialism of today, yesterday and tomorrow has no place in Zen, nor can man be represented by a series of events surrounding his life.'[2] Suzuki's overall attitude towards the biographical, and hence towards the personal and individual, is rooted in the idea that individual personality is ultimately inconsequential and superfluous precisely because it is accidental: the historical, as that which is shaped and formed in time, is accidental, having neither necessity nor universality. With such a premise it is not surprising, then, that Suzuki cannot attribute the same weight to Jesus, his predecessors, or his followers as does the Christian tradition, where history and biography are of overwhelming and decisive significance. So it is that Suzuki is concerned, not so much with the particular events, activities and personages which constitute the Bible, as he is with how such a world of events, activities and personages, all of whom are caught up in, subject to, constituted by and, indeed, identified with the story of their *time*, could acquire such crucial and consequential significance in the first place.

Though our reflections thus far may have offered us an initial insight into the question as to why Suzuki did not focus upon Jesus and other biblical figures as primary points of reference for Christianity, we still must press the question as to why he did focus upon *Genesis*. I would like to suggest that in a certain sense our brief examination of the first question begins to answer the second. Quite simply, in *Genesis*, Suzuki found the key to what he saw as the baffling importance of *time, time-serialism* and *individuating differences* for the Christian world-vision.

... and why the Book of Genesis?

The *Book of Genesis,* whatever else we may say about it, portrays time as built into, and even constitutive of, the very fabric of the Judaeo-Christian Creation. Indeed, considering

---

safe to declare that he has outdistanced any other among the Buddhist scholars of eastern origin in history for his constant quotations, allusions, and dealings with biblical concepts, ideas and thoughts', in Ki-bum Han, 'Zen and the Bible', (unpublished doctoral dissertation), Temple University, Philadelphia, 1975: 1-2.
2 See D.T. Suzuki, *The Essence of Buddhism,* London, Buddhist Society, 1957[2]: 81f.

that God's first reported activity consists in the distinction between light, as 'Day', and darkness, as 'Night', one could claim that, in effect, time is the first creation. Though I have written 'the first creation', Suzuki would tend to say 'the first *division*', for, as Suzuki reads the Genesis account, creation and division are essentially synonymous. That is to say, in creating a this as *this,* and thus distinguishing it from a *that,* the process of creating a world of diverse and discrete things, events and entities is essentially the process of breaking-up what had originally been a whole and, *via time,* setting it on a linear, serial, inexorably forward-thrusting track and making a return to the primordial whole effectively impossible. Time, once created, serves as the framework within which the Creator establishes the world: each new event, each new phenomenon, is embedded within an essential cut of temporality: 'on the First Day', 'on the Second Day'... 'on the Seventh Day...' Even the idea of *new* events and *new* phenomena cannot be thought without a dynamic conception of the forward movement of time underlying them: one after another, after another, each one 'newer' than the preceding ones. A Western Christian or Jew might take that for granted, but this serial element is far from indispensable to a story as to how the universe arose, and cosmogonies of many other cultures do very nicely without a particular conception of time at all, as Suzuki well knew.

Yet, for Suzuki, Christianity's attachment to time is simply one aspect of a much larger problem; indeed, this is the overriding problem with Christianity. The logic behind his choice of *Genesis* as the hermeneutical point of departure for an analysis of the Christian spirit comes yet more clearly into focus when one considers what Suzuki held to be the central and defining feature of the Christian message. This is not 'Love Thy Neighbour' or 'Love Thy Enemy', nor is it the revelation of Yahweh as 'the Compassionate Father', or the hope of *eudaemonia* in God's Kingdom, or any other of the conceptions generally associated (at least by Christians) with Christian teachings. For Suzuki, the hallmark of the Christian attitude is *dualism*, a thoroughgoingly dualistic world-vision which from the very genesis of the world expresses itself in division, rupture, and progressive otherness.[3] Indeed, the Judaeo-Christian God's creation *is* dualistic thinking. For Suzuki, the story of Creation in *Genesis* and the West's dualistic way of experiencing the world are inseparable from one another.

Dualistic thinking and its Consequences

Now, of course Suzuki could have presented this tendency to separate and divide as simply 'Western'. Dualistic thinking certainly pre-dates not only the emergence of Christianity but also the composition of the relevant chapters of *Genesis*. Instead, however, Suzuki identified it as decisively and quintessentially Christian, and saw it, not only as built into the Judaeo-Christian tradition, but also as forming the very foundation of the Judaeo-Christian tradition and providing the paradigm according to which the Christian life is to be lived and the world to be perceived and interpreted.

---

3 Upon closer consideration, the much-touted (by Christians) 'love of neighbour' or 'love of enemy' is itself but a manifestation of and testimony to the almighty rule of dualistic thinking in the Jewish-Christian tradition. Suzuki holds that the concept of 'enemy' arises only where particular relationships are fostered; where the idea of personal love is at work, then personal hate must be reckoned with as well. This is contrasted with the a-personal ideal of the Bodhisattva, where one finds simply 'compassion going out', see D.T. Suzuki and Tucker N. Callaway, 'Dialogue: Christian and Buddhist', in *The Eastern Buddhist* (NS) 3,1 (1970): 109-121.

Suzuki begins, then, with *Genesis*, because the key problem with Christianity and, indeed, with Western civilization as he saw it, begins there. It finds its foundation and source in the Genesis story, inasmuch as it is God's *fiat* which sets off the whole chain of discrimination which ultimately divides and sub-divides reality, making the human being *other* than God and *other* than nature. The genesis of the Judaeo-Christian world not only indicates the genesis of the Christian-Western problem, it *is* the genesis of the Christian-Western problem. It bodies forth a world whose building blocks are divisions, bifurcations, separations, and gives rise to human beings characterized and beset by divisions, bifurcations, separations. Its Creator has established the world upon the discrimination of *this* from *that*, which results in the all-but-insurmountable *otherness* at the heart of the biblical vision. And this vision, in turn, both causes and perpetuates the dis-ease of the Western psyche, especially in its modern neurotic manifestations: alienation from oneself, alienation from one's fellow human beings, alienation from Nature, alienation from God or Being.

The relationship (or lack thereof) between the human being and God, the constitution of the universe as a web of 'others' and the concomitant frustration, if not neurosis, which follows, are all pre-programmed in Genesis.

Divisions, splits, separations and 'the human condition'

Suzuki sees Western peoples as taking dualistic thinking as their starting point. Eastern peoples, on the other hand, start 'further back', where 'further back' is not intended in any strictly chronological sense but rather refers to 'a primordial state before we think, before we divide ourselves'.[4] And Zen holds that it is indeed possible to *return* there. This 'returning' is Enlightenment. And it is called returning because one goes back before Genesis.[5]

> Ordinarily we go out of ourselves to seek a place of ultimate rest. We walk on and on until we reach God who is at the head of a long tedious series of bifurcations and unifications. Zen takes the opposite course and steps backwards, as it were, to reach the undifferentiated continuum itself. This means that Zen wants us to face the world into which time and space have not yet put their cleaving wedges.[6]

Zen, Suzuki is saying, is grounded in the premise that there must be something which has not yet been divided.[7]

> The West lives in a world separated into two terms: subject and object, self and not-self, yes and no, good and evil, right and wrong, true and false... where yes cannot be no and no cannot be yes, where a square is not a triangle, where one is not two, where 'I' and 'thou' are eternally separated and can never be merged, where God creates and the creature forever remains created, where 'our Father ... art in Heaven' and we mortals are grovelling on earth.[8]

Suzuki never tired of censuring the dualistic way of experiencing the world as an infection all too characteristic of Christianity and, *via* Christianity's all-permeating influence, of the West.

---

4 Callaway and Suzuki, 'Dialogue': 109.
5 See Suzuki, *Essays in Zen Buddhism*, First Series, New York, Grove, 1961: 154.
6 'Satori', in Abe, *A Zen Life*: 47.
7 Of course, the Jewish-Christian tradition also acknowledges this, but calls it *tôhû wābôhû*, or chaos.
8 Suzuki, 'Basic Thoughts Underlying Eastern Ethical and Social Practice', in *The Eastern Buddhist* (NS) 31,2 (1998): 153-178: 155.

In the *Genesis* story, Suzuki locates the foundation and source of the epidemic Western penchant for endless intellectual analysis, inasmuch as it is God's *fiat* which sets off the chain of discriminations which effectively divide and subdivide reality, thus erecting an ultimately unbridgeable distinction between the human being and God, and between the human being and nature – with fateful consequences for Western civilization.[9]

God's *fiat* is the objectification of something *other*. It results in *two:* God here, and the world there – the first and decisive dualism.[10]

In an important sense, the most significant 'division' which took place in the Creation was not so much light from darkness, day from night, water from land, and so on, but rather 'God' from 'the world'. Moreover, the human being's separation from God did not begin with human sin; rather, it is built into Creation. Suzuki tells us that the 'separation of God from the world is the source of all our troubles.'[11] To be part of the Judaeo-Christian Creation is to be separated from that which is supposed to give it meaning.

From *Genesis*, then, Suzuki derived not only his conception of 'God' and of the human being which this God created, but also his analysis of the psychological maladies and problems which beset the modern Western person. Suzuki repeatedly and categorically pointed to and repudiated the effects of dualistic thinking both in his writing and lecturing for Western audiences.[12] He drew further implications out of the *Genesis* story: because Ultimate Reality is *other*, the Christian tradition must approach it as somehow 'hidden' and, thus, it becomes an object of 'faith', to be clearly differentiated from the ordinary reality of the world as we inhabit and experience it everyday. Suzuki was intensely critical of the Christian/Western belief that something about reality is inaccessible to us, concealed from us; for Zen, he told his readers and listeners, nothing is hidden. It is all here, now.

According to Suzuki's observation of the state of Western society, the ruptures which the biblical narrative builds into the constitution of the universe have had disastrous effects upon the psychological and emotional wellbeing of the human beings who have inherited this perspective, a perspective which is the source of so much and such unnecessary grief, most especially in its unnecessary and discouraging insistence on the severance of the human being from God. The Christian God always remains an 'other' for the Christian and, as such, says Suzuki, the Christian God always frustrates the heart. No accumulation of intuitions of God's presence amassed across time will ever bring Westerners to an apprehension of the wholeness of their God's reality.[13] Thus, the presence of God can only be inferred: 'we see God's works, not God'.

---

9 Suzuki is aware that Christ is seen by Christians as having bridged the gap, but Suzuki finds that unsatisfactory in view of the Christian understanding that Jesus Christ still remains an *other*. Thus, even when Suzuki speaks of Jesus, it is generally as an instance, or as a victim, of dualistic thinking.
10 See D.T. Suzuki, *The Field of Zen*, London, Buddhist Society, 1969: 75-77; also Suzuki's review of Heinrich Dumoulin, *A History of Zen Buddhism*, in *The Eastern Buddhist* (NS) 1,1 (1965): 123-126: 125.
11 Suzuki, *The Field of Zen*: 15-16.
12 Thus, though his initial response upon discovering the work of Meister Eckhart was heartily affirmative, he later came to reject Christian mysticism and retracted his earlier assertion that it was in any important way similar to Zen Buddhism. He came to see mysticism as positing a 'higher', hidden knowledge of truth beyond whatever we say and see, whereas Suzuki maintained that, for Zen, all is already open, present.
13 Augustine's panting and thirsting for God as expressed in 'Late, late have I loved Thee…', and John of the Cross's desolate yearning for God in the Dark Night, reflect the separation between

If one sustains, as Suzuki does, the unshakeable vision of an absolute seamless whole, then the choice of *Genesis* as the key to understanding the Christian world-view is no longer so puzzling. For Suzuki, the unrelieved *otherness* entrenched in Christian thinking and perception – light as opposed to darkness, eternity as opposed to time, good as opposed to evil, 'nature' as distinct from the human being, God as distinct from the human being – do not merely reflect philosophical or hermeneutical developments in the course of world history; rather, all flow inexorably from the story of Creation. Indeed, separation and distinction constitute Creation.

Suzuki's Zen Antidote

Already in the early 1930s, and up to his death in 1966, Suzuki held out to his public a prelapsarian state of consciousness in which no 'otherness' had yet arisen.

> [W]e have a persistent desire to return to the state of innocence prior, epistemologically speaking, to creation, to the state where there is no division, no knowledge – prior to the subject-object division, to the time when there was only God as he was before he created the world. The separation of God from the world is the source of all our troubles. We have an innate desire to be united with God.[14]

I would contend that these last two sentences are key for Suzuki's success in the West: 'The separation of God from the world is the source of all our troubles. We have an innate desire to be united with God.' Against the backdrop of that statement, Suzuki can describe most effectively the peace of mind and heart offered by Zen as he proposes it:

> Our spiritual yearnings are never completely satisfied unless this ... undifferentiated knowledge is awakened whereby the whole field of consciousness is exposed, inside and outside, to our full view. Reality has now nothing to hide from us.[15]

Suzuki's representation of the Christian world served him as a most effective foil against which he was able to present Zen's apparent wholeness both forcefully and cogently to his audience in the West. Over and against Christian dualities, Suzuki was able to offer the seamless experience of *advaita* as the antidote for the dis-ease and malaise which he found in the West. And, that he struck a nerve in the West, with his analysis of what he saw as Christian thinking as well as with what he understood as authentic Zen Buddhism, cannot be doubted. As Masao Abe observed:

> It was in the midst of the waves of sudden change in world history, with the order of Western society so shaken to its roots by the [Second World] War, that the luminous body of Zen ... began to emit its own original light. In those days, when many people in Europe and America were seized with anxiety, doubt and despair over the failure of their traditional system of values, Zen emerged to suddenly impress a large segment of the intellectual community, and began to provide new hope for people's broken spirit. Many individuals sensed in [Suzuki's] Zen the light of an entirely new life, and set out determinedly to grope towards this vision.[16]

---

belief, on the one side, and what is believed in, on the other. Suzuki would see such experiences as corroborating his depiction of the Christian's dilemma. The Christian cannot be with God in the Absolute Present.
14 Suzuki, *The Field of Zen*: 15-16.
15 'Satori', in Abe, *A Zen Life*: 56.
16 Masao Abe, 'The Influence of D.T. Suzuki in the West', in Abe, *A Zen Life*: 111.

Fuelled, then, by an astonishingly acute reading of the situation and the needs of his post-World-War 2 Western public, and with his particular unpacking of the story of *Genesis* providing the key to the problems of the Christian West and his particular presentation of Zen 'wholeness', Suzuki became one of the greatest makers and shapers of 20th century religious life. As we noted at the beginning of this article, Suzuki's status as a Buddhist scholar is certainly a subject of debate. But, then, Buddhist scholarship was not really the goal to which he aspired. We conclude with his own words; at the age of 93 he observed:

> I have devoted my entire life to the task of making Zen Buddhism known and comprehensible in the Western world. To this one goal all my strength and my labour have been given.[17]

---

17 See Gerta Ital, *Der Meister, die Mönche und Ich. Eine Frau im Zen-Buddhistischen Kloster*, Heidelberg, 1966: 53. The author spoke with Suzuki in 1963, and reports Suzuki's words in German, which Suzuki could not speak, as follows: 'Ich widme mein ganzes Leben der Aufgabe, den Zen Buddhismus der westlichen Welt nahe zu bringen und verständlich zu machen. Nur diesem Ziel gehört meine Kraft und meine Arbeit seit je.' (Re-translation into English is by Carolina Weening.)

Part 4

Peace Studies as Ecumenics

Theodor Ahrens

Reconciliation – Leitmotif of Christian Mission

It was from the early 1980s onwards that John D'Arcy May shared with the author an interest in the interaction between religion and society in the South Pacific, particularly in Melanesia. The following contribution is given as a sign of gratitude and appreciation for many an inspiration received throughout those years.

A scarce resource

How different people will be able to get along with each other in spite of their differences is a question which reaches far into the future of Christian missions and mission studies just as much as it reaches far back to the beginnings of the modern Ecumenical Movement.[1] Likewise, the question reaches far into the field of international politics just as much as it reaches deeply into the core of any human heart. What is at issue here is the question of reconciliation, of how one person, or one group or nation, is reconciled with another.

Ius or law has been a formative power shaping European culture and cultural self-awareness. A great cultural achievement, *ius* is, nonetheless, variable. On the one hand, amidst European societies, which perceived themselves as the peak of social, cultural and religious evolution, hell broke loose in the 20th century...repeatedly, e.g., Fascist Germany, Stalinist Russia, 'ethnic cleansing' in the Balkans. In each, people killed and were killed on ideological grounds, and destructiveness, violence and insanity reigned. On the other, in our present context we are also confronted with sharp social conflicts, e.g., between immigrants and residents, employers and employees, young unemployed and older well-established people, individual freedoms and state control. In some cases *ius* does not apply at all. Though it is not used in these contexts, reconciliation may yet have something to offer.

From the fringes to the centre of ecumenically committed mission

The word reconciliation is enigmatic. The scope of its possible meanings range from a settlement of outstanding debts, *reconciliation of accounts*, via the termination of physical violence, to a policy which – in order to regain political leeway – ceases to hold former enemies hostage to bad collective memories. Leaving the past behind, former enemies can deal rationally with their current interests and do together what is politically needful. Though the word reconciliation is moving with ease into the political sphere, its Christian roots are being forgotten. Reconciliation implies forgiveness, gratuitously and freely granted, and not motivated by any political interest. What can churches contribute from their particular resources?

---

1 Wolfgang Lienemann, *Frieden: vom 'gerechten Krieg' zum 'gerechten Frieden'*, Göttingen, Vandenhoeck & Ruprecht, 2000; Wolfram Weiße, *Praktisches Christentum und Reich Gottes, Die ökumenische Bewegung Life and Work 1919-1937*, Göttingen, Vandenhoeck & Ruprecht, 1991; Wolfram Weiße, *Reich Gottes*, Göttingen, Vandenhoeck & Ruprecht, 1997.

The Conference on World Mission, which the World Council of Churches held in Athens last year, took up the issue of reconciliation as a plea: *Come Holy Spirit – Heal and Reconcile!* Reconciliation appears as a gift from beyond, shared by the Spirit, impossible to grasp or to fabricate, yet of vital concern everywhere and for everyone. The WCC picked up a train of thought from the plenary, in 1991, in Canberra, Australia,[2] and from the plenary of the Conference of European Churches in Trondheim, Norway, in July 2003.[3] The Trondheim texts claim that Christianity's unique contribution, as far as reconciliation is concerned, is Jesus, the revelation of God's presence amidst human suffering. The risen Reconciler works within the sphere of personal lives, but will also be witnessed to as the beginning of a cosmic transformation towards the kingdom of God.[4]

While the use of the word reconciliation is not widespread in the Bible, as an issue it is broadly and deeply rooted, for instance, in the Old Testament narration of the reconciliation of the two estranged brothers, Jacob and Esau, or in Jesus's famous response to Peter's question, how many times should one forgive the trespasses of one's neighbour?

Concerning an explicit use of the word in the New Testament, three texts especially suggest themselves. In 2 Corinthians 5:17, Paul writes about reconciliation as an act of God: *God was in Christ reconciling the world with himself.* This is a cosmic event, irreversible, and Paul's own existence is inextricably linked with these events. In Christ's stead he appeals: *Let yourselves be reconciled with God.* Offering the *word* of reconciliation, Paul is stand-in for the Messiah.[5] In Ephesians, a post Pauline document, the reconciliation of different religious cultures is brought back to its Christological foundations (2:12-16). A third reference in Colossians (1:15-20), also post Pauline, expands the scope of the word reconciliation: human destructiveness, projected onto the firmament of the Hellenistic cosmos as hostile and dangerous powers, is said to have already been 'reconciled', hence, since the Jesus event, it is soteriologically irrelevant.

Thus, for Paul, reconciliation is a divine and not a human endeavour. Humankind, with God's creation, is part of a new reality and we are invited to acknowledge the givenness of that reality which God has brought about – *without* making human repentance a precondition for being part of it. Two questions arise. What was the substance of this divine reconciling act? And, how can we bridge the gulf between reconciliation as God's act and our awareness that human communities need reconciliation for their very survival? To answer these I draw on two Protestant theologians, Karl Barth (1886-1968) and Gerhard Ebeling (1912-2001).

The Doctrine of Reconciliation lies, according to Karl Barth, at the very centre of our understanding of Christianity.[6] In Jesus Christ God the Creator takes up the lost case of humankind, making it God's own business and leading it to its goal.[7] Reconciliation is understood as a movement arising from God's innermost being towards the lowness of a human being and, at the same time, an elevation of the human being Jesus to the 'right hand' of the Father. The divine self-abasement corresponds to the elevation of the

---

2   Jacques Matthey, 'Versöhnung im ökumenischen missionstheologischen Diskurs', in *Zeitschrift für Mission (ZMiss.)* 3 (2005): 174-191.
3   Konferenz Europäischer Kirchen (KEK) (ed.), *Jesus Christus heilt und versöhnt, Unser Zeugnis in Europa*, Geneva, mimeo, 2002.
4   KEK, *Jesus Christus heilt und versöhnt*, numbers 11, 18, 19, 20, 22.
5   Cf. Cilliers Breytenbach, *Versöhnung. Eine Studie zur paulinischen Soteriologie*, Neukirchen-Vluyn, Neukirchener Verlag, 1989: 2ff., 107ff., 220ff.
6   Karl Barth, *Kirchliche Dogmatik*, Zollikon and Zürich, Ev. Verlagshaus, 1955ff.
7   Barth, *KD IV*, 1, § 57, Das Werk Gottes des Versöhners: 1.

human being. We may not think highly enough of the human being.⁸ Incarnation as a theological concept is placed centre stage and no theological train of thought may bypass its criteriological function. In Jesus Christ is a reality valid for each and all⁹ – an inclusive story of reconciliation.¹⁰ He *is* Immanuel, God with us. This does not cancel the human but, rather, reconstitutes humans as subjects.¹¹ The triumph of grace comes to fruition as people have faith in God's victory over evil and against this background refuse to take evil more seriously than actually necessary.¹² Consequently, Barth unfolds the human condition in terms of cooperating with the Kingdom of God.¹³ Reconciliation and commitment to the cause of the Kingdom go together.¹⁴

Hence, Barth's notion of mission is firmly rooted in his notion of reconciliation. Mission is participating in Christ's prophetic ministry, though not, as liberation theology holds, a continuation of the incarnation. The witnesses of Jesus Christ address their fellow human beings as people who have already been reconciled by God. Such is the basis of ecumenical solidarity. Mission, then, tells of salvation but is not salvation itself.

Let us now turn to Gerhard Ebeling.¹⁵ Ebeling sees reconciliation as relevant today. On the one hand, people are interested in processes of reconciliation where there are verifiable results. On the other, people feel a sense of resignation before the powers of destructiveness. What causes such resignation before the truth of reconciliation? Where Barth emphasized *'You are reconciled'* as an anthropological *a priori*, and relegated concern for sin, evil, and destructiveness to second place, Ebeling discusses reconciliation along with the common experience of destructiveness. Before the latter, reconciliation is questioned. The Gospel as the Word of the Cross addresses the tension between what each and everyone experiences and what is not experienced by one and all.¹⁶ In situations overshadowed and shaped by strife, the Word of the Cross bears witness to a love which was truly lived by God.¹⁷ This Word is a word of reconciliation; it evokes faith that God's love may reach into the deepest depth of destructiveness and suffering;

---

8 Jörg Dierken points out that Barth does not continue to further interpret his understanding of reconciliation in the sense of a mutual *communicatio idiomatum*, see Jörg Dierken, 'Karl Barth (1886-1968)', in Friedrich Graf (ed.), *Klassiker der Theologie, Von Richard Simon bis Karl Rahner*, München, Beck, 2005: 223-257, 246ff.
9 Barth, *KD IV*, 1, § 50, 55ff.
10 Cf., for a reaction to this theory of reconciliation, Katsumi Takizawa, *Das Heil im Heute, Texte einer japanischen Theologie*, Göttingen, Vandenhoeck & Ruprecht, 1987: 25ff, 181ff.
11 Sauter, *'Versöhnung' als Thema der Theologie*: 209.
12 Barth, *KD II*, 1, 566; *KD II*, 280f; *KD III*, 3, 4: 102ff.
13 Sauter, *'Versöhnung' als Thema der Theologie*: 117ff.
14 Sauter, *'Versöhnung' als Thema der Theologie*: 204.
15 Gerhard Ebeling, 'Zum Begriff der Versöhnung', in his *Dogmatik des christlichen Glaubens*, volume 2, Tübingen, Mohr, 1979: 219-228.
16 Gerhard Ebeling, 'Zu "meiner Dogmatik christlichen Glaubens"', in *ThLZ* 105,10 (1980): 722-733: 730.
17 When Ebeling emphasizes the *word* of the reconciliation as being the word of the cross and as such as being the special and particular feature of Christianity, he is aware of the following: those, who in the face of the power of sin identify themselves with the will of God and who dare represent God in the face of the world, come to the place where God is in this world of sin, the place of being outcast. And someone, who dares not only to represent God before the people but also the people to God, in one and the same person, in order to take the people as seriously as God does and God as seriously as the people do and in order to live God's love in this way and to reconstruct true life, makes sin visible, namely, as destruction of true life, see Ebeling, *Dogmatik des christlichen Glaubens*: 186.

it announces such faith as the restoration of true life. Reconciliation with God gains a social dimension only indirectly, i.e., in one's conscience. Thus, the Word, reconciling people at odds with themselves, with God and with their situation, creates the preconditions for reconciliation as a social process.

Both Barth and Ebeling emphasize the one-sidedness of reconciliation that is brought about by God. In contrast, reconciliation between human beings calls for the participation and cooperation of more than one party. Of course, neither in Barth's nor in Ebeling's understanding does faith in God as the reconciler of the world entail a blueprint for social action – as if God's reconciling act could be *imitated* on a level of human actions. For a clue to how they might bridge the gap, we look to Romans 5:1-10 where Paul aligns *reconciliation* and *justification*, a correlation taken up by both Barth and Ebeling. Supposing one is prepared to acknowledge *reconciliation* and *justification* respectively as appropriate decoders of the Christ event, then an indirect link may be established between God reconciling the world of humans and human efforts to settle conflicts. In Barth's perspective, God has disclosed Godself in Christ as the keeper of human dignity and the companion of human freedom. Each and every human being is invited to let himself or herself be drawn into God's good purpose for creation. Ebeling's approach focuses our awareness on the point that our conscience is the very forum where it is decided how people allow themselves to be affected both by the Word from God and by their fellow human beings.

Reconciliation and forgiveness as elements of political hermeneutics?

Faith in the all-pervading power of love cannot be transferred one-to-one to the political discourse.[18] How can the woman whose brother was killed by her neighbour, in the massacres in Rwandi-Burundi, forgive that neighbour? Yet, the term reconciliation has been charged with a political mission, putting to the test the interpretative scope of a Jewish-Christian leitmotif in the political sphere all around the globe.

Political endeavours to establish a new order in Europe, after the barbarisms of fascism and World Wars I and II had almost destroyed Western civilization, were marked symbolically. For instance, president de Gaulle and chancellor Adenauer visiting a church together for prayer, or German chancellor Brandt kneeling in front of the memorial in the former Warsaw ghetto, or Kohl and Mitterand hand in hand on the cemeteries of World War II. Former enemies cease to hold each other hostage to bad collective memories. Politicians realize that to regain the leeway needed for political manoeuvre today memories of conflictual encounters of the past have to be left behind. The word reconciliation is increasingly being used for that.[19] Nevertheless, such 'markers' are not the whole story. For, there is no reconciliation without justice, John de Gruchy suggests.[20] How do these two go together? The establishment of the Commission for Truth and Reconciliation gave a signal to society at large of South Africa's commitment to publicly confront the upheavals of the past, to acknowledge the injustice, the wrongs and the terror of the apartheid regime and to try and bring society to a threshold leading beyond that time.[21]

---

18 John de Gruchy, *Reconciliation: Restoring Justice*, London, SCM, 2002: 18.
19 Hermann Lübbe, *'Ich entschuldige mich', Das neue politische Bußritual*, Berlin, Berliner Taschenbuch, 2003.
20 De Gruchy, *Reconciliation*: 13ff.
21 Joachim Braun (ed.), *Versöhnung braucht Wahrheit, Der Bericht der südafrikanischen*

When Bishop Desmond Tutu declared that without reconciliation no future would be possible for South Africa and, for that matter, for any other society torn apart by terror and violence, he drew first and foremost on his Christian convictions.[22] The Nigerian writer Wole Soyinka objected. In Soyinka's view reconciliation – in the sense of a re-establishment of acceptable social relationships – cannot be achieved without compensation.[23] Generally, apart from rather extreme cases, Soyinka considers a transfer of the concept of reconciliation to the socio-political field as rather disquieting.[24] Instead, Soyinka recommends returning to traditional African methods of straightening things out. He suggests that conflicts should be settled by payments of compensation, after which the opposing parties may – following the style of traditional initiation rites – jointly step over the threshold of the gate to a new future.

One would assume, though, that precisely this was the concern of those who decided to establish the South African Commission for Truth and Reconciliation. The government-controlled judicial system could not have brought about a balanced situation. Legal action could have produced neither justice nor reconciliation. The forces of the old system were still too strong and, as the preservation of the unity of the country was the overriding concern, a new way had to be found. On its side, perhaps the work of the South African Commission for Truth and Reconciliation here and there gave the impression that social reconciliation would not only be possible but could, in fact, be easily achieved.[25]

The key for the work of the commission was that it abstained from retaliation and that it granted amnesty not to all, but only to some of those who publicly confessed their crimes.[26] The wish to retaliate was relegated to second place in favour of the need to look forward to the future and to establish a background against which acceptable social relationships could grow. If the truth sought was not always told sufficiently, was this a useless procedure, then? John de Gruchy counters by asking whether normal trials would have brought the truth into the open to a greater or more complex degree and thus would have contributed more effectively towards that goal of bringing the nation to the threshold of a communally shared future. He suggests that the demand to say nothing but the truth is limited wisdom: exploration of the past is often more than people are able to bear. Yet, the work of the commission enabled many people to realize that they need not consider themselves to be forever captives of their past and, perhaps, allowed society as a whole to move a step forward. Looked at in this way the commission made an important contribution to a moral regeneration in South Africa.[27]

Wahrheitskommission, Gütersloh, Kaiser/Gütersloher Verlagshaus, 1999; Charles Villa-Vicencio and Wilhelm Verwoerd (eds.), *Looking Back – Reaching Forward, Reflections on the Truth and Reconciliation Commission in South Africa*, Cape Town and London, Cape Town University, 2000; Robert I. Rotberg and Dennis Thompson (eds.), *Truth versus Justice: The Morality of Truth Commissions*, Princeton, Princeton University, 2000.

22 Cf. Desmond Tutu, *Keine Zukunft ohne Versöhnung*, Düsseldorf, Patmos, 2001: 211-234.
23 Wole Soyinka, *Die Last des Erinnerns, Was Europa Afrika schuldet – und was Afrika sich selbst schuldet*, Düsseldorf, Patmos, 2001.
24 Soyinka, *Die Last des Erinnerns*: 102.
25 Tinyiko Sam Maluleke, 'Sechs Thesen zum südafrikanischen Experiment der Versöhnung und innergesellschaftlichen Vergebung', in *Ökumenische Rundschau* 49,4 (2000): 462-470: 464 (author's translation).
26 As a matter of fact, only a small minority of perpetrators who confessed were granted amnesty.
27 Cf. Johnny de Lange, 'The Historical Context, Legal Origins and Philosophical Foundation of the South African Truth and Reconciliation Commission', in Villa-Vicencio and Verwoerd, *Looking Back – Reaching Forward*: 14-31.

As a rule, and following Soyinka, forgiveness shall not get in the way of justice. The state under the rule of law operates on the assumption that individuals are to be held accountable for their actions: 'I could have acted differently.' The state under the rule of law will either pronounce someone guilty or will acquit someone of guilt. In this way the perpetrators are put beyond revenge. The state under the rule of law re-establishes order but does not grant forgiveness.

Forgiveness does not feed on the logic of an equivalence of justice but on the abundance of love. It proves itself in the sphere of personal relationships.[28] However, at a very thin edge, as Klaus-Michael Kodalle has pointed out, the judicial system of the state is linked to mercy and forgiveness, namely, in the sovereign's privilege to grant amnesty. Forgiveness then is *not completely* beyond the processes of reciprocity of the judicial system, or, in fact, beyond our daily interactions where we try to strike a balance between love and justice. Thus, we presuppose a dependency on forgiveness and, in reality, have been living in such dependency all along. Forgiveness, then, could be the secret centre of ethics, pointing to the beyond of an apparently untraceable territory.[29]

Unreliable witnesses of a trustworthy word

Churches take a stance in societal conflicts – one way or another. Churches as well as other humanitarian and religious multinationals have at times played a role in prolonging conflicts (Serbia, Bosnia-Herzegovina, Northern Ireland, Rwanda-Burundi, Fiji and South Africa). Yet, it is also true that churches have time and again helped to reduce violence and to back people and institutions that further mutual understanding. There are tendencies to exaggerate both views.

One instance of the role the church can play in conflict situations is provided by Bishop Sanangke Dole of the Melpa Lutheran Church in the Highlands of Papua New Guinea. Bishop Dole has repeatedly and successfully mediated between groups involved in violent conflicts.[30] Together with a team of church elders and pastors the bishop will establish a camp within the fighting zone and stay there – if need be – for weeks. Decision-makers and opinion-leaders moving behind the scene, if not otherwise known, need to be identified. So, the bishop keeps moving between the warring parties until he has been able to gain the support of those opinion-leaders and decision-makers, identifying those willing to support a non-violent settlement of the conflict. Usually, thoughtful and constructive people can be found on both sides. It is more difficult, the bishop reports, to get the hotheads and opinion-leaders, who are interested in keeping the conflict going, involved. Those people must not be allowed to stay behind when peace negotiations are eventually opened. Before joint talks can actually take place the bishop will have moved many times back and forth between the groups in order to hear and to understand the often irreconcilable reconstructions of their conflict.

---

28 Julia Kristeva, 'Forgiveness, An Interview', in *Publications of the Modern Language Association of America*, 2002: 278-287; cf. also Ruth Kluger's 'Forgiving and Remembering', in *Publications of the Modern Language Association of America*, 2002: 311-313.

29 Klaus-Michael Kodalle, 'Verzeihung des Unverzeihlichen, Mut zur Paradoxie bei Ricoeur, Derrida und Lögstrup', in Thomas Buchheim and Rolf Schönberger and Walter Schweidler (eds.), *Die Normativität des Wirklichen, Über die Grenze zwischen Sein und Sollen*, Stuttgart, Klett-Cotta, 2002: 414-438: 426ff, 438.

30 Cf. Melpa Lutheran Church in Papua New Guinea (ed.), *Reconciliation – A Paradigm of Mission*, Mt. Hagen, mimeo, 2006.

Once the leaders of the warring parties get together the hard facts have to be brought to the table. This may take time and, in fact, may also produce bitterness on both sides. However, being exposed to the other side's version may also kick off learning processes by all the parties. It may appear that churches are part of the problem or that some church leaders played a role in the emergence of a conflict.

The bishop has several times been successful in settling tribal fights. He is well-known and well-respected locally. Not a professional diplomat, he has acquired relevant cultural and political competencies. He knows regional politics and how to deal with traditional modes of interaction. He acts without being afraid of being denounced by others. Outwardly, there is no indication of partiality on his part; within meetings, however, frank words may be said to one or other group.

There are other factors. The national government is far away, the provincial government has practically given up trying to uphold law and order, and the police do not dare to enter the fighting zones. Under such circumstances it is more likely that churches, unions and other non-government organizations, which operate on an intermediate, regional level, do have a chance to mediate, not least because they are more firmly rooted than other institutions at the level where people actually live and strive.[31] The institution getting involved should have earned some trust and respect; yet, it seems to be more important that the persons acting as mediators need to be people who are known and have earned public trust.

Such mediation may differ somewhat from other forms of mediation, e.g., of professional diplomats who, for a limited period of time and somewhere outside of the actual crisis area, consult with only some of the representatives of the opposing parties, with the goal of initiating negotiations between the groups. It goes without saying that in both types of mediation it would be crucial to be well-acquainted with the present situation and the history of a conflict. Further, an attitude of unpretentious objectivity is called for on the side of the mediators, not a keeping of the eye on one's own prestige or other personal interests. In both approaches, though, a threshold has to be established where a shared interest in securing one's future and an interest in leaving behind the destructiveness of the past can be balanced out.[32]

Sanangke Dole insists on drafting a written agreement, a *contract*, a public declaration, so to say. This document will be signed in the presence of the representatives of both groups as well as of high-ranking politicians and police officers, representatives of churches and others. On the spot where the agreement is signed, a large wooden or metal cross will be erected – *a reminder for future generations*. After that *gifts* are being *exchanged*. And, finally, a worship service will be *celebrated*, involving all the people present at that moment. Thus reference is being made to that untraceable point beyond our attempts at striking a balance between the establishment of justice and the practice of love. Each group presents the other with a Bible and with a promise: 'Never again'. While in a number of cases such agreements to terminate violence have been quite durable, in other cases violence has erupted again. At the back of such peace ceremonies there always lingers the question how long the peace, which has just been confirmed, will, in fact, last.

---

31 Cf. Klaus Wilkens, 'Der Beitrag der Kirchen zum Friedensprozess in El Salvador', in *ZMiss*. 3 (2005): 192-200.
32 John Paul Lederach, *Building peace: sustainable reconciliation in divided societies*, Washington DC, United States Institute of Peace, 1997: 29.

Conclusion

More is needed, of course, than a formal termination of armed conflict, as in South Africa, El Salvador or Northern Ireland.[33] Opposing groups often maintain quite different, even irreconcilable, reconstructions of the conflict's history – be it Protestants and Catholics in Northern Ireland, the Serbs and Albanians in the Kosovo, the indigenous inhabitants in West Irian and the people from Java whom the government settled there, or the groups Bishop Sanagke Dole was and is trying to bring together. Established strategies for reconstructing or forgetting the past, strategies for the use or abuse of recollections need to be worked upon.[34] Of course, the past is constantly being re-interpreted. That is true for the memory of an individual no less than of a group.[35] It is vital that, in the interest of getting along with each other in a less destructive way, such reconstructions of the past have to be critically analyzed, i.e., they have to be de-mythologized.[36] What, then, is a memory that is fair to both sides?

I suggest, with the help of Gesine Schwan,[37] that, first, it is necessary to acknowledge what the facts are. Certain things happened, certain people were involved; the past is not a totally arbitrary construction. But, there is also reconstruction; what were the motives and reasons why somebody did, or did not do, something to somebody else?[38] The myths of the past are also part of the hard facts that have to be brought onto the table. Second, what is the moral significance of what happened? Third, and most difficult, how does one side listen to the stories of the other? Fourth, for a later-born generation, confrontation with the past will result in a conflictive emotion between the positive feelings towards one's parents' generation and what one now learns about the past. All of this will have to be integrated into one's self-awareness, into the knowledge of who one really is and wants to be.[39]

The worlds of politics and economics provide no space for a sacrament of forgiveness. The churches, however depraved or trustworthy they may appear, do cultivate spaces where we remember that, in the name of God, guilt may not only be crossed out but erased, i.e., forgiven, as if it never had occurred. Making reconciliation present is what makes the church a special place.[40]

I should like to thank Andrea Ehlers for her help in straightening out a rough English draft of this manuscript. TA

---

33 Cf. Alan D. Falconer (ed.), *Reconciling Memories*, Dublin, Columba, 1988; The Faith & Politics Group (ed.), *Forgive us our Trespasses...? Reconciliation and Political Healing*, Belfast, The Faith & Politics Group, 1996.
34 See Paul Ricoeur, *Das Rätsel der Vergangenheit, Erinnern – Vergessen – Verzeihen*, Göttingen, Wallstein, 2002: 131-156.
35 See Ricoeur, *Das Rätsel der Vergangenheit*: 76ff.
36 Cf. Richard Kearney, 'Myth and the Critique of Tradition', in Falconer, *Reconciling Memories*: 4-24.
37 Cf. Gesine Schwan, *Politik und Schuld, Die zerstörerische Macht des Schweigens*, Frankfurt a.M., Fischer, 1997.
38 Ricoeur, *Das Rätsel der Vergangenheit*: 117.
39 Cf. Wulf-Volker Lindner, 'Vergessen. Verdrängen. Durcharbeiten, Zum Umgang mit der eigenen Geschichte', in *ZMiss*. 3 (2005): 201-212; Schwan, *Politik und Schuld*: 161ff.
40 Cf. Magdalene L. Frettlöh, 'Der Mensch heißt Mensch weil er ... vergibt?' Philosophisch-politische und anthropologische Vergebungsdiskurse im Lichte der fünften Vaterunserbitte', in Jürgen Ebach and Hans-Martin Gutmann (eds.), *Wie? Auch wir vergeben unseren Schuldigern?' Mit Schuld leben*, Gütersloh, Gütersloher Verlagshaus, 2004: 179-215.

Iain Atack

NGOs as agents of Cosmopolitan Values or Parochial Interests

Introduction

I have worked with John D'Arcy May as my teacher and colleague since I arrived in Dublin to begin my Peace Studies degree at the Irish School of Ecumenics. I was looking for an opportunity to reflect upon and learn from my work with development and peace NGOs (non-governmental organizations) in both Canada and Sri Lanka. This required a combination of philosophical and ethical probing with social and political analysis to help me develop a critical understanding of the kind of peace and justice work in which I had been involved. John May's lectures during that year provided me with many of the concepts and theories I needed to engage in such reflection. While some of my fellow students found this combination of the philosophical and the political, and the ethical and the social somewhat baffling, I found his interdisciplinary approach to issues novel and refreshing.

One of the many lectures given to us by John May was on the theme of development ethics. Development agencies often give the impression of viewing development as largely a technical issue, associated with determining the best methods for achieving laudable and unproblematic goals such as economic growth and poverty alleviation. John May, however, encouraged and expected us to ask fundamental questions about the nature and purpose of development as an embodiment of Western models of modernity and instrumental thinking applied to all corners of the human world. This breadth of scope together with a capacity to deal with foundational issues is a prerequisite for multidisciplinary fields of inquiry such as Peace Studies. We must continue to ask basic and sometimes uncomfortable questions about the types of values implicit or explicit in development activities, and the types of organizations best suited to implementing them or putting them into practice.

Cosmopolitanism, as a normative theory connected to international politics, involves a commitment to global distributive justice, a value that is central to development. Furthermore, non-governmental organizations (NGOs) can be seen as vehicles or instruments for the achievement and implementation of cosmopolitan values, including global distributive justice. There is, nonetheless, a tension between NGOs as agents of cosmopolitan justice and as representatives of local groups and special interests, even where such groups are considered marginalized in some way.

This apparent tension between community representation and cosmopolitan values, or between the local and the global, involves a false dichotomy, however, because specific local grievances are so often connected to broader cosmopolitan themes. Marginalized groups within any society often campaign on the basis of supposedly universal values or norms such as human rights or distributive justice and not merely to defend or promote their immediate special interests. In other words, a commitment to cosmopolitan values such as global distributive justice can provide an essential normative basis for NGO action on even highly local issues.

Cosmopolitanism and global distributive justice

Cosmopolitanism refers to the view that all human beings are part of a universal moral community. As such, cosmopolitanism has both an ethical or normative dimension, and political or institutional implications. In normative terms, cosmopolitanism allows us to ask questions about our moral responsibilities to other human beings regardless of political, cultural or geographical boundaries. 'The crux of the idea of moral cosmopolitanism is that each human being has equal moral worth and that equal moral worth generates certain moral responsibilities that have universal scope.'[1]

In political or institutional terms, cosmopolitanism allows us to move beyond an exclusive emphasis on state sovereignty as the central component of international or global politics. It suggests instead a more polycentric approach to global issues and global governance. This includes a role for the organizations of transnational civil society, including social movements and NGOs for example.

Cosmopolitan ethical theories can be said to share three important characteristics: egalitarianism (or impartiality), individualism and universality (or inclusiveness). In other words, the focus of cosmopolitanism is the human individual as a member of a universal moral community, and all individuals are held to be equally valuable in moral terms. David Held refers to this as 'the principle of individualist moral egalitarianism or, simply, egalitarian individualism'.[2]

Furthermore, the equal and inalienable dignity of every human being exists independently of and prior to any particular legal or political order.[3] As Held writes, the 'first principle' of cosmopolitanism 'is that the ultimate units of moral concern are individual human beings, not states or other particular forms of human association'.[4] The state has, at best, a purely instrumental value, derived from its capacity to facilitate the exercise of individual moral choice and to serve human ends. This implies that: '[a]llegiance is owed, first and foremost, to the moral realm of all humanity, not to the contingent groupings of nation, ethnicity, and class.'[5] In other words, 'egalitarian individualism' as a normative principle of cosmopolitanism underlies or implies a more polycentric approach to issues of global governance in institutional terms than conventional state-centred approaches to international politics. Richard Falk, for instance, has characterized the contemporary global order as 'a composite reality, reflecting the persisting influence of states...yet, also exhibiting the effects of voluntary associations and social movements that are motivated by the law of humanity and situated in civil society'.[6] The 'law of humanity', for Falk, reflects the cosmopolitan principle of 'treating each person on earth as a sacred subject'.[7]

---

1 Gillian Brock and Harry Brighouse, 'Chapter 1: Introduction', in Gillian Brock and Harry Brighouse (eds.), *The Political Philosophy of Cosmopolitanism*, Cambridge, Cambridge University, 2005: 4.
2 David Held, 'Chapter 2: Principles of Cosmopolitan Order', in Brock and Brighouse, *The Political Philosophy of Cosmopolitanism*: 12.
3 A. Honneth, 'Is Universalism a Moral Trap? The Presuppositions and Limits of a Politics of Human Rights', in J. Bohman and M. Lutz-Bachman (eds.), *Perpetual Peace: Essays on Kant's Cosmopolitan Ideal*, Cambridge MA, MIT, 1997: 167.
4 Held, 'Principles of Cosmopolitan Order': 12.
5 Held, 'Principles of Cosmopolitan Order': 10.
6 Richard Falk, 'The World Order between Inter-State Law and the Law of Humanity: the Role of Civil Society Institutions', in Daniele Archibugi and David Held (eds.), *Cosmopolitan Democracy: An Agenda for a new World Order*, Cambridge, Polity, 1995: 164.
7 Falk, 'The World Order': 172.

Individualism, egalitarianism and universality (or 'egalitarian individualism') are the three formal characteristics of cosmopolitanism as an ethical theory. In terms of the substance or the content of our moral responsibilities or duties to other human beings, Andrew Linklater suggests that at a minimum, members of this universal moral community have an obligation of non-maleficence, or 'fundamental, perfect or non-optional duties not to harm one another'.[8]

It has also been suggested that a commitment to cosmopolitan law, as distinct from both domestic law and international law (following Kant), can be translated in contemporary terms to a commitment to universal human rights. Domestic law governs relations between citizens within the boundary of a sovereign state, while international law (where it exists) governs relations between sovereign states. Cosmopolitan law, or a 'law of peoples', on the other hand, governs those obligations we have towards any human being, and not merely our fellow citizens.

Thus, 'human rights must be the domain of cosmopolitan law, which institutionalizes basic rights of individuals and the rule of law at the supranational level'.[9] In other words, the human rights of each individual have a moral, and legal, status that transcends their position as citizens of a particular country or state. Richard Falk also characterizes human rights as the embodiment of 'the law of humanity', which he distinguishes quite clearly from inter-state law.[10]

A number of cosmopolitan theorists refer to different dimensions of justice as the concept that exemplifies the moral content of cosmopolitanism. Catriona McKinnon, for instance, summarizes the 'cosmopolitan ideal' as: 'A world in which some fundamental principles of justice govern relations between all persons in all places.'[11]

Thomas Pogge has developed a version of global distributive justice in response to the problem of world poverty on the basis of cosmopolitan values. Global distributive justice concerns normative principles governing the distribution of access to material resources and basic goods. In particular, Pogge combines these themes of non-maleficence or non-harm, human rights and justice to provide a cosmopolitan response to issues of world poverty.

Pogge explicitly identifies justice with the fulfillment of basic human rights when he interprets the 'justice...of any institutional order' as depending upon 'its success in affording all its participants secure access to the objects of their human rights'.[12] Pogge defines the objects of human rights in terms of secure access to a fairly conventional list of basic goods, including 'basic freedoms and participation, of food, drink, clothing, shelter, education, and health care'.[13]

---

8   Andrew Linklater, 'The Problem of Harm in World Politics: Implications for the Sociology of States-systems', in *International Affairs* 78,2: 324n18.
9   J. Bohman and M. Lutz-Bachman, 'Introduction', in Bohman and Lutz-Bachman, in *Perpetual Peace*: 1997: 18.
10 Falk, 'The World Order': 163.
11 Catriona McKinnon, 'Chapter 15: Cosmopolitan Hope', in Brock and Brighouse, *The Political Philosophy of Cosmopolitanism*: 235.
12 Thomas Pogge, 'Human Rights and Human Responsibilities', in Pablo de Greiff and Ciaron Cronin (eds.), *Global Justice and Transnational Politics*, Cambridge MA and London, MIT, 2002: 165.
13 Thomas Pogge, *World Poverty and Human Rights: Cosmopolitan Responsibilities and Reforms*, Cambridge, Polity, 2002: 51.

Furthermore, Pogge interprets human rights in explicitly cosmopolitan terms because 'human rights are...universal...in the...sense of having global normative reach: human rights give persons moral claims not merely on the institutional order of their own societies, which are claims against their fellow citizens, but also on the global insitutional order, which are claims against their fellow human beings'.[14] Justice, in other words, can be applied to coercive social institutions, assessed in terms of their contribution towards the fulfillment of human rights. Pogge also associates human rights with issues of global distributive justice because 'most of the current under-fulfillment of human rights is more or less directly connected to poverty'.[15]

Pogge emphasizes the minimum negative duty of non-maleficence in regard to this human rights based version of global distributive justice. In other words, it is 'the responsibility of the affluent states and their citizens' to ensure that 'the global economic and political order they impose' on the rest of the world, and from which they benefit, does not impede the realization of human rights in other parts of the world[16], particularly in the form of absolute poverty. That is, 'we are not to collaborate in the coercive imposition of any institutional order that avoidably fails to realize human rights'.[17] Pogge's argument 'conceives, then, both human rights and justice as involving solely negative duties: specific minimal constraints...on what harms persons may inflict upon others'[18] through collaborating with or benefitting from coercive institutional orders. Thus, according to Pogge, we must think about global distributive justice in terms of protecting the poor 'from the effects of global rules whose injustice benefits us and is our responsibility'.[19] The principle of non-maleficence concerns our obligation not to contribute to coercive institutions preventing access to basic goods by the poor and thus engage in a violation of their human rights.

In other words, Pogge argues for a cosmopolitan commitment to global distributive justice not merely on the basis of some putative positive (or 'imperfect') duty to do good to others, but on the basis of some minimum negative duty not to actively harm them, no matter where in the world or in what country they might live. He derives this commitment to global distributive justice from such a cosmopolitan duty of non-maleficence because he claims that the relative positions of the better and worse off, or the affluent and the impoverished, in the global economy have resulted from the same historical process, instigated by massive wrongs such as slavery and colonial exploitation,[20] and perpetuated, for instance, by unequal trade relations and continuing 'structural violence'. The institutional dimension of this interpretation of the cosmopolitan principle of non-maleficence is important because, as Andras Miklos points out, according to this argument it is through 'imposing unjust institutions on the poor – that is, institutions that predictably lead to outcomes that are worse from the point of view of justice than those of the best available insitutional scheme – [that] the rich harm them'.[21]

---

14 Pogge, 'Human Rights and Human Responsibilities': 169.
15 Pogge, 'Human Rights and Human Responsibilities': 151.
16 Pogge, 'Human Rights and Human Responsibilities': 185.
17 Pogge, 'Human Rights and Human Responsibilities': 182.
18 Pogge, *World Poverty*: 13.
19 Pogge, *World Poverty*: 23.
20 Thomas Pogge, 'Chapter 7: A Cosmopolitan Perspective on the Global Economic Order', in Brock and Brighouse, *The Political Philosophy of Cosmopolitanism*: 96-97.
21 Andras Miklos, 'Institutions in Cosmopolitan Justice', in *Global Society* 20,3 (July 2006): 243.

One of the reasons Pogge suggests restricting ourselves to a deliberately modest cosmopolitan understanding of human rights and justice in terms of this negative duty of non-maleficence is that it remains compatible with 'an international diversity of institutional schemes',[22] such as forms of government, legal systems and so on, as well as different versions of the precise content or substance of the 'good life' for human beings. This helps minimize the tension between the demands of cosmopolitan justice and the diversity of cultural norms and expectations at regional, national or local level.

Similarly, Andrew Linklater agrees that this emphasis on non-maleficence or 'international prohibitions of harm suggest that although states have proved incapable of agreeing on any particular conception of the good which they should try to promote together, they have succeeded in reaching a global moral consensus about certain forms of harm that should be eradicated from international society'.[23] There are shared 'basic human vulnerabilities...to mental and physcial harm' that 'make it possible...to develop a global ethical consensus that straddles divergent conceptions of the good'.[24]

The important point is that for Pogge 'world poverty' exemplifies the violation of the fundamental human rights of the poor, through denying them access to the basic goods to which they are entitled as human beings. Global distributive justice, on the other hand, exemplifies the fulfillment of these human rights, and requires those of us who benefit from the current global order to rectify those institutions or structures which prevent access to basic goods by the poor in accordance with the principle of non-maleficence. Finally, this vision of global distributive justice can be defined in explicitly cosmopolitan terms, since it involves an equal commitment to all human beings as members of a universal moral community (or 'egalitarian individualism').

NGOs and cosmopolitan values

Non-governmental organizations (NGOs), as entities within civil society more generally, can provide both a normative and an institutional basis for cosmopolitanism. In institutional or organizational terms, civil society represents the political space available for autonomous political or social action independently of the state. Some definitions of civil society stress its voluntary character, in the sense that individuals choose to participate in or become members of civil society groups 'as part of a completely free choice'.[25] The voluntary character of civil society is sometimes contrasted with the coercive realm of state sovereignty, which involves the right to command and to be obeyed. The increased prominence and influence of NGOs at multiple levels, from the local to the global, has been well-documented. Richard Falk, for example, claims that 'the historical potency of the international law of human rights is predominantly a consequence of its implementation through the agency of civil society'.[26] NGOs also address a huge range of issues, from human rights to economic and social development to environmental concerns, to name just a few. They also employ different strategies to

---

22 Pogge, *World Poverty*: 36.
23 Linklater, 'The Problem of Harm': 330.
24 Linklater, 'The Problem of Harm': 330.
25 Marina Ottaway, 'Civil Society', in Peter Burnell and Vicky Randall (eds.), *Politics in the Developing World*, Oxford, OUP, 2005: 120-135: 122.
26 Falk, 'The World Order': 162.

deal with these issues, from direct engagement with them as operational NGOs, for example, to campaigning and lobbying as advocacy NGOs.[27]

Furthermore, civil society, as the arena within which NGOs operate, is a highly-contested political space. As Vivien Collingwood points out, civil society is characterized by a wide variety of hugely divergent and even contradictory 'political viewpoints and outlooks, from cosmopolitan to fascist, secular humanist to religious fundamentalist'.[28] Similarly, according to Marina Ottaway:

> Organizations citizens develop voluntarily are not always 'civil' in the normative sense of the word. The realm of civil society comprises organizations that promote human rights and vigilante groups that prey on the people they are supposed to protect.[29]

Or, as Jan Art Scholte phrases it, 'civil society is not an intrinsically virtuous space'.[30]

Nonetheless, NGOs as entities within civil society provide an opportunity for individuals to express themselves collectively as rational and autonomous moral agents. Thus, according to Mary Kaldor, 'the concept of transnational civil society...is used to refer to self-organized groups which are non-governmental'. Furthermore, such 'self-organized groups...represent, in effect, a public pressure for cosmopolitan right',[31] or those rights we can claim simply in virtue of being human, and members of a universal moral community. As Collingwood suggests:

> Many transnational NGOs' justifications of their international activities are rooted in notions of universal human dignity or global justice. NGOs that lobby for respect for human rights by governments worldwide, or specialise in getting food and shelter to war refugees, explain and justify these activities in terms of our shared moral commitment to treating every human being equally, or our responsibility to raise awareness of and reduce suffering around the world. From this perspective, national borders and the notion of 'across the border' activity have little moral or practical relevance.[32]

In other words, NGOs can provide the normative and institutional space for action upon cosmopolitan values. As entities within global civil society, their activities can transcend or at least cut across state or government defined boundaries in order to help fulfill the shared basic rights or material needs of human beings anywhere in the world.

Although he does not deal with the role of NGOs or civil society organizations as agents of global distributive justice in much detail, Thomas Pogge does suggest that such organizations can provide a useful bridge between the individual and a global order dominated by affluent and powerful states. In particular, civil society organizations provide an avenue for citizens of these states to challenge and change a global order they otherwise seem powerless to affect. Thus, 'thanks to international human rights

---

27 Cf. Anton Vedder, 'Questioning the Legitimacy of Nongovernmental Organisations', in Anton Vedder (ed.), *The Involvement of NGOs in International Governance and Policy: Sources of Legitimacy*, Leiden, Brill/Martinus Nijhoff, (forthcoming 2007): 4.
28 Vivien Collingwood, 'Non-Governmental Organisations, Power and Legitimacy in International Society', in *Review of International Studies* 32 (2006): 441.
29 Ottaway, 'Civil Society': 134.
30 Jan Art Scholte, 'Civil Society and Democracy in Global Governance', in Rorden Wilkinson (ed.), *The Global Governance Reader*, Oxford and New York, Routledge, 2005: 335.
31 Mary Kaldor, 'Introduction' to Mary Kaldor and B. Vashee (eds.), *Restructuring the Global Military Sector, Volume 1: New Wars*, London and Washington, Pinter, 1997: 23.
32 Collingwood, 'Non-Governmental Organisations, Power and Legitimacy': 447.

organizations like UNICEF, Oxfam, or Amnesty International we can also help prevent or mitigate some of the harms caused by the global order, thereby making up, as it were, for our contribution to their production'.[33]

In other words, NGOs as civil society organizations can fulfill a vital role in both mitigating and changing unjust institutions and structures responsible for violating the human rights of the poor through depriving them of access to basic goods, in accordance with the cosmopolitan principle of non-harm or non-maleficence. NGOs can be agents of cosmopolitan values through promoting global distributive justice, poverty alleviation and the fulfillment of fundamental and universal human rights.

Local values and global justice

Questions are sometimes raised about the ability of NGOs to understand and express the interests and values of those they claim to represent. Collingwood suggests, for example, 'that due to insufficient representation and democracy within NGOs the latter often fail to accurately reflect their clients' values and are disconnected from the communities that they attempt to help'.[34] This can be an issue for international development NGOs, for instance, which are based in the so-called 'developed' countries of the North, but claim to work on behalf of economically impoverished communities in the global South.

Even where NGOs are successful in identifying and representing a particular constituency, however, this raises further questions concerning their connection to and promotion of cosmopolitan values. As Collingwood points out, for example, many NGOs are designed to represent the interests and values of specific groups, such as refugees, children in poverty and abused women.[35] Although such groups are considered marginalized in some way, their interests and values could be presented as highly specific and in competition with the interests or objectives of other social groups. This may be particularly true of 'less formal, local groups, sometimes referred to as community-based organizations (CBOs),' which 'are usually concerned about local level development and welfare issues, focusing on service delivery or simply self-help'.[36] Thus, the suggestion is that 'NGOs will always represent particular groups and constituencies, however passionately their claims to global representation are expressed'.[37]

In other words, NGO success in becoming genuinely representative of specific local norms and objectives may not connect them to a coherent set of cosmopolitan values. There may be tensions between the requirements of environmental protection and the economic ambitions of particular impoverished groups within specific communities, for instance.[38] As Vedder suggests, NGOs are designed to deal with specific issues and not to reconcile competing normative claims, on cosmopolitan or any other grounds. 'Because NGOs – just like multinationals – are usually single issue organizations, they lack in many respects the degree of impartiality ideally needed to deal with situations in which normative conflicts occur.'[39]

---

33 Pogge, 'Human Rights and Human Responsibilities': 170-171.
34 Collingwood, 'Non-Governmental Organisations, Power and Legitimacy': 449.
35 Collingwood, 'Non-Governmental Organisations, Power and Legitimacy': 448.
36 Ottaway, 'Civil Society': 123.
37 Collingwood, 'Non-Governmental Organisations, Power and Legitimacy': 450.
38 Cf. Collingwood, 'Non-Governmental Organisations, Power and Legitimacy': 449.
39 Vedder, 'Questioning the Legitimacy': 10.

Marina Ottaway also questions the analytical accuracy or usefulness of a definition of civil society 'that separates a democratic, virtuous civil society acting in the public interest from a non-democratic, uncivil one, selfishly promoting narrow interests' because 'all societies are made up of groups with different and often conflicting interests'.[40] Civil society is a realm of competing interests just like other components of society such as the market or the state as an instrument of political power.

This emphasis on the local dimension of NGO representativeness also raises the possibility that the meta-ethical framework for their legitimacy is communitarian rather than cosmopolitan. Communitarianism is the position, in direct opposition to cosmopolitanism, that norms and values are both generated within and justified by reference to specific moral communities. In other words, even where NGO action has a normative basis in shared values and norms, these norms occur and are justified within a specific culture or community. The more successful NGOs become in representing specific constituencies or particular local interests, the less relevant cosmopolitan (as distinct from communitarian, perhaps) ideals and values become for defining and establishing the normative basis of their work.

I would suggest, however, that this apparent tension between community representation and cosmopolitan values, or between the local and the global, is a false dichotomy. Marginalized groups within any society often campaign on the basis of supposedly universal values or norms such as human rights or distributive justice and not merely to defend or promote their immediate specific interests. Furthermore, the use of such cosmopolitan language can often be strategically important in terms of widening the constituency for a campaign, to include other groups both nationally and internationally who may have no direct interest in or benefits to be accrued through the campaign. Such groups can include the wide variety of NGOs who also claim or aim to be committed to cosmopolitan values or norms.

Campaigns or action around local issues can originate within affected or aggrieved social groups or communities who then recruit outside NGOs as allies on the basis of their commitment to a shared set of cosmopolitan values. As McKinnon suggests, although for slightly different reasons, 'there can be as many paths to global principles of justice as there are local contexts'.[41] Specific local issues around land or income or gender or caste provide the content or substance of, or embody or exemplify, cosmopolitan principles of distributive justice, for instance.

Pogge's emphasis on non-maleficence as providing a modest or minimum cosmopolitan core for human rights and global distributive justice, to which Linklater's emphasis on 'the harm principle' corresponds, may be useful in furnishing a shared set of norms that NGOs and other civil society organizations can use as a basis for action while remaining sensitive to the specific requirements, values and 'goods' of the communities they claim to represent. The cosmopolitan impetus for action around poverty alleviation and human rights violations depends on a universal concern with human vulnerability and the prevention of harm, but this can be pursued within a diverse range of social and political arrangements reflecting the ways of life and the values of specific local communities. As Sylvie Loriaux suggests, one can act to ensure that the basic

---

40 Ottaway, 'Civil Society': 134.
41 McKinnon, 'Cosmopolitan Hope': 246.

human needs that form 'the very precondition of all possible conceptions of happiness' are met, without prescribing any 'particular conception of happiness'.[42]

In other words, Pogge's cosmopolitan approach to the problem of world poverty through a combination of non-maleficence or non-harm, human rights and justice may help to resolve tensions between NGO claims to represent local and community needs and their appeal to cosmopolitan or universal values to justify and motivate their work. Conversely, NGOs can provide both a normative and an institutional space through which world poverty can be addressed on cosmopolitan grounds. They can exemplify such cosmopolitan ideals as global distributive justice and human rights, while providing the opportunity to act on these ideals through more polycentric, non-hierarchical and transnational forms of social and political organization that connect us more directly to other human beings as members of a universal moral community.

Conclusion

Non-governmental organizations (NGOs) can be an important vehicle for implementing or putting into practice such cosmopolitan values as global distributive justice. NGOs, as civil society organizations, are well-placed to help rectify and challenge the harm caused to the world's poor by the current coercive global economic order in accordance with Pogge's cosmopolitan agenda, for example. Finally, this appeal to cosmopolitan values can strengthen rather than undermine NGO representation of the interests or concerns of specific local groups or communities.

---

42 Sylvie Loriaux, 'Beneficence and Distributive Justice in a Globalising World', in *Global Society* 20,3 (July 2006): 261.

Thomas Bremer

Peace-Building in the Balkans – Do the Churches Contribute?

Some personal observations and experiences

It was in the early 1990s that I participated in a conference on war and conflict in different European contexts; it took place in a small German university. This was in the time when the European public was shocked by what was going on in former Yugoslavia – people who seemed to have lived together peacefully now killed each other, nations claimed territories for their own members and expelled everyone who belonged to another nation, and people who were mostly seen as 'Yugoslavs' in Western Europe proclaimed identities as Croats, Serbs or Bosnian Muslims (Bosniacs). At the conference mentioned, John D'Arcy May spoke about the situation in Northern Ireland, and he said how he as an Australian, a Catholic and living in Dublin, saw the Irish conflict. At one point, he mentioned that when speaking with people involved in the conflict, he had frequently to listen to the dismissal that 'someone who is not from here cannot understand our troubles'.

This phrase struck me when I heard it. Since the 1970s, I had been many times in what was then Yugoslavia, had spent a year of my studies there, spoke the language, had written a lot on the religious situation in the country, and I knew exactly this kind of argument: 'if you are not from here you can't understand it'. In fact, of course, this phrase tries to exclude the other from any insight into a difficult situation. It proposes that for understanding and analysing a situation, it is not so important to have intellectual skills, but is necessary to come from a certain area, namely, the area involved. Of course, this argument does not make any sense; otherwise, we could not understand any political or conflict situation in the world except those in our own countries.

However, there is more. The example shows that there are structural similarities between conflicts which take place within a country. One of them, which we can see in this small example, is the idea that the 'true' understanding of the conflict has to be kept within the particular group. It is the idea that only 'we' have the monopoly of knowing and interpreting what has been going on, and why. Such an attitude also helps to preserve the integrity of the particular identity; it contributes to homogenizing the convictions of one's own group's members.

The question of the identity of a collective is an issue of special interest when churches and religious groups are involved. They are of central importance for group identities, on the one hand, and they are expected to foster peace, reconciliation and mutual understanding, on the other. As known, they do not always succeed in this task, above all not in situations when they form a part of the problem, i.e., when they are one of the main identity builders in a society.

I shall try to develop some thoughts on the interconnection between religious communities and peace building based on my experience in the Balkans. I presume that some of them might also be of interest for other contexts, as my small example may have shown.

1. Churches and Identity

In many cases, belonging to a certain church or religious community also implies belonging to a certain nation, and vice versa. Many nations identify themselves traditionally as Catholic, Orthodox or Protestant. In most cases this does not present a problem. Actually, nations which traditionally belong to several religious convictions are, in Europe, an exception (if we do not take into account the results of modern migration processes). One could name some such cases: Germans, Dutch, Swiss, Czechs, Hungarians, Albanians, Romanians and Ukrainians. Among these nations, the Reformation had an decisive influence, though there also exist Catholic churches of the Eastern rite ('Uniates') which means that we can find Orthodox Christians as well as Eastern Catholics. Frequently, we also find here a late development of national consciousness and nation states. Nevertheless, in some of these cases, one of the religious belongings played – at least historically – an important role in the respective national consciousness, for instance, Lutheranism among Germans, Calvinism among the Dutch, or Islam among Albanians.

In the other cases, however, national and religious belonging are narrowly linked to each other. The vast majority of a nation belonged (or belongs) to the same religion. In order to be a good Pole, one should be a good Catholic. In several cases, there were and are even state churches (England, Scandinavia). In the Orthodox world, the relationship between church and state was described with the notion *symphonia* which means that the two entities were closely related to each other, although not formally linked. The term avers that both have common interests. We should not be astonished that it happened, for instance, several times in Byzantium that a high-ranking state official like the Imperial Chancellor became Patriarch while a layman – and had to be ordained deacon, priest and bishop within a few days. As well, decisions of synods had the character of state laws and were enforced by the authorities with police means.

This connection between religion and nation is especially important when it comes to a situation where one community has to differentiate itself from another by stressing the differences. Religion is a homogenizing factor: it forms a group identity, offers values, and, most importantly, it does not follow the logics 'of this world' since it deals with questions which are beyond arguments. If it is necessary for my eternal salvation – and that is what religion deals with! – to belong to a certain church, this belonging cannot be subject to discussion or compromise. With people who are convinced that only their religion can lead to salvation, one can argue about belonging to a political or social group, on living in a certain place or on driving a certain car – but hardly on changing one's religious conviction. Of course, we know that the ecumenical movement has also brought along insight into the possibility of keeping one's own conviction while nevertheless respecting that of the other. We must be aware that historically, though, religion has not been so open for dialogue with the other.

Under these circumstances, it can be easily understood that in social or political confrontation, when the strengthening of group identity was needed, the use of religion for this purpose was attractive. That means that in most cases it was not religion which formed a national identity, but rather national ideas which used religion. Since 'nation' is not a theological category at all, it was not religion's inner logic which was used, but the social phenomenon of cohesiveness which is typical of religious communities. Nevertheless, there is a very important question, and a field of research to be pursued, concerning how and why religious groups have been so obviously ready to be used (or better, misused) for political purposes. The explanation, that in a period of secularization it was possible for religion to gain importance, is not sufficient since we know this phenomenon also in periods and in societies with a very low degree of secularism.

Interestingly, religion offers also a group identity of its own, i.e., an identity which is not linked with political issues. The local Catholic churches in Germany, Poland, Italy and the Netherlands differ very much from each other; the mainstreams of these churches are quite different due to several reasons. However, an average German Catholic who would enter a Catholic church in one of the other countries would recognize it immediately as 'my' church, as a service which is 'my own', etc. Although in many questions German Protestants would be much closer and much more familiar to him or her than other Catholics in other countries, this average Catholic would most probably feel at home in a 'foreign' Catholic church; he or she has a group identity which was created by his or her church and which created feelings of belonging to it. Such an identity is not dangerous for others, it was not formed by the desire to be different, but is just the normal result of a group which offers to its members a feeling of belonging. One could argue that the mere existence of such group identities makes it easier to use religious groups for political and other purposes. If this were true, then the religious communities have failed to make sure that their members understand the religious dimension of their identity, and to limit it to this identity they should not allow other people to use the advantages of an already existing community for things far from issues of religion.

2. Churches in a Situation of War

In the case of armed conflict and war, 'normal' conditions are no longer valid. For the question of group identities, this means that it is even more difficult to see their double-bind character, the cohesive power of religious belonging and the possibility of misuse. In a crisis, it seems to be even easier to convince groups that they are endangered and that a certain political option is the best (or, the only) way to keep them existing. It needs self-distance and frequently an outside perspective in order to have full insight into the challenges of such a situation. Obviously, in an acute crisis, the view from outside is even more helpful than a perspective from within – this, of course, contradicts the phrase quoted in my introductory remarks, thereby showing its more polemical character and self-serving defence than its putative analytical value.

However, if an outside perspective can understand a given situation more comprehensively, how can this understanding be transferred to the churches involved? The Balkans experience shows the difficulties. In the beginning of the clashes, in spring 1991, the Catholic bishops of Croatia sent a letter to all Catholic bishops in the world to explain to them the local situation and to ask for solidarity and support. Indeed, many bishops from abroad, above all from Italy, Germany, Austria, and the United States, were concerned and began to deal with the issue. There were lots of visits, statements, meetings, etc. However, in a lot of these utterances, beside solidarity with the Catholic church in the region, there was also expressed the need for mutual understanding, negotiations, and ecumenical efforts towards the Serbian Orthodox Church. This was a surprising result for the Catholic church in the region. It had requested support for its own side and yet received calls for encounters and contacts with a church which seemed to represent the enemy, the very people who – in Croatian perceptions – bore the sole guilt for the war. The result was a certain attitude of mistrust which could frequently be noted in representatives of the Catholic church in Croatia when they were in contact with church people from abroad, even with fellow Catholics.

One can easily find similar examples also within the Serbian Orthodox Church and within the Muslim Community. This shows that groups behave differently in difficult situations. The challenge for people from abroad is then to find ways of dealing with this, taking into account the specific needs and views of each of the groups involved, but also having in mind the goals of peace, justice, and reconciliation.

The wars on the territory of what once was Yugoslavia constitute the conflict that has had the largest involvement of churches, church representatives and church bodies, all trying to intervene and to mediate, ever in history. There were dozens of missions, delegations, meetings, etc., sponsored mostly by CEC and CCEE, by the WCC and by single churches and church organizations (e.g., Pax Christi, the peace movement within the Catholic church). And, astonishingly, there were lots of meetings between representatives of the churches in the region – which itself is something almost completely new; in other wars it was unthinkable that representatives of the churches that were at least indirectly involved would be brought together. When judging the small outcome of the engagement of the churches during the post-Yugoslav wars, one must not forget the precedent that had been set and that for sure was a result of the peace theme being present for such a long time in the ecumenical movement, especially in the Justice, Peace and the Integrity of Creation (JPIC) process in Europe.

Frequently, the mediating churches and organizations were accused of not being neutral, but of siding with one of the churches in the region. The alliance between Orthodox churches in the world and the Serbian Orthodox Church, and local Catholic churches with the Catholic church in Croatia, however, was not completely convincing. Interconfessional church bodies also intervened, and a common mission undertaken by a Catholic cardinal, an Orthodox metropolitan and a Lutheran archbishop does not fit into these categories. Additionally, it is too simplistic to ascribe the solidarity which could be observed only to confessional belonging. One has to take into account also political and other circumstances.

The international church organizations undertook some interesting activities, although not all of them resulted in a melioration of the situation. For example, editors and journalists from church newspapers were brought together for meetings. During the years of war, these papers usually wrote in a very critical and sometimes ugly manner about the other side and about the other church. Another attempt was the idea of bringing church historians together in order to discuss issues of common history and, above all, their different interpretation. This resulted in a number of volumes which will show effect most probably only after some time.

These remarks show that in the case of the Balkans, similar phenomena as in other cases of the involvement of churches in conflicts could be seen, but there were different and new attempts to overcome these phenomena. One can be pessimistic concerning the outcomes of the Balkan wars, but the mere fact that a rapprochement took place must not be neglected.

3. Churches and Reconciliation

The reconciliation issue was put forward by the JPIC process, and especially with the 1997 European Ecumenical Assembly in Graz, Austria. This made clear that fostering reconciliation after conflicts is a main task and issue for churches. As the Graz Assembly was influenced by the events and developments in the former Yugoslavia, many representatives there felt that the churches had failed to act appropriately in the Balkan wars and therefore they stressed the need for church engagement in reconciliation.

What is the contribution that the churches can make to reconciliation, after a war in which they were at least perceived as clearly belonging to one of the conflict parties? First of all, it must be said that in such cases a great step forward, or rather a turn in direction, is necessary. They must come to the conclusion that the position they have held so far has to be revised. As long as any community, and this is valid also for churches, adheres narrowly to an outer ideology such as nationalism, there cannot be a development towards reconciliation since this term means to accept the other (which is here, the other church) as someone who is different, and to accept him or her in his or her difference.

This also means that empathy for the other side is to be developed. In the case of the churches in the former Yugoslavia, we find very frequently that statements of empathy are expressed almost solely for one's own side. One could hardly find any kind of understanding for the suffering of the others, be that caused by fellow nationals or by a third party. It is understandable that such a shift of perception cannot be expected immediately. There must be a lot of preparatory work on the grass-roots level, i.e., activities which help members of the respective church to get into contact with believers from the other one. There were (and frequently still are) virtually no contacts between members of the congregations. That means that they do not know each other and that they mostly rely on prejudices and stereotypes. Encounters could contribute to building a perception of the other that is based on experience of personal contacts; this would enable the human being behind what was presented thus far as just a member of a different nation to be seen. It is clear that such meetings are a challenge and must be prepared for well.

What has happened in the area of former Yugoslavia in the years after the fighting, i.e., after 1995? On the one hand, one can notice that the relations between the churches have become much better, even better than ever, at least on the official level. Was there just one official meeting between the heads of the Catholic church in Croatia and the Serbian Orthodox Church between 1945 and 1990, namely in 1968, in a time of growing tensions and of armed conflict? In fact, several such meetings took place; at least the first two came from an initiative within the churches themselves, and not from abroad. Interestingly, after the end of the wars, such meetings continued, and one may say that relations between those two churches are today better than ever before. This is partly due to individuals who came to bear responsibility in the churches and who had another approach than that of their predecessors, but partly also to the growing consciousness about the task of the church to promote reconciliation and even to feel shame about what had happened in the war years.

One important difference in the situation nowadays is that the two countries, Croatia and Serbia, are now distinct states, neighbouring, and, though burdened with a difficult past, are nevertheless urged to develop mutual relations. During the war, there were completely different perceptions of whether it was one country (Yugoslavia) and the clashes were a civil war, or two countries engaged in an international war. Of course, these perceptions had consequences for the political judgement of the situation and therefore influenced also the churches. Today, there is clarity that we are dealing with separate states.

Nevertheless, there are different views on what the war was really about. In both societies, and in both churches, the idea prevails that 'my' side was completely or almost completely innocent, and that 'we' were victims of the other side. This means that in the interpretation and evaluation of some central aspects of history, there are two different discourses. This concerns almost all aspects of a common history, beginning with the settling of the Slavs in the Balkans throughout the Middle Ages, through the communist era until the question of responsibility and guilt for the wars of the 1990s. It is questionable, whether a real reconciliation can take place when the parties involved have a completely different vision about what they have to reconcile. It is a precondition for successful reconciliation processes at least to recognize the perception of the other side as valid, even if the sides cannot agree on what has happened. We still do not know very much about how groups can reconcile, but if we juxtapose the results from research on reconciliation between individuals, then we must be aware that this is a precondition also for churches which were – though indirectly – involved in conflicts. Each church must develop a feeling for the needs and for the perceptions of the respective other churches. Regrettably, in the Balkans area, almost no such compassion can be noticed so far. Therefore, the progress in the relations between the churches in the Balkans must be noted with caution; for, behind this progress are still big problems which are not yet solved.

* * *

These observations may have shown how similar are some characteristics of churches in different conflict situations. It would be worthwhile to research these common phenomena in order to further the role of religious communities in future conflicts. Northern Ireland and the Balkans seem not to have so very much in common, but maybe a comparative study of these cases (including, perhaps, others as well) would be highly significant for us in preventing the religious factor from becoming so decisive in conflicts. Religious communities should become motors of peace and of reconciliation. As long as they seem to be part of the problem, but not part of the solution, there is still a lot to do both for people engaged in churches and for scholars.

Jude Lal Fernando
God of Plentitude and Meditation on Conscience
Subverting Religious Narratives for Peaceful Coexistence

Introduction

This paper attempts to critique some interpretations of certain religious narratives that have constructed the other as the eternal enemy. These interpretations have emerged within imperialism, colonialism and postcolonial nation-building, consequently giving rise to conflicts in our societies today. The critique will focus on some narratives in monotheistic traditions that are interpreted as 'One God – One People', excluding the other, and on some narratives in non-theistic traditions like Theravada Buddhism in Sri Lanka which are given an ethnocentric interpretation.

In modern times, Christianity as a monotheistic religion and Theravada Buddhism as a non-theistic tradition have encountered each other within the Western imperialist project. I would like to examine how certain cultural forms interacted with particular material conditions under imperialism and colonialism in bringing about exclusivist interpretations of cultures and religions. This examination will show us how to subvert the same narratives in order to include or accept the other, instead of excluding him or her. Re-reading religious narratives in view of a moral re-visioning that challenges us to bear responsibility for the other would provide a basis for inter-religious dialogue while giving us a paradigm to overcome exclusivist ethno-religious and national identities. In critiquing the monotheistic traditions, the work of the biblical scholar Regina Schwartz in *Curse of Cain: The Violent Legacy of Monotheism*[1] will be taken as a major resource; and, in the critique of ethnocentric Theravada Buddhism, the work of the anthropologist Gananath Obeysekara in *Meditation on Conscience*,[2] will be our reference point.

Critique of Monotheistic Traditions

While Aloysius Pieris suggests justice for the oppressed as the 'canon within the canon' of the critique of racist, ideological contamination in the Bible,[3] Regina Schwartz suggests the notion of plentitude, which is found in the Bible, as an antidote to the notion of scarcity which she argues provides the basis for violence. Schwartz shows how history in the Bible, though treated as a continuous development to support nationalist projects, is in fact full of ruptures rather than a continuous process. Even though there is a tendency to fix identity in these narratives themselves, Schwartz, referring to a vast number of other narratives that run throughout more than a thousand years, shows the

---

1 Regina M. Schwartz, *The Curse of Cain: The Violent Legacy of Monotheism*, Chicago and London, University of Chicago, 1997.
2 Gananath Obeysekara, *A Meditation on Conscience*, Colombo, Social Scientist's Association of Sri Lanka, 1988.
3 Aloysius Pieris, 'Faith-Communities and Communalism: The Role of Religion and Ideology', in *Dialogue* (NS) 29 (2002): 111-131: 123.

impossibility of fixing such definitive identities: '[t]he Hebrew Bible depicts a history that stubbornly resists any notion of fulfilment or completion.'[4]

Although one uniform fixed identity is attempted, Schwartz shows how the notion of Israel is an inconsistent, fractured and multifarious concept: the wilderness is glorified when fixity is built, and the land is glorified when exile is experienced. There is always a tension between tents and houses, nomadism and agriculture, the wilderness and Canaan. In other words, in settled times the wilderness is glorified as it is opposed to the corruption of the state, and in unsettled times the land is glorified in order to enkindle hope of a new rule. The biblical narratives, she notes, are interested in exploring the 'questions of definition' rather than in fixing them. Fixing of an exclusivist identity where the deity is depicted as possessing land and people, generates conflict. 'When truth is multiple instead of single, when memories are plentiful instead of scarce', Schwartz suggests, rather than as contradictory they can be treated as complimentary and as stories illuminating each other so that 'creativity could be generated by many'.[5]

Recent studies show how the biblical myths of Chosen People and Promised Land have shaped the histories of Britain for over four centuries and North America for over three centuries. Anthony D. Smith, Linda Colley and Clifford Longely show us that these religious myths are not mere metaphors.[6] Smith notes how, from one angle, 'Victorian Britain's imperial mission' was 'merely an extension' of belief in the biblical myth of chosenness.[7] Schwartz shows how 19th century biblical scholars, who critiqued the biblical narratives as having being written by human beings who are culturally and historically conditioned and who thereby promoted secularism, forgot that these narratives were influencing German nationalism at the same time.[8] Selective reading of these myths not only has conditioned the histories of these imperial powers but also has lingered into the current secular discourse of Western hegemony (particularly, North American).[9] At the heart of such interpretations lie the issues of wealth and power.

In the nationalist adaptations of the narratives we see that ruptures in their history were totally suppressed. Otherness in the narratives was overlooked. Memories that are treated as certain and fixed have become so by suppressing other memories. It is by referring to the ruptures and suppressed memories that we can critique such fixity and recover an alternative vision. Possession of the land which all monotheistic religions claim as the will of God, Schwartz points out, is critiqued by an inbuilt narrative in the Bible itself. She writes:

> Their [biblical writers] alternative vision embraces the values of nomadism, is suspicious of settled agriculture and even idealizes the wilderness. A closer look

---

[4] Schwartz, *The Curse of Cain*: 124.
[5] Schwartz, *The Curse of Cain*: 173.
[6] Anthony D. Smith, *Chosen People*, Oxford, OUP, 2003; Linda Colley, *Britons: Forging the Nation, 1707-1837*, New Haven and London, Yale University, 2005; Clifford Longley, *Chosen People: The Big Idea that shapes England and America*, London, Hodder & Stoughton, 2002.
[7] Smith, *Chosen People*: 48.
[8] Schwartz, *The Curse of Cain*: 10-11.
[9] Michael Northcott, analyzing the vote base of George Bush, shows how the Southern Baptists, evangelical mega-churches and conservative religious groups backed him not because his policies were different from the other candidate but because of their world-view, especially the messianic certainty that their world-view is the right one, see Michael Northcott, 'The Triumph of Imperial Politics', in *Tablet* 6 November 2004: 5.

at the etymological relation between man, Adam, and land, adama, reveals that it is between human beings and all land.[10]

She asks the question whether the people own land or whether the dynamic is the more possessive idea of land owning people, and shows how the story of the tower of Babel offers a critique against nation building.[11] In this sense, then, supporting the building of a Western or an American empire, a Jewish state or an Islamic state in the name of God is highly questionable. Referring to the story of Joseph, she shows how narratives of scarcity and violence give way to those of plentitude and reconciliation, and how recovery of memory brings reunion; unlike the story of Cain's treatment of Abel, the brothers of Joseph realize that he is their brother (the Egyptian is their brother). Schwartz states: 'Plentitude proliferates identities without violence. Scarcity obliterates the other with violence.' In conclusion, and instead of a deity characterized by scarcity who favours Abel over Cain, Jacob over Esau, Sarah over Hagar, Israelites over Canaanites, we can discover a biblical God of plentitude whose first command is to uphold multiplicity, who opposes the possessing of land and the building of nations. Rodney Stark, from a sociological perspective, shows how the human images of God in the Hebrew Bible evolved from a moody to a touching one, from terror to loving transcendent being.[12] This God is not a possessive deity who subdues peoples and lands, but the God of plentitude who delivers justice to the poor and respects diversity.

Critique of Theravada Buddhism in Sri Lanka

Ancient myths play their part in constructing identities in Sri Lanka, too. The ethnocentric character of Theravada Buddhism in Sri Lanka, which provides the ideological basis for the present Sinhala Buddhist nationalism, has its roots in the construction of the identity of the Sinhala people as one chosen to safeguard Buddhism. Chosenness here is part of a historical consciousness, mainly supported by post-canonical Pali literature – especially, the *Mahavamsa*[13] – which, in one of its clauses, justifies killing for the sake of religion. As Gananath Obeysekara puts it:

> The moral dilemma resulted from the particularization of a universal religion like Buddhism as the religion of a specific nation, and the definition of the nation in terms of a dominant ethnic group. The *Mahavamsa* sees the destiny of the nation, the Sinhalese and that of the religion as inextricably linked. If so, then is killing and violence for the sake of the religion justified? The *Mahavamsa* says 'yes'.[14]

---

10 Schwartz, *The Curse of Cain*: 43.
11 Schwartz, *The Curse of Cain*: 38.
12 Rodney Stark, *One True God: Historical Consequences of Monotheism*, Princeton and Oxford, Princeton University, 2001: 28.
13 *Mahavamsa* was written by Mahanama Thera in the 6th century CE. It depicts the work of the rulers who patronized the Mahavihara monastry and covers the domain controlled from Anuradhapura by these patrons. As K. Indrapala notes, *Mahavamsa* could be described as the chronicle of the Mahavihara monastery; also, the domain of the rulers of Anuradhapura that the chronicle covers was never the whole island that we call Sri Lanka today, see K. Indrapala, *The Evolution of an Ethnic Identity: The Tamils in Sri Lanka, c.300 BCE to c.1200 CE*, Sydney, MV Publications, 2005: 16.
14 Obeysekara, *A Meditation on Conscience*: 19.

The present war in Sri Lanka against the Tamils, which has cost so many lives, is meant to safeguard the Sinhala Buddhist state.[15] The cultural influence of the *Mahavamsa* narrative in justifying war (which also has Western interests) is clear, though the complicity between the interests of the West and the Sinhala Buddhist nation-state will be discussed later.

Although Sinhala Buddhist nationalism attempts to interpret the history of the land as a conflict between the Tamils and Sinhalese based on the post-canonical texts, there are ruptures in history as well as in the texts themselves that do not support such claims.[16] The *Mahavamsa* teaching which says that it is not sinful to kill non-Buddhists is radically different from the central teaching of Buddhism as found in canonical literature, as well as some of the post-canonical literature like *Saddharmarathnavaliya* (13th century CE). Nevertheless, the *Mahavamsa* itself is unable to deviate fully from the central teaching of Buddha and support the ethnocentric nationalist claims of Sri Lanka today, which is itself revealing. As I counteracted the exclusivist claims of monotheistic traditions based on the notion of scarcity, let me now show how the *Mahavamsa* and other-post canonical Buddhist texts attempt to address the historical 'conscience' of ethical commitment to the other and thereby counteract the exclusivist nationalist claims of a historical consciousness. As Regina Schwartz deconstructs the exclusivist historical consciousness in monotheistic traditions, Gananath Obeysekara in his reflections on the narrative of the conscience of the king in the *Mahavamsa* deconstructs the exclusivist Sinhala nationalist claim in history. And, as Schwartz demonstrates the proliferation of narratives in the Bible, so Obeysekara points out how the *Mahavamsa* narrative of the Duttagamini-Elara conflict has other, different versions. For instance, in the *Deepavamsa*, written in the 4th century CE, the defeat of the just king Elara by Duttagamini is mentioned only in a few lines, whereas it becomes the central narrative of the *Mahavamsa*, which was written in the 6th century CE. According to the Duttagamini-Elara conflict depicted in the *Mahavamsa*, the enemy king Elara himself is treated as a just king. He is praised for his just rule, in which he attends to the needs of the people in compassionate and just ways. There is no indication that he is anti-Buddhist; instead, he is said to have revered Buddhism. There were Buddhists in his army and cabinet. Moreover, Duttagamini orders that Elara be revered, and builds a tomb for him. Yet, by the time we come to the *Pujawaliya*, written in the 14th century, King Elara is depicted as a wicked king.

Today, in Sinhala Buddhist nationalism, Elara is identified with the Tamils, who are considered a national threat; in this reading the good and just king Elara who was deified is missing. Obeysekara notes a consistent theme in the chronicles in the following way:

> Wherever Duttagamini is presented as having a conscience Elara appears as the just king, and when Duttagamini is portrayed as doing his duty untroubled by his conscience, Elara is ignored or presented as evil.[17]

---

15 The Sri Lankan conflict has claimed 68,000 lives, displaced 1.2 million people (1 million of whom are Tamils), and devastated the Northern and Eastern regions of the country. Moreover, 50,000 children were made orphans. 40,000 women were made widows and over two million palmyra trees were destroyed, see Kithusara Group, *With the Eyes of Faith*, Kalutara/Sri Lanka, Kithusara Publications, 2002.

16 Out of 2000 years of written history only 200 have been under one rule. It had been a land of kingdoms which was invaded by South Indian dynasties several times, as shown by the *Mahavamsa* itself.

17 Obeysekara, *A Meditation on Conscience*: 144.

In this way, Obeysekara reiterates the need to read the narrative in a symbolic way, rather than taking a historic approach: 'The moral significance of a myth helps it transcend a specific historical rootedness.'[18] He points out how the myth-model of the narrative of the troubled conscience of the king who killed millions is peculiar to similar situations in the life of Arjuna in the *Bhagavad Gita* and Emperor Asoka. The narratives imply in all these cases that the king was consoled. Obeysekara asks, '…but might not the king's conscience reflect the conscience of other persons made uneasy by the reply of the Arahats?'[19] Both Walpola Rahula Thera[20] and E.W. Adikaram,[21] two Sri Lankan Buddhist scholars, in their writings voice this conscience. Another Buddhist scholar, Ven. Dhammavihari, suggests changing the *Mahavamsa* and rewriting history.[22]

Can we not say it is the conscience of the *Mahavamsa*'s author-monk himself that is troubled? The text reflects an ideological contamination of a religious tradition emerging as a result of a monastic order's close relationship to the power politics of the land. Although the author-monk himself is in a dilemma in reinventing history to suit his own ends, he himself cannot hide the conscience of the king, the goodness of the enemy and his much revered tomb. (What happened to the Canaanites? What happened to the Tamils?) In fact, highly moral aspects of Buddhist tradition, articulated in the form of mythical stories of Buddha's self-sacrificial rebirths – *Saddharmarathnavaliya* (13th century) and *Jatakapotha* – have been popular among the ordinary peasants in the land, forming their conscience for ages. How can such a community of people tend to justify a war in the name of their religion?

As Obeysekara notes, the dismantling of the Buddhist conscience begins with the rejection of the popular tradition of *Jataka* tales that formed the conscience of the society. It was replaced with a Western intellectual interpretation of Buddhism as a rational theosophy (Olcott), over against Christianity's belief in an omnipotent god of creation, and the parallel socio-political movement (of Anagarika Dharmapala) of the 19th century, which resurrected the 'king without conscience' idea. Ironically, we can see how the Sinhala Buddhist nationalist movement, while undermining the moral tradition of *Jataka* tales, also treats the myth of Duttagamini as history. 'The dark underside of Sinhala Buddhism', without its age-old 'mitigating humanism of conscience',[23] may be seen today in both the devastated homes and villages of Tamils in the North and East of the country, and in the thousands of monuments to Sinhala dead soldiers in the South.

An Orientalist-Occidentalist Alliance

It should also be noted how the *Mahavamsa* narrative became a cultural basis for the nationalist struggle against colonialism, which itself was based on another ethnocentric

---

18 Obeysekara, *A Meditation on Conscience*: 27.
19 Obeysekara, *A Meditation on Conscience*: 20.
20 Walpola Rahula acknowledges how Buddhism began to lose its original spirit of renunciation and simplicity when the monks, for the first time, officially entered the politics of the state by accompanying Duttagamini's army, see Walpola Rahula, *The History of Buddhism in Ceylon*, Dehiwala, Buddhist Cultural Centre,1993: 76-80.
21 E.W. Adikaram, *Jathivadaya saha Budu Dahama saha Venath Lipi*, Nugegoda, Adikaram Padanama, 1993: 19-47.
22 Ven. Dhammavihari, 'Recording, Translating and Interpreting Sri Lankan Chronicle Data', in *Journal of Buddhist Ethics* 10 (2003). Available online at http://www.buddhistethics.org/bath-conf.html (accessed 4 August 2007).
23 Obeysekara, *A Meditation on Conscience*: 40.

religious nationalism, namely, Western Christian imperialism. Ironically, it was the British who discovered the *Mahavamsa* and translated it into English even before it was translated into Sinhala in the latter half of the 19th century. From a postcolonial perspective, Pradeep Jeganathan argues that this helped to bolster a division between the Sinhalese and Tamils as Aryans and Dravidians respectively, depicting the Sinhalese as having a civilizational superiority like the British. Marisa Agnell shows how the Royal Asiatic Society in Colombo started to publish articles in their journals tracing the Aryan origins of the Sinhalese in opposition to Dravidians.[24] Jeganathan notes that the British were interested in the chronicle because it contained narratives of the grandeur of an ancient kingdom (Sinhala kingdom?) that fought against India.[25] For the British Raj, India was the 'Jewel of the Crown' and the island of Lanka was a strategic location in the ruling of it. As Kumari Jaywaredene shows, the material basis of the Sinhala Buddhist nationalist movement was provided by the emerging commercial classes who were loyal to the British Crown but were competing with the Muslim and Indian traders.[26] This colonial practice which is associated with essentialist representations of cultures and religions has given rise to a process of polarization of diverse ethnic and religious communities.

Sinhala Buddhist nationalism is culturally supported by the narratives of *Mahavamsa* (narrative reinvented without the conscience of the king) and politically structured in the image and likeness of the unitary state of the West (one people and one nation). The cultural influence of monotheism reflected in the ideology behind nations – one people, one nation – can also be seen in the formation of the unitary state structure in Sri Lanka, which is inextricably linked to the Sinhala Buddhist identity. Today, Sinhala Buddhist nationalists are ready to align with the Western powers (particularly, the United States of America) to suppress the Tamils' own movement toward self-determination. The reluctance to recognize this movement both by the Sri Lankan state and the international community of states reflects the absolutism of the present system of nation-states. In the maintenance of the international order of nation-states (which is hegemonic both locally and globally) it is an 'Orientalist-Occidentalist Combine'[27] that generates conflicts both locally and globally.

A Historical Transcendental!

The phenomenon of the nation-state which appears to function as a transcendental reality over and above civil society is a historical construction which first emerged in the West in a context of imperial conquests, competing economies and religious reformations. Michael Hardt and Antonio Negri note how the absolutist theological definition of transcendence that formed the foundations of the monarchical nation-state was replaced

---

24 Marisa Agnell, 'Understanding the Aryan Theory', in Mithran Tiruchelvam and Dattathreya C.S. (eds.), *Culture and Politics of Identity in Sri Lanka*, Colombo, International Centre for Ethnic Studies, 1998: 41-71.

25 Pradeep Jeganathan, 'Authorizing History, Authorizing Land: The Conquest of Anuradhapura', in Pradeep Jeganathan and Qadri Ismail (eds.), *Unmaking the Nation: The Politics of Identity and History in Modern Sri Lanka*, Colombo, Social Scientists' Association, 1995.

26 Kumari Jayawardene, *Nobodies to Somebodies: The Rise of the Colonial Bourgeoisie in Sri Lanka*, Colombo, Social Scientists' Association of Sri Lanka, 2003: 263-274.

27 This is a term that I borrowed from Aloysius Pieris who critiques both 'ism's and introduces a liberative interpretation of religions, see Aloysius Pieris, 'The Asian Reality and the Christian Option: A Plea for a Paradigm Shift in Christian Education in Asia', in *Dialogue* (NS) 32-33 (2005-2006): 158-196.

by an equally absolutist, secular definition of state (the republican nation-state).[28] Transcendence of the rational state is as absolutist as its predecessor. This absolutism is predicated upon 'the deity of scarcity' who possesses and dominates. This is also the absolutism of 'the king without conscience'. Absolutist transcendence constructs the other. As Schwartz puts it, '[v]iolence is not only what we do to the Other. It is prior to that. Violence is the very construction of the Other'.[29] Using the words of Pierre Bourdieu we could say that the phenomenon of nation-state is a *habitus* which is a 'historical transcendental bound up with the structure and history of a field'.[30] *Habitus* is both structured and structuring at the same time. This perspective recognizes the importance of human agency while ruling out deterministic absolutism in both political or theological concepts and structures of the nation-state.

Today, within the economic field, the notions of scarcity and plentitude have to be analysed within an international system regulated by the rule of market forces that are dominated by a few powerful countries and transnational corporations. The present global order upholds a system, as Zigmunt Bauman puts it, where 'riches are global and the miseries are local'.[31] The misery and uncertainty experienced by the 'Global South' is generated by the absolutist logic of capitalist globalization which claims to have no other alternative. In this sense the neo-liberal economic policies that determine the present world order reflect a practice of belief in a deity of scarcity. Its claims to a hybrid culture is elitist while in reality the very capitalistic logic of market forces continues to polarize many people who belong to diverse ethnic and religious communities. The logic of the market itself is a historical transcendental. The fundamentalist reactions such as the Sinhala Buddhist and Hindutva ideologies in South Asia[32] that have emerged against this system reflect the same image of the deity of scarcity (or the king without conscience) whose divine body is the nation-state which is characterized by exclusivist ideologies of political centralization and ethnic homogenization. This way of thinking is an ideology which rules out plurality based on belief in a God of plentitude. We see how political, theological or philosophical and economic fields imbricate each other. As these historical transcendentals are results of a historical process of interactions between material and cultural fields they cannot be transformed by adhering to a purely normative approach to religions. As Richard King writes, '...power, indeed, is constituted in particular cultural forms. Equally, cultural forms are embedded in a field of power relations'.[33] The very recognition and close examination of this interplay will not only throw light on to the path towards transformation but also will suggest new alternatives.

The notion of plentitude that opens up to plurality as found in the Bible, and the reawakening of the deep moral significance of the conscience of the king in the face of

---

28 Michael Hardt and Antonio Negri, *Empire*, London, Harvard University, 2000: 94-95.
29 Schwartz, *The Curse of Cain*: 5.
30 Pierre Bourdieu and Loïc J.D. Wacquant, *An Invitation to Reflexive Sociology*, Cambridge, Polity, 1992: 189.
31 Zygmunt Bauman, *Globalization: The Human Consequences*, Cambridge, Polity, 1998: 74.
32 See Peter Schalk for further analysis of these ideologies and for analogies drawn from German nationalism, in his 'Operationalizing Buddhism for political ends in a martial context in Lanka: the case of Simhalatva', in John R. Hinnells and Richard King (eds.), *Religion and Violence in South Asia: Theory and Practice*, New York, Routledge, 2007: 139-153.
33 Richard King, *Orientalism and Religion: Postcolonial Theory, India and 'The Mystic East'*, New York, Routledge, 1999: 1.

the millions killed in war could provide us with a moral re-envisioning of our socio-political life. In fact, the Buddhist tradition itself promotes the right to life, and the plurality of all. Mahinda Thera, who was the first to preach *dhamma* or Buddhist teachings to the inhabitants of Lanka in an encounter with the king of the land who was hunting, said: 'Put down your arrow. All those others should live in this land. You are not the owner but only the caretaker'. Is it possible to possess the land? Does not possession mean domination and construction of the other's identity for them?, which is violent? In the peace movement in Sri Lanka, a group of Sinhala Buddhist artists from the city of the battle between Duttagamini and Elara (Anuradhapura) and some Christian peace activists who join them, in their rallies quoting Mahinda Thera, interpret the saying in the context of the militarization of the Tamil areas by the Sinhala Buddhist state. The theme of the campaign for peace is 'letting the millions of Tamil refugees (including Muslims) live in their villages and go to their places of worship as the Sinhalese who also want to live peacefully in the land.' This is the path shown to the king of the land and to his people by Mahinda. The Sinhala Buddhist farmers from the same ancient city of Gamini and Elara retrieved the same words of Mahinda Thera in their campaign to protect one of their richest natural manure (phosphate) resources from an American private company. During the time of the peace process the official paper of the political wing of the Tamil Tigers published an open letter written by an old Tamil father from Jaffna (who has become a refugee due to the acquisition of his land by the Sri Lankan military) addressing a Sinhala youth as his son, Gamini. It is *Gamini* or *Duttagamini*'s conscience which is addressed by the letter.[34] On the other hand, in the movement against privatization of land and sea, among the fishermen and women who are mostly Christian, the notion that the land cannot be possessed by anyone is stressed against the interests of certain Western and other regional powers. The fisherfolk, with the eyes of faith, perceive the God of the Bible not as a deity of scarcity who is depicted as a conqueror and a possessor, but someone who identifies herself with the landless and the refugees. It is in this context of re-conceiving the different faiths within a particular socioeconomic and political context that the interreligious dialogue can and will become a reality.

Conclusion

The first commandment of the Bible as reinterpreted by Regina Schwartz is not belief in one God but rather the command given to Eve and Adam: 'Go forth and multiply.' This means 'be plural'. It is the notion of plentitude and plurality which is implied. The first *dhamma* or the Buddhist teaching that the people in the land of Lanka heard was to give room to the other to live, violation of which troubles the king's conscience. As John May puts it:

> Religion could even be defined as the capacity to create space for *the* Other, the absolute Stranger who is nevertheless closer than one's own Self: God or the equivalent symbol of the transcendent in the non-theistic religions...[35]

Belief in transcendence therefore becomes basically an ethical commitment to the other, the totally different other where the artificial demarcations between transcendence and immanence get utterly blurred. As Rabbi Jonathan Sacks puts it:

---

34 Appa, *Vanniye Sita Liyami*, Killinochchi, Political Wing of the LTTE, 2004.
35 John D'Arcy May, *Transcendence and Violence: The Encounter of Buddhist, Christian and Primal Traditions*, New York and London, Continuum, 2003: 127.

> The test of faith today is whether I can make space for difference. Can I recognize God's image in someone who is not in my image, whose language, faith and ideals are different from mine?... Difference does not diminish. It enlarges the sphere of human possibilities.[36]

What is therefore needed is the rediscovery of the moral visions of our traditions which have been suppressed by the authoritative knowledge exemplified in constructing the other in conflict situations. There needs to be a reawakening to the potentialities (God of plentitude, meditation on conscience) in our own traditions and an articulating of them in each concrete situation. In each situation it is of vital importance to emphasize the mutual interaction between cultural and socioeconomic and political fields. In so doing we would help initiate a movement for justice and peaceful coexistence.

---

36 Jonathan Sacks, *The Dignity of Difference: How to Avoid the Clash of Civilizations*, New York, Continuum, 2003: 201, 209.

Gladys Ganiel
Religious Dissent and Reconciliation in Northern Ireland

Introduction

For Protestants in Ulster, Calvinism and evangelicalism have formed the basis for religious dissent and political action during various periods in history. This essay is concerned with comparing periods when the tradition of religious dissent seemed a contributing factor in transcending sectarianism between Protestants and Catholics: the United Irish movement, the radical evangelical wing of the labour movement of the early twentieth century, and the radical evangelical wing of the contemporary peace movement. A comparison of the United Irish, labour and peace movements is instructive because of their historical prominence, including their often idealized places in folk history. It is important to understand why the first two movements failed, and to evaluate the peace movement's prospects for contributing to reconciliation.[1]

In the case of the United Irishmen, it seemed that republican ideology would transcend sectarianism. Here, the New Light Presbyterians carried the banner of religious dissent. Likewise, it seemed that the working class cooperation, manifested in the 1907 dock strike, represented an opportunity for socialism to transcend sectarianism. Here, evangelicals like Lindsay Crawford in the newly formed Independent Orange Order spoke out as dissenters. In the peace movement, it is the 'cross community' groups which are said to be transcending sectarianism. Here, organizations like Evangelical Contribution on Northern Ireland (ECONI) – now called the Centre for Contemporary Christianity in Ireland (CCCI) – have provided a dissenting voice from traditional evangelicalism. While these movements have been rooted in the social, religious and political configurations of the times, it is possible to discern some common characteristics of the religious dissenters who have participated in them:

1. *Cooperating* with others outside of their tradition. The ability of the movements they are involved in to hold together disparate groups has been hailed as the transcending of sectarianism.

2. *Challenging* the theology of their own and articulating alternative theologies to justify socio-political change.

Despite their self-conscious non-sectarian aims, the United Irish and labour movements descended into sectarian conflict. This can be tied to historical circumstances, such as the failure of the French to aid the United Irishmen, tensions surrounding home rule in the period around the 1907 Belfast dock strike, and British military intervention in both cases. Circumstances, however, were not the only culprits. The inability of these movements

---

1 Frank Wright's *Two Lands on One Soil: Ulster Politics Before Home Rule,* Dublin, Gill and Macmillan, 1996, examines eras when Liberalism seemed to be transcending sectarianism. He calls it a story marked by 'hopeful beginnings and eventual disappointments' (21). He looks at a number of incidents, not dealt with here, saying that 'the importance of these episodes is to look at occasions in the past when people of the two traditions have worked and hoped together' (21). This essay is written in that spirit.

to last can be traced to the internal contradictions in the theologies, philosophies, and ideologies of the dissenters and those with whom they were temporarily allied. Tensions inevitably arose about attitudes toward Catholicism, and the related issue of the perceived Catholic threat to Protestantism. Anti-Catholicism, coupled with what seemed to be Catholic gains, played a significant role in the breakdowns of both movements. It is not clear if the theologies and philosophies that motivate participants in the peace movement will hold it together, or if it will meet a fate similar to the other movements. Like the United Irish and labour movements, participants in the peace movement do not share a clearly defined common philosophy. These tensions could prove problematic, although the movement is more likely to drift into irrelevance than to implode. Of ECONI/CCCI, internal tensions over Catholicism will probably not prove to be as significant as challenges arising from traditional evangelicals who oppose their innovative application of religion to politics.

This essay proceeds as follows. First, it outlines Calvinist and evangelical concepts, exploring how they can be drawn on to challenge their own traditions. Next, it compares the United Irish, labour and peace movements. It concludes with an evaluation of the prospects of the peace movement to transcend sectarianism, arguing that whilst a common, overarching goal (such as self-government, workers' rights, or the end of the 'Troubles') is important for this process, it is not enough. Transcending sectarianism involves focused reconciliation amongst Protestants and Catholics, rather than a simple setting aside of differences to pursue common interests.

Calvinism and Evangelicalism

Scholarship has confirmed the significance of both Calvinism and evangelicalism for Ulster Protestants.[2] Numerically, churches in the Calvinist tradition (Reformed or Presbyterian) are the largest of the Protestant denominations and have been since the migration from the lowlands of Scotland in the sixteenth and seventeenth centuries. The Calvinist conception of the covenant was significant for these Ulster-Scots, whose Scottish forbears had entered into a series of religious-political covenants with the English crown. In 1912 Ulster Protestants harked back to that idea of the covenant when they initiated the Solemn League and Covenant to resist home rule. Evangelicalism, an international, pan-denominational, overwhelmingly Protestant movement, was a later development, dating from the mid-eighteenth century. Evangelicalism spread rapidly in Ulster in the nineteenth century, forming a 'sacred canopy' for Protestants in nearly every denomination. The evangelicalism of this period was associated with spirited opposition to Catholicism, and upholding the values of the British Empire. Today, it is estimated that about 25 per cent of Northern Ireland's Protestants are evangelicals.[3]

---

2 Alwyn Thomson, *Fields of Vision: Faith and Identity in Protestant Ireland*, Belfast, Centre for Contemporary Christianity, 2002; Liz Fawcett, *Religion, Ethnicity and Social Change*, Basingstoke, Macmillan, 2000; John Brewer and Gareth Higgins, *The Mote and the Beam: Anti-Catholicism in Northern Ireland, 1600-1998*, Basingstoke, Macmillan, 1998; Donald Akenson, *God's People: Covenant and Land in South Africa, Israel and Ulster*, Ithaca, Cornell University, 1992; David Hempton and Myrtle Hill, *Evangelical Protestantism in Ulster Society 1740-1890*, London, Routledge, 1992; Steve Bruce, *God Save Ulster! The Religion and Politics of Paisleyism*, Oxford, Clarendon, 1986.

3 Claire Mitchell and James Tilley, 'The Moral Minority: Evangelical Protestants in Northern Ireland and their Political Behaviour', in *Political Studies* 52,4 (2004): 585-602.

Calvinism and evangelicalism are notoriously difficult 'isms' to define. However, some concepts are especially important in Ulster. For example, a Calvinist conception of the relationship between church and state is that government should reflect God's laws. Ulster Protestants have associated this with maintaining Ulster's place in the United Kingdom, believing that political union with the Republic of Ireland would eliminate their ability to practice right religion. Several implications follow. If the state is not fulfilling its part of the covenant, then the Christian citizens living within it may resort, firstly, to non-violent agitation for change. If that does not work, armed resistance may be justified. However, it is possible for dissenters to reject the idea that the state should recognize God's laws and enter into covenants with the church. Believing that this concept is flawed, they draw on the Calvinist imperative to dissent rather than accept this interpretation.

Evangelicalism, on the other hand, has not developed a conception of the relationship between church and state. Indeed, some evangelicals believe that converting others is the best way to change society and politics. This leads them to be socially active, believing that when a sufficient number of the population are 'born again', they will lead moral lives. This will produce a better, more just society. In nineteenth century Ireland, the development of evangelicalism was associated with the culture and values of the British Empire, and the boundaries between conversion, Godliness, and Britishness were often confused. Spiritual conversion – even if it was supposed to be an internal matter – implied political and cultural conversion as well. The equation of 'right religion' and 'right politics' continues to be held by some evangelicals today. However, recent research has demonstrated that other evangelicals in Northern Ireland are rejecting this interpretation.[4] Because evangelicals are so active, it is not surprising that, if some of them become convinced that the outworking of faith in society is flawed, they will dissent from their tradition and seek to change it.

The United Irishmen

The union of Presbyterians and Catholics in the United Irish rebellion of 1798 has been interpreted as the transcending of sectarianism. It is assumed that classical republican ideology held the movement together. This, however, was not the dominant motivating factor for everyone involved. The United Irishmen included people who embraced conflicting and contradictory conceptions of the society that they wanted to create. The unity of the United Irishmen – and the hope that they could ultimately transcend sectarianism – was more apparent than real.

It is impossible to quantify the overall influence of the politics of religious dissent on the United Irish movement, given the range of ideologies employed by the revolutionaries. Certainly, the New Light Presbyterians were prominent in the movement, and contemporaries associated them with the rebellion. Wolfe Tone is known to have said that the 'genius of their religion' motivated their involvement. That said, those whom Tone

---

4 Gladys Ganiel, 'A New Framework for Understanding Religion in Northern Irish Civil Society', in Christopher Farrington (ed.), *Global Change, Civil Society and the Northern Ireland Peace Process: Implementing the Political Settlement*, Basingstoke, Palgrave, 2008; Gladys Ganiel, 'Emerging from the Evangelical Subculture in Northern Ireland: A Case Study of the Ikon and Zero28 Community', in *International Journal for the Study of the Christian Church* 6,1 (2006): 38-48; Patrick Mitchel, *Evangelicalism and National Identity in Ulster, 1921-1998*, Oxford, Oxford University Press, 2003; Glenn Jordan, *Not of this World: The Evangelical Protestants of Northern Ireland*, Belfast, Blackstaff, 2001.

praised, the New Lights, were not unified in their religious beliefs. Indeed, one of the most striking aspects of New Light theology is the vagueness of its position. Frustrated New Light critics tried to brand them as heretics, but they often could not figure out just what they believed. Clearly, however, the New Lights questioned the accepted Calvinist conception of the relationship between church and state.[5] This was articulated in William Steel Dickson's series *Three Sermons on the Subject of Scripture Politics*, which McBride calls 'a United Irish manifesto.'[6] Dickson argued that the idea that Christian principles should inform the conduct of the state was wrong. Rather, the only group that was bound to associate on the basis of Christian principles was the church. But the theology of some of the New Lights' United Irish partners – the Covenanters – harked back to the traditional ideals of a Calvinist commonwealth. They believed that the 1643 Scottish Solemn League and Covenant was binding, and should be applied to Ireland. Their theology incorporated the traditional Calvinist interpretation of when a revolt against the state was justified. Further, some New Light ministers articulated a millenarian interpretation of events, including the demise of the Catholic Church. The French Revolution had been widely interpreted as a victory for Protestantism and Reason over Antichrist (identified with the Catholic Church), which implied that the Catholicism would soon wither away. Thus, the unity of Dissenter and Catholic was at least partly predicated on the belief that Catholics would cease, as it were, being Catholic.

In sum, the United Irish republic of the New Lights would have been one in which freedom of conscience and rationality reigned supreme. There would have been no established church. The Catholic Church, regarded as an upholder of irrationality and superstition, could not have survived in this environment. The 'United Irish' republic of the Covenanters would have been 'a militant Calvinist state in which both civil and ecclesiastical authorities would be mobilized in the suppression of heresy and idolatry'.[7] The Catholic Church would not have been allowed to survive in this environment. These were both positions with which the Catholics in the United Irish movement, for obvious reasons, would not have been able to agree. Elements within New Light theology that might have contributed to a transcending of sectarianism were not held widely enough to provide a bulwark against the military failure of the rebellion, its descent into sectarian fighting, and the resurgence of the Catholic Church in Ireland after the turn of the century.

The Labour Movement

The early twentieth century labour movement has been celebrated as an example of non-sectarian collaboration in which Protestant and Catholic cooperated to present a socialist challenge to the British Empire. The 1907 Belfast dock strike is held up as an example of what could have been. The politics of religious dissent was articulated by the radical evangelical wing of the movement, as exemplified by Lindsay Crawford in the Independent Orange Order (IOO).

---

5   Ian McBride, *Scripture Politics: Ulster Presbyterians and Irish Radicalism in the Late Eighteenth Century*, Oxford, Clarendon, 1998; Finlay Holmes, 'The Reverend John Abernethy: The Challenge of New Light Theology to Traditional Irish Presbyterian Calvinism', in Kevin Herlihy (ed.), *The Religion of Irish Dissent, 1650-1800*, Dublin, Four Courts, 1996.
6   McBride, *Scripture Politics*: 99.
7   McBride, *Scripture Politics*: 83.

However, a complex configuration of philosophies, ideologies and theologies motivated those who took part in the labour movement. The most visible evangelical participants in the labour movement – leaders of the newly formed IOO – harboured different motivations and conceptions of the society they wished to create. Crawford developed a liberal vision that echoed that of the United Irishmen. Alex Boyd championed socialism, and Thomas Sloan articulated a traditional evangelical outlook that hoped to achieve a 'Protestant democracy'. That socialism, or at least the same kind of socialism, was *not* the dominant strain of thought for all those who participated in the movement is clear. Moreover, much Protestant (including evangelical) participation in the labour movement depended to a large extent on the 'absence of home rule' from the political agenda.[8] This meant that Protestant fears of domination by Catholic Ireland could be momentarily set aside and Protestants could focus on the plight of the workers. The unity of the labour movement – and the hope that socialism could ultimately transcend sectarianism – was just as tenuous as the unity of the United Irishmen.

It is as impossible to gauge the influence of evangelicalism on the labour movement as it is to gauge the influence of the New Lights on the United Irishmen. It seems, however, its influence on the overall movement was not as great. An accurate analysis of the IOO must admit that Crawford was often a voice crying in the wilderness and did not represent the majority of its membership. Moreover, the IOO did not initiate the 1907 dock strike, and not all of its members were enthusiastic about it.[9] That said, the evangelical wing was a particularly important part of the labour movement because it challenged the evangelical tradition, which had been developing during the nineteenth century. After the United Irish rebellion, evangelicalism had become a badge of identity for many Ulster Protestants, and served as an important element in transcending class differences. It was significant that the prevailing Protestant order, which was underpinned by evangelicalism, was being challenged by the dissent of evangelicals. There is a crucial distinction, though: Crawford dissented from an evangelicalism that promoted a Protestant democracy; whilst Sloan dissented from an evangelicalism that was seen as failing to promote a Protestant democracy.

As was the case with the United Irishmen, there were many tensions within and between the theologies of evangelicals in the IOO and the philosophies and ideologies of their temporary allies amongst the labour leaders. Each had a different vision of what could be accomplished by a triumph of labour. Sloan wanted a Protestant democracy that would recognize the needs of the labourers and keep the Catholic enemy at bay. Crawford, while starting from a position similar to Sloan's, became a political liberal who challenged the basis of that Protestant democracy. Connolly and Larkin wanted a socialist Irish nation. The dominant voices of Belfast labour wanted socialism within a progressive Protestant empire. Elements within evangelicalism that might have contributed to a transcending of sectarianism were not held widely enough to be sustained in the face of the failure of the 1907 strike, and its descent into sectarian riots. Just as the United Irishmen could flourish because the Catholic Church no longer seemed a threat, labour could flourish because home rule did not seem a threat. Finally, the home rule crisis would move Protestant Ulster to resurrect the covenant – in the form of the

---

8 John Gray, *City in Revolt: James Larkin and the Belfast Dock Strike of 1907*, Belfast, Blackstaff, 1985; Henry Patterson, *Class Conflict and Sectarianism: The Protestant Working Class and the Belfast Labour Movement 1868-1920*, Belfast, Blackstaff, 1980.
9 Gray, *City in Revolt*: 89.

Solemn League and Covenant of 1912 – seemingly putting to rest indefinitely not only the labour movement, but the prospects for transcending sectarianism.

The Peace Movement

The proliferation of Peace and Conflict Reconciliation Organizations (PCROs), both secular and religious, since the beginning of the Troubles, has been interpreted as another means to transcend sectarianism. There is little agreement about how vital the PCROs have been to the peace process, but some scholars and journalists have credited PCROs for the role they played in the run-up to the negotiations that produced the Belfast Agreement, and in the yes campaign.[10] In these accounts the peace movement is juxtaposed to the ineffectiveness of elected officials in solving problems. The peace movement, it is said, is developing a philosophy of reconciliation that is based on inclusiveness, respect for difference, and dialogic democracy.

The Christian contribution to the peace movement is not necessarily Calvinist or evangelical; indeed, the dominant ethos of Christian participants in the peace movement is ecumenical.[11] The most prominent example of evangelical involvement in the peace movement is Evangelical Contribution on Northern Ireland, now renamed the Centre for Contemporary Christianity in Ireland (ECONI/CCCI). This group is not explicitly cross-community. However, like the Independent Orange Order in its early association with the labour movement, it has associated with other groups in the peace movement – including Catholic and ecumenical groups. Its decision to change its name to CCCI in 2005 may reflect its commitment to inclusive dialogue. It practices a variety of dissent that is particularly important because it challenges specific aspects of traditional evangelicalism and Calvinism and, like the New Light Presbyterian ministers, develops alternative models of involvement in society and politics.[12] For example, ECONI/CCCI has dissented from its evangelical tradition in its God, Land and Nation project, which critiques the way Protestants have applied the concept of the covenant. Reflecting on the phrase, 'For God and Ulster', ECONI/CCCI concluded that some evangelicals had put loyalty to Ulster and the UK ahead of loyalty to the kingdom of God. ECONI/CCCI also has developed a position on the relationship between church and state that differs from Calvinism. It has been influenced by Anabaptist theology, which denies that the church should have a covenantal relationship with the state. This position parallels the one articulated by Dickson two centuries before in his sermons on Scripture politics. Further, the church's role is seen as a model for society: exhibiting forgiveness, servant-hood, and nonviolence. Thus, ECONI/CCCI's Forgiveness Project sought to highlight

---

[10] Adrian Guelke, 'Civil Society and the Northern Ireland Peace Process', in *Voluntas: International Journal of Voluntary and Nonprofit Organisations* 14,1 (2003): 61-78; Feargal Cochrane and Seamus Dunn, *People Power? The Role of the Voluntary and Community Sector in the Northern Ireland Conflict*, Cork, Cork University, 2002.

[11] John Brewer, 'Northern Ireland: Peacemaking Among Protestants and Catholics', in Mary Ann Cejka and Thomas Bamat (eds.), *Artisans of Peace: Grassroots Peacemaking Among Christian Communities*, Maryknoll, Orbis, 2003; Joe Liechty and Cecelia Clegg, *Moving Beyond Sectarianism*, Dublin, Columba, 2001; Ronald Wells, *People Behind the Peace: Community and Reconciliation in Northern Ireland*, Grand Rapids, Eerdmans, 1999.

[12] Gladys Ganiel and Paul Dixon, 'Religion, Pragmatic Fundamentalism and the Transformation of the Northern Ireland Conflict', in *Journal of Peace Research*, 2007 (forthcoming); Ganiel, 'Emerging from the Evangelical Subculture'.

the importance and implications of forgiveness in Christian traditions, and asked how forgiveness might be applied to the situation in Northern Ireland.[13]

ECONI/CCCI's religio-political dissent must be set in the context of the peace movement, a defining characteristic of which is its lack of commitment to particular philosophies in favour of a dialogic, democratic process.[14] Participants in the peace movement know they disagree, and they are searching for ways to manage their disagreements. It is not clear that the United Irish and labour movements frankly acknowledged their disagreements, or sought to manage them the way the peace movement does. However, agreeing to disagree could prove paralysing to the peace movement – a case of all talk and no action. There is evidence that after the Belfast Agreement, some groups have become less active, thinking they have played their part.[15] These factors could doom the peace movement to irrelevance, even as it begins to emerge that Protestants and Catholics at the grassroots have been drifting further apart since the agreement.[16] This might demand more, not less, local level reconciliation efforts. As for ECONI/CCCI, it also acknowledges its disagreements. It does not have an agreed position on Catholicism and it is not clear if tensions over Catholicism have hindered or may hinder its efforts.[17] This agreement to disagree may make ECONI/CCCI less likely to divide round the Catholic question. When past dissenting movements divided over Catholicism, it often was because one faction had a vision of a Protestant democracy in which Catholicism would be eliminated, or in which Catholics would become like Protestants. ECONI/CCCI's Anabaptist model expressly rejects a Protestant democracy, or even a government informed by Protestant principles. This, in effect, eliminates questions about whether Catholics could be good democratic citizens; it potentially could eliminate the significance of the question of Northern Ireland being part of the UK or the Republic.

Another factor that has contributed to the disintegration of non-sectarian movements is what seemed in each context to be an increased Catholic threat. Wright, in his analysis of times when Liberal politics came close to transcending sectarianism, argues that these movements were only possible when the weakness of Catholicism opened up enough 'political space' for cooperation to occur.[18] According to this logic, we should look at the present circumstances to try and ascertain if Catholicism is 'weak.' Then, the increased secularization in the Republic of Ireland and the disillusionment caused by clerical abuse scandals might seem 'favourable' conditions. However, for the transcending of sectarianism to rely on the weakness of one partner seems a bleak, even perverse, conclusion. As Wright realized, this sort of transcendence could only be temporary unless non-power based relationships could be established between Catholics and Protestants. That requires accepting that the other is not a threat – no matter how 'strong' the other may seem to be.

---

13 See http://www.contemporarychristianity.org.
14 Cochrane and Dunn, *People Power?*
15 Guelke, 'Civil Society and the Northern Ireland Peace Process'.
16 Peter Shirlow and Brendan Murtagh, *Belfast: Segregation, Violence and the City*, London, Pluto, 2005; Bernadette Hayes and Ian McAllister, 'Ethnonationalism, Public Opinion and the Good Friday Agreement', in Joseph Ruane and Jennifer Todd (eds.), *After the Good Friday Agreement*, Dublin, UCD, 1999.
17 Liechty and Clegg, *Moving Beyond Sectarianism*: 182-183.
18 Wright, *Two Lands, One Soil.*

The ability of ECONI/CCCI to ally with the peace movement and contribute to transcending sectarianism depends on the extent to which it can convince other evangelicals to dissent from their tradition. It is not certain how widely ECONI/CCCI's positions are accepted by Northern Irish evangelicals.[19] There are traditional, evangelical action groups advocating the familiar interpretations of the relationship between church and state, and highlighting the threat of Catholicism.[20] ECONI/CCCI must articulate its position in such a way that evangelicals no longer feel threatened by Catholicism. Further, the wider peace movement must affirm its commitment to reconciling Catholic and Protestant. In the United Irish and labour movements, Catholics and Protestants were brought together in pursuit of a common goal, or perceived a common enemy. To some extent this is the case with the peace movement, with the common goal being 'peace.' However, as this essay has demonstrated, a common goal is not enough. Relationships which can withstand the tensions and contradictions of competing ideologies and visions of the future are required. This means renewed dedication to quality, cross-community contact at the grassroots – including a willingness to live with difference.

---

19 Claire Mitchell, *Religion, Identity and Politics in Northern Ireland: Boundaries of Belonging and Belief*, Aldershot, Ashgate, 2006

20 Gladys Ganiel, 'Ulster Says Maybe: The Restructuring of Evangelical Politics in Northern Ireland', in *Irish Political Studies* 21,2 (2006): 137-155. These groups include the present-day IOO, the Caleb Foundation and the Evangelical Protestant Society.

Elizabeth J. Harris

Transforming Conflict: Can Religion Help?

John D'Arcy May's concern for issues surrounding religion and conflict is well known. I offer this essay in appreciation of that interest.[1] For it is one we share. Between 1986 and 1993 I lived in Sri Lanka, studying Buddhism. Three conflicts burned whilst I was there: the long-standing ethnic conflict;[2] a conflict between the government and a southern militant group of insurgents;[3] and conflict between Buddhists and Christians, and Hindus and Christians, over what was coming to be known as 'unethical conversions'.[4] My study of Buddhism was therefore carried out against a background of war and mistrust between religions. Since returning to Britain, as part of my work as Secretary for Inter Faith Relations for the Methodist Church in Britain, I have visited several other places where there has been internal war or interreligious tension: Israel-Palestine; Gujarat in India; Pakistan; Cambodia; Bosnia.

Questions about the relationship between religion and conflict, and religion and peacemaking arose for me in all these contexts but I start with the words of a religious leader in Bosnia. I visited Bosnia in 1999 with a small Muslim-Christian non-governmental organization called SANA. At one point, we asked a religious leader whether religion was the cause of the conflict that had wracked the country. He replied, 'Religion is not the cause of the conflict. But religion is not innocent.' I agreed with him. Religion is rarely the primary cause of violent conflict. The main causes are more often economic or political – access to land, water and other resources, or the failure of parliamentary structures to give a voice to minorities. In conflict after conflict, however, religious factors are present, contributing to cycles of violence. Religion is not innocent in Sri Lanka. It is not innocent in Northern Ireland, Israel-Palestine or the Balkans. Particularly disturbing for me is that religion is a contributory factor in some of the world's most intractable conflicts.

In situations where religion is not innocent, can religion or people of religious faith contribute to conflict transformation? Some people would immediately say, 'No'. I have

---

1   This contribution draws from two lectures I have given in the last year: 'Religion and Peacemaking' at the international conference of the International Association for Religious Freedom (IARF) in Taiwan, 2006; and, 'Understanding Violence: How can Buddhism help', given at the Sion Centre for Dialogue and Encounter, London, February 2007. Neither has been published.
2   There are many books on Sri Lanka's ethnic conflict, one of the most recent and trustworthy being Mahinda Deegalle (ed.), *Buddhism, Conflict and Violence in Modern Sri Lanka*, London and New York, Routledge, 2006.
3   The insurgents belonged to the Janatha Vimukti Peramuna (JVP – People's Liberation Party). In 1971 and again in the late 1980s the party attempted to gain political power through violence and the manufacture of fear. The latter was eventually crushed viciously by the Sri Lankan Government with the loss of many innocent lives, see, for example, Rohan Gunaratne, *Sri Lanka A Lost Revolution?: The Inside Story of the JVP*, Kandy, Institute of Fundamental Studies, 1990.
4   See Elizabeth J. Harris, 'Confrontation over Conversions: A Case Study from Sri Lanka', in John D'Arcy May (ed.), *Converging Ways: Conversion and Belonging in Buddhism and Christianity*, Sankt Ottilien, EOS, 2007: 37-54.

friends in Sri Lanka who have rejected religion because they believe it has done nothing to solve the long-standing ethnic conflict there. I would like to argue, in contrast, that people of faith can and must be part of the solution to conflict. To be part of the solution, however, recourse to religious texts is not enough. Insights from many quarters are necessary, using what John Paul Lederach, an American Mennonite, has called 'the moral imagination'.[5]

To explore this, I will use examples from some of the conflict-torn countries I have visited to reflect on three interlinked areas that I believe are crucial to understanding and transforming conflict:

1. Breaking cycles of contempt
2. Passing over to the side of 'the other'
3. Imagining peace and taking risks.

In daring to speak about these things, I owe debts to many peace activists and spiritual teachers in countries such as Cambodia and Sri Lanka: Venerable Maha Ghosananda, Bob Matt, S. Balakrishnan, Rev Yohan Devananda, Audrey Rebera and Aloysius Pieris SJ to name a few.

Breaking Cycles of Contempt

I start with 'contempt' because it is often the unrecognized key to understanding a conflict. Anger, resentment and violence very often have their roots in the conviction that contempt is being directed towards one's ethnic, linguistic or religious identity. When a community believes that it is viewed with contempt, the defence of self-respect and dignity becomes all important – and violent ways of doing this can so easily be judged the only option. Let me use the example of the tension caused by the perceived threat of 'unethical conversions' in Sri Lanka. The accusation is that Christians are bribing poverty-stricken Buddhists and Hindus to become Christians through promises of material benefits. It has resulted in attacks on churches and the tabling, but not so far the passing, of anti-conversion legislation in Parliament. The roots of this, according to research I have done over several years,[6] go back to the nineteenth century when Sri Lanka was under British rule and evangelical Christian missionaries were seeking to convert Buddhists and Hindus.

My understanding of what happened when missionary and Buddhist met in nineteenth century Sri Lanka grew when I came across this record of a conversation between an Anglican Bishop and a Buddhist monk in 1863, written by the former:

> They were moved when I said that I came to them as the teachers of the people, feeling sure that if they could be convinced that my Religion was true they would wish to teach it instead of their own. They told me that nothing had more turned them against Christianity than finding themselves treated with marked contempt by its professors.[7]

---

5 John Paul Lederach, *The Moral Imagination: The Art and Soul of Building Peace*, Oxford, Oxford University, 2005.
6 See Elizabeth J. Harris, *Theravada Buddhism and the British Encounter: Religious, Missionary and Colonial Experience in Nineteenth Century Sri Lanka*, London and New York, Routledge, 2006.
7 Bishop Claughton writing to Rev. E. Hawkins from Colombo, 13 January 1863, Ceylon Letters Volume II (SPG Archives), as quoted in Harris, *Theravada Buddhism and the British Encounter*: 189.

The eventual cause of conflict between Christians and Buddhists, and between Christians and Hindus, during the British colonial period was not that Christians preached Christianity, or that they gained some converts. It was not the differences between Christian and Buddhist belief and practice. It was that the Christian missionaries rejected the respect-filled co-existence Buddhists and Hindus sought, by contemptuously seeking to undermine what Buddhists and Hindus held precious. The consequence was that some Buddhists and Hindus, in defence of their self-respect and identity, threw away their wish for co-existence and adopted the competitive methods of the missionaries. It was a move that led to revival both in Buddhism and Hinduism, a revival predicated on opposition to Christianity. And the experience of contempt is an important key to understanding it.

To move to the twenty-first century, contempt was an important factor in the reactions of Muslims to the cartoons of the Prophet Muhammad that were published by the Danish broadsheet, *Jyllands-Posten*, and then in other European papers.[8] Most people of faith can tell jokes against themselves and Muslims are no exception to this. There is a difference, though, between humour and contempt. The cartoons showed contempt for Muslim self-understanding in a world where many Muslims already felt vulnerable. One of them, for instance, showed the Prophet with a bomb under his turban. As one Christian expert on the Muslim world told me, an equivalent cause of offence for Christians would be a cartoon of Jesus sexually abusing a child.

The conflict in Israel-Palestine is another example of a situation where contempt is an important factor. The Government of Israel declares that the wall between Israel and the West Bank is necessary if suicide bombers are to be deterred; and it cannot be denied that bombings have decreased since its erection. Most Palestinians, however, struggling to reach their own fields and olive groves on the other side of the wall, see it as an embodiment of contempt for Palestinian livelihoods, well-being and identity. Similarly, the refusal of Hamas and Iran to recognize the State of Israel is seen by Israelis as an expression of contempt for their Jewish identity and the horror of what happened to the Jews in Nazi-controlled Europe.

How can people of faith transcend, or help others to transcend, this element in conflict and the resentment, anger and self-assertive action it nurtures? There are no easy answers. Any path away from the experience of contempt demands change both in those accused of acting contemptuously and in those who feel dehumanized by contempt. However, this is where the idea of moral imagination can come in. According to Lederach, it is the kind of imagination that can take what is present in any situation and create what is new. It is a force that possesses 'peripheral vision', a vision that is curious, and open to the unexpected. It requires, he stresses, the capacity 'to imagine ourselves in a web of relationships that includes our enemies' and to step 'into the mystery of the unknown that lies beyond the far too familiar landscape of violence.'[9] One way to enable 'peripheral vision' to develop in situations of conflict, I believe, is to create spaces where people involved in conflict are helped to imagine what it is like to be on the side of the 'other' in the conflict.

---

8   Twelve cartoons, most of which were of the prophet Muhammad, were published in *Jyllands Posten* (The Jutland Post) on 30 September 2005, and in other European newspapers in subsequent days. This led to violent protests by Muslims in Europe and elsewhere.
9   Lederach, *The Moral Imagination*: 118 and 5.

Passing over to the side of 'the other'

The kind of imagination that can pass over to the side of 'the other' is not easy to evoke, especially where the experience of contempt is present. For parties to conflict are usually imprisoned within different 'constructed realities', different ways of perceiving the past and the present. For instance, in a number of the conflicts I am familiar with, where contempt is present as a factor, there is also a competition in comparative suffering, in which each side claims that it is they who have suffered the most and that it is they who are the victims. In Sri Lanka, there are three main ethnic groups. The Sinhala people, predominantly Buddhist and speakers of Sinhala, are about 73% of the population. The Tamil people, mainly Hindu and speakers of Tamil, are about 18%, and there is a Muslim presence of about 8%. Christians form about 8% also, some Sinhala, some Tamil. In the ethnic conflict that has caused suffering in the country since the 1950s, most particularly after 1983, all these groups consider themselves to be the victims in the conflict and a minority under threat. Muslims look to 1990 when the militant Tamil group that then controlled the North of the country, the Liberation Tigers of Tamil Eelam (LTTE), gave Muslims living in the North only a few hours to leave, in a blatant example of 'ethnic cleansing'. Many are still in refugee camps. Tamils see themselves as the victims of a centralized Parliamentary structure that cannot be other than Sinhala-dominated. They refer to numerous state-inspired incidents of discrimination, oppression and violence. Both Tamils and Muslims see themselves as minorities in the country. The Sinhala majority also see themselves as victims, for example, of the numerous LTTE suicide bomb attacks that have killed innocent civilians in the South. Some also see themselves as a minority in the face of more than 62 million Tamils in Tamil Nadu in south India.

When I visited Israel-Palestine, I found a similar dynamic. Both the Israelis and Palestinians see themselves as the side who has suffered the most and both consider themselves to be the threatened minority, the Palestinians in the face of the might of Israel, the Israelis in the wider geo-political area of Syria, Lebanon and Iran.

In these contexts, how can people be helped to move imaginatively over to the other side so that they can glimpse how people on that side see themselves? I find help in a Buddhist concept: gradual training or skilful means. This stresses that people must be met where they are and that one step must be taken at a time. Let me use some examples from Sri Lanka. In June 1998, Ven. Dr. Kadurugamuve Nagitha Thero, then Head of the Linguistics Department at the University of Kelaniya, arranged a Tamil Day, where students sang, danced and staged dramas in Tamil. Yet, the participants were not Tamil. They were all Sinhala, some of them Buddhist monks. All had taken a certificate course in Tamil and so had glimpsed the linguistic and cultural world of 'the other'. When Ven. Nagitha was asked about his reasons for encouraging Sinhala students to learn Tamil, he replied, '[w]hen you understand the other side better, you learn to respect the other's cultural identity. Just as much as we are Sinhalese and proud of it, we must learn to respect Tamil culture and their way of life.'[10] Learning the Tamil language was the first step towards empathy, the first step in a gradual process of awareness-building.

---

10 T. Dissanayaike, '"Malar Kothu" from Sinhala students', in *The Sunday Times Plus*, 14 June 1998: 1, as quoted in Elizabeth J. Harris, 'The Cost of Peace: Buddhists and Conflict Transformation in Sri Lanka', in Philip Broadhead and Damien Keown (eds.), *Can Faiths make Peace? Holy Wars and the Resolution of Religious Conflicts*, London and New York, I.B. Tauris, 2007: 149-162.

Even when the language is not known, song, music and drama can play a part in gradual training. In February 2006, the Anti-War Front, a coalition of groups, both religious and secular, organized a commemoration in Colombo to mark the fourth anniversary of the Ceasefire Agreement. About 10,000 people gathered for a rally that included music, song and drama. In preparation for this, three caravans of cultural activists had travelled around the country, helping local groups with District-level events. They performed street theatre and music with four focal points: opposition to a return to war; condemnation of all acts of violence by parties to the Ceasefire Agreement; and a call for the government and opposition parties to work together in the Peace Process. About 25 such events were held, some in Buddhist and Hindu temples. Central to this initiative was the awareness that it is easier for people to 'pass over' into the experience of groups considered 'other' through music, art and drama than through speeches. Although the goals were political, people could enter what was happening in different ways.

Sometimes, however, people are unable to move over to the other side simply because they lack information about what 'the other' is suffering. Some multi-faith peace organizations in Sri Lanka organize workshops on the ethnic conflict in Buddhist villages. The organizers usually find that when villagers hear Tamils speaking of their experiences – not being able to communicate with government bodies in Tamil, hiding in the jungle for fear of attacks, seeing religious buildings and schools bombed or losing their children to the war – their reaction is, 'we have never been told this before! Why didn't we know this!' Knowledge then gives birth to empathy, as they compare their own experiences of economic hardship and bereavement with the lives of Tamil villagers.

Imagining peace and taking risks

Let me move to my last area. I begin with a well-known example from Cambodia: the Dhammayietras or Pilgrimages of Truth pioneered by the Buddhist monk, Ven. Maha Ghosananda. (May I apologize to anyone who has read my book, *What Buddhists Believe* for using the same material again.) The first Dhammayietra took place in 1992, soon after a UN-brokered peace treaty had brought four of the warring factions together. The second came in 1993, on the eve of UN-brokered elections, in a most volatile situation. I use the description of it given to me in 1995 by Liz Bernstein, who was working with the Ven. Maha Ghosananda at the time. She began by stressing that fear was widespread in 1993. Some doubted whether elections would ever happen or, if they did, whether people would vote. She continued:

> The walk began from Angkor Wat [a complex of temples] and went through one of the heaviest areas of conflict to Phnom Penh. On the eve of the walk there was a fire-fight between the Khmer Rouge and the government soldiers right in the grounds of the temple. As everyone huddled in the temple and rockets and grenades were flying, one grenade came into the temple where three or four hundred people were huddled and landed next to the Buddha image. It didn't explode.

Afterwards, the walkers decided to continue. There had been two or three walkers injured and they sent messages from their hospital beds that the walk must continue. So the walk left Siem Reap and went through areas where the UN peace-keepers were stationed but where they did not leave their bases; they didn't walk five hundred metres from their bases because of the conflict between the government and the Khmer Rouge.

So, people along the road saw that even where the peace-keepers wouldn't go, here was this line of five hundred monks and nuns walking for peace. Again we had an incredible welcome from the people. 'We have never', they said, 'seen peace. We have heard on the radio that they have signed a peace accord but we are lying in our bunkers at night. We have never seen peace until we have seen this walk.' At the bridges the soldiers who were guarding laid down their weapons and came to Maha Ghosananda and said, 'Give us a blessing so that our bullets don't hit anyone and so that their bullets don't hit us.'

> So the walk went on. When we were about to arrive in Phnom Penh it was just the day before elections and the city was very tense with fear. The UN had ordered their staff to send their families abroad because the situation was unstable. They were expecting attacks from the government or the Khmer Rouge and people were very, very frightened. When the walk entered the city, tens of thousands joined the walk and just kept walking around Phnom Penh calming people down, stopping at monuments and temples to meditate in silence for fifteen minutes. We then appealed for peace and for calm.[11]

Since 1993 there have been yearly walks.

One reason why the 1993 Dhammayietra in Cambodia worked was because it called people back to what was already in their Buddhist culture: non-violence and fearlessness in the face of outside threat. According to Lederach, protracted conflict can be seen as 'a narrative broken'. Using this concept, the 1993 Dhammayietra restored a narrative already present in the culture.[12] It helped people reconnect with values and traditions long known. For, in the Buddhist tradition there are many stories of violence being met with non-violence. For instance, there is the story of the Buddhist monk, Venerable Punnovada, who was to travel to a district where people were known to be hostile. Before he goes, the Buddha questions him about how he will deal with abuse and violence, listing the possible violence he might receive, from verbal abuse to physical harm. After each one, Punnovada says that he would be thankful that the abuse was not even more serious. When the Buddha eventually mentions murder, Punnovada says:

> If the people of Sunaparanta deprive me of life with a sharp knife, revered sir, it will be thus for me there; I will say, 'there are disciples of the Lord, who, disgusted by the body and the life-principle and ashamed of them, look about for a knife. I have come to this knife without having looked for it.[13]

I like this image of narrative broken and narrative restored. In Sri Lanka, a narrative exists of all peoples living harmoniously. I have so often been told, 'before this war happened, we lived so peacefully.' The forming of the state of Israel was accompanied with the ideals of the Kibbutzim – the communal settlements that were set up in the 1950s – such as the sharing of resources, joint decision-making and encouraging the desert to bloom through manual labour. In many situations of conflict there are narratives, which are often religious, that speak of harmony and non-violence. Imagining peace involves finding the spaces where people can re-connect with these narratives and inject new meaning into them. Offering symbolic images of these narratives is one method. Five hundred Buddhist monks and nuns walking for peace in Cambodia in 1993 was a symbolic image of fearlessness and peace. However, there was risk for the participants. Several were injured. There was risk for the Christian Peacemaker Team of four that went to Iraq in 2005 to offer the Iraqi people an image of the West and

---

11 Elizabeth J. Harris, *What Buddhists Believe*, Oxford, Oneworld, 1998: 116-117.
12 Lederach, *The Moral Imagination*: 146.

Christian-Muslim relations that was unconnected with aggression and violence. Norman Kember, a British Baptist, and his colleagues were abducted on 26 November 2005. One member of the Team, Tom Fox, was killed; the others were released in March 2006. There was risk for the Sri Lankan Roman Catholic priest, Fr Michael Rodrigo OMI, when, in his sixties, he went to live in a remote and poor Buddhist village in his country, seeking to roll back over a hundred years of mistrust between Buddhism and Christianity there. He was killed, not by the villagers but by other interests opposed to his actions.[13] Using 'moral imagination' involves risk.[14]

To re-make and restore narratives of peace is, therefore, no easy task. One reason for this is that narratives of peace often compete with narratives of conflict, embedded in past centuries or in religious texts. In the Balkans, alliances made in World War II still affect relationships between Muslims, Orthodox Christians and Roman Catholics. In Sri Lanka, some Sinhala extremists have drawn on stories of conflict in the ancient historical chronicle, the *Mahavamsa*, and on material from the Theravada Buddhist canon, to justify their view that the threat to Buddhism posed by the LTTE can only be eradicated through military means.[15] Even the circulation of a pamphlet drawing attention to a narrative of conflict that happened hundreds of years ago can be enough to re-start violence in the present. Furthermore, fearlessness can be present for more than one end. A suicide bomber may be able to develop just as much fearlessness as the dedicated peace-maker.

I have learnt much from Buddhism about why peace-making is so difficult. In November 2005, I gave a talk at the launch of a new educational centre at the Dhammatalaka Buddhist Pagoda in Birmingham, England, on 'What can Buddhism offer a violent world?' Let me quote two paragraphs from that presentation:

> One popular reaction to extreme violence whether perpetrated by an individual or a group is: 'How could any human do that?' Of suicide bombers we exclaim, 'How can a human blow himself and others up?' Of those in the Third Reich who helped Hitler's genocide we cry, 'How could ordinary men – husbands, fathers, lovers – carry on with their everyday life and at the same time send thousands of Jews to be killed in gas chambers?' It is as though the violent ones are placed in a sub-human category, far away from us, the civilized, peaceful ones.

I continued:

> We will never understand violence if we stay at this level. Buddhism can help here in two ways. First, it can teach us that violence is to be expected in a world that is in the grip of greed, hatred and delusion. Second, it can force us to see that the perpetrators of violence are not aberrations within the human race. They are formed by a web of conditioning factors that implicate many more people than the actual perpetrator.[16]

---

13 See, e.g., Sr. Milburga Fernando, *Harvest Dreams of Fr. Mike: Coming to Fruition*, Colombo: Centre for Society and Religion, 1998; Michael Rodrigo, 'The Hope of Liberation Lessens Man's Inhumanity: A Contribution to Dialogue at Village Level', in R.S. Sugirtharajah (ed.), *Asian Faces of Jesus*, London, SCM, 1993: 189-210.

14 *Punnovadasutta, Majjhima Nikaya*, iii, 269 (*Sutta Pitaka* of the Theravada Buddhist Canon).

15 See, e.g., Elizabeth J. Harris, 'Buddhism and the Justification of War: A Case Study from Sri Lanka', in Paul Robinson (ed.), *Just War in Comparative Perspective*, Aldershot, Ashgate, 2003: 93-108.

16 A shortened form of this was published as Elizabeth J. Harris, 'What can Buddhism offer a violent world?', in *Interreligious Insight* 4,1 (2006): 54-66.

In brief, what I was trying to say in Birmingham was that the arising of conflict should not surprise us completely, although it may horrify, disturb and grieve us. For we live in a world that is in the grip of greed, hatred and delusion and these forces have considerable power. This means that those involved in conflict – and also in peace-making – are not free agents. Even those who seek to exercise moral imagination can make mistakes. They can be compromised and can experience lack of courage. They can become victims of their own 'constructed realities' and to their own greeds and hatreds. Setbacks in peace-making are therefore without number, as the peace processes in Sri Lanka, Israel-Palestine or the Balkans show.

Conclusion

In conclusion, let me turn again to narratives of peace. All religions and cultures contain them. I believe that most ordinary people aspire to them, however far away they may seem. Conflict resolution theory sometimes speaks of developing a 'critical mass' of support for peace, a critical number of people who can tip the balance away from conflict and towards peace. However, there is another picture that comes from several of our religions – that of one or two people who can work against the gravity of conflict. Lederach speaks of 'critical yeast' rather than 'critical mass',[17] echoing the words of Jesus in the Christian tradition that the Kingdom of God is like yeast which, when mixed with flour, eventually leavens the whole, even though it is the smallest ingredient.[18] Lederach's point is that a few people, strategically placed, can sometimes do more for peace than hundreds of people believing the same thing.

I have mentioned three factors in peace-making: breaking cycles of contempt; passing over to the side of 'the other'; imagining peace and taking risks. It is not necessary to be religious to realize how important they are; but they all have spiritual content. They are rooted in qualities central to most religions: empathy; compassion; fearlessness for self; transforming the mind and heart; and the willingness to take risks in faith. My hope is that these qualities will increase and that people of faith will be at the forefront of this, bringing good news to our world.

---

17 Lederach, *The Moral Imagination*: 92-93.
18 Luke 13:20-21.

Gerhard Köberlin

Coming Home: The Place of the Other in Religious Peace Work

The Jewish Buddhist from Berkeley, Eliyahu McLean, decided to live with the Peace Maker Community of the American Zen Buddhist Bernie Glassman in Israel/Palestine. There he met the Palestinian Muslim, Ibrahim AbulHawa, who lives on the Mount of Olives in the Occupied Territories. Both believe in the power of peace in the Middle East. One year after 9/11 they toured the USA. Standing in front of the altar of the Methodist Glide-Memorial Church in San Francisco at an interreligious gathering in 2002, they concluded the evening by saying: We have come the long way to California to tell our story of how a Buddhist, who was born a Jew, came home in a Muslim's heart. And the weathered Muslim gave the young Jewish Buddhist a warm and uncompromising hug: yes, we have come home, in each other's heart.

How can it happen that the hearts of people who are at war widen so much that they become the home of the 'enemy'? How, indeed, can 'coming home' mean not to be at home 'with me', but 'with the other'? In the following I relate some experiences that I have been part of in order to reflect on what these questions entail. Beginning with an interreligious organization that grew from the Bosnian war situation I go on to detail a growing phenomenon in Buddhism, namely, engaged Buddhism. Finally, I argue that the two form part of one understanding of being at home with the other that is open to the future rather than being determined by and in the past.

A Bosnian Experience

The war in Bosnia ended through the Dayton Agreement, and NATO forces, in 1995. Since then foreign troops patrol the streets. Slaughter-houses like Srebrenica and Tuzla remain in our memories. Sarajevo was besieged for 22 months by Serbian nationalists. Many trees on the boulevards of Sarajevo were felled to provide fuel as the capital had neither coal nor electricity for two winters.

A young Serbian Orthodox Bosnian, Ljubinka Petrovic, called her friends to meet together. She was supported by her German husband, the pastor Christof Ziemer, former dean of the Protestant church in Dresden. She trusted that there was a way into the heart of the other, a way of faith. In time a group of young Bosnian Christians, Orthodox Serbs and Roman-Catholic Croats, and Bosnian Muslim Bosniaks, and Bosnian Jews met together and founded their own interreligious NGO, called 'ABRAHAM', in 1998.[1]

Until March 1992, Bosnia had been a multicultural state, with a multi-religious history of more than 500 years. A glance at the ethnic map of this Yugoslavian state showed a great variety of colours, like a carpet, woven of Christians, Muslims, and Jews, who, though not necessarily at home in one another's heart, lived next to each other.

A look at the map of Bosnia today gives a shock. There is no more a colourful web of different identities living together, but, rather, a uniformity enforced by violence:

---

1 See *Ökumenischer Dienst. Schalomdiakonat für Gerechtigkeit, Frieden und Bewahrung der Schöpfung*, 10 Jahre Ökumenischer Dienst, Diemelstadt-Wethen, Shalomdiakonat, 2002: 24-26.

Bosnia for the Serbs! Bosnia for the Croats! And what is there for the Bosniak Muslims? Or the Bosnian Jews? Or the Bosnian 'atheists' (who don't want to be identified by religion)? Today's map shows the artificial creation of three major uniformly coloured patches of 'Serbs', 'Croats', and 'Muslims'…a uniformity made possible by turning millions into refugees.

Abraham – traveller into the unknown

The Bosnian friends established ABRAHAM beyond their religious, ethnic and cultural belonging. They looked to the biblical story of Abraham in order to ground the group's spirituality.[2] Abraham's story is one of leaving certitudes behind. He had to leave his nomadic North-Syrian home, to follow his invisible God into a foreign promised land, agricultural Canaan. Nevertheless, the great story does not find its climax in the fulfilment of a dream of arriving home. Instead, Abraham's faith rested on the opening of the horizon through God, and its high point was in his leaving home.

Abraham embodies the dream of travelling into the unknown – into the unknown of the other, the unknown of the fellow enemy and the fellow neighbour. The other is like an unknown territory. So any human – and religious – encounter is like putting one's feet on new ground, different ground, holy ground. Encounter is travelling into the unknown, whether of friend or opponent.[3]

With their vision in place the ABRAHAM group began by publishing a magazine for the four religions together. Their varied opinions were put side by side on paper. Here everybody could see for himself or herself the actual thinking among 'opponents'. Listening to each other was both their foremost and most difficult peace practice. They also provided physical and spiritual space in the urban society of Sarajevo to have monthly meetings, dialogues, and events. In this open space the other could be encountered without suspicion and fear.

The first test of their work turned out to be a 'peace training' in non-violent action. Help was given by the Shalom Diaconate, or Ecumenical Service, in Wethen, Germany: a young couple would give the appropriate training, a young Croatian couple.[4] The results were exciting. Members of the different communities had to enter into the role of the other. This proved to be very difficult, and led at times to a break-down of communication. Yet, the basic experience of trying to see with the eyes of the other, to hear with the ears of the other, breaks up one's hitherto narrow identity.

Since May 2002, the group started a research project on 'space for the other in our faith and life'. In the regions of Bosnia, Herzegovina, Croatia, Serbia and Montenegro, the group studies theological texts and positions as well as personal and local experiences that illustrate the space of the 'other' in one's own tradition. They found that religions had actually contributed to the ideological legitimation of the conflict by radically denying any space for the other in their own tradition, which they did, as the group says, 'through discrimination, expulsion and annihilation'. Since 2007 the results of the work are being studied.[5]

---

2   See Karl-Josef Kuschel, *Streit um Abraham. Was Juden, Christen und Muslime trennt – und was sie eint*, München, Piper, 1994.
3   The term opponent, in the modern non-violent movement, is borrowed from Gandhi. It indicates somebody to whom one is opposed but who is not considered an enemy.
4   See note 1.
5   The group could not hold their momentum and closed down in 2006.

The spiritual formation of identity

While I was staying with the ABRAHAM group in Sarajevo we had the chance to reflect on the moment of turning from hatred to peace. The stories found resonances in each other. Often it was a story of a particular moment in life when the enemy was suddenly seen as fellow human being who was sharing the same suffering, sharing the same life. Common humanity was the common ground. I would call these stories conversion stories. Most of these stories of being 'converted' to peace were stories of an encounter; this corroborated the experience that Christians of different and differing traditions have in their dialogues and which they call 'ecumenical learning'.

Conversions take place in missionary contexts, but also in many stages of any personal development, even in the sudden stages of mental and physical development in early childhood, often marked with great joy, relief, enlightenment. The make up of identity can thus be described as a spiritual process. Conversions cannot be produced. They are experienced, they are given. Muslims in ABRAHAM reported that becoming a Muslim was experienced as an act of liberation from nationalism and from the majority mind-set. One of my Muslim hosts in Sarajevo emphasized that he is now able to say, first I am a Muslim, and second I am a Bosnian, and that is why I cooperate with Christians and Jews. This statement runs contrary to the war-time creed of Sarajevo. At that time what counted first of all was the side you were on, whether Bosniak or Serbian. Then this was equated with religious identity: Are you Muslim or are you Orthodox? I find it important to understand such personal confessions as that of my Muslim host above as constituting an act of peacemaking. My Muslim friend says: I am Bosnian just as the Orthodox is Bosnian, as the Roman-Catholic is Bosnian; my religious identity now empowers me to fight the idolatry of ideological, national belonging.

Religious faith thus liberates us to take the first step into the unknown territory of the other: we bridge our nationalist separations. It empowers us to overcome the fear of insecurity when we are in a minority situation. My identity no longer rests on the majority who share my beliefs. Identity is no longer guaranteed by belonging to the good, and white, and just, side of the world, but can accept the black and white, the good and evil, the just and the unjust, both in the world and in oneself. Identity is then marked by an ability to reach stability through integration, not through exclusion. This conversion to become a Muslim is thus an act of coming home: coming home in God, who is creator of all different individuals, and coming home in this common humanity, even coming home in the heart of the other.[6]

An American Experience

My second example of coming home with the other concerns the Buddhist Peace Fellowship, in which I served as a volunteer in 2002. The Fellowship is a child of the Vietnam war. It derives its name from another fellowship which also expresses the international peace movement, namely, the International Fellowship of Reconciliation (IFOR). The latter was founded in Great Britain during the First World War, in 1916, and was one of

---

6 A missiological note: Japanese Christians often declare vis-à-vis their fellow countrymen that they are first Christians, then Japanese. They have been liberated from Japanese nationalism and militarism, from the ideology of Tennoism (emperor myth, Yasukuni Shinto-shrine), by becoming Christians. It is also remarkable that this independence of national ideology helped many Japanese Christians to contribute to the peacemaking effort of Japan towards her Asian victims after World War II.

the first Christian and interreligious organizations for world peace. In 1966 IFOR's US-branch sponsored a lecture tour by Thich Nhat Hanh, the Buddhist monk from South Vietnam, who pleaded with the American people to bring an end to the war of their government in his country. A year later, the American peace activist and Zen Buddhist from Hawaii, Robert Aitken, joined IFOR. During World War II, though himself a pacifist, he had been held in a Japanese internment camp, where he became exposed to Zen practice. Later, in 1974, he received Dharma-transmission, or the right to teach, from Yamada-roshi in Japan. He came to be the founder of the Zen community on Maui.

It was at his Zen community in Maui/Hawaii that he met with a group of Buddhist friends and decided to start a new chapter of the Fellowship of Reconciliation, which they called the Buddhist Peace Fellowship, in 1977. Why did they find it necessary to form an organization which could attract Buddhists in the USA from all groups, and lineages, and traditions?

Two years after the end of the Vietnam War in 1975, they had been very concerned that the Buddhist centres and groups in the USA were 'entirely removed from the social and political issues of the day',[7] such as the growing nuclear armament and the massive build-up of the US military. As there was no place for discussion and action among Buddhists a network would enable them to act together, one that should be ecumenical in nature. Using the membership cards of the Fellowship of Reconciliation, Nelson Foster, the assistant of Aitken-roshi and the first corresponding secretary, established an initial mailing list of Buddhists, mostly from Hawaii and the San Francisco Bay area. Among them were Jack Kornfield, Joanna Macy, Richard Baker, Gary Snyder, Al Bloom, Ryo Imamura, later followed by Fred Eppsteiner, Arnie Kotler. Their office was set up in Berkeley, California, in 1981. The network soon comprised several hundreds of members, with chapters in some cities. They began, in 1979, with a newsletter, now the *Turning Wheel* magazine, and the vigils in front of the entrance gate of the nuclear test site in Nevada.

Buddhist Peace Fellowship (BPF)

The newsletters of the Buddhist Peace Fellowship (BPF) used 'engaged Buddhism' to describe their approach. This term was a term coined by Thich Nhat Hanh when he articulated the need for monks and nuns in the forest monasteries and temples of South Vietnam, to both meditate and to take care of their village people during the US-bombing raids. BPF and its newsletter came to be the leaders of engaged Buddhism in the West. They shaped the identity of Buddhist activists, and drew on the traditions of Theravada, Zen, Pure Land, and Tibet; they intertwined action and meditation practice, and laid a foundation for a Buddhist approach to activism and non-violence, as well as inter-religious cooperation.

In 1985 the first collection of articles on engaged Buddhism in the West was published by Fred Eppsteiner, *The Path Of Compassion (*Berkeley, Parallax Press*)*. In the same year BPF sponsored the first tour of Thich Nhat Hanh in the USA after the Vietnam War.

When in 1991 war was again being waged by the United States the BPF offered Buddhists and others a vehicle with which to oppose this Gulf War. New members joined the BPF. They opposed the war of their government, and in many town meetings this dissenting voice of Buddhists was made manifest. Alan Senauke, the new director

---

7 Judith Simmer-Brown, 'Speaking Truth to Power: The Buddhist Peace Fellowship', in Christopher Queen (ed.), *Engaged Buddhism in the West*, Boston, Wisdom, 2000: 67f.

of BPF and himself a Zen priest in Berkeley, gave a clear profile to this understanding of Buddhism: being an engaged Buddhist means working in a non-violent way, and in collaboration with non-violent allies. BPF has never supported armed struggle though Buddhism must deal with suffering, personal and social and international. Alan Senauke, together with Tova Green (board president, 1996), helped BPF to become a place in US society, and in the world, where the sources of violence could be contemplated. The debate on the Gulf War was vital to this development.

BPF helped engaged Buddhists to address human rights issues, national and international, refugees, disarmament, war. It became a leading member of the International Network of Engaged Buddhists (INEB), founded 1989 in Bangkok, Thailand, by Sulak Sivaraksa, with Maruyama Teruo from Japan, and having as chairpersons Buddhadasa, Thich Nhat Hanh and the Dalai Lama, representing the Buddhist traditions of Theravada, Mahayana and Vajrayana respectively.[8]

As there is no national organization of Buddhists in the USA, such as the Buddhist Union in Germany, issues of Buddhist communities also had to be dealt with. In 1997 the BPF first published a guideline in ethics.[9] Also in 1997 a new programme was developed to deal with the death penalty and with prisoners in the growing prison sector of US society, and with US industry. Today BPF has more than 6,000 members, of which some 70% live in California, and 30% on the East Coast. The magazine *Turning Wheel* has a circulation of more than 7000, of which 1000 copies are being read in prisons as a gift of BPF.

BPF and war

The senior friends of the Buddhist Peace Fellowship like Robert Aitken and Nelson Foster began by demonstrating in front of nuclear sites. Though the BPF has always supported the inter-faith coalition of the national and global network to abolish nuclear weapons, through the Fellowship of Reconciliation, it has not been very articulate about its own contribution. The classical instruments and issues of peace work have not been so prominent within the BPF.[10] However, the board of the Fellowship agreed recently to put more emphasis on the Buddhist understanding of peace work.

Buddhists will have to work very diligently with a complex tradition. Buddhists often stress the fact that they are the foremost religion of peace because their first 'precept' is not to take life. They also stress that their understanding of life is substantially broader than the Abrahamic, as it includes all sentient beings, not only humans. However, this approach cannot be an absolute principle, as Buddhists reject any absolute principles. Instead, they insist on the essential one-ness of the relative and the absolute. That is why, in preserving life, there is some taking of it, e.g., eating, taking Penicillin. It is also known that Buddhists, and Buddhist countries, have engaged in

---

8 For greater detail, see Gerhard Köberlin, 'Friede sein. Ein Netzwerk engagierter Buddhisten entsteht', in Andreas Heuser and Wolfgang Weiße (eds.), *Neuere religiöse Bewegungen in internationaler Perspektive. Festschrift für Erhard Kamphausen*, volume 34 in Perspektiven der Weltmission, Aachen, Verlagshaus Mainz, 2005: 83-93.
9 Alan Senauke (ed.), *Safe Harbour*, Berkeley, BPF, 1997.
10 Such issues include: nuclear and conventional disarmament, abolishment of land mines, conscientious objection to military service, abolishment of the NATO, civil defence concepts as alternatives to the military, support of the United Nations and its peace keeping role including the provision of troops, support of war prevention through cooperation with peace groups in areas of conflict.

war: the Buddhist king Ashoka in ancient India and his many followers among the Theravada kingdoms; Sri Lankan nationalists against the Tamils today; and Japanese Buddhists as uncritical followers of Tennoism in World War II.[11]

A Buddhist contribution to the understanding of peace work will have to be very clear on any non-violent solution of conflicts, but at the same time will always have to be open to each single situation of conflict, and to each single agent involved, without any preconceived judging. As yet, I do not see a Buddhist contribution to the ongoing debate about belligerent and pacifist positions, the (Augustinian) concept of just war, or the latest concept of *realpolitik* on unilateral 'humanitarian military intervention', or even the world wide 'war on terrorism'.

Without suspicion or fear

The Abrahamic concept that we have looked at described coming home in the heart of the other as an opening of one's own identity. This opening is made possible through sharing faith in God who is 'greater', expressed by the Muslim cry of 'Allahu akbar', for God is greater even than the known territory of 'home' and of 'identity'. Faith in God opens one's identity without suspicion or fear of the other's religious, and ethnic, and political, identities. This is work for peace that is founded on the religions themselves.

The peace work of the Buddhist Peace Fellowship grew out of a situation of war and violence, as ABRAHAM did. However, the BPF's peace work rests on the Buddhist practice of meditation. The consequence of this practice can be seen in the primary mode of action of BPF. The members of the fellowship began by sitting down in front of the entrance gate of the nuclear testing site in Nevada. They practise sitting vigils in front of prison gates to protest against capital punishment in the USA. Experienced members offer meditation classes in prisons, with the expressed aim to contribute to transforming hatred against the staff, the system, oneself, into the possibility of (re-)connecting with life.[12]

I want to link this Buddhist practice to my first point. Buddhist meditation is a training in developing identity without the need to secure it against the other. It is a training in *sunnata*, the voidness or emptiness of self. This essentially critical approach to identity prepares us to integrate 'the other side', even the other who is my enemy. It opens us up to relate to the other without 'knowing' and without judging (*upekha*), in practising giving (*dana*) and not taking; it is the raft (*paramita*) we use to gain the other shore. The basic practice while sitting in vigils is the *metta* meditation, sending love or *metta* to the enemy, the opponent, identifying with the other. This practice is an exercise of inclusion, not exclusion.[13] Going this path of inclusion to the final goal is also to be

---

11 Ulrich Dehn, *Den Buddhismus verstehen. Versuche eines Christen*, Frankfurt a.M., Otto Lembeck, 2004: chapter 11 ('Buddhismus und Gewaltfreiheit – mit einem Blick auf das Christentum').
12 In October 2001, when the US military started bombing Afghanistan, Buddhists started to organize weekly meditation vigils on public ground to count the days of the war. At the time of writing the days of war on Afghanistan add up to more than 2000! BPF also supports the Zen Peace Maker Community in Israel-Palestine to find ways of transforming decades of hatred and violence into reconciliation; it has invited Eliyahu McLean and Ibrahim AbulHawa to the USA.
13 On the international Buddhist debate, see *ReVision* 26,2 (*Identity and Peace*), (Fall 2003): esp. Jonathan Watts, 'Storytelling, Structural Analysis, and Ethical Praxis: A Buddhist Response to Modern Violence': 22-30; and Jonathan Watts, 'Karma for Everyone: Social Justice and the Problem of Re-Ethicizing Karma in Theravada Buddhist Societies', in *World Fellowship of Buddhists Review* (*Rethinking Karma: The Dharma of Social Justice*) XLI,4 and XLII,1 (Bangkok, October 2547/2004 – March 2548/2005).

expressed as coming home with the other. Meditation cultivates openness of identity. The starting point of this practice is the meditation of the common experience of suffering – including the suffering of the other, the prisoner, the enemy.

I think this is a very special contribution by Buddhists to the overcoming of violence; it is the practice of a non-dualistic attitude beyond good and evil. At the same time, too, it is a contribution to interreligious dialogue.[14]

Christians, for their part, can contribute beyond dialogue and peace making in the Abrahamic fold by developing a 'theology of religions' to describe a place for the other. To achieve this they will have to deal with their own deeply engraved exclusivism. In Germany this theological task has only begun. Reinhard von Kirchbach, the late Lutheran dean of Schleswig-Holstein, can be regarded as a forerunner in this theology of religions. He had a deeply rooted fearlessness towards the different other. In his remarkable 'Project on Inter-religious Dialogue' of 1979 he stated: 'You cannot tell your neighbour: We know the way, you don't know it... We belong to God, we are doubtful about you... With us is justice and peace, not with you. With us dwells the fullness of truth, not with you. We are sustained by love, not you. If you speak like this, you don't know what you are saying. Did you not read, what is said: I am the way, I am the truth, I am the life?'[15] Christians can root their religion in an openness that is ahead of where they are today. Christians can be open to otherness by their preparedness to listen to the other and unite their hearts to those of others. With Muslims and Jews and many others Christians can learn a way of peace from Buddhist understanding. Thus, in the days after 9/11, when the now famous Thich Nhat Hanh was asked what he would have done if he had met Osama bin Laden after the attacks, he reflected and answered: first, I would have listened to him.

---

14 The European Buddhist-Christian dialogue of June 2007 in Salzburg focused on the Buddhist understanding of the religious 'other'. This is a study conference of the European Network of Buddhist Christian Studies under the chairmanship of John May, see www.buddhist-christian-studies.org.

15 Joachim Wietzke, 'Reinhard von Kirchbach – Grenzgänger des Glaubens', Hamburg, (typescript), 2007: 22.

Kristin Kwasniewski

Developing a Muslim Modernity
Integrating Mu'tazilite Philosophy with Progressive Principles to Implement Change

Discordant relations between the West and Islam are not a new phenomenon. The Muslim and the Western world have long endured a mutually antagonistic co-existence. Assumptions of a violent and uncompromising *other* on the part of both the West and Islam have engendered insular cultural systems, each wholly precluding the other. It is only by common necessity that Islam and the West have begun to move toward developing relations. Globalization has created a need for interdependence, evident in current concerns about oil production and distribution and global migration. Mutually exclusive Muslim and Western domains are no longer viable on a global scale: ours is now a world that requires cooperation – and thus mutual respect and understanding.

In recent years, academic discussion about relations between Islam and the West has become synonymous with examination of the events of 11th September 2001.[1] The attacks expedited an already developed mutually enforced rhetoric of oppositional dialectics. Discussion of the actual nature, diversity and identity of the *other* (be it Islam or the West) was replaced with a sense of fundamental incompatibility. To Islam, the West embodied a morally bankrupt global power that threatened the very existence of the Muslim world. To the West, Islam represented a single combative and vengeful entity.

Yet, the tragedy of 9/11 also drew Western public attention to the acrimonious relationship between Islam and the West, while arousing Muslim interest in engendering a positive Western view of Islam. As discussions about why and how 9/11 occurred became the focus of both public and private spheres, Western queries regarding Islam as a whole began to take shape. Further, the question of 'what is Islam?', posed by so many Western students, media sources and politicians in the wake of the events of 11th September 2001, inspired the far more profound question of whether Islam is compatible with Western socio-political ideals. Both positive and negative responses to that question have emanated from the West and from Islam, from academic and political, fundamentalist and apologetic sources. However, attempts at developing positive relations are also being made.

Despite some opposition, the desire to establish mutual understanding and an amicable relationship is evident in both civilizations. While the need for discussion and acceptance has been recognized by both traditions, it is the *means* by which such discussion and acceptance may be reached that remains in doubt. It is this issue, therefore, which must be our primary concern. This essay will argue that the most effective means of establishing mutual respect and understanding is to recognize the world-views of both Islam and the West *via their respective philosophical systems*. Islam cannot be measured by Western concepts of development and modernism. Therefore, a uniquely Muslim concept of modernity must be established. This author suggests the develop-

---

[1] Further information regarding the implications of 9/11 on Muslim-Western relations may be found in Ron Geaves, Theodore Gabriel, Yvonne Haddad and Jane Idleman Smith, *Islam and the West Post 9/11*, Aldershot and Burlington VT, Ashgate, 2004.

ment of a *Muslim modernity*, through which current Islam may re-access and rejuvenate itself, and establish an equal and alternative world-view in interreligious and international relations.

Redefining Modernity

The concept of a Muslim modernity begs a re-examination of the assumed definition of modernity. That term's connection with secularity and with the distinction between the private and public spheres, (and the associated implication that democracy assumes – if not necessitates – secularity) suggests total incompatibility with an Islamic world-view. From a western sociological standpoint, modernity connotes secularism, de-contextualization and individualism – a world-view based almost entirely in the rational where the religious is stripped of authority.[2] Western understanding of modernity is also linked to a direct comparison to post-modernity, a term emphasizing alternate concepts of 'diversity, differentiation... decentralization and internationalization', as well as a re-acknowledgment of tradition.[3] Most importantly, the very concept of modernity (in the context of a modern versus a pre-modern or a post-modern era) is a Western creation, formed from Western value structures and Western philosophy. By contrast, the philosophical developments of Ancient Greece (which serve as a foundation for current Western socio-political systems) while certainly recognized by Muslim scholars (and in some instances integrated into Muslim philosophy), do not serve as the basis for Muslim socio-political systems.[4] Western modernism measures the development of the West via the creation of a secular culture that draws divisive lines between the private and the public spheres. By this standard, Islam's non-secular, integrated system is pre-modern. However, the current Western socio-political question of how to pull Islam into modernity fails to consider what the application of this understanding of modernity means to Islam. The overarching rationalism that characterizes the Western modern era loses much of its universality when applied to a civilization that, at its core, is based in the divine. However, the subjective relativity characteristic of post-modernity and its focus on the local rather than the universal can have no place in a civilization that, while remarkably diverse, maintains a unifying spiritualism centered in Islam.

In order properly to understand the relationship between Islam and modernity, we must redirect our assessment of current Islam. Rather than attempting to super-impose a Western concept upon Islam, we must examine current Islam for what it truly is, without forcing Western concepts. In doing so, we find that aspects of current Islam are indeed modern: the essence of modernity is in the traditional that remains relevant in the contemporary.[5] It is in this foundation in tradition that we may find the beginnings of a Muslim modernity.

---

2 *Merriam-Webster Dictionary*, Merriam-Webster, 1998^{10}.
3 Alex Callinicos, *Against Postmodernism: A Marxist Critique*, Cambridge, Polity, 1989: 4.
4 Majid Fakhry, *A Short Introduction to Islamic Philosophy, Theology and Mysticism*, Oxford, Oneworld Publications, 1998: 2. Influential works such as Aristotle's *De anima, Categories, Hermeneutica* and *Secrets of Secrets* were transcribed into Arabic by a number of noted translators, yet perhaps the two most important translations – both of which were erroneously attributed to Aristotle – were Ibn Na'imah of Emessa's paraphrase of Plotinus' last three Enneads (or, *De Causis*, books IV, V and VI), and the *Theologia Aristotelis* which was translated into Arabic under the direction of al-Kindi (considered the first purely philosophical Arab writer).
5 *Merriam-Webster Dictionary*.

Islam has developed its own modernity which lies somewhere between the Western concepts of modernity and post-modernity. It is a form of truly Muslim modernity that embraces both the universality of modernity and the relativism and individualism of post-modernity. This modernity reconciles the global and the local and allows religion and rationalism to co-exist as mutually authoritative sources. However, as a uniquely Muslim concept, Muslim modernity must move beyond an amalgamation of the Western modern and post-modern, and establish itself as a new and authentic means of understanding Islam. Anchored in tradition (and the Qu'ran) but still amenable to adaptation, the concept of Muslim modernity provides a means of balancing the spheres of the religious and the rational, and thereby creates a viable Muslim alternative for approaching current global society.

Supporting a Progressive Philosophy

To achieve this alternative, a Muslim modernity will incorporate the core values and tradition-centered self-critique of the Progressive Muslims,[6] and will be founded on the central philosophical concepts of the Mu'tazilites, an early Muslim school of philosophy. A Muslim modernity must at once be rooted in purely Muslim tradition and recognize the need for adaptation in a changing world.

The Progressive Muslims suggest a new means of approaching the question of how to reconcile Islam and Western modernity by proposing an examination of Islam that champions the traditional but critiques current problems – a combination of both religious and rational approaches to developing a system of governing Muslim societies. This development may answer the question of how to reconcile with the West without surrendering a faith-based social and political system, as well as, the question of how to establish both innovation and continuity within tradition. In examining the development of a Muslim modernity – and thus a purely Islamic moral and socio-political system – Islam may be infused with a source of internal power (that would combat the negative after-effects of colonialism) and also establish a new means of assessing Islam that does not depend on Western standards of modernization.[7] To this end, Progressive Muslims provide a philosophy of positive change that is corroborated in a Muslim modernity.

In the essential concerns of Progressive Muslims, as described by Omid Safi, a new means of approaching Islam – as well as a new means of perceiving Islam from a global perspective – may be found. His interpretation of 'progressive' does not imply modernist progressivism, nor does it (entirely) suggest an Islamic revolution.[8] Rather, Safi's 'progressive' refers to 'a relentless striving towards a universal notion of justice in which no single community's prosperity, righteousness, and dignity comes at the expense of another'. Safi's Progressive Muslims seek to establish a just morality that originates entirely from within Islam, championing a strong basis in human rights and opposing Western hegemony via a multiple critique – thus reestablishing an Islamic morality and reasserting power, while also addressing the negative aspects of current Islam. Revelation and rationality function together to shape a society that is based in religious tradition,

---

6 For the purpose of this essay, Omid Safi's description of Progressive Muslims (as those Muslims who share a similar desire for the reassessment of Islam in light of human rights and gender equality and a re-evaluation of Muslim morality) will be used, despite the existence of alternative concepts of Progressive Muslims and Progressive Islam.
7 Khaled Abou El Fadl, 'The Ugly Modern and the Modern Ugly: Reclaiming the Beautiful in Islam', in Omid Safi (ed.), *Progressive Muslims,* Oxford, Oneworld, 2005: 33-77.
8 Omid Safi, *Progressive Muslims*: 3.

but which is governed by a rational approach to that tradition. From this stems a truly Muslim modernity: a form of Islam that acknowledges and champions both reason and religion in an equilibrium that allows each authority structure (rationalism and religion) to balance one another.

At the centre of a Progressive Muslims' philosophy lies the belief in the equal intrinsic worth of all humanity – a concept that echoes the Divine unity of the Mu'tazilites (which will be discussed later).[9] From this fundamental belief stems a focus on social and gender justice.[10] These values are paired with an active endeavour to effect pluralism – through the restoration of 'interpersonal ethics (*adab*)', and a need to engage tradition through the consideration of Islamic philosophical and theological writings as well as the Qu'ran and Hadith.[11] Further, Progressive Muslims strive for a reclamation of the concept of *jihad* as the struggle to improve both oneself and the world; they link this with *ijtihad* – *jihad* is etymologically related to *ijtihad* – which refers to a principle of intellectual and progressive interpretation in Islam; thus, they oppose Wahhabism and avoid an apologetic approach to interpreting Islam.[12] The tenets of Progressivism require not only a re-evaluation of current Islam, but the establishment of a new historical, hermeneutical and social approach to Islam, in which alternative philosophies and Qu'ranic verses (and alternate readings of these verses) are considered.

Progressive Muslims are 'mindful and critical of the arrogance of modernity'.[13] Given the current, Western understanding of modernity, rejection of a perceived 'Hegelian, unidirectional, and inevitable march towards the end game of modern Western civilization' is an understandable aspect of a Progressive Muslim's philosophy.[14] Unlike Muslim modernists, Progressive Muslims do not see Western modernity as a goal to be reached and in which a complete imitation of Western modernity is the next step in Islam's evolution.[15] Rather, Progressive Muslims strive to reinvigorate Muslim morality specifically through Muslim tradition. Perhaps then the 'next step' is a Muslim modernity. A Muslim modernity champions the values of progressive Muslims while maintaining a traditional source. The establishment of a Muslim modernity would act to coalesce Progressive Muslims: creating a socio-political philosophy that is equivalent to Western modernity yet establishing a philosophy still rooted in revelation. It would provide an alternate morality where reason and reassessment of tradition acted as an equal counterpart to Divine revelation. In the principles of the Mu'tazilites and their delicate balance of reason and religion we may find a basis for a Muslim modernity, as well as traditional support for Progressive Muslims.

Integrating Mu'tazilites Philosophy

The balance between religious and rational interpretations of Islam is central in the development of a Muslim modernity. In establishing such a balance, one may also establish a bridge between Islam and the West. The theme of 'religious' *versus* 'rational' suggests

---

9 Omid Safi, *Progressive Muslims*: 3.
10 Omid Safi, *Progressive Muslims*: 9-10.
11 Omid Safi, *Progressive Muslims*: 13.
12 Omid Safi, *Progressive Muslims*: 9: 'Wahhabism is a reactionary theological movement that originated in eighteenth century Arabia'. Wahhabism is generally associated with a fundamentalist, literalist interpretation of doctrine.
13 Omid Safi, *Progressive Muslims*: 4.
14 Omid Safi, *Progressive Muslims*: 4.
15 Omid Safi, *Progressive Muslims*: 4.

the possibility of a dualistic societal authority, where revelation maintains its sacredness while remaining grounded by rationality. The challenge of this balance is evident throughout Muslim philosophical and theological history, and indeed is paralleled in Christianity and the Western world – though the Western secular currently outweighs the religious. Most notably, a balance of reason and religion is championed in the Muslim Mu'tazilite philosophy of the 9th century. It is through an understanding and development of this balance between faith and reason that the foundations of a new Muslim concept of modernity, and perhaps a means of establishing an Islamic philosophical basis for the application of this modernity, may be built.

Despite a variety of disagreements within the Mu'tazili, the concepts of Divine unity and Divine justice served as philosophical foundation.[16] Essentially, Mu'tazilite Divine unity held that God is an entirely unified One *Tawhīd*: God's attributes are integrated in Divine Oneness (thus, God's knowledge of something is an attribute and does not originate from external knowledge).[17] In order to maintain this concept, any anthropomorphic aspects of the Qu'ran or the Hadith were read as metaphorical. The concept of Divine justice stemmed from the concern that God does not create evil, nor does God cause evil; therefore, any evil in the world was of human origin. Free will thus became an important aspect of Mu'tazilite philosophy, as it is only from human acts that evil may be derived. For the Mu'tazili, free will bestowed on human beings the unique ability 'to listen to God's created speech. They are capable of rational activity and above all, they are able to initiate their own acts and bear moral responsibility for them' – humanity is capable of rationality while maintaining a connection to the Divine.[18] Human reason is responsible for differentiating between good and evil, as it is through reason that humanity recognizes morality.[19] Though there is some debate about the true nature of goodness (and the degree to which human reason is responsible for its identification),[20] the Mu'tazili generally distinguish two classes of moral obligations: those known by revelation and those known by reason, where reason allows us to recognize general morality and revelation provides the guide for following that morality.[21] Hence, Mu'tazilite philosophy established a moral structure that was equally dependent on reason and revelation. Each of these authoritative sources functioned to balance the other: reason was applied to the interpretation of doctrine when the morality or meaning of the passage was not direct, while revelation was subject to rational elucidation, preventing strict literal interpretation.[22]

---

16 W. Montgomery Watt, *Islamic Philosophy and Theology*, Edinburgh, University Press, 1987. The following explanation of Mu'tazilite philosophy is necessarily brief; within the philosophical school there are many disputed concepts as well as varying degrees of rationalism. For the purposes of this essay, however, only those concepts that are nearly universally accepted within the Mu'tazilite school will be noted.
17 Seyyed Hossein Nasr and Oliver Leaman, *History of Islamic Philosophy*, London, Routledge, 2001: 105, 126.
18 Eliot Deutsch and Ron Bontekoe, *A Companion to World Philosophies*, Malden and Oxford, Blackwell, 1999: 465.
19 Eliot Deutsch and Ron Bontekoe, *A Companion to World Philosophies*: 484.
20 Eliot Deutsch and Ron Bontekoe, *A Companion to World Philosophies*: 485; the most notable of these differences were in the interpretations of 'Abd al-Jabbar, Al-Ghazzali and Al-Ash'ari. Further information may be found in Richard C. Martin, and Mark R. Woodward, *Defenders of Reason in Islam, Mu'tazilism form Medieval School to Modern Symbol*, Oxford, Oneworld, 2003.
21 Eliot Deutsch and Ron Bontekoe, *A Companion to World Philosophies*: 486.
22 Eliot Deutsch and Ron Bontekoe, *A Companion to World Philosophies*: 485-490. It bears mention-

Mu'tazili philosophy provides a means of implementing these values via the practice of *Kalam*. The Mu'tazilite school of philosophy developed through the practice of *Kalam:* the Muslim tradition of 'seeking theological principles through dialectic' – a definition evident in the literal translation of the term as the act of 'speaking'.[23] More specifically, *Kalam* refers to a 'discussion', 'argument' or 'debate', as *Kalam* focused on the forbidden discussion of delicate topics; the proponents of *Kalam* countered traditionalist disapproval by associating *Kalam* with *'ilm al-tawhid* – 'the science of [affirming God's] unity'.[24]

Early *Kalam* placed equal importance on rational and traditional arguments, emphasizing the Mu'tazilite balance of rationalism and religion.[25] To this end, *Kalam* often focused on the relationship between God's intervention and activity and humanity's free will.[26] The early scholar Wasil ibn 'Ata best defined the Mu'tazilite understanding of *Kalam* in his assertion of four key sources of truth: 'the Qu'ran, agreed Hadith, rational argument, and *ijma*.'[27] This statement recognizes the significant connection between rationalism and tradition, as well as the mutual importance of utilizing traditional and external sources when engaging in *Kalam* – an insight that is evident in the values of the current Progressive Muslims. Thus, if we are to resurrect the principles of the early Mu'tazili for incorporation in the foundation of a Muslim 'modernity' we must also develop a model of *Kalam* that has the capacity to be re-established in contemporary Islam. To achieve this, the work of H.M. Al-Safi'i (a present-day authority on *Kalam*) may be of use: he explains that the Qu'ranic middle position refers to the rational proofs – *Kalam* – that are evident within the verses of the Qu'ran.[28] The *Kalam* found within the Qu'ran 'treated theological issues supported by rational proofs.'[29] Yet, in the development of a Muslim modernity, the slightly liberal *Kalam* of the Mu'tazili may be more applicable. To the left of the Qu'ranic centre lies the Mu'tazili focus on *'ta'wil* (interpretation) and *tanzih* (transcendence)' as well as an adherence to rational proof, or *'aql'*.[30] When we incorporate this Mu'tazilite *Kalam* into a Muslim modernity, a hermeneutical approach to tradition and texts becomes available. A Mu'tazilite system of establishing morality (in the form of human rights, gender equality and pluralism) is posited, resulting in a moral system that is rooted in tradition yet can be adapted in ways applicable to current issues.

Considering the Obstacles of a Muslim Modernity

The creation of a distinctly Muslim modernity is both a promising and a dubious concept. While this modernity may provide a new means of approaching Western relations with Muslim countries, as well as a more objective means of accessing current Islam, it

---

ing in conjunction with this concept that the Mu'tazili believed that, while God's speech is wholly Divine, the Qu'ran was created.
23 http://www.muslimphilosophy.com/ip/rep/H009.htm, accessed on 28 January 2007.
24 http://www.muslimphilosophy.com/ip/rep/H009.htm, accessed on 28 January 2007.
25 Nasr and Leaman, *History of Islamic Philosophy*: 81.
26 Ninian Smart, *World Philosophies*, London, Routledge, 1999: 159.
27 Nasr and Leaman, *History of Islamic Philosophy*: 81. The term *ijma* refers to the consensus of the Muslim community, though its literal translation refers only to the consensus of Islamic scholars with regard to Islamic law.
28 Nasr and Leaman, *History of Islamic Philosophy*: 82.
29 Nasr and Leaman, *History of Islamic Philosophy*: 82.
30 Nasr and Leaman, *History of Islamic Philosophy*: 82.

also raises significant questions regarding the authenticity of modern Islam. Despite the careful insistence that a Muslim modernity be drawn entirely from Muslim tradition and religious texts, the more liberal, rational aspects of this modernity do necessitate a self-critique that is prone to substantial fundamentalist opposition. Further, the authenticity of a *purely* Muslim modernity must be questioned, as we cannot assume that a Muslim modernity is an eventuality. Here is the challenge of a Muslim modernity: the latter's reliance on the recognition of historical development as well as historical context may have consequences for the question of whether modern Muslims are authentically Muslim. While this new conception of Islam is indeed entirely founded in tradition, while its philosophies are wholly Islamic, its sources genuine and its central basis still the Qu'ran, a problem remains in that the selection and assigned dominance of one interpretation of Islam above all others (with the philosophies, verses, and writings that support that interpretation) is prone to develop a narrow understanding of Islam. Such a fate is evident in Wahhabism, where strictly literal readings and isolated Hadith are used to negate the vast and varied interpretations of Islam that do not support the specific concept of Islam that is embraced. It is with this hazard in mind that a Muslim modernity must be developed – with care not to attenuate or constrict Islam by condemning alternative interpretations. In venturing into new interpretations of Islam, Omid Safi rightly warns that we must 'seek to locate ourselves as part of that broader conversation, not to collapse the spectrum.'[31]

Conclusion

The creation of a truly Muslim modernity may provide a unique means of reconciling Muslim-Western relations. Once we stop accessing Islam via Western standards, we may begin to see the *other* not as a threat, but as gift, and from this context, we are challenged to find alternative inter-relational approaches to globalization. However, the establishment of a fully objective understanding of the *other* is difficult. Is it possible for the West to recognize in Islam a modernity that is not governed by Western standards? Perhaps still more difficult a challenge is for two concepts of modernity to co-exist without negating or absorbing each other. Undoubtedly, there are limitations to the application of a Muslim modernity. However, if accepted, this Muslim modernity may be a most promising contribution to the restoration of contemporary Islam. In offering a viable and uniquely Muslim alternative to Western morality, the development of a Muslim modernity may provide a means of re-evaluating international relations, the current supremacy of the Western secularized world-view and the necessity of secularity for democracy. A Muslim modernity maintains a progressive approach to Islam while preserving the potency of revelation. Here is a catalyst for change.

---

31 Omid Safi, *Progressive Muslims*: 6.

Aasulv Lande

Dialogue, for Heaven's sake

Dialogue – including interreligious dialogues – might well be classified as the completed stage in a process. It is something to dream of or look forward to, the end of conflict. Conflicts may at last turn into dialogue. The place of 'dialogue' is heaven, the state of fulfilment. Heaven *is* actually dialogue. What is then the earlier, the intermediate dialogue, dialogue as an ongoing process among humans? What is particularly inter-religious dialogue? Might it be more than a step towards peace and understanding, possibly a joyful foretaste of heavenly consummation?

Existence Alongside: Basis for Interreligious Dialogue

The atmosphere of the West in the 1950s and 1960s was decisively influenced by existentialist ideas. Gunnar Skirbekk, a fellow Norwegian student of mine from the late 1950s, wrote a challenging essay called *Nihilisme*.[1] His essay did not provide a Christian solution to the question of meaning of life. He was attracted by French existentialists such as Jean-Paul Sartre, Simone de Beauvoir and Albert Camus. Working himself through a number of theological and philosophical positions he ended up with what he considered the only certain fact of life: *death*. In awareness of death he discovered a basis from which to approach existence. However, he was not alone. Names such as Martin Heidegger, Hannah Arendt, Karl Jaspers, Rudolf Bultmann, Paul Tillich, Karl Barth and others elaborated on the idea of existence. I could formulate the existential dogma of the time as follows: *Existence is what counts, we are existing – and that is where we start. Furthermore, existence should be embraced; that embrace is the meaning of life.* In Christian circles this existentialism, however, attained a *kerygmatic* shape.

Already prior to this period, in the 1940s, the German Lutheran theologian Dietrich Bonhoeffer had opened up a theology of Christian presence. God was primarily to be found in the midst of life processes rather than in the realm of ecclesiastical traditions. This trend inspired above all the dialogue with secular society. Urban and rural mission projects grew up, not at least in Western cities. Christians were called to be present where God was at work – in society and religion outside of church. Roman Catholic French worker priests were particularly early in getting alongside secular workers in a society where religion had become alienated. Listening and being present were crucial parts and starting points of their dialogue with secular and urban France.[2]

Church Missionary Society general secretary, Max Warren in Britain had introduced the concept of 'Christian presence' with a more religious flavour. He edited the 'Christian Presence series' which introduced Christian presence in the religious world. A standard work was the sensitive study of Islam by Anglican Kenneth Cragg, *Sandals at the Mosque: Christian Presence Amid Islam*.[3] Many religiously committed people grasped

---

1 Gunnar Skirbekk, *Nihilisme*, Oslo, Tanum, 1958.
2 See *Student World* 3 (1965) and 4 (1965).
3 Kenneth Cragg, *Sandals at the Mosque: Christian Presence amid Islam*, London, SCM, 1959.

similar ideas. In the religious world of Roman Catholicism persons such as Thomas Merton, Aloysius Pieris, William Johnston, KADOWAKI Kakichi, Enomiya Lassalle and others practised interreligious Christian presence. These people had especially worked with the great religions of the East, namely, Buddhism and Hinduism. They emphasized listening and dialogue and the willingness to learn.

What was the relationship between the concern for existence and the Christian presence theology? Was the group of people starting from a Christian presence theology also starting from a concern with existence? Was there – beyond the concerns of Christian presence theologians such as Merton and Johnston – a fresh embrace of existence in the contemporary world, in one's own time? They did not want to achieve or produce; primarily they wanted to exist then and there. I suggest – I cannot prove it but at least I can raise it as a hypothesis – that those of us who related to Christian presence thought were existentialists in our hearts. This is not to say that we were not all existentialists in the way the kerygmatics were. We chose another existentialist route than the one of Barth and Bultmann. We tried to grasp existence in presence. Was 'Christian presence' essentially a Christian application of the existential dogma of the age? Was it an 'existence alongside'?

From an 'existence alongside' the road to interreligious dialogue was short. Western ecclesiastical and political dominance was coming to an end. In Christian interreligious relations humility of learning substituted for the dominance of teaching. Using ears substituted for use of the mouth. The existential dogma guided Christian outreach into humble listening to others. Interreligious dialogue commended itself as a fresh appreciation of existence alongside other faiths. Mission was transformed into the interreligious dialogue. Christians should be present; in attentive concern and dialogue.[4]

Transcending Instrumental Dialogues?

As admitted in my introductory lines, dialogue may be a final stage of bliss, but it could also be seen as a preliminary tool. It is at times instrumental. Dialogue – if considered a tool – is in other words used for some purpose.

It has become standard, particularly in missionary circles, to classify religious dialogues in accordance with their purpose. Two main categories are dialogues for social improvements and dialogue aiming at truth. *Social dialogue* implies dialogue for social improvement, reconciliation and peace. It connects a mostly theoretical or contemplative procedure with a social purpose. *Truth dialogues* might also proceed as contemplative and theoretical projects. Their aim is, however, to reach new levels of understanding, leading others and oneself towards deeper levels of truth.

Is it possible to transcend the difference between these two categories of dialogue? Guided by the philosophical perspectives of Martin Buber and others I look for an interreligious dialogue which transcends these two purpose-oriented dialogues. I seek an interreligious dialogue beyond instrumentality, drawing from the realm of fulfilment. I do not plead for a dialogue of fulfilment that substitutes for the instrumental approaches. Nonetheless, is there not a need to focus on the dimension of fulfilment in interreligious dialogue?

---

4 See *Student World* 3 (1965) 4 (1966).

The Instrumental Dialogue for Peace

I have found the clearest arguments for a socially oriented, instrumental dialogue in groups affiliated with the World Conference of Religion and Peace (WCRP), established 1970 in Kyoto, Japan. The arguments and theologies in WCRP relate to different religious contexts and traditions. There is a particularly well-articulated concern in the Japanese new religious organization of Rissho Kosei Kai, founded in 1938. Religiously, its background might be traced to the Buddhist prophet Nichiren, of 13th century Japan. Rissho Kosei Kai interprets the world as governed by Buddhist laws or karma. To establish peace is thus completely dependent upon an intimate correspondence with karmic principles which have to be mobilized for peace. In accordance with the globalized and universal ideas of Rissho Kosei Kai these principles are not considered the sole property of Buddhism. Various religious traditions provide different approaches to the karma of cosmos. If leaders of different religions meet and make peace between themselves, cosmic karma is mobilized and peace-conductive forces are activated in the world. In other words, interreligious dialogue is a vital, cosmic premise for world peace. Interfaith dialogue is a seed of peace – which in due time will yield a peaceful life, peaceful societies, and in the end a peaceful world.

This karma thinking links interestingly to the 'model-thought' in Buddhist inspired, Japanese Omoto and its offspring Sekai Kyusei Kyo. Omoto thinks as follows: It is a fruitful peace work to create models of peace in the world. This might be a 'garden', a centre of beauty or a milieu where peace reigns. Artistic performance is of utmost importance as efficiently working models of peace. By performing classical folk arts, for instance in music or painting, such dynamic models are established. Omoto emphasizes the significance of interreligious worship. Common interreligious rites have not only been performed in Omoto's own sanctuaries (Ayabe and Kameoka) near Kyoto, Japan, but even in cooperating Christian Churches outside the home country. Strikingly parallel to Rissho Kosei Kai's religiously pluralist understanding of karma, Omoto emphasizes interreligious cooperation with a promising initiation of world peace.

Within Christian traditions, noted initiatives have been promoted by German theological professors Hans Küng and Karl-Josef Kuschel. The Global Ethic project led by Hans Küng is founded on the conviction that world religions have similar ethical norms. On this basis, religious peoples have to cooperate; because there will be no peace in the world without cooperation between religious people – although this cooperation cannot be considered sufficient for peacemaking – there is here a necessary project. The Global Ethic project is not exclusively religious – people from a humanistic background are also invited to participate. There is also a contextual European version led by Karl-Josef Kuschel: Children of Abraham – also supported in countries like Sweden and Germany.[5] Kuschel sees the cooperation and joint efforts for peace among the Abrahamic faiths as a promising peace process.[6]

Küng and Kuschel are convinced that Christ is present in these interreligious efforts and in the foundation of world culture, thus connecting world peace projects to the

---

5 See Karl-Josef Kuschel, 'The Open Covenant. The Need for a "Theology of the Other" among Jews, Christians and Muslims', in Werner G. Jeanrond and Aasulv Lande (eds.), *The Concept of God in Global Dialogue*, Maryknoll, Orbis, 2005: 63-88.
6 See Karl-Josef Kuschel, *Streit um Abraham. Was Juden, Christen und Muslime trennt – und was sie eint*, München, Piper, 1994; Hans Küng (ed.), *Yes to A Global Ethic*, London, SCM, 1996.

universal effects of Jesus Christ. The belief in a cosmic Christ dynamism might explain Küng and Kuschel's interreligious cooperation.

There are similarities between the dynamics of peace based on a cosmic Christ principle and on interreligious, dynamic karma. From the Christian perspective one might look at the cosmic Christ strategy for peace in the light of 'Christian presence'. Christ is *present* in the whole world as a logos which corresponds with fundamental insights of world religions. This present logos – with which the world saviour Jesus Christ identifies – furthermore promotes redemption and world peace. In the Buddhist context as seen by Rissho Kosei Kai, the basic interest in interreligious dialogue is based on a multi-religiously oriented view of Buddhist karma. This karma is in principle working in all world religions and thus is indeed present worldwide. One might possibly talk of 'Buddhist presence'. The implications of these two 'presences' are considered in similar terms in the Buddhist and Christian theologies referred to. Both traditions share an awareness of the presence and recommend practical strategies of religious cooperation towards global reconciliation and peace.

As a first comment on the use of social dialogues for peace I would ask: do they work? My answer is somewhat hesitant. I have serious doubts about the practical efficiency of religious dialogues for peace. They may be conducted in a spirituality of high level concern and enthusiasm – but do they really solve the problems of power, self interests and the dynamics of suppression? Do they reduce the number of wars? Do they solve or substantially counteract conflicts over property and financial interests? Whatever might be said in favour of interreligious dialogues, there is little doubt that such initiatives alone do not solve the problems of conflict and the tensions between financial, political and military competitors. The interreligious dialogues apparently do not offer working solutions to serious conflicts. These dialogues are generally weak or powerless; but, in spite of their fragile character one has to ask: do they not after all, offer hope and optimism – attitudes without which peace hardly can be established? I recently sat down with the Japanese Zen Buddhist NISHIMURA Eshin and talked about problems confronting us. We were particularly worried about the dramatic changes in world climate. Professor Nishimura had seen and had been deeply touched by the documentary *An Inconvenient Truth*. The movie, illustrating an urgent message about global warming from previous US presidential candidate Al Gore, had rung an alarming bell. Japan had, for instance in 2006-2007, recorded the warmest winter for one hundred years. What did it, and similar developments, signify? We were immediately united in a common concern for the well-being of humanity and for the preservation of life on our globe. It was an element of existential interreligious dialogue on preservation of life. We were thrown back on our different spiritual traditions and shared spontaneously a common hope for world wellbeing and peace.

The *social, interreligious dialogue* performed in order to obtain reconciliation and peace had in Christian circles evolved out of spirituality of Christian presence. In a Buddhist environment the dialogue had a similar origin, for instance in a humble, Japanese post war concern for peace, a 'Buddhist Presence Theology'. By small or large scale interreligious initiatives a hope for an all-embracing harmony and peace have been enkindled. Immediate effects on peace work are questionable and incomplete. However, a concentration on our common needs of existence in interreligious dialogue may open religious treasures of powerful visions and hopeful perspectives.

Dialogue for the Sake of Truth

When dialogue leads to the establishment of hope and visions it approaches the perspective of truth. Truth is here not necessarily a powerful truth, it might be contested. It has a strong personal character. Truth transcends factuality and centres on what is trustworthy. It contains an existential dimension. Is dialogue possibly, then, on a fruitful track when it works to attain and establish truth?

During the last decades dialogue has focused on *learning* – it has been a dialogue for the sake of truth – for the extension and the deepening of truth. Not to propagate truth, but to attain truth. The dialogue of learning has appeared in two significant and substantial forms. One was the *theoretical dialogue* for the sake of truth. The great ecclesiastical organizations engaged in theoretical dialogues. In Protestantism, Stanley Samartha from Bangalore became instrumental in working out a theoretical dialogue programme. One met for conferences – a pioneer conference took place in Ajaltoun in 1967 (Christian-Muslim) – and a number of theoretical conferences on interreligious issues emerged in the 1970s. In the Lutheran World Federation, the Indian theologian Paul Rajashekar initiated similar developments. They were 'theoretical dialogues' but they had a serious motivation. They were undertaken in order to achieve truth.

The dialogues of experience, a substantial part of which were the *contemplative dialogues*, also offered dialogue for the sake of truth. They largely took place in Roman Catholic circles after the second Vatican Council 1962-1965. Some of the names mentioned above (Kakichi Kadowaki, Thomas Merton) engaged in this dialogue where the Benedictine, monastic tradition took an active lead. Christian-Zen encounters developed in particular between Buddhist monasteries in Japan and Western Europe/USA. The German, Benedictine monastery of St Ottilien played an important role in this particular outreach. Christian monks and nuns meditated for a period in Buddhist surroundings and together with Buddhists. Buddhist religious practitioners visited in return Christian monasteries and meditated together with their religious partners or counterparts. Participants testified to experiences pointing at a truth not yet completely grasped and which somehow completed and extended the boundaries of one's own faith so far.[7]

Here is room to include *missional* dialogue as a genuine, truth dialogue. By missional I mean that truth is proclaimed in the form of a *kerygma* or a message. Missional dialogues have a significant history. The Socratic dialogues were 'missional', based on leading the partner to an understanding of truth. It is questionable whether they should be termed dialogues in the modern meaning of the term. Agents of dialogue in post-war Christianity or Buddhism have followed a more subtle and humble line of listening than the analytical, therapeutic dialogues for which Socrates is known. Many post-war preachers transcended the Socratic norms, making proclamation dependent upon, even secondary to, listening. Such were the ways of e.g., Thomas Merton and Kakichi Kadowaki. The Episcopal missionary Kenneth Cragg ushered in a new Christian missionary enthusiasm by 'leaving his sandals outside the mosque', recognizing the presence of God outside the Church. Young scholars like Japanese Emi Mase Hasegawa and Swedish Ann Aldén have in their doctoral works illustrated how a Christian message can be transmitted in a genuine spirit of open dialogue.[8] Although the dialogues in

---

7 See Aasulv Lande, 'Recent Developments in Interreligious Dialogue', in Jeanrond and Lande, *The Concept of God*: 32-47 and Katrin Åmell, *Contemplation et dialogue. Quelques exemples de dialogue entre spriitualités après le concile Vatican II*, Uppsala, SIM, 1998.
8 See Emi Mase-Hasegawa, *Spirit of Christ Incarnated: A Theological Theme Implicit in*

principle were instrumental on the way towards truth, they were conducted in a spirit of listening humility. They were shaped in an awareness of 'Christian presence', and eventually of 'Buddhist presence'.

In 'missional dialogue' it is of utmost importance to respect the other, to admit and support the freedom of the other. This respect constitutes a most sublime feature of missional dialogue. A representative of 'another' faith might never in the name of dialogue be forced into one's own faith or, indeed, into any particular faith. Dialogue presupposes the freedom of the other and it works contrary to force, manipulation or suppression. In missional dialogue worthy of the name, instrumentality is highly conditioned by the approval of the partner. However, if conducted under these restrictions, dialogue might offer to both or all participants hope and vision based on the dignity of human beings.

The humble dialogue for truth emerges from an awareness of what I have termed 'presence' which might be related to various religious traditions. It contains a learning attitude and a sharing of convictions (missional) while honouring the rights and the dignity of the other. Dynamic religious presence, stemming from Buddhist, Humanist, Christian or other faiths, promotes the freedom and personal dignity of humankind. The insights into truth fostered by this dialogue offer a unique spirituality, which I have characterized as vision, hope and a fundamental respect of the other human being.

Towards an Ultimate Dialogue

These reflections on the character of instrumental dialogues lead to certain preliminary suggestions. Interreligious social dialogues as well as truth dialogues arise from an awareness of religiously conditioned presence. The efficiency of an interreligious dialogue for peace is doubtful, if measured in terms of immediate, positive results. However, visions and hopes for peace emerging from interreligious encounters on questions of social crises contribute towards a spirituality of reconciliation and peace. Such an outcome points towards truth dialogues, in which religious partners seek existential and 'trustworthy' truth. In terms of mutual understanding, existential hope and convictions interreligious dialogue offers unique contributions to the participants. The truth dialogues might thus also contribute towards the interreligious dialogues for social purposes. Truth-dialogues and social dialogues thus work interactively and cannot actually be sharply distinguished. They are, however, vulnerable and intermediate attempts to reach determinate aims. I therefore look for an 'ultimate' dialogue, one that fundamentally reflects human existence and connects us with the ultimate, with God. This is not a dialogue to obtain peace and truth; it is rather a dialogue which reveals ultimate peace and truth. One might say that this dialogue presupposes the unified peace and truth. It does not mean that an instrumental search has come to an end. Truth and peace remain unfulfilled. One might, however, establish and practise dialogue models of peace and truth as expressions of trust in humanity and as signs of hope.

I am constantly impressed by the Buddhist priest Nishimura Eshin, whom I met in 2007 and to whom I have referred above. 'We are getting old', he said. 'It is good to meet and to have conversations. Perhaps we meet for the last time. Personally', he said,

---

Shusaku Endo's Literary Works, Lund, Lund University, 2005; Ann Aldén, *Religion in Dialogue with Late Modern Society: A Constructive Contribution to a Christian Spirituality Informed by Buddhist-Christian Encounter*, Lund, Lund University, 2005.

'my Buddhist faith has constantly grown in encounter with Christians. The first group of believers I met in Christendom were Quakers, and my later experiences extend to Roman Catholics and mainline Protestants as well. Interreligious dialogue is a deep dimension of my own faith.'

I have a similar perspective myself. My Christian Church contains a radical experience of otherness and surprise which can be encountered in persons of non-Christian faith traditions. I do not expect them to cut their roots – but I do welcome them in a community of truth seekers where they listen and try to share our Christian joy and grief. I appreciate that my 'church' offers an interreligious opportunity to 'meet and to greet' believers in different traditions of faith.[9]

Permit me to indicate a philosophical position by referring to Martin Buber in *I and Thou*.[10] He states that the human being in dialogue does not receive a content but *presence*, and that presence as power. He finds three elements in this powerful presence: first, he accepts its *fullness of true mutuality*. One belongs together, one is accepted. This does not make life easier but heavier. The second element is subsequently *the inexpressible confirmation of meaning*. Nothing is hereafter void of meaning. The question of the meaning of life, then, simply disappears: the meaning of life will be *done* by us, not interpreted, neither proved nor demonstrated. This is the third element and it means that the 'meaning of life is here'. It is to be fulfilled and practised in this world and on this earth, and is not something beginning in a life outside this one. The dialogue is ultimate as we approach God in it, though we are neither offered any solution to the riddle of the world nor any disclosure of the secrets of existence. Thus, Martin Buber in *I and Thou* embraces a dialogue that recognizes a divinely-based human existence and the freedom of 'the other'.

Let me return to my erstwhile fellow student Gunnar Skirbekk. He began his reflections on existence on the basis of an awareness of death. From this radical negation of existence he felt safe and secure in approaching and even disclosing the mystery of existence. He now talks of the philosophical *unrest (uroa)*, which means a certainty implying acceptance of a basic existential uncertainty.[11] In the terminology of this article it corresponds to the simultaneous recognition of ultimate interreligious dialogues and instrumental dialogues at an intermediate stage.

In conclusion, the instrumental dialogue for peace and truth cannot and should not be suspended. Although interreligious dialogues lack the power to enforce peaceful solutions, they convey hope and vision. A most challenging and significant perspective of dialogue occurs, however, when the dialogue for peace and truth interacts with the ultimate dialogue springing out from divinely-based, human existence. *Truth is doing* – as Buber says. This pronouncement of dialogue as consummated existence is at the same time a call to action. Interreligious dialogue is therefore indeed 'a joyful foretaste of heavenly consummation'.

But, it takes place in the here and now – and at times one gets dirty hands.

---

9 See Kenneth Cragg, *To Meet and to Greet*, London, Epworth, 1992.
10 Martin Buber, *jeg og du*, [Danish edition] Århus, Munksgaard, 1964 [1922]: 145.
11 Gunnar Skirbekk, *Den filosofiske uroa*, Oslo, Universitetsforlaget, 2005: 183.

Fiachra Long

The Challenge of Tactility

It is a testimony to John D'Arcy May that I never quite know whether he is a Buddhist or a Christian. He always seems highly committed to both religions and both ways of life. Perhaps my quandary comes from the fact that he is not an either/or kind of man but one who understands from his own experience of cultures and religions what it means to be an inculturated person. By this I mean someone who values what is to be valued highly in different religions in the light of a more basic commitment. Since it takes a particular type of education to produce someone with these capacities, an education in the pluralism of cultures, one that focuses clearly on what it is to live in an inhabited world (*he oikoumene ge* 'the inhabited world'), then the ecumenical fruits of this type of education is a cause of wonder. Educational systems in general seek only to reproduce themselves and the cultures of learning they recognize as valid; they do not spend much time and certainly could not politically justify spending any resources on the development of world citizens without any clear economic purpose for doing so.

These pages will attempt to explore the plausibility of the claim that there is one education that produces globalized individuals and another education that produces individuals who learn to live in the inhabited world. To make this claim we will have to suggest that, whereas in the past, globalization could ally itself to total mindsets that could be recognized through one kind of ideology or another, today globalization allies itself to tactility as its preferred orientation. Tactility not only describes a temporal orientation towards reality but also a pattern of relation between individuals, groups and nations. It seems that speedier contacts only promote the totalizing mindset. They further the interests of a global economy bent on persuading everyone that they are the same, that their tastes and values are the same and hence that the products on the market have universal appeal, that differences in these matters merely act as obstacles to world progress. I will argue here that what is needed today is a mindset that learns to live with differences, differences of culture, differences of religion, differences even of economy and that this latter task is proving too difficult a challenge for education systems in the developed world. Rather than carefully weighing up the significance of intractable differences in culture and mindset that are features of the inhabited world, young learners, subject to socio-cultural neglect, fail to break down the norms of childhood, and simply enhance the static, black and white picture that children use to understand themselves and others.

Still using these black and white views, knowledge becomes a matter of consumer opinion, personal choice and meaning making. Under such conditions, peace is easily identified with war or with secularization and the abolition of religions. In other words, talk of one world leads to a suppression of important differences rather than to a type of learning that accommodates these differences. Underlying all this there is a deep seated resistance by the young to accepting limitations of any kind, thus at once echoing and enhancing the omnipotent claims of childhood. While in the past, ideologies may have served to consolidate these omnipotent claims – colonial empire building, national socialism, Communism and now widespread Democratic capitalism, there are signs that none of these ideologies matter in a culture dominated by tactility.

I. From Globalization to Tactility

The marginalization of pluralism is not new in itself, but the speed of today's world is new. Marshall McLuhan gave us a hint about a global mindset in 1964 when he described the world as being 'compressed into a single space' and this same judgement might be made with even greater plausibility about society today. While an increase in speed and global availability of communications has made access to ever increasing streams of information much more possible, it has also made the effect of this exposure much more superficial. Understandably, the news industry is not too worried by this trend. It is not perturbed if the ozone layer of news itself is thinning out and it has come to accept that we, as consumers of news, are more impressed by daring reporters flying over volcanoes than by what they actually say. So while we might believe that there has never been a better informed generation than ourselves, we have to admit that the surplus of poorly digested (if digested at all) information points to the precipitation of this culture into what Jean Baudrillard calls a crisis of meaning:

> Our culture of meaning is collapsing beneath the excess of meaning, the culture of reality collapsing beneath the excess of reality, the information culture collapsing beneath the excess of information – the sign and reality sharing a single shroud.[1]

The most negative effect of this excess of meaning, or this thinning out, or weightlessness, is that it leads to a simulated kind of consciousness. Explained quite simply, a simulated consciousness *plays* at being aware of the world but it is basically not very bothered by it. The result is an awareness that does not impinge on our set values, perspectives or prior prejudice. It is not that a simulated consciousness does not know what is going on, quite the contrary, but it knows everything so poorly, so fast, so timelessly, that any depth sense of what is happening lies beyond the common understanding and is of interest to fewer and fewer people. Hence, because the language-game[2] involving news is becoming speedier and shallower, news items pass us by without effect. Bombings, child kidnappings, road crashes trail off into insignificance. They create an impact, perhaps even globally significant for a brief moment, but they disappear without any trace since they do not affect our consciousness.

None of these trends cause children to question the tactility of what they learn and they overlook the cultural function of knowledge in traditional societies, part of whose primary function is to reproduce the culture itself. In the new set up, consciousness without the mediation of local culture turns into a simulacrum, something that seems on the surface to retain the transformational qualities of mediated knowledge but in reality simply establishes a simulation of consciousness. This situation is made worse by the promotion of uncritical progressive teaching methods that can readily combine the dominant centralist trends of national assessment tools, commonly known as the 'points race', with a proclamation to make children the centre of their own learning. This contradiction heralds children as agents in their own educational project and while this child-centeredness is preferable to the unscrupulous mediations of adult societies that, in

---

1 Jean Baudrillard, *The Perfect Crime*, translated by C. Turner, London and New York, Verso, 1966: 17.
2 Ludwig Wittgenstein, *On Certainty* #315, see his *On Certainty (Über Gewissheit)*, edited by G.E.M. Anscombe and G.H. von Wright, translated by Denis Paul and G.E.M. Anscombe, Oxford, Blackwell, 1969.

the case of the child-soldiers of the Sudan, turned boys into killers or, condemned children caught in the poverty trap to reproduce the same poverty in their adult lives, there is also a case to be made that child centeredness is inferior to the more harmonious mediations of adult culture. These issues matter little in a tactile culture, however, as Baudrillard has remarked.[3]

Two results follow from this issue. First information that is so easily accessed gives children a different primal experience of its density. It is easily gathered; it falls easily off the lips; even diagrams of amazing complexity are immediately explained or presented as explicable. A combination of factors influences children to glance over information and not to treat knowledge as something that needs to be digested. Tactility has reversed the old adage taken up in the Book of Wisdom and in Augustine's *Confessions*, namely, that everything needs to be filtered by number, measure and weight and the result is that the traditional role of mediators within a culture, namely, teachers and the elderly, have been set aside. In the west, this means that the normal pyramid has been reversed, and children are now teachers of the old.

Second, one has a right to be worried about an environment where consciousness itself is not culturally mediated and even more so where the simulation of consciousness is so closely centred on children themselves that it is never deconstructed or critiqued. Pressed for time, a simulated consciousness will be more impressed by the instant – instant pop stars, instant heroes, instant solutions, and by the tactile, by contacts and strategies that make or break contact, by multi-tasking, hopping about and the general joy of switching off. Break off contact if the going gets tough, it whispers. Relate without giving an account of yourself, it advises. Lose yourself in a kind of giddiness, it suggests.[4] Jump from one thing to the next without expecting to make connections, for tactility alone makes or breaks the contact with reality and a click of the mouse moves you on to the next thing.[5]

It is clear that if we agree with Baudrillard's account about the tactility of postmodern culture and if global exchange now uses a system of single-hit contacts as its preferred means of communication, then it follows that a child's 'contact' with the developing world will remain somewhat superficial, especially after the computer has been switched off. If the gentlest hit on an internet site is preferable to the more fraught experience of learning from other humans, then there is less likelihood of developing that reflection on murkiness and incompletion that is the essential mark of human experience in the inhabited world. There is also a widening gap between this attitude and the majority attitude of more traditional societies. More traditionally minded people who value custom, built up around the slow and deliberate assembly of stories and

---

3 'We are closer in effect to the tactile than we are to the visual universe, where there is greater distance, and reflection is always possible', see Jean Baudrillard, *Symbolic Exchange and Death,* London and New Delhi, SAGE, 1993: 65.

4 'We're condemned to effects of giddiness – in all the games as well. There's no more pleasure, no more interest, but a kind of dizziness induced by the connections, the switching operations in which the subject gets lost. You manipulate all you want, without any objective, with the effect of aleatory giddiness of the potential systems where anything can happen', see Jean Baudrillard, *Forget Foucault, Forget Baudrillard*, New York, Semiotext(e), 1987: 77-78.

5 Baudrillard also speaks of the end of panoptic space and the abolition of the spectacular: '[w]e are witnessing the end of perspective and panoptic space (which remains a moral hypothesis bound up with every classical analysis of the objective essence of power), and hence the *very abolition of the spectacular*', see Jean Baudrillard, *Simulations*, translated by Paul Foss, Paul Patton and Philip Beitchman, New York, Semiotext(e), 1983 [1981]: 54.

memories, mediated by local authorities, will not be able to communicate with this tactility mindset and a gulf begins to form between the west and traditional cultures. Stories by the camp fire in the jungle or over a cup of tea with the smell of turf in the nostrils, illustrate a contrast with this tactile mindset. Arguably the tactile mindset wants to leave an impression and to be impressed in turn. It hops about like Francis Bacon's much lauded bee (*Novum Organum*, XCV) but its value to civilization becomes as accidental as the bee's action is to the plants it unwittingly pollinates. In such a context, there are no values or any meaning either.[6]

If educated in this way, human beings only make an accidental appearance in the inhabited world and this feature rather undersells their intellectual capacity and leaves them unhappy. To form intelligent society with such a tactile mindset means that protracted conversations are impossible. The ability to form friendships becomes compromised as does the ability to share cultural or religious beliefs. Clearly, the fall of the Twin Towers is an advanced warning of this gap between a tactile culture and a culture of memory, despite the image of the collapsing towers embedding itself ironically in the memory of Americans. Islamic culture, however misguided these particular actions in the name of Islam, stands as a public critique of the trivialization of human cultures in the name of individualism and consumerism.

In sum, one has to note that this problem is not a west *versus* east problem or a west *versus* Arab problem. At base, this is a battle between two ways of *being in time* and two startlingly different ways of exercising *human memory*. The argument here is that tactility imprisons the human being in successive moments of time, each disconnected from the previous – a state of affairs that, if it applied to the brain would cause neurologists to think of disease. It also throws people back on their imaginations as a way of escaping from the world. Hence, tactility produces a totalized mindset that is not based on ideology, as one might expect, but rather on time itself and the absence of all ideology.

II From Tactility to Totalities

Let us look briefly at the classical notion of totalitarianism developed so carefully and with such personal energy by Hannah Arendt.[7] Asking herself the question about spaces of political action in the context of recent memories of the Holocaust and with the memory of Hitler so vividly etched on her Jewish memory, Arendt's classical work on totalitarianism could be used as a resource text in support of the claim advanced here, namely, that totalitarianism is but one modulation of a totalized mindset and that a totalized mindset bases itself on a particular understanding of the temporal significance of human action.

While many people historically recognize the malevolent intentions of the Nazi regime and hoped constantly that life would not get much tougher, ordinary Germans had to live without intellectual assent to much of what they saw written in public places. They learned to turn their beliefs inwards away from public gaze and to centre them instead on their own imaginative lives. Most people could see the idiocy behind antisemitic propaganda; yet, they felt compromised to accept what appeared at first to be

---

6 Baudrillard, *Simulations*, 37. Also, 'Our culture of meaning is collapsing beneath the excess of meaning, the culture of reality collapsing beneath the excess of reality, the information culture beneath the excess of information – the sign and the reality sharing a single shroud', see Baudrillard, *The Perfect Crime*: 17.
7 Hannah Arendt, *The Origins of Totalitarianism*, New York, Harvest Harcourt Brace Jovanovich, 1979.

rather shallow curtailments of civil liberties as a gesture of support for the fatherland. As long as their imaginations could offer them access to a purer cleaner world, they could tell themselves that these were extraordinary times and that extraordinary times needed extraordinary measures. Halbestram mentions how the Nazi regime continued to enhance this fictitious turn in the images it engendered – *das deutsche Volk* – using films of idyllic maidens in the countryside which then came to replace the real world in the imaginations of most people.[8] As a consequence, this option to take refuge in a private space of thought made the public more vulnerable to lies, irrespective of prevailing ideology.

Another modulation of the totalizing mindset could be seen in the 'national socialism' of the German Democratic Republic (GDR) of East Germany. A new modulation of the totalized mindset had occurred with a supporting ideology that abhorred the ideology of Nazis and promoted a public stance of peace and goodwill to all. The thought form had mutated slightly but, to an outsider visiting the GDR in the 1980s, the society seemed still organized along Nazi-like lines. As in the Nazi era, private opinions stood apart in their own space, far removed from the ice-cream shops frequented by smiling workers and fully uniformed Russian soldiers, once the factory hooters sounded at 15.00 hours. Here too, elaborate billboards, located in the main square in front of the Hotel Elephant, proclaimed freedom and the brotherhood of man, as the daily squadron of military helicopters flew overhead. Here too an élite rewarded those who were willing to commit to the Party and to spy on others, not because they believed in anything themselves, but rather because they were not prepared to set any limits to the types of action their loyalty could demand. Here too influence, measured in hard currency, was only available to those who stood above the law. The political result was once again the same. The common people took refuge in their imaginations and dreamed of a better life elsewhere, although no one seemed able to see it coming in their lifetime. Instead, at home they enjoyed West German television and resisted bitterly whenever the authorities tried to block out these signals. Finally, the authorities understood that access to West German television would only enhance their centralized power. Better sustain public cynicism about the billboards than actual political resistance. Consequently, citizens of the GDR mismatched a dull grey exterior with a rich colourful interior both in their dwellings and in their imaginary lives, their mandated retreat from the public sphere, except perhaps for the underground churches, simply serving the regime better than it served themselves.

A further modulation of the totalized mindset and yet another example of simulated consciousness can be seen in American thinking about Iraq where the dominant ideology, different from the Nazis and from National Socialism, is support for peace and democracy. The education of Private Lynndie England of Fort Ashby Kentucky, reservist with the 372nd MP Company might be an example of Hannah Arendt's idea of a totalized individual, having apparently surrendered the very capacity for *personal* experience in order to 'provide the forces of nature with an incomparable instrument to accelerate their movement.'[9] In this case, US military operations in Iraq had enhanced the relentless movement of nature invoked by classical totalitarianism and applied now

---

8 Michael Halbestram, 'Hannah Arendt on the Totalitarian Sublime and its Promise of Freedom', in Steven E. Aschheim, *Hannah Arendt in Jerusalem*, Berkeley, University of California, 2001: 108.
9 See Halbestram, 'Hannah Arendt': 106, and references, too, to Arendt, *The Origins of Totalitarianism*: 303, 459, 466, 474, 476, 478.

to the democracy movement. The effect of a concealed totalized mindset on this soldier was to place her under the influence of a domineering commander, caught up in a line of obedience where no one needed to take the ultimate responsibility for actions undertaken. Her behaviour in tugging the naked prisoner by the leash seemed at odds with advice she might have been offered by one West Point instructor who declared that the 'office of personhood is a natural, inalienable one that all humans hold; it is always more fundamental than other offices that individuals might occupy concurrently, such as that of soldier, (or judge, or police officer).'[10] That advice, however, could only ever be listened to by a critical mind. Private England in these photos showed no evidence of being critically aware. Her consciousness was more simulated than real, caught up as it was in an obediential military culture and trained not to question or think in West Point terms. Nor was thinking a particular feature of many in her home town of Fort Ashby who, despite abhorring the sexual explicitness of the images, continued to support this soldier in the execution of her duties, for was it not the case, as one account mentioned, that the prison torture in Abu Ghraib faded in significance compared to the savagery of being beheaded and, besides, were not the Iraqis behind the atrocity of the World Trade Centre?[11]

A fourth modulation of this general totalizing mindset can be seen in current attempts to vaporize universities. The universities had once traditionally been independent from the obeisance owed to Kings, Princes and Popes, all pomp and ceremony notwithstanding, but they are less successful now in refusing to curtsy before capitalist economics. As there is a current attempt to redefine all third level learning and research in terms of a general matrix which, like a giant plasma television, offers itself to the ionizing action of research grants, while the lighted elements are then identified, clustered and ranked using the model of Mendeleyev's periodic table. This ranking contains explicit and implicit judgements about the entropic state of elements in the system and a judgement of Darwinian proportions is never far away. Not only are students ranked but so are teachers; not only are teachers ranked but so are programmes; not only are programmes ranked but so are the universities; not only are universities ranked but so are countries. In this context, true educators have to exercise their trade in secret, for neither the replication of culture nor its critique is possible in a well orchestrated totalizing context. Local cultures are also to be rendered silent, hidden behind what a totalizing culture always considers normal progress.

III Stepping back from the Brink

Stepping back from these particular examples of totalized mindsets, mindsets that slip easily into totalitarian practices, irrespective of cultural context or dominant ideology, the difficulty now facing educators is how to cope with an expected disconnection of the global from the inhabited world. Children, with a totalized mindset made worse by a wash of images that mimic consciousness in them so that they think with borrowed thoughts, can delude themselves into believing that everyone is the same. They can readily accept an image of themselves as contact points or nodes within a global matrix or mindset. Similarly, learners, switched on by tactile culture may be vulnerable to the

---

10 See Paul Christopher, *Ethics of War and Peace*, 1990: 153, as quoted in Mark J. Osiel, *Mass Atrocity, Ordinary Evil and Hannah Arendt: Criminal Consciousness in Argentina's Dirty War*, New Haven and London, Yale University, 2001: 144.

11 See Sara Daniel, 'Lynndie England, 21 ans, tortionnaire...' in *Le Nouvel Observateur* 13-19 (Paris, mai 2004): 63.

totalitarian twists of thought already promoted by totalizing cultures. When educators then place the onus on learners to make their own sense of contact-knowledge in this climate of relativism and ignorance, they do nothing to counter this weakness but simply make the young more viable as economic players. The real educational work still has to be done.

In my view, liberalism is a false saviour in these matters. While on the face of it, talk of individuals seems to counter totalization or what Dana Villa, echoing Hannah Arendt, terms the totalitarian tendency 'to replace human plurality and spontaneity with a kind of oneness...while moving us ever closer to rhythms of nature and necessity'[12], there is little liberalism can do to prevent the abolition of differences on a world scale. This is because individualism does not value differences; it simply cancels these differences out by making all differences subject to a law or a rule agreed by all for the welfare of the majority. It limits all differences to this perspective.

On the other hand, one feature of Arendt's account is important, viz., the view that even the lowliest individuals need to distinguish themselves and to communicate themselves in freedom.[13] Individualism might not need to be embraced in order to achieve this result. The opportunity to appear is the key point, for when Baudrillard talks about contemporary culture being nihilistic, he seems to imply that this type of distinctiveness cannot be achieved and that a radical indifference of human action to systems designed to be transparent and inevitable,[14] the failure to allow individuals to appear, damages educational polities, including universities, religious communities, cultural and ethnic groups. Not only has meaning been replaced in such cultures by a kind of totalizing technospeak but there is a preoccupation, almost a fascination with the disappearance of mankind under these conditions, or as Baudrillard explains, 'a nihilistic passion par excellence...a passion proper to the mode of disappearance',[15] a melancholia that has turned into 'our fundamental passion'.[16] The result is a failure to do what education in traditional societies has always done, namely, to hand on to a new generation the values and visions of the past. Those 'educated' into being individuals with a totalized mindset and who have been induced into believing that the old ways are irrelevant to current life seem strangely incapable of recognizing the importance of pluralism itself. For this reason, totalized children no longer see the need for dialogue or respect for differences because they believe that ultimately everyone is the same: differences simply get in the way of progress and peace.

A telling example of this *indifference* can be seen in a contrast between the use of information technology in western schools. The Four Directions Project is an indigenous education model for American Indians who live geographically isolated lives in Reservations extending across sixty-three locations in the U.S. Left behind by the information age up to now, the culture of these Indians has been dying, but connected to each other by the web, they have established a new sense of themselves, and now collaborate on a new curriculum for Indians. From a situation where school paradigms were imposed from the outside, resulting in demoralization and a high level of drop-out among the

---

[12] Dana Villa, 'Totalitarianism, Modernity and the Tradition' in Aschheim, *Hannah Arendt*: 132.
[13] Hannah Arendt, *The Human Condition*, Chicago, University of Chicago, 1958: 176.
[14] Jean Baudrillard, *Simulacra and Simulations*, translated by Sheila Faria Glaser, Ann Arbor, University of Michigan, 1994: 160.
[15] Baudrillard, *Simulacra and Simulations*: 160.
[16] Baudrillard, *Simulacra and Simulations*: 162.

46,600 or so students registered as school-goers, isolated groups can now communicate with other groups, design their own curricula to take account of their own stories and resist negative assimilations into the majority culture.[17] Similarly, immigrants at a Further Education college in Belgium were encouraged to use I.T. projects to write their own stories and adjust to the complexities of living in a western country with a large multi-cultural population.[18] When a Dublin primary school came to use this technology in 2004, it centred its interest on the technology itself and remained blind to its cultural implications or the socio-cultural context. Pupils ended up thinking that the technology was 'cool'. They could manipulate the levers but no one involved in the project thought of using the technology as an aid for understanding the high number of newcomer children in the inner city of Dublin. Is this an example of the totalized mindset that continues to find local issues irrelevant to the main thrust of education?

Now while this query may not be exactly fair in this case or indeed typical of primary schools in Ireland at the moment, where many newcomer children have now taken up places, the decoupling of technology (and the possibility it offers for greater tactility) from culture is worrying. It is an example of local multi-cultures dropping from sight in favour of a totalized mindset. An ecumenical education would value the opportunity to do something different, to assert the value of local socio-cultural experience over totalized experience, to insist on the validity of community readings, to encourage the rubric of gaze rather than touch in human relations and to sustain a way of being in time that depends crucially on the exercise of memory. One can see how deeply we miss some sprinkling of an ecumenical attitude that is happy to explore the human dimension in all its limits in opposition to the totalizing mindset whose frittering effects can be seen everywhere in the contemporary world.

---

17 See http://4directions.org/community/abstract.html.
18 See http://www.thedigitalhub.com/community_learning/index.php, for details of Netdays projects facilitated in Irish Primary Schools in 2004.

David R. Loy

The Attention-Deficit Society
Awareness Fragmented, Commodified, and Controlled

> *No wisdom can we get hold of, no highest perfection,*
> *No Bodhisattva, no thought of enlightenment either.*
> *When told of this, if not bewildered and in no way anxious,*
> *A Bodhisattva courses in the Tathagata's wisdom.*
> *In form, in feeling, will, perception and awareness*
> *Nowhere in them they find a place to rest on.*[1]
>
> *Should your mind wander away, do not follow it, whereupon your wandering mind will stop wandering of its own accord. Should your mind desire to linger somewhere, do not follow it and do not dwell there, whereupon your mind's questing for a dwelling place will cease of its own accord. Thereby, you will come to possess a non-dwelling mind – a mind that remains in the state of non-dwelling. If you are fully aware in yourself of a non-dwelling mind, you will discover that there is just the fact of dwelling, with nothing to dwell upon or not to dwell upon. This full awareness in yourself of a mind dwelling upon nothing is known as having a clear perception of your own mind, or, in other words, as having a clear perception of your own nature. A mind, which dwells upon nothing, is the Buddha-mind, the mind of one already delivered, Bodhi-Mind ...*[2]

Do we miss the nature of liberated mind, not because it is too obscure or difficult to understand, but because it is too obvious? Perhaps, like Poe's purloined letter, we overlook it: rummaging around hither and thither, we cannot find what we are searching for because it is in plain sight. Or, to employ a better metaphor, we look for the spectacles that rest unnoticed on our nose. Mind seeks for mind.

'Let your mind come forth without fixing it anywhere', says the most-quoted line from the *Diamond Sutra*, prompting the great awakening of the sixth Chan patriarch Hui-neng, whose *Platform Sutra* makes and remakes the same point: '[w]hen our mind works freely without any hindrance, and is at liberty to "come" or to "go", we attain liberation.' Such a mind 'is everywhere present, yet it "sticks" nowhere.' Hui Neng emphasized that he had no system of Dharma to transmit: '[w]hat I do to my disciples is to liberate them from their own bondage with such devices as the case may need.'[3]

---

1 *Astasahasrika Sutra* 1: 5-7, 10, in *The Perfection of Wisdom in Eight Thousand Lines and Its Verse Summary*, translated and edited by Edward Conze, Bolinas CA, Four Seasons Foundation, 1973: 9.
2 *The Zen Teaching of Hui Hai*, translated by John Blofeld, London, Rider, 1969: 56.
3 *The Platform Sutra of the Sixth Patriarch*, translated and edited by Philip B. Yampolsky, New York, Columbia University, 1967: 133. The Dunhuang version that Yampolsky translates does not mention this particular line from the *Diamond Sutra*, only that Hui Neng awakened when he heard the sutra expounded to him.

These teachers are pointing to the same realization:

> Delusion (ignorance, samsara): attention/awareness is trapped (attached to forms);
>
> Liberation (enlightenment, nirvana): attention/awareness is liberated from grasping.

Although the true nature of awareness is formless, it becomes trapped when our attention is conditioned – that is, when we learn to identify with particular forms. Such identifications happen due to ignorance of the essential 'non-dwelling' nature of our attention. The familiar words 'attention' and 'awareness' are used to emphasize that the distinction being drawn refers not to some abstract metaphysical entity ('Mind') but simply to how our everyday awareness functions. To appropriate Hakuin's pregnant metaphor in *Zazen Wasan*, the difference between Buddhas and other beings is that between water and ice: without water there is no ice, without Buddha no sentient beings – which suggests that deluded beings might simply be 'frozen' Buddhas.

Most Zen students are familiar with such teachings, so this point does not need to be belaboured. Yet, an important implication is not usually considered: the danger of what might be called *collective attention-traps*. Meditation practices make me more sensitive to my attachments: the places where my awareness is fixated. But my problems with attachment are not just my own. We tend to have the same problems because as members of the same society we are subjected to similar conditioning and tend to get stuck in similar ways. How different is our present conditioning from social conditioning in the time of the Buddha, and in other Asian Buddhist societies? How has the development of the modern/postmodern world affected human attention generally? Not only what we attend to, but how we attend to it. The constriction or liberation of awareness is not only a personal, individual matter. What do contemporary societies do to encourage or discourage its emancipation?

This issue is an important one for Buddhists because today our awareness is conditioned in at least three new ways that did not afflict previous Buddhist cultures and practitioners.

The Fragmentation of Attention

Media coverage suggests that one of our major concerns about attention is the lack thereof. Attention-deficit hyperactivity disorder has become a serious medical issue in the U.S., originally among schoolchildren but now among young adults as well. According to the *New York Times*, the use of drugs to treat attention-deficit disorder in young adults in the U.S. doubled between 2000 and 2004; one percent of adults aged 20 to 64 now take them. In the same period, the share of children using such drugs increased from 2.8 to 4.4 percent, despite increasing concern about their side-effects.[4] What are we to make of this?

Buddhist practice evokes images of meditation with minimal distractions. The IT revolution – personal computers, the internet, email, cell phones, walkmans and iPods, etc. – encourages an unremitting connectivity that pulls us in the opposite direction, as Catie Getches conveys in a recent *Washington Post* article:

---

4   Gardiner Harris, 'Use of Attention-Deficit Drugs is Found to Soar Among Adults', *New York Times* 15 September 2005, see http://www.nytimes.com/2005/09/15/health/15/disorder.html, accessed 16 September 2005. No doubt the lobbying of pharmacological companies has also been a factor in this increase.

> All it takes is a little time alone, especially late at night, to confirm how much technology has transformed culture and how it has changed the way we relate to each other. That's because being alone is not what it used to be. These days, even momentary solitude seems like something to be avoided at all cost. And technology makes it possible; thanks to cell phones, no one has to face that stroll down the street, the five-minute commute or the lunch line without companionship.
>
> However, the more technology we turn on, the more relationships we have to manage simultaneously – and the more likely we are to ask our best friends if they can hold. I have programmable phone lists and speed dial at my fingertips, and yet I feel more disconnected than ever – somehow, it is easier than ever to be two places at once but nearly impossible to, as my mom says, just 'be here now.' Yet, being in two places at once has become strangely familiar. You don't just go out to lunch with a friend anymore; you go out to lunch with the friend and the friend's cell phone book.
>
> It is so common now to correspond by e-mail alone, it is easy to go for days without actually interacting with a real live human.[5]

As we become attentive to so many more people and so many more possibilities always available, is less attention available for the people and things most important to us?

Consider, for example, how MP3 players are changing the ways we listen to music. A century ago, you are part of a live audience, and once you are there you are *there*, so you settle down and focus on the music being performed. For me today, strolling along with my iPod, the decision to listen to any particular 'selection' is never completely settled in the sense that I can instantaneously change what is playing if I become dissatisfied with it, for any reason at any time, simply by pressing a button. I must, in effect, continually decide to listen to this particular song. Does awareness of these other possibilities distract my attention from the music I am actually hearing?

Of course, this point applies just as much to many other aspects of our lives, e.g., TV channel-surfing, the surfeit of books and DVDs (Amazon's one-click orders!), video games, surfing the net, etc. Our old foraging habits were based on info-scarcity, but suddenly, like Mickey Mouse the sorcerer's apprentice, we find ourselves trying to survive an *info-glut,* and the scarcest resources have become *attention* and *control over our own time.* Thomas Eriksen formalizes this relationship into a general law of the information revolution:

> When an ever-increasing amount of information has to be squeezed into the relatively constant amount of time each of us has at our disposal, the span of attention necessarily decreases.[6]

Eriksen's insight can be expanded to include the near-infinite range of consumption possibilities that also attract our attention and proliferate our cravings. This gives us the following reformulation:

> (same amount of time) ÷ (more possibilities [info-glut + digital shopping mall])
> = shorter attention span

---

5 'Wired Nights: In the 24-Hour Universe, There's No Winding Down', *The Washington Post* Sunday, 17 October 2004: B1.
6 Thomas Eriksen, *Tyranny of the Moment: Fast and Slow Time in the Information Age*, London, Pluto, 2001: 19-22, 69.

This way of 'liberating' attention tends to scatter it. Even if we ignore for the moment the consumer alternatives, such an avalanche of information (and therefore shorter attention spans) challenges our ability to construct narratives and logical sequences, putting pressure on traditional ways of thinking that involve cause/effect and organic development. In its very form, 'the World Wide Web inculcates a strong and almost reflex-like preference for heightened visual stimuli, rapid changes of subject matter, and diversity, combined with simplicity of presentation.'[7] Sherry Turkle has noticed that some of her MIT students now reason and arrange their ideas differently. 'There is this sense that the world is out there to be Googled', she says, 'and there is this associative glut. But linking from one thing to another is not the same as having something to say. A structured thought is more than a link.'[8] A cascading glut of de-contextualized signs, with an inelastic amount of attention to make them meaningful, results in association-glut. No wonder, then, that so many people turn to chemicals for a little help in concentrating.

In place of the usual Buddhist warnings about clinging and attachment, many of us now have the opposite problem: an inability to concentrate. An attention that jumps from this to that, unable to focus itself, is no improvement over a clinging attention. Yet, they are not really opposites: to jump from one perch to another is not an escape from clinging, but a different type of clinging.[9]

The Commodification of Attention

For most of us in the developed world, the greatest 'attention trap' is consumerism, involving sophisticated advertising that has become very good at manipulating our attention. Today, the big economic problem is not production but keeping us convinced that the solution to our *dukkha* is our next purchase. As the pioneering advertising executive Leo Burnett (1891-1971) put it, '[g]ood advertising does not just circulate information. It penetrates the public mind with desire and belief.'[10] That penetration may have been lucrative for his clients; however, Ivan Illich is perceptive about its spiritual consequences: 'in a consumer society there are inevitably two kinds of slaves, the prisoners of addiction and the prisoners of envy.'[11] Whether one is able to afford the desired product or not, one's attention is captured.

---

7 Lorne Dawson, 'Doing Religion in Cyberspace: The Promise and the Perils', in *Council of Societies for the Study of Religion Bulletin* 30,1 (February 2001): 3-9: 7.
8 Quoted in Oliver Burkeman and Bobbie Johnson, 'Search and You Shall Find', in *The Guardian*, 2 February 2005.
9 Another Buddhist perspective on modern technology is offered by Peter D. Hershock in *Reinventing the Wheel: A Buddhist Response to the Information Age*, Albany, SUNY, 1999.
10 This remark has been widely quoted, see, for example, http://thinkexist.com/quotes/leo_burnett/, accessed 12 January 2007.
11 Ivan Illich, *Tools for Conviviality*, New York, Harper & Row, 1973, online at http://todd.cleverchimp.com/tools_for_conviviality/, accessed 3 May 2006. In one of his last papers, 'Guarding the Eye in the Age of Show' (2000), Illich traces 'the route on which the image mutated to the point of becoming a trap for the gaze... An ethics of vision would suggest that the user of TV, VCR, McIntosh [sic] and graphs protect his imagination from overwhelming distraction, possibly leading to addiction.' He contrasts the earlier tradition of ocular *askesis*: '[d]uring the Middle Ages and well into modern times, it dealt primarily with protecting the heart from distracting or destructive images. The question that is profoundly new today is a different one: How can I eschew not pictures, but the flood of shows?', http://homepage.mac.com/tinapple/illich/, accessed 26 August 2005.

Recently, it has become more evident that attention is the basic commodity to be exploited. 'The new economy is not an information or a knowledge economy... It is an attention economy', according to a writer in South Africa's *Financial Mail,* coining a meme that has proliferated in business circles.[12] Ben Franklin's old adage needs to be updated: not *time is money* but *attention is money*. Jonathan Rowe expands thus:

> The basic resource of this new economy is not something they provide us. It's something we provide them – 'mindshare,' in the charming idiom of the trade. Now ask yourself this: What if there's only so much mind to share? If you've wondered how people could feel so depleted in such a prosperous economy, how stress could become the trademark affliction of the age, part of the answer might be here.[13]

Rowe is concerned about the commodification of what he terms *cognitive space*, the corporate response to the fact that people might sometimes be concerned about something else besides buying and consuming. This has led to 'the ultimate enclosure – the enclosure of the cognitive commons, the ambient mental atmosphere of daily life', a rapid development now so pervasive that it has become like the air we breathe unnoticed, or the contact lens that focuses our perceptions. Time and space, he argues, have already been reconstructed: holidays (including new commercialized ones such as Mother's Day) into shopping days, the 'civic commons of Main Street' into shopping malls. Now advertising is infiltrating into every corner of our conscious (and unconscious) awareness. Sports stadiums used to have ads; now renamed stadiums are themselves ads. TV shows used to be sponsored by ads; today insidious product placement makes the whole show an ad. The jewellery company Bulgari sponsored a novel by Fay Weldon that included over three dozen references to its products. A 2005 issue of the *New Yorker* did not include any ads because the whole magazine was a promotion for the retail chain Target. Children are especially vulnerable, of course, and while half of four-year-old children do not know their own name, two-thirds of three-year-olds recognize the golden arches of McDonald's.[14]

In the past one could often ignore the ads, but enclosure of the cognitive commons now means that they confront us wherever our attention turns. Unless meditating in a Himalayan cave, we end up having to process thousands of commercial messages every day. And they do not just grab our attention, they exploit it:

> The attention economy mines us much the way the industrial economy mines the earth. It mines us first for incapacities and wants. Our capacity for interaction and reflection must become a need for entertainment. Our capacity to deal with life's bumps and jolts becomes a need for 'grief counselling' or

---

12 The *Financial Mail* quotation is from Jonathan Rowe, 'Carpe Callosum' [Latin, 'seize the brain'], *Adbusters* November/December 2001 [no page number]. For Michael Goldhaber, 'obtaining attention is obtaining a kind of enduring wealth, a form of wealth that puts you in a preferred position to get anything this new economy offers', in 'The Attention Economy and the Net', http://www.firstmonday.org/issues/issue2_4/goldhaber/, accessed 25 September 2005. See also Thomas H. Davenport and John C. Beck, *The Attention Economy: Understanding the New Currency of Business*, Cambridge, Harvard Business School, 2001, and the online discussion of it at http://www.alamut.com/subj/economics/attention/attent_economy.html, accessed 25 September 2005.
13 Rowe, 'Carpe Callosum'. The rest of this section summarizes Rowe's argument.
14 The child references are from Jonathan Freedland, 'The Onslaught', in *The Guardian* http://media.guardian.co.uk/site/story/0,14173,1600020,00.html, accessed 25 October 2005. The other examples cited in this paragraph, except for the special *New Yorker* issue, are mentioned by Rowe.

Prozac. The progress of the consumer economy has come to mean the diminution of ourselves.[15]

Consumerism requires and develops a sense of our own impoverishment. By manipulating the gnawing sense of lack that haunts our insecure sense of self, the attention economy insinuates its basic message deep into our awareness: the solution to any discomfort we might have is consumption. Needless to say, this all-pervasive conditioning is incompatible with the liberative path of Buddhism.

The Control of Attention

Dictatorships control people with violence and the threat of it, to restrain what they do. Modern democracies control people with sophisticated propaganda, by manipulating what they think. The title of one of Noam Chomsky's books sums it up well: *Manufacturing Consent*.[16] We worry about weapons of mass destruction, but we should be as concerned about weapons of mass deception, which may be more insidious and more difficult to detect. To cite only the most obvious example, the disastrous 2003 invasion of Iraq would never have been possible without carefully orchestrated attempts to make the public anxious about something that did not exist. It was easy to do because September 11th made many Americans fearful, and fearful people are more susceptible to manipulation.

Rulers and ruling classes traditionally used religious ideologies to justify their power. In pre-modern Europe the Church supported the 'divine right' of kings. In Buddhist societies karma offered a convenient way to rationalize both the ruler's authority and the powerlessness of his oppressed subjects: you should accept your present social status because it is a consequence of past actions. In modern secular societies, however, acquiescence must be moulded in different ways.

According to Alex Carey, the 20th century was characterized by three important political developments: the growth of democracy, the growth of corporate power, and the growth of propaganda as a way to protect corporate power against democracy.[17] Although corporations are not mentioned in the U.S. Constitution – the founding fathers were wary of them – corporate power in the United States began to expand dramatically towards the end of the 19th century, so successfully that today there is no longer any effective distinction between major corporations and the federal government. Both identify wholeheartedly with the same goal of continuous economic growth, regardless of its social or ecological effects. (We are repeatedly told that any unfortunate consequences from this growth obsession can be solved by more economic growth.) This often requires foreign intervention, for our access to resources and markets must be protected and expanded, usually under the guise of 'defending ourselves'.

Continual economic growth requires that we define ourselves primarily as workers and consumers, while accepting that our present government and economy are natural and 'the best in the world'. Instead of raising questions about this orientation, the

---

15 Rowe, 'Carpe Callosum'. This does not amount to an argument for Marxism. For Buddhism, capitalism and Marxism share the same delusion insofar as they imply that there is an economic (or technological) solution to human *dukkha*.
16 Edward Herman and Noam Chomsky, *Manufacturing Consent: The Political Economy of the Mass Media*, New York, Pantheon, 2002.
17 Alex Carey, *Taking the Risk Out of Democracy: Corporate Propaganda Versus Freedom and Liberty*, Urbana, University of Illinois, 1997: 18.

mainstream media – our collective nervous system – have become powerful profit-making corporations that buy into the same belief system and serve to rationalize it. (We will never see a light-hearted TV series about a family successfully 'downsizing', simplifying their lives in order to have more quality time.) Only a very narrow spectrum of opinion is considered acceptable, 'realistic'; and whatever problems arise require only a few minor adjustments here and there. As the earth begins to burn, as ecosystems start to collapse, the media focus our collective attention on the things that really matter: the Superbowl, the price of gas, the latest murder or sex scandal…

The liberation of collective attention?

Who owns our attention, and who should have the right to decide what happens to it? Rowe concludes that we need a new freedom movement, to 'battle for the cognitive commons. If we have no choice regarding what fills our attention, then we really have no choice at all.' From a Buddhist perspective, however, it seems doubtful that any social protest movement could be successful without an alternative understanding of what our attention is and what alternative practices promote more liberated attention. It is not enough to fight against billboards and internet banner ads; one must also consider what it really means for awareness to be here-and-now, deconditioned from attention traps, both individual and collective. Is awareness to be valued as a means to some other end, or should we cherish its liberation as the most valuable end? The Buddhist answer to such questions is clear. What is less clear is what role that answer might play in our collective response to the challenge.

Bill McSweeney

In Praise of Fuzzy Boundaries

In June 1963, five months before he was killed in Dallas, John F. Kennedy gave the Commencement Address at American University. Famous not just for the rhetoric deployed, nor only for the worthy sentiment it expressed so close to his death, the Address bears scrutiny by all who share a commitment to the pursuit of peace in its broadest, humanistic dimensions.

'What kind of peace do I mean?', the president asked. 'Not a Pax Americana enforced on the world by American weapons of war. Not the peace of the grave or the security of the slave. I am talking about genuine peace, the kind of peace that makes life on earth worth living, the kind that enables men and nations to grow and to hope and to build a better life for their children – not merely peace for Americans but peace for all men and women – not merely peace in our time but peace for all time.'

For President Kennedy, peace was not an end amenable to technical fix nor was it, from an intellectual viewpoint, a topic of analysis which could be reduced to the narrow, observable, absence of war. Furthermore, his idea of world peace stood in sharp contrast to the residual category of classical realism still in vogue in the 1960s, which saw peace as the gap between wars, the pause when the world drew breath before continuing on its natural, violent course.

For Kennedy, war is not humanity's default characteristic; nor is peace an ideal that is beyond human striving. 'Too many of us think [peace] is impossible', he said. 'Too many think it unreal. But that is a dangerous, defeatist belief. It leads to the conclusion that war is inevitable – that mankind is doomed – that we are gripped by forces we cannot control. We need not accept that view. Our problems are manmade – therefore, they can be solved by man.'

I cite the speech by Kennedy because attention was drawn to it by the eminent economist, Jeffrey Sachs, in his opening Reith Lecture this year. Facing an audience of sceptical diplomats and academics, most of them critical of his optimistic view of our capacity to change, Sachs stood his ground. 'We live in a world of choice', he insisted, pointing for support to Kennedy's speech in 1963. 'It's not right to say the world doesn't change, and even if human nature doesn't change our institutions can change. So I believe that we can create the kind of world that we want...'

What has this to do with John D'Arcy May and the work he accomplished at the Irish School of Ecumenics? At base it has to do with the attitude of interdisciplinarity which had been a core component of the School from its earliest days, but which John held and encouraged as an article of faith. Peace was not just an ideal for the churches, but for the whole *oikoumene*, as he liked to say, referring to the international order. John is one of those rare academics who can tolerate fuzzy boundaries. Perhaps it is his Buddhist interests that lead him to make connections, to link unlikely ideas and disparate approaches to academic inquiry. It was this instinct for the eclectic – for the 'ecumenical' one might say – that he brought to the School just at the time when the new programme of Peace Studies was on the agenda for final decision.

How could a programme of secular studies be integrated into an institute founded and flourishing on essentially theological criteria? That was the intellectual problem. Just as worrisome for some friends and supporters of the School was the question of integrating not just the new range of concepts but the new kind of students. It was here that John May's instinct for bringing people and things together without having to wait for a cast-iron guarantee of success played its part. Yet, it was more than instinct, more than tossing the bits in the air optimistically and hoping they would land together.

There was, first, the fact that John brought to the School an intellectual background in both theology and the social sciences. He is as much at home teaching some of the core disciplines of Peace Studies – sociology in particular – as he is in teaching world religions. More important, perhaps, was his understanding that a stronger bond linked the ecumenical programme to Peace Studies than the factors which seemed to separate them. This was the common ethic underlying both programmes – the commitment to justice and peace throughout the world. And he held and advocated – with Kennedy and Sachs – the philosophical principle underlying that moral ideal: we live in a world of choice, not of necessity.

It seems appropriate, and of interest, as we approach the twentieth anniversary of the M.Phil. programme in Peace Studies, to reflect further on the ethical ideal which links the academic programmes of the School and to relate that ideal to the philosophical claim that our world is made by humans and can be changed by them.

Peace Studies and the wider community in international relations

It was fortuitous, but is not without relevance, that the start of the School's graduate programme in Peace Studies coincided with the end of the Cold War. Mikhail Gorbachev and Ronald Reagan probably hadn't heard of the word 'ecumenics' or the School which carried its banner in Dublin as they began the talks that led to the end of the nuclear confrontation in 1988. Yet, their talks changed the world dramatically and in ways which challenged the institutes of Peace Studies throughout the world, including the nascent programme in Dublin.

Peace Studies began in the 1960s and throughout the early decades its focus and rationale was dictated largely by the relations of the superpowers and the threat of nuclear war. Further, its approach to research was heavily influenced by its more prestigious rival in the field of international relations (IR). Since the 1960s, institutes of Peace Studies have claimed the same territory as IR but felt at some disadvantage to it in the competition for resources; it has never been easy to define their distinctive area of interest and competence in contrast to that of the IR community. During the Cold War, when the major question demanding attention revolved around the nature, number and deployment of weapons constituting mutual deterrence, peace institutes enjoyed an easy demarcation of their role for students and practitioners, by virtue of their self-chosen function as critics of the mainstream. For four decades following the end of World War II, the discipline of IR provided a relatively unitary and simple target for the Peace Research community, permitting the latter to rest comfortably with its definition as the official opposition in the academy. In the problem-area of nuclear deterrence posed by IR scholars, peace researchers found a target adequate to the demands of their constituency of academics peers, students and peace activists.

However, they were always the junior partners, the poorer cousins, seen by some as lacking a theoretical foundation and sniping at the margins of mainstream international concerns. In an academic community where the canons of natural science established the measure of scholarly worth, Peace Research scholars struggled bravely to keep up with the scientific pretension of the mainstream, which pressed home its advantage by labelling its research domain 'political science'. In this community, moreover, even the whiff of idealism or moralizing was deemed in bad taste. The scientific standard for the study of international relations was set by the school of classical realism, and that made it a dubious bedfellow for Peace Researchers. It was obviously a prescriptive exercise concerned with changing the status quo from one of endemic violence to one where war and violence were seen as deviant. In the eyes of traditional IR scholars, that was more than enough to condemn the exercise to the backbenches reserved for the loopy left.

In the early years of Peace Research, its proponents defended the normative aspect of their research orientation by recourse to analogy with medicine. This was intended to illustrate the compatibility of ethical commitment with dispassionate objectivity. Like the ethic of medical scientists in respect of disease and physical suffering, peace researchers saw violence and war as an evil to be controlled or eliminated. If the moral impulse to improve the lives of the sick did not impugn the scientific competence of medical researchers, the same must be true for peace researchers engaged in the life-saving enterprise of discovering and developing a cure for violence and war. Or, so it seemed at the time.

It was a clever analogy in its day. It raised peace researchers to the level of scientists at a time when the fallacies of applying the method of natural science to social action were scarcely on the horizon. Who could deny that ethics entered into the choice of the research topic and did not thereby distort the objectivity of the research process? If medical research was not compromised as a scientific discipline by the moral choices which directed its study, why should Peace Studies have any case to answer?

Thus fortified against the misplaced criticism of the IR community, peace researchers consolidated their position as the loyal opposition, working to the same principles, following the same rules of method, as the dominant school of realism. Support for the new status of peace research was bolstered – indeed to a large extent initiated – by the infectious enthusiasm of Johan Galtung, the Norwegian father of peace research, who led a team of researchers at the University of Essex in the quest for a Science of Peace, developing peace games to combat the think-tanks of the war industry playing war games. The strong moral conviction which Galtung brought to his research in no way inhibited his equally strong conviction that scientific laws governed the social order, and could be discovered and explained in essentially the same way as the positivistic methods of natural science prescribe. In international relations as in Peace Research, to subscribe to positivism made scientists of them all. Galtung was a sociologist as well as a mathematician. Had he cultivated his intellectual roots in sociology, rather than mathematics, the retreat of Peace Studies into positivism might have been arrested at an earlier stage, and its recovery of the normative dimension of politics facilitated. The pretensions to construct a science of the social were dominant in sociology also until the 1970s. The crisis in that discipline, though, at the end of that decade generated a radical reassessment of its foundations.

Already in the late 1960s, sociology had begun to turn away from the amoral, value-free illusions cultivated in its American homeland for decades previously, and to begin the task of constructing an alternative body of theory capable of incorporating human agency and moral choice into the analysis and characterization of the social order. It was only in the mid-1980s that this development spread from sociology to international relations and raised the hope that a theory of the international order, which placed moral choice at the centre rather than the periphery of social action, might be possible both for the discipline of Peace Research and International Relations.

The sudden end of the Cold War in the late 1980s was a major factor in forcing the rethinking which led to this development. Such was the preoccupation of Peace Research with the Cold War and the overriding need to provide a critique to academic supporters of the status quo, that its demise left the formal organization of Peace Research bereft of a clear focus. Like Sovietology from 1991, researchers and students found themselves deprived of their familiar surroundings.

Armed at last with a theory of the international order which made moral choice central to its object of study, Peace Research no longer needed to flog the dead horse of the medical analogy. Medical research implied a moral impulse, certainly, but the normative choice was external to the object of research. Now Peace Research, like IR generally, has a theoretical basis for exploring the whole area of moral choice as a central feature, not a marginal one, of the object of inquiry. It is not just in the desire to make a better world that the normative element can be identified in the study of peace; it is both in the insistence that all arrangements in the social order are the consequence of moral choice, and in the focus on exposing the moral in the areas of inter-community and inter-state relations. Like churches, secular states and communities are moral constructs, 'built by man' as John F. Kennedy put it, edifices of ideas which were not forced on us by the necessity of religious truth or human nature. It is by showing that no ideas are literally infallible and no state structures are mandated by the nature of our material environment that ecumenical theology and Peace Research come together in a common subscription to a social theory of fuzzy boundaries – or, to give it a more respectful title, social constructivism. In a nutshell, the real world may not be *our* choice but it only exists as human choice, and it can be changed.

This is the antithesis of fundamentalism, either in its evangelical Protestant form, which gave rise to the term, or in the Catholic variety, which replaces the literal truth of the bible with the unerring tradition of the magisterium. It embraces the cardinal error, in the view of both fundamentalist traditions, of leaving open the door of every set of ideas and institutions to later revision. In the often-repeated accusations of conservative political and religious leaders, it is the embrace of relativism.

Neither ecumenical studies nor peace research need blush at this charge. Relativism is thinking for grown-ups. In the sphere of ethics, too, and not just of theory and doctrine, we do well to respect the influence of culture and context over time and space on what we judge to be ethically right or wrong. Of course, at a certain level of generality and abstraction, which is still within the boundary of the meaningful, there is a way of delineating an ethic common to both areas of study in the School which comes as close to a universal value as we are likely to find.

If the aspiration built into the ecumenical programme at its foundation was oriented to the resolution of conflict between religious communities, it became immediately clear that such a peace could not be confined to communities of religion and it could not be predicated solely on the virtue of tolerance. For an obvious example, peace today between Muslims and Christians cannot be pursued without consideration of peace between the political communities which house the religions. Also, peace between Hindus and Buddhists in India cannot be reduced to the absence of war or to tolerance, while neglecting the demands of social justice which is invariably the ethical question at the heart of conflict in the first place.

What constitutes an ethic common to the ecumenical and peace studies programmes in the School can, then, be stated thus: it is the commitment to a process of social change which rejects violence and war as the inescapable consequences of human nature and promotes more equitable and cooperative relationships between all the collectivities which comprise the *oikoumene,* or international order.

John May's major contribution to the work of the School lay in providing enthusiastic support for openness to these ideas, in accepting the fuzzy boundaries which they entailed, and in promoting a high level of integration between the ecumenical and peace studies programmes without stifling the creative tension which came with the changes.

Eda Sagarra
Dumb Believers and Clever Jesuits
Anti-Catholic Polemics in Nineteenth-Century Germany

In the summer of 1848, a cartoon appeared in the short-lived Munich satirical paper *Leuchtkugeln*[1] depicting the head and shoulders of a young male wearing an open shirt and sporting a badge on his jacket. In common with most of his kind as depicted in similar ephemera of the time, this young man is evidently registering a protest. However, whereas other young males portrayed during that heady spring and summer of the 1848 Revolution represent in various guises the contemporary stereotype of Germany, *der deutsche Michel* ('Mick the German'),[2] this particular cartoon is different. The many graphic images in satiric papers or broadsheets in 1848-1849 featuring Michel present him taking an active part in the early months of the Revolution. Athletic in build and gesture, and with a frank open countenance, he challenges the forces of tyranny in the guise of a courageous young artisan, demanding a constitution for Germany[3], or as a student resting on the banks of 'Father' Rhine, hailing the rising sun of Liberty.[4] Virtually all such cartoon figures wear Michel's characteristic accoutrement: the peaked cap or *Michelsmütze*, its upward thrust conveying the wearer's sense of optimism for the success of his mission.[5] No such cap adorns the head of the ignorant-looking young peasant whose face and form contrast so evidently with the dynamic body language of revolutionary Michel. The superscript identifying him as *Ein Mitglied des Pius-Vereins* is an eloquent example of liberal media 'spin' on Catholic associations: members of such Catholic organizations are dumb peasants, in thrall to their priests. Yet, the Pius Association[6] was founded not by clerics, as was often alleged, but by a group of professional and commercial laymen at Mainz in March 1848. Modelled on similar organizations in France and more particularly in O'Connell's Ireland,[7] the *Pius-Verein für religiöse Freiheit*,

---

1 *Leuchtkugeln* ('bolts of light') was published in Munich from late 1847 to early 1849. The Bavarian State Library holds a complete run. As with many such illustrated satirical papers and broadsheets in the 1848 Revolution, *Leuchtkugeln* was not dated, apart from the year, but followed a sequential (page) numbering. The cartoon in question appears on page 24 of volume 2 (1848).
2 Michel is the oldest national stereotype, far older than France's Marianne or Paddy the Irishman and predating even John Bull by almost two centuries. His name derives from Germany's patron saint, the Archangel Michael (as befitting the imperial status of the 'Holy Roman Empire of the German Nation').
3 As in the much-reproduced cartoon where the stick-wielding Michel demands for a 'Reichsverfassung' from the king of Prussia and his advisors, Germanic National Museum Nuremberg HB 152729/1316.
4 *Leuchtkugeln* 2,5: 40.
5 Michel's cap in its revolutionary form points clearly back to its origins in the Phrygian cap of the freed Roman slave and the *bonnet rouge* of the French revolution.
6 It took its name from Pope Pius IX (reigned 1846-1878) who from the time of his election to his expulsion from the Vatican in the summer of 1848 was known as a reforming pope, see Heinz Hürten, *Geschichte des deutschen Katholizismus 1800-1960*, Mainz, Matthias Grünewald, 1986: 83ff.
7 Geraldine Grogan, *The Noblest Agitator: Daniel O'Connell and the German Catholic Movement 1830-50*, Dublin, Veritas, 1991: 79ff.

the first and most important of a host of local and national associations serving the politicization and self-organization of German Catholics, had initially a dual agenda. Later known as 'the spiritual parliament of the Catholic people' [of Germany],[8] it initially sought to promote reform within an authoritarian church and to defend religious freedom of all Christian churches against the encroachment of the secular state. The following months saw the establishment of hundreds of local branches across Germany, but now with a specifically confessional agenda – in the south-western state of Baden alone some 400 local associations were founded. A particular feature of Catholic associations from the outset was their democratic social composition. The Pius Association actually afforded women a(n indirect) role in the proceedings. Although prohibited under German law from being members of political associations, women had seats regularly reserved for them in the galleries of the halls where the local associations met. By the time of its first general assembly in October 1848, in response to attacks in the media and as part of the general polarization of political life in the course of the Revolution, the *Pius-Verein* had changed its name to *Deutscher Katholikenverein* or German Catholic Association. Bismarck's *Kulturkampf* in the 1870s, directed against political Catholicism, would paradoxically complete the process of mass mobilization of German Catholics.

The context of such developments helps the observer to interpret the emblematical nature of what is being presented in the crudely sketched figure of the anonymous protester of the *Leuchtkugeln* cartoon. 'Catholic' protesters are 'different'. In evident contrast with young Michel's open countenance, this creature's forehead is hidden by a thick shock of hair. Sporting a coarse earring, his facial expression manages to be at once sly, smug and stupid as he hurls his scarcely articulate insults at his opponents. The badge on the young man's jacket gives a clue to the artist's negative stereotyping: it features a squirrel. The squirrel is an iconic figure of Vormärz political caricature, image and text, signifying authoritarian domination or, as here, blind subservience to the dictates of Rome. The caption reads: *Ös Lumpen, jetzt hat halt uns're heilige Religion doch g'siegt – ös Lumpen! Und der Papst ist auch wieder in Rom – ös Lumpen!* ['Ye dirty rotters, our holy religion has triumphed after all – ye dirty rotters! And the Pope is back in Rome: so there!'] More significantly, by exaggerating his subject's receding forehead and large protruding chin, the (anonymous) cartoonist associates this scion of Bavarian Catholicism with the many prognathous figures of mid- and later nineteenth-century defamatory political caricature, designed to indicate their subjects' membership of inferior races. A familiar figure of Anglo-Saxon caricature on both sides of the Atlantic in the mid- and later nineteenth-century was the simian Paddy the Irishman[9]. Alongside this brutish representative of the (Irish) Celtic race, Latins and Slavs too were regularly depicted by the disciples of popular phrenology, self-styled orthognathous spokesmen of the master races, as kinds of 'white negroes'[10].

The loud-mouthed yokel and Pius-Association member disappears from the columns of *Leuchtkugeln* as suddenly as he had appeared. Most of these satirical journals in the revolutionary year tended merely to reflect topical concerns, many of which proved as ephemeral as themselves. But it raises a question central to understanding the pheno-

---

8 Thomas Nipperdey, *Germany from Napoleon to Bismarck 1800-1866*, Dublin, Gill and Macmillan, 1996: 365.
9 Lewis Perry Curtis, *Apes and Angels. The Irishman in Victorian Caricature*, Newton Abbot, David & Charles, 1971, especially the chapter 'Simianizing the Irish Celt': 29-57.
10 The phrase was coined by the Belgian political economist Gustav de Molinari (1819-1912) in his articles on Ireland in the *Journal des Débats* of 1880, as quoted in Curtis, *Apes and Angels*: 1.

menon of anti-Catholic polemics in nationalist Germany. Why the invective, and why use it of fellow German citizens? On what basis could German Catholics be described, as they so frequently were in mid- and later nineteenth-century cartoons, and in poems, prose tales and pamphlets up to the time of Bismarck's *Kulturkampf* in the 1870s and beyond, as intellectually and morally inferior to their compatriots, as if belonging to a lower order of beings, and as anti-national?

The course of the 1848 Revolution in Germany taught its political leaders, whether of the liberal centre or the democratic left, that the greatest danger lay in their own disunity. The 'double loyalty' of Catholics, in Germany as elsewhere, to Rome and to their local secular ruler, made them inevitably suspect, both to members of the (state-based) Protestant churches and to the increasingly secularized political classes. To their spokesmen in the media, the problem with Catholics, including revolutionary Catholics, was a perennial one: for them 'freedom of religion' always took precedence over freedom for the nation. Moreover, few critics of the ultramontane and increasingly clericalized Roman church in mid-century believed in Catholics' democratic credentials. Yet in the crucial debates in the Frankfurt Assembly in late July of 1848 on what became known as the 'Polish Question,'[11] it was the spokesmen of a new brand of chauvinistic German nationalism who denied their own liberal and democratic consciences. When it came to a choice between unity and freedom, between the vision of a united Germany and equal rights to national self-determination for all, including Germany's large Polish (and Catholic) minority and the Danes in Schleswig, the most vocal element of the German revolutionaries chose the former. Furthermore, Catholic deputies' support for their fellow Catholic Poles' national aspirations at the Frankfurt Parliament was branded in the new mood of Germany's revolutionary nationalists as treason. In a profound sense, German Catholics served as a scapegoat for the unresolved dilemma between German liberals' constitutional and national aspirations which the Frankfurt Parliament laid bare. At all events, from the summer of 1848 forward and in the decades following the collapse of the Revolution and the installation of a neo-absolutist state in Catholic Austria, the idea that German Catholics were somehow less dependable German citizens gained credence in educated as well as popular circles in Protestant Germany. It was Bismarck, the so-called *Reichsgründer* or architect of German unity, who gave respectability to prejudice when in his Reichstag speech of 1st April 1871 he went as far as to label Germany's Catholics, together with her Poles, Danes and Alsatians, as 'enemies of the state' (*Reichsfeinde*). So too, it was Bismarck who successfully re-invoked the quasi-mythical power of that ancient stereotype of anti-Catholic polemics: the sinister Jesuit. Germany's Catholics, predominantly from a rural or small-town background as they were, might be less well-educated than their Protestant counterparts. That, implied Bismarck, was not the problem. The real danger for Germany, so recently united (to the chagrin of her enemies), following the expulsion of Catholic Austria from Germany in 1866, was, he suggested, the way in which it laid Germany's millions of remaining Catholics open to the manipulation by the Pope's own secret emissaries, the Jesuits. Confident in his reading of the public mind, he introduced in 1872 a series of anti-Jesuit measures, the so-called May Laws, into Prussia's parliament, which led to the banishment, for almost half a century, of Germany's 737 Jesuits. The response was an extraordinary outburst of popular polemics in support of the Chancellor but directed against 'Rome' and the Society. The texts appeared in a wide variety of genres, as stridently polemical poems,

---

11 Wolfram Siemann, *The German Revolution of 1848-49,* Basingstoke, Macmillan, 1998: 145.

many by highly visible public figures, anthologized for easy reference,[12] in plays and in some one hundred and eighty contemporary historical novels, as well as in articles in the regional and national press. A particular feature of the years 1872 and 1873, which witnessed the harshest state measures against bishops, priests and Catholic journalists, along with a small number of tacitly condoned incidents of mob violence in Prussia unleashed against Catholic convents and institutions, was a series of defamatory and at times semi-pornographical pamphlets and broadsheets elaborating Jesuit excesses against the 'German nation'. Even an emerging feminist voice identified the struggle for women's liberation with a notional crusade against 'Jesuitism in the household', as in the redoubtable Hedwig Dohm's *Der Jesuitismus im Hausstand. Ein Beitrag zur Frauenfrage* of 1873. Of these ephemeral texts, the only survivor today is the grotesque but thoroughly entertaining mock-heroic epic with matching illustrations on the subject of Germany's latter-day Tartuffe, the Jesuit *Pater Filucius* (1872) by the artist writer Wilhelm Busch.[13]

Anti Jesuit hysteria,[14] somewhat akin to early modern witch-crazes (with which they were sporadically associated), dates from the era of seventeenth-century Germany's religious wars. Deriving from the Jesuits' key role in the promotion of the Counter-Reformation, anti-Jesuit polemics drew on a long-established iconographical arsenal. Exemplified in tracts with titles such as J. Cambilhom's *Nova novorum jesuitica: das is historische und außfürliche Beschreibung von den verborgensten Geheimnüssen und schrecklichsten Thaten der Jesuwider*[15] (Gera, Martin Spiess, 1611), the stereotype of the 'wicked Jesuit' with his 'diabolical' associations proved surprisingly easy to resurrect. While the revival of grotesque bogeymen such as the sinister Jesuit in the *Vormärz* or pre-March era (1830-1848) by university-educated journalists as a weapon against one's opponents might seem to sit uneasily with the rational credentials of the 'liberal era', it is useful to recall that crass stereotyping of the Other was a tried and accepted form of entertainment (which Catholic polemicists in their turn did not hesitate to use). The Jesuits exercised very considerable influence within the German Catholic Church in mid-century, notably by way of appointments to key positions, including several bishoprics, of graduates of the Jesuit-run *Collegium Germanicum*, which had been re-founded in Rome in 1824. Two incidents in neighbouring Austria and (German-speaking) Switzerland in the late 1830s provided the occasion for the re-entry of 'the Jesuits' into political polemics. The first, the expulsion by the local bishop of the small Protestant population of the Alpine Ziller valley in 1837, acquired a national dimension through its exploitation in the popular media. An example is the poem, *Der Jesuit*, by the Innsbruck civil servant, Hermann von Gilm (1812-1864), who describes his subject as one who 'brings the dark night back into a land where dawn was about to break.'[16]

---

12 See Ernst Scherenberg (ed.), *Gegen Rom. Zeitstimmen deutscher Dichter*, 1874⁴. Scherenberg was a cousin of the Hohenzollern court poet, Christian von Scherenberg; his collection was reprinted several times. It contained poems by prominent (Liberal) members of parliament, university professors, senior civil servants and other high-profile citizens.

13 Eda Sagarra, 'Der neue krumme Teufel der Kulturkampfzeit. Der Jesuit Pater Filucius im Zeitkontext', in Marijan Bobinac (ed.), *Literatur im Wandel. Festschrift für Viktor Žmegač*, number 5 in Zagreber Germanistische Beiträge, Zagreb, University, 1999: 119-129.

14 As early as 1904, Bernard Duhr SJ provided a massive documentation of anti-Jesuit fables in his *Jesuitenfabeln*, Freiburg i.B., Herder.

15 Note the clumsy pun on the term 'Jesuiter' as 'Jesu – wider', i.e., 'opposed to Jesus'.

16 '…und bringt die Nacht zurück ins Land / Wo schon die Dämmrung war", in Jost Hermand (ed.), *Der deutsche Vormärz. Texte und Dokumente*, Stuttgart, Reclam, 1969: 156f. Also, 'Die Vertreibung der Zillerthaler' by the Austrian Adolf Pichler, in Scherenberg, *Gegen Rom*: 66-68.

Gilm's poem resonated with admirers of Goethe's much-read domestic idyll, *Hermann und Dorothea* (1796-1797), based on the expulsion of Austrian Protestants by the Archbishop of Salzburg in 1731. The second event, the imposition of the Jesuits on the university of Lucerne in 1838, received its exemplary and national character only in the following decade, in the context of the debate on the new liberal constitution for Switzerland. This had been promoted by the mainly Protestant and urbanized cantons but was opposed by the conservative rural Catholic cantons of central Switzerland. The Lucerne affair owed its exemplary status to the far more significant power game played out in 1837-1838 in the (Catholic) Rhineland, which had been assigned to Prussia in the post-Napoleonic settlement. The conflict, known as the Cologne Incident, erupted over the issue of mixed marriages (spearheaded by the frequency of unions between Prussian officials and local Catholic women), and the demands of the newly elected archbishop Droste-Vischering that the children be brought up as Catholics. Episcopal obduracy in refusing the diplomatic channels preferred by his predecessor in these matters resulted in a serious tactical error on the part of the Prussian authorities: the arrest and fortress imprisonment of the septuagenarian churchman galvanized believers. While the Young German and voice of secular liberalism, Karl Gutzkow, in his witty polemic *Red Caps and Black Hats* (1838), conjured up an image of world divided into the forces of human progress and clerical repression, Joseph Görres, in one of the most brilliant pamphlets of the age, *Athanasius*,[17] turned the tables on the church's critics by basing his stance on a human rights agenda: the right of believers to freedom from state interference in the 'private' areas of worship, marriage and education. In the events leading up to the Swiss civil war of 1844-1847, it was in fact the canton of Lucerne and not the church that had imposed the Jesuits on the local university. But it was the literary exploitation of the affair and of the Jesuits' key role in overseeing the Catholic cantons' resistance to the invading armies from the Protestant cantons which gave the affair seminal importance in subsequent anti-Catholic polemics in Germany right up to the era of Bismarck's Kulturkampf of the 1870s.[18] In the brief civil war, which claimed one hundred lives, the Catholic cantonal resistance was soundly defeated and the Society of Jesus expelled from Switzerland in 1847. The young Zurich poet Gottfried Keller and disciple of Ludwig Feuerbach conjured up half-forgotten images of diabolical association between Jesuits and witches and other powers of darkness from the arsenal of seventeenth-century zealots, in his denunciation of the fearsome conspiracy against reason and progress in *Loyola's Wild, Bold Hunt* (1845). Part of the poem's appeal lay in its title's reference to that icon of German national resistance to (Napoleonic) tyranny, Theodor Körner's poem: *Lützows wilde Jagd* of 1813 and in its explicit coupling of Jesuitical threats to human liberty with national resurgence. Keller casts Switzerland in the role of 'fair bride' (*schöne Braut*), about to be ravished by the Jesuits who come, riding on snakes, behind them (image of a witches' Sabbath!), dragons and pigs, stinking 'infernally'. With cross and flag aloft, they bear venom in their train, while fanaticism and stupidity are their agents. Even the child in her mother's womb (*Wohl graut im Mutter-*

---

17 The age's appetite for extended rhetoric may be gauged by the immense success of this 170-page pamphlet, which sold more than 7000 copies (and sparked some 300 pamphlets in the following year), see Franz Schnabel, *Deutsche Geschichte im 19. Jahrhundert*, Freiburg i.B., 1949-59: volume 1: 139.

18 Georges Andrey in Ulrich Hof et al. (eds.), *Geschichte der Schweiz und der Schweizer*, Basel, Helbing & Lichtenhain, 1986: 627f.

leib das Kind), trembles in fear of her future fate at the hands of these devilish creatures. This extraordinary text of nine four-line verses became a kind of blueprint for contemporary and future anti-Jesuit literature. In far-away Berlin, Theodor Fontane and his aristocratic officer friend, Bernhard von Lepel, tried their hand at 'Jesuit' verse, to be read aloud to their literary club, the Tunnel across the Spree.[19] It was indeed, as Fontane somewhat wryly observed half a century later, 'a somewhat polemical age'.[20] The stereotyping of the figure of Martin Luther in nationalist circles in Germany had already established the Reformer as the courageous and defiant liberator of the people (*das Volk*) from the thrall of clerical/papal aggression.[21]

Anti-Jesuit polemics, whether as image or text, derived a vigorous impulse from the fashion for a (vulgarized) study of physiognomy, 'that ancient half-science and half-art,'[22] adding both to their dynamic and their entertainment value. The 'Jesuit', whether as image or as a character in a text, is immediately recognizable by his physical appearance and body language. While his height betokens his desire to manipulate, like some sinister puppet-master, his skeletal figure clearly derives from the 'inhuman' asceticism of his training. This successfully aims to kill all forms of emotion in himself and in those, notably the young, in his charge. An example from English literature is Charlotte Brontë's novel *The Professor* (1851), set in Belgium, where education was largely in the hands of the Jesuits, which contrasts the 'pale blighted image, where life lingered feebly...the foster-child of Rome, the protégée of Jesuitry' with the healthy happy 'daughter of Albion and nursling of Protestantism'.[23] In German literature, the most notorious example is Conrad Ferdinand Meyer's short story, *Das Leiden Eines Knaben* (1883), about a boy who dies from the harsh treatment received at the hands of his Jesuit mentors. The Society of Jesus is to its critics a secret society, and therefore to be feared. The Jesuit does not walk; he creeps and slinks. He does not appear in the open, but lurks rather, in dark corners or shadowy passages. Like the devil, he fears the light, for it might reveal his eyes, no 'mirror of the soul' they: the glassy, impenetrable eyes of a Jesuit betray his fanaticism. Where the *bonnet rouge* of the young revolutionary, *der deutsche Michel*, left his face and forehead free to the beholder, the Jesuit's face is hidden by his stereotypical broad-brimmed hat. Thus, he prevents those with a passing understanding of phrenology – and who in mid-nineteenth-century Germany did not trust his own competence in these matters? – from being able to 'read' the Jesuit's evil intentions towards those whom he would deceive. Obscurity is the element in which he operates, spinning, like a spider, his horrid network of agents world-wide.[24] He never

---

19 For example, Theodor Fontane, 'An den Orden Jesu', in Joachim Krüger and Anita Golz (eds.), *Gedichte* volume 2: *Einzelpublikationen. Gedichte in Prosatexten. Gedichte aus dem Nachlaß*, Weimar, Aufbau, 1989: 258f.
20 'Es war … eine polemische Zeit', Theodor Fontane, *Von Zwanzig bis Dreißig. Autobiographisches*, München, dtv, 1973: 278.
21 Peter Sprengel, *Von Luther zu Bismarck. Kulturkampf und nationale Identität bei Theodor Fontane, Conrad Ferdinand Meyer und Gerhart Hauptmann*, Bielefeld, Aisthesis, 1999. Germany's greatest satirist, Heinrich Heine, opportunistic Jewish convert to Lutheranism, made frequent play of Luther as national leader and human liberator in his prose texts from the 1830s to the early 1850s.
22 Curtis, *Apes and Angels*: viii.
23 See Charlotte Brontë, *The Professor*, edited Margaret Smith and Herbert Rosengarten, Oxford, Clarendon, 1987.
24 The image of the spider anticipates, as so much of Jesuit stereotypy, anti-Semitic conspiracy theories. See the images of the Jewish manipulation of world financial markets in the 1920s, represented graphically in the image of the spider straddling the globe, in Norman Cohn,

stands upright, his curved spine articulating his deviousness and determination to ingratiate himself with the rich and powerful or those whom he seeks to control. Just as his master, Satan, the Jesuit's claw-like hands seek to control and manipulate the human race.[25]

A theme which surfaced sporadically in German anti-Jesuit literary polemics is the Jesuit's lasciviousness, directed at innocent young girls. Both Gottfried Keller's seminal poem of 1845 and Wilhelm Busch's *Pater Filucius* exploit the motif. The same Satanic fantasies, in essence pornographical with an eye to reader appeal,[26] would feature prominently in later anti-Semitic polemics.[27] It is in this regard that the host of anti-Jesuit pamphlets which streamed from the press in the years 1872-1873, including that of leading publishing houses such as Otto Wigand in Leipzig, deserve particular attention. Thus, the 120-page *Der Jesuitismus, getreu nach der Natur gezeichnet und den Männern des Staates und des Volkes zur Betrachtung vorgestellt von einem bekehrten Jesuiten* (1872), purported to be a factual analysis of the Society.[28] Others, such as *Teufelsbündler, Zauber und Hexenglauben und dessen kirchliche Ausbeutung zur Schändung der Menschheit* (1873) or *Der Teufel im Beichtstuhl. Jesuiten-Schliche* (1873), appealed directly to the popular appetite for unsavoury revelations. Utterly ephemeral as these pamphlets were, they may well have significance far beyond the occasion of their publication or indeed the tradition of anti-Jesuit and anti-Catholic polemics which provided their immediate context. It is the metaphorical arsenal of these texts which gives pause for thought, notably to the student of anti-Semitism in Germany. The 'standard' evocation in all of these pamphlets is of a conspiracy of evil against the German nation and people, now couched in biological images. Thus, invisible 'parasites' (*Gewürm*) secretly gnaw away at the 'roots of the human tree', 'the tree of life', eager for their work of debilitating and destroying, while the 'caterpillars' (*Raupen*) and the moths into which they 'metamorphose' devour the trees' source of life, their 'leaves and blossoms'. The author calls on the people to 'eradicate' (*vertilg[en]*) the 'whole brood' (*die ganze Brut*) of vermin.[29] In hindsight, familiar terms indeed! With the expulsion of the Society completed within a year of the May Laws, the anti-Jesuit pamphlets disappeared from the scene as suddenly as they had appeared. Was it a coincidence or was there a link between these texts and the emergence at the end of the same decade of anti-Semitic, chauvinistic nationalist pamphlets and brochures directed against Germany's Jews? The metaphorical arsenal, the Social-Darwinistic biological images of the *Kampf ums Dasein* on which the latter would draw, did not need to be invented. In their anti-Catholic and anti-Semitic pamphlets, whose back pages usually included advertisements for similar texts, respectable

---

Warrant for Genocide: The Myth of the Jewish World Conspiracy and the Protocols of the Elders of Zion, Harmondsworth, Penguin, 1970.

25 Eda Sagarra, '"Entfamter Jesuwiter!" Zur Dämonisierung der Jesuiten in der Literatur des Vor- und Nachmärz bzw. der Gründerzeit', in Anita Bunyan et al. (eds.), *Kulturkritik, Erinnerungskunst und Utopie nach 1848. Deutsche Literatur vom Nachmärz bis zur Gründerzeit in europäischer Perspektive*, Bielefeld, Aisthesis, 2003²: 165-182.

26 As distinct from the 'good clean fun' of clerical hypocrisy, beloved of comic writers from medieval times to Rabelais, Molière (*Le Tartuffe*) and beyond.

27 It had constituted, of course, a significant part of the appeal of early modern anti-Jesuit polemics, in which Jesuits were assigned the devil's role as partner of sex-crazed females in the witches' Sabbath. And does not Goethe draw on such sources for much of Mephisto's body-language in *Faust. Part I*, more particularly his frolics in the *Hexensabbat*?

28 *Der Jesuitismus, getreu nach der Natur gezeichnet und den Männern des Staates und des Volkes zur Betrachtung vorgestellt von einem bekehrten Jesuiten* (1872).

29 *Der Jesuitismus*: 112.

German publishing houses employed the sophisticated salesmanship characteristic of the contemporary German capitalistic literary market to promote the emergence and popularization of such vituperative language, while at the same time conferring highly acceptable nationalist credentials on the sentiments they expressed.

Unlike other countries where one Christian confession had been dominant for centuries, anti-Catholic polemics in Germany's age of nationalism were not of their essence sectarian. It is true that the purveyors, usually educated men, who evoked the credentials of enlightened 'Protestantism' to legitimize their stance, had generally been baptized and brought up as members of the Lutheran/ Reformed churches, but few were followers of Luther more than in name only. Devout German Protestants generally showed considerable unease at Bismarck's measures against the Catholic clergy and religious orders and by extension their flock, even if they shared his concern for national unity, in the light of what they interpreted as the Vatican's claims on the consciences of Catholics as epitomized in the strident triumphalism of Pius IX's *Syllabus of Errors* (1864) and the promulgation of the dogma of papal infallibility at the Vatican Council in 1870. Since '"cultural Protestantism" was an extraordinary powerful force among the middle classes' and 'since "German culture" *was* Protestant,'[30] anti-Catholic polemics from mid-nineteenth-century Germany forward had an evident 'nation-building' function. This did not quite mean, as many German Catholics of the time saw it,[31] 'a Protestant state for a Protestant people' but it identified even nominal membership of the Protestant church as evidence of 'true' German national identity in a way no 'Roman' Catholic could ever aspire to share. The unification of Germany by Prussia in 1871 and the propaganda invested in vaunting the values of the centralized nation state involved no small degree of denial, particularly of the federal traditions of German history which most German Catholics supported. Moreover, unity was effectively bought at the cost of a diminution of constitutionalism. The Second Reich suffered from a lack of democratic legitimacy, which polemics, directed at the dissentient minorities, whether national, Polish, Alsatian, Danish, or confessional, Catholic or Jew, sought to deny. The very success of the ultramontane and anti-liberal Catholic Church in Germany in mobilizing the faithful, and the unified face which German Catholics presented to their critics as a consequence of the Kulturkampf,[32] exacerbated a sense of grievance in the majority. Equally, envy at the remarkable and continuing success of Germany's newly emancipated Jewish minority, in education and the professions, in industry, finance, commerce and the creative arts, was relentlessly cast in nationalist discourse as a provocation of the 'German *Volk*'. Thus, anti-Catholic and anti-Jewish polemics, both among the educated and the populace in the emerging German national state, reinforced the judgement of historians of national stereotyping, and indeed of human nature generally, that 'the

---

30 David Blackbourn, *The Long Nineteenth Century 1780-1918*, London, Fontana, 1997: 293.
31 Such as the article in the orthodox but respected Catholic journal *Historisch-politische Blätter* 58 (1866), 'Die Katholikenhetze während des deutschen Krieges gegen die Festlegung deutscher Katholiken auf die Seite der Österreicher', as quoted in Jutta Osinksi, *Katholizismus und deutsche Literatur im 19. Jahrhundert*, Paderborn, Schöningh 1993: 307.
32 As reflected not only in Catholic organizations, a flourishing Catholic newspaper and periodical press, and in support for the Catholic Centre Party, which attracted 83% of the adult male Catholic vote in the mid 1870s; this only decreased from the mid 1890s, when Catholic voter behaviour and national sentiments began to align themselves with prevalent trends in the state, see Thomas Nipperdey, *Deutsche Geschichte 1866-1918* Part I: *Arbeitswelt und deutscher Geist*, München, C.H. Beck, 1990: 439f.

refracted image worked at the same time to enhance the self-confidence of the beholder at the expense of those being stereotyped.'[33] By the end of the century, German Catholics had gradually begun to assimilate to the majority,[34] both in terms of voter behaviour and national sentiment, despite a lingering residue of popular prejudice enshrined in common parlance.[35] By contrast, similar and more self-conscious efforts by Germany's Jews in the Second Empire to do likewise foundered on the bedrock of endemic European anti-Jewishness, now, however, in its far more virulent, racist anti-Semitic guise.

---

33 Curtis, *Apes and Angels*: 14. The same process but in reverse was true of those who liked to establish their 'Catholic' and 'nationalist' credentials by defamation of Protestants, such as, for example, in Franco's Spain or in certain circles in chauvinistic 'Gaelic' Ireland. See also Blackbourn, *The Long Nineteenth Century*: 392, on 'clerical demonology'.
34 Including anti-Semitic prejudice.
35 Catholics 'were' 'falsch', see the various derogatory meanings of 'katholisch' in popular phrases, such as 'katholisch schauen', implying malice or 'katholisch gucken' (deceitfulness) or even 'es ist zum Katholischwerden', it is (so awful) it would make you want to turn Catholic, Lutz Röhrich, *Sprichwörtliche Redensarten* volume 2, Freiburg i.B., Herder, 1977: 492.

Sulak Sivaraksa
No River Bigger Than *Tanha*

The word development in Pali is *vaddhana*, which means messiness or making messiness; it can be messy with good things or messy with problems, sufferings, or chaos. In the modern world, development means the world is 'flooded with material things neglecting the spiritual aspects.' These are the words of Buddhadasa Bhikkhu, a renowned Buddhist monk and thinker of Siam. Following on this, I feel that consumerism has become a new religion of sorts, demonic in essence. This paper focuses on the effects of consumerism in Siam and alternative visions and initiatives based on the work of Ven. Buddhadasa Bhikkhu and others within the Engaged Buddhist movement in Siam. The structure of this essay is based on the teachings of the Four Noble Truths: this means identifying problems, looking at causes, envisioning solutions, and outlining a path from the present reality to the desirable situation.

The Perils of Consumerism

Four countries in Southeast Asia — Laos, Cambodia, Burma, and Siam — face conflict between Buddhist and capitalist values. Each is of Theravada Buddhist background and at different stages of Western-style development. To explore the First Noble Truth, identifying the problems, we will look at how consumerism affects traditional Buddhist societies in Southeast Asia. At one extreme is Siam, wholeheartedly following the Americanization process over the last fifty years. At the other extreme is Burma, trying to close the country to every form of Western influence.

If we visit Shwedagon Pagoda in Yangon, the most important pagoda of the country, we see Burmese of all ethnic backgrounds — monks, nuns, and laypeople — paying homage to the Buddha. Some pray and meditate; others perform devotions. The pagoda is crowded all day, every day of the year, from as early as 5:00 A.M. until 9:00 P.M. In Bangkok, the capital of Siam, if we visit the Emerald Buddha Temple, we see it is crowded all day, nearly every day of the year, with foreign tourists. Only a few Thais are there paying homage to the Buddha. Instead, Thai people crowd the big shopping malls in Bangkok, such as Central, Lotus, Tesco, and Robinsons, every day from opening until closing time. For most Thais these shopping malls are the new temples and consumerism is their religion, even though if asked they will say they are Buddhist.

What does it mean for the Thais to have consumerism as their religion? It means they define who they are by what they buy: wearing the right brand of dress, owning the most expensive wristwatch, driving the right car, eating at Japanese or Western restaurants, and for the neo-middle class, speaking English to each other. This devotion to consumerism is putting many Thais into debt, especially through the use of credit cards. Credit card companies encourage people to take on debt and then charge them interest that sucks away at their income.

With few exceptions, the monks of Siam naively welcome this new religion, blending it with Buddhism as an unavoidable friend. The Thai Buddhist *sangha* that is supposed to generate Buddhist values of simplicity, generosity, and compassion is now, too, almost completely under the spell of consumerism. Many monks compete with each other to possess consumer goods such as mobile phones, BMWs, and portable computers; others are obsessed with raising money from their newly rich parishioners to build ever-larger Buddha statues and superfluous religious halls.

Whatever your social status in Siam, you have to climb to the top. If you are from a farming family, you must not be content with being a farmer. You have to buy education to escape from being a farmer to become someone else. If you are a monk, you have to climb up the *sangha* hierarchy or make yourself famous and have many followers. The whole ethos of Thai consumer society, especially the media and the education systems, inflicts a sense of inferiority. No matter who you are, you are never good enough. From a Buddhist perspective, this is a basic form of alienation. This existential sense of not being good enough (*vibhava-tanha*) has been stimulated by Western-dominated media and advertising to such an extent that young people in Siam reject who they are. Helena Norberg-Hodge explains this phenomenon of cultural alienation very clearly and powerfully in her book *Ancient Futures*.[1] Such alienation stems from the illusion of self competing and comparing with others to define who you are (*mana*). The consumer monoculture feeds on this human weakness. To have consumerism as a religion means that the aim of individual life and of society is to gain unlimited wealth, power, recognition, and sensual pleasure. The Buddha warned his followers not to cling to these four worldly temptations. Yet, the present social structures supporting consumerism encourage people to run after them madly.

In contrast to Siam, Burma has been greatly damaged by an authoritarian military junta and, luckily or unluckily, closed to the outside world for more than half a century. This means that, except for the few corrupt top military families and some leaks through the Chinese and Thai borders, consumer monoculture has touched the lives of ordinary people very little. The Buddhist values of simplicity, generosity, compassion, and detachment from worldly success are still intact for most Burmese. Meditation practice is widespread, not only among the monks but also throughout the lay community. The Burmese are proud to wear colourful wraps rather than the Western trousers and skirts that have been adopted in Bangkok and many other parts of Southeast Asia. Yangon street markets are full of producers selling indigenous vegetables, largely home-farmed and grown without chemicals.

Of course, with any small opening to the outside world, the big multinational corporations rush in and pollute the beautiful cities with advertising for Marlboro, Tiger Beer, Philips, and Sony, thus spoiling the cultural landscape. We do not know whether future democratic leadership in Burma will be aware enough of the dangers of consumerism to stop this trend. It is also a big question whether Americanization in Siam and the Philippines will rush into Burma once the country is opened. At least at this moment, Yangon, with its charming old buildings and greenery, is much more beautiful than Bangkok, one of the most polluted cities in the world. Once renowned as the Venice of the East, a mystical city of canals and golden spires, Bangkok today is full of unfinished construction sites, ugly new buildings, superhighways, and shopping malls that are tearing the heart out of local communities.

In Siam, development over the past fifty years has overemphasized economic growth without adequate consideration for environmental sustainability, social justice,

---

1 Helena Norberg-Hodge, *Ancient Futures: Learning from Ladakh*, Introduction by Peter Matthiessen, Preface by HH the Dalai Lama, London, Rider and Co., 2000^{revised}.

cultural diversity, and spiritual well-being. This economic growth has been possible only by gradually challenging the traditional Buddhist world-view and replacing it with consumerism. During the Vietnam War, when Americans wanted to prevent Siam from becoming communist, they sent 'experts' to advise the various Thai government departments. They urged the Thai government to request the Buddhist *sangha* to stop giving teachings on contentment (*santosa* or *santutthi*). If people were content and happy, they wouldn't want American-style development. To follow the new economic path of consumerism, they would need to feel that their way of life was inferior, underdeveloped, not good enough. Unfortunately, almost the entire Buddhist *sangha* was tamed to follow this heretical suggestion – except for Buddhadasa Bhikkhu, who saw the dangers of consumerism more than fifty years ago.

The government, business circles, and multinational corporations have used the education and mass media systems and gradually become very successful in uprooting basic Buddhist values from Thai society. Many thousands of self-reliant villages were persuaded to join the cash crop economy, and most are now in debt due to lack of control over the price and costs of their production. After decades of development, more and more farmers have lost their land to absentee landlords or to middlemen who trade their products. Debt-ridden villagers are migrating en masse to the big industrial areas to work in factories and the building trades. As rural communities disappear, people are robbed of their sustainable livelihoods as well as the social security of traditional ways of life. Children of even the better-off farmers are now leaving the countryside for big cities where they will face further alienation and loss of community. In an abortive attempt to fill this void, the estranged turn to the instant gratification of consumerism, including abusive use of drugs and sex.

A few rural people and poor urban dwellers manage to join the middle class and live a material life with modern conveniences such as private cars, televisions, mobile phones, DVD players, modern houses, and so on. As competition is the name of the game, urban consumers are never satisfied with what they have. Soon, the new car will be unfashionable and the new computer must be upgraded. Many business executives live a stressful life, going to bed with a handful of drugs to help them sleep.

From a Buddhist perspective, this cannot be a healthy way of life, as one is always driven by greed (*lobha*), anxiety and aggression (*dosa*), and the delusions of individualism and competition (*moha*). Moreover, this way of life is a life without community. In Buddhism, a person cannot grow without a supportive community. A higher quality of life based on generosity (*dana*), compassion (*karuna*), and respect for others (*samanttata*) cannot be developed in an individualistic society. Without the maturity of these healthy qualities (*kusalamula*), however successful you are in terms of wealth, power, and recognition, you still experience a deep sense of lack, loneliness, and isolation.

Craving and Consumerism

We turn now to the Second Noble Truth to look for causes of the problem. According to Buddhist analysis, craving is the root cause of all suffering. The very core of consumerism is the amplification of craving, or *tanha*. Traditionally, *tanha* is classified with three aspects: craving for sensual pleasure, craving for existence, and craving for non-existence. In other words, *tanha* manifests in the three unwholesome roots (*akusalamula*): greed (*lobha*), hatred (*dosa*), and delusion (*moha*). Seen in the context of consumerism, *lobha* is the need to acquire the four worldly states of unlimited wealth, power, recognition, and sensual pleasure. *Dosa* is the anxiety to acquire these, the fear of losing them, the anger, sadness, and depression (which can turn into aggressive violence) when they are lost or not attainable. *Moha* is the individualism and competition to attain these four states, the pride when one has them, and defining who you are according to what you have. These modern states of delusion also include endemic low self-esteem and feelings of not being good enough when you don't attain these four states, as well as jealousy when others get them and you do not.

In Siam we can see clearly that *tanha* manifests itself not only on the individual level, as seen in accepted social values. It also manifests as structural violence in the form of the free-market economy, the control of media by transnational corporations, and state mechanisms that favour the rich over the poor. Another form of structural violence is the industrialization process that overuses natural resources for excessive human consumption without compassion towards other beings.

Of course, *tanha* has existed in all societies at all times since history has been recorded. However, in nonconsumeristic societies past and present, people have learned to curb *tanha* so that harm to individuals, community, and nature is kept to a minimum. It is only in today's consumer monoculture that *tanha* has been eulogized as a desirable value. In contrast to the consumerist world-view, Buddhist teachings advocate reducing and eliminating *tanha* as the path to happiness.

Happiness can be increased either by satisfying *tanha* more often or by reducing *tanha* itself. While consumerism chooses the former solution, Buddhists attempt to embrace the latter. The Buddhist argument is that the more you try to satisfy *tanha*, the more it will increase. 'There is no river bigger than tanha', said the Buddha. This implies that *tanha* is something ultimately insatiable. A society where *tanha* is encouraged is Mara's playground, with few winners and many losers. In this process the winners are not real winners, for, on the road to acquisition, they create oppression and inflict great suffering on many people. The processes of colonization, industrialization, development, and globalization are *tanha* operating on the macroscale of structural violence.

As *tanha* becomes globalized, the scale of suffering has amplified immensely around the world through the spread of consumerism. It is clear from the Buddhist point of view that *tanha* in the minds of the people works in tandem with violent social structures to reinforce unprecedented suffering in the present society.

Vision For Alternatives

Turning now to the Third Noble Truth, the Buddhist way of peace and happiness (*santisukkha*) is to reduce unwholesome aspects of life and society (*akusala*) and encourage growth of the wholesome qualities. In other words, the greed, violence, individualism, and competition that presently dominate society must be curbed, and generosity, compassion, cooperation, and interconnection must be promoted. These wholesome values must be encouraged at both individual and structural levels.

During the left-right political debate of the 1970s, Buddhadasa Bhikkhu voiced the strong criticism that the present mode of development was the path to madness and messiness. He proposed that the *sangha* model be used as an ideal for social reconstruction. He coined the term Dhammic Socialism as an alternative to the present system. He not only presented a theoretical framework but also experimented with creating and living in an alternative community for monks and nuns, which became the famous Suan Mokkh (Garden of Liberation). In contrast to Marxism, Dhammic Socialism sees human beings as part of the natural system, not as the dominating agent. Hence, human beings should live very simply and devote their energy to cultivating the Buddha potential within.

Buddhadasa's Dhammic Socialism would produce a society that provides an environment for individual growth so that one can be fully human. Buddhadasa spoke about 'simple living, higher thinking' as a more attractive ideal than gaining wealth and power. To live this good life he offered detailed methods of self-training and meditation, developing ways to look at the world with a free mind. Buddhadasa felt that a life with limited, but enough, material well-being was more conducive to fully developing human potential than a life of too much material concern.

Buddhadasa also felt it was important for human beings to live a life close to nature: people should be friends with nature and not try to conquer nature. His favourite saying was that the Buddha learned, lived, taught and died in nature. For him, a good society is not one full of artificial artifacts that separate us from the natural environment. Rather, the ideal habitat for Buddhist culture is the rural life such as at Suan Mokkh. In his own life, close to nature, Buddhadasa observed his natural surroundings and came to the conclusion that nature works in a cooperative way. To prove this to visitors, he always pointed to a big tree in front of his hut, where many small trees and plants grew together with the tree, along with a number of wild animals such as birds, squirrels, and lizards. He suggested that human society should be organized in this cooperative spirit. Nature operates under specific laws; the most important of these is the law of interdependence. So, he would say, as human beings we have to understand this and behave accordingly if we want to have a good life and good society. For Buddhadasa, the cultivation of a free mind, cooperative spirit, and living close to nature are practices in harmony with the laws of nature.

Buddhist thought advocates that, whether you are stupid or clever, man or woman, black, brown, pink, white, or yellow, rich or poor, powerful or powerless, believer or nonbeliever, you have intrinsic Buddha-nature within you. You do not have to be someone else to be valuable — hence the primacy placed on self-respect (*hiri-ottappa*). Any society with a structure that undermines this self-respect is an unhealthy society. You cannot be 'more who you are' by rejecting what you are. This does not mean strictly adhering to traditional roles and responsibilities. It means rejecting the notion of belonging to a lesser race, class, gender, religion, culture, or civilization. Once one is firmly rooted in self-respect, it is possible to make healthy and critical choices from among the options offered both by what we inherit from our past and from Western modernity. Working for a sustainable future through political and economic structural change alone is not enough. A new kind of Asian cultural revolution is required to liberate Asia from Western cultural imperialism and from the colonized mentality. This kind of thinking is debilitating and must stop.

Initiatives on the Path to Reduce Suffering

The Spirit in Education Movement (SEM) was launched in 1995. This movement is designed to develop a comprehensive educational movement to counter the trends of globalization and consumerism, using spiritual strength to empower individuals and communities to choose alternative ways of development with confidence and full awareness. This approach is rooted in cultural appropriateness and indigenous wisdom to confront the trends of cultural imperialism that belittle people of non-Western origin.

One SEM programme, the Grassroots Leadership Training (GLT) programme, has been ongoing for nearly ten years. The GLT works with marginalized communities in Siam, Burma, Laos, and Cambodia, running three-month training courses with follow-up sessions. The aim of the courses is to empower communities to be self-reliant in terms of basic needs while maintaining their cultural integrity and sustaining a healthy environment. These are examples of the Fourth Noble Truth.

The empowerment education approach of GLT applies critical self-awareness in a far broader context. This starts with a community-needs analysis to highlight the structural injustices of the modernization process. Tools are given to help communities identify problems and develop sustainable solutions. The real 'experts' are seen as those who know and care for their local environment. Staff facilitate problem analysis and reflection, especially in relation to the connection between local and global problems. GLT also offers study tours to innovative projects, introducing appropriate solutions such as sustainable technology and microcredit.

As communities begin to recognize the oppressive forces in society and how they are mirrored within themselves, they move beyond these trends, finding renewed belief in traditional wisdom and regaining their self-confidence and community confidence. This becomes a starting point for locally sustainable futures. GLT alumni are now involved in hundreds of small-scale, appropriate development projects and training initiatives that focus on local production for local consumption. At best, they hope to help traditional communities not yet marred by the consumer monoculture to protect themselves from the negative forces and to make use of the positive elements to revitalize a healthy community life. The idea is to bypass the mistakes of other victimized traditional communities that opened up to modernization without critical awareness.

Though GLT works with participants of several faiths, encouraging spiritual practice according to their own beliefs, the content and process of the training reflect the basic essence of Buddhist education—the Noble Eightfold Path. A large part of the training is to cultivate right view and right thought about internal and external development. Right thought is unselfish, nonviolent, and free of hatred and excessive desire. In order for individuals and communities to develop properly, generosity (or sharing of wealth), power, and recognition are crucial. When conflict arises, a compassionate and nonviolent approach is encouraged.

To practise right speech, GLT students learn methods of reconciliation and mediation and develop understanding of the structural violence of the present media system. Right action refers to the five basic precepts for ethical conduct. The first precept, abstaining from killing, is applied to understanding the cruelty of the industrial production of meat and breeding of animals for consumption. GLT discussions also address the arms industry that supports powerful societies and is linked to many wars around the world. The second precept, abstaining from stealing, takes up the injustice of a national and international economic order that allows the rich to steal from the poor with legal and political legitimacy. GLT participants also learn about alternative economic systems. As for the third precept, abstaining from sexual misconduct, GLT courses investigate the global structure of male dominance and exploitation of women and how the structures of patriarchal greed, hatred, and delusion relate to violence in the world. To address right livelihood. GLT organizes exposure trips to self-reliant communities that practise both cooperation to prevent exploitation as well as sustainable agriculture and handicraft production.

The last three spokes of the Eightfold Path — right effort, right mindfulness, and right concentration — are related to meditation. In order to encourage these aspects, the GLT courses include a weeklong retreat, integrating meditation, prayer, or puja practice into the daily schedule. Alumni are encouraged to do regular retreats and daily practice when they return to their communities. In the long term, the Spirit in Education Movement aspires to establish a residential college of sustainable communities for Southeast Asia. It is planned that courses will then devote about one-third of the time to meditation and other serious spiritual practices.

A Future with Less Suffering

Consumer monoculture is able to dominate contemporary society because individuals have become alienated from their Buddha-nature, from their culture, and from each other. Driven by greed, hatred, and illusion, we need to find ways to see this *tanha* to avoid destruction of soil, soul, and society. Empowerment education for grassroots communities and individuals from all social strata, providing tools to counteract these trends, is crucial. It must address both inner and outer landscapes in understanding *tanha* in order to give alternative thinking and behaviour a chance.

In Buddhist society it is believed that every being embodies Buddha-nature, the potential to attain the highest understanding, and that we should all strive for this. The poor and marginalized are entitled to the same dignity as everyone else in their struggles. These grassroots initiatives are a light for the future, as they emphasize the importance of critical examination, localization of power, and economic activity growing from, rather than deriding, indigenous local wisdom. The GLT and other similar initiatives in the region are a vital proactive approach, and the signs are that these will make a real difference to coming generations.

How much healthier would all our societies be if they were based on value systems that truly advocated sustainability rather than unlimited growth! A society where people help each other out in hard times. A society where power is shared rather than fought over, that reveres and respects nature rather than controlling and using it as a resource. A society unsullied by the poisons of *tanha*. A society with values steeped in spirituality and wisdom.

Concrete steps are being taken to manifest this vision through initiatives inspired by spirituality in general, and Buddhism specifically. A good number of committed people are working on these initiatives. They do not have all the answers, but they have a clear awareness of structural violence and a strong determination to work with the violence within the structures of their minds. They take the path of contemporary *bodhisattvas* confronting the suffering in themselves and in society in order to work for the liberation of all sentient beings. It is a very challenging yet enriching path — a combination of contemplation and activism, spirituality and politics, humour and seriousness. These committed people are returning to the very roots of traditional Buddhist teaching and using this power to move toward a wholesome and sustaining future.

Jørgen Skov Sørensen

Modernity, Diversity and Coexistence in Contemporary Society

A liberal theological view

Setting the scene: Someone – Somewhere

Nicholas Lash has reminded us that no discourse can 'speak of everywhere from nowhere in particular'.[1] No academic work – in fact, no activity at all – exists by itself but is always contextually situated. Some of the most obvious impact factors pertain to the individual researcher, the societal circumstances under which the work has been conceived and written, the personal inclinations of the author, and his or her social, national and gender related situation...religious affiliation, too, by the way.

Most important, indeed, as presupposition for the current paper, is the fact that I speak as a Christian theologian. I also speak from within a deep-rooted tradition of critical and questioning analysis of my surroundings. In particular, I am determined to bring about critical knowledge on the issue of 'modernity, diversity and coexistence in contemporary society'. I also wish to give readers an impression of current diversities, dynamics and trends in a liberal intra-Christian theological discourse as I see them from my particular place, situation and research findings.

Furthermore, I must underline that what is expressed here is not an official statement of my church. For, although I am employed by the Lutheran Church in Denmark in order to undertake certain international, ecumenical and theological responsibilities, what I am about to say on the nature of diversity and modernity is not endorsed by my church. Neither am I in any official way representing my church nor the church unit, the Office on International Relations of the Danish Lutheran Church, which is the unit where I spent my current professional life. Many colleagues in my church would not agree with my ideas. What I offer is, as indicated, a liberal view. It is also about diversities.

I address you as an individual researcher who has studied issues of 'diversity' and 'modernity' at some length and who wish to share my thesis and suggestions with like-minded as well as not-so-like-minded. If I represent anything or anyone it would be the long tradition of critical theological research done by theologians who have always challenged the mainstream theological convictions from the margins of the established church.

This said, my rather simple thesis or suggestion with this paper is that 'modernity' as a mindset we have known since the Enlightenment – as a way of looking at the world – *seems to have difficulties in coping with radical plurality as we encounter it in today's globalizing world*. Or, in other words, modernity as a pattern of perceiving and understanding the world, a pattern which has been dominant in Europe and the Western world as such for a couple of centuries, seems to run counter to radical plurality, or 'deep' plurality as David Ray Griffin has recently expressed it,[2] as an emerging factor in contemporary societies.

---

1 Nicholas Lash, *The Beginning and End of 'Religion'*, Cambridge, Cambridge University, 1996: 197.
2 David Ray Griffin (ed.), *Deep Religious Pluralism*, Louisville, Westminster John Knox, 2005.

What's on our mind? Modernity is!

In order to prove this point, let me take you through a few examples of modernity as a mindset. Also, I would like to give a few examples of emerging alternatives. However, most of all I would like to move on from here knowing that my contribution gave rise to a constructive academic discussion on the nature of modernity – a discussion which brings us just that little bit further in our collective, limited and fractioned understanding of the world around us.

How, then, is my thesis to be dealt with? What, in fact, are the indicative parameters of modernity? Can we speak of an Enlightenment or modernity project as if modernity is a given construction, set in stone? Gregor McLennan, in an article on the nature and characteristics of the Enlightenment and that which we subsequently have termed modernity, indicates rather strongly that it may not be quite as appropriate to talk about the 'Enlightenment Project' or the 'Project of Modernity' as scholars at times tend to do. The plethora of voices that belong to the modern period and which identify themselves with the Enlightenment and, later on, with modernity are by no means unified in their understanding of what their presuppositions are. However, McLennan also makes the observation that what we in general term 'modernity' does indeed have certain coherent features, which are typical of a certain standpoint or foundation from which modernity finds its starting point and builds itself up as a concrete expression. So, even if there is 'something slightly misleading' about the 'project' terminology so often employed both within and outside modernity's own ranks, McLennan, when he looks to his own professional field of social science, believes that there is a

> cluster of underlying assumptions and expectations about the nature of modern social theory which are shared by a significant number of social scientists and which stem from classical eighteenth- and nineteenth-century scientific aspirations.[3]

What exactly, then, is it that modernists have in common? Can we derive certain underlying assumptions and expectations that are typical for modern reasoning? If Peter Hamilton is correct in giving the Enlightenment and later modernity such comprehensive attributes as 'belief-system', 'world-view', and '*Zeitgeist*',[4] then surely there ought to be something that constitutes modernity, a frame of reference that is assumed when we act under modern presuppositions in the modern paradigm.

Illustration: The case of Habermas *versus* Lyotard

Illustrative of an attempt to identify more clearly what is the world-view derived from modernity we turn to the social sciences; here, we find one of the best examples of the dialogue on modernity as it has emerged in Western philosophy over the last 20–30 years. The debates between German philosopher Jürgen Habermas and French thinker

---

3 Gregor McLennan, 'The Enlightenment Project Revisited', in Stuart Hall, David Held and Tony McGrew (eds.), *Modernity and its Futures, Understanding Modern Societies Series*, Cambridge, Polity, with Blackwell and Open University, 1992: 328-372: 328. McLennan employs social science for his illustration. However, the general impression is that this is an observation that is not restricted to his own area of concern, but is found in all spheres of specialist research as well as lived (modern) life in general.
4 Peter Hamilton, 'What was the Enlightenment', in Stuart Hall and Bram Gieben (eds.), *Formations of Modernity*, Cambridge, Polity, 1992: 22-34: 22.

Jean-François Lyotard mainly took place in the 70s and 80s of the 20th century. The debates problematize the relationship between modernity and plurality in a previously unseen way. Simultaneously, they illustrate a profound change in attitude to 'plurality' and 'diversity' and situate the discussion in a context derived from questions on coexistence in a globalizing world.

Although I believe Jürgen Habermas can only be seen as a promoter of a modern mindset, it is fair to say that in the 70s he was aware of modernity's difficulties with deep plurality. He also takes a critical stand towards many thinkers on modernity and some of the activities carried out by a powerful Western world and legitimized by a modern mindset and view of the other. However, Habermas still opts for modernity as the only possible way of dealing with the diversities of the world as he makes the notion of 'consensus' into a cornerstone in his thinking: the peoples of the world need to adhere to consensus.[5]

The question is, rather, are the notions of unity and consensus too simplistic to describe a much more complex world? And, anyway, exactly whose consensus are we talking about? Does Habermas really imply a 'value-neutral' and 'non-contextual' consensus model? Jean-François Lyotard argues that Habermas did believe in such a 'value-neutral' and 'non-contextual' consensus model and, hence, he critiqued Habermas's notion of consensus, pointing to the profound complexity and deep diversity of our globalizing world.

As an alternative, Lyotard came up with the substitute notion of 'paralogy'. Contrary to the 'consensus' project launched by Habermas, Lyotard's notion of paralogy indicates, rather, a 'process' with a free flow of dissimilar ideas that allows for a deeper global diversity. Lyotard opts for an exchange of ideas that is not from the outset governed by a consensus-seeking mindset, one that is not seeking consensus as the end goal. Lyotard's claim is that his model provides a better option for peaceful coexistence that does the patronising consensus model promoted by Habermas.[6]

No doubt, my presentation of the philosophical debate, Habermas *versus* Lyotard, is overly simple. However, it does set the scene for a much wider discourse, one that in many and diverse ways finds its starting point in the background to the Habermas-Lyotard dispute. As a theologian, I am tempted to look at Christian theology, and add a few examples of theologies that, in comparable ways, seriously critique the modern mindset prevalent in much Christian theology since the Enlightenment.

Turning theological: Grace as a bridge builder

As a bridge builder between sociology and theology, we turn to the British sociologist of religion, Grace Davie. Davie, in her monograph, *Europe: The Exceptional Case*, makes an indirect, though rather significant, observation on the nature of a Europe whose mindset has been shaped by centuries of modernity.[7] Speaking of religious development and secularism in a European setting, Davie asks whether modern Europe, compared to other traditions of the world, is a special – a particular – case. Is Europe the exceptional case?

---

5 This is illustrated, e.g., in Jürgen Habermas, 'Modernity – An Incomplete Project', in Hal Foster (ed.), *The Anti-Aesthetic: Essays on Post Modern Culture*, Port Townsend, Bay, 1983: 3-15; see also his 'Modernity versus Postmodernity', in *New German Critique* 22 (Winter 1981): 3-14.

6 The term 'paralogy' is introduced in Jean-François Lyotard, *The Postmodern Condition: A Report on Knowledge*, Manchester, Manchester University, 1984.

7 Grace Davie, *Europe: The Exceptional Case: Parameters of Faith in the Modern World*, in Sarum Theological Lectures series, London, Darton Longman and Todd, 2002.

Davie is here giving voice to what must be seen as part of a larger landmark observation, which the West has witnessed recently. Whereas Europeans have tended to see their societal, religious and other standards as natural (one might even be tempted to say, 'God-given') worldwide principles, the recognized reality of globalization, along with emerging, strong postcolonial voices, cannot but question the legitimacy of this very viewpoint.[8]

From a non-Western theological perspective, the Malaysian Christian theologian Emanuel Gerrit Singgih expresses the case well. He speaks about the lack of 'context consciousness' in former Christian mission theology:

> Many Christians in the Third World received an image of their reality as being the same as the reality of Christians in the First World. Or better, Christians in the First World tend to see the world as being the same everywhere, and passed along this assumption to their Christian counterparts in the Third World, so that the latter see the world in the same way as them. The result is that Christians in the Third World have never seen the reality of their own world. It is only in recent times that Christians in the Third World become aware that Christianity in its western mould has a context, namely the context of Western Europe and the USA, which belongs to the First World.[9]

Here, though mainly speaking to an Asian or perhaps a Third World audience, Singgih has an important message for Europeans, too. He calls on them to realize that they themselves are trapped in their historical and cultural context or mindset. European theology is indeed a contextual notion and has always been. This fact, highlighted for me as a European by a Malaysian, brings us still closer to the core subject matter of what modernity can be more easily identified with, namely, a universalizing project.

In case this could not be seen from within Europe, voices from outside Europe, tabling their viewpoints in cross-cultural conversations, clearly tell us that modernity is basically a universalizing project. Let's look at this from an internal, European theological point of view.

To tame, to master, to take control... Seeking consensus?

German theologian and historian Werner Ustorf, in his and Hugh McLeod's book *The Decline of Christendom in Western Europe, 1750-2000*, remarks that 'We can only work in the culture we have got'. This refers to the fact that 'Christian Faith is in a constant conversation with the realities of the past' and that '[t]he the European past is that of the Enlightenment'.[10] Here, again, is highlighted the particularity of the European context: the modern mindset has been shaped by the Enlightenment.

---

8 Davie uses the example of Peter Berger's secularization theories that claimed an eventual and inevitable secularization of all cultures, see Davie, *Europe*: 17). This theory today seems obsolete in the light of thriving religiosity in most parts of the world including rapidly developing countries, e.g., the Newly Industrialized Countries (NICs) in East Asia, but also large parts of affluent contemporary USA. Berger most recently relates to the secularization question in his article 'Secularization and de-secularization', in Linda Woodhead et al. (eds.), *Religions in the Modern World: Traditions and Transformations*, London and New York, Routledge, 2002: 291-298. Here Berger challenges his own thesis through the empiric suggestion that 'secularization now appears to be the exception' (296).
9 Emanuel Gerrit Singgih, 'Globalization and Contextualization: Towards a New Awareness of One's Own Reality', in *Exchange. Journal of Missiological and Ecumenical Research* 29,4 (October 2000): 361.
10 Werner Ustorf, 'A Missiological Postscript', in Hugh McLeod and Werner Ustorf (eds.), *The Decline of Christendom in Western Europe, 1750-2000*, Cambridge, Cambridge University, 2003: 218-225: 224.

Ustorf attempts, elsewhere and in a more detailed manner, to identify the modernity project initiated by the Enlightenment philosophers and carried out by various European institutions including the Christian Church. He writes:

> [European churches] had repackaged the knowledge of God, putting it within the safe confines of a modern interpretation of Christianity as an absolute religion, and came to see themselves as the executors of divine history. This divine mandate included the conversion of anybody who might think differently [...]. At the centre stood a desire to tame any independent or local designs for life and religion, and with this to take control of their social forms. The intention was to master the ambiguity and fuzziness of the world by applying a universal religious rationality.[11]

Ustorf here is hinting at the close relationship between the world-view – or mindset – of the Christian churches and the modern mindset which he characterizes with phrases like 'safe confines', 'absolute religion', 'tame', 'to take control', 'to master', and 'universal rationality'. These words are used as constitutive labels for an ethos of modernity as, in Ustorf's example, it has emerged, born and bred in modern Western society. His argument takes him, eventually, to conclude that Christianity was ambiguously inculturated in the European drive to unify the world through a twofold process involving modernization and Christianization.[12]

In this light, one of the most significant missiological publications in recent years is Brian Stanley's *Christian Missions and the Enlightenment*. The publication is significant due to the way it comprehensively deals with the 'alliance' between modern Christian mission and modernity as a mindset. It has long been commonplace to identify the modern missionary movement with an anti-modern and anti-enlightenment ethos.[13] However, implicitly supporting Ustorf's point of view, Stanley points out that the missionaries of the traditional churches of the West represented a movement 'whose origins and contours owe an immense debt to the philosophical and cultural patterns of the Enlightenment'.[14] In our terminology: the modern mission movement was thoroughly shaped by the mindset of modernity.

Stanley's thesis is supported by Daniel W. Hardy. Hardy maintains that the modern missionary movement was limited by and governed by what he terms 'Enlightenment orthodoxy', which Hardy mainly associates with the universalizing ideas of the European modernity project. In this way, modern mission was made possible not only through the newly developed means of transport and communication, although they indisputably also made their mark on it, but, and importantly, by 'the enhanced sense of unity and potential of humanity that Enlightenment thought and practice embodied'.[15]

---

11 Werner Ustorf, 'Protestantism and Missions', in Alister E. McGrath and Darren C. Marks (eds.), *The Blackwell Companion to Protestantism*, Oxford, Blackwell, 2004: 392-402: 397-8.

12 Ustorf, 'Protestantism and Missions': 392.

13 That is, allegedly and hypothetically, due to the devastating impact of the Enlightenment on traditional Christianity. Lesslie Newbigin, as an explicit and influential mission thinker who turned against modernity and its secularizing understanding, has underscored and popularized this view; see e.g., Lesslie Newbigin, *The Gospel in a Pluralist Society*, London, SPCK, 1989.

14 Brian Stanley, 'Christian Missions and The Enlightenment: A Reevaluation', in Brian Stanley (ed.), *Christian Missions and The Enlightenment*, in Studies in the History of Christian Mission series, Grand Rapids, William B. Eerdmans, and, Cambridge, Curzon, 2001: 2.

15 Daniel W. Hardy, 'Upholding Orthodoxy in Missionary Encounters', in Stanley, *Christian Missions and The Enlightenment*: 215.

These few illustrations show an apparent interconnection and deep penetration by modernity of the modern mission movement as the world has come to know it since the Enlightenment. They illustrate how modernity's decisive marks have been added on to the way the West perceived and acted upon the rest of the world and upon the 'otherness' inherent within global realities such as these were laid bare for the Western powers and ecclesial principalities. However, they also show how modernity with its belief in global unity fails to recognize deep religious diversity and plurality; and with this we come back to the theme of this article, i.e., modernity, diversity and coexistence in contemporary society, and to my thesis that modernity has a problem in not being able to recognize profound and deep plurality and diversity.

A postmodern theology of diversity: Liberal theological voices

Our final question is now: Is Western Christianity approaching a change in perceptions? Is there a theological development taking shape, along with voices critical to modernity as we have here met them through Jean-François Lyotard? Is there a growing awareness also in Western theological thinking that the world is larger that what can be contained within one single framework, i.e., that of a modern mindset? And, maybe more importantly, will such changes towards an acceptance of plurality help us move into a more legitimate, a more reachable coexistence among the various elements of global plurality?

Let me bring two voices to the table: feminist theologian Rita Gross and John D'Arcy May. One of my favourite aphorisms in the current discourse is Rita Gross's, in which she describes her unease with the hierarchical structures of the Western mindset. She says:

> Why is it so difficult to deal with [religious] diversity and disagreement? My own suggested answer is that the difficulty is, in large part, due to a deeply entrenched tendency in Western thinking to turn difference into hierarchy [...]. If we are different, then one of us must be better.[16]

In this passage, Rita Gross points in a more or less veiled way to problems associated with the critique we have seen launched on modernity above: the Western modernity mindset as an 'either-or' one, and not a 'both-and' one. Therefore, differences are treated in a hierarchical manner. Gross represents here a feminist voice that not only runs counter to hierarchies of traditional masculinity and the patriarchy of Christian theology, she also analyses and launches an internal critique against modernity, 'a deeply entrenched tendency in western thinking'.

The second voice that I would like to bring forward is that of John D'Arcy May. May is even more straightforward in his critique of a universalizing religious project. He writes:

> The 'meliority principle,' the conviction of uniqueness and superiority based on divine revelation or the exclusive possession of higher truth, [...] in the end makes [the universalist religions] impossible, because their purported universality is in fact *someone's* particularity projected onto all. All the religions are having difficulty in grasping that the time when this may have been conceivable has passed.[17]

In his monograph *Transcendence and Violence* May points out that what once was possible, viz., to live out one's religious tradition in isolation from other traditions, is no

---

16 Quoted from memory.
17 John D'Arcy May, *Transcendence and Violence: The Encounter of Buddhist, Christian and Primal Traditions*, New York and London, Continuum, 2003: 149.

longer tenable. As quoted above, he alludes to this condition, hinting at the fact that in today's interconnected and globalized world, a system of complete and unambiguous truth always represents '*someone's* particularity projected unto all'.[18]

Critical of various attempts to create a 'global ethic', arguing that such attempts are extremely 'thin' and eligible for the critique associated with an alleged but questionable universalism, May implies that neither a withdrawal in a separatist fashion of segregated local traditions, nor aggressive and competitive scenarios based on religious assumptions of uniqueness and superiority are viable options in a globalizing world.[19]

May confirms the global religious traditions as distinct contextual expressions. At the same time, however, he acknowledges the role of globalization as a force which affects the variety of religious traditions which 'in the new context of globalization […] need to be mutually translatable without the threat of alienation or identity loss'.

May's conclusion from this insight is that, whereas the traditions until recently could (and did) live relatively isolated lives as traditions in their separate cultural contexts, and clarifying their identities for their own sake, so to speak, 'in the new context of globalization they can only do [that], if at all, together'.[20]

Is this back to the consensus model promoted by Habermas? No, it is not. May suggests and works with a more acceptable and more reconciling understanding of deep diversity among religious traditions than a traditional consensus model would allow. Also, if we combine May's critique of the 'meliority complex' of many religious traditions with Gross's pointing towards a tendency to make hierarchies out of differences in Western thinking, then we may get even closer to Lyotard's 'paralogy' model. Thus, we do not look for consensus, but for interconnected and reconciled diversity. I venture to say that we turn from modernity to post-modernity.

Does this turn have potential as a vision for religious coexistence in the 21st century? And if it does, is it a viable model to be applied to wider society through 'interconnected and reconciled diversity? Is it naïve to suggest that liberal religious voices make this their particular contribution to a world that is tormented by both patronising consensus-seekers and desperate religious extremists?

---

18 May, *Transcendence and Violence*: 149.
19 May, *Transcendence and Violence*: 150 and 149.
20 May, *Transcendence and Violence*: 151.

David Stevens
Look if You Like But You Will Have to Leap
The position of Ulster Protestants

Introduction

I know John D'Arcy May primarily through the Faith and Politics Group, of which we were both members. The Group began when a motion was passed at the 1983 Greenhills Ecumenical Conference calling for the setting up of a Christian Centre for Political Development to analyse the relationship of churches to politics in Ireland. A steering group was established and a number of people co-opted in an individual capacity. It quickly became clear that a Centre was not a realistic goal and the best role for the group was as an unofficial think-tank, reflecting concretely on the relationship of faith and politics through the particularity of the Northern Ireland conflict.

Around 30 people were involved for varying lengths of time from 1983 to 2002. John was part of the mix and he, in particular, was able to bring a wider international view to Northern Ireland's 'narrow ground'. This piece is offered to John in the spirit of our working together in the Faith and Politics Group.

Historic Fault Lines

Northern Ireland lies on a British/Irish fault line. In consequence, insecurity and anxiety have permeated Ulster Protestant existence. Fear of being annihilated, derived from settler/native opposition, has haunted Ulster Protestants. So also has fear of 'political popery'; indeed, anti-Catholicism has underpinned Protestant identity. These feelings, however, have co-existed with a sense of superiority: of religious superiority; of the Ulster Protestant community being imbued with divine approval; of Britain being more progressive and modern than Ireland; of Northern Irish/British/Protestant values being superior to Irish Catholic ones. All this has led to a recognition of Catholic Nationalists based on fear and mistrust, which, in turn, has led to a relationship founded on defensive living, injustice, dominance and exclusion, and an absence of trust, mutuality and equality. Uneasy 'peace' based on deterrence has often given way to violence.

As Irish Catholic power increased and the Irish national project developed in the 19th century, a mode of Protestant strength and protection was sought. What emerged was partition, and with it the protection of a British State and the control exercised as a majority in Northern Ireland.

After partition, the Northern Ireland State became the focus of Protestant communal identification and its policies helped to sustain community solidarity. Nationalist hostility and periodic Republican violence also helped to maintain solidarity (as well as anxiety). Community solidarity had to contain and manage considerable religious and class differences, as well as an East/West geographical divide.

The main cultural foci of the new State were Protestantism and Britishness. Indeed, Protestant faith and Britishness meshed into one common fabric. The Government identified with a Protestant public culture and the Protestant churches in turn identified with the new State and supported it. The political manifestations of Protestantism, for example, the Orange Order, were important and influential. Political Protestantism was a sustaining and bonding force for many.

Identity was given a stronger British focus by the experience of the Second World War and by the post-war integration of Northern Ireland into the British Welfare State. Indeed, the benefits of the Welfare State were to provide some of the elements in the desire for change among the nationalist minority that was to lead to Northern Ireland being transformed beyond recognition. In the 1960s some Unionists and others within the Protestant churches realized that there had to be a change – a perception shared to some extent by the then Prime Minister, Terence O'Neill. This need for change was strongly resisted by many other Unionists and by figures within Protestantism – a key person being Ian Paisley, who came to embody political and religious resistance. Meanwhile, Northern Ireland society moved towards crisis, incapable of significant internal reform.

The Crisis since 1969

The crisis was precipitated in the late 1960s by the Civil Rights movement, led to the dismantling of the alliance between the Unionist community and the British State, culminating in the end of the Northern Ireland Parliament in 1972. After that date the British State sought a new approach to the government of Northern Ireland. These British policies deepened Unionist divisions. In reality, political divisions and strains had always been there – between loyalists at one end of the spectrum and liberal Unionists at the other. However, they intensified in the early 1970s with the creation of the Democratic Unionist Party at one extreme and the Alliance Party at the other.

Since the mid-1970s there has been a fundamental strategic question facing Unionists, namely, how the Union (of Great Britain and Ireland) should now be protected. Was it through full integration with the rest of the UK, or, was it through devolved institutions over which Unionists might exercise some control? If it were the latter, should power sharing be accepted? If so, with whom? No one view gained the upper hand. In fact, political fragmentation and incoherence increased. Unionists also had to increasingly face the reality that while they could bring down particular political settlements they could not impose their own.

The Problematic of Britishness

At an even more fundamental level, however, British intervention and policies widened Unionist divisions by discomforting a major aspect of Northern Irish Unionist identity: its Britishness. The signing of the Anglo-Irish Agreement in 1985 was a huge shock and added enormously to the discomfort and disillusion of many Unionists; it was, in the words of poet Tom Paulin, 'the defenestration of Hillsborough'. It increased in them, a sense of betrayal and abandonment by a British Government apparently unwilling to put down terrorism. Some began a search for other sources of identity, e.g., Ulster Scots.

Northern Ireland Protestants differ in their reasons for valuing the Union and in what Britishness means to them. Some value the Union because they have a deep sense of belonging and loyalty and affinity with Britain – to its institutions, culture and people. They wish to be part of a British world or way of life. Others value particular British institutions and traditions or the British economic subvention. There are also those for whom the Union serves a defensive function: it is a defence of Protestant interests against Roman Catholicism and a United Ireland. For many, indeed, there is a strong conditional quality to their support. While for some, being British is their primary identity, for others it is an addition to a more specific communal identity. Whatever these differences, there has been a distinctive Ulster variety of British political identity.

What has become clear, however, is that the meanings traditionally given to Britishness by many Ulster Protestants are no longer a sustaining or an adequately bonding force. Britishness itself has changed over the past half century: secularization, which has meant that Protestantism has waned as a key ideological component in Britishness, the end of empire, the huge and increasing importance of Europe and the parallel decline in the authority of the British state, as well as the ebbing of respect for the institution of monarchy are all elements of that change. What is also clear is that, since 1920, the deep structure of British policy has been to insulate Northern Ireland from British politics, in consequence of which there is an increasingly tenuous relationship with the wider British community. All this has created a sense of Northern Ireland being on the edge of the Union.

The deep insecurities and vulnerabilities of this position are a reality and the consequences have to be acknowledged, for instance, the sense of precarious belonging. The fragile political base of their British identity is one reason which leads Unionists to resist any moves that would dilute the Britishness of Northern Ireland. This accounts for why flags, emblems and anthems are so important: they express and focus people's sense of belonging.

Political Protestantism

Political Protestantism, too, is no longer a sustaining or bonding force. Partly this is because of secularization (particularly in working class communities) and partly because of a critical 'reserve' by the mainstream Protestant churches. The latter have been unwilling to support or condone violence, or, to approve or condemn the idolatry of 'for God and Ulster'. Another factor has been the developing of relations with the Roman Catholic Church. The Orange Order, the exemplar of Political Protestantism, sought, through contestations around parades, to recover the 'old realities'; these realities were challenged by nationalist residents groups and, when it picked a battle with the British State at Drumcree, the Order ultimately lost. Thus, the Orange Order finds itself marginalized and leaderless, particularly in urban areas.

Melting into Air

There is a sense for Unionists of 'everything solid melting into air', which the Good Friday Agreement is accelerating. The Agreement created a fluidity and malleability about the Northern Ireland State; the whole framework of society is altering. Further, the State and its institutions are being remodelled and this is most evident in the changes in the security forces and policing. Reform of the Royal Ulster Constabulary (RUC) and the phasing out of the Royal Irish Regiment (RIR) also raise the issue in its most potent form: who will protect us now? We have now reached the end of the Protestant tradition of armed militia (or the echo of them) that began with the Plantation of Ulster four hundred years ago. No wonder, then, that there is an unwillingness by loyalist paramilitaries to decommission.

Furthermore, the release of paramilitary prisoners has offended a community's sense of right and wrong. Many perceive that 'unrepentant' perpetrators are rewarded and innocent victims of violence are not; that the sacrifices of the heroic protectors from unjustified violence are devalued; and, that virtue and restraint are not given recognition. A party with paramilitary links is allowed to enter government. Thus, it appears, the moral universe is turned upside down.

Continuing paramilitary violence (although at a much lower level) and the refusal of the Provisional IRA to decommission weapons until recently have meant that the promise of peace has not come. There is the fear of a mafia society and of general lawlessness. Insecurity remains. There has been a disenchantment with the peace process and an impression that the British Government is prepared to do deals with Republicans to defend British interests but to concede on issues of importance to Unionists.

The Unionist community has been profoundly disorientated by the Provisional IRA cease-fire – 'all changed, utterly changed' as a result of it. Lives have been profoundly shaped by violence. The paradoxical solidarity created by violence disappears. Loyalist paramilitary turns on loyalist paramilitary and areas fragment. The world changes. We had a script, we had a language by which we have described ourselves and the situation. Now, there is a huge empty space that the old story occupied. Now, we have to discover who we are again. Of course, change can be denied and we can seek to hang on to the old enemy. However, when they – Irish Catholic Nationalists, Northern Republicans – change, we have to change or be plunged into crisis:

> And now what shall become of us without any barbarians?
> Those people were some kind of solution.[1]

The reconvening of the Northern Assembly in May 2007, with Ian Paisley as First Minister, and Martin McGuinness as the Deputy First Minister, opens a new chapter in the story of relations between the communities in Northern Ireland. What it will mean for the Unionist community, in particular, is too early to say.

Socio-Economic Change

Protestant economic power has declined significantly over the last 30 years and there has been a significant change in demography over the same period. There is a profound re-balancing of power and resources going on between the two main communities.

The collapse of industrial Belfast (which existed for over 100 years), in particular, has had profound consequences. The socio-economic basis for a working class Ulster-British community has been eroded by industrial decline, political change and defeat, by demographic shift and by a collapse in narratives of Britishness and Political Protestantism. These are communities experiencing a gradual but accelerating process of breakdown – a hollowing out. The riots and widespread mayhem which swept Belfast, and other places in Northern Ireland in the second week of September 2005, and which had its immediate triggers, must be seen in this light. Of course, industrial decline is a feature of other cities in other places: Glasgow, Liverpool, Swansea, Dresden, Detroit. Yet, the particular intensity of the crisis in Belfast is made more acute because of where Ulster Protestants find themselves at this time. Here are people who have been rendered defenceless by economic, social, cultural and political change – the only (dysfunctional) protection being provided by paramilitary organizations. History is flowing in the wrong direction.

---

1 From Constantine P. Cavafy's poem 'Waiting for the Barbarians'.

There is a painful process of adapting to change and the loss of dominance. Some want to return to an imagined yesterday, to retreat from a future which looks more and more unpalatable. Some have a sense of apocalyptic threat. Others seek to re-negotiate their identities, perhaps to emphasize the religious over the political. Many opt out and seek to coast along in a private world of material prosperity (increasing numbers of Unionists in East Ulster, for instance, no longer vote). There is defensiveness, pain, denial, despair and numbness.

In this context the DUP has emerged as the largest Unionist Party, in an apparent triumph of Political Protestantism. This triumph may prove empty. The reality is the weakness of Political Protestantism and a movement in the tectonic plates on the fault line: of industrial decline, of changed demographics and power balances in Northern Ireland, of a transformed British/Irish relationship, of changed relationships on the island with a vibrant economy and society in the South, of secularization, of a changed relationship with Britain.

The struggle within contemporary Unionism involves not just constitutional issues and the compromises required by the Good Friday Agreement but also attitudes to modernity and social change, and the moral issues thrown up by modernity and social change.

The challenge will be to give leadership and to tell a narrative of reality, rather than to reflect peoples' fears, hurts, grievances and sense of loss. If reality is not faced up to, actions are likely to get more desperate, logic more twisted, and rhetoric more rabid and paranoid. The choices are difficult but as W.H. Auden warns, 'look if you like, but you will have to leap'. And the DUP and Ian Paisley are having to take the decision to leap.

A Broken Story

What is being described above is the breaking of a story, or at the very least a story under severe strain. If a foundational story of who we are as a people is broken then meaning, identity and a place in history are lost. It may be that a literal place is lost as well. The crisis of a broken story is played out in repetitive, and often destructive and violent, loyalist activity and in self-pitying victimhood, and in other parts of the Unionist community, in frozen denial or diversionary activity. This crisis cannot be answered by trying to talk people into rationality or into pursuing pragmatic self-interest, or by throwing money at supposed or actual problems, or by asking people to let go of the past they hold dear. Nor can it be found by the invention of a differentiating language like Ulster-Scots.

The challenge is to 'restory', to find a narrative that gives meaning to community life and ongoing relationships. It will link the past with the future and create purpose in the present. It is not any 'restorying' however. It is about constructive expression (so it *is* about finding a language), and it is about positive interaction with others. They have to be included in the story too. And within a reality of inter-dependence, this story has to find its place with other people's stories. A lot of this necessary work will be hidden from the eyes of pragmatic politics and the world of quick fixes which often seeks immediate solutions to complex problems. It is at the point of brokenness that work needs to be done, so that new and positive energy will come.

Losing a Sacred

If you take away something sacred from people you are taking away part of the binding and organizing power that gives identity, meaning, togetherness, security and a sense of good and bad. Over the last 30 years 'sacred' things – Britishness, Stormont, the RUC – have come under threat or been lost. One of the natural reactions of people who are in the process of losing their identity, their security and togetherness is violent anger. We have been containing and navigating the violent anger of the loyalist paramilitaries for a long time now. Another reaction is to look for new victims so as to bring back unity, identity and togetherness – and so, racial and ethnic minorities can be a convenient target. Yet another reaction can be numbness, lostness, depression and withdrawal.

The loss of a 'sacred' has to be worked through. It took Protestants in the Republic of Ireland two generations to do so and in that the role of the Church of Ireland in supporting people was important. It might be that the Protestant churches could play a similar role in Northern Ireland. Also, people need to be given space and time in order to allow new possibilities and relationships to develop. Old 'sacreds' cannot be brought back; they do, however, have to be mourned and memorialized.

Part 5

John D'Arcy May
and Ecumenics

Heinz-Günther Stobbe
Between Melancholy and Anger – Looking Back on Common Days

'We are all getting older.' You frequently hear this statement or pronounce it yourself – and the older you get, the more often. This would actually be superfluous; after all, it seems a mere banality. However, that is just what it is not. 'We' does refer to us, to both of us. We do not talk about humankind in general, we talk about us. When conducting a logico-linguistic analysis – this, John, is your special field – there is a considerable difference between the (in this case popular) statement that 'all humans are mortal', or 'I am mortal', or even 'I am dying'. It is all about the 'pragmatic use' (Habermas) of this statement in a certain context, not just about its objective content. However, you know this better.

It is about time to make a confession: I was a bit startled to use the statement, '[w]e are all getting older' on this occasion in your honour. It is not your age startling me, but the sudden awareness of how long we have known each other, and that it is already a long time since we both studied and did our doctorates at the chair of Peter Lengsfeld and became assistants at the Institute for Ecumenical Theology afterwards. This, too, makes me think of a popular idiom: it was ages ago! Unfortunately, this also applies to our common days. I do not remember the exact date of our first meeting, but I am still aware of the place and occasion: it was in the library of our institute, and we took part in a seminar of Peter Lengsfeld's dealing with the linguistic analysis of ecumenical documents. I had to present a seminar paper on using adjectives in such texts. At that time, none of us had any idea of the extent to which these questions would shape our work to come. Thinking of these days makes me feel as if everything has happened in a different life! Yet, this forms just one part of my memory, the one slowly fading away. At the same time, remembering these days gives rise to strong emotions, especially to overwhelming melancholy. Although the following years, in the course of which we pursued different ways through life, give no reasons for complaint, there has never been again such excitement, intensity and creativity as in our common days.

Of course, in getting older we gloss over the time when we were young, and I do not underestimate the worries which were burdening us, especially professional ones. For certain reasons, the academic career we were striving for receded more and more into the distance. At least, this was the impression for a long wearisome while. During the first years we did not really care about this, though. We were enthusiastic about ecumenical theology, which – without exaggeration – made us, with Peter and some other companions, break new ground. Peter was the one providing the impetus, simultaneously granting us space to talk, think and do research. Within this space, our different talents and starting points enabled us to pursue his basic idea concerning a theory for ecumenical processes. The first step he took was an essay entitled 'Macht als Faktor in ökumenischen Prozessen' (Power as a Factor in Ecumenical Processes), which was published in *Una Sancta* in 1973. I do not know whether this essay was meant to be programmatic, but indeed it was, as it already contained all the important thoughts and subjects we would deal with later on: a plea for an interdisciplinary ecumenical theology as a theory for ecumenical processes, based on central notions such as 'truth', 'identity' and 'sociality'. The missing theoretical frame was added later in the form of 'Collusion Theory' (J. Willi).

In 1980, Peter published a substantial book entitled 'Ecumenical Theology', which we referred to as 'the blue book' due to its cover. In numerous articles, the innovative concept was unfolded and explained in detail. Still today, i.e., nearly thirty years later, I consider this joint work as pioneering. Needless to say, after having made enormous efforts, we all felt relieved and rightly proud of this result. However, even before publication, we had to realize that our honest intention to serve the ecumenical movement and to promote its theology would not find the appreciation we hoped for. Due to its size, the publisher was prepared to print the book solely with a substantial monetary contribution. Therefore, we 'did door-to-door canvassing' to raise the amount necessary; one could also put it like this: we went begging. It soon emerged that no ecclesiastical authority was prepared to invest a single Deutschmark (which was then the national currency). This was not due to any financial crisis; they just did not want to sponsor 'such a book'. According to the Deutsche Ökumenische Studienausschuss (DÖSTA, German Ecumenical Studies Commission) it was neither sound nor helpful to the ecumenical movement to support 'such severe criticism of the Roman Catholic Church'. I well remember the disappointment and our slowly rising anger when it became clear that the publication was doomed to failure. However, a certain degree of anger can turn out to be positive. Without it, I would have never hit upon the idea of taking the money out of our private purses. And so it happened: the members of the institute pooled whatever money they could and the 'blue book' was published.

This – at least from our point of view – happy ending could make us easily forget this episode. However, we had some more negative experiences, too. To our surprise, the Katholische Nachrichtenagentur (Catholic News Agency) reacted very quickly; this would have been pleasant had the criticism not been so devastating or without either fairness or understanding. It was not merely stupid but malicious and so insulting that we seriously considered taking legal steps. When both editor and publisher refused to give any comment, we let the matter rest out of self-esteem, though we did not resign. Afterwards, there was dead silence. One day, this seemed to change. We learned that the DÖSTA (!) had dealt with the blue book exclusively during one of its meetings. This should have pleased us. However, there was a small but important drop of bitterness: we had not been invited to, or even informed of, the meeting, even though Peter was a member of the DÖSTA and the office of its chairman was next to our institute. One might say that this is what, in ecclesiastical fields, is commonly known as 'excommunication'. I do not exaggerate when I say: the blue book was completely hushed up, and one could only find scattered quotations from single articles. There was neither a detailed review nor a reception. And this is still the situation. Recently, two introductions to ecumenical theology were published in Germany, and in both of them the blue book is not even part of the bibliography. I most readily admit that this is when the old anger rises again. I would like to laugh about this, because in the cold light of day the fate of our book teaches an important lesson concerning truth, power and identity. Still, I simply am unable to face this with the relaxed calmness of old age. I am still concerned about the ecumenical movement, and I am arrogant enough to think that the theory of ecumenical processes is suitable for understanding the standstill we have seen in the past few years. I do not want to say that the theory is perfect. For, already in 1980, when the blue book first saw the light of day, we were both convinced of the constant need for clarification.

It has always been correct to put the different dimensions and levels of the ecumenical movement into one comprehensive theory. You just need to look at world politics, where struggles over identity, conviction, and power often occur, to realize that we have been on the right path. Of course, according to some persons dealing with ecumenical theology, this very kind of comparison should be ruled out. Our concept critically considered aspects of the social sciences and linguistic analysis in ecumenical fields, but while we thought this an advantage, some persons blamed us for doing so. Nonetheless, I say that none of us seriously assumed we had come up with 'just the thing'. We thought that in comparison to other concepts, ours had slightly better possibilities for analyzing complex and sometimes contradictory ecumenical events. However, we did not succeed in precisely grasping how different factors 'interact' (collusion). We were determined to do some more work on this aspect, but it turned out differently, though for reasons not pertinent to the issue and related to events that happened 'ages ago'. After leaving Münster with Margret you ended up in quite a remote corner of the world, at least from a Münsteranean point of view: Papua New Guinea. However far away this place may be geographically, concerning ecumenical matters, it is very close to us. When I take the blue book and read your article about finding the way from the inner-Christian to the interreligious dialogue, then it seems as if Providence was playing a part. You have written and spoken of quite a few aspects of your activities, and I have always had the impression that, in spite of all adversities, you really found your mission: promoting a global ecumenical movement. At the same time, however, the 'spirit of Münster' has been perceptible; it has been our common 'inspiration', and we have tried to remain true to it in our new and different areas of work and life. Returning, then, to a comparatively provincial Europe – in your case, Ireland – has not changed anything. Whenever we met, it was very easy to overcome the distance between us. May I see this as a sign of true friendship linking us – Margret, you and me – together although we rarely meet?

If both of us were younger and lived closer together (and if I was healthier), I'd love to write another book with you. If it were up to me, it would deal with the global importance of the ecumenical movement, with the 'consensus of those who suffer' and with the Church as a conciliar community. Perhaps this book, too, would be ignored, just like the blue one. But, as John Wayne puts it: 'A man's got to do what a man's got to do'. I am just afraid that this dream will not now come true. It must be sufficient to have come to know you, to have learnt with you and from you and to dream of our common days of long time ago. As the Bible puts it, everything has its season. The 'beautiful days of Aranjuez' are irrevocably over. I would like to place special emphasis on my deep gratefulness for our cooperation and everything linked with it, especially for the friendship with you and Margret, the passionate debates in the graduates' colloquium and not forgetting the celebrations. This does not need to be over, especially as you are now going into your 'restless retirement', releasing you from many burdens. I am sure you will not be bored; perhaps you will write another book, a summary of your experience and studies. This would be nice, but only if you frequently quoted the blue book and our (common) essays. Once in a while, we all need to be praised and if other people do not do so, then we have to do it ourselves. As far as you are concerned, this short flashback is meant to be a beginning.

Translated by Judith Wegener

Robyn Reynolds
Australian Accent

Recently, remembering John, a Melbourne friend recalled, 'You know after all these years, he never lost his Australian accent.'

And there's the heart of it! From his earliest years, grounded in the Grampians, land of the Gunditjmara Aboriginals, and nurtured in the profound love and wisdom of parents, Frank and May, John held and developed that Australian accent. As the years passed, he shaped his own tones and resonances certainly, and discovered his own pitch and style; but in recognizing and celebrating that basic 'home chord', his far-reaching intellect perhaps often found – and shared – a particular focus or inspiration drawn from the deep waters and mysteries of the billabong.

John's playfulness, his awe in the wonders of our universe, his keen mind and contemplative spirit were already apparent in childhood years. In the 50s in Hamilton back-yards and on Monivea paddocks, seeds for the interreligious and inter-cultural encounter were being firmly planted. And now: what a courageous, gifted thinker we are honouring! And a man of peace: gentle, hardworking, humble – and prophetic!

In *Transcendence and Violence*, John invites us to celebrate 'the sacrament of the Stranger' (154). Today, many countries, religions, traditions, can call him 'friend'. Fundamentally, in his person as well as his writings, John is about 'transcending violence' through peace.

> *Brilliant soft light, Morning Star shine!*
> *Didgeridoo earth-beat remain!*
> *Ghostly gum whisper your deepest wisdom*
> *And Grange River flow again...*

Published Work by John D'Arcy May

Publications – Books

2007 (ed.), *Converging Ways? Conversion and Belonging in Buddhism and Christianity*, Sankt Ottilien, EOS

2003 *Transcendence and Violence: The Encounter of Buddhist, Christian and Primal Traditions*, London & New York, Continuum

1999 *After Pluralism: Towards an Interreligious Ethic*, Münster, Hamburg and London, LIT Verlag [lectures delivered under the inaugural Ethel Hayton Fellowship, University of Wollongong, Australia, July-August 1994]

1998 (ed.), *Pluralism and the Religions: The Theological and Political Dimensions*, London and Herndon VA, Cassell

1990 *Christus Initiator. Theologie im Pazifik*, Düsseldorf, Patmos

1989 (co-editor, with Bernard Narokobi, R.G. Crocombe, Paul Roche) *Lo bilong yumi yet: Law and Custom in Melanesia*, number 12 in Point Series, Goroka, The Melanesian Institute; Suva, University of the South Pacific

1985 (ed.), *Living Theology in Melanesia: A Reader*, number 8 in Point Series, Goroka, The Melanesian Institute

1984 *Meaning, Consensus and Dialogue in Buddhist-Christian Communication: A Study in the Construction of Meaning*, volume 31 in Studies in the Intercultural History of Christianity, Berne and New York, Peter Lang

1976 *Sprache der Ökumene – Sprache der Einheit. Die Einheit der Menschheit: Zukünftige Grundlage der theologischen Ethik der Katholischen Kirche und des Ökumenischen Rats der Kirchen?*, number 12 in Forum Theologiae Linguisticae, Bonn, Verlag Linguistica Biblica

Publications – Articles, conference papers, extensive reviews, etc.

2007 [with Linda Hogan] 'Social Ethics in Western Europe', in *Theological Studies* 68: 154-171

2007 'Education Then and Now: Reflections on the 50th Anniversary of Monivae College, Hamilton', in *Journal of Religious Education* 55,1: 38-40

2007 'Nothingness-*qua*-Love? The Implications of Absolute Nothingness for Ethics', in Jerald J. Gort, Henry Jansen and Hendrik M. Vroom (eds.), *Probing the Depths of Evil and Good: Multireligious Views and Case Studies*, Amsterdam and New York, Rodopi: 135-150

2007 'Europe's God: Liberator or Oppressor? The Postcolonial Mediation of Transcendence', in Norbert Hintersteiner (ed.), *Naming and Thinking God in Europe Today: Theology in Global Dialogue*, Amsterdam and New York, Rodopi: 69-92

2006 'Buddhists, Christians and Ecology', in Perry Schmidt-Leukel (ed.), *Buddhism, Christianity and the Question of Creation: Karmic or Divine?*, Aldershot, Ashgate: 93-107

2006 'Muslims in the Free Society', in *Doctrine and Life* 56,6: 22-28

2006 'Rootedness: Reflections on Land and Belonging', in Werner G. Jeanrond and Andrew D. Mayes (eds.), *Recognising the Margins: Developments in Biblical and Theological Studies. Essays in Honour of Seán Freyne*, Dublin, Columba Press: 146-159

2006 'Human Dignity, Human Rights, and Religious Pluralism: Buddhist and Christian Perspectives', in *Buddhist-Christian Studies* 26: 51-60

2006 'Interreligious Studies in the University: Help or Hindrance to Peace?', in Toh Swee-hin and Virginia Cawagas (eds.), *Cultivating Wisdom, Harvesting Peace*, Brisbane, Multi-Faith Centre, Griffith University: 291-298

2006 [with Linda Hogan] 'Gender and Culture as Dimensions of Bodiliness', in Harm Goris (ed.), *Bodiliness and Human Dignity: An Intercultural Approach / Leiblichkeit und Menschenwürde. Interkulturelle Zugänge*, Münster and Berlin, LIT Verlag: 45-57

2006 'The Space in Between: Mission as Reconciliation', in *Norsk tidsskrift for misjon* 60 [Spiritualitet og dialog: Festskrift til Professor Dr. Notto Reidar Thelle]: 205-216

2005 'On Trying to be a Theologian', in Gesa E. Thiessen and Declan Marmion (eds.), *Theology in the Making: Biography, Contexts, Methods*, Dublin, Veritas: 112-120

2005 'Alternativa a Dio? Le religioni nella sfera pubblica globale', in Antonio Autiero (ed.), *Teologia nella Città, Teologia per la Città: La dimensione secolare delle scienze teologiche*, Bologna, Edizioni Dehoniane: 95-109

2005 'Nothingness-qua-Love? The Loss and Recovery of "God" in Buddhist-Christian Dialogue', Free University of Amsterdam, 17-19 March; Joint conference of Irish Theological Association and (British) Society for the Study of Theology, St Patrick's College, Drumcondra, Dublin, 29 March – 1 April

2005 'Guided Diversity? Interreligious Dialogue and Education for Peace', Multi-Faith Education for Harmony and Peace, Faculty of Education, State Islamic University, Jakarta, Indonesia, 1-3 February 2005

2005 'The Religions and the Powers in West Papua', in Michael Biehl and Amélé Adamavi-Aho Ekué (eds.), *Gottesgabe. Vom Geben und Nehmen im Kontext gelebter Religion. Festschrift zum 65. Geburtstag von Theodor Ahrens*, Frankfurt a.M., Lembeck: 199-213

2004 'Visible Unity as Realised Catholicity', in *Swedish Missiological Themes*, 92,1: 55-61

2004 'The Dialogue of Religions: Source of Knowledge? Means of Peace?', in *Current Dialogue* 43: 11-18

2004 'A Catholic Theology of Religious Pluralism: The Recent Work of Jacques Dupuis SJ', in *Priests and People* 18,1: 28-30

2004 [co-authored with Linda Hogan] 'Gender and Culture as Dimensions of Bodiliness', Bodiliness and Human Dignity: An Intercultural Approach, Conference of the Centre for Intercultural Ethics, University of Tilburg, Netherlands, 19-21 November

2004 'Whose Universality? Which Interdependence? Community, Ecology and Human Rights', Second conference on 'Thinking God in Europe Today', Leuven, Belgium, 2-12 September 2004

2004 'The Space In Between: Mission as Reconciliation', in Geraldine Smith OP (ed.), *Distance Becomes Communion: A Dominican Symposium on Mission and Hope*, Dublin, Dominican Publications: 76-87

2004 'Loving Nothingness? Possibilities of Prayer in Buddhism and Christianity', in *Swedish Missiological Themes* 92,3 [*The Dynamics of Mission and Dialogue: Studies in Honour of Aasulv Lande*]: 371-381

2004 'Universalität oder Partikularität der Menschenrechte? Eine interreligiöse Perspektive', in Jan Jans (ed.), *Für die Freiheit verantwortlich. Festschrift für Karl-Wilhelm Merks zum 65. Geburtstag*, Freiburg, Academic Press Fribourg / Freiburg and Wien, Herder: 148-161

2004 'Cosmic Religion and Metacosmic Soteriology: The "Completion" of Interreligious Dialogue by Primal Traditions', in Robert Crusz, Marshal Fernando and Asanga Tilakaratne (eds.), *Encounters with the Word: Essays to Honour Aloysius Pieris SJ on his 70th Birthday*, Colombo, Ecumenical Institute for Study and Dialogue: 351-364

2004 'Alternative a Dio? Le Religioni nella Sfera Pubblica Globale', in *ITC Informa. Periodico dell'Istituto Trentino di Cultura* 19,2: 19-20

2003 'God in Public: The Religions in Pluralist Societies', in *Bijdragen: International Journal in Philosophy and Theology* 64,3: 249-262

2003 [review article] 'The Elusive Other: Recent Theological Writing on Religious Pluralism', in *Studies in Interreligious Dialogue* 13,1: 114-124

2003 [co-authored with Linda Hogan] 'Constructing the Human: Dignity in Interreligious Dialogue', in *Concilium* 2003,2 [Regina Ammicht-Quinn, Maureen Junker-Kenny and Elsa Tamez (eds.), *The Discourse of Human Dignity*, London, SCM]: 78-89

2003 'Interreligious Dialogue and the End of Ecumenism', in David W. Chappell (ed.), *Socially Engaged Spirituality: Essays in Honor of Sulak Sivaraksa on His 70th Birthday*, Bangkok, Sathirakoses-Nagapradipa Foundation: 476-485

2003 'God in Public: The Religions in Pluralist Societies', in *Bijdragen: International Journal in Philosophy and Theology* 64,3: 249-264

2003 'Internalising the Primal Other: Aboriginal Religion and European Christianity', in Andrew Pierce and Geraldine Smyth OP (eds.), *The Critical Spirit: Theology at the Crossroads of Faith and Culture. Essays in Honour of Gabriel Daly OSA*, Dublin, Columba Press: 79-96

2003 'The Postcolonial Mediation of Transcendence', at the American Academy of Religion Annual Meeting, Atlanta, Georgia, November

2002 'Living Buddha, Living Christ? Interreligious Dialogue and the Crisis of Christology', in *South Pacific Journal of Mission Studies* No. 26: 25-31 [Polding Lecture, St John's College, University of Sydney, 27 August 2001]

2002 'Education as Initiation? Some South Pacific Perspectives', in *Journal of Religious Education* 50,2: 45-52

2002 'Ethic of Survival or Vision of Hope? The Aim of Interreligious Dialogue', in *Dharma World* 29 (Sept.-Oct.): 25-28

2002 'Der Osten des Westens. Europa vor der Herausforderung des interreligiösen Dialogs', in *Ost-West. Europäische Perspektiven* 3: 243-253

2002 [thesis report] 'The Theology of Aloysius Pieris', in *Swedish Missiological Themes* 90,3: 413-417

2001 'Mehr als Schulung. Religiöses Lernen als Identitätsstiftung im Südpazifik', in Engelbert Gross and Klaus König (eds.), *Religiöses Lernen der Kirchen im globalen Dialog. Weltweit akute Herausforderungen und Praxis einer Weggemeinschaft für Eine-Welt-Religionspädagogik*, Münster, Hamburg and London, LIT Verlag: 107–121 [paper read at International Religious Education Congress, Catholic University of Eichstätt, Bavaria, 13-16 October 1999]

2001 'Catholic Fundamentalism? Some Implications of *Dominus Iesus* for Dialogue and Peacemaking', in Michael Rainer (ed.), *"Dominus Iesus": Anstössige Wahrheit oder anstössige Kirche?*, Münster, Hamburg and London, LIT Verlag: 112-133

2001 'A Rationale for Reconciliation', in *Uniting Church Studies* 7,1: 1-13

2001 'Verantwortung *Coram Deo?* Europa zwischen säkularer und interreligiöser Ethik', in Karl-Wilhelm Merks (ed.), *Verantwortung – Ende oder Wandlungen einer Vorstellung? Orte und Funktionen der Ethik in unserer Gesellschaft*, Münster, Hamburg and London, LIT Verlag: 193-207 [paper read at 29th International Congress of German Moral Theologians and Social Ethicists, Tilburg, Bovendonk, 20-24 September 1999]

2001 'Economics and Culture in the South Pacific', in Lucia A. Reisch (ed.), *Ethical-Ecological Investment: Towards Global Sustainable Development*, Frankfurt a.M., IKO-Verlag für Interkulturelle Kommunikation: 117-122

2001 'Catholic Fundamentalism? Some Implications of *Dominus Iesus* for Dialogue and Peacemaking', in *Horizons* 28,2: 271-293

2001 'Response to Rabbi Sidney Brichto', in Tony Bayfield, Sidney Brichto and Eugene J. Fisher (eds.), *'He Kissed Him and They Wept': Towards a Theology of Jewish-Catholic Partnership*, London, SCM: 228-232

2000 'Strange Encounters: On Transcending Violence by Transcending Difference', in *Studies in World Christianity* 6,2: 224-244

2000 'The Millennial Mission of South Pacific Christianity', in *Neue Zeitschrift für Missionswissenschaft* 56: 204-211; also, *Zeitschrift für Mission* 26: 163-171

2000 'Economics and Culture in the South Pacific: Some Presuppositions of Ethical Investment in Aboriginal and Melanesian Contexts', in Project Group Ethical-Ecological Rating Frankfurt-Hohenheim (eds.), *Intercultural Comparability of the Ethical Assessment of Enterprises According to Criteria of Cultural, Social and Environmental Responsibility*, München, ökom Verlag: 70-76

2000 'So What Was the Point? Reflections During and After the BIAMS Conference', in Timothy Yates (ed.), *Mission – An Invitation to God's Future*, Hope Valley, Cliff College: 117-118

2000 'Jesus Through Buddhist Eyes: Third Conference of the European Network of Buddhist Christian Studies, St Ottilien, Germany, 26 February – 1 March 1999', in *Buddhist-Christian Studies* 20: 257-259

2000 'European Union, Christian Division? Christianity's Responsibility for Europe's Past and Future', in *Studies* 89: 118-129 [Christian Unity Week lecture, Trinity College Dublin]

1999- [Series Co-editor of 'Religion and Theology in the Asia-Pacific Context', Münster, Hamburg and London, LIT Verlag]

1999 'Contested Space: Alternative Models of the Public Sphere in the Asia-Pacific', in Neil Brown and Robert Gascoigne (eds.), *Faith in the Public Forum*, Adelaide, Australian Theological Forum: 78-108 [paper read at a conference on 'Faith in the Public Forum', Australian Catholic University, Strathfield, Sydney, 2-5 January 1998]

1999 'The Heavy Hand of the German State: An Open Letter to Richard Hutch on Attitudes to Scientology', in *Australian Religious Studies Review* 11,2: 134-136

1999 'The Loss and Rediscovery of Initiation in the South Pacific', in *Catalyst* 29,1: 32-47

1999 'Empowerment and Powerlessness: Minorities and Majorities in a Pluralist Society', in Ruth Weyl (ed.), *Unity Without Uniformity: The Challenge of Pluralism. Proceedings of the International Consultation of the International Council of Christians and Jews, 23-26 August 1998, Erlbach, Germany*, Heppenheim, Martin Buber House: 151-154

1999 'Realised Catholicity: The Incarnational Dimension of Multiculturalism', in *The Australasian Catholic Record* 76: 419-429

1999 'Jesus Through Buddhist Eyes: Third Conference of the European Network of Buddhist Christian Studies, St Ottilien, Germany, 26 February – 1 March 1999', in *Current Dialogue* 33: 68-70: and *Studies in Interreligious Dialogue* 9,2: 226-228

1999 'Initiation, Initiationsverlust und Initiationsersatz im Südpazifik', in Thomas Schreijäck (ed.), *Menschwerden im Kulturwandel. Kontexte kultureller Identität als Wegmarken Interkultureller Kompetenz: Initiationen und ihre Inkulturationsprozesse*, Luzern, Edition Exodus: 456-471

1999 'Religion, Morality and Society: A Chinese Perspective', in *Irish Theological Quarterly* 64: 385-387

1998 'Piety and Politics: An Encounter with Rissho Kosei-Kai', in *Dharma World* (Tokyo) 25, Sep.-Oct.: 8-10

1998 [review article] 'Paul F. Knitter, *Jesus and the Other Names*, and S. Mark Heim, *Salvations*', in *Mid-Stream* 37,1: 108-113

1998 'Zen With Teeth: The Contributions of Buddhists and Christians to Preserving the Earth', in *Buddhist-Christian Studies* 18: 213-215

1997 'Aboriginal Religion and Australian Culture', in *Nelen Yubu* (Sydney) 65: 1-12

1997 'Development Without Violence: Some Buddhist and Christian Sources for Development Ethics', in *Seeds of Peace*, (Bangkok) 13,1: 18-25 [paper read at international conference of the Society for Buddhist-Christian Studies, De Paul University, Chicago, July 27 – August 3, 1996]

1997 'Ecology and the Religions: A Marriage of Convenience?', in *Future Generations Journal* 22,1: 18-21

1997 'Gibt es eine buddhistische Wirtschaftsethik?', in Maria Hungerkamp and Matthias Lutz (eds.), *Grenzenüberschreitende Ethik. Festschrift für Prof. Dr. Johannes Hoffmann anlässlich seines 60. Geburtstages*, Frankfurt a.M., IKO-Verlag für Interkulturelle Kommunikation: 65-82

1996 'Ecology: Our Newest Religion?', in *Doctrine and Life* (Dublin) 46: 578-585

1996 'Pomirenje I oprostaj u Irskoj' ['Nationalismus und Religion. Das Beispiel Irland'], in Nobosja Popov (ed.), *Trauma i katarza u istorijskom pamcenju*, Beograd, Srpska Strana Rata: 713-725 [paper contributed to a conference of the New Serbian Forum, Belgrade, 8-10 December, 1995]

1995 'The Ethics of Multiculturalism: An Ecumenical Challenge for Australia', in *St Mark's Review* (Canberra) 160: 25-31 [Inaugural Ted Arblaster Memorial Lecture, St Mark's National Theological Centre, Canberra, August 1994]

1995 'Transforming Pluralism and Dialogue', in *Doctrine and Life* 45: 524-533 [Irish School of Ecumenics annual Academic Council lecture, November 1995]

1995 'Instrumentalisierung des Christentums durch die Politik? Das Beispiel Nordirland', in *Una Sancta* 50: 141-150

1994 'What do Socially Engaged Buddhists and Christian Liberation Theologians Have to Say to One Another?', in *Dialogue* (Colombo) 21: 1-18 [paper read at annual conference of the Australian Association for the Study of Religions, University of Melbourne, July 1992]

1994 '"Rights of the Earth" and "Care for the Earth": Two Paradigms for a Buddhist-Christian Ecological Ethic', in *Horizons* 21: 48-61 [paper read at international conference of the Society for Buddhist-Christian Studies, Boston University, July 1992]

1994 [review article] 'Ministry Reconsidered', in *Doctrine and Life* 44: 150-152

1994 'Menschenrechte als Landrechte im Pazifik. Vier Fallstudien', in Johannes Hoffmann (ed.), *Universale Menschenrechte im Widerspruch der Kulturen. Das eine Menschenrecht für alle und die vielen Lebensformen* II, Frankfurt a.M., IKO-Verlag für Interkulturelle Kommunikation: 213-237

1994 'Reconciliation in Buddhism', in Michael Hurley (ed.), *Reconciliation in Religion and Society. Proceedings of a conference organised by the Irish School of Ecumenics and the University of Ulster*, Belfast, Queen's University, Institute of Irish Studies: 177-182

1994 'Australien: I. Allgemeine Einführung; III. Kirchengeschichte; IV. Kirche und Theologie in der Gegenwart; V. Theologie und Theologen in Australien; VI. Statistik', in *Lexikon für Theologie und Kirche*, Freiburg, Herder: 1273-1284

1993 'Human Rights as Land Rights in the Pacific', in *Pacifica: Australian Theological Studies* 6: 61-80

1993 [review article] '100 Years of Global Interfaith Dialogue: 1893-1993', in *Doctrine and Life* 43: 61-80

1993 'Is Interfaith Dialogue Undermining Interchurch Dialogue? Ecumenics as the Framework for an Integral Ecumenism', in Oliver Rafferty SJ (ed.), *Reconciliation: Essays in Honour of Michael Hurley*, Dublin, Columba Press: 159-175

1993 'Sulak and the King of Siam', in *Five Cycles of Friendship, by Friends of Sulak Sivaraksa to Honour his Sixtieth Birthday*, Bangkok, Suksit Siam & Kled Thai Co.: 53-54

1993 'Australien VI. Kultur, Religion, Bildung', in *Staatslexikon*, Freiburg, Basel and Wien, Herder, (7th edition): 838-840

1993 'The Trinity in Melanesia: The Understanding of the Christian God in a Pacific Culture', in James Byrne (ed.), *The Christian Understanding of God Today. Theological Colloquium on the Occasion of the 400th Anniversary of the Foundation of Trinity College, Dublin*, Dublin, Columba Press: 154-165

1992 'Reporting Religion: A Response to Greg Bailey', in *Australian Religion Studies Review* 5: 42-43

1991 'Syncretism or Synthesis? An Anticipatory Sketch of Religious Change in the Pacific', in *South Pacific Journal of Mission Studies* 1,4: 18-21

1991 'Is Theology a Social Science?', in *Doctrine and Life* 41: 458-464

1991 'Papua-Neuguinea', in *Evangelisches Kirchenlexikon* III, Göttingen, Vandenhoeck & Ruprecht, (3rd edition): 1035-1037

1991 'A Pacific Assembly? The Significance of the WCC's Canberra Assembly for Religion in Australia', in *Australian Religion Studies Review* 4: 22-24

1991 'Synkretismus oder Synthese? Eine antizipatorische Skizze des religiösen Wandels im Pazifik', in Hermann Pius Siller (ed.), *Suchbewegungen. Synkretismus – kulturelle Identität und kirchliches Bekenntnis*, Darmstadt, Wissenschaftliche Buchgesellschaft: 185-192

1991 'Wind and Fire: An Interpretation of the VIIth Assembly of the WCC', in *Doctrine and Life* 41: 226-232

1991 'The Dance of the Spirit: A Theological Interpretation of the VIIth Assembly of the WCC', in *Doctrine and Life* 41: 305-311

1991 'Beginn eines ernsthaften interkulturellen Gesprächs', Rapport der Sektion III: Menschenrechte im multireligiösen Kontext Asiens, in Johannes Hoffmann (ed.), *Begründung von Menschenrechten aus der Sicht unterschiedlicher Kulturen. Band I des Symposiums Das eine Menschenrecht für alle und die vielen Lebensformen*, Frankfurt a.M., IKO-Verlag für Interkulturelle Kommunikation: 151-155

1990 'The Economics of Ecumenics', in *Search: A Church of Ireland Journal* 13: 32-36

1990 'Political Ecumenism: Church Structures and the Political Process', in *Studies: An Irish Quarterly Review* 79: 396-405

1990 'Ökumene im Übergang: Gedanken zur Grundlegung ökumenischer Theorie und Praxis aus westkirchlicher Sicht', in *Una Sancta* 45: 274-280 [keynote address at 30th anniversary celebrations of Catholic Ecumenical Institute, University of Münster, June 1990]

1990 'Teaching Ecumenics in a New Europe: Irish School of Ecumenics Celebrates 20th Anniversary', in *Ecumenical Trends* 19: 116-119

1989 'Die kleineren "Glaubensmissionen"', in H. Wagner, G. Fugmann, H. Janssen (eds.), *Papua Neuguinea: Gesellschaft und Kirche. Ein ökumenisches Handbuch*, Neuendettelsau, Freimund-Verlag; Erlangen, Verlag der Ev.-Luth. Mission: 216-218

1989 'Ökumenische Zusammenarbeit', in Wagner-Fugmann-Janssen, *Papua Neuguinea*: 219-226

1988 'Integral Ecumenism: Sri Lanka, Papua New Guinea and Ireland', in *Doctrine and Life* 38: 190-198 [inaugural lecture, Irish School of Ecumenics, November 1987]

1988 '"The Only Great Ecumenical Question": Christian-Jewish Relations', in *Studies* 77: 300-308 [lecture, Irish Council of Christians and Jews, Dublin, November 1987]

1988 'Integral Ecumenism', in *Journal of Ecumenical Studies* 25: 573-591

1988 'Response to Patrick O'Farrell', in *Australian Religion Studies Review* 1: 15-18

1987 'Kontextuelle Theologie in Melanesien', in *Zeitschrift für Missionswissenschaft und Religionswissenschaft* 71: 279-291 [guest lecture at the University of Frankfurt a.M., May 1986]

1987 'Contextual Theology in Melanesia', in *Theology Digest* 35: 25-29

1987 'The Religious Studies Saga in Melanesia: Some Historical Background', in *Melanesian Journal of Theology* 3: 9-21 [paper read at a consultation on tertiary level religious education in Melanesia, Goroka, April 1987]

1987 [report] 'The Ethics of Development: 17th Waigani Seminar, University of Papua New Guinea, 7-12 September, 1986', in *Melanesian Journal of Theology* 3: 54-63

1987 'Towards the Development of Ethics', in *Catalyst: Social Pastoral Magazine for Melanesia* 17: 235-251

1987 'Dialogue between Religions', in Max Charlesworth and Peter Fenner (eds.), *Religious Investigations: Study Guide*, Deakin University, Australia: 81-100

1987 'Einheit der Menschheit', 'Glaubensbekenntnis', 'Leiden', 'Symbol', 'Tod', 'Volk Gottes', in Adel Theodor Khoury (ed.), *Lexikon religiöser Grundbegriffe. Judentum, Christentum, Islam*, Graz, Wien and Köln, Verlag Styria

1986 'The Autonomous Church in Independent Papua New Guinea', in H. Wagner and H. Reiner (eds.), *The Evangelical Lutheran Church in Papua New Guinea: The First Hundred Years, 1886-1986*, Adelaide, Lutheran Publishing House: 307-326

1986 *Christian Fundamentalism and Melanesian Identity*, Goroka, The Melanesian Institute, Occasional Paper No. 3 [paper read in the section 'Melanesia, Australia and Oceania', XVth International Congress, International Association for the History of Religions, University of Sydney, August 1985]

1986 'Ministerial Training for Australian Aborigines', in *Melanesian Journal of Theology* 1: 200-204

1985-1987 [Founding Editor of the *Melanesian Journal of Theology: Journal of the Melanesian Association of Theological Schools*]

1985 'Theologies of the "Third Church"', in *Melanesian Journal of Theology* 1: 65-71

1985 'Whatever Happened to the Melanesian Council of Churches? A Study in Ecumenical Organisation', in *Melanesian Journal of Theology* 1: 138-157

1984 'Einige Voraussetzungen interreligiöser Kommunikation am Beispiel Buddhismus und Christentum', in *Neue Zeitschrift für Missionswissenschaft* 40: 26-35

1984 [report] 'Melanesian Theology: Melanesian Theologians at Work', in *Catalyst* 14: 181-186 [also in *Journal of Ecumenical Studies* 21: 414-415]

1984 'Essence – Identity – Liberation: Three Ways of Looking at Christianity', in *Religious Traditions* 6: 30-41 [paper read at VIIth Annual Conference, Australian Association for the Study of Religions, University of Melbourne, August 1982]

1984 'The Prospects of Melanesian Theology', in *Catalyst* 14: 290-301

1984 '"Lokalisierung": Selbsthilfe oder Überforderung?', in M. Sollich (ed.), *Probezeit ausgeschlossen. Erfahrungen und Perspektiven der personellen Entwicklungsarbeit*, Mainz, Grünewald / München, Chr. Kaiser: 105-109

1983 'Dialog und Befreiung. Versuch einer Vermittlung zwischen "pazifischen" und "atlantischen" Theologien', in *Junge Kirche* 44: 165-170 [valedictory lecture at the Catholic Ecumenical Institute, University of Münster, February 1983]

1982 'Vom Vergleich zur Verständigung. Die unstete Geschichte der Vergleiche zwischen Buddhismus und Christentum, 1880-1980', in *Zeitschrift für Missionswissenschaft und Religionswissenschaft* 66: 58-66 [guest lecture at University of Bremen, May 1981]

1982 'Probleme einer Untersuchung zur "Sinnkonstruktion" im frühen Buddhismus und Christentum', in *Linguistica Biblica* 50: 33-39 [research report, section on *Semiotik der Religionen*, Deutsche Gesellschaft für Semiotik, IIIrd Congress, University of Hamburg, October 1981]

1982 'Christian-Buddhist-Marxist Dialogue in Sri Lanka: A Model for Social Change in Asia?', in *Journal of Ecumenical Studies* 19: 719-743

1981 '"Making Sense of Death" in Christianity and Buddhism: Towards a "Pragmasemantic" Analysis of 1 Thess 4:13-5:11 and Sutta-Nipata III,8 ("The Dart Sutta")', in *Zeitschrift für Missionswissenschaft und Religionswissenschaft* 65: 51-69 [paper read at the IVth annual conference of the Australian Association for the Study of Religions, University of Sydney, August 1979]

1981 '"Volk Gottes" als Grundlage einer Theologie der Religionen: Ein katholisches Votum', in H.H. Hendrix (ed.), *Unter dem Bogen des Bundes. Beiträge aus jüdischer und christlicher Existenz*, Aachen, Einhard: 235-249 [paper read to the *Gesellschaft für christlich-jüdische Zusammenarbeit,* Krefeld, October 1980]

1980 'Consensus in Religion: An Essay in Fundamental Ecumenics', in *Journal of Ecumenical Studies* 17: 407-431

1980 'Sprache der Einheit – Sprache der Zwietracht. Der Rassismus als Testfall ökumenischer Kommunikation', in P. Lengsfeld (ed.), *Ökumenische Theologie. Ein Arbeitsbuch*, Stuttgart, Kohlhammer: 251-284

1980 [co-authored with H.-G. Stobbe] 'Übereinstimmung und Handlungsfähigkeit. Zur Grundlage ökumenischer Konsensbildung und Wahrheitsfindung', in Lengsfeld *Ökumenische Theologie*: 301-337

1980 'Vom innerchristlichen zum interreligiösen Dialog', in Lengsfeld, *Ökumenische Theologie*: 426-432

1980 'Buddhist and Christian Responses to Social and Technical Revolution', in *Dialogue* 7: 23-40 [paper read at Marga Institute, Colombo, August 1979]

1980 'Religious Symbolisations of Nature in Ethical Argumentation: A 'Pragma-semantic' Analysis of Romans 8:18-25 and a Buddhist Comparison', in *Linguistica Biblica* 48: 19-48 [paper read at XIVth International Congress of the IAHR, Winnipeg, August 1980]

1980 [review article] 'Menschenrechte als ökumenische Frage', in *Una Sancta* 35: 182-184

1979 'Fehlt dem Christentum ein Verhältnis zur Natur? Eine Analyse der Seligpreisungen (Mt 5,2-12) und der Feuerpredigt des Buddha (Samy. XXXV,28)', in *Una Sancta* 34: 159-171 [abridged in *Anstösse aus der Arbeit der Evangelischen Akademie Hofgeismar* 2, 1979: 68-75]

1978 'Der Lotos in der Wüste. Der Aufbruch der Religionswissenschaft in Australien', in *Zeitschrift für Missionswissenschaft und Religionswissenschaft* 62: 134-143

1978 'Ökumene vor der Barriere Angst', in *Una Sancta* 33: 190-195

1977 'Kulturelle Identität und wirtschaftliche Abhängigkeit als Probleme ökumenischer Kommunikation', in *Una Sancta* 32: 70-83 [English summary in the *Journal of Ecumenical Studies* 15 (1978): 358]

1977 'The Religious Construction of Meaning: Christianity and Buddhism as "Problem-Solvers"', in Victor C. Hayes (ed.), *Australian Essays in World Religions*, Adelaide, Australian Association for the Study of Religions: 106-115 [paper read to the Adelaide chapter of AASR, March 1977]

1977 'From Ecumenical Theology to Fundamental Ecumenics', in *Journal of Ecumenical Studies* 14: 304-312

1977 'Vorbereitende Überlegungen zu einer Konsenstheorie der Konziliarität', in *Una Sancta* 32: 94-104 [English summary in the *Journal of Ecumenical Studies* 15 (1978): 777-778]

1976 'Ökumene jenseits der Kirchen? Die "neue Religiosität" in soziologischer und ökumenischer Hinsicht', in *Una Sancta* 31: 188-204 [English summary in the *Journal of Ecumenical Studies* 14 (1977): 351-352]

1976 'Strategien der Ökumene. Eine Problemanalyse', in *Test – Katholische Studentenzeitschrift* 17,2: 48-53

1976 'Was sagen "Glaubensaussagen" aus? Ein Versuch mit dem Sinnbegriff', in *Linguistica Biblica* 39: 5-36

1974 'Die Funktion der Rede von der Einheit der Menschheit in den neueren Dokumenten der Katholischen Kirche und der Ökumenishen Bewegung: Ein Versuch zu Anspruch und Leistung der Sprache der Ökumene', [doctoral dissertation], Westfälischen Wilhelms-Universität, Münster in Westfalen

1971 'The Infallibility Debate in Germany', in *Compass Theology Review* 5: 55-59

1970 'What is Political Theology?', in *Compass Theology Review* 4: 88-94

Contributors' Biographies

THEODOR AHRENS is emeritus Professor for Missiology and Ecumenics at the University of Hamburg, having been a colleague of John D'Arcy May at the Melanesian Institute (Goroka, Papua New Guinea). He has published *Gegebenheiten. Missionswissenschaftliche Studien* (Frankfurt a.M., Lembeck, 2005).

ANN ALDÉN is a Minister in the Church of Sweden and member of the European Network of Buddhist Christian Studies. Her PhD is *Religion in Dialogue with Later Modern Society* (Frankfurt a.M., Peter Lang, 2006).

IAIN ATACK is Lecturer and Coordinator of International Peace Studies in the Irish School of Ecumenics TCD. His most recent book is *The Ethics of Peace and War* (Edinburgh, University Press, 2005).

URSULA BAATZ is an academic and journalist, working in the University of Vienna and in the national media. Her PhD was on the Zen Jesuit Hugo Lassalle, *H. M. Enomiya Lassalle. Jesuit und Zen-Lehrer, Brückenbauer zwischen Ost und West* (Freiburg i.B., Benziger, 2004).

RAQUEL BOUSO GARCÍA is Adjunct Professor of the History of Ideas in the Universitat Pompeu Fabra (Barcelona). She translates works of the Kyoto School into Spanish. Her PhD was 'The Religious Experience of Emptiness in Nishitani Keiji' (in Spanish, Barcelona, UPF, 2005; forthcoming, Barcelona, Fragmenta, 2007).

FRANÇOIS BOUSQUET is Professor of Fundamental Theology and Dogmatics at the Institut Catholique de Paris, and Director of the Institute for Science and Theology of Religions. He is editor, with Philippe Capelle, of *Dieu et la raison* (Paris, Bayard, 2005).

THOMAS BREMER is Professor of Ecumenics and Peace Studies in the Catholic Theological Faculty of Münster University. He is a specialist in the Eastern Churches and he has just published *Kreuz und Kreml. Kurze Geschichte der orthodoxen Kirche in Russland* [Cross and Kremlin: Short History of the Orthodox Church in Russia] (Freiburg i.B., Herder, 2007).

LESLEY CARROLL is Minister of Fortwilliam Park Presbyterian church, Belfast and member of the Eames-Bradley consultative group on dealing with Northern Ireland's past 'troubles'. Her PhD is 'Divided Loyalties – A Reconciliation Ethic for Churches in Northern Ireland' (ISE TCD, 2006).

GABRIEL DALY OSA is retired from lecturing in theology in Trinity College Dublin, the Milltown Institute of Philosophy and Theology and the Irish School of Ecumenics. A founding member of ISE, he is well known for his *Transcendence and Immanence: A Study in Catholic Modernism and Integralism*, Oxford, Clarendon, 1980).

TMG DUFFY is on the staff of the International Peace Studies programme of the Irish School of Ecumenics TCD. He also works in peacekeeping and human rights with the UN, OSCE, and Red Cross. His report on human rights education has been published (UNESCO and EPU, Stadtslaining, 2007).

GEORG EVERS is recently retired from Missio (Aachen), where he worked at the Asia desk. He took his PhD under Karl Rahner SJ, edited *Theologie im Kontext/Theology in Context* for many years, and is author of *The Churches in Asia* (New Delhi, ISPCK, 2005).

ALAN FALCONER is Minister of St Machar's Cathedral (Aberdeen). He is a former Director of ISE and of the Commission on Faith and Order (World Council of Churches). Responsible for the *Eighth Forum on Bilateral Dialogues* (WCC, 2002), he and Joseph Liechty revised their *Reconciling Memories* (Dublin, Columba, 1998).

JUDE LAL FERNANDO is a graduate student of ISE and now pursues a PhD under John May. In his native Sri Lanka he was National Co-ordinator of All Ceylon Fisherfolk Trade Union. His *A Paradigm for a Peace Movement* (Dublin, Columba, 2007) is forthcoming.

ANTJE FETZER is the theological speaker of the Diakonisches Werk Württemburg. She is a graduate of ISE. Her PhD was published as *Tradition im Pluralismus. Alasdair MacIntyre und Karl Barth als Inspiration für christliches Selbstverständnis in pluralen Gesellschaften* (Neukirchen-Vluyn, Neukirchener Verlag, 2002).

FRANK FLETCHER MSC has a ThD from the Melbourne College of Divinity. He has devoted his pastoral and theological work to helping Aboriginal people, especially in Sydney. He published 'Faith Seeking the Heart' in the *Australasian Catholic Record* 83,4 (October 2006).

KIERAN FLYNN is a member of St Patrick's Missionary Society, of which he is Interfaith Advisor; he has worked for many years in Nigeria. He is undertaking a PhD in ISE. He has just published *Communities for the Kingdom* (Eldoret, Kenya, GABA, 2007).

GLADYS GANIEL is Lecturer in Reconciliation Studies at the Belfast campus of the Irish School of Ecumenics TCD. Her most recent book is *Evangelicalism and Conflict in Northern Ireland* (New York, Palgrave, forthcoming).

ROBERT GASCOIGNE is Professor at the School of Theology, Australian Catholic University (Strathfield), and a past president of the Australian Catholic Theological Association. He is author of *Freedom and Purpose: An Introduction to Christian Ethics* (New York, Paulist, 2004).

GIDEON GOOSEN was Associate Professor of Theology, Australian Catholic University (Strathfield) until his recent retirement. He has been visiting lecturer at ISE and has published *Bringing Churches Together* (Geneva, World Council of Churches, 2001^2).

NORMAN C. HABEL is Professorial Fellow at Flinders University (Adelaide). He is initiator, editor and contributor of The Earth Bible series, and initiator and coordinator of The Season of Creation (www.seasonofcreation.com). For the last 20 years he has been mentor of a programme for Dalits and Tribals in South India.

ELIZABETH J. HARRIS is Senior Lecturer in the Comparative Study of Religion at Liverpool Hope University. She is on the editorial board of Buddhist Studies Review and the executive of the European Network of Buddhist Christian Studies. She is author of *Theravāda Buddhism and the British Encounter* (London and New York, Routledge, 2006).

CATHY HIGGINS is Lecturer in Education for Reconciliation, in the Northern Ireland campus of ISE. She has co-authored *Communities of Reconciliation* (Belfast, Colourpoint, 2002) and is designing a programme on Women and Peacebuilding in Northern Ireland and Border Counties.

LINDA HOGAN is Professor of Ecumenics and Head of the Irish School of Ecumenics TCD. In addition to her *Confronting the Truth* (London, DLT, 2001) she has recently published 'A Different Mode of Encounter' (*Political Theology* 7,1 (2006): 59-73), and has co-authored a number of papers with John May.

MAUREEN JUNKER-KENNY is Associate Professor of Theology (practical theology and Christian ethics), Trinity College Dublin, and is on the Board of Concilium. She edited, with Peter Kenny, *Memory, Narrativity, Self and the Challenge to Think God* (Münster, LIT Verlag, 2004).

PAUL F. KNITTER is the Paul Tillich Professor of Theology, World Religions and Culture at Union Theological Seminary (New York). Having written *Introducing Theologies of Religion* (2002), he edited *Myth of Religious Superiority* (2005; both: Maryknoll, Orbis).

GERHARD KÖBERLIN is a founder member of the European Network of Buddhist Christian Studies and has held appointments in Mahidol University (Bangkok) and the Academy of Mission (University of Hamburg). He has edited, with Erhard Kamphausen, *Gewalt und Gewaltüberwindung. Stationen eines theologischen Dialogs* (Frankfurt a.M., Lembeck, 2006).

KRISTIN RABLING KWASNIEWSKI is a graduate of ISE and is pursuing her PhD under John May; she is working on the development of a Muslim modernity through the implementation of Mu'tazilite philosophy and Progressive objectives.

AASULV LANDE is emeritus Professor of World Christianity and Religious Relations at Lund University. An expert on Japanese interreligious dialogue, he is a former President of the European Network of Buddhist Christian Studies. He edited, with Werner G. Jeanrond, *The Concept of God in Global Dialogue* (Maryknoll, Orbis, 2005).

BRENDAN LEAHY is Professor of Systematic Theology in St Patrick's College (Maynooth). He is secretary of the Advisory Committee on Ecumenism of the Irish Bishops' Conference and a member of the Irish Three Faiths Forum. Among his recent publications is a co-edited work, *Vatican II Facing the 21st Century: Historical and Theological Perspectives* (Dublin, Veritas, 2006).

FIACHRA LONG is a Lecturer in Education in University College Cork (Ireland). He works in the crossover areas between education, theology and philosophy. He is author of *Maurice Blondel: The Idealist Illusion* (Dordrecht, Kluwer, 2000) and 'The Alpha and the Omicron' (*The Furrow*, February 2007).

DAVID R. LOY is Besl Family Professor of Ethics/Religion and Society at Xavier University (Cincinnati). His books include *A Buddhist History of the West* (Albany, SUNY, 2002) and *The Great Awakening: A Buddhist Social Theory* (Boston, Wisdom, 2003).

JOHNSTON MCMASTER is Lecturer in, and Programme Coordinator of, Education for Reconciliation in the Northern Ireland campus of the Irish School of Ecumenics TCD. His book *Celtic Spirituality and Contemporary Social Ethics* is forthcoming.

BILL MCSWEENEY is Research Fellow at the Irish School of Ecumenics TCD, having retired from leading the Peace Studies programme there. He has published *Security, Identity and Interests* (Cambridge, CUP, 1999).

KARL-WILHELM MERKS is emeritus Professor of Moral Theology at Tilburg University (Netherlands), where he was also Director of the Centre for Intercultural Ethics. He wrote *Gott und die Moral* (1998) and edited *Modèles d'unité dans un monde pluriel* (2003; both: Münster, LIT Verlag).

HEDWIG MEYER-WILMES is Associate Professor for Gender Studies in Religion at Radboud-University of Nijmegen (Netherlands), and a past president of the European Society of Women in Theological Research (ESWTR). She wrote *Rebellion on the Borders: Feminist Theology between Theory and Praxis* (Kampen, Pharos-Kok, 1995).

PAUL O'GRADY is a Lecturer in Philosophy and Fellow of Trinity College Dublin. He is author of *Themes in Modern Philosophy* (Dublin, Priory Institute, 2006).

JOHN O'GRADY is a teacher and lecturer in ecumenical theology. He is on both the Trust of the Irish School of Ecumenics and the executive of the European Network of Buddhist Christian Studies.

GERRY O'HANLON SJ is a staff member of the Jesuit Centre for Faith and Justice, and Associate Professor at the Milltown Institute. As Jesuit Provincial he was President of the Academic Council for Research (ISE). He is author of *The Immutability of God in the Theology of Hans Urs von Balthasar* (Cambridge, CUP, 1990).

JOSEPH S. O'LEARY is Associate Professor, Department of English Literature, Sophia University (Tokyo). Widely published also in religious studies, he is associated with the Nanzan Institute for Religion and Culture. He wrote *Religious Pluralism and Christian Truth* (Edinburgh University, 1996).

ANDREW PIERCE is Lecturer and Programme Co-ordinator in the ecumenics programme of the Irish School of Ecumenics TCD. His recent articles reflect his present research into the theological significance of religious fundamentalism.

ALOYSIUS PIERIS SJ is an Indologist and theologian. He is director of Tulana Research Centre (Colombo), where he has profoundly influenced a number of the contributors and John D'Arcy May. He has recently published *Studies in the Philosophy and Literature of Pāli Ābhidhammika Buddhism* (2004) and *Prophetic Humour in Buddhism and Christianity* (2005; both: Colombo, Ecumenical Institute for Study and Dialogue).

Contributors' Biographies

ROBYN REYNOLDS OLSH is a Lecturer in Missiology at Yarra Theological Union (Melbourne). She is a member of the Daughters of Our Lady of the Sacred Heart and has worked with indigenous people for many years in Australia's Northern Territory. Her PhD was on Catholic sacrament and Wadeye ritual (2000) and she publishes regularly in *Pacifica*.

JOHN ROBINSON is a graduate of the Irish School of Ecumenics TCD, and is pursuing his PhD under John May on the possibilities afforded by transcendental Thomism as in integrative framework in Buddhist-Christian encounter.

MARTIN RÖTTING is a graduate of the Irish School of Ecumenics TCD. He is the Secretary of the European Network of Buddhist Christian Studies. His PhD has been published as *Interreligiöses Lernen im Buddhistisch-Christlichen Dialog* (St Ottilien, EOS, 2007). Currently, he is a lay pastoral worker in Freising (Germany).

EDA SAGARRA is Pro-Chancellor of the University of Dublin (TCD), and emeritus Professor of German (TCD). Her most recent book is *Germany in the Nineteenth Century. History and Literature* (New York, Peter Lang, 2003).

JOSEPH SALIHU is a graduate of the Irish School of Ecumenics TCD, completing his PhD under John May. He is a school principal, parish priest, and chair of the interreligious Dialogue Commission in Northern Nigeria.

PETER SCHERLE is Professor of Church Theory and Cybernetics at, and Director of, the Theological College, Herborn. A graduate of ISE, he now lectures there yearly. His PhD was published as *Fragliche Kirche* (Münster, LIT Verlag, 1998) and he is editor of *Herborner Beiträge* volumes 1-3 (2002, 2004, 2007; Wuppertal, Foedus).

JACQUES SCHEUER SJ is Professor of Asian Philosophies and Religions, Louvain University (Louvain-la-Neuve, Belgium). He is founder and director of the 'Voies de l'Orient' (Brussels). He is author of 'The Bhagavad Gîtâ as "Spiritual Exercises"' in C. Cornille (ed.), *Song Divine: Christian Commentaries on the Bhagavad Gîtâ* (Leuven, Peeters, 2006).

PERRY SCHMIDT-LEUKEL is Professor of Systematic Theology and Religious Studies and Chair of World Religions for Peace (Glasgow). He is a member of the European Network for Buddhist Christian Studies. He has, among many recent books, edited *Buddhism, Christianity and the Question of Creation* (Aldershot, Ashgate, 2006).

SIMONE SINN is a former graduate student of John May. Currently, she has been seconded by her church to work as theological assistant for the Lutheran World Federation (Geneva). She has published *The Church as Participatory Community – on the Interrelationship of Hermeneutics, Ecclesiology and Ethics* (Dublin, Columba, 2002).

SULAK SIVARAKSA is one of the world's foremost engaged Buddhists. A trained academic he is, like Buddhadasa his fellow-Thai mentor, dedicated to practical endeavours, e.g., founding the Satheirakoses-Nagapradipa Foundation (1968), and the International Network of Engaged Buddhists (1988). In 1998 he published *Global Healing*.

GERALDINE SMYTH OP is Senior Lecturer in Ecumenical Studies in the Irish School of Ecumenics TCD. A former Director of the Irish School of Ecumenics, she is Board member of Healing Through Remembering and Chair of INCORE. She has published *Distance Becomes Communion* (Dublin, Dominican, 2004).

JØRGEN SKOV SØRENSEN is General Secretary of the Council on International Relations of the Evangelical Lutheran Church in Denmark. His PhD is in ecumenics and missiology and he is author of *Missiological Mutilations – Prospective Paralogies: Language and Power in Contemporary Mission Theory* (Frankfurt a.M., Peter Lang, 2007).

DAVID STEVENS is currently Leader of the renowned Corrymeela Community. He is author of *Land of Unlikeness: Explorations into Reconciliation* (Dublin, Columba, 2004).

HEINZ-GÜNTHER STOBBE was Professor for Systematic Theology and Theological Peace Studies at Siegen University before his retirement. He published 'Religion und Gewalt. Systematisch-theologische Überlegungen' (*Zeitschrift für Theologie und Gemeinde 9* (2004): 207-229).

EUGENE STOCKTON is a priest of the Parramatta diocese and is now retired from lecturing and archaeological fieldwork. One of his books is *Wonder: A Way to God* (Homebush, St Paul's, 1998).

PARICHART SUWANBUBBHA is Assistant Professor at Mahidol University (Thailand), where she works on the Comparative Religion and Contemplative Education graduate programmes. Her PhD, in English, was *Grace and Kamma* (Chicago, Lutheran School of Theology, 1994).

DAVID THOMAS is Professor of Christianity and Islam at the University of Birmingham. He is also Visiting Lecturer at ISE. He is joint editor of the journal *Islam and Christian-Muslim Relations*, and senior editor of the book series *The History of Christian-Muslim Relations*.

GARRY W. TROMPF is Professor in the History of Ideas, University of Sydney. Founder of Studies in World Religions, he is also executive Director of the Centre for Millennial Studies, Sydney. He has written *Religions of Melanesia* (Westport CT, Praeger, 2006).

ABRAHAM VÉLEZ DE CEA is Assistant Professor of Philosophy and Religion, Eastern Kentucky University. He did his PhD under Raimon Panikkar and is an expert in Theravāda Buddhism. He wrote 'A New Direction for Comparative Studies of Buddhists and Christians' (*Buddhist-Christian Studies* 26, 2006).

CAROLINA WEENING is an associate of the European Network of Buddhist Christian Studies. She recently completed her PhD, 'Whose Truth? Which Rationality?' on John Hick's strategies for managing conflicting truth claims. It will be published by Peter Lang in late 2007.

MARTIN WILSON MSC is in active retirement at Chevalier Resource Centre (Sydney), after decades teaching philosophy (John May was a student of his), researching in social anthropology, lecturing, etc. He established the Nelen Yubu Missiological Unit for Research in 1977.

Diakonie und Ökumene – Diakonia and Ecumenics
hrsg. von Prof. Dr. Bernd Jochen Hilberath (Universität Tübingen) und Rob Mascini

Bernd Jochen Hilberath; Rob Mascini (eds.)
Diakonia and Diaconate as an Ecumenical Challenge
At present, both the social and the ecumenical situation call for a renewed attention to the relationship between faith and life, between evangelisation and *diakonia*, which arise from and culminate in liturgy, from which they also draw their strength. The essays published in this collection call attention to the diaconal structure of every Christian action and to the theology underlying *diakonia*. The present book sums up the results and reflections of the first ecumenical theological symposium on the diaconate, which took place in Stuttgart in November 2003. The participants represented the Church of England, the Church of Sweden, the Episcopalian Church in the USA and the Roman Catholic Church. All of the symposium's material is summed up in this first book of the series and gives an impetus for interesting on-going discussion.
Bd. 1, 2006, 184 S., 19,90 €, br., ISBN 3-8258-7268-8

LIT Verlag Berlin – Hamburg – London – Münster – Wien – Zürich
Fresnostr. 2 48159 Münster
Tel.: 0251 / 620 32 22 – Fax: 0251 / 922 60 99
e-Mail: vertrieb@lit-verlag.de – http://www.lit-verlag.de

Ökumenische Studien / Ecumenical Studies

hrsg. von Prof. Dr. Ulrich Becker (Universität Hannover), Prof. Dr. Erich Geldbach (Marburg), Prof. Dr. Ulrike Link-Wieczorek (Universität Oldenburg), Prof. Dr. Gottfried Orth (TU Braunschweig, Ernst Lange-Institut Rothenburg) und Prof. Dr. Konrad Raiser (Genf/Berlin) in Verbindung mit dem Ernst Lange-Institut Rothenburg

Lena Lybæk; Konrad Raiser; Stefanie Schardien (Hg.)
Gemeinschaft der Kirchen und gesellschaftliche Verantwortung
Die Würde des Anderen und das Recht anders zu denken.
Festschrift für Professor Dr. Erich Geldbach

Leben, Wirken und Lernen in der Ökumene gehen einher mit der beständigen Herausforderung, sich neben dem und den Anderen auch der eigenen, kirchlichen wie gesellschaftlichen Gemeinschaft zu stellen. Der vorliegende Band zu Ehren Erich Geldbachs weist dessen zahlreiche ökumenische Kontakte und Freundschaften aus und entspricht dem breiten Interessenspektrum, dem er seine Forschung gewidmet hat: Von der Untersuchung der Geschichte der Freikirchen und Sondergemeinschaften sowie des Holocausts über die Beobachtung des interkonfessionellen Dialogs und der weltweiten Ökumene bis hin zur Beschäftigung mit Religionsfreiheit und den „dissenting voices" unter den „dissenters".
Bd. 30, 2004, 600 S., 34,90 €, br., ISBN 3-8258-7061-8

LIT Verlag Berlin – Hamburg – London – Münster – Wien – Zürich
Fresnostr. 2 48159 Münster
Tel.: 0251 / 620 32 22 – Fax: 0251 / 922 60 99
e-Mail: vertrieb@lit-verlag.de – http://www.lit-verlag.de